EUROPE, 1783–1914

EUROPE, 1783–1914

William Simpson and Martin Jones

Routledge
Taylor & Francis Group

LONDON AND NEW YORK

FLIP

First published 2000
by Routledge
2 Park Square, Milton Park, Abingdon, OX14 4RN

Simultaneously published in the USA and Canada
by Routledge
270 Madison Avenue, New York, NY10016

Reprinted 2005, 2007

Routledge is an imprint of the Taylor & Francis Group, an informa business

Typeset in Garamond by RefineCatch Limited, Bungay, Suffolk
Printed and bound in Great Britain by
Bell & Bain Ltd, Glasgow

British Library Cataloguing in Publication Data
A catalogue record for this book is available from the British Library

Library of Congress Cataloging in Publication Data
Simpson, William, 1932–
Europe, 1783–1914 / William Simpson & Martin Jones.
p.   cm.
Includes bibliographical references and index.
1. Europe – History – 1789–1900. 2. Europe – History – 1648–1789. 3.
Europe – History – 1871–1918. I. Jones, Martin (Martin Desmond) II. Title.
D299 .S48   2000
940.2′8 – dc21   99–087727

ISBN 10: 0–415–22659–7 (hbk)
ISBN 10: 0–415–22660–0 (pbk)

ISBN 13: 978–0–415–22659–2 ((hbk)
ISBN 13: 978–0–415–22660–8 (pbk)

• CONTENTS •

• ILLUSTRATIONS •

• ACKNOWLEDGEMENTS •

The authors and publishers gratefully acknowledge permission from the following to reproduce from copyright material:

From *The French Revolution* edited by J. Hardman, Edward Arnold (Publishers) Limited, 1991; From *Documents in the Political History of the European Continent* by G. Kertesz, 1968, by permission of Oxford University Press; from *A Sourcebook for Russian History from Early Times to 1917*, edited by G. Vernadsky, 1972, by permission of Yale University Press.

The authors wish to acknowledge the following works from which the tables in the book have been adapted: 1.1 *European Urbanisation 1500–1800*, Jan de Vries, London, Methuen, 1984; 2.3 *The French Revolution: an economic interpretation*, F. Aftalion (citing E. Labrousse, J. Dupâquier, M. Lachiver and J. Meuvret), Cambridge, CUP, 1990; 5.1 *The Longman Companion to Napoleonic Europe*, C. Emsley, London, Longman, 1993; 7.1 and 15.2 *The Unbound Prometheus*, D.S. Landes, Cambridge, CUP, 1969; 10.1 *The 1848 Revolutions*, P. Jones (citing *A Dictionary of Statistics*, M. Mulhall, 1892), London, Longman, 1981; 10.2 *The French Second Republic*, R. Price, Batsford, 1972; 15.1 and 15.3 *Barricades and Borders: Europe 1800–1914*, R. Gildea, Oxford, OUP, 1996; 15.4 *La Population active et sa structure*, P. Bairoch, Brussels, 1968; 15.5 *Industrial Growth and World Trade*, A. Maizels, 1963; 15.6 *An Economic History of England, 1870–1939*, W. Ashworth, London, Methuen, 1972; 20.1 *Reaction and Revolution in Russia 1881–1923*, M. Lynch, London, Hodder and Stoughton, 1992; *The Russian Peasant Movement 1906–17*, L. A. Owen, London, 1937; 22.1 and 22.2 *The Rise and Fall of the Great Powers*, P. Kennedy, London, Fontana, 1988.

• CHAPTER ONE •

The Condition of Europe c. 1789

• CONTENTS •

EUROPE'S EXTENT AND THE CONCEPT OF EUROPE

Europe is both a place and an idea. Most of us, if challenged to do so, could produce a reasonably precise description of its boundaries: to the west the Atlantic coastline, stretching from Cape Finisterre (Finis terrae – the end of the land) to Ireland and the Outer Hebrides, but also including island groups such as the Faroes and the Azores; to the north the coasts of Norway, Finland and Russia; to the south the Mediterranean, and to the east, less assuredly perhaps, the Ural mountains.

A much more difficult question to answer is when and why the concept of Europe came into common use. The Ancient Greeks were the first to use Europe as a geographical term, denoting first the Greek mainland, and by 500 BC the northerly landmass that lay beyond it in contrast to Asia to the east and Libya to the south. The first recorded use of European in Latin (Europeenses) has been traced to AD 732, when it was used with reference to Charles Martel's victory over the followers of Muhammad at the battle of Tours. The word European occurs for the first time in English in the seventeenth century, the *Oxford English Dictionary* citing a play, written in 1632, *The City Madam*, by Philip Massinger: 'You are learned Europeans and we worse than ignorant Americans.'

Thus the origins of the term Europe are shrouded in mystery and it has a long and complex ancestry. More important from our point of view is to establish why those who occupied what we now think of as Europe came to feel that they belonged to a distinct continent and what it was that they had in common. One obvious answer to the first question is that Europeans came to be distinguished from the inhabitants of other continents by recognition of differences between them. In the case of Charles Martel's contemporaries, it is the religious difference between Christian and Muslim, and Europe's southern boundary became that dividing line. In the case of Philip Massinger's, it is the technological superiority which Europeans enjoyed over the Native Americans whom they colonised – and in many cases slaughtered.

But there was much more to being a European than Christianity or technical knowledge. Those who lived in Europe shared certain fundamental historical experiences. At one time or another most of western Europe at least had been part of the Roman empire, and as a consequence of that experience Europeans were also heirs to the world of Greek and Latin culture. Latin became the language of educated discourse in Europe until at least the end of the seventeenth century. Two of the greatest minds of that century, Thomas Hobbes (1588–1679) and Isaac Newton (1642–1727), wrote their main works in Latin. Until the end of the eighteenth century the study of the classical world of Greece and Rome was the staple diet of university education from Cracow to Aberdeen and from Bologna to Salamanca.

With the fall of the western Roman empire in the fifth century AD came the so-called Dark Ages, and the breakdown of the existing political structures in many areas. A common response to the threat of anarchy was the emergence of local leaders who would guarantee protection, land and office to their followers in return for services, whether in the form of military service or forced labour, often commuted into payments in cash or in kind. Historians have coined the term 'feudalism' to describe societies organised in this way, the 'feodum' or 'fief' representing the office or property conveyed by the lord to his vassal. Feudalism never extended to the whole of Europe (Norway remained an exception) and it rarely existed in its purest form. But it was sufficiently widespread to generate a powerful landowning class based on the principle of inheritance and even where this class lost its exclusiveness, as in England, its distinctive privileges remained. One of the most successful plays in the late eighteenth century, *The Marriage of Figaro*, by Beaumarchais, concerned the thwarting of Count Almaviva in his attempt to exercise his *droit de seigneur* by sleeping with the bride of his valet Figaro on their wedding night. Though the play was written in 1778 public performance was censored in France until 1784. Mozart's equally successful opera, based on the play, had to be toned down before Emperor Joseph II would permit its performance in Vienna in 1786.

A third shared experience was the spread, and imposition, of Christianity throughout Europe. This was a long process, eventually achieved with the conversion of Hungary in the fourteenth century and the conquest of the Moors in Spain in the fifteenth. The term Christendom came into use in the eleventh century to denote the territory subject to the Catholic Church; the extent to which Christianity was conceived of as a European religion, at any rate by Protestants, is well illustrated by this 1625 comment:

Europe is taught the way to scale heaven, not by mathematical principles, but by divine verity. Jesus Christ is their way, their truth, their life; who hath long been given a bill of divorce to ungrateful Asia, where He was born, and Africa, the place of his flight and refuge, and is become almost wholly and only European. For little do we find of this name in Asia, less in Africa, and nothing at all in America, but later European gleanings.
(cited by J.M. Roberts, *The Triumph of the West*, London, BBC, 1985, p. 200)

Before equating Christendom with Europe, however, two important qualifications have to be made. Europe, until the twentieth century, did not include much of the Balkan peninsula, which remained part of the Ottoman empire. Eastern Christianity began to diverge from western as early as the ninth century. In 1054 each branch of the Church issued anathemas against the other, and divisions hardened with the Fourth Crusade, when Constantinople was sacked by Latin Crusaders. When Constantinople fell to the Turks in 1453 the eastern Church came under Turkish rule; while Christianity was still permitted, Christians in the Balkan peninsula continued to be subject to sporadic bouts of persecution and their welfare continued to be a matter of concern to neighbouring Christian states. Western Christendom was itself irretrievably split with the coming of Protestantism in the sixteenth century and the religious wars which ensued.

A fourth and arguably the most significant shared experience was the exploration and settlement of other continents by Europeans. In 1492 Columbus crossed the Atlantic ocean. In 1499 Vasco da Gama reached India by sailing round the Cape of Good Hope. In 1519 Magellan set out on the first circumnavigation of the globe, completed by one of his captains, Sebastian del Cano, in 1522. From these initial ventures sprang the empires of Portugal, Spain, Holland, Britain and France which by 1750 extended to North and South America, India, Africa and the Far East. Though the empires of Portugal and Spain had already passed their zenith by this date European domination of the world was already assured.

Thus by the end of the eighteenth century the concept of Europe denoted a distinct geographical area whose inhabitants inherited from the past a fund of common experiences, and which enabled them to feel a common identity when they faced Muslims and races of other colours. But when they faced each other they were only too conscious of what divided them. Local and national sentiment was to be for many years to come a much more powerful force than any sense of belonging to Europe. The history of Europe thus has to be written not only in terms of developments which affected the continent as a whole, the Renaissance, the Enlightenment, the industrial revolution, imperialism, for instance, but also in terms of individual states and nations – by no means identical – and the conflicts to which the divisions between them gave rise. Another characteristic feature of European history was the urge by one state or another to dominate the continent. France dominates the first part of this book, Germany the second.

THE SOCIAL AND ECONOMIC BACKGROUND

Population

Accurate population statistics date from the nineteenth century. Sweden was the first country to have a national census, in 1749, followed by Britain and France in 1801 and other countries thereafter. Thus all population figures for the eighteenth century are at best based on careful guesswork, and are subject to considerable margins of error. In the case of France, for instance, estimates for the population in 1789 range between 25 million and 28 million. There is little dispute however over the main trends, which show that Europe's population was rising constantly from about 1750 onwards, if not at a uniform rate (Table 1.1).

Table 1.1 Total population of Europe by country, 1750–1850 (in millions)

Country	1750	1800	1850
Britain (including Ireland)	10.6	16.1	27.4
Austria and Bohemia	5.7	7.9	12.9
Russia	35.0	49.0	79.0
Belgium	2.2	2.9	4.4
Germany	17.0	24.5	34.4
Scandinavia	3.6	5.0	7.9
Switzerland	1.3	1.7	2.4
Spain	8.9	10.5	15.0
France	21.7	27.0	35.8
Italy	15.3	17.8	24.0

For the first time in its history, Europe's population was on a rising trend that was not seriously interrupted by events such as the Black Death. The Irish potato famine from 1845 to 1848 and the Russian famine of 1921 were exceptional events. Any growth in population has to be explained by a change in the relationship between birth and death rates. If these match each other the population will remain stable. An increase in population will occur whenever there is a rise in the birth rate or a fall in the death rate, or where both occur simultaneously. All these conditions seem to have been present in eighteenth century Europe. In England the age of marriage fell, resulting in a rise in the birth rate. In France it appears that in some parts of the country at least, there was a fall in the death rate as famine became less common. While demographers continue to debate the precise explanation for the population rise, it was sufficiently evident to contemporary observers to cause alarm. In 1798 an English clergyman, Thomas Malthus, wrote his celebrated *Essay on Population* in which he argued that population unless unchecked has a tendency to double itself every twenty-five years (a geometrical progression, 1, 2, 4, 8, 16 . . .) But the means of subsistence could not be increased more than arithmetically (1, 2, 3, 4 . . .). Malthus posed in stark form the problem encountered by any country with a rising population. Unless resources could be increased to match the extra mouths to be fed the natural checks of famine, disease and war would inevitably operate to bring population and resources back into balance. This was the demographic background confronting Europe at the end of the eighteenth century, and it had inescapable consequences not only for living standards, but also for the supply of labour. Much would hinge on whether Europeans could apply their inventiveness to ensure that the rise in employment kept pace with the rise in population.

Agriculture

'Agriculture was the principal source of employment and wealth, the most significant sector of the economy, the basis of the taxation, government, ecclesiastic and seigneurial, that funded most other activities' (J. Black, *Eighteenth Century Europe*, London, Macmillan, 1990, p. 19). In some parts of France, it has been calculated, 74 per cent of the population were engaged in agriculture. In rural parts of Poland or Russia the ratio would have been even higher. In England it was rather lower.

Patterns of landownership and production varied so widely then, as they do today, that they defy meaningful generalisation. Certain tendencies can be identified, however. In much of western Europe, Britain and the Low Countries in particular, a landlord–tenant relationship was the characteristic feature of ownership. Landless agricultural labourers, who in England formed an increasing element in the agricultural population, were still free in the sense that they were not tied to a single owner. In much of eastern Europe and in Russia particularly, serfdom not only persisted but also was becoming more extensive.

Historians are now inclined to doubt whether anything as dramatic as a revolution occurred in agriculture, even in England in the eighteenth century. There were certainly improvements in stock breeding, new crop rotations were introduced to improve fertility and there was a switch to high yield crops such as maize and potatoes in areas such as western Ireland, Bavaria and Alsace. The landowning class founded agricultural societies and had access to a wide range of books and pamphlets on agriculture: 1,214 such works were published in France alone in the eighteenth century. But the implementation of the practices and improvements recommended was very haphazard, and where peasant proprietorship persisted almost non-existent. The general picture is one of gradual increase in food production as more land was brought into cultivation and new techniques were applied which still failed to meet the needs of a rising population. Agricultural prices tended to rise throughout the century while wages lagged behind. In France a rise of 65 per cent in food prices between 1760 and 1789 was offset by a rise of only 22 per cent in wages (O. H. Hufton, *Europe: Privilege and Protest*, London, Fontana, 1980, p. 34). In many parts of Europe, it has been calculated, as much as 90 per cent of the population did not have enough to live on.

INDUSTRY AND TRADE

As with the agricultural revolution, historians have cast an increasingly sceptical eye at the pace and scale of industrial development in the eighteenth century. Throughout Europe industry was mainly small scale and rural in 1800, as it had been in 1700. Even in Britain, while there was spectacular growth in the iron, cotton and coal-mining industries from the 1780s onwards, agriculture retained its pre-eminence as the main source of employment well into the nineteenth century. In Europe as a whole there were some isolated pockets of industrial development. The Russian iron industry grew rapidly and its arsenal at Tula produced 14,000 muskets a year between 1737 and 1778, even if they could fire only five or six times without breaking. In Flanders, half the rural population were engaged in weaving linen and spinning flax. The coal-mines near Liège used steam engines for pumping purposes as early as 1725. The use of coke rather than charcoal for smelting iron was introduced in Prussia in 1776. In Bohemia Count Joseph Kinsky set up mirror factories in 1761. The first mechanised textile factory at Düsseldorf was opened in 1783. But these were much less typical than the handlooms to be found in weavers' cottages all over Europe. The factory system had still to come.

The extent to which industrial production remained mainly rural is reflected in the low level of urbanisation. In no European country did town-dwellers exceed 20 per cent of the population except the Austrian Netherlands, where in Flanders and Brabant they reached 24 per cent, and in Sicily where towns like Palermo attracted huge numbers of displaced peasants.

Industry and commerce were mutually dependent. Without markets and the financial institutions needed to sustain them, industry could not prosper. Equally, without an adequate system of communications, buyers and sellers could not be brought together. The eighteenth century saw limited improvements in all these areas. It has been calculated that a carriage pulled by four horses could transport 4,000 lb. of goods 20 miles in a day over adequate roads. A cart pulled by a single horse could manage 1,120 lb., a pack horse with panniers 280 lb. Until the coming of railways these limitations remained in force, except in those areas where rivers or canals could be used. Roads improved sporadically, most significantly in Britain where turnpike trusts ensured that by 1780 large parts of the country were linked by an adequate road system. In Russia, by way of contrast, it still took two weeks to cover the 825 kilometres between Moscow and St Petersburg as late as 1760. There was a spate of canal building in Britain between 1760 and 1800 which produced 3,000 miles of canal. Canal building also took place in France, Prussia, Russia and Spain if not on the same scale. Sea transport remained dependent on wind power until well into the nineteenth century but improvements in ship design increased the capacity of merchant ships though not their speed. Even in 1815 it took on average six weeks to cross the Atlantic from east to west.

These developments enabled the volume of trade to expand significantly both within and between countries. The number of ships passing through the Sound between Denmark and Sweden, leading to the Baltic, doubled between 1730 and 1795. There was a rapid increase in the colonial trade between France and the French West Indies, and between Britain and her colonial possessions in the West Indies, North America and India. Of the increase in British exports between 1707 and 1800, 95 per cent went to areas outside Europe. Trade was still subject to many barriers, some self-imposed, others due to circumstance. Internal tolls were lifted in the Habsburg territories only in 1776, and on cereals in Spain in 1765. Where external trade is concerned most European countries subscribed to the mercantilist doctrine that tariffs should be imposed to safeguard domestic industries and employment, and laws were passed to keep trade with their colonies firmly in the hands of the mother country. Such were the British Acts of Trade and Navigation. It was not until the publication of Adam Smith's *The Wealth of Nations* in 1776 that the cause of free trade gained an effective advocate.

The difficulties of securing agreement to a single European currency today illustrate the problems of international finance in the eighteenth century. There was a permanent shortage of bullion to act as a medium of exchange. In some countries there was no uniform currency. Spanish silver dollars circulated in Scotland. Paper money, even when backed by governments, was universally distrusted, especially after the collapse of John Law's experiment in France in 1720. Central banks such as the Bank of England, established in 1694, and the Bank of Amsterdam in the Netherlands provided rare examples of financial probity and solvency. Nonetheless, these handicaps were overcome and the wheels of commerce continued to turn more rapidly as the century progressed, at least until interrupted by twenty years of warfare.

To sum up, it may be said that in 1789 the European economy was still heavily dependent on its own agriculture, which was the staple industry; that a rising population was imposing an increasing strain on resources, but at the same time providing a growing market for the products of industry and a surplus of workers for the jobs to be created by the incipient industrial revolution; and that in Britain particularly improvements in agriculture, industry, communications and financial management were more advanced than elsewhere, and thus she was already prepared for her future role as 'workshop of the world'.

THE STATES OF EUROPE

The characteristic political unit in Europe throughout much of the twentieth century has been the sovereign, unitary state, that is to say a state with clearly defined frontiers which recog-

nises allegiance to no external authority and whose central government exercises its powers unchecked by provincial institutions. With the advent of the European Union the position has changed, but the idea of national sovereignty still retains a powerful appeal, as recent events in the Balkan peninsula have made all too clear.

Prior to 1789 the sovereign, unitary state was far from typical, and generally became less and less common the further east one went (see Map 1.1). Great Britain was closest to the ideal. Wales was fully incorporated with England in 1536, gaining the right to send Members of Parliament (MPs) to Westminster in that year. The thrones of England and Scotland were united in 1603, with the accession of James VI of Scotland to the English throne. The two parliaments were united under the Act of Union in 1707. Ireland remained, as it still does, a special case, but it too was fully integrated with England by the Act of Union in 1800. Until 1922 when the Irish Free State came into existence the writ of the Parliament at Westminster ran unchallenged throughout the British Isles and was subject to no external authority.

France's frontiers, too, in 1789, though soon to be radically altered as a consequence of the French Revolution, were much as they are today. Bordered by the Atlantic to the west, the Mediterranean and the Pyrenees to the south, France's northern frontier abutted on to the Austrian Netherlands (present-day Belgium). It was only to the east that changes were to come. The Rhine remained a disputed boundary. Lorraine was acquired as recently as 1766, and would pass, with Alsace, into German hands in 1871 before returning to France in 1918. Nominally the authority of the French crown was undisputed throughout France, but in the more recently acquired provinces such as Languedoc, Brittany and Burgundy provincial Estates still retained the power to vote taxes and provincial feeling was still a factor to be reckoned with. The papal enclave of Avignon remained outside French jurisdiction until the Revolution.

In the Iberian peninsula geography and the long campaign in the fifteenth century against the Moors, known as the Reconquista, had combined to give a precocious unity both to Spain and Portugal. Surrounded by sea on three sides and protected by the Pyrenees on the fourth, the Iberian

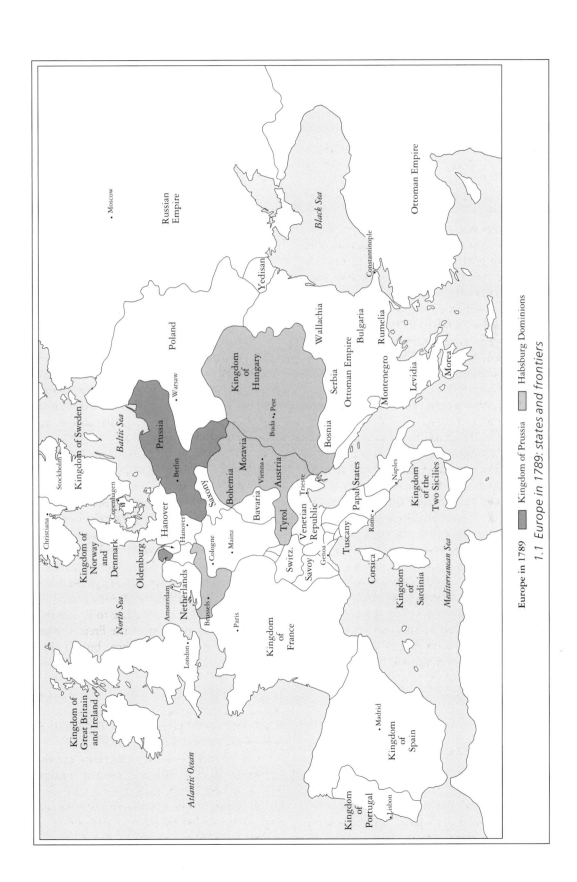

Europe in 1789 | ▨ Kingdom of Prussia | ▨ Habsburg Dominions

1.1 Europe in 1789: states and frontiers

peninsula was well defended by natural frontiers. A militant Catholicism stimulated by the warfare against the Moors helped to unite the Christian inhabitants even if it divided them from Jews and Muslims. The crowns of Castile and Aragon were formally united with the marriage of King Ferdinand of Aragon to Queen Isabella of Castile in 1469. But local loyalties were still powerful. There was a serious revolt in Catalonia in the 1640s, and it was not until the *Nueva Planta* (New Plan) in 1716 that Spain was transformed 'from a collection of semi-autonomous provinces into a centralized state' (J.H. Elliott, *Imperial Spain*, London, Arnold, 1963, p. 372). Portugal emerged with her present boundaries in the fifteenth century, and was sufficiently advanced to lay the foundations of her great commercial empire in Africa, the Far East and Brazil in the sixteenth. Spain, covetous of her wealthy neighbour, seized the opportunity of a disputed succession to lay claim to the Portuguese throne in 1580, but after a lengthy struggle which began in 1640 and lasted until 1665, the Portuguese regained their independence.

The Italian peninsula, despite its historic role as the centre first of the Roman empire and then of the Catholic Church, had lost all of its political cohesion and much of its religious pre-eminence. Italy retained her cultural attractions, and the cities of Venice, Florence, Rome and Naples drew intellectuals like Goethe as well as English gentry doing the Grand Tour. But a succession of invasions by the Spanish, the French and the Austrians had reduced most of the peninsula to foreign rule. The territorial changes that took place in the eighteenth century alone show just how little control Italians had over their own destiny.

By the treaty of Utrecht in 1713 Milan, Naples and Sardinia were handed over to the Habsburg emperor, Charles VI, while Sicily went to the Duke of Savoy. In 1718 Savoy acquired Sardinia in exchange for Sicily, which went to the emperor. In 1734 Don Carlos, eldest son of Philip V of Spain, gained Naples from the Habsburgs and by the treaty of Vienna in 1735 he also acquired Sicily. In compensation, Tuscany went to Leopold, second son of the Habsburg empress Maria Theresa. In central Italy the Papacy still exercised its temporal authority over the Papal States, which stretched from Rome almost to Venice. Though all eighteenth century popes were Italian, it was only in the republics of Genoa and Venice that native Italian governments survived, and they were too small and vulnerable to survive the external pressures brought by the French Revolution.

The Low Countries (present-day Belgium and Holland) had long been the focus of rival attentions from their more powerful neighbours. They were acquired by Spain as the result of a dynastic marriage in the sixteenth century, but the insensitivity of Spanish rule provoked a revolt in 1566 which continued, despite a twelve-year truce from 1609 to 1621, until 1648. The seven northern provinces gained their independence and became the United Provinces, otherwise known as the Netherlands. The southern provinces, predominantly Catholic, remained under Spanish rule until the treaty of Utrecht in 1713, when they were transferred to Austria and became part of the Habsburg inheritance. The Low Countries had been fought over so often that the area became known as the cockpit of Europe, a description that was to be equally apt in the nineteenth and twentieth centuries.

To the north, the kingdom of Denmark was joined to Norway, but in other respects occupied much of the territory she does today. Sweden made a determined bid to become a great power in the seventeenth century by expanding into Europe south of the Baltic into much of present-day Poland and Germany. But she had been forced into retreat in the wars of the eighteenth century, chiefly by Russia and Prussia, and by 1789 had been reduced to her present boundaries.

It was to the east that the map of Europe bore least resemblance to the present one. Much of central Europe came under the nominal authority of the Holy Roman Empire. Founded by Charlemagne, it owed the first word of its title chiefly to the occasion on Christmas Day 800 when Charlemagne was crowned in St Peter's Rome by Pope Leo III. Charlemagne was evidently unprepared for the Pope's action, and asserted that he would not have entered St Peter's had he known the Pope's intentions. Be that as it may, he took upon himself the obligation to be the secular head of the recreated Roman empire in the west as the Pope was its spiritual head. In a famous gibe Voltaire declared in 1756 that the empire was 'neither holy, Roman nor an empire' (*Essai sur les Moeurs et l'Esprit des Nations*). Successive emperors had certainly not embraced Charlemagne's religious obligations, though most of them remained loyal to the Catholic faith. By 1789 any links with the Roman empire were at best tenuous. But the empire still had some life in it. Though the emperor was formally chosen by eight electors, the imperial title had been vested in the house of Habsburg since 1356. True, Maria Theresa's accession had been challenged in 1740, because she was a woman; but she had made good her claim, and Habsburgs continued to rule the empire until its end. What weakened the empire were its multifarious divisions. It consisted of no fewer than 2,303 territories, ranging from large states like Prussia and Saxony to bishoprics such as Mainz, Imperial Cities such as Regensburg and individual dukedoms or cathedral chapters. In the Imperial Diet or Reichstag sixty-five ecclesiastics, forty-five dynastic princes and fifty to sixty imperial cities were entitled to representation. These divisions were exacerbated by the religious split which had been a consequence of the Reformation. In 1555 the Peace of Augsburg had given to all rulers the right to determine the religion of their subjects under the formula *cuius regio, eius religio* (let the subject conform to the religion of his sovereign). The controversies to which this formula led helped to spark off the Thirty Years War (1618–48), and though religious animosities died down in the eighteenth century it was still possible for the archbishop of Salzburg to expel Protestants from his domain in 1731.

The emperor's authority over his many subjects was mediated through the rulers of the states, cities and bishoprics over which he presided. When one of them, Frederick II (the Great) of Prussia attacked Silesia in 1740, Maria Theresa despite her many efforts to do so was unable to get it back. Significantly, prayers for the emperor ceased to be said in Prussian churches in 1750.

A distinction must be drawn between the territorial extent of the Holy Roman Empire and the Habsburgs' own possessions, some of which were in the empire and some of which were not. Inside were Austria, Bohemia, Silesia (until 1740) and Moravia; outside were Hungary, Milan, Parma and Piacenza, and the Austrian Netherlands. In these latter territories, the emperor's powers were greater, if not unchallenged. Both Maria Theresa and her son Joseph II attempted to draw these scattered lands into some kind of administrative unity; they all came under the authority of the Geheimrat (the conference or secret council) and the Hofkammer or council of finance (Hufton, *Europe: Privilege and Protest*, p. 157). Significantly many of the reforms which Joseph II attempted to implement ran into such localised opposition that he was forced to withdraw them.

By 1789 Habsburg power within the empire had already been challenged by Prussia. Unlike most of the other states, Prussia had grown in extent, population and power. Between 1713 and 1780 she had acquired 76,000 square miles, made up of Silesia, West Prussia and a few possessions in the Rhineland. Her population had risen from 2.2 million to 5 million. Frederick the Great could put an army of 150,000 men in the field. Though her territories in the east and the west were widely separated, an efficient civil service, largely staffed by a loyal nobility, and an effective tax system gave to Prussia a leverage that was disproportionate to her resources or land area.

Further to the east lay the country whose claim to be a European power was most in doubt. Despite the westernising policies of Peter the Great (1689–1725), Russia's destiny lay in Asia as much as it did in Europe. Russia experienced neither the Renaissance nor the Reformation. Her religion and political system owed more to the Byzantine than to the Roman empire. When Prince Vladimir returned to Kiev from Constantinople in 988 it was the Greek Orthodox rather than the Roman Catholic variety of Christianity that he imposed on his subjects. In consequence the Russian Tsar was to be the religious as well as the secular ruler of his subjects.

By the end of the eighteenth century the kingdom of Kiev had expanded to take in Muscovy, Estonia, Latvia and the territories bordering the Gulf of Finland, mainly during the reign of Peter the Great. Under Catherine the Great (1762–96) the process of expansion was extended into Poland, the Ukraine and the Crimea. At the same time Russian explorers and settlers moved east into Siberia. A Russian had reached the Bering straits as early as 1649. Lacking natural frontiers to the east or to the west, Russia was prey to invasion from both directions, but equally, when strong and united, capable of expansion as well. At the end of the eighteenth century Russian ambitions impinged on Europe from two directions: control of Poland on the west and control of the straits which linked the Black Sea to the Mediterranean, the Dardanelles.

To the south of Russia lay the Ottoman empire, which both encroached on to the European continent (see Map 1.1) but extended far beyond it. The Ottomans established themselves as the ruling tribe in Anatolia in the fourteenth century, taking their name from one of their early rulers, Osman I (1281–1326). From Anatolia they spread southeast to the Persian Gulf, north-east to the Caspian Sea, westwards into the Mediterranean and northwest into the Balkan peninsula. At its greatest, under Suleiman the Magnificent (1522–66) the empire extended up to Budapest in the Balkans, to Tiflis in Georgia to Algiers in North Africa and Baghdad in the Middle East. The Ottoman empire differed most notably from European states through its devotion to Islam. The Sultan was both the religious and political leader of the empire. His authority was not limited by any constitutional checks. He had a large standing army, stiffened by a corps of Janissaries, recruited from his conquered Christian subjects. In the sixteenth and seventeenth centuries they were regarded as the most formidable soldiers in Europe. But the empire also suffered from certain intrinsic weaknesses. Disputes over the succession were frequent, so long as Sultans were allowed to have more than one wife. Much hinged upon the capacity of the man who eventually gained the throne. So long as the empire was expanding, the loyalty of the landowning class could be bought with the promise of further rewards, but once the process of expansion was halted, as it was by the end of the seventeenth century, internal revolts were all too possible. The empire never developed the strong centralised administration and fiscal system needed to ensure its survival. Local chieftains and elites were constantly usurping the Sultan's authority.

Every attempt to modernise the country by adopting western styles of dress, technology and methods of government was apt to arouse opposition from Islamic fundamentalists. The Grand Vizier Halil Hamid was assassinated in 1785, attacked as an enemy of Islamic law for having accepted French military advisers. When Sultan Selim III employed western educated young men with the aim of reforming the army, the financial system and the administration, they too became victims of a savage purge by conservative elements in 1807. These efforts to imitate the west, and the opposition they aroused, were to be a continuous theme in Ottoman history and illustrate the ambivalent character of the empire, at once part of Europe and in conscious opposition to it.

European attitudes to the Ottoman empire showed a similar ambivalence. On the one hand voices were frequently raised in condemnation of Turkish atrocities, particularly when they concerned the Christian subjects of the empire. Gladstone's furious pamphlet in 1876 after suppression of the Bulgarian revolt alleged that 'no government ever has so sinned; none has proved itself so incorrigible'. On the other hand the Ottoman empire could prove a welcome obstacle in the face of Russian expansion into the Balkan peninsula and towards the Dardanelles. Austria, France and Britain were all at one time or another to come to the Ottoman empire's assistance when faced with this threat.

A succession of Russo-Turkish wars in the second half of the eighteenth century raised such fears. Under the treaty of Kutchuk Kainardji (1774) Russia gained the right to protect Christians in the Ottoman empire and her merchant ships were granted free extract into the Mediterranean. In 1783 Russia annexed the Crimea and established a protectorate over much of Georgia. In 1792 they acquired the powerful fortress of Ochakov, just west of the Crimean peninsula, provoking British and Prussian opposition.

The Ottoman empire became proverbially known as 'the sick man of Europe' (the phrase was first coined by Tsar Nicholas I in 1853) and suggestions for its partition were made as early as 1782 by Catherine the Great. In practice it did not lose the last of its Balkan possessions until the Balkan wars of 1912–13 or its Arab provinces until 1923. The weakness of the empire was to be a constant source of tension, mainly because while Russia hoped to gain from the empire's dissolution, the other powers of Europe had a vested interest in its survival.

Forms of government

The varieties of state which characterised Europe in the late eighteenth century were reflected in their differing forms of government. No state had a written constitution except Sweden, which acquired one in 1772. There was no common constitutional pattern, and no ideal model to which states might seek to conform. Some generalisations are still possible, however. For the great majority of states, the norm was a hereditary monarchy, vested in a well-established ruling house: in Britain the Hanoverians; in France the Bourbons; in Spain, the Bourbon family had also secured the succession in 1701; in the Holy Roman Empire the Habsburgs; in Russia the Romanovs and in Prussia the house of Hohenzollern. There were struggles over the succession, notably the 1715 and 1745 rebellions in Britain; the attempt to exclude Maria Theresa from the succession to the empire in 1740–48; and the deposition and murder of Peter III of Russia in 1762. But by comparison with the wars of the Roses in England in the fifteenth century, the French wars of religion in the sixteenth century and the challenges to monarchy all over Europe in the seventeenth century, eighteenth century monarchs looked reasonably secure, at any rate until 1789.

Exceptions were to be found, notably in Poland and in the United Provinces. In Poland 'aristocratic constitutionalism had run amok' (Hufton, *Europe: Privilege and Protest*, p. 134) with the consequence that the elected king was little more than the nominee of a foreign ruler, and dependent on the support of a self-interested nobility. In the United Provinces, while the house of Orange had a hereditary claim to the stadtholderate of Holland, and to command of the army, real power rested with the Estates General, on which all seven provinces were represented.

The terms absolute monarchy and enlightened despotism have often been applied to eighteenth century government. But even where there were no constitutional restraints, every ruler operated within certain constraints. Taxes were universally

unpopular; changes, even when well intentioned, were certain to be resisted by vested interests likely to be damaged by them; poor communications, lack of adequate information and the general absence of a trained civil service meant that reforms were difficult to implement even when they had been agreed.

In some countries there were effective barriers to royal authority. In Britain the 1688 Revolution, which replaced James II with William III, and the Act of Settlement of 1701 vesting the succession in the Hanoverian dynasty meant that the king owed his position to parliamentary statute rather than hereditary right. Parliament's powers over taxation ensured that it was summoned annually and gave it significant influence over policy. In Sweden, the United Provinces, the Austrian Netherlands and in parts of France such as Brittany, elected assemblies retained a similar right to vote taxes. By comparison there were no such checks in Spain, Portugal, Russia or in most of the Italian peninsula. At one extreme, Catherine the Great of Russia was an unashamed apologist for absolute monarchy: 'There is no better form of government than autocracy for it combines the strength of law with the executive despatch of a single authority' (Brendan Sims, 'The eastern empires from the ancien regime to the challenge of the French Wars, 1780–1806', in P.M. Pilbeam (ed.) *Themes in Modern European History*, London, Routledge, 1995, p. 67). At the other extreme, a British House of Commons voted in 1780 that 'the influence of the Crown has increased, is increasing and ought to be diminished.' But except across the Atlantic where the American colonists took pride in establishing a republic in 1783, monarchy was generally accepted as the most appropriate form of government.

Whatever the constitutional checks, all monarchs except arguably the British one retained control over appointments, foreign policy and the initiation of change. They had at their disposal standing armies, and in some cases navies, which increased rapidly as the century progressed. By its end Prussia could put into the field an army of 190,000, the Habsburg empire an army of 300,000, Russia one of 458,000 and France one of 187,000. Britain and the United Provinces had regular forces of about 25,000 and in Britain's case a navy of 84,000 to man 173 ships (1783). Such forces were there for a purpose. Frederick the Great was a successful exponent of his own maxim: 'The first task of a prince is to survive, the second to expand'. But he was imitated by most of the other crowned heads of Europe. Catherine pushed Russia's frontiers southwards into the Crimea. Joseph II of Austria spent his final years trying to absorb Bavaria and in war against the Turks. The rulers of France and Britain were engaged in a contest for territory in the New World and in India throughout most of the century, which was punctuated by wars of conquest: the war of the Spanish succession, 1701–13; the war of the Polish succession, 1733; the war of the Austrian succession, 1741–48; the Seven Years War, 1756–63; the War of American Independence (in which France, Spain and the United Provinces joined), 1776–83 and the Russo-Turkish war of 1768–74. These wars inevitably imposed huge financial strains and absorbed the lion's share of taxation. Where taxes did not suffice loans had to be raised. By 1789 60 per cent of France's revenue was being used to pay interest on the national debt. Thus while in theory and in practice European monarchies enjoyed considerable powers, these had to be exercised in an increasingly difficult environment to which they themselves had often contributed by their aggressive policies.

THE ENLIGHTENMENT

This survey of Europe before the French Revolution concludes with a brief examination of the ways in which their world was interpreted, at least by the literate elite who thought about it. The term Enlightenment has long been used to describe their leading ideas and attitudes, and whatever limitations now attach to the term it still provides the best key to understanding the intellectual atmosphere of the late eighteenth century. The Enlightenment embraced so many different thinkers and institutions that it is impossible to describe it as a movement. It is perhaps better seen as a change in the climate of opinion when many received ideas were attacked and new ones came to the fore. In 1784 in a famous essay, the German

philosopher Immanuel Kant addressed the question *Was ist Aufklärung?* (What is Enlightenment?). Kant's response was that Enlightenment was the

emergence of man from his self-imposed infancy. Infancy is the inability to use one's reason without the guidance of another. It is self-imposed, when it depends on a deficiency, not of reason, but of the resolve and courage to use it without external guidance. Thus the watchword of the Enlightenment is: *Sapere aude!* [Dare to Know!] Have the courage to use one's own reason!
(quoted in Peter Gay, *The Enlightenment: An Interpretation, The Science of Freedom*, London, Wildwood House, 1973, p. vii)

As a consequence, men were ready to reject the dual authority of monarchy, as divinely ordained, and of a Church endowed with the monopoly of truth. But there was a constructive side to the Enlightenment, too. Many of its representatives believed in the possibility of progress or improvement through the application of reason to human concerns and institutions.

The destructive, critical side of the Enlightenment is best seen in the attack mounted on revealed religion in general and on the Roman Catholic Church in particular. In 1757 David Hume, the Scottish philosopher, published *The Natural History of Religion*, in which he explained religious belief as a response to the primitive fears and aspirations of ancient man. Hume also challenged the existence of miracles in his *Essay on Human Understanding* in 1748. In 1770 Baron d'Holbach went so far as to produce a defence of atheism in his *Système de la Nature*. The Catholic Church came under particular attack from the French writer Voltaire, who in 1763 in his *Traité sur la Tolérance* made a notable plea for religious toleration following the notorious Calas case, when a Protestant father had been broken on the wheel, supposedly for killing his son to prevent his conversion to Catholicism. It should be stressed that such literature evidently did little to affect the practice of Christianity until the outbreak of the French Revolution. The eighteenth century also witnessed the last great age of church building, of which the magnificent baroque churches of southern Germany are a prime example; they, and the religious music of Haydn and Mozart, much of it dating from the 1780s, should warn us against assuming that the critics of Christianity had it all their own way. Nonetheless in France criticism of the Church was so strong that when the Revolution came it would be a prime target.

Absolute monarchy and the world of privilege also came in for critical scrutiny. Again, it was French authors who were most influential. In *L'Esprit des Lois* (The Spirit of the Laws), published in 1748, Montesquieu attacked despotism and expressed his preference for a balanced constitution in which executive power would be checked. In the Encyclopédie, launched by Diderot and d'Alembert in 1751, the article on Political Authority stated categorically: 'No man has received from nature the right to command others. Liberty is a present from Heaven' (Black, *Eighteenth Century Europe*, pp. 211–12). A much more radical attack on existing forms of government was launched by Rousseau, who in 1762 published *Du Contrat Social* (Of the Social Contract). It began with the electrifying sentence 'Man was born free, but now he is everywhere in chains.' Its central message was that in a civil society men could retain their freedom only by acting in conformity with the general will, the will of the majority.

The constructive side to the Enlightenment is best represented by the Cameralist writers in Germany such as Christian Wolff. In his book *Rational Thoughts on the Social Life of Mankind*, first published in 1721, Wolff argued for state intervention to provide better education and welfare services such as hospitals and orphanages. One of the most influential books written in the eighteenth century was Cesar Beccaria's *Dei delitti e dell pene* (Of Crimes and Punishment). Published in 1765, it was translated into all the major European languages, and led to the reform of many criminal codes. Torture was abolished in most European countries by the end of the eighteenth century. Religious toleration came to be seen as desirable for its own sake, not just as expedient.

Most eighteenth century monarchs were influenced by the new ideas that were circulating and tried to translate some of them at least into action. Frederick the Great of Prussia described the role of the enlightened monarch in these terms: 'Idleness, pleasure-seeking and imbecility are the causes which keep princes from the noble task of securing

the happiness of their people. The sovereign is the first servant of the state' (S. Andrews, *Eighteenth Century Europe, the 1680s to 1815*, London, Longman, 1965, p. 119). Joseph II, Holy Roman Emperor from 1765 to 1790, embarked on an ambitious programme of reform which included the extension of religious toleration to Jews and Protestants, the dissolution of many contemplative religious orders with the aim of using their resources to provide a properly paid priesthood, the abolition of censorship and the ending of serfdom. In practice, many of these reforms had to be abandoned in the face of opposition from the vested interests affected and provincial resentment, notably in Hungary and the Austrian Netherlands. That they were attempted at all is witness to the influence of the Enlightenment.

Catherine the Great of Russia corresponded with Voltaire and Diderot, whose library she acquired. In 1767 she summoned a legislative commission to Moscow for which she published her own Instructions. These included statements approving equality before the law, condemning the excessive use of capital punishment and calling for the restriction of serfdom. In practice the achievements of the legislative commission were meagre. Pugachev's rebellion in 1773–74 called for the abolition of serfdom and posed a severe threat to Catherine's authority. With its suppression her reforming instincts gave way to a more reactionary stance and in the Charter of Nobility, issued in 1785, she formally recognised the nobles as a separate estate and confirmed their traditional privileges, including the right to own serfs. By the end of the century it has been estimated that out of a population of 36 million, 19.5 million were privately owned serfs, and 14.5 million were serfs owned by the Church or the state.

The Enlightenment and the role and status of women

Growing interest in women's history has rightly reminded men that for women in the eighteenth century opportunities were limited and their natural inferiority to men, at least in some respects, widely assumed. Women were denied the right to take any part in political life, unless through the accident of birth they inherited a throne. Maria Theresa of Austria and Catherine the Great of Russia were the great exceptions that proved the rule, and were viewed as such. Employment opportunities were equally limited, as Olwen Hufton points out in her remarkable and ground-breaking book, *The Prospect before her: a History of Women in Western Europe, vol. 1, 1500–1800*: 'When in the late eighteenth century women sell their labour in the market, they cook, clean, work in textiles, sew and perform skilled but finicky work, or they teach, tend the sick and cater to the needs of the least privileged members of society' (O.H. Hufton, *The Prospect before her*, London, HarperCollins, 1995, p. 497). The old professions, the Church, the law and medicine were barred to women, but so were the new ones, the civil service, banking and finance, tax collecting and engineering. Marriage remained the goal of upper and lower class women alike, as Jane Austen's novels so clearly indicate. Once married, a wife was expected to obey her husband and to hand over to him all her property and any money she might earn.

The Enlightenment, while it did much to end the slave trade and improved the treatment of criminals and the insane, did very little to alter the status of women. Diderot, despite his readiness to challenge authority, believed that 'women were essentially savages; the veneer of civilization remained skin deep and he firmly believed that they needed to be trained to respect convention as a means of control but also as the way to contentment' (Hufton, *The Prospect before her*, p. 433). Rousseau, a revolutionary thinker in so many ways, urged women to be content with their domestic lot as wives and mothers: 'Her dignity depends on remaining unknown; her glory lies in her husband's esteem, her greatest pleasure in the happiness of her family' (*Émile*, 1770, cited in Linda Colley, *Britons*, London, Pimlico, 1991, p. 240). Only Condorcet among French Enlightenment thinkers was prepared to give women the vote, and then only when they qualified as property owners. Of English writers and thinkers before 1800, only Mary Wollstonecraft and her husband William Godwin were ready to argue that women as well as men should enjoy the rights and duties of citizenship (see her *A Vindication of the Rights of Women*, 1792). The French and industrial revolutions were

to have a limited impact on the roles and status of women, to which reference will be made in subsequent chapters; but it would not be until the latter half of the twentieth century that anything approaching equality would be achieved.

Thus as the eighteenth century drew to a close the established order, while under threat, showed a degree of resilience which indicated just how powerful vested interests continued to be, even in the face of supposedly absolute monarchs bent on reform. While the ideas fostered by the Enlightenment would help to promote revolution in France, elsewhere in Europe their impact outside the charmed circle of the court was much less in evidence.

Further reading

The New Cambridge Modern History, vols 7 and 8 (Cambridge University Press, 1957), is most useful for purposes of reference. C. Cook and J. Stevenson, *The Longman Handbook of Modern European History, 1763–1991* (London, Longman, 1992) is an invaluable compendium of factual information, chronologies, bibliographies and so on. J.M. Roberts, *The Triumph of the West* (London, BBC, 1985) is a magisterial explanation of Europe's emergence to dominance, superbly illustrated.

Norman Davies, *A History of Europe* (Oxford University Press, 1996) is a recent attempt to write the history of the continent from the Stone Age to the twentieth century. It is particularly good on the concept of Europe and in its treatment of eastern Europe. Cultural aspects are generously covered, and there is a wealth of unusual and stimulating detail. The eighteenth century is well summarised in S. Andrews, *Eighteenth Century Europe, the 1680s to 1815* (London, Longman, 1965). J. Black, *Eighteenth Century Europe* (London, Macmillan, 1990) is a sophisticated interpretation, particularly good on social and economic aspects.

O.H. Hufton, *Europe: Privilege and Protest 1730–1789* (London, Fontana, 1980) is good on individual countries as well as general themes. P.M. Pillbeam (ed.) *Themes in Modern European History* (London, Routledge, 1995) has stimulating essays, especially useful on eastern Europe. E.N. Williams, *The Ancien Regime in Europe* (London, Bodley Head,

1979) is another thorough country-by-country survey.

For the Enlightenment, see H. Dunthorne, *The Enlightenment* (London, Historical Association, 1991) a masterly summary of recent research; N. Hampson, *The Enlightenment* (London, Penguin, 1968), a general survey; and J. Yolton *et al.* (eds), *The Blackwell Companion to the Enlightenment* (Oxford, Blackwell, 1990) which is useful for reference purposes. For the role and status of women see O.H. Hufton, *The Prospect before her: a History of Women in Western Europe, vol. 1, 1500–1800 (London, HarperCollins 1996).*

• CHAPTER TWO •

The French Revolution, 1785–89

• CONTENTS •

Key dates

SECTION A

The collapse of the *ancien régime*, 1786–89

The year 1789

SECTION B – SOURCES

Poverty or prosperity as explanations for the French Revolution

KEY DATES

1774		Louis XVI's accession to the throne
1778		France enters American War of Independence against Britain
1781		Necker's Compte Rendu, a statement of government finances
1787	Feb.	Assembly of Notables rejects Calonne's taxation reforms
	May	Assembly of Notables rejects de Brienne's taxation reforms
	July	Paris *parlement* rejects taxation reforms
	Aug.	Paris *parlement* exiled to Troyes
	Nov.	Royal Session of reinstated Paris *parlement*
1788	May	Paris *parlement* demands Estates General
		Lamoignon's Six Edicts suspends all *parlements*
	June	'Night of Tiles' in Grenoble
	Aug.	Government promises Estates General for May 1789 and recalls *parlements*; de Brienne and Lamoignon resign; Necker appointed Comptroller-General of Finances
	Sept.	Paris *parlement* convokes Estates General on 1614 precedent
	27 Dec.	Louis XVI grants double representation to the Third Estate
1789	4 May	Estates General opens at Versailles
	10 June	Third Estate votes for the common verification of credentials
	17 June	Third Estate votes itself 'The National Assembly'
	19 June	First Estate votes to join the Third Estate
	20 June	Tennis Court Oath
	23 June	Royal Session of the Estates General
	12 July	Rising in Paris sparked off by news of Necker's exile
	13 July	National Guard of 48,000 formed in Paris
	14 July	Fall of the Bastille
	17 July	Louis XVI visits Paris
	4/5 Aug.	National/Constituent Assembly abolishes feudalism
	11 Aug.	Decree abolishing feudalism
	26 Aug.	Declaration of the Rights of Man and the Citizen passed by Assembly
	15 Sept.	Assembly grants King a suspensive veto
	5 Oct.	Women's march to Versailles
	6 Oct.	Royal family escorted to Paris and placed in the Tuileries
	20 Oct.	Constituent Assembly moved to the Manège in Paris

SECTION A

THE COLLAPSE OF THE *ANCIEN RÉGIME*, 1786–89

The Bastille, the symbol of the *ancien régime*'s authority, was taken by the Parisian crowd on 14 July 1789. This confirmed that the royal power of the Bourbons had already collapsed. In fact, a power vacuum had appeared before 1789 with clear signs that the government was economically, politically and militarily bankrupt. Things had not been the same since the reign of Louis XIV (1643–1715), which is usually regarded as the highwater mark of the Bourbon dynasty. The Palace of Versailles was built to embody the authority of 'the Sun King' who could proclaim 'L'état c'est moi' (I am the state) with a brash confidence that was completely missing under his great-grandson, Louis XV (1715–74), and Louis XV's own grandson, Louis XVI (1774–93). How had this decline come about?

The influence of the Enlightenment

There were several factors involved, and of course they interacted to erode the authority of the Bourbon government. Perhaps the most difficult to pin down in terms of its results is the general intellectual climate of the eighteenth century Enlightenment. The writers and philosophers of the Enlightenment such as Voltaire, Diderot and Rousseau questioned everything in the spirit of rational enquiry. Inevitably the unchanged teaching of the Church was challenged. The whole approach relied upon the individual's ability to question, to reason and to make choices; in the process an absolutist government whose King claimed the God-given right to rule by heredity was challenged as well.

But French society under the *ancien régime*, and indeed the government itself, proved strangely slow to see the danger in this new thinking. Although Voltaire was exiled, he was allowed to return in 1778 in triumph. Montesquieu wrote *The Spirit of the Laws* in 1748 and argued that despotism could be avoided by having a constitution containing checks and balances; the functions of government should be divided between a legislative, an executive and a judiciary. Despite his criticism of the *ancien régime*, Montesquieu was a nobleman who was very well received in the salons of Paris. Rousseau's *Social Contract* (1762) itself became in a way the pattern for the Jacobin dictatorship (1793–94), yet the language of the general will was actually used by the sovereign legal courts (called *parlements*) whose function was to operate the government of the *ancien régime*. It was, as Rudé has noted, fashionable to be sceptical, and the *ancien régime* appears to have encouraged a movement which helped to damage its own authority: 'that the total impact of their ideas was considerable seems hardly open to doubt' (G. Rudé, *Revolutionary Europe*, London, Fontana, 1964, p. 35; see also G. Rudé, *The French Revolution*, London, Phoenix, 1994, p. 7).

Demographic and economic problems

The demographic and economic problems of eighteenth century France proved hostile to the regime as well. By 1789, the population had grown by about 30 per cent (D.G. Wright, *Revolution and Terror in France, 1789–1795*, London, Longman, 1990, p. 7). In the absence of an industrial revolution as Britain was by then experiencing, great pressure was building up on land and food supplies in what remained mainly an agricultural, peasant economy. Economic growth did occur, the van Rabais textile works employed an exceptionally large workforce of 12,000, and Bordeaux's prosperity reflected the growing trade with the American continent. Marxist historians like Lefebvre and Soboul have drawn attention to the economic ambitions of the capitalist, bourgeois class in transforming the land-based economy of the *ancien régime* into one based upon commerce and industry and dominated by the new entrepreneurial class. But revisionist historians have disputed the class divisions on which much of the Marxist version is based, Blanning for instance concluding: 'With so many bourgeois behaving like nobles and so many nobles behaving like bourgeois, it is difficult to find much evidence of class-conflict between the two' (T.C.W. Blanning, *The French Revolution: Aristocrats versus Bourgeois?*, London, Macmillan, 1989, p. 13). What may be argued with less controversy is that the treaty of Paris in 1763, which concluded the Seven Years War with Britain, deprived France of her colonial empire in Canada, the West Indies, India and Louisiana, and in the process removed an important social and economic escape valve for a France which was becoming overpopulated for her limited economic base. Furthermore, prosperity, tax revenue and the stability of the regime became highly dependent upon trade with America and Europe, which was in turn highly vulnerable to disruption by unrest at home, or by war.

It was in this context that made the government's decision to enter the American war on the side of the colonists and against Britain in 1778 highly dangerous for the survival of the Bourbon regime. For France it held out the prospect of settling the score with Britain, the hated victor of 1763, depriving her of her imperial advantage and recovering some French colonial or at least commercial business across the Atlantic. But it was a high risk strategy, and it did not pay off. In the first place, siding with the American colonists' pursuit of liberties, which the Bourbon monarchy denied its own subjects, dangerously exposed the double standards of the regime and its own confused attitude to the values of the Enlightenment. Second, trade was disrupted and French trade gained little or no post-war benefit, and the British empire was not mortally wounded. Finally, the cost of the war amounted to 1,066 million livres (W. Doyle, *The Oxford History of the French Revolution*, Oxford University Press, 1990, p. 68) and dwarfed the costs of previous wars. This started an indebtedness problem which was to end in government bankruptcy.

Financial weakness

Government indebtedness was perhaps inevitable for a regime which built the Palace of Versailles. The court remained extravagant: ten thousand people lived and worked at Versailles by the time of Louis XVI's reign. Expensive naval projects such as the fortification of Cherbourg by cones (sort of vast naval forts) towed out to sea in the 1780s in what Schama calls 'an expensive fantasy, even perhaps a ruinous fiasco' cost 28 million livres even as they collided, became worm-eaten and sank (S. Schama, *Citizens*, London, Penguin, 1989, p. 59). All of this, together with the funding of the American war, had to be financed by a very narrow tax base, principally the peasantry (see Figure 2.1). The nobility (the Second Estate) had generous tax

A faut esperer q'eu se jeu la finira bentot

2.1 *The peasant's burden: here a peasant woman supports a nun and a noblewoman in this 1789 cartoon*

Source: Musée Carnavalet, Paris

exemptions, although they paid the capitation tax on their revenues and the vingtième tax (of 5 per cent) on their net landed revenues, and the clergy (the First Estate) traditionally paid by *don gratuit* (free gift) an amount decided every ten years; they were exempt from ordinary taxation.

In this delicate situation the government borrowed money by simply selling the right to collect the taxes to Farmers General, who became the most wealthy group within the Third Estate on the proceeds. Of course this procedure relied upon the government appearing creditworthy, and during the American War of Independence the Comptroller-General of Finances, Necker, hit on a clever method of giving this reassuring impression; in 1781 he published the Compte Rendu which showed a healthy surplus of 10 million livres by hiding the 'extraordinary items' of the loans raised to finance the war. Necker's reputation as a brilliant financial wizard was made. However, he had complicated the task of his successors, who had to challenge Necker's honesty before the urgent need to reform the tax system was accepted. This task fell initially on Calonne, who succeeded Necker as Comptroller-General of Finances (1783–87), and who warned that by 1786, with a deficit of 112 million livres on a total revenue of 475 million livres, bankruptcy was looming. In the immediate future half the revenue would be needed just to pay the interest on the loans, most of which had been raised to finance the war and were soon due for capital repayment (Doyle, *French Revolution*, p. 69).

Sweeping reform of the tax system was necessary therefore if the regime was to survive. As Lefebvre points out: 'Technically the crisis was easy to meet: all that was necessary was to make everybody pay' (G. Lefebvre, *The Coming of the French Revolution*, 1939, trans. R.R. Palmer, Princeton University Press, 1989, p. 23). The trouble was that such a change meant overturning the privileged status of the nobility and the clergy. However, the regime depended upon these orders for its authority and its inherited, God-given status. No doubt a despotic regime, energised by a capable monarch, well equipped with the power of a loyal army, could attempt such a change. But the authority of Louis XVI's government proved inadequate for such a task.

The failure of reform

There were several causes of this political weakness. The King himself was conscientious but he was not a decisive or authoritarian character. Fond of hunting and eating and a keen locksmith, he was something of a practical joker (he enjoyed turning on the fountains at Versailles without warning to drench the elegantly dressed strollers) and some of his habits made him a figure of fun in the formal, courtly and traditional environment. It was a talking point that, in an age when the health of France was seen to be represented in the person of the King, his marriage to the Austrian princess Marie Antoinette in 1770 failed to produce an heir until 1778. The Queen was disliked, widely seen as frivolous and interfering. She became the target of the gutter press especially over the 'Diamond Necklace Affair' of 1785 which, probably unfairly, confirmed that she was vain, greedy and extravagant in the eyes of the public (see Schama, *Citizens*, pp. 203–10). One by-product of the Enlightenment was a literacy rate of 50 per cent (Wright, *Revolution*, p. 13) and as a result there was a wide market for stories and cartoons which developed Marie Antoinette's reputation as 'The Austrian Whore', damaged the credibility of the court and the regime, and which were on sale from newsvendors just outside the Palace of Versailles.

Calonne, on becoming Comptroller-General in 1783, was forced by the state of government finances to set out his reform package to the King in 1786. The vingtième was due to expire in 1787 and Calonne proposed that it should be succeeded by a land tax (up to 5 per cent of the value of the holding) which would be assessed by Assemblies of taxpayers. It would involve the privileged orders fully, which would bring in considerably more revenue. A stamp tax would be introduced, government economies enforced, and the economy stimulated by allowing free trade in grain, dismantling internal customs barriers and changing the corvée (a labour requirement) into a tax. Politically, Calonne's problem was that his proposals challenged so many vested interests and threatened the privileged hierarchy of the regime itself for reasons which few saw as essential. Furthermore, Louis XVI lacked the authority to enforce them, and Calonne invented the device of the Assembly of Notables in order to strengthen the hand of the royal government.

The aristocratic revolt

When Calonne's Assembly of Notables met in February 1787, all had been hand-picked by the King and his Comptroller-General. However, the result was a catastrophic failure of political management, one delegate for example arguing that: 'The King does not have the competence to institute a percentage tax but only to ask for a fixed sum to meet specific requirements. Such a tax could not be accepted by the parlements . . . only the Estates General could give the necessary consent to such a tax.' (extracts from the debates of the Assembly of Notables, cited in J. Hardman, *The French Revolution*, London, Arnold, 1991, pp. 36–37).

Calonne's whole purpose in calling the Assembly of Notables had been to avoid submission to the *parlements* and admitting government weakness by convening the Estates General. Far from helping, the Notables demanded precisely what he was hoping to avoid. He was duly replaced as Comptroller-General by de Brienne.

Formerly the archbishop of Toulouse, de Brienne seized the opportunity that his appointment gave him to move to the more lucrative archbishopric of Sens. Much was riding upon his competence; Marie Antoinette herself supported him, he was believed to be a good administrator but Lefebvre adds that he 'was an incompetent ignoramus' (Lefebvre, *Coming of the French Revolution*, p. 28). Although he altered Calonne's reform plan, restricting in particular the land tax, the Assembly continued the so-called 'Noble Revolt' by politely refusing support for his proposal in May 1787. In July de Brienne's plan was considered by the Paris *parlement* in the vain hope that it might give the King's government the authority to implement the tax changes.

The *parlements* were sovereign legal courts, staffed by the 'nobility of the robe'. All laws needed to be registered by the *parlements*, and the jurisdiction of the Paris *parlement* covered about one-third of France, making it by far the most important. Although the monarch could attend the *parlement* in person and dictate registration of a law by *lit de justice*, since the reign of Louis XIV the *parlements* had followed the lead taken by the Paris *parlement* in making demands on the King and obstructing the registration of laws. Worse still for the authority of the *ancien régime*, the *parlements* had made themselves tribunes of public opinion and were using the language of popular government which the Enlightenment had generated. Thus the *parlement* of Toulouse asserted in 1763 that the law must be subject to 'the free consent of the nation', and in 1788 the *parlement* of Rennes would echo the American Declaration of Independence in asserting that 'man is born free, that originally men are equal, these are truths that have no need of proof' (Rudé, *Revolutionary Europe*, p. 75). Such identification by the privileged *parlementaires* with the writings of Rousseau and the constitution of the American Republic would become absurd after the storming of the Bastille (1789), but for the *ancien régime* to eat humble pie and appeal to the *parlement* of Paris in 1787 shows clearly how desperate the King's government had become.

True to form, the Paris *parlement* not only rejected de Brienne's land tax and stamp duty as 'contrary to the rights of the nation' (Wright, *Revolution*, p. 18) but opened wide the whole issue of monarchical power; convening an Estates General was recommended. In August 1787 Louis XVI took up the challenge. By *lit de justice* he exiled the *parlement* of Paris to Troyes. Popular protest was met by the closure of clubs, restrictions on publications and the use of troops to patrol the streets of Paris. De Brienne and the King then made concessions. In September the Paris *parlement* was reinstated and a new, less controversial, plan was announced; the land tax and the stamp duty were abandoned, the *vingtième* prolonged, and the government promised full public accounting. Meanwhile, new loans would be needed to tide the government over and a Royal Session of the Paris *parlement* was called for 19 November to hear the proposal to borrow 420 million livres over the next five years. Government economies were promised. Confident that by 1792 all would be well, de Brienne and the King even promised an Estates General for then. But Louis XVI seems to have destroyed his chances of victory. He shattered the conciliatory session by ordering the registration of

the loans, using the *lit de justice* procedure, and he answered the challenge by declaring 'it's legal because I wish it' (Doyle, *French Revolution*, p. 80).

Confrontation followed quickly. In May 1788 the *parlement* of Paris asserted that only the Estates General had the authority to alter the taxation system. Arrests followed, and the Chancellor, Lamoignon, issued the Six Edicts which suspended all the *parlements* and created a Plenary Court to register laws instead. But again it seems that the government did not have the stomach for a monarchial coup. Pamphlets circulated, full of references to representative government and the general will, and in Grenoble in June soldiers had roof tiles rained upon them. More significantly the army refused to confront rioters in other cities. Furthermore, the harvest of 1788 was very poor, compounding not only the deep-seated economic problems of France but also threatening the government's tax revenue further.

In August 1788 the government backed down. The *parlements* were recalled, Lamoignon and de Brienne resigned and an Estates General was promised for May 1789. Apparently the 'aristocratic revolt' had triumphed. Politically, the *ancien régime* had declared itself at an end, and left the seat of power empty for the successor authority to fill.

THE YEAR 1789

The meeting of the Estates General

The year 1789 saw the passing of the *ancien régime* and the beginning of the new political order, focused upon Paris itself. There, by the end of the year, an uneasy relationship was emerging between the national authority, seeking to establish a constitutional monarchy, and the Parisian authority, the Commune, which championed the rights of the citizen to exercise popular sovereignty if necessary at the point of a pike, the favoured weapon of the *sans-culottes*.

Necker was reappointed as Comptroller-General in September 1788 in the hope that his reputation would enable him to handle the Estates General, which was to be convened on the precedent set in 1614. With firm expectations of the dawning of a new era, political activity exploded; pamphlets, debates and political clubs multiplied as France prepared to elect delegates to the Estates General and to draw up *Cahiers de Doléances* for consideration. A great deal of activity focused not on the clergy (the First Estate) or the nobility (the Second Estate), but upon the claims of the Third to represent the nation as a whole. The social and economic situation had changed since 1614. Commerce had become more important, and the burdens on the peasantry more evident. The tax exemptions allowed the First and Second Estates were more challenged by the thinking of the Enlightenment. The confidence of the opinion-formers in the Third Estate such as Mournier and Barnave from Grenoble, Mirabeau, Duport, Volney and Robespierre (from Artois) was strong. Many were lawyers, and they objected furiously to the adoption of the 1614 precedent for the Estates General because it meant that the Third, who were the bulk of the population, should have only the same number of deputies as each of the Second and First Estates. Furthermore, the Estates would vote by order so allowing the First and Second always to outvote the Third. On 27 December 1788, Louis XVI and Necker granted double representation to the Third Estate against the opposition of five of the seven Princes of the Blood, but as no promise was made to replace voting by order with voting in common, the campaign continued, reaching its most forceful statement in Sieyès's pamphlet of May 1789 entitled *What is the Third Estate?* This argued that it was indeed the nation and it should be able to outvote the other two Estates by voting in common. It should be noted, however, that Sieyès was no democrat and he did not suggest that women or the poor should be active, voting members of the nation. Louis XVI had encouraged the Third by one gesture, while avoiding the kind of alliance which Mirabeau advocated and which would have antagonised the nobility and senior clergy. His efforts at appeasement created the grounds for distrust, and Barentin, the Keeper of the Seals, encouraged this by preventing communication between the King and the Third Estate in May and June 1789.

Following an election procedure of unprecedented scope, the Estates General opened on 4 May 1789 with a procession of the eleven hundred deputies at Versailles. Most of the Third were lawyers or government officers, and only 13 per cent were businessmen (Wright, *Revolution*, p. 23). Among the deputies of the First were only 22 *parlementaires*, their pose as champions of popular government had been destroyed when they supported the 1614 precedent which denied the Third double representation. More significantly, of the 303 deputies of the First Estate, 192 were parish *curés*, many of whom proved eager to support the claims of the Third Estate and to disassociate themselves from the canons and bishops who sought to preserve their privileges.

The King's speech to the expectant assembly was relatively brief, but neither he nor Necker had anything of substance to propose (see Figure 2.2). Necker's minute exposure of the state of the government's accounts lasted for three hours and drove even the King to yawning, and in the weeks that followed events began to assume a momentum of their own. Louis XVI fidgeted and hunted, but then withdrew to Marly to mourn the death of the Dauphin. Meanwhile the Estates General wrangled about voting procedure and the Third, which continued to meet separately, became increasingly exasperated by its exclusion. On 10 June the Third Estate voted by 494 in favour and 41 against for the common verification of credentials, which was to say the voting of all the deputies together. This would enable the double representation of the Third to outvote the combined deputies of the First and Second Estates once some of the *curés* joined them, as they did from 13 June. On 17 June the deputies of the Third voted themselves the 'National Assembly' and claimed that any dissolution would make taxation invalid. By these steps the deputies of the Third Estate were seeking to fill the power vacuum through claiming to embody popular sovereignty.

Even as the First Estate climbed aboard the bandwagon and voted to join the Assembly on 19 June, rumours of a confrontation with the King's fading power circulated. Troop movements were reported, a Royal Session of the Estates General was scheduled for 23 June and it seemed that Marie Antoinette and her tough-minded brother-in-law, the Compte d'Artois, were stiffening the King to face down the revolutionary claims to

2.2 Louis XVI (top left) presides over the first meeting of the Estates General, 5 May 1789. To his right sit 291 clergy, to his left 270 nobles, and facing him are the 578 deputies of the third estate. Painted by Charles-Auguste Couder in 1839

Source: Chateau de Versailles et Trianon © Photo R.M.N.

sovereignty. But events were to develop further before this could be staged.

No one seems to have told the deputies of the Third Estate that their meeting place of the *Salon des Menus Plaisirs* was closed on 20 June merely in order to prepare it for the Royal Session to come. Sinister fears that a monarchical coup was in progress took hold, and the deputies took themselves off to the building which housed the royal tennis court where all but one swore not to disperse until a constitution had been drafted. This was the oath that bound them to defiance, and some members of the clergy joined the deputies of the Third Estate in their revolutionary act.

Coming after such gestures, the Royal Session of 23 June was bound to ring hollow. The King rejected the claims of the 'National Assembly', decreed that the Estates should meet and vote separately, but acknowledged that the Estates General's consent was required for any changes to the taxation system. The session was then declared closed. Mirabeau, however, rallied the Third to

remain in session and the King left the deputies in possession of the hall, untroubled by any military action.

Events in Paris

It was events in Paris which now advanced the claim of popular sovereignty to fill the space that the King's government had so plainly left empty. Troops, probably unpaid, were refusing to fire on the demonstrators who protested at Necker's apparently enforced resignation of 23 June, and on 27 June the King reinstated Necker and instructed the First and Second Estates to join the Third in a common Assembly. Many at Versailles were worried by the disorder in Paris, and compromise was desired. But suspicion that the King, no doubt pressed by the Queen and Artois, was preparing for a show of force was fuelled by troop movements from the frontier to Paris where a force of 20,000 was mustered by early July (Doyle, *French*

Revolution, p. 108). As they were not actually used, presumably because their loyalty was doubted, Louis XVI's explanation that they were necessary for public order has left his real attitude ambiguous.

The government certainly possessed sufficient power to provoke, but not to deter Paris. This became clear when on 11 July Necker was exiled, evidently due to a plot by the Queen and Artois. The next day the capital exploded in fury and support for its adopted hero of the moment. Hunger played a part – by early 1789 89 per cent of the average wage was spent on bread – but the primary motive of the Parisian mob appeared to be to gather arms to defend itself from the expected military assault. During the night of 12–13 July the *tocsin* (alarm bell) sounded and the abbey of Saint Lazare was raided early the next day; the discovery of substantial stocks of grain proved to many that there was a 'famine plot' and that the food shortages were created by the government to control the population. Hampson comments that what 'transformed the movement from a riot into a revolution was the readiness of the bourgeoisie to take control instead of turning to the king for protection against the threat to property' (N. Hampson, *A Social History of the French Revolution*, London, Routledge, 1988, p. 71). Later on 13 July the electors of Paris, who had represented the sixty electoral districts of the capital in May but had continued to meet, took the important step of setting up a National Guard. This citizens' militia of 48,000 was intended to maintain order, but it was also an act of open defiance to the King, who had forbidden such a step, and it carried with it the clear message that government troops and plans were not trusted in Paris.

If ever a government needed to call upon force, it was now. But the army was demoralised, a prey to revolutionary ideas and disintegrating. Furthermore the government's ability to pay its troops, so long in doubt, disappeared with its last shred of creditworthiness on 13 July when a severe hailstorm destroyed the ripening harvest in the Paris basin. With the crop ruined, few taxes could be paid, and no financier would advance a loan to the regime on the security of future taxation. Bankruptcy followed in August.

In its continuing quest for gunpowder, the Parisian crowd besieged the fortress of the Bastille on 14 July. This eight-towered fourteenth century fortress with walls towering 70 feet above the Faubourg Saint-Antoine had for long been a state prison, but its location and its grim reputation made it the embodiment of the repressive government of the *ancien régime*. Thinly defended and besieged by the angry crowd, including a sizeable proportion of defecting soldiers, the Governor of the Bastille, de Launay, surrendered. Eighty-three besiegers died in the battle to seize the large supply of powder, liberate all seven prisoners and, symbolically, all of France. The victors of the day were principally the Parisian *sans-culottes*, the artisans and labourers, reinforced by some proprietors (who would soon lay claim to being *sans-culottes* as the revolution made this status desirable) and the defecting French Guards who had brought up cannon. De Launay was hacked down outside, his head stuck on a pike and paraded through the streets together with the severed hand of another which still clasped a key to the gate of the fortress. The storming of the Bastille was the first of the revolution's *journées*, the direct intervention of popular sovereignty in affairs, and Schama makes much of the gory triumphalism which accompanied its celebration as the forerunner of the mob violence and Terror to come (Schama, *Citizens*, pp. 404–06).

Power now rested in Paris in the hands of the Commune. This was the municipal authority comprising representatives from the forty-eight Sections of the city under Mayor Bailly, and the National Guard, led by the veteran of the American war, Lafayette. At Versailles, the consequences were rapid. Necker was recalled, Louis XVI recognised the National Assembly and courageously journeyed to Paris on 17 July. Even as he was demonstrating his acceptance of the new political order by appearing at the Hôtel de Ville with Bailly and Lafayette, wearing the revolutionary cockade of red, white and blue, Artois was in flight to the frontier; the Court party was defeated, but it did not suffer the humiliating popularisation which the Bourbon King faced in Paris.

Revolutionary changes followed. Municipal authorities were replaced and suspicion of the nobility and senior clergy became clear in some cities. Events in Paris sparked an explosion of peasant disturbances in the countryside. These expressed a mixture of desperation at the harvest failures, a traditional belief in the existence of a landowners' conspiracy to starve them into submission, and the interesting view that in attacking the nobility, burning the records of feudal obligations and sometimes chateaux as well, the peasants were following the wishes of the King who had himself confronted the nobility. This rural uproar was followed by 'the Great Fear' when peasant communities expected aristocratic vengeance to descend upon them.

Constitutional changes

The response to the disturbances was less spectacular. The property owners who dominated the new authorities feared the disorder particularly, and the National Guard was used in some areas to restore the situation. More shrewdly the National Assembly in an all-night sitting on 4–5 August proclaimed that it 'abolishes the feudal system entirely' (The August Decrees, cited in Hardman, *French Revolution*, p. 108). Of course much lay behind this gesture, and the decree of 11 August made clear that redemption payments would be required from the peasantry instead of some of the feudal obligations, but in reality it was merely an insurance. The Assembly was recognising that the feudal system had already ceased to function and hoped that this grand gesture would ensure the survival of their own property. Thus the National Assembly was showing itself already to be the prisoner of events rather than their author.

The National Assembly was now clearly a Constituent Assembly, addressing the task of drawing up a constitution for the new revolutionary order. On 26 August the Assembly finally concluded its lengthy debate and voted through the Declaration of the Rights of Man and the Citizen. The rule of law was central, and this was defined with a clear echo of Rousseau as 'the expression of the general will'. Sovereignty resided in the nation, a clear rejection of the hereditary principle of the *ancien régime*, and 'the natural and imprescriptible rights of man' were defined as liberty, security and resistance to oppression, and property – a point particularly dear to the hearts of the well-off deputies who were at the centre of affairs at this time. Freedom of religion was established despite the opposition

of the Church (Declaration of Rights, cited in Hardman, *French Revolution*, pp. 114–17). The double purpose of the Declaration was to forestall both counter-revolution and anarchy, but in the process the Assembly established the ringing affirmation of individual rights of French citizens who were no longer the subjects of an absolute monarch.

Despite his effort in July to come to terms with the new order, Louis XVI was opposed to the Assembly's decrees on feudalism and rights. By September debate centred upon the question of what authority the King should be allowed to retain, and the King's attitude coloured the discussion considerably. The proposal was to give the King power to delay decrees for three years, that is a suspensive veto. The Assembly supported the lead given by the Patriot group, led by Barnave, Duport and the Lameth brothers, and followed the hint dropped by Necker that granting this would speed up the King's approval for the August decrees, and passed the suspensive veto by 673 votes to 352 on 15 September.

The Constituent Assembly's vote immediately prompted the active mistrust of popular opinion. In Paris Marat's journal *L'Ami du Peuple* was breathed into life by the reaction, and Desmoulins' pamphlet *The Lantern's Tales* made great play of the threat to lynch from lamp-posts the 'aristocrats' who sought to preserve the power of the monarch. Significantly, one of the deputies who had argued that the Constituent Assembly itself embodied the general will and should not be impeded by any royal veto was heard with increasing respect; his name was Maximilien Robespierre.

The march to Versailles

It was in part this growing political distance between Versailles and Paris which launched the second great *journée* of the year, but there were other provocations too. Food shortages provoked disturbances in the capital. Louis then ordered the Flanders Regiment to Versailles, and the loyalty of these troops was beyond doubt. Soon after their arrival he announced on 18 September that he did not support some parts of the decree abolishing feudalism, and on 4 October he objected to the Declaration of Rights. It seemed that the *ancien régime* was poised to act against the revolution, and the *tocsin* greeted the morning of 5 October in some districts of Paris. The market women played a leading role. Traditionally they believed that they had a right to riot if food was not available at a 'just price', and it seemed to them that the revolution had lost its way if there were still shortages months after the Bastille had fallen. Rudé quotes a witness saying: 'These women said loudly that the men didn't know what it was all about and they wanted a hand in things.' (cited in G. Rudé, *The Crowd in the French Revolution*, Oxford University Press, 1967, p. 69).

Crowds of market women and some menfolk converged on the Hôtel de Ville, gathered some arms including cannon, and set out in the pouring rain for Versailles. Their apparent aim was to bring home to the King the dire shortages being experienced in Paris, and to replace his bodyguard with those who were more in tune with the revolution. According to Olwen Hufton, this was a 'time honoured' and unoriginal purpose. However, she goes on to point out: 'The chief baker [the King] must know what is going on. He must be made to leave the artificiality of the court. Here, the movement assumed originality' (O.H. Hufton, 'Voilà la citoyenne', *History Today*, May 1989). This purpose involved a readiness to threaten force, and it was to be decisive with the help of the National Guard. Lafayette had been obliged to lead his National Guard after them, in the process giving the 'women's march to Versailles' the status of a metropolitan coup against the government of France at Versailles.

Arriving at Versailles on the evening of 5 October, the peaceful stand-off was threatened early the next morning when the royal bodyguard killed a number of the crowd who had entered the palace. The enraged mob was appeased only by the appearance of the Royal family on the balcony with Lafayette, and by their agreement to come to Paris immediately. For good measure Louis sanctioned both the decrees on the abolition of feudalism and the Declaration of Rights.

The King and his family were escorted to the Tuileries palace in Paris on 6 October by the triumphant crowd of some 6,000, and two weeks later the Constituent Assembly followed them, taking up residence in the nearby riding school,

the Manège. The government of France had been taken prisoner less by the Parisian authorities than by the *menu peuple*, the common people who had forced Bailly and Lafayette to support their great intervention. The political clubs and the associated journals were far more in tune with their real power than the Assembly itself, and the fate of the monarchy looked increasingly insecure as support for a republic developed. Paris, the *sans-culottes* and those who could appeal to them, were now in control of events.

SECTION B – SOURCES

POVERTY OR PROSPERITY AS EXPLANATIONS FOR THE FRENCH REVOLUTION

In the orthodox or Marxist view of the coming of revolution, the condition of poverty among the urban and rural poor, the *sans-culottes* and the peasantry, made them both desperate for bread and resentful at the burdens of taxation imposed by the regime (extract D). Their display of power was the 'popular revolution' identified by Lefebvre and symbolised by the storming of the Bastille. The bourgeoisie, the most vocal group within the Third Estate, were resentful at the taxation from which the privileged orders were exempt, and eager for the power and status to which their numbers and wealth entitled them, sparked off the process by challenging the regime at the Estates General (extract E).

More recent work has revised (hence the 'revisionist' label) this Marxist orthodoxy. Blanning has drawn attention to the difficulty of separating nobility from bourgeoisie which makes the class-based analysis simplistic, and there is evidence that the Third Estate's attitudes were also to be found within the First and Second Estates (extract C). The role of the bourgeoisie has been developed by the revisionists such as Hampson who argues 'their intention was to replace the *ancien régime* by a society based on the political and economic ideas of the Enlightenment' (Hampson, *Social History*, p. 63). Certainly, the Declaration of the Rights of Man (extract F) seems to reflect both Enlightened ideas and bourgeois, property-owning self-interest, which, rather than producing a wholly new intellectual explanation of the coming of the revolution, takes the argument back to take in the orthodox view of poverty and prosperity as being the cause. No explanation can be complete without considering government poverty and the difficulties the *ancien régime* faced in changing the taxation system in order to pay its way (extracts A and B); was the political-constitutional crisis which caused the power vacuum political or economic in nature?

A From Calonne's speech at the opening of the Assembly of Notables, 22 February 1787

Yes, gentlemen, abuses . . . are defended by self-interest, influence, wealth and ancient prejudices which seem to be hallowed by time. . . .

His Majesty has judged that the way of remedying these defects simply by the rules of a strictly distributive justice, of restoring the original intentions behind the tax . . . to replace the *vingtièmes* with a general land tax which . . . would consist of a proportion of all produce. . . .

The churchlands would necessarily be included.

(*Archives parlementaires* I, pp. 189–98, cited in J. Hardman, *The French Revolution*, London, Arnold, 1991, pp. 24–26)

B The final budget of the *ancien régime* for fiscal year 1788

The state's budget of 629 million livres was divided as follows:

Expenses	
Finances (costs of collection etc.)	6.04%
Court expenditure	5.67%
Administration, justice, police, highways	3.03%
Welfare in state regions, towns and districts	2.80%
Public economy	3.68%
Public education and welfare	1.94%
War	16.83%
Navy and colonies	7.18%
Foreign affairs	2.28%
Servicing of the regular debt	29.59%
Various expenses linked to this debt	5.03%
Repayment of capital	11.70%
Pensions	4.32%

Income	
Loans	21.37%
Lotteries	2.62%
Various items	4.20%
Direct taxes (including the *taille*: 154.7 million)	24.60%
Indirect taxes, including *Fermes Générales* (150.1 million) and customs dues (51 million)	32.47%
Monopolies and industrial ventures	2.23%
Produce of royal lands	7.86%
Dues from state districts (direct taxes)	4.64%

(reconstruction by F. Braesch, cited in F. Aftalion, *The French Revolution: An Economic Interpretation*, Cambridge University Press, 1990, pp. 196–97)

C L'Abbé M. Lavassor on division within the clergy

None are so wretched and so oppressed as the lower clergy. While the Bishop plays the great nobleman and spends scandalous sums . . . the parish priest has not the wherewithal to buy himself a new cassock. The burden of collecting the tithe falls on him, but the Prelates, not he, pocket it.

(L'Abbé M. Lavassor, 'Les Soupirs de la France esclavé, qui aspire après la liberté', in L. Ducros, *French Society in the Eighteenth Century*, trans. de Geijer, 1926, cited in L.W. Cowie, *The French Revolution*, London, Macmillan, 1988, p. 10)

D The cost of food

(i) From G. Lefebvre's analysis of what mobilised the masses

In 1789 a Paris workman earned on the average some 30 to 40 sous a day. For him to live, it was estimated that bread should cost no more than 2 sous a pound. In the first half of July the price was twice this figure. In the provinces it was much higher, reaching 8 sous or more, because the government, fearing disturbances in Paris, had no hesitation in selling there, well below the current price, the grain which it imported from abroad. Bread had never been so dear since the death of Louis XIV. How can one fail to suspect a connection between this ordeal and the fever of insurrection that gripped the population at the time?

(G. Lefebvre, *The Coming of the French Revolution*, 1939, trans. R.R. Palmer, Princeton University Press, 1989, p. 105)

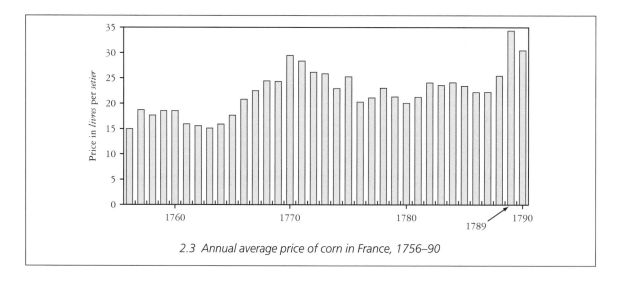

2.3 Annual average price of corn in France, 1756–90

(ii) The price of corn (Figure 2.3)

E From Sieyès's pamphlet, *What is the Third Estate?*, 1789

Such are the labours which sustain Society. Who undertakes them? – the Third Estate. Public undertakings similarly comprise four recognized classes – the Sword, the Robe, the Church and the Government. It would be unnecessary to consider them in detail to show that the Third Estate together forms nineteen-twentieths of those who serve Society, with this difference, it is engaged in everything that is truly laborious, in all the duties that the privileged Order refuses to undertake.

(Cowie, *French Revolution*, p. 12)

F From the Declaration of the Rights of Man, 26 August 1789

1 Men are born free and remain free and equal in their rights. Social distinctions can only be founded on public utility.

2 The aim of every political association is the maintenance of the natural and imprescriptible rights of man. Those rights are those of liberty, property, security and resistance to oppression.

3 The fundamental source of all sovereignty resides in the nation. . . .

6 The law is the expression of the general will. . . .

12 An armed public force is required to safeguard the rights of man and the citizen . . .

13 General taxation is indispensable for the upkeep of the public force and for the expenses of government. It should be borne equally by all citizens in proportion to their means.

17 As the right to property is inviolable and sacred, no one may be deprived of it except when public necessity . . . evidently demands it and this on condition of being paid fair compensation in advance.

(cited in Hardman, *French Revolution*, pp. 114–16)

Questions

1 What does Calonne mean in extract A by 'ancient prejudices which seem to be hallowed by time'?

2 Why does Sieyès argue in extract E that only the Third Estate's role is 'truly laborious'?

3 Assess the value of extracts C and D (i and ii) in supporting the view that the Revolution was caused by poverty.

4 What importance should be attached to Calonne's reform proposal (extract A) and to the final budget of the *ancien régime* (extract B) in explaining the coming of the Revolution?

5 How far does the Declaration of the Rights of Man (extract F) reflect the view of Sieyès (extract E) about the importance of the Third Estate?

Further reading

W. Doyle, *The Oxford History of the French Revolution* (Oxford University Press, 1990) provides an invaluable, clear and detailed account which draws upon many studies. D.G. Wright, *Revolution and Terror in France, 1789–1795* (London, Longman, 1990) offers a very concise text which refers to a documentary collection at the back of the book and to a long list of works. An orthodox or Marxist interpretation is provided by G. Lefebvre's classic, *The Coming of the French Revolution*, trans. by R.R. Palmer (Princeton University Press, 1989), developed in G. Rudé, *The French Revolution* (London, Phoenix, 1994) and revised by N. Hampson's important

study, *A Social History of the French Revolution* (London, Routledge, 1988) and T.C.W. Blanning, *The French Revolution: Aristocrats versus Bourgeois?* (London, Macmillan, 1989) in a clear and economical booklet. Useful historiographical discussion is provided by A. Forrest, *The French Revolution* (Oxford, Blackwell, 1995).

The role of women during the Revolution is treated concisely by O. Hufton's 'Voilà la citoyenne', in *History Today*, May 1989, and with authoritative depth by the same author in *The Prospect before her: a History of Women in Western Europe, vol. 1, 1500–1800* (London, HarperCollins, 1995). S.E. Melzer and L.W. Rabine follow the same perspective in *Rebel Daughters: Women and the French Revolution* (Oxford University Press, 1992).

Two editions of selected documents, L.W. Cowie, *The French Revolution* (London, Macmillan, 1988) and J. Hardman, *The French Revolution* (London, Arnold, 1991) provide editorial introductions which open the way to detailed study of the sources.

• CHAPTER THREE •

The Collapse of the French Monarchy and the International Response, 1789–92

• CONTENTS •

Key dates

SECTION A

The constitutional monarchy, 1789–92

The international response and the outbreak of war

SECTION B – SOURCES

Why did the experiment in constitutional monarchy fail?

Key dates

SECTION A

The constitutional monarchy, 1789–92

Reforms of the Constituent Assembly

During the months that followed the King's removal to the Tuileries, much of the political activity in Paris took place outside the Constituent Assembly. Political clubs such as the Society of Friends of the Constitution, which soon took its new name from the premises of the former Jacobin order which it occupied, became well attended by the general public, and by July 1790 some two hundred deputies from the Constituent Assembly were members. The municipal government of Paris, the Commune, was totally reformed by July 1790. It became a vehicle of direct democracy for the male citizens and comprised representatives from each of the forty-eight Sections of Paris (see Map 3.1). Inevitably, it had much influence with the Parisian crowd. The politics of the Commune, the street and the clubs influenced and intimidated the Constituent Assembly where deputies who advocated a role for the King in the new constitution were jeered from the public gallery, while those who sat on the left of the debating chamber, such as Pétion and Robespierre, were cheered for their increasingly republican and anti-clerical views.

The early reforms of the Constituent Assembly changed the structure of local government. The old patchwork of ecclesiastical, royal, military and judicial units of administration which had no relation to each other were replaced and the Comité de Division based everything on the new unit, the Department. Districts and communes also had their own elected councils. The franchise was based upon the idea of active citizenship, so that men who paid the equivalent of three days' labour in taxation had the vote, while counsellors and deputies had to pay more in taxation. Robespierre's fears that the result would be too exclusive do not seem to have been realised, for in many rural areas 90 per cent of the men could vote although, according to Wright, only 1 per cent of the population qualified to be deputies (D.G. Wright, *Revolution and Terror in France, 1789–1795*, London, Longman, 1990, p. 37). No consideration was given to allowing women to vote; their role was

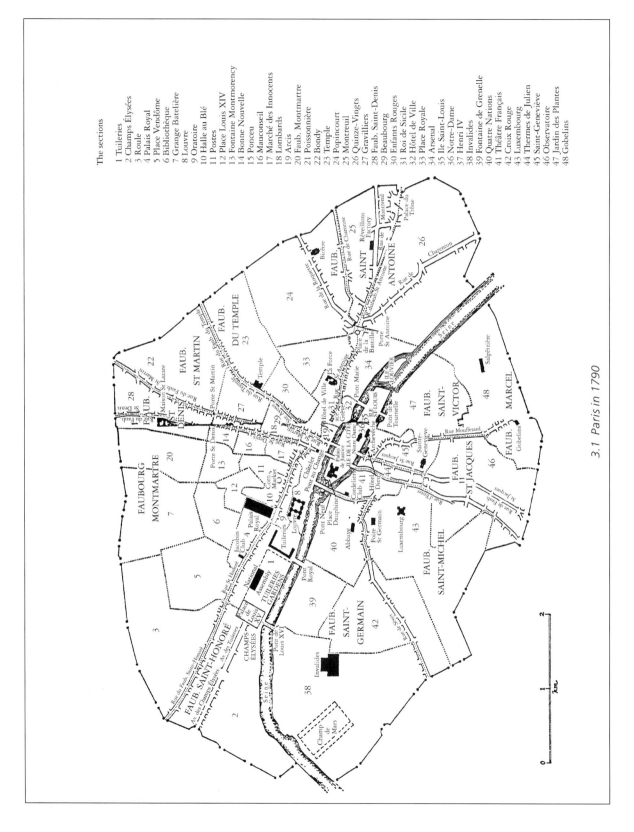

3.1 Paris in 1790

The sections

1 Tuileries
2 Champs Élysées
3 Roule
4 Palais Royal
5 Place Vendôme
6 Bibliothèque
7 Grange Batelière
8 Louvre
9 Oratoire
10 Halle au Blé
11 Postes
12 Place Louis XIV
13 Fontaine Montmorency
14 Bonne Nouvelle
15 Ponceu
16 Mauconseil
17 Marché des Innocents
18 Lombards
19 Arcis
20 Faub. Montmartre
21 Poissonnière
22 Bondy
23 Temple
24 Popincourt
25 Montreuil
26 Quinze-Vingts
27 Gravilliers
28 Faub. Saint-Denis
29 Beaubourg
30 Enfants Rouges
31 Roi de Sicile
32 Hôtel de Ville
33 Place Royale
34 Arsenal
35 Ile Saint-Louis
36 Notre-Dame
37 Henri IV
38 Invalides
39 Fontaine de Grenelle
40 Quatre Nations
41 Théâtre Français
42 Croix Rouge
43 Luxembourg
44 Thermes de Julien
45 Saint-Geneviève
46 Observatoire
47 Jardin des Plantes
48 Gobelins

expected to be domestic and supportive to the politically active menfolk. These changes followed the direction started by convening of the Estates General. The King was no longer an absolute monarch, but as Forrest comments: 'He was still King, of course, but was he sovereign?' (A. Forrest, *The French Revolution*, Oxford, Blackwell, 1995, p. 36). Increasing the participation of citizens in government meant that sovereignty now lay with the nation.

The campaign against the church

It was anti-clerical measures which marked the increasing extremism of the Revolution and helped remove any pretence that Louis XVI still had a sovereign role to play. Faced with the same shortage of revenue which had helped to destroy the King's government, the Constituent Assembly in November 1789 decreed that church lands should be sold for the benefit of the nation. The buyers tended to be well-off bourgeoisie, who became anti-clerical in the defence of their new property. The government issued a new paper currency, the *assignat*, based upon the value of the church lands which the government had taken over for future sale. But if the motive behind this measure was fairly obviously economic, a stronger political purpose became evident in 1790.

In June the Assembly abolished hereditary nobility and the use of titles, and in September the *parlements* were abolished, their earlier role in challenging royal authority failing to save them in the new circumstances. Inevitably, the Church was to be reorganised too and republican anti-clericalism gave an important edge to the process. In July 1790 the Assembly announced the Civil Constitution of the Clergy; the Church was to be reorganised upon departmental lines, the number of bishoprics and parishes reduced, monastic orders were to be closed in the following March, and the state was to take over from the Church responsibility for education and poor relief. Clerical stipends were to be paid by the state, making the humble *curé* better off as a state employee. Some thirty bishops in the Assembly demanded that the Pope's authority was needed for such changes, and the consequence was to polarise opinion. The Jacobin Club in Paris, and its sister clubs in the provinces, became stridently anti-clerical. In November the Assembly enacted the Civil Constitution of the Clergy and demanded an oath of allegiance from the clergy to prove their loyalty to the state whose decree so many had questioned. Many priests became non-juring, but the refusal to take the oath varied strongly from one region to another; opposition was very strong in the Vendée for example. Increasingly the government authorities regarded the 'Refractory priests' as enemies of the revolution; some went into hiding, some into exile, and in May 1791 the Papacy condemned the direction of events by withdrawing the Papal Nuncio (the Catholic Church's ambassador) from France.

The flight to Varennes

Although Louis XVI sanctioned the decree, it was with 'death in the soul' (cited in J. Hardman, *Louis XVI*, New Haven, CT, Yale University Press, 1994, p. 182) and the bishop of Clermont gave him little sympathy for having acted under duress. Hoping to take his Easter communion from a non-juring priest, the King and his family prepared to leave the Tuileries in April 1791 for the nearby palace of Saint-Cloud, but a crowd prevented their departure. This event helped convince the King of the need to escape what had become imprisonment in a city where, he complained, the 'mentality of the clubs dominated and pervaded everything . . . and pushed the public in the direction they wanted to lead it' (Louis XVI's Declaration on leaving Paris, 20 June 1791, cited in J. Hardman, *The French Revolution*, London, Arnold, 1981, p. 133). Apparently from the evidence of his Declaration on leaving Paris, and from the testimony of his close supporters, the King did not want to restore the *ancien régime* nor to launch an attack on France with an army of émigrés. Louis XVI's intention seems to have been to set himself up at Montmédy, on the frontier with the Austrian Netherlands, from where he could negotiate his place in the new constitution beyond the power of the Parisian crowd and the hothouse atmosphere generated by the republican clubs.

The flight of the King and his family in June 1791 got to Varennes, about 40 miles short of

Montmédy. Their identity was revealed and they were returned to a Paris under instructions to show calculated but sombre disrespect. The constitutional monarchy, which the Assembly was seeking to bring to life, was mortally wounded by the King revealing his real attitude to the Revolution. The fiction advanced in the Assembly that he had been kidnapped against his will was poor first-aid. Doyle calls it 'the Revolution's second great turning-point. Like the oath of the clergy, it forced Frenchmen to make choices that most would have preferred not to face' (W. Doyle, *The Oxford History of the French Revolution*, Oxford University Press, 1990, p. 152).

The pressure on the King to abdicate was contained by his agreement to be limited by a constitution, and by the efforts of the Feuillants Club (led by Brissot and Barnave) which feared the republicanism of Paris. The division came to a head on 17 July 1791 when the third great *journée* took place. A crowd of 50,000, organised by the Jacobin and Cordelier clubs to demand a republic, was dispersed on the Champ de Mars by Lafayette's National Guard. Some fifty demonstrators were killed and it is interesting to note the Constituent Assembly in July 1791 making use of the military power of the state when some two summers earlier Louis XVI had been unable or unwilling to control Paris in this way. Although Desmoulins and Marat went into hiding, and Danton prudently fled to England, republicanism was not destroyed and the Jacobins were well placed to exploit the resentment of the Parisian *sans-culottes* in future.

The 1791 Constitution

The Constitution of September 1791 limited the King's powers to delaying legislation for four years (a suspensive veto), while making the Legislative Assembly the centre of government. This Assembly was to be indirectly elected by active citizens (who paid the equivalent of three days' labour in taxes each year) every two years. Deputies of the expiring Constituent Assembly were not allowed to serve in the Legislative Assembly, nor to hold executive office for four years, due to the motion which Robespierre had carried in May

3.1 *Lafayette's oath at the Festival of the Federation, 14 July 1790*

Source: Musée Carnavalet, Paris © Photothèque des Musées de la Ville de Paris

1791 and which his supporters argued demonstrated his own 'sea-green incorruptibility'. Another consequence was that the new Legislative Assembly which met in October 1791 contained no clerics or former nobles, and all 745 were comfortably off local figures, propertied men and lawyers, not obviously well qualified for politics in a teeming Paris which paid such attention to the Jacobin and Cordelier clubs with their republican passions.

What was Louis XVI's real attitude to a constitution embodying the Declaration of the Rights of Man and stating that the 'law is the expression of the general will' (Hardman, *French Revolution*, p. 114)? Counter-revolutionary supporters abroad alleged that the King was forced into accepting the constitution and in August 1791 Austria and Prussia issued the Declaration of Pilnitz which promised a crusade to restore his powers. The Prince de Condé's émigré army at Coblenz presented a potential challenge to the new regime and both the King and Queen kept in contact with sympathisers abroad to the extent of intriguing with them. The Feuillants (constitutional monarchists) numbered some 345 of the 745 deputies in the Legislative Assembly (Doyle, *French Revolution*, p. 175) but their debates were held in private and they failed to attract a popular following, while the Paris Commune became a real focus of popular government in Paris. Furthermore, about one-quarter of the new Legislative Assembly were members of the Jacobin Club, and support for the republicanism of the Jacobin and Cordeliers clubs in Paris continued to develop due to the exclusion of many *sans-culottes* from the franchise and as a result of the massacre of the Champs de Mars. In these circumstances the British ambassador reported that the 'present Constitution has no friends and cannot last'. (Doyle, *French Revolution*, p. 158). The manner of its collapse, however, is revealing of Louis XVI's attitude and showed his growing defiance as his position became more hopeless.

Louis XVI and the Legislative Assembly

The Legislative Assembly's strict law requiring émigrés to return or lose their estates, and refractory priests to swear the oath within eight days or become suspected of being in revolt, provoked Louis XVI to use his veto late in 1791. While Louis XVI argued that he was merely acting constitutionally, his republican critics saw things differently and some of the constitutionalists were embarrassed at this use of the power they had given him.

In this situation war against France's enemies became an attractive way for the King to restore some popularity with the Assembly, although he feared the stresses it would cause. A quarrel was provoked with the Austrian empire and in March 1792 Louis XVI appointed a new ministry from the ranks of Brissot's supporters, now called Girondins after one of the regions from which they came. They were enthusiasts for the war which was declared with Austria in April. The attraction for the ministry, the Assembly in which only seven deputies voted against the war, and for the King in this popular course was to cash in on the patriotic anger at Austria's threats and expose any traitors at

home. Robespierre, however, had warned against such a course before the revolution was securely established, and he rightly suspected that the King and Queen hoped that a rescue or a restoration would result from war with the Duke of Brunswick's formidable Austrian and Prussian forces.

France's forces were quickly in retreat, food riots broke out in the cities and the *assignat* fell to 63 per cent of its original value. The atmosphere in Paris became still more turbulent with the arrival of new troop levies from the provinces, called *fédérés*. Stories of an 'Austrian Committee' in the Tuileries circulated, and Marie Antionette's Austrian birth made her widely suspected of conspiring to cause France's defeat on the battlefield; her letters sent to the Austrians in July revealing the plan of attack were discovered later. Fear of a military coup and a witch-hunt for scapegoats prompted the Jacobin Club to organise the break-in at the Tuileries by a crowd of ten or twenty thousand Parisian *sans-culottes* on 20 June 1792. Louis XVI, beleaguered for several hours by the mob, calmly defended his use of the veto and protested his loyalty to the constitution from the safety of a window seat, while the Queen was treated with less respect in another room. Such clear evidence of the Royal family's perilous situation in the capital prompted much sympathy in the provinces, and caused the Duke of Brunswick to issue a manifesto warning that 'exemplary and forever memorable vengeance' would be dealt out if any harm befell them.

The storming of the Tuileries

War and the Brunswick manifesto triggered the end of the constitutional monarchy. Parisian fury made it easy for the Jacobin Club to set up an Insurrectionary Commune, formed from the central committees of the Sections, which replaced the regular Commune and paralysed the Legislative Assembly as it prepared to overthrow the monarchy. On 10 August 1792 the Tuileries was stormed by a force of twenty thousand in another *journée*, and this decisive intervention of direct popular sovereignty, as the Jacobins saw it, forced the Royal family to take refuge in the Assembly building itself as their palace was ransacked and the Swiss Guard butchered.

The Legislative Assembly immediately bowed to Parisian force and suspended the monarchy. New elections were called on the basis of universal manhood suffrage for a Convention, a move which the Paris Sections loudly demanded. This would replace the Legislative Assembly and constitutional monarchy with a republic. In a process which began with the *journées* which stormed the Bastille and brought the King to Paris in 1789, the elected government of France and the remaining power of the monarchy had been finally eclipsed on 10 August by the power of the Parisian *sans-culottes*, assorted *fédérés* and National Guardsmen from Paris. The republican stage of the French Revolution was set to continue according to their demands, or rather according to the wishes of those among the Jacobin and Cordelier clubs who could direct the politics of the capital city.

THE INTERNATIONAL RESPONSE AND THE OUTBREAK OF WAR

Britain's initial welcome

To an England still celebrating the centenary of the Glorious Revolution, events in France in 1789 seemed to be a welcome imitation of her own parliamentary liberty. Coleridge put in verse a typical reaction in 1789:

Shall France alone a Despot spurn?
    Shall she alone, O Freedom, boast thy care?
    . . . wider yet thy influence spread,
    Nor e'er recline thy weary head,
    Till every land from pole to pole
    Shall boast one independent soul!
And still, as erst, let favour'd Britain be
First ever of the first and freest of the free!
    (from Samuel Taylor Coleridge, 'Destruction of the
    Bastille', in *Coleridge: Poetical Works*, ed. E.H. Coleridge,
    Oxford University Press, 1969, p. 11)

Fox, the leader of the Whig party, aristocratic 'friends of the people', exclaimed of the falling of the Bastille: 'How much the greatest event that ever happened in the world, and how much the best' (cited in V.H.H. Green, *The Hanoverians*,

London, Arnold, 1970, p. 387). While the Tory government of William Pitt was much less enthusiastic, its sense of safe detachment stemmed from the initial view that France was at long last modernising her political institutions along the lines pioneered by England. However, pressures for the reform of parliament were stimulated and in 1790 they spanned a wide spectrum from Henry Flood's case for householders to elect a hundred additional Members of Parliament, through to Thomas Spence's demand for the confiscation and reallocation of land. Ultimately more worrying for the government was the widening of the political debate to include tradesmen and artisans; John Cartwright revived the Society for Constitutional Information which in 1791 and 1792 engineered the distribution of over 200,000 copies of Thomas Paine's pamphlet *The Rights of Man*, and numerous corresponding societies (such as Hardy's London Corresponding Society) developed the case for reform and an admiration for the French Revolution's beginnings.

When the Whig philosopher Edmund Burke published his *Reflections on the Revolution in France* in November 1790 his critical and carefully argued opposition to the revolution was most unusual. He argued that the granting of double representation to the Third Estate when the Estates General was convened was a dangerous departure from precedent which opened the way for inferior men to take power, 'the stewards of petty local jurisdictions, country attornies, notaries, . . . the fomentors and conductors of the petty war of village vexation' (E. Burke, *Reflections on the Revolution in France*, London, Penguin, 1986, p. 130). The consequence of so ignoring and uprooting the past and of giving everyone a say in government, he predicted, would be intoxication with power, the destruction of order, anarchy and violence. Britain would not be left unscathed. Thomas Paine's pamphlet *The Rights of Man* appeared in 1791 in response, pointing to the achievement of American independence in 1776 and arguing the supremacy of reason over blind obedience to the authority of the past. A new generation in France therefore could claim sovereignty and overthrow monarchical government. Many in the Whig party became alarmed by the popularity of Paine's ideas, and Burke's views earned growing respect after the flight to

Varennes. In July 1791 rioters in Birmingham burned Dr Priestley's house and laboratory in an expression of anti-revolutionary views; as an opponent of Burke and as a Dissenter, he was regarded as a friend of Revolution. Burke's public break with Fox in May 1791 divided the opposition to Pitt's government, and Burke increasingly achieved the status of a prophet as events in France developed in 1792.

Habsburg distractions

In continental Europe the French Revolution came as a surprise. Hungary and the southern Netherlands, dominions of the Habsburg Emperor Joseph II, were in turmoil as a result of his drive to create a streamlined military despotism, and it was his throne which looked least secure, rather than that of the Bourbons in France. But signs that France's power was crumbling were unmistakable when in September 1787 she failed to uphold her promises to the Dutch patriots and allowed the Prussians to march into the Dutch Republic. All Louis XVI offered was refuge and pensions to the 1,500 Dutch exiles from Prussian and Orangist power. Most of the Dutch patriots, numbering perhaps 40,000, stayed in the Austrian Netherlands or the principality of Liège. They welcomed the revolution in France which they saw as bringing into power a like minded group of patriots.

It seemed to many educated people that the fall of the Bastille proved that reform and regeneration was possible on the European side of the Atlantic also. In Habsburg-controlled Belgium there was resistance to the Emperor's reforms and a strong desire to be allowed the independence to maintain their existing political order. This Brabant Revolution came to a head in 1789 and seemed to be in parallel with the French Revolution and the resistance of the Dutch patriots. Van der Noot, an exiled lawyer from Brussels, with the help of fellow lawyer Vonck, organised an invasion in October from bases in Holland and Liège which destroyed Austrian power. In January 1790 an independent United States of Belgium was proclaimed. However, this statist regime wanted to maintain the systems and privileges of the Church and the nobility which were increasingly attacked in

France, but this difference was not noticed initially by the crowds in Brussels, who took to wearing their own national cockade of black, yellow and red.

Emperor Joseph II died on 20 February 1790 and was succeeded by his brother Leopold. Initially welcoming towards the French Revolution, he showed a readiness to accept the statist regime in Belgium if it acknowledged his sovereignty. This gesture came to nothing. War was declared on the rebels once Leopold had reached an agreement with King Frederick William II of Prussia, who controlled Liège and access to Belgium. By December 1790 the United States of Belgium was no more, and Habsburg control was extended to Liège as well. Neither Britain nor the French National Assembly, who now recognised the distance separating them from the Belgium statists, were concerned to intervene.

Growing concern over events in France

The continental powers seemed quite content at this stage to leave France preoccupied with her domestic upheaval and to take advantage of her weakness beyond her borders. Poland became the focus of attention after the diet, having shown itself to be outside Russian control by January 1789, was itself challenged in May 1791 by popular demands for non-noble representation, majority voting in the diet, and a new constitution which included a hereditary monarchy. Catherine II of Russia perceived French Jacobinism at work here and was poised to recover control of Poland during 1792. This kind of awareness of the contagious influence of the French Revolution which Burke had foreseen grew up slowly. In Spain, early action was taken and events in France were not reported in the official press after May 1789, but in Sweden censorship did not reach such a level until 1792 and even Russian censorship increased only after April 1790.

More alarm was generated by the plight of the French Royal family, reduced to prisoners in the Tuileries first by the *journée* to Versailles in October 1789 and then by the flight to Varennes in June 1791. Governments were made uneasy as Paris became the centre for many political exiles who called for revolutions throughout Europe, and in June 1790 the National Assembly had allowed Anarcharsis Clootz, an exiled Prussian nobleman, to speak on behalf of an international delegation of revolutionaries.

The émigrés and their supporters

None of these developments explain the outbreak of war between France and the former opponents Austria and Prussia in April 1792, although they help to make it understandable. The courtiers such as the Comte d'Artois, the Condés and the Polignacs who fled in the summer of 1789 established themselves in Turin with the purpose of organising a counter-revolution. The October days brought more nobles into exile, and the émigré community grew during 1790 as the army broke up. However they were without money, allies or military force at this stage, and the King refused to join in any planned rescue. But German nobles resented the abolition of feudal rights in France which deprived them of property there, and early in 1791 Artois and his followers moved to Coblenz, the capital of his uncle the Prince-Archbishop of Trier. From here the émigrés would be well placed to gather support and strength. After the flight to Varennes, the Comte de Provence and thousands of new émigrés gathered there, including perhaps two-thirds of the officer corps of the army. The émigrés' presence and hopes were an important ingredient in the cauldron of war, but it was not as yet at boiling point.

On 10 July 1791 the Emperor Leopold II issued the Padua Circular, inviting fellow monarchs to join a campaign to restore the French monarchy. Only Frederick William II of Prussia responded and the joint Declaration of Pilnitz was issued on 27 August promising 'to put the king of France in a state to strengthen, in the most perfect liberty, the bases of a monarchical government'(cited in Doyle, *French Revolution*, pp. 156–57); but the tough-sounding commitment was undermined by the condition that prompt action would require the agreement of other powers. Gustavus III of Sweden was all for intervention, concluding peace with Russia in readiness for the crusade, but Catherine II was more interested in restoring her rule of

Poland, and Leopold was not prepared to follow up the Declaration once Louis XVI accepted the constitution in September 1791.

French enthusiasm for war

War was inching nearer, however, partly because of the response in the Legislative Assembly to the émigrés and the Declaration. One of the last acts of the Constituent Assembly in September 1791 had been to vote the annexation of the papal enclaves of Avignon and the Comtat in defiance of international opinion. The fighting which ensued in Avignon between the annexationists and the papal supporters encouraged the Legislative Assembly to pursue the émigrés and refractory priests who were also seen as opponents and conspirators. Louis XVI vetoed the measures against émigrés and priests, the former on 11 November 1791 and the latter on 19 December. His authority was boosted because, on 14 December, the King had attended the Legislative Assembly and announced that he had issued an ultimatum to the Electors of Trier and Mainz demanding that they instantly expel the émigré armies from their territories. Louis XVI earned enthusiastic popularity with the Assembly which had pressed him to act, and he was surely aware that war with some German principalities would quickly prompt Austrian intervention, the destruction of France's depleted army and the restoration of his own authority.

Although the Electors of Trier and Mainz quickly expelled their émigré visitors, Leopold was persuaded that the counter-threat he issued on 21 December, that Austrian forces would resist a French attack on the Electors, would have a sobering effect in Paris. Instead it acted as an incitement.

Why had French revolutionary politics become so intoxicated with war fever? In purely pragmatic terms, Brissot and his supporters were confident that an army of free men fighting for their cause would be more than a match for the mercenary and conscripted ranks of the *ancien régime*. Lafayette and Narbonne, who was appointed Minister of War in December 1791, believed that war would reinvigorate the army of 150,000 which they began to mobilise. Practical calculations really demanded an understanding with Britain that she would remain neutral, and Talleyrand was sent to see Pitt. The results were inconclusive, but Pitt declared soon afterwards to the House of Commons that 'there never was a time in the history of this country when from the situation of Europe we might more reasonably expect fifteen years of peace than we may at the present moment' which suggested a comfortable isolation from the threat of war (cited in I.R. Christie, *Wars and Revolutions*, London, Arnold, 1982, p. 212).

But above all it was aggressive rhetoric and not calculation which made war such a popular cause; Brissot argued that it was necessary for external and internal security 'for the malcontents . . . are insolent only because Coblentz exists', it was necessary for the stability and credibility of the government, and to put an end to counter-revolution everywhere (cited in L. Kekewich and S. Rose, *The French Revolution*, London, Longman, 1992, p. 134). It would solve all the problems with an outpouring of revolutionary enthusiasm. A self-sacrificing and crusading element was added when Austria's warning confirmed the breadth of the conspiracy against France; in January 1792 Vergniaud told the Assembly:

You have renounced conquests but you have not promised to suffer such insolent provocations. . . . led by the most sublime passions beneath the tricolor flag that you have gloriously planted on the ruins of the Bastille, what enemy would dare attack you . . . follow the course of your great destiny that beckons you on to the punishment of tyrants.

(cited in S. Schama, *Citizens*, London, Penguin, 1989, pp. 594–95)

Amidst the thunderous applause that such views attracted, Robespierre's warnings that 'armed missionaries' would not be welcomed, and that the motives of the King in supporting war were self-serving, left him isolated. He had to drop his objections when the war began.

The outbreak of war in 1792

In March 1792 the King dismissed the ministry which had come under severe criticism from the Assembly, appointing in its place Brissot's supporters. Dumouriez, a professional soldier and veteran of campaigns against the Austrians, became Foreign Minister and promptly appeared at the Jacobin Club in the red cap of liberty, symbolically combining revolutionary appeal with the patriotic cause of war. News of Leopold's death on 1 March failed to check the direction of French policy, and on 20 April 1792 Louis announced to the Assembly that France was now at war with the King of Hungary and Bohemia (Francis II had yet to be proclaimed Emperor); only seven deputies voted against.

What drove France's opponents to war? Ideological opposition to the revolution is an unconvincing explanation in view of Leopold's initial attitude, Catherine II's greater concern for Poland, and Britain's response. Blanning argues that wars were started to obtain limited advantages when Austria and Prussia were no longer distracted by disputes in Turkey or Poland, and when they perceived France's ability to resist was low (T.C.W. Blanning, *The Origins of the French Revolutionary Wars*, London, Longman, 1986, cited in A. Forrest, *The French Revolution*, Oxford, Blackwell, 1995, p. 114). Hence in December 1791 Leopold at last supported claims of the German princes to their feudal privileges in Alsace, and the Prussian government, having signed a pact with Austria in February 1792, rejected Dumouriez's overtures for neutrality in March.

To start with it seemed that Austrian and Prussian calculations were correct. In April 1792 the French advance into Belgium was greeted not by a welcome from the victims of Austrian oppression but with resistance; French forces fled, and murdered their own commander, General Dillon. Prussia joined hostilities on 21 May, and her steady advance during July under their commander the Duke of Brunswick compounded the sense of demoralisation in the ranks of the French armies. Robespierre's earlier warnings seemed justified and his popularity was restored and enhanced. Amidst the turbulence caused by the slide in the value of the *assignat* and the summoning to Paris of the *fédérés*, troops levies from the provinces, the hunt for scapegoats focused quickly upon an 'Austrian Committee' in the Tuileries. Consequently, the monarchy itself became in August an early victim of the war that it had sponsored in a final risky bid for popularity or restoration.

SECTION B – SOURCES

WHY DID THE EXPERIMENT IN CONSTITUTIONAL MONARCHY FAIL?

The situation changed in so many ways between the storming of the Bastille in 1789 and the storming of the Tuileries in 1792 that it is not possible to single out one factor in the failure of the constitutional monarchy without first considering several others. The King at first travelled along the path of constitutionalism willingly enough for some observers, yet he appointed Breteuil to be his Minister in Exile and charged him secretly to restore his authority in November 1790 (extract A (i)); was this a plea to restore the *ancien régime* in the light of the more extreme direction events were by then taking, or merely a gesture to keep the forces of counter-revolution obedient?

The flight to Varennes and the Declaration which Louis XVI left behind (extract C) are usually regarded as revealing of his true attitude to developments by 1791, and perhaps reflect his growing decisiveness, or desperation, by this stage. Yet the failure of the escape bid exasperated the British ambassador and, perhaps when combined with reverses in war and the use of the veto, sealed the fate of the monarchy. What were the King's intentions in fleeing? Bouillé's memoirs (extract A (ii)) offer a sympathetic view, and Louis, in writing to his brothers (extract E), confirms his anxiety to avoid civil war, yet he eventually sponsored war with the Habsburg empire during which the Queen repeatedly betrayed military information to France's enemies. Possibly Louis XVI was driven by the mounting influence of the republican clubs exemplified in Desmoulins' journalism (extract B) which helped convert the poorer sections of Paris (extract F), but the assault on the Church which the Assembly initiated also encouraged Louis XVI to show his hand and confront the direction in which politics was moving (extract D).

A Louis XVI's intentions

(i) The King to the Baron de Breteuil, 20 November 1790

You know my intentions and I leave it to your discretion to make such use of it as you think necessary for the good of my service. I approve of everything that you do to achieve my aim, which is the restoration of my legitimate authority and the happiness of my peoples.

(*Annales historiques de la révolution française*, 1962, p. 40, cited in J. Hardman, *The French Revolution*, London, Arnold, 1991, p. 122)

(ii) From the memoirs of the Marquis de Bouillé

I had therefore to suppose that once the King had recovered his liberty he would have based his conduct on the dispositions of his people and of the army and that he would only have employed force in the eventuality of his not having been able to come to a suitable arrangement with the Assembly, which several leading members of the Assembly – including Mirabeau, Duport and even the Lameths – desired, realizing all the vices of their constitution, which tended towards a republic they did not want and anarchy which they dreaded.

(M.F. Barrière (ed.) *Mémoires du Marquis de Bouillé*, 1859, pp. 123–24, cited in Hardman, *French Revolution*, p. 123)

B Camille Desmoulins' newspaper report on the Jacobin Club, 14 February 1791

In the propagation of patriotism, that is to say philanthropy, this new religion which is bound to conquer the universe, the club or church of the Jacobins seems destined for the same primacy as that of the church of Rome in the propagation of Christianity. . . . it is also the great investigator which redresses all abuses and comes to the aid of all citizens. It seems that in reality the club acts as a public ministry alongside the National Assembly.

(*Les Révolutions de France et de Brabant*, cited in D.G. Wright, *Revolution and Terror in France 1789–1795*, London, Longman, 1990, p. 122)

C From the King's Declaration on leaving Paris, 20 June 1791

... one of the main clauses in all their *cahiers* providing that *legislation would be carried out in conjunction with the King*. In contempt of this clause, the Assembly has denied the king any say in the Constitution by refusing him the right to grant or withold his assent to the articles which it regards as constitutional. ...

This form of government, so vicious in itself, has become even more so for the following reasons:

(1) The Assembly, by means of its committees, constantly oversteps the limits which it has itself prescribed ...

(2) In nearly all the cities ... associations have been founded with the name of *Société des amis de la Constitution* [Jacobin Clubs]: in defiance of the laws, they do not permit the existence of any other clubs that are not affiliated to themselves, thus forming an immense corporation more dangerous than any of those which existed previously. ...

... The National Assembly never dared check this licence, far removed from true liberty; it has lost its influence ... It can be seen from the dominant mentality in the clubs and the way in which they are seizing control of the new primary assemblies what can be expected of them and if one can detect any disposition on their part to go back on anything, it is in order to destroy the remains of the monarchy ...

(cited in J. Hardman, *French Revolution*, pp. 127 and 132–33)

D The view of two contemporary historians

There is little doubt that the schism in the Church did indeed provide the issue around which the forces of counter-revolution could rally. Furthermore, the King's reluctant and grudging acceptance of the Civil Constitution served only to deepen the suspicion which already existed concerning his attitudes and motives, thus further weakening his position.

(L. Kekewich and S. Rose, *The French Revolution*, London, Longman, 1990, p. 49)

E From Louis XVI's secret memorandum to his brothers, 25 September 1791

... I have carefully weighed the matter and concluded that war presents no other advantages but horrors and a continuance of discord. ... therefore ... I should try once more the sole means remaining to me, namely the junction of my will to the principles of the Constitution.

(F. de Conches, *Louis XVI*, vol. 2, pp. 365–75, cited in Hardman, *French Revolution*, p. 138)

F From the address of the Section Mauconseil to Parisians, 31 July 1792

For too long a wretched tyrant has played with our destiny; let us not delay to punish him lest he gains his triumph. ... Let us all unite to pronounce the disposition of this cruel king. Let us say with one accord: *Louis XVI is no longer King of the French*. Public opinion alone gives kings their power. Very well! Citizens, employ opinion to depose him, for public opinion makes and unmakes kings.

(*Archives parlementaires* XLVII, p. 458, cited in L.W. Cowie, *The French Revolution*, London, Macmillan, 1987, p. 86)

Questions

1 Explain the meaning of the following in their contexts:
   (a) Louis XVI's phrase 'the restoration of my legitimate authority' (extract A (i))
   (b) Desmoulins' phrase 'this new religion' (extract B)
   (c) Louis XVI's phrase 'the junction of my will to the principles of the Constitution' (extract E).

2 How far does Desmoulins in extract B support the views of the King about the role of the clubs expressed in his Declaration on leaving Paris (extract C)?

3 Using extracts A (i and ii), B and C, assess how realistic the Marquis de Bouillé's comments (in extract A (ii)) were of finding a 'suitable arrangement' between the King and the Assembly.

4 Is the judgement of the British ambassador fair in saying that: 'If this country ceases to be a monarchy it will be entirely the fault of Louis XVI. Blunder upon blunder ... a total waste of energy of mind accompanied with

personal cowardice have been the destruction of his reign'? Use the extracts and your own knowledge in your answer.

(quoted in J.M. Thompson (ed.) *English Eye Witnesses of the French Revolution*, 1938, cited in L. Kekewich and S. Rose, *The French Revolution*, London, Longman, 1990, p. 51)

5 What are the causes behind the popular expression of republicanism in extract F? Use the extracts and your own knowledge in your answer.

Further reading

D.M.G. Sutherland, *France 1789–1815: Revolution and Counterrevolution* (London, Fontana, 1990) provides an up-to-date, detailed and clear account of the whole period which picks out the theme of counter-revolution as well. T.C.W. Blanning, *The French Revolutionary Wars 1787–1802* (London, Arnold, 1996) gives an authoritative analysis which stresses pragmatic calculations above ideological motives, and goes on to argue the distorting effect the war had on the Revolution. S. Schama, *Citizens* (London, Penguin, 1989) is an immense chronicle of the collapse of the *ancien régime* and the descent of the Revolution into the violence of war, civil war and terror; it is full of illuminating anecdotes and readable detail, but it ends with Robespierre's execution in 1794 and is in some ways a return to an old-fashioned, narrative version of the Revolution. J. Hardman, *Louis XVI* (New Haven, CT, Yale University Press, 1994) is a useful, sympathetic biography of the King, whose dignity and courage seems to have grown as his plight became more hopeless, and L. Kekewich and S. Rose, *The French Revolution* (London, Longman, 1990) is a valuable textbook with a good selection of documentary extracts and essays. G. Rudé, *Revolutionary Europe 1783–1815* (London, Fontana, 1964) provides a concise and readable survey, as does I.R. Christie, *Wars and Revolutions: Britain 1760–1815* (London, Arnold, 1982). A more detailed analysis of the British response is H.T. Dickinson (ed.) *Britain and the French Revolution 1789–1815* (London, Macmillan, 1989); some of his analysis is to be found in his article in *Modern History Review*, vol. 6(4), April 1995.

Documentary collections covering this period are mentioned at the end of Chapter 2.

• CHAPTER FOUR •

The Revolution at War

• CONTENTS •

Key dates

SECTION A

The radicalisation of the French Revolution under the pressure of war

The reign of Terror

The Directory

SECTION B – SOURCES

Why did Republican France wage war, and what effect did war have on the Revolution?

KEY DATES

1792	2–7 Sept.	September Massacres
	20 Sept.	French victory at Valmy
	22 Sept.	Convention proclaims Republic
1793	21 Jan.	Louis XVI guillotined
	Feb.	France at war with Britain, Holland and Spain
	10 March	Enragé rising demands price controls
	April	General Dumouriez deserts; Committee of Public Safety set up
	May	Convention decrees Maximum price of bread; Hébert and Varlet arrested
	2 June	Convention sortie; arrest of Girondins; provincial revolt; major cities as well as Vendée now; Republican Constitution suspended
	July	Robespierre voted on to Committee of Public Safety
	Aug.	Mainz taken by Prussian army
	Oct.	Lyon recaptured; to be subjected to 'exemplary justice'; Convention decrees a new calendar and passes decree of revolutionary government (19 Vendémiaire); official Terror beginning
	Dec.	Vendée revolt suppressed by Carrier
		Law of 14 Frimaire increases authority of committees
1794	March	Purge of the Hébertists; 'Great Terror' beginning; Laws of Ventose authorise the confiscation of property of suspects
	April	Purge of the Indulgents, Danton and his followers
	8 June	Festival of the Supreme Being
	10 June	Law of 22 Prairial removes right of defence before Revolutionary Tribunal
	23 June	Maximum on wages
	26 June	French victory at Fleurus
	27 July	9 Thermidor; Robespierre arrested
	29 July	11 Thermidor; Robespierre captured and guillotined
	Aug.	Revolutionary Tribunal purged, committees' powers cut
	14 Nov.	Jacobin Club closed
	Dec.	Carrier guillotined; Girondin deputies reinstated; Maximum price controls abolished
1795	1 April	Germinal Rising of hungry Parisians collapses
	April	Peace signed with Prussia and Holland
	21 May	Prairial Rising; Deputy Feraud murdered; repression followed
	Aug.	Constitution of Year III (the Directory)
	Oct.	Vendémiaire Rising of Royalist sympathisers protesting the Law of two-thirds defeated
1796	March	Babeuf's Conspiracy of the Equals betrayed
1797	June	Bonaparte creates Cisalpine Republic in Italy
	Sept.	Coup of 18 Fructidor; Royalists purged from legislative Councils; Treaty of Campo Formio with Austria
1798	May	Coup of Floréal; Jacobins purged from legislative Councils
	1 Aug.	Battle of the Nile; Nelson destroys Bonaparte's fleet
1799	March	War of the Second Coalition begins against France
	Nov.	Coup of Brumaire; Bonaparte and Sieyès abolish Directory and become Consuls with Ducos

SECTION A

THE RADICALISATION OF THE FRENCH REVOLUTION UNDER THE PRESSURE OF WAR

Between the storming of the Tuileries on 10 August 1792 and 'Thermidor', the fall of Robespierre and the Jacobins, in July 1794, the centre of political activity moved to the left with great speed. The Jacobins, who represented the more radical and hard-line Republicans, dominated the government through their control of Paris. Their ruthlessness built a centralised system of *gouvernement révolutionnaire* which waged war with vigour against foreign enemies and the rebellious provinces, while managing the war economy and changing many aspects of life. They even invented a new religion. The desperate energy of this period could not be sustained beyond a certain point. When the most pressing war emergencies passed the Jacobin dictatorship became a victim of the plots, suspicions and violence which it had earlier been able to manage to its advantage.

The birth of the Republic

Only one person in five of the 7 million eligible to vote for the new Convention delegates did so on 27 August and 2 September 1792. Many in the provinces felt remote from Parisian politics which had

just destroyed the monarchy, but there were other distractions as well. The threat from the Prussian and Austrian armies caused panic. Spies and traitors were suspected everywhere, an Extraordinary Criminal Tribunal was set up to sift out counter-revolutionary suspects and the Minister of Justice, Danton, took the lead in getting house-to-house visits authorised. Three thousand people were detained on the night of 30–31 August. News that Verdun had fallen reached Paris on 2 September, increasing the sense of desperation. Over a thousand prisoners were butchered in the prisons of Paris during the next few days to safeguard the capital from treachery while the *sans-culottes* went off to fight the advancing enemy (see Figure 4.1). There was a dangerous blood-letting fanaticism in the September massacre too. Among the many atrocities, the Queen was invited to look on the severed head of her lady-in-waiting as it

4.1 A British view of the Terror: Gillray's cartoon appeared shortly after the September massacres in 1792

Source: J. Brooman, *Revolution in France* (London, Longman, 1992)

bobbed up and down on a pike outside her window, and the Commune of Paris paid those who took part in the massacres for their loss of earnings as a gesture of thanks for their efforts in cleansing the city of its suspects.

The battle of Valmy on 20 September 1792 halted the Austrian and Prussian advance and with it the immediate threat of counter-revolution. French forces had been given the mocking motto 'not to conquer but to run' by the Austrians, but when the morning fog lifted to reveal the well-disciplined French formations, and General Kellerman's encouraging shout of 'Vive la Nation!' was taken up and yelled by his whole army, Frederick William II and the Duke of Brunswick reconsidered their plans. After further fighting, the Prussian and Austrian forces accepted that the French could not be moved. The French Revolution had survived its baptism of fire, and Goethe offered cold comfort to his fellow Prussian officers: 'From here and today there begins a new epoch in the history of the world, and you can say that you were there' (J.W. von Goethe, *Campagne in Frankreich*, 1898, p. 74, cited in T.C.W. Blanning, *The French Revolutionary Wars 1787–1802*, London, Arnold, 1996, p. 78).

The new Convention which met on 21 September acted with the confidence which victory brought. The Republic was proclaimed the next day. In November the Convention threw down another challenge to all Europe by its Decree of Fraternity (see extract A (iv)), and on 27 November annexed Savoy. This was an early sign that the war of revolutionary principles and defence would become one of conquest.

The trial of the King

It was inevitable that the new Republic would take the decision on 3 December 1792 to put Louis Capet, as Louis XVI was now humiliatingly called, on trial. An iron cabinet had been discovered in the Tuileries containing secret correspondence with France's enemies and looked certain to condemn him for treachery, at the same time as making Louis carry the blame for the disasters of the war. The Girondin ministers were in a delicate position as they too had urged war, and the Jacobin

members of the Convention, who were called Montagnards as they sat high up on the left of the banked amphitheatre, accused Minister of the Interior Roland of suppressing those letters which implicated his friends. The Jacobins were able to take an influential and idealistic attitude to all this because, with the exception of Danton, they did not control the ministries of government and in January 1792 Robespierre had opposed the war (see extract A (ii)). Robespierre argued for punishment rather than trial: 'He has been judged, or else the Republic is not blameless. To suggest putting Louis XVI on trial . . . puts the revolution itself in the dock' (*The Principal Speeches of the Statesmen and Orators of the French Revolution*, vol. 2, Oxford, 1892, p. 359, cited in W. Doyle, *The Oxford History of the French Revolution*, Oxford University Press, 1990, p. 195).

However, Louis's defence was heard, but on 7 January 1793 his guilt was voted by 693 deputies with no votes against. An attempt by the Girondins to call a referendum on his guilt, and allow a reprieve, were defeated. On a sombre grey morning of 21 January Louis was guillotined, his final words to the crowd drowned out by the roll of drums.

This act of regicide, together with the proclamation of the Republic and the Decree of Fraternity, convinced European governments that peace or coexistence with the Revolution was impossible. English opinion was horrified by stories of French atrocities, and Pitt's government feared the advance of the French to the Dutch frontier after the victory over the Austrians at Jemappes (6 November 1792). Holland was Britain's commercial and naval ally, now endangered by French talk of expansion to her 'natural frontiers', the Rhine, the Alps and the Pyrenees. The Convention declared war on Britain and the Dutch Republic on 1 February 1793. No dissenting voice was raised against hostilities with the industrial, financial and naval power of Britain which would so damage French ambitions in Europe in the long term.

The maximum price of bread

The Montagnard deputies and orators of the Jacobin Club were clever manipulators of Parisian passion. In the Convention they were increasingly influential over the majority, called 'the Plain' (because they sat in the centre), while the Girondins, whose strength lay in the provinces and in the government ministries, had been damaged by the war they had started.

All deputies had believed in a free market, that is they were against any price controls. However, by February 1793 the *assignat* has slipped to 50 per cent of its original value and Santerre had to use the National Guard to police food riots in Paris (see Figure 4.2). On 10 March the Enragés, a group led by Jean Varlet and Jacques Roux, organised a rising in Paris and demanded that a maximum price for bread should be fixed. Speculators who hoarded or profited from the shortages should be arrested. The Paris Commune refused to help and the National Guard suppressed the trouble, but the Jacobins took the hint and moved quickly to accept the need for price controls. On 4 May they persuaded the Convention to set a Maximum on the price of bread to cheers from the public gallery. The Jacobins had pragmatically shifted their position, hijacking the popular cause from the Enragés and justifying it by talk of 'popular sovereignty'. The provincially popular Girondins, who were still free-marketeers, had been outmanoeuvred and the importance of Paris in directing the Revolution was shown again, furthering

the power of the Jacobins who seemed able to ride the tiger of popular opinion there. A police report commented acidly: 'The Jacobins know only too well that the people cannot be resisted when one needs them' (quoted in A. Schmidt, *Tableaux de la révolution française*, vol. 1, Leipzig, 1867, p. 174, cited in Doyle, *French Revolution*, p. 229).

The purge of the Girondins

The Girondins' position weakened steadily. In March 1793 Belgium revolted against the French 'liberators'. The eighty-two Representatives on Mission dispatched by the Convention to recruit for the army helped to provoke a revolt in the Catholic and Royalist Vendée, where this demand for men was too much coming from a remote government which had persecuted their priests and executed their king. General Dumouriez, closely associated with the Girondins, was defeated at Neerwinden on 18 March and confirmed Jacobin suspicions of him by deserting on 6 April.

These events boosted the authority of the new Committee of Public Safety which began work in April. Robespierre turned down his own nomination and Danton dominated the nine-man team, elected monthly by the Convention, charged with overseeing and checking all aspects of the

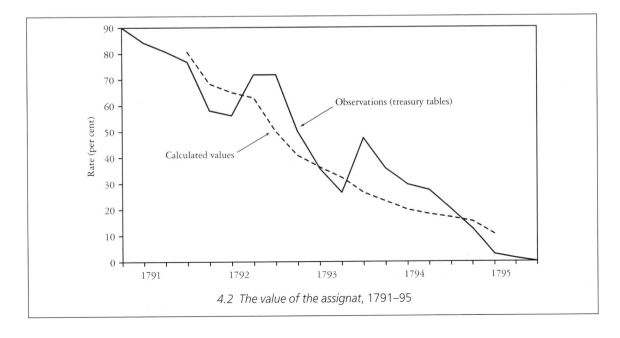

4.2 The value of the assignat, 1791–95

management of the war – in the Vendée, at the front, through recruitment and the supply of food. Such zeal and authority was seen by many in the Convention as a means of harnessing and institutionalising mob violence; the radical Jacobin journalist Marat's talk of 'the despotism of liberty' and his view that 'liberty must be established by violence' were worrying to those who owned windows which might be smashed.

The Girondins tried to reassert themselves, and on 12 April 1793 they voted to impeach Marat for publishing threats against the Convention. Thirty-three Sections of Paris came to the defence of their hero by demanding the arrest of the twenty-two deputies who began the move, and their demands were strengthened when Marat was acquitted by the Revolutionary Tribunal. The Convention set up a Commission of Twelve to investigate 'plots' against it; the arrest of Varlet and Hébert (deputy *procureur* of the Commune) was ordered. A tremendous row broke out in the Convention on 25 May when Danton demanded that the protest from Paris Commune should be heard, and the President of the Convention, the Girondin Isnard, unwisely threatened Paris with provincial retaliation in words which reminded everyone of the Duke of Brunswick's threat: 'If, as a result of one of these constantly recurring insurrections, the National Convention were to suffer attack, I declare to you . . . in the name of all France: Paris will be annihilated . . . Soon people would search along the banks of the Seine to determine whether Paris had existed' (P.J.B. Buchez and P.C. Roux, *Histoire parlementaire de la revolution française*, 1834–38, XXVII, pp. 224–25, cited in J. Hardman, *The French Revolution*, London, Arnold, 1981, p. 156).

Robespierre now helped to organise an insurrection against the Girondins before a provincial revolt developed. This meant using the Jacobin authority in Paris to intimidate the Convention, which consisted of the elected deputies of all France. On 2 June 1793 Hanriot's National Guard, together with a crowd of about twenty thousand, surrounded the Convention building while the Commune demanded the arrest of thirty Girondin deputies. Cannon were primed and pointed at the Chamber, and Hanriot on horseback and ranks of armed men barred the way to deputies who came outside. The Jacobin deputy Couthon, speaking from his wheel-chair, piloted the Convention towards the good sense of surrender; they had mingled with the guards so they were free and they all wanted suspects to be removed. So it was that the Convention voted for the arrest of twenty-nine Girondins, including all of the Twelve, and two ministers. Roland was detained later. The Jacobins were in control, but their power rested on Paris and they depended upon the National Guard, the Commune and popular insurrection; they would need great skill to remain in the saddle.

THE REIGN OF TERROR

Gouvernement révolutionnaire

A new constitution was voted in June 1793 which gave the vote to all adult men, established freedom of the press and the rights of property ownership. There was no provision for the economic controls (and the implied redistribution of wealth) which the Enragés demanded. But Robespierre warned that democratic republicanism would be too liberal during the war emergency. The constitution was duly suspended in a box above the chamber, awaiting calmer times, while the fall of the fortress of Mainz to Prussia in August and the slide of the *assignat* to 22 per cent of its original value emphasised the need for tough and decisive government.

One casualty of the trend to emergency government was the political equality of women. The Cordeliers Club had welcomed women, and their rights were advocated by various societies such as the Fraternal Society of Citizens of Both Sexes, the Revolutionary Republican Citizenesses, and by personalities such as Théroigne de Méricourt and Olympe de Gouges. However, the Jacobin Club was open only to men and some Sections excluded women. When women demanding the right to hold public office and to bear arms were attacked by market women (who disliked Revolutionary government which had imposed price controls on their sales) in October 1793, the Jacobins and the Convention moved against the women's clubs. Their radical demands seemed too close to the Enragés'. Thereafter, the role of women was confined to supporting the political and military work of the menfolk, despite the female embodiment given to the Republic in much art work.

Tough, emergency authority would be supplied by the Committees of Public Safety and General Security, which became the core of government by October 1793 and allowed the Jacobins to dominate the Convention totally until the fall of Robespierre the following July. In July 1793 Danton and Delacroix were voted off the Committee of Public Safety as they were seen to be too mildly tempered for the times. Robespierre was voted on to the Committee over which he seems to have presided, but as no minutes were kept, its meetings were held in secret and the decision of a group would stand for the decision of all twelve members, historians have debated the real extent of his power. Among the key members were Barère, Billaud-Varenne, Collot d'Herbois, Couthon (more blood-thirsty in his words than his deeds), the military strategist Carnot, and Lindet, who masterminded the logistics of food supplies most effectively. Saint-Just terrified many by his cold, youthful idealism (he was aged 25), and he was devoted to Robespierre, who never left Paris 'on mission' as did his colleagues.

The Convention empowered the two Committees by the decree of 19 Vendémiaire (10 October 1793) and the Law of 14 Frimaire (4 December) (see extract C (iii)), but the most important element in their authority were the Representatives on Mission. These were members of the Committees or the Convention sent out by the Committees to the armies, to cities and to the provinces with sweeping authority. Saint-Just, on mission in Alsace, had General Isambert shot in front of his troops for showing insufficient determination in the face of the enemy, and Carrier had 1,800 rebels from the Vendée chained together and drowned in holed barges in the Loire (see Map 4.1).

The other key element supporting the authority of the Jacobin Committees were the Revolutionary Tribunals. These dispensed revolutionary justice and implemented the Law of Suspects (17 September 1793) throughout France. About 30,000 died 'officially' by the 'sword of liberty' or the 'national razor', as the guillotine was called, but many more died in custody or by lamp-post lynchings. Revolutionary justice came to mean that a citizen became guilty simply by allowing his conduct to make him suspect to anyone who would denounce him or her. In April 1794 only the Revolutionary Tribunal in Paris, where Fouquier-Tinville presided, was trusted to hear conspiracy cases. The doomed victims were brought in from all over France to the already bursting prisons of the city. By the Law of 22 Prairial (10 June 1794) the right of defence was removed and the purpose of the Tribunal was simply to confirm the death sentence on all the suspects brought before it. Overall some 9 per cent of the victims were nobles, and 7 per cent clergy, although during the Great Terror of the spring and summer of 1794 they featured more prominently; the vast majority were, as Doyle points out, 'ordinary people caught up in tragic circumstances . . . who made the wrong choices in lethal times, when indifference itself counted as a crime' (Doyle, *French Revolution*, p. 259).

War on all fronts

Did the Terror evolve naturally from the Revolution, was it just '1789 with a higher body count' as Schama put it (S. Schama, *Citizens*, London, Penguin, 1989, p. 447)? Blanning argues that the Terror 'needed the strains of war to be activated' (Blanning, *French Revolutionary Wars*, p. 139). These strains were enormous. By the late summer of 1793 Spain was victorious in Rousillon, Prussia was holding Mainz, the Austrians had won the battle of Valenciennes and a British and Dutch force was besieging Dunkirk. On the home front the rebels in Toulon handed the port over to the British navy on 27 August, and the Vendée was defiant having defeated government forces at Chatillon and Villiers in July. But the increasingly powerful authority of the Committees gave direction and energy to the holding strategy, combined with maximum effort in the north, which was probably Carnot's idea. Houchard defeated the allied force besieging Dunkirk on 6 September, but while the British government allowed the Duke of York to soldier on for another year, Houchard was guillotined in November for failing to press home his victory. In Alsace two new generals, Pichegru and Hoche, under the watchful eye of Saint-Just,

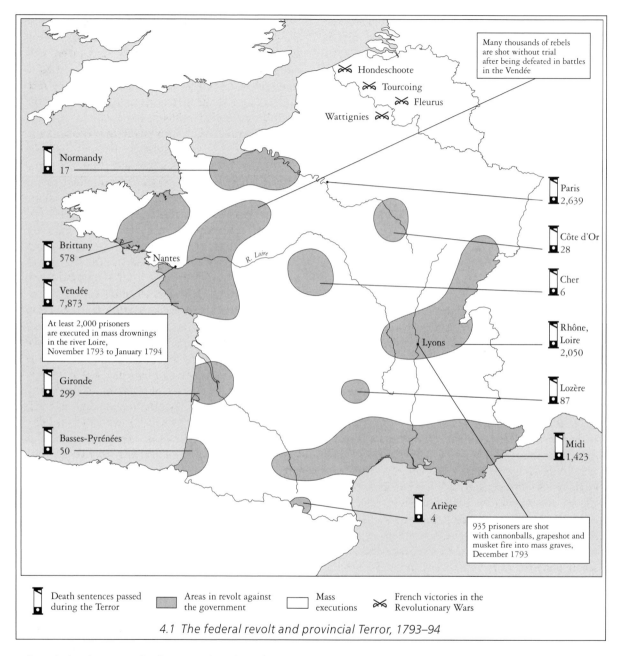

Many thousands of rebels are shot without trial after being defeated in battles in the Vendée

Hondeschoote
Tourcoing
Fleurus
Wattignies

Normandy
17

Paris
2,639

Côte d'Or
28

Brittany
578

Nantes

R. Loire

Cher
6

Vendée
7,873

At least 2,000 prisoners are executed in mass drownings in the river Loire, November 1793 to January 1794

Rhône, Loire
2,050

Lyons

Gironde
299

Lozère
87

Basses-Pyrénées
50

Midi
1,423

Ariège
4

935 prisoners are shot with cannonballs, grapeshot and musket fire into mass graves, December 1793

Death sentences passed during the Terror

Areas in revolt against the government

Mass executions

French victories in the Revolutionary Wars

4.1 The federal revolt and provincial Terror, 1793–94

forced the Austrians back across the Rhine by the end of 1793. Although Austria continued to hold most of Belgium, and the allied armies were unbroken, the French forces had bought a breathing space.

The arrest of the Girondins sparked off further provincial revolts in June in the major cities of France. Five of those arrested came from Bordeaux, which declared itself in revolt against the Conven-tion. In Marseilles two Representatives on Mission were imprisoned. Lyon began raising an army to fight the Convention and it took four strokes of the blunt guillotine to execute the local Jacobin leader, Chalier. The Jacobin Committees moved against the rebels with growing energy. In October Tallien entered Bordeaux with troops, guillotined 104 but himself fell under suspicion for acquitting more; Jullien (who was known to be close to Robespierre) arrived and more heads rolled. Marseilles was recaptured in August but many of the rebels fled to nearby Toulon, which was in British hands; it took the artillery of a young officer named Bonaparte to help to drive the Royal Navy out and recapture the port on 20 December. Between October and December Lyon was subjected to 'exemplary justice'; Couthon asked to be transferred, Fouché and Collot d'Herbois took over and used artillery grape-shot to blast the suspects into open graves as the guillotine could not cope with the numbers. By April 1794, 1,880 had been condemned, many buildings levelled and the city renamed Ville Affranchie. Carrier, later joined by Jullien, set about reducing the Vendée in October. The rebels failed to meet up with a British force in the north at Granville, and retreated into their heartland, which was good country to fight a guerrilla war. Not until 12 December at Le Mans were they defeated in open battle, with the remnant destroyed at Savenay on 23 December. Any survivors were hunted down. Nantes became the centre for the Terror which followed; 3,548 death sentences were given, and many were carried out in the *noyades* (drownings).

By the turn of the year, therefore, the Jacobin authorities seemed to be fairly secure on the home front. The value of the *assignat* had risen to 48 per cent, helped by raising a forced loan from the wealthy. In September 1793 the Law of the General Maximum set general price controls (but not on wage levels), and by February 1794 Lindet's Subsistence Commission had established a nationwide schedule of maximum prices for most goods; severe penalties awaited anyone who sold for more. Bread supplies to Paris soon became so relatively plentiful that checks were made at the gates to prevent people smuggling bread out of the city to sell for a black-market price.

The Habsburg Emperor Francis II arrived in Brussels in April 1794 to drive the war forward, but after the reverse at Tourcoing in May he returned to Vienna, leaving Austrian forces holding the line of the river Sambre. The French General Jourdan's repeated attacks in this sector met with defeat after defeat, but two days after having to abandon 3,000 men and retreat he was urged in person by Saint-Just to make a seventh attempt. On 25 June the city of Charleroi surrendered, and

this gave the French force an important edge in the day-long struggle of 26 June at Fleurus. Coburg eventually disengaged and French forces were left victorious. The door to Belgium, Holland and a frontier on the Rhine was now open to France and exploited over the next seven months; Brussels itself fell on 10 July 1794.

Why had the Revolutionary forces won through? A unified command structure, centralised lines of communication and clear strategic aims were in marked contrast to the allied force. Often the allies preferred a defensive strategy which allowed the French the initiative. The *levée en masse* (extract B (ii)) produced large forces of indisciplined and inexperienced soldiers who got on rather badly with the professionals. The solution to this, decreed in January 1794, proved to be the *amalgame*, the unit which combined volunteers and regulars in the ratio of two to one. The importance of morale was considerable, and propaganda at the front was plentiful. French generals who failed were executed, and all knew that they were fighting with their backs to the wall against a Europe which had declared its hatred of the Revolution. Channelling all this was the ruthless authority of the great Committees which implemented what was, after all, the decision of the Convention on 5 September to make Terror 'the order of the day'.

The Republic of Virtue

Was victory on all fronts the product of the Terror, or did the Jacobins extract an unnecessarily high price? In December 1793, Robespierre argued to the Convention: 'The revolution is the war of liberty against its enemies; the constitution is the regime victorious and peaceful. Revolutionary government requires extraordinary activity, precisely because it is at war.' In February 1794 he was adding another justification for revolutionary vigour:

What is the end to which we are striving? The peaceful enjoyment of liberty and equality. . . . What then is the fundamental principle of democratic or popular government . . . ? It is virtue . . . this sublime sentiment supposes a preference for the public interest above all particular . . . what is immoral is impolitic, and what corrupts is counter-revolutionary.

(*Robespierre: textes choisis*, ed. J. Poperen, vol. 3, Paris, 1957, pp. 99 and 112–15, cited in Doyle, *French Revolution*, pp. 263 and 272–73)

As the Committees became more successful, they became more remote, isolated and fearful. Robespierre developed something of an obsession for cleansing the Republic so that in some sense which Rousseau might understand the natural virtue of man could shine uncorrupted. Others like Fouché, a former priest, attacked the Church with zeal, forcing priests to marry or adopt orphans, and desecrating graveyards in Nievre where he was on mission. In October 1793 the Convention authorised a new calendar dating not from the birth of Christ but from the birth of the Republic, and allowed Notre Dame to be turned into the Temple of Reason where an actress personified Liberty. Robespierre, worried that the closure of churches would create further enemies, argued that atheism was aristocratic and that people believed in the existence of a Supreme Being. In May 1794 the Cult of the Supreme Being was launched to back this up. By this stage Robespierre was being accused of dictatorship, so when he had to lead the procession in person (as President of the Convention) his status as Supreme Being seemed ridiculously clear.

'The Republic of Virtue' was not really a war aim, but it stood for a kind of totalitarian control more typical of the twentieth century. Fearful of sliding from power, the Committees eliminated those they feared and tried to tighten their control. The Law of 14 Frimaire (extract C (iii)) forbade dechristianisers and Representatives on Mission to interpret – or develop – laws themselves. Revolutionary Armies, which had been set up by local authorities, were abolished by this law, and Representatives on Mission with their overwhelming powers were increasingly replaced by the National Agents who had to report every ten days to the Committees.

The Committees arranged two bloody purges of factions which they feared in the spring of 1794. Hébert, an important figure in the Paris Commune and author of the *Père Duchesne*, which was highly influential with the *sans-culottes*, argued for an intensification of the Terror, further dechristianisation and the redistribution of wealth. He had allies in the War Ministry, including Vincent and Ronsin, and Collot d'Herbois and Billaud-Varenne, the hard-line members of the Committee of Public Safety, were sympathetic. On the other side a group around Danton and Desmoulins, the author of the influential *Vieux Cordelier*, became known as 'Indulgents' because they argued that the terror should be relaxed. While the one faction might be played off against the other up to a point, Robespierre's links with the Dantonists, the sympathy of some of the Committee members with the Hébertists, and the possibility that one or other group might raise an insurrection in Paris, made doing nothing too risky.

On 14 March 1794 Hébert, Ronsin, Vincent and seventeen more were arrested, accused of plotting insurrection, famine and a prison massacre, and guillotined on 28 March after a show trial before the Revolutionary Tribunal. Paris was kept quiet by a special grant of food, and the Laws of Ventose which authorised the confiscation of suspects' property (by implication it would be distributed among the faithful patriots who denounced the victims). All passed off quietly and the *sans-culottes* were either convinced of the treason or too exhausted to protest.

The Dantonists were potentially a tougher proposition. Although they were a less close-knit group than the Hébertists, they had power in the Convention and the huge figure of Danton was recognised as one of the original great movers in the Republic. He would speak without notes, but his words would flow with passion and like a torrent, and he could prove a dangerous opponent for the Committees. Robespierre was reluctant to move against his former friend and had two secret meetings with him, presumably trying to persuade him to show in public his loyalty to the Committees. But it was fruitless and on 30 March Danton and his supporters were arrested. Robespierre was energetic in assembling evidence against him and rumours of how he had received money gave weight to Saint-Just's accusations. But in the Tribunal itself, Danton's oratory overwhelmed Fouquier-Tinville. The Convention, persuaded by Robespierre to place its trust in the Committees and bar Danton from any special right of defence (he had demanded to call witnesses), allowed the show trial to be completed in his absence. On 5 April Danton, Desmoulins, Delacroix, Philippeaux and twelve others were guillotined. Paris did not rise to rescue the great revolutionary, and it is possible that Parisians had become punch-drunk by stories of treachery. The necessity of his removal was clear only in the minds of the members of the Committees and the Tribunal who arranged it; they were terrified of what he might do rather than angered by any 'crime' he had committed.

Thermidor

The Festival of the Supreme Being and the victory at Fleurus in June 1794 were hollow triumphs because the Great Terror carried on. Having consumed Hébertists and Dantonists, Robespierre continued to make accusations of conspiracy. It was said that sixty deputies were so fearful of arrest that they would not sleep at home. The Committees were dividing, technocrats like Carnot confronting the idealist Saint-Just, while Robespierre laid himself open to a charge of conspiracy by speaking only at the Jacobin Club and refusing to attend the Convention over the month before his fall.

Would Robespierre be able to call upon the forces which had put him in power? The loyalty of the *sans-culottes* and the Commune had accepted the destruction of the factions. But the maximum on wages, which came into force on 23 June (the Le Chapelier Law was approved in April), threatened to destroy the loyalty of the Sections of Paris. The extension of economic controls to wages in order to limit purchasing power was vital sooner or later if price controls were to remain effective, otherwise wage inflation would fuel a black market. The necessity of this step shows that the Jacobin dictatorship, given power by the *sans-culottes*, was no longer able to uphold their interests; it was reaching the end of the road.

On 26 July 1794 Robespierre spoke to the Convention, warning in a rambling speech that there was a conspiracy afoot. A majority of the deputies, no doubt bent upon self-preservation, mustered the courage to refuse permission for the speech to

be published. Later that day the Jacobin Club expelled any members who had voted with them. Billaud-Varenne, Collot d'Herbois, Fouché and Tallien were prominent among those who believed that either Robespierre or they must die, and they prepared for the battle on 9 Thermidor (27 July). Saint-Just, deciding to court martyrdom like his master, debated vigorously for Robespierre. Tallien's and Billaud-Varenne's counter-denunciations were cheered, and Robespierre's attempt to speak was drowned by shouts of 'Down with the tyrant'. His arrest was voted, along with Saint-Just, Couthon and Hanriot (the commander of the Paris National Guard), but the Commune later ordered their release and on 10 Thermidor Robespierre and his supporters gathered at the Hôtel de Ville. However, popular insurrection could not be restaged now. Only seventeen of the forty-eight Sections answered Hanriot's call to arms, and by the early morning of 11 Thermidor they had drifted away. The Convention's force under Barras entered the Hôtel de Ville and found Robespierre with his jaw shattered from an attempt at suicide with a pistol. He and his companions were guillotined as outlaws without a trial later that day, and over the days that followed the Commune was exterminated. As Robespierre's head fell into the basket the crowds shouted 'Down with the Maximum', apparently confirming one reason why the *sans-culottes* failed to come to his aid.

Robespierre's fall ended the rule of the Committees and the Jacobin dictatorship, and many of those who had contributed to it had also turned to bring it down. They would be lucky to survive the witch-hunt against former Terrorists. Both Robespierre and Danton have their defenders and detractors among the historians, and it is recognised by some that Robespierre was made to carry the blame for a system of government by Terror which the Convention had set up (and in due course dismantled). As Carrier said, when he was put on trial for the drownings at Nantes, all of the Convention were guilty 'down to the President's bell' (Doyle, *French Revolution*, p. 285). Whether all the Representatives on Mission were only obeying orders or not, the reputation of the 'sea-green incorruptible' Robespierre as 'a man of pure integrity, a true republican' as Barère later called him, or as a fussy provincial lawyer who over-achieved, remains to be resolved (Barère, cited in A. Cobban, *A History of Modern France*, vol. 1, London, Penguin, 1967, p. 222).

THE DIRECTORY

After Robespierre's fall the Convention reasserted its authority. During the Thermidorian regime (July 1794–October 1795) the machinery of Terror was dismantled, and with it the economic controls which had kept the cities fed. A new constitution was created to prevent a return to any form of monarchy (as the 1791 constitution allowed) and to stand more firmly against Jacobinism than the Republican constitution of 1793. The constitution of Year III created the Directory of five and tried to produce a regime which would have its centre of gravity firmly in moderate Republicanism. It was destabilised by war, financial pressures and unpopularity in a way which suggested that history was repeating itself, and it was removed in the virtually bloodless coup of 18 Brumaire (November 1799) by Napoleon Bonaparte, at that stage in cooperation with some of the former Directors.

Dismantling the Terror

In August 1794 the Convention repealed the Law of 22 Prairial, purged the Revolutionary Tribunal (Fouquier-Tinville followed his numerous victims to the guillotine in May 1795), and ended the role of the Committees in supervising government. Authority had been taken back by the Convention and rested in the hands of the men of Thermidor who had brought Robespierre down. In December seventy-one Girondin deputies, purged before the reign of Terror but saved from death then by Robespierre's influence, were reinstated to the Convention, giving the Thermidorian regime the character of a Girondist revival. Former Terrorists tried to distance themselves from Jacobinism, 'they condemned themselves in the person of their former friends' commented a contemporary (from Levasseur's memoirs cited in Hardman, *French Revolution*, p. 223). Freron (once Representative on

Mission at Toulon) started a newspaper *L'Orateur du Peuple* to encourage the 'Gilded Youth' lynch mobs to seek out former Terrorists; Tallien's *L'Ami du Citoyen* followed suit in October 1794 and encouraged an attack on the Jacobin Club which the Convention quickly closed 'for provocation' in November! The trial of Carrier for his conduct in the Vendée sent a powerful message to the provinces where the Terror had lingered well after Thermidor. 'Companies of the Sun' hunted down former Jacobins, and many who had only recently been handing down death sentences found the tables turned. Barère, Billaud-Varenne and Collot d'Herbois enjoyed their triumph over Robespierre until their arrest in March 1795; they were exiled to 'the dry guillotine' of Devil's Island.

The Constitution of Year III: the Directory

The moderate Boissy d'Anglas took a leading role in drafting the constitution which was approved by the Convention in August 1795. It safeguarded equality before the law, and the ownership of property, thus avoiding any move towards the redistribution of wealth. An elaborate system of checks and balances was created. The bicameral Legislature comprised a Council of Five Hundred to initiate legislation, and a Council of Elders which could only pass or reject laws. The executive was to be five Directors (chosen by the Elders from a list drawn up by the Five Hundred), one of whom would be chosen for retirement annually by lot.

But the Convention did not trust its new constitution entirely and feared that the first elections would produce a Royalist majority – so many had fallen out of love with the Republic, and Royalism embraced both constitutional monarchists and out-and-out counter-revolutionaries. It tried to protect its new creation by approving the law that two-thirds of the Councils had to be former members of the Convention. While the constitution was approved by over 1 million votes as against 49,000 (4 million citizens did not bother to vote), the two-thirds law was approved by only 205,498 while 108,754 voted against it. In Paris the response of seven Sections was to declare insurrection to prevent the implementation of the law of two-thirds, and a crowd of 25,000 descended on the Convention on 13 Vendémiaire (5 October). The Convention's 6,000 men under Barras had a hard time of it in the fight which followed, but the artillery of the 26-year-old General Bonaparte delivered what he called the 'whiff of grape-shot' and carried the day. Hundreds lay dead, and the ability of Paris to dictate to the government of France was ended.

The *sans-culottes* and the value of money

Soon after Robespierre's fall the Maximum on wages was abolished and the *assignat* fell to 34 per cent. On 24 December price controls were abolished and many in France starved through an icy winter. Few had the fuel to cook the emergency supplies of rice, and many citizens froze on the streets or committed suicide. By May 1795 the *assignat* had collapsed to 8 per cent and the daily bread ration, for those who were able to obtain it, was 2 ounces.

On 1 April 1795 the Convention had faced down a crowd of 10,000 who besieged them in protest at the shortages in what was called the Germinal Rising. It was a leaderless affair without a clear set of demands which embarrassed the remnant of Montagnards (mockingly called 'The Crest') who were painfully keen to show that they disliked popular insurrection. But the rising of 1 Prairial (20 May) was more purposeful. The *tocsin* sounded in the eastern faubourgs of the city, the marchers demanded 'bread and the constitution of 1793', the re-establishment of the Commune, and shouted 'Vive le Montagnard'. Deputy Feraud's head was hacked off and carried into the debating chamber, and 'The Crest' became carried away and took up the demands. But the next day the crowds were persuaded to leave a petition and go home. Retribution soon followed. The eleven Montagnard deputies were arrested and condemned, the Faubourg Saint Antoine surrounded by troops until Feraud's assassins were surrendered, and a further 3,000 arrests symbolised the Thermidorian regime's triumph over Paris.

Hunger remained the powerful reason for protest in the Vendémiaire rising in October, and the Directory failed to cure the problem too. The economic system was collapsing along with the *assignat* (the floor of the printing house symbolically collapsed in October 1795 from the pounding of the presses), and the new currency of 1796 lost all of its value within months. 'Robespierre didn't let us waste away, he only brought death to the rich; this lot are letting people die every day,' a woman was overheard saying in the street (Schmidt, *Tableaux*, vol. 3, p. 95, cited in Doyle, *French Revolution*, p. 325). The resurgence of Jacobinism was a haunting possibility to the Directory, and Babeuf's Conspiracy of the Equals, betrayed in March 1796, lent substance to the threat of popular insurrection and a return to 1793.

War

In April 1795 France made peace with Prussia and Holland, and with Spain in July. War continued against Britain but her expedition to land an émigré force at Quiberon Bay in southern Brittany failed badly in July 1795, and French attempts to turn Ireland into a 'British Vendée' by the Bantry Bay expedition of 1796 and General Humbert's landing in County Mayo in 1798 (defeated at Ballinamuck in September) showed the precariousness of Britain's naval power and kept her on the defensive. Austrian power was damaged severely by Bonaparte's campaign in Italy in 1796. In 1797, with the French forces only 62 miles from Vienna, Austria began negotiating and in September signed the treaty of Campo Formio. Belgium was ceded to France, Venetia partitioned and France's position recognised in Northern Italy. Bonaparte's reputation soared in France, and the Directory began to fear a man who could set up the Cisalpine Republic in June 1797 out of Bologna, Ferrara, Modena and Lombardy as a sister state of the 'Great Nation', as France was now calling herself.

Britain alone had to be brought into line and, in 1798, Bonaparte got the approval of the Directors to strike at her route of imperial communications with India by attacking Egypt. This was less costly than a cross-Channel invasion, and undoubtedly the Directors were eager to get rid of the ambitious young general. Malta, Alexandria and Cairo fell to the French force in June and July, while Nelson's fleet scoured the Mediterranean for week after week in desperate pursuit of the French plan. Late on 1 August the Royal Navy found the French fleet in Aboukir Bay, near Alexandria, and engaged immediately with unconventional tactics in what became celebrated as the Battle of the Nile. Of the thirteen French ships of the line, nine were captured, two burned, and two escaped (to be hunted down later); 218 British seaman died, and over 2,000 Frenchmen. Bonaparte and his army were cut off in Egypt and British naval supremacy established. In addition the Second Coalition was brought to life, with Austria, Russia, the Ottoman empire and Naples all joining Britain in a new phase of war in March 1799. Before the summer was over French gains in Italy were in deadly peril and Bonaparte hurried home, leaving his army in Egypt to defeat in 1801.

Government by *coup d'état*

The cost of these wars was vast and led to the Directory renouncing two-thirds of its debts in September 1797 and making a token paper payment. Taxation was increased, and troops were billeted on those who did not pay. Indirect taxation reminiscent of the *ancien régime* was levied on a range of items from tobacco to windows. The Directory looked to the generals to pay for the wars and finance the government by raising loans or indemnities from the conquered nations. This increased the dependence of the government on the army, and created growing resentment and disloyalty in the territories 'liberated' by the French from Belgium to Naples. In the sequence of war, conscription, taxation, military emergency and resistance, the Directory seemed doomed to repeat the blunders of its predecessors. Furthermore, the Directors did not trust either the Jacobin left or the Royalist right to provide a constitutional opposition, and they had little faith that the moderate centre could endure without the army. Peace might bring stability and time for consolidation (as Lenin would perceive over a century later), but a lasting peace would involve giving up some hard-won conquests which the army would not allow.

The Directors tried to ensure that the elections to the Councils in April 1797 favoured approved candidates of the moderate centre without success; 182 Royalists took their seats. Three of the

Directors who became known as the Triumvirs, Reubell, La Révellière and Barras, had General Hoche move his troops to the capital and in September staged the coup of 18 Fructidor. Fifty-three deputies were arrested, many newspapers closed, and Barthélemy and Carnot replaced as Directors by Neufchâteau (an anti-clerical) and Douai, who ironically had helped to draft the constitution in the first place. There was no opposition to this coup which set aside the results of the election.

With 437 Council seats to fill in 1798, the government redoubled its efforts to prevent another Royalist swing. Propaganda sought to damage both extremes by talking of 'Royalism in a red cap'. The election in April showed Jacobinism's growing popularity with 162 former members of the Convention (including 71 who voted for the King's death) being returned. Under the provision of the Law of 22 Floréal the election of 127 deputies was overturned; among those 'Floréalised' by the coup were eighty-six known Jacobins. Again there was no serious protest.

In the elections of March 1799 the few who bothered to vote returned only sixty-six of the government's 187 approved candidates, and it seemed clear that the Directory was unable to win popularity. This time the Councils called the Directors to account for the recent failures in the war, and raised the charge of corruption at the 'dilapidations' suffered by the country. The newly nominated Director Sieyès saw his chance to alter the system of government into one with a stronger executive. Another new Director, Gohier, and the Director Barras, the former nobleman, 'an unparalleled cynic, "surrounded by crooked men and fallen women",' as Gordon Wright describes him (G. Wright, *France in Modern Times*, New York, Norton, 1987, p. 62), planned with Fouché and Talleyrand to use Bonaparte, who returned to Paris in November. Under the pretext of a Jacobin threat in the city, the Councils moved to Saint-Cloud under the protection of Bonaparte's soldiers, and the Directors resigned in order to highlight the need for a strong executive. Bonaparte then confronted the Councils and compelled some deputies to adjourn the Legislature, appoint a committee to draw up a new constitution and entrust the government meanwhile to three Consuls – Ducos, Sieyès and Bonaparte.

In the coup of 18–19 Brumaire Year VIII (9–10 November 1799), the Directory had fallen to the military whose power it had done so much to increase. With French armies just beginning to turn the tide against their opponents in Holland and Italy, it is hard to escape the conclusion that the revolutionary decade had come full circle. Paris had ceased to be the pacemaker of events, the hopes of the *sans-culottes* for a better life had been crushed by economic hardship and conscription, while continuing wars of conquest drained resources, made a mockery of the ideal of 'liberty and fraternity', and left the country teetering on the brink of proclaiming '*La patrie en danger*' as the Terrorists had done in 1793. An authoritarian government was poised to emerge; would it develop or destroy the Revolution?

SECTION B – SOURCES

WHY DID REPUBLICAN FRANCE WAGE WAR, AND WHAT EFFECT DID WAR HAVE ON THE REVOLUTION?

The war which began early in 1792 generated great enthusiasm, as Gaudet's speech (extract A (i)) illustrates, and Robespierre was in a tiny minority in voicing his suspicions of the motives and likely results of war at this stage (extract A (ii)). The war escalated quickly into a crusade to extend 'liberty' beyond France's borders (extracts A (iii and iv)), and quickly demanded a new level of national involvement and effort which the *levée en masse* (extract B (ii)) symbolised; the era of total war had arrived. The defeats which France suffered early in the war created panic (extract B (i)), sealed the fate of the monarchy, damaged the reputation of the Girondins who had urged war, and magnified Robespierre's stature as the incorruptible prophet of Republican virtue. War was to be waged on all fronts by the Jacobin Committees, which became all powerful by the autumn of 1793 (extracts C (i–iii)); against speculators who profited from scarcities, against first price inflation and later wage inflation, against those in revolt in the provinces, against the European coalition which saw no prospect of coexistence with such a fanatical

regime, and against even those who failed to demonstrate proper enthusiasm for the Republic (extracts C (i–iii) and E). Many died in the Terror, which was part of the strong, centralised government's machinery of power, and many more died in the various fronts of the war, but it is difficult to imagine the Revolution surviving the enormous challenges without the Jacobin dictatorship. On the other hand, the increasing spiral of violence and intolerance within France probably suggests that the original principles of the Revolution were destroyed in the process. Did the treatment kill the patient?

A Attitudes to war

(i) From Gaudet's speech to the Legislative Assembly, 14 January 1792

the French nation has decided to maintain its constitution in its entirety; we shall die here . . . (members of the Assembly) – *Yes, we swear it! . . . We shall live in freedom or we shall die, the constitution or death!*) . . . In a word, let us mark out in advance a place for traitors, and that place will be on the scaffold.

(*Archives parlementaires* XXXVI, p. 406, cited in T.C.W. Blanning, *The French Revolutionary Wars, 1787–1802*, London, Arnold, 1996, pp. 65–66)

(ii) From Robespierre's speech to the Jacobin Club, 2 January 1792

The court and the factions have no doubt reasons for adopting their plan for war; what should be ours? 'The honour of the French name,' you say. Good heavens, the French nation dishonoured by this mob of fugitives, as ridiculous as powerless, . . . Ah! The shame of being deceived by the unscrupulous artifices of the enemies of our liberty. Magnanimity, wisdom, liberty, fortune, virtue, there is our honour.

(H. Morse Stephens (ed.) *The Principal Speeches of the Statesmen and Orators of the French Revolution*, vol. 2, pp. 306–16, cited in L.W. Cowie, *The French Revolution*, London, Macmillan, 1987, p. 81)

(iii) From the declaration of war on Austria, 29 April 1792

The National Assembly declares that the French nation, faithful to the principles enshrined in the Constitution 'not to undertake any war with the aim of making conquests and never to employ its forces against the liberty of any people,' only take up arms to maintain its liberty and independence.

(*Archives parlementaires* XLII, pp. 217–18, p. 406, cited in Cowie, *French Revolution*, p. 82)

(iv) From the Decree of Fraternity, 19 November 1792

The National Convention declares, in the name of the French nation, that it will grant fraternity and assistance to all peoples who wish to recover their liberty, and instructs the Executive Power to give the necessary orders to the generals to grant assistance to these peoples and to defend those citizens who have been – or may be – persecuted for their attachment to the cause of liberty.

(*Archives parlementaires* LIII, pp. 472–74, cited in Blanning, *French Revolutionary Wars*, p. 92)

B Mobilisation

(i) Mme Roland to Bancal des Issarts, 2 September 1792

Our mad Commune hampers everything. . . . Even as I write the alarm cannon is fired, the drums beat out the call to arms, the tocsin is tolled and everyone rushes to his Section. On whose orders? No one has given any. But the Commune has said that this evening the people must assemble in the Champs de Mars.

(*Roland*, vol. 1, Perroud, pp. 432–34, cited in J. Hardman, *The French Revolution*, London, Arnold, 1981, p. 153)

(ii) From the levée en masse decree, 23 August 1793

From this time until the enemies of France have been expelled from the territory of the Republic, all Frenchmen are in a state of permanent requisition for the army. The young men will go to fight; married men will forge arms and transport food and supplies; women will make tents and uniforms and work in hospitals; children will find old rags for bandages; old men will appear in public places to excite the courage of the warriors, the hatred of kings, and the unity of the Republic.

(cited in translation in D.G. Wright, *Revolution and Terror in France 1789–95*, London, Longman, 1990, p. 125)

(iii) Official figures showing the size of the army

1793	February	361,000
1794	January	670,900
	April	842,300
	August	1,075,000

(S.T. Ross, *Quest for Victory: French Military Strategy 1792–99*, New York, 1973, p. 61, cited in Blanning, *French Revolutionary Wars*, p. 120)

C The setting up of *gouvernement révolutionnaire* in 1793

(i) From Saint Just's speech to the Convention, 10 October 1793

You can hope for no prosperity as long as the last enemy of liberty breathes. You have to punish not only the traitors but even those who are neutral; you have to punish whoever is inactive in the Republic and does nothing for it: because, since the French people have declared its will, everyone who is opposed to it is outside the sovereign body; and everyone who is outside the sovereign body is an enemy.

(ii) From the Law of 19 Vendémiaire Year II (10 October 1793)

1 The provisional government of France is revolutionary for the duration of the war.
2 The Provisional Executive Council, the ministers, the generals and constituted authorities are placed under the surveillance of the Committee of Public Safety which will report every week to the Convention.

(iii) From the Law of 14 Frimaire Year II (4 December 1793)

1 The National Convention is the only centre of impulse on government.
2 All the constituted authorities and public functionaries are placed under the immediate supervision of the Committee of Public Safety for measures concerned with government . . . for everything relating to individuals and to general and internal police, this particular supervision belongs to the Convention's Committee of General Security . . . these two committees are obliged to give an account of their

operations to the National Convention at the end of each month. . . .

6 Surveillance . . . in the Departments is exclusively attributed to the Districts, who are obliged to give a faithful account every ten days to the Committee of Public Safety . . . and to the Convention's Surveillance Committee. . . .

11 It is expressly forbidden for any authority or public functionary to issue proclamations or to take measures which extend, limit or contradict the literal meaning of the law, on the pretext of interpreting or expanding it.

(Gouvernement révolutionnaire, Mautouchet, pp. 196–202 and 233–43, cited in Hardman, *French Revolution*, pp. 180–82)

D G. Rudé's judgement on *Gouvernement révolutionnaire*

The Terror remained [following Law of 14 Frimaire], but it was to be institutionalized and directed from the centre. It was the end of anarchy, but it was the beginning of the end of popular initiative as well.

Thus, strong government had at length emerged and it is doubtful if the Republic's achievements could have been realized without it. Yet, by its very nature, it could hardly fail to provoke a chorus of protests from former supporters and injured parties.

(G. Rudé, *Revolutionary Europe, 1783–1815*, London, Fontana, 1972, p. 148)

E From Saint Just's speech to the Convention, 26 February 1794

Oh, do not allow yourselves to become soft-hearted! . . . To see the indulgence that is advocated by a few, you would think that they were the masters of our own destiny and the chief priests of freedom. Since the month of May last, our history is a lesson about the terrible extremities to which indulgence leads. In that period, Dumouriez had abandoned our conquests; patriots were being assassinated in Frankfort; Custine had abandoned Mainz, the Palatinate and the banks of the Rhine; Calvados was in revolt; the Vendée was victorious; Lyon, Bordeaux, Marseille and Toulon were in arms against the French people; . . . our armies were being

beaten in the Pyrenees and around Mont Blanc. You were being betrayed by everyone.

(Wright, *Revolution and Terror in France*, pp. 134–35)

F S. Schama's view of the Revolution

From the very beginning – from the summer of 1789 – violence was the motor of the Revolution. . . . 'There must be blood to cement revolution', said Mme. Roland, who would herself perish by the logical application of her enthusiasm. While it would be grotesque to implicate the generation of 1789 in the kind of hideous atrocities perpetrated under the Terror, it would be equally naive not to recognize that the former made the latter possible . . . all the features of what historians have come to designate the 'political culture of the Revolution' – were the products of the same morbid preoccupation with the just massacre and the heroic death.

(S. Schama, *Citizens*, London, Penguin, 1989, p. 859)

Questions

1 Read extracts A (i–iv). To what extent do the extracts show that the original reasons taking France to war had changed?

2 How useful are extracts B (i–iii) for showing the war mobilisation of France at this time?

3 In what ways do extracts C (i–iii) suggest that government became more authoritarian and intolerant before the end of 1793?

4 To what extent is Rudé's analysis (extract D) about the nature and results of *Gouvernement révolutionnaire* supported by the evidence? You should refer to extracts B (iii) and C (i–iii), as well as using your own knowledge, in your answer.

5 Does extract E provide an explanation for *Gouvernement révolutionnaire* and the Terror, or is Saint Just simply preparing an attack on Danton?

6 Use the extracts and your own knowledge to evaluate Schama's argument that 'violence was the motor of the Revolution' (extract F).

7 Compare and contrast the views of Rudé and Schama (extracts D and F) on the French Revolution.

Further reading

Several of the works mentioned in the previous chapters go on to cover this period well. The great controversy about Robespierre, Danton and the Terror may be approached through Norman Hampson's very accessible biographies, *Danton* (Oxford, Blackwell, 1988) and *The Life and Opinions of Maximilien Robespierre* (Oxford, Blackwell, 1988). J.M. Thompson's classic *The Leaders of the French Revolution* (Oxford, Blackwell, 1965) is very readable. The Historical Association pamphlet by Hampson, *The Terror and the French Revolution* (London, Historical Association, 1981), debates the issues. Another pamphlet by G. Rudé, *Interpretations of the French Revolution* (London, Historical Association, 1961), reviews the histiography of the whole Revolution very concisely, from Burke and Carlyle, Michelet, Taine and Aulard, to Mathiez, who constructed a great defence of Robespierre in the 1920s and 1930s. The later works of G. Lefebvre modified the starkness of the Danton–Robespierre debate, but readers today may find more accessible Gwynne Lewis, *The French Revolution: Rethinking the Debate* (London, Routledge, 1993), or perhaps François Furet, *Interpreting the French Revolution* (Cambridge University Press, 1981) and Jacques Solé, *Questions of the French Revolution* (New York, Pantheon, 1989). An intriguing study of the Terror at its most gruesome is Daniel Arasse's *The Guillotine and the Terror* (London, Penguin, 1989). M.J. Sydenham's *The Girondins* (London, Athlone Press, 1961) remains a helpfully focused study, as does Charles Tilly's *The Vendée* (Cambridge, MA, Harvard University Press, 1964).

Documentary collections covering this period include J. Hardman, *The French Revolution* (London, Arnold, 1991), L.W. Cowie, *The French Revolution* (London, Macmillan, 1992) and D.G. Wright, *Revolution and Terror in France 1789–1795* (London, Longman, 1990), which contains some source material.

• CHAPTER FIVE •

The Rule of Napoleon

• CONTENTS •

KEY DATES

1799	9–10 Nov.	Coup of 18–19 Brumaire
	15 Dec.	Constitution of Year VIII; Napoleon is First Consul
1800	June	Napoleon defeats Austrians at Marengo, after crossing the Alps
	Dec.	Moreau defeats Austrians at Hohenlinden
1801	Feb.	Peace of Lunéville with Austria
	July	Concordat with the Pope
1802	25 March	Treaty of Amiens with Britain; war of the Second Coalition ends
	April	Concordat published with the Organic Articles
	Aug.	Napoleon made Consul for life
1803	18 May	Britain declares war on France
	Dec.	Boulogne invasion force assembled
1804	March	Royalist conspiracy; Cadoudal arrested; Duc d'Enghien kidnapped and shot
	Dec.	Napoleon crowned Emperor
1805	August	Napoleon abandons plan to invade Britain; war of the Third Coalition begins
	Oct.	Nelson's victory at Trafalgar Austrian surrender to Napoleon at Ulm
	Dec.	Napoleon's victory at Austerlitz over Russian and Austrian force; Austria signs Peace of Pressburg
1806	Oct.	Prussia defeated at Jena and Auerstädt
	Nov.	Berlin Decrees establish Continental System
1807	Feb.	Inconclusive battle of Eylau with Russia
	June	Napoleon defeats Russian army at Friedland
	July	Treaty of Tilsit with Russia; alliance, and Grand Duchy of Warsaw established; Treaty of Tilsit with Prussia; forced to pay indemnity and join Continental System; Third Coalition destroyed
	Oct.	French army moves through Spain into Portugal to extend Continental System
1808	Feb.	French forces occupy Rome
	July	Joseph Bonaparte made King of Spain; French army defeated at Bailen by Spanish force
	Dec.	French under Napoleon's command recapture Madrid
1809	July	Napoleon defeats Austrians at Wagram
1812	June	*Grande Armée* advances into Russia
	Sept.	Russian defeat at Borodino; French army enters Moscow
	Oct.	French begin retreat from Moscow
	Dec.	French survivors return to Germany
1813	Feb.–July	Fourth Coalition formed by Russia, Prussia, Austria and Britain
	Oct.	Battle of the Nations, Leipzig; defeated Napoleon retreats to the Rhine
1814	March	Paris occupied by allies
	11 April	Napoleon abdicates
	May	Bourbon restoration; Louis XVIII (Comte de Provence) King; Napoleon exiled to Elba First treaty of Paris imposed on France
1815	1 March	Napoleon returns for the One Hundred Days
	20 March	Napoleon arrives in Paris; Louis XVIII flees
	18 June	Waterloo; Wellington's stand and Blücher's arrival defeats Napoleon's army decisively
	22 June	Napoleon abdicates again
	8 July	Louis XVIII is restored again
	15 July	Napoleon leaves France for exile on St Helena
	Nov.	Second treaty of Paris

SECTION A

Napoleon Bonaparte was born in Corsica in 1769, the son of minor Corsican nobility, which enabled him to train and qualify as an artillery officer in France in 1785. Following his success with the recapture of Toulon in 1793, he became a general, his rapid promotion helped by the way that war and revolution had thinned down the officer corps of the regular army. He survived the fall of the Jacobin dictatorship in 1794, having been imprisoned briefly, and he re-established himself by his part in crushing the Vendémiaire rising. He was appointed commander of the Army of the Interior by the grateful Directory. In 1796, following his marriage to the widow and fashionable celebrity Josephine de Beauharnais, he took the Army of Italy through a spectacular series of victories over the Austrians, which he made sure were colourfully reported. By 1797 he had the status of a hero at home. In 1798 he led an expedition to Egypt as part of the strategy to dislocate the British empire, but he was stranded there after Nelson's victory at the Battle of the Nile in August 1798. The next year Napoleon abandoned his army and slipped home to France where he involved himself with Sieyès and others in the Brumaire coup of 1799. He had not been the first or even the second choice accomplice in the coup, which owed its final success mostly to his brother, Lucien, who was President of the Council of Five Hundred.

This record reflects the combination of luck, ability and opportunism which is at the heart of 'Bonapartism'. Once he became First Consul in 1799, Napoleon proceeded carefully but with growing authority and confidence to order and control France. In the process the decade of Revolution was developed, or halted, or reversed, the analysis depending upon the definition of the Revolution and its end-point. Success in war was crucial, as it had been for the Jacobin dictatorship, and the second Italian campaign and the ending of the war of the Second Coalition in 1802 helped to consolidate the Napoleonic regime. He crowned himself Emperor in 1804. Military triumphs continued and helped to bring prosperity to France, lending 'Bonapartism' a glory and a glow that would burn throughout France's nineteenth century. But the tide began to turn as the war in Spain dragged on after 1808. The disastrous Russian campaign of 1812 created enormous strains on French manpower and the economy. Defeat and abdication followed in 1814, followed by

Napoleon's extraordinary One Hundred Day comeback in 1815. Napoleon's reception on his return from Elba proved the attraction of 'Bonapartism', and his narrow defeat at Waterloo arguably added tragedy to the Napoleonic legend, rather than guilt for the loss of 32,000 French and 22,000 allied casualties. Perhaps strangely to a modern era which is accustomed to war crimes trials, Napoleon was allowed to retire in exile to St Helena and develop the glamour of 'Bonapartism'. He died on the island in 1821, but in 1840 his remains were reburied with great reverence beneath the dome of the Invalides in Paris.

NAPOLEON'S RULE IN FRANCE

The Constitution of Year VIII (1799)

After the Brumaire coup a constitution was drawn up quickly. Sieyès wanted a rigid separation of powers between the legislature and the executive, and a complex system of elections to produce 'confidence from below, authority from above' (cited in D.M.G. Sutherland, *France 1789–1815: Revolution and Counterrevolution*, London, Fontana, 1990, p. 338). Napoleon took exception to being made Grand Elector while two Consuls held executive power. With the mixture of pressure and persuasion for which Napoleon became famous, Sieyès's scheme was greatly changed and he had to console himself with the presidency of the Senate and a large country estate.

The new Constitution of Year VIII was ready in December 1799. The key position was that of First Consul, and Bonaparte was appointed for ten years. The other two Consuls, Cambacérès and Lebrun, had the power to advise only, and make proposals for the budget and for legislation which only the first Consul could amend. Cobban's verdict on the legislative shows that there were no checks here to the new dictator's powers either: 'The simulacrum of representative institutions was preserved as a sop to revolutionary tradition, with an advisory Senate, a Legislative Body which could vote but not speak, and a Tribunate which could speak but not vote' (A. Cobban, *A History of Modern France*, vol. 2, London, Penguin, 1970, pp. 19–20). A Council of

State was appointed by Napoleon to advise, prepare legislation, and act as the administrative hub of this highly centralised government. All this seemed a far cry from the hopes of democracy which the Revolution had brought in, and Napoleon's proclamation that the 'Revolution is ended' (extract A (i)) had a suitably deadly ring to it. But popular sovereignty was acknowledged by the plebiscite, which officially produced over 3 million votes in favour of the new constitution and only 1,562 against. However Lucien Bonaparte, the Minister of the Interior, added half a million votes from the army which had not been polled, and many other inventions, so the real vote was about 1.5 million in favour. In Paris only 23 per cent of those who had the vote bothered to exercise it, perhaps explaining Napoleon's comments about the lack of interest in liberty (extracts B (i–iii)). Certainly political participation no longer had the power to intoxicate Paris as it had done ten years earlier.

Changes to the Constitution

It is easy to overlook the fragile nature of the regime during the first two or three years because of its later strength. Until later in 1800 bands of brigands, draft-dodgers and deserters made large areas of the countryside very dangerous and in places they attacked tax officers and fought National Guardsmen. Unrest was often provoked by former nobles, who aimed to restore a king and Catholicism. Those who had bought lands which once belonged to the Church or to nobles were often targeted, and many bourgeois property owners feared that a restoration of the *ancien régime* would threaten the prosperity which the Revolution had brought them. An assassination attempt on Napoleon in December 1800 heightened these fears, and prompted the Senate to offer Napoleon the Consulship for life, with the right to nominate his successor. This step towards hereditary rule would help to entrench the regime against a restoration of the Bourbons. Another plebiscite duly approved this change, but this time the army did vote and caught the authorities by surprise; 40 per cent of the 8,374 votes against the change were cast by Napoleon's soldiers!

Other changes to the Constitution followed.

The Senate and its powers were enlarged as Napoleon wanted. This cut down the role of both the Legislative Body and the Tribunate, which met less and less often and whose membership included many of Napoleon's nominees. The reduction in the power of these two representative bodies was paralleled by a change in the electoral system in 1802. Sieyès's complicated system was abolished. In its place every five years adult men (there was no enfranchisement of women) chose a departmental electoral college from a list of the wealthiest men in the department. These electoral colleges produced lists of candidates for election to the Legislative Body and the Tribunate. Far from being the representatives of their constituents, the wealthy men selected were Napoleon's clients, given posts and contracts in return for using their influence in the government's interests. The property owners and the Napoleonic regime were tied tightly together in mutual self-interest.

The Concordat, 1802

The assassination attempt in the rue Nicaise in December 1800 was used as a reason to deport a number of Jacobin suspects, although royalists had been responsible. Royalists were executed in 1801 for other conspiracies, and Napoleon aimed to remove one reason for royalist popularity by arranging a reconciliation with the Catholic Church. From December 1800 Sunday worship was permitted and churches were reopened. However, there is much evidence to show that priests were already active and churches busy under the Directory, making the Concordat with Pope Pius VII in 1801 (it was published in 1802) little more than an official acceptance of a Catholic revival which was already under way. The Pope accepted the Revolution, the loss of Church lands, and that the clergy were appointed by, paid and bound by oath to the government. In return the government merely accepted Catholicism as the religion of the majority, and Napoleon angered Rome by adding the Organic Articles giving him tight control over the Bishops and requiring church teaching to reinforce the authority of the state. In 1806 Napoleon increased his hold by imposing a standard catechism for all churches (extract C (ii)). It was clear that Napoleon regarded religion simply as another mechanism for controlling the people and for producing obedient soldiers (extract C (i)).

Crowning the Emperor, 1804

When a royalist agent had his fingers crushed under a musket hammer during interrogation in 1804 he betrayed a royalist plot to kidnap or kill Napoleon. Cadoudal, Pichegru, the former Jacobin, Moreau, and many suspects from Brittany were arrested. Napoleon decided to send an unmistakable message to all conspirators by arranging for the Duc d'Enghien (grandson of the Prince of Condé) to be kidnapped from neutral Baden, brought before a tribunal in Paris and shot in a ditch that night. His connection with the plotters was not proven, but the action was doubly successful. It deterred further conspiracies, and it emphasised the seriousness of the threat; as Sutherland points out, the 'plot seemed to show that only Bonaparte stood between a restoration and the preservation of what remained of revolutionary achievement' (Sutherland, *France 1789–1815*, p. 364). This made the argument that only the full-blooded adoption of the hereditary principle would stop further assassination attempts seem plausible, and the Council of State, Legislative Body, Tribunate and Senate agreed without controversy that Napoleon should be crowned Emperor.

The ceremony in December 1804 was attended by the Pope, and made memorable because Napoleon took the crown himself and placed it on his head, showing symbolically that he was creating a dynasty. Josephine did not produce an heir, however, and she was divorced in 1809. The way was cleared for Napoleon's marriage the next year to Marie Louise of Austria. Although she was unpopular as the niece of Marie Antoinette, she gave birth to the necessary son and heir, Napoleon II, King of Rome, in 1811.

Controlling the people

The carrot and stick method for keeping power was used effectively not just with the Church. Local government was taken out of the hands of the citizens in 1800, and departments were to be run by a prefect who was appointed by Napoleon and who answered to the Minister of the Interior. Sub-prefects (of arrondissements) and mayors (of communes) executed the prefect's instructions. Not only was this a highly centralised system like the way *intendents* operated under the *ancien régime*, but also it gave Napoleon a vast system of patronage. The grateful office-holders became his loyal supporters and formed part of the class which is called the notables, comprising men of wealth and ability from a variety of backgrounds. In the army, too, promotion on merit opened the way for former royalists and Jacobins to rise, and Ney became a Marshal of France from very humble family origins.

Although liberty in the sense of a free press and popular participation in government was removed, Napoleon recognised the appeal of equality, even if it was only allowed as equality of opportunity or 'a career open to talent' (see extracts B (i–iii)). The awarding of the Legion of Honour (introduced in 1802) and the many ranks and titles which followed under the Empire helped to create the new elite which was based less upon birth but merit (it is true that merit was sometimes measured as wealth). The educational system was reformed with the creation of the selective *lycées* after 1802. These provided an excellent education for the new meritocrats who would in their turn run the regime, and they were free to the sons of army officers. Other schools were set up, but primary education was often left in the hands of the Church, and women were not considered to need much of an education as their primary role was to serve their husbands and produce children.

Fouché's career revived when he was placed in charge of the police, and he operated an extensive surveillance operation to catch conspirators and also to feed back public opinion to his master. Napoleon had other sources. In Paris he ran an independent (and much feared) secret police, which checked up on Fouché's operations as well, and all of Napoleon's many appointees throughout France and the empire were expected to report back secretly.

Censorship was extensive and political reporting and comment quickly became a government monopoly. Between 1799 and the end of 1800 the number of newspapers in Paris had fallen from seventy-three to ten, and by 1811 there were only four. Each Department was allowed one paper, and the official *Le Moniteur* had no rival for reporting. Bulletins (usually from the war front) were a major vehicle for propaganda, which Napoleon developed thoroughly from the days of his victories in Italy under the Directory; 'to lie like a bulletin' became a common simile. No criticism of Napoleon was permitted, and one poet who dared to rhyme 'Napoleon' with 'chameleon' was placed in a lunatic asylum for implying a comparison. The effect of these controls, and spectacles such as David's portrait of the First Consul leading the crossing of the Alps on a rearing horse (in fact he followed his troops on a mule) was to glorify Napoleon and help to make many people feel secure and confident with the regime. The Napoleonic legend began here.

The Code Napoleon, 1804

By and large the police and the administration operated within the law, and the regime made important changes to the system. Judges became government appointees rather than elected officials. The Civil Code of law (*Code Napoleon* as it was called later) was a development of the work of previous Revolutionary governments. It attempted to reconcile the customary law which operated in the north of France with the more patriarchal Roman law of the south in a unified and streamlined system. Napoleon was closely involved in shaping the final result. The authority of the male head of the household was strengthened, following Roman law, and while the husband could have his adulterous wife imprisoned, a wife could obtain a divorce (a very expensive process) only if her husband kept his mistress in the family house. Among the other illiberal features of the Code, workers had to hold a *livret* for the police to check their employment record, and slavery was reintroduced in the colonies. On the other hand, changes made by the Revolution were included. The abolition of feudal obligations and the title to church and other lands which had been sold off were established, and land was to be divided equally between legitimate sons on the father's death. Codes of Commercial Law,

and tough Criminal and Penal codes, followed. While the prison population tripled during Napoleon's period in power, it is clear that property owners and those appointed to the numerous posts in the judiciary benefited greatly from the system of law and order.

Taxation and the economy

The reintroduction of a metal currency brought a painful return of confidence in the system after the inflation of the mid-1790s, and Napoleon's regime reaped the benefit of this achievement. A Bank of France was founded in 1800, and taken under state control in 1806 to control the issue of paper currency. This was needed for commerce, but the notes were restricted to high value denominations only to avoid mass circulation and the risk of inflation.

Of more urgent concern to the new regime was the shortage of tax revenue. Gaudin was appointed to the Ministry of Finance in 1799 and ran the government's revenue-raising operations until 1814. The taxation system was completely overhauled, new registers drawn up for the land tax and the tax on personal income. Indirect taxes raised nearly five times the revenue, and they were more burdensome to the poorer classes; many items attracted a duty including salt in 1806, recalling the hated *gabelle* of the *ancien régime*. Barbé-Marbois and (after 1806) Mollien ran the treasury's spending controls. Expenditure had to be authorised by law or by a ministerial instruction, and thorough accounts were kept, giving the executive tight control for the first time since long before the Revolution.

The reforms benefited the bourgeoisie most. The *sans-culottes*, controlled by the *livret*, taxed and conscripted, were kept fed but hardly prosperous. The peasantry suffered similarly, and often resented the subdivision of the landholding into uneconomic units among several sons. However, Napoleon's regime remained preferable and infinitely more glamorous than a Bourbon restoration which might bring back the burdens of feudalism.

It was the progress of war which really determined the buoyancy of the economy. While France's imperial and commercial borders expanded, the economy prospered and other nations shared the military costs. When the empire began to contract after 1812 the costs of defence and the burden of conscription fell on France alone. The first poor harvest for some time was gathered in 1811, and the yield in 1812 was poor also, but bourgeois discontent focused on Napoleon's failures in Spain and Russia, and the cost of the trade war with Britain, and this class began to desert the Emperor.

WAR, 1803–08

Napoleon's regime was almost continuously at war. Except for the uneasy peace with Britain between March 1802 and May 1803, France under Napoleon was always embattled on one or many fronts between 1799 and 1814, and of course she faced the final show-down on the battlefield of Waterloo when Napoleon returned in 1815 (see Map 5.1). Success in battle had brought Napoleon to prominence before Brumaire, then it was vital to defeat the Austrians in Italy to establish the regime, and the expansion of the empire and its later contraction regulated the prosperity of France and the glamour of her leader. Although Napoleon remarked in 1800 that, were he to die in three or four years, France should choose a civilian government, he was more truthful about the nature of his power once he was on St Helena: 'In the last analysis, in order to rule one must be a soldier: without spurs and boots, no government' (translated in J.C. Herold, *The Mind of Napoleon*, New York, Columbia University Press, 1955, p. 77).

The end of the Second Coalition

The coup of Brumaire gave Napoleon the concentrated authority over resources and strategy which he had not had before, and which his adversaries never had. In May 1800 he took the risky step of marching the new reserve army across the Alps (see Figures 5.1 and 5.2). Descending from the St Bernard Pass onto the plains of Piedmont, he took the Austrian forces in the rear and defeated them at Marengo on 14 June. Napoleon then returned to Paris, secure as the heroic First Consul.

Meanwhile, Moreau crossed the Rhine in April and drove the Austrian army back; after the armistice expired in November, Moreau defeated the Austrians at Hohenlinden (in Bavaria) on 3 December. Defeated to the north and south of the Alps, Austria signed the treaty of Lunéville with France in February 1801. French control of her sister republics in Italy and Switzerland (Cisalpine, Ligurian, Batavian and Helvetic) was confirmed, and Austria retained Venetia only. Tuscany became the kingdom of Etruria, and the Pope was confirmed as the ruler of the Papal States. In the north, French control of lands to the west of the Rhine was confirmed, including Belgium and Luxembourg. The Second Coalition against France was finished; Tsar Paul had pulled out in October 1799, and Austria's humiliation left only Britain at war. British forces defeated the remnant of Napoleon's Egyptian expedition in March 1801, and Nelson mortally damaged the Danish fleet (allied with France in the Armed Neutrality League, aimed against British trade) at Copenhagen in April, clearing the way for an uneasy balance of power to be struck. In March 1802 Britain and France signed the treaty of Amiens. Britain returned all of her colonial gains except Ceylon and Trinidad, while France agreed to respect the commercially sensitive independence of Naples, the Batavian Republic (Holland) and Portugal.

The Napoleonic war

Britain's colonial losses under the peace of Amiens caused uproar in Britain: 'Peace in a week, war in a month', Lord Malmesbury remarked, but it was destroyed within fourteen months by Napoleonic ambition as well (F. Markham, *Napoleon*, New York, New American Library, 1963, p. 103). Napoleon raised tariffs against British imports, retained control in Holland and the Helvetic Republic, and made a threat to recapture Egypt, while the British government kept hold of Malta and allowed the press to ridicule 'Boney'. Why did Napoleon not call a halt to war at this stage? As with the other turning-points that lay ahead, notably his offensive against the Spanish peninsula in 1807 and Russia in 1812, the answer lies in the nature of the man himself. Napoleon's aims were

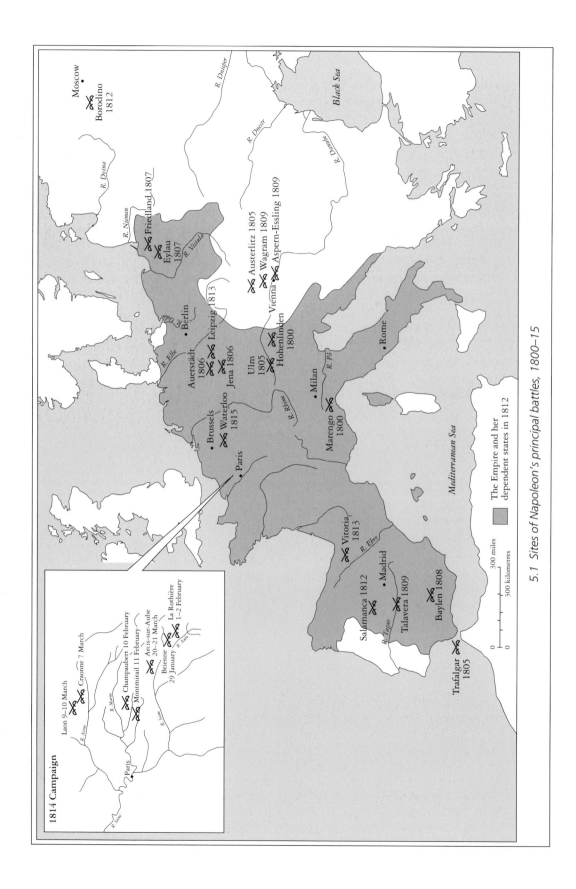

1814 Campaign

Laon 9–10 March

Craonne 7 March

Champaubert 10 February

Montmirail 11 February

Arcis-sur-Aube 20–21 March

La Rothière 1–2 February

Brienne 29 January

Paris

R. Seine

R. Aisne

R. Marne

R. Aube

Moscow

Borodino 1812

Black Sea

R. Dnieper

R. Dniestr

R. Danube

R. Dvina

Friedland 1807

R. Niemen

Eylau 1807

R. Vistula

Austerlitz 1805

Wagram 1809

Vienna · Aspern-Essling 1809

Berlin

Leipzig 1813

R. Elbe

Auerstädt 1806

Jena 1806

Ulm 1805

Hohenlinden 1800

· Rome

R. Po

· Milan

R. Rhine

Brussels

Waterloo 1815

· Paris

Marengo 1800

Mediterranean Sea

The Empire and her dependent states in 1812

Vitoria 1813

R. Ebro

Salamanca 1812

· Madrid

R. Tagus

Talavera 1809

Baylen 1808

Trafalgar 1805

0   300 miles

0   300 kilometres

5.1 Sites of Napoleon's principal battles, 1800–15

5.1 Napoleon crossing the Alps, May 1800, painted by J-L. David in 1800–1

Source: Charlottenburg Castle, Berlin, Stiftung Preußische Schlösser und Gärten Berlin-Brandenburg/Bildarchiv.

5.2 Napoleon crossing the Alps, May 1800, painted by P. de la Roche in 1837

Source: The Board of Trustees of the National Museums and Galleries on Merseyside (Walker Art Gallery, Liverpool)

never defined, so his war was simply 'the maximisation of his power' as Blanning says; he quotes Schroeder saying that 'his whole character and career were fundamentally wrong: he always went too far' (P. Schroeder, *The Transformation of European Politics 1763–1848*, Oxford, Clarendon Press, 1994, p. 284, cited in T.C.W. Blanning, *The French Revolutionary Wars, 1787–1802*, London, Arnold, 1996, p. 261).

After war between Britain and France resumed in May 1803, Napoleon began to assemble an enormous fleet and army at Boulogne. But before an invasion of the British Isles could be launched, the Royal Navy would have to be defeated, or at least lured across the Atlantic and split up. Spain declared war on Britain in December 1804, but the attempt by the combined French and Spanish fleets to draw Nelson to battle in the West Indies during 1805 failed. Instead, Nelson engaged the fleet off Cape Trafalgar on 21 October, crossing and breaking their line-of-battle formation. The short-range 'carronades', cast in the advanced Carron iron-

works, proved capable of firing a broadside down the length of a French ship's hull and killing up to 250 men, helped to inflict a decisive defeat. British supremacy of the seas could not be challenged again, and her navy proceeded to gather up many colonies.

Austerlitz and the defeat of the Third Coalition

On the European continent, however, Napoleon would prove himself the master against the Third Coalition of Austrian and Russian armies, financed by Britain. In September 1805, as Austrian forces prepared offensives in Bavaria and Italy, Napoleon moved with decisive speed. Abandoning the British invasion plan, he left some forces at Boulogne in August to disguise his withdrawal. By the end of September he had 190,000 troops across the Rhine. His 'lightning war' caught the Austrian

General Mack by surprise, forcing him to surrender 33,000 troops at Ulm in October. The Russian force, under Kutusov, prudently tried to avoid
a pitched battle and pulled back, gathering new
Austrian forces as it went. Vienna was occupied by
Napoleon on 15 November. With an increasingly
exhausted army and extended lines of communication, Napoleon pressed on northwards, hoping for
a decisive encounter with the Russian and Austrian
forces. This he achieved at Austerlitz on 2 December 1805 in an engagement which had all the
ingredients of Napoleon's genius as a commander.
He selected the battlefield where his stronger
opponent could be lured, ambushed and destroyed.
He encouraged his tired *Grande Armée* with skill,
strolling into the light of many of his soldiers'
campfires on the eve of battle. He deluded the Tsar
into thinking that he was ready to surrender by
discussing terms. And on the day of battle itself,
he used the discipline of his veteran army to stand
firm, outmanoeuvre and attack, with overwhelming results.

The Tsar and the remnant of his army went
quickly home, and Austria signed the Peace of
Pressberg in December 1805; Napoleon ruled
supreme in northern Italy and in the German
states. Negotiations with Prussia about Hanover
and the blockade of Britain broke down in 1806,
and French forces defeated her at Jena and Auerstädt in October, moving on to occupy Berlin.
Napoleon then gave chase to the Russian army,
advancing through Poland. In February 1807, in a
snowstorm, French and Russian forces fought the
bloody but indecisive battle of Eylau. In June,
Napoleon and Marshal Lannes defeated the Tsar's
army at Friedland, and a cease-fire was agreed. In
July Alexander I and Napoleon met. The treaties of
Tilsit were signed; Russia and France actually
became allies, and the Duchy of Warsaw was created as a French controlled state. The treaty of
Tilsit with Prussia bound her to occupation until
she paid an indemnity, and compelled her to join
the Continental System against British trade.
Napoleon was at the height of his power. In Italy,
where he had taken the title of King in 1805 and
annexed the Ligurian Republic, he went on to
crown his brother King of Naples the next year,
while in 1808 French forces occupied Rome. This
was surely the point to call a halt to war.

Defeat, 1808–15

Napoleon believed that there was more to win. His
decision to continue the struggle against the
commercial power of the British empire has made
'Bonapartism' stand for increasingly reckless military campaigning which risked and lost all it
had won.

The Continental System and the Peninsular War

Having failed to destroy British naval supremacy,
Napoleon aimed to undermine his opponent by
preventing her from trading with Europe. In
November 1806 the Berlin Decrees set up this
blockade. It was a dangerous step because its
enforcement would stretch the empire to breaking
point. Internally, protection of the French economy against British competition helped, but even
the textile industry remained more of a cottage-
based affair than anything on the scale of Lancashire's mills (see Table 5.1). Coastal areas of France
were badly hit by the British counter-blockade,
and unrest and smuggling became common. The
French authorities resorted to issuing licences giving permission to some areas to trade with Britain.

It was France's imperial possessions, and her
allies, who came to resent the Continental System,
and their opposition presented the greatest problem. Napoleon's occupation of Rome in 1808 was
to force the Pope to operate the blockade, and the
opening of the Peninsular campaign in 1807 was
aimed at stopping Portugal's trade with Britain.
Not only did this fail (the value of British exports
through Portugal doubled), but also the campaign
provoked quarrels with Spain. Joseph, King of
Naples, was also made King of Spain in 1808 and
nationalist feelings were awoken there which were
quite comparable to those that the Revolution had
started in France. Open war broke out and a French
army was defeated by a Spanish force at Bailén on
21 July, prompting the intervention of Napoleon
himself with a powerful army. A British force
arrived in Portugal and opened a new theatre of
war there, while Madrid fell to Napoleon's forces
in December and Zaragoza followed in February
1809 after a grisly siege. Napoleon himself left

Table 5.1 British and French economic statistics (annual averages) *c.* 1750–1815

	Britain	*(period)*	*France*	*(period)*
Output of grain crops (million quintals)	35	(*c.* 1790)	98.1	(1781–90)
	43	(*c.* 1810)	94.5	(1803–12)
Output of coal and lignite (million metric tons)	11.2	(1800)	0.8	(1811)
	16.2	(*c.* 1815)	0.9	(*c.* 1815)
Output of pig iron (thousand metric tons)	69	(1788)	141	(1781–90)
	127	(1796)		
	248	(av. 1800–13)	200	(av. 1803–12)
Raw cotton consumption (thousand metric tons)	8.1	(1781–90)	4	(1781–90)
	13.9	(1791–1800)		
	31.8	(1801–14)	8	(1803–12)

his armies in 1809 to attend to a new Austrian threat, but the 'Spanish ulcer' had already begun to drain France's strength and show that French armies were not invincible. By the time that Wellington eventually drove the French across the Pyrenees in 1813, about half of the 600,000 French soldiers committed to the Peninsular war had been lost.

To Moscow, and back

Napoleon confronted the Austrian army in 1809. The new commander, Archduke Charles, had learned much from Napoleon's earlier successes; although he lost the first encounter at Eckmühl in April, he inflicted a defeat on Napoleon at Aspern the following month. But in July Napoleon again, and arguably for the last time, showed his mastery of the battlefield at Wagram. Although Austria lost 40,000 and was compelled to sign the severe treaty of Schönbrunn, the French sustained 32,000 casualties. Had Napoleon been prudent, he would surely have tried to make this and the Peninsular campaign his last.

But tensions with Tsar Alexander I were allowed to grow, for example over French influence in the Duchy of Warsaw. At the end of 1810 Russia imposed new tariffs favouring British goods at the expense of French trade. This was an open challenge to the Continental System, and Napoleon began assembling a *Grande Armée* of over half a million men, roughly half of whom were French. In

June 1812 the army crossed into Russia. As usual, Napoleon planned an early and decisive battle, and his soldiers were not equipped for a campaign which lasted into the winter. Due either to chaos or a grand strategy, the Russian forces avoided an encounter, retreating and drawing Napoleon ever onwards. The 'scorched earth' retreat left nothing for Napoleon's troops to live off, as they had been accustomed to do in the fertile Italian and European theatres, and hundreds of cavalry horses and some 60,000 men were lost before any real battle had been fought.

The Russian commander Kutusov made a stand in September 1812 at Borodino, 60 miles to the west of Moscow. The Russians were defeated, but Napoleon's battered army (now below half-strength), which entered a deserted and burning Moscow a week later, still could not get the Tsar to agree to negotiate peace. The French invaders had stirred Russian patriotism to feats of heroic and brutal resistance, and the *Grande Armée* which set out from Moscow on the dangerous road home on 19 October had succeeded in breathing life into nationalism in Russia as had happened in Spain. Skirmishing attacks and ambushes, together with the icy winter weather, hunger and disease, made the retreat from Moscow a disaster and a humiliation. While the legend of 'Bonapartism' would later emphasise the way the indomitable Emperor marched with his men and encouraged them through their shared suffering, the fact that only 25,000 men survived the campaign meant that it was the turning-point of empire. More defeats than victories lay ahead now.

The Fourth Coalition

Early in 1813 Tsar Alexander I secured Prussian support and pursued Napoleon into Germany. Although Napoleon was victorious in May 1813 at Lützen and Bautzen against Russian and Prussian armies, he was sufficiently realistic about his shortages of men and horses to agree to a cease-fire to last for two months, until August. Within France, the burden of defence began to be felt. Tax levels were raised, and the loss of French domination in Europe restricted her markets and caused the economy to falter. Conscription had been handled sensitively, with married men excused, 'buying out' by paying a substitute permitted, and heavier requirements being levied from the eastern departments than from the more rebellious western areas. But in 1813 the Arch-Chancellor Cambacérès advised that married men should be recruited, and there had been a wild surge in marriages from 14 per thousand of the population in 1811 to 26.5 in 1813 (cited in M. Lyons, *Napoleon Bonaparte and the Legacy of the French Revolution*, London, Macmillan, 1994, p. 48) which showed growing fear and opposition to the needs of empire now. The losses of the Russian campaign had not been adequately hidden from the people.

Austria and Britain (who pledged subsidies) joined Prussia and Russia in the Fourth Coalition in July 1813, and hostilities began in August. In terms of army size, Napoleon was now at a disadvantage. Bravely or foolishly, Napoleon had refused the offer of mediation which the Habsburg Emperor Francis I and Metternich (the Chancellor) had made at a meeting in Dresden on 26 June. The clash came in October at Leipzig. The 'Battle of the Nations' confronted Napoleon's 195,000 with 365,000 Austrian, Russian, Prussian and Swedish soldiers. Napoleon was outmanoeuvred and defeated, taking 73,000 losses to the allies' 54,000, and retreated to the Rhine.

France had lost the Duchy of Warsaw to Russia, and now her empire in Germany had crumbled. Her armies were in retreat in Spain. Holland now rose in revolt, leaving France master only in Belgium and Italy. French people seemed unwilling to respond to the threat of invasion, yet Napoleon stalled for time when peace talks were offered on the basis of France's 'natural frontiers'. Early in 1814 the war resumed. Napoleon's forces were pushed back from the Rhine, and the allies entered Paris at the end of March. On 11 April 1814, Napoleon abdicated as the Emperor of France and King of Italy, and the Senate invited the Comte de Provence to become King Louis XVIII.

The One Hundred Days

After his abdication, Napoleon took the poison he had carried on the Russian campaign. But the concoction had lost its potency and he survived, encouraged that Fate had spared him for some reason. He was allowed to retire with the title of Emperor to the Mediterranean island of Elba on a large pension (which the restored Bourbon King failed to pay). Meanwhile the victorious allies met at the Congress of Vienna to discuss the future of post-Napoleonic Europe.

The restored Bourbons had to accept a constitutional charter, which meant that the *ancien régime* was not to be fully restored. However, many people were suspicious, especially about the ambitions of the King's brother, the Ultra-royalist Comte d'Artois. The revival of courtly etiquette and the white flag of the Bourbons, together with the discontents of so many demobilised soldiers and former officers now without careers, made the new regime widely unpopular. Increasingly, Napoleon's defeat was put down to betrayal, and tales began to circulate that he was about to return to France.

On 1 March 1815, Napoleon did precisely that. Eluding the British navy, he landed with 1,100 fellow adventurers near Cannes. He gathered forces and supplies as he marched north, and Marshal Ney, who promised to capture him in an iron cage, joined him too. The Bourbon King and his court fled across the border, and Napoleon arrived in Paris by 20 March. The Bourbon Charter of 1814 was echoed in the Additional Act of the Imperial Constitution, adding a liberal dimension to Napoleon's rule probably to encourage support. Failing in his attempt to strike deals with the allies separately, he made ready to do battle. The coalition had held together, and its leaders and military commanders had hurried away from Vienna to resume their posts.

The encounter happened on 18 June 1815, near the village of Waterloo, where 67,000 British and allied soldiers under the Duke of Wellington withstood the repeated attacks of the 72,000 under Napoleon's command. At the crucial stage, later in the day's fighting, Marshal Ney launched the giant cavalry charge of 5,000, uphill. Ney believed wrongly that Wellington's army was withdrawing, and he had seized the moment without telling Napoleon. Ney's cavalry regrouped, and charged again. Then Kellermann's cavalry charged, and another 9,000 French infantry surged forward. Wellington's forces formed squares, the infantry loading and firing in ranks, their artillery firing until some gun muzzles bent with the heat. 'Hard pounding this,' remarked Wellington, 'let us see who will pound the longest' (Edward Cotton, *A Voice from Waterloo*, 1852, p. 311, cited in A. Schom, *One Hundred Days*, London, Penguin, 1994, p. 286). The squares were engulfed and weakened, but they held, and Wellington's confidence in the disciplined firepower of this defensive tactic was justified. Huge losses were sustained on both sides, but the main Prussian forces were arriving in increasing numbers and the tide of battle was turning against Napoleon. Rather than disengage and salvage what was left, he staked all on a final attack, perhaps hoping that Grouchy would arrive in time to help. Grouchy did not arrive (adding to the legend of Napoleon's defeat through betrayal), and the charge of Napoleon's Imperial Guard was broken. Napoleon fled the carnage of his last gamble.

Napoleon abdicated for the second time on 22 June. On 8 July Louis XVIII returned to Paris for the second time, thanks to the speedy action of Talleyrand, Fouché and Wellington preventing the allies finding an alternative ruler, and on 15 July Napoleon left France for the remote south Atlantic island of St Helena. The second treaty of Paris, imposed on France in November 1815, punished her for Napoleon's last adventure; she was reduced to her 1790 frontiers, occupied by a garrison of 150,000 for five years, and required to pay an indemnity.

THE NAPOLEONIC IMPACT ON FRANCE

With a Bourbon back on the throne, a damaged economy and casualties amounting to about 1 million men, Napoleon left France far worse for the giddy imperial adventure. Or did he?

France had been changed by the Napoleonic regime. Popular sovereignty had been replaced by a centralised administration, departmental prefects, appointed judges and a structure for suppressing free speech. The taxation system collected revenue efficiently, expenditure controls were good and the currency stabilised with a central Bank of France. Put in these terms, Napoleon's lasting legacy seems to have been a return to the *ancien régime* at full efficiency.

However, some of the changes brought by the Revolution were also made secure. The Civil Code guaranteed equality before the law, and safeguarded property rights including the ownership of former church and crown lands. The Concordat settled relations between the state and the church for the rest of the century by entrenching a position somewhere between that which existed before 1789 and what the most extreme Jacobin dechristianisers had tried to fix. As Stendhal's novel *Scarlet and Black* showed, Republicanism and Catholicism continued to hate each other in the nineteenth century, but the state was better equipped to survive the quarrel.

Who was better off thanks to Napoleon? The matter is much debated by historians, but it seems that neither the *sans-culottes* nor the peasantry had much to show for the years of Empire. But the peasantry in particular developed an extraordinary fascination for the idea of Napoleon as the great protector, the 'Emperor of the common man', and souvenirs of the regime became treasured on many a cottage wall for years to come. The bourgeoisie had much to thank Napoleon for; he protected their property, and for many years reduced the burden of direct taxation and helped French industry and trade. The *lycées* gave an excellent education to the more able and helped many of the bourgeoisie to join the Napoleonic elite of 'notables'. While the school system survived, and while many of the most powerful and wealthy of Napoleon's elite remained prominent in France, the bourgeoisie had grown tired of Napoleon's wars and left it to the peasantry to remember him most fondly.

Therefore some of Napoleon's domestic reforms survived his fall. The legacy of war and empire on France herself is, on the face of it, wholly negative. The losses were enormous. About 7 per cent of the population were killed by war, mostly from the generation of young men, and this damaged the birth rate, although by how much is not certain; the evidence shows that it began to fall before the Revolution, and the pattern of later marriages continued to affect the birth rate too. But the most important legacy of Empire and war on France, and perhaps the most important of all the things that Napoleon left, was in the minds of the people of France. For some he would be the 'ogre' whose personal ambition murdered many, or the Corsican upstart who mocked the thrones of Europe, or the ridiculous dictator who killed off the Revolution. However, many others believed in the Napoleon of legend, the inspirational commander who brought power and glory to France, the ordinary man who rose thanks to the Revolution and his own genius to shake a Europe which would never be the same again. This legend was developed by the version of history produced during the St Helena period, by a selective memory of Napoleon's record, and by the often dreary and shabby record of French governments in the nineteenth century by comparison with 'the good old days'. This became the basis of the appeal of 'Bonapartism'.

SECTION B – SOURCES

NAPOLEON'S RELATIONSHIP TO THE FRENCH REVOLUTION

Napoleon wrote, or rather dictated, between 54,000 and 70,000 letters during the fifteen years he was in power; as J.M. Thompson points out, this average of ten to twelve per day kept his secretaries busy and always at his side. In exile on St Helena, Napoleon dictated his memoirs and commentaries to a group of companions which included Captain Las Cases, generals Gourgaud, de Montholon and Bertrand, and doctors O'Meara and Antommarchi. Napoleon never edited or

ordered his memoirs, and several of his companions also published their own journals as well as their record of what the former Emperor had said. Besides all this primary material there exist the numerous proclamations, official documents and records of discussion from 1799 to 1815.

It is unsurprising to find that Napoleon's views altered between the time when he was the successful general under the Directory (extract B (v)), through the period when he consolidated his hold on power as First Consul (1799–1804) (extracts A (i–iv)), and then as Emperor (extracts A (ii and iii) and B (i and iv)). In exile he was concerned, like most retired leaders, to put his actions in the best light for posterity, and extracts A (iv) and B (ii and iii) perhaps show this. Once power had left him, Napoleon laboured to show how he had combined the best of what the Revolution had achieved with earlier French history, and it is possible to see something of this reconciliation in Napoleon's treatment of the Catholic Church and his attitude to 'liberty, equality and fraternity' when he was in power. On the other hand it can be argued that Napoleon developed French nationalism well beyond anything the Revolution had invented, and that he used it cynically to support his own ambitions to rule throughout Europe.

Napoleon continues to have his admirers and critics among historians, and the debate is complicated by the 'Napoleonic Legend' which his exile and memoirs helped to create. The unsettled history of nineteenth century France added lustre to the Napoleonic legend of glory, stability and reconciliation because the century seemed doomed to complete a feeble recycling of the past with a failed Bourbon restoration, two Republican regimes and the Second Empire of Napoleon III, Napoleon I's nephew.

A Napoleon's attitude to the Revolution

(i) Napoleon's proclamation, 15 December 1799

Citizens, the Revolution has been made fast to the principles that started it. The Revolution is ended.

(translated in J.C. Herold, *The Mind of Napoleon*, New York, Columbia University Press, 1955, p. 72)

(ii) Napoleon to the Council of State, 1804

The Emperor, the Senate, the Council of State, the Legislative Body, and the Tribunate together make up the entire governmental machinery. Together, they can do anything they like. They represent the nation. The Emperor, who is the head of all, is hereditary because a choice has to be made among various disadvantages, and there are fewer disadvantages in his being hereditary than in his being elective – otherwise he would be elective.

(ibid., pp. 81–82)

(iii) Letter, Napoleon to his brother Louis, King of Holland, 1809

You must understand that I make no distinction between myself and my predecessors; that, from Clovis to the Committee of Public Safety, I consider myself in solidarity with everything that has been done.

(ibid., p. 83)

(iv) From the memoirs Napoleon dictated on St Helena after his final abdication in 1815

The Constituent Assembly . . . committed two errors, which might have produced the ruin of the nation. The first was to establish a Constitution [1791] . . . whose mechanism was contrived not to strengthen social order and promote national prosperity but to restrict and annul the public power, which is that of government. . . . the second – that of persisting in re-establishing Louis XVI on the throne after the affair of Varennes. What then ought the Assembly have done? . . . to have proclaimed Louis XVII king; and to have created a regency.

(cited in S. de Chair (ed.) *Napoleon on Napoleon*, London, Brockhampton Press, 1992, p. 71)

B From several of Napoleon's conversations on liberty and equality

(i) In the early 1800s

I have come to realise that men are not born to be free.

. . . Liberty means a good civil code. The only thing modern nations care for is property.

. . . Liberty is a need felt by a small class of people

whom nature has endowed with nobler minds than the mass of men. Consequently, it may be repressed with impunity. Equality, on the other hand, pleases the masses.

. . . What must be done, then, is to give everybody the hope of being able to rise.

(ii) In 1815

My motto has always been: A career open to all talents, without distinctions of birth.

(iii) In 1816, on St Helena, related by Las Cases

old orders of chivalry tended to strengthen caste divisions, whereas the single decoration of the Legion of Honour and the universality of its application was the symbol of equality.

(translated in Herold, *The Mind of Napoleon*, pp. 73–74)

(iv) Napoleon to the Council of State, 20 December 1812

These errors were bound to, and in fact did, bring about the reign of terror by the blood-stained men. Who indeed proclaimed the principle that rebellion was a duty? Who fawned on the people by proclaiming its sovereignty, which it was incapable of exercising? Who destroyed the order and sanctity of the laws by making them depend, not on the sacred principles of justice, . . . not on civil law, but merely on the will of the assembly whose members were ignorant of civil, penal, administrative, political, and military laws? . . .

(ibid., p. 69)

(v) Napoleon to Mme de Rémusat on his part in suppressing the Vendémiaire rising (1795)

They began deliberating whether it was right to meet force with force. I asked them, 'Are you waiting for the people to give you permission to fire on it?'

(ibid., p. 70)

C The place of Christianity in the Empire

(i) Napoleon's view of the role of religion

No society can exist without inequality of fortunes; and

inequality of fortunes cannot exist without religion. When a man is dying of hunger beside another who is stuffing himself with food, he cannot accept this difference if there is not an authority who tells him, 'God wishes it so'. . . . It is religion alone that gives to the state a firm and durable support.

(ii) The official school catechism

Q: What are the duties of Christians towards princes who govern them? In particular what are our duties to Napoleon, our Emperor?

A: Christians owe to princes who govern them, and we, in particular owe to Napoleon I, our Emperor, our love and respect, obedience, loyalty and military service, and the taxes ordered for the defence of the Empire and his throne.

(cited in translation in A. Stiles, *Napoleon, France and Europe*, London, Hodder and Stoughton, 1993, pp. 90–91)

D M. Lyons's appraisal of Napoleon

Napoleon's individual trajectory cannot be understood outside the historical forces which helped to direct it. . . . The revolutionary ideals of freedom and equality, the notion of popular sovereignty, the goal of rational administration and the rule of law, the liberation of Europe from feudal oppression, and above all the poisoned legacy of war – all these inheritances formed the basis of his power, and at the same time limited his options.

. . . In 1793 Napoleon was a Jacobin . . . in 1796–7, he had mellowed into Bonaparte the republican, supporter of the Directory, but discovering in Italy the possibilities of military glory. As First Consul, Bonaparte's persona was that of the creative statesman, the lawgiver who brought France peace, reconciliation. . . . After 1804, he was transformed into the Emperor Napoleon, more authoritarian, concerned to protect his dynasty . . . a final transformation occurred in 1815, when the circumstances of the Hundred Days forced a new metamorphosis into Napoleon the liberal.

Throughout this evolution, two main themes stand out. Napoleon was . . . the founder of the modern state. His regime was also the fulfilment of the bourgeois revolution of 1789–99.

The new state, which emerged from the Revolution and was shaped by Napoleon, was a secular state, without a trace of the divine sanction which had been one of the ideological props of the old régime monarchy. It was a state based on a conscripted army and staffed by a professional bureaucracy.

(M. Lyons, *Napoleon Bonaparte and the Legacy of the French Revolution*, London, Macmillan, 1994, pp. 294–95)

Questions

1 Explain Napoleon's meaning in the context:
   (a) 'They represent the nation' (extract A (ii))
   (b) 'I consider myself in solidarity with everything that has been done' (extract A (iii))
   (c) 'the principle that rebellion was a duty' (extract B (iv))
   (d) 'the sacred principles of justice' (extract B (iv)).
2 Read extracts A (i–iv). In what ways did Napoleon's attitude to the Revolution appear to alter between 1799 and his exile on St Helena?
3 How consistent was Napoleon's attitude to liberty, equality and popular sovereignty in extracts B (i–iii) with the principles of the Revolution?
4 How useful are extracts C (i and ii) for revealing Napoleon's attitude to religion? How does it compare with the attitude of the Jacobin dictatorship of 1793–94?
5 Look at the paintings of Napoleon crossing the Alps by David and De la Roche earlier in the chapter. Which is the more useful portrayal to a historian investigating Napoleon?
6 In extract D, does Lyons suggest that, in the end, Napoleon shaped the Revolution rather more than it shaped him? Explain your answer using the extracts and your own knowledge.

Further reading

There are fewer recent scholarly works available in English on Napoleon than there are on the Revolutionary decade, but the studies in French are made accessible by G. Ellis in *The Napoleonic Empire* (London, Macmillan, 1991). M. Lyons provides an important and focused study in *Napoleon Bonaparte and the Legacy of* the French Revolution (London, Macmillan, 1994), as does J. Tulard in *Napoleon: the Myth of the Saviour* (London, Weidenfeld and Nicolson, 1984). D.M.G. Sutherland provides a good and detailed survey in *France 1789–1815: Revolution and Counterrevolution* (London, Fontana, 1990), and volume 2 of A. Cobban's *A History of Modern France* (London, Penguin, 1970) is highly readable. F.L. Ford's *Europe 1780– 1830* (London, Longman, 1989) is another useful text. To make Napoleon come alive, however, use *Napoleon on Napoleon*, which contains a selection of his St Helena memoirs edited by S. de Chair (London, Brockhampton Press, 1992), or read A. Schom, *One Hundred Days: Napoleon's Road to Waterloo* (London, Penguin, 1994) or, perhaps best of all, F. Markham's biography *Napoleon* (London and New York, New American Library, 1963) or F. McLynn's *Napoleon* (London, Pimlico, 1997).

Documentary collections are not easy to come by, and J.M. Thompson's translations of *Letters of Napoleon* (Oxford University Press, 1934) and J.C. Herold's *The Mind of Napoleon* (New York, Columbia University Press, 1955) contain important material. Two concise and very helpful texts make use of some of the primary sources: A. Stiles, *Napoleon, France and Europe* (London, Hodder and Stoughton, 1993) and D.G. Wright, *Napoleon and Europe* (London, Longman, 1989). Both of these works are analytical, concise and detailed surveys, and C. Emsley, *The Longman Companion to Napoleonic Europe* (London, Longman, 1993) is a usefully comprehensive reference book.

• CHAPTER SIX •

The Impact of the French Revolution and Napoleon on Europe and the Congress of Vienna

• CONTENTS •

Key dates

SECTION A

The varied impact of French rule

The making of the peace settlement

SECTION B – SOURCES

The Treaty of Vienna: a backward looking settlement?

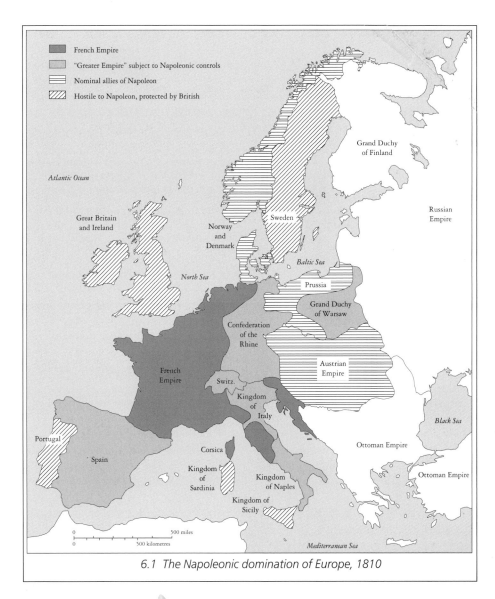

Legend:
- French Empire
- "Greater Empire" subject to Napoleonic controls
- Nominal allies of Napoleon
- Hostile to Napoleon, protected by British

6.1 The Napoleonic domination of Europe, 1810

In areas not contiguous to France (*pays conquis*) French rule was exercised less directly up to 1805 through republics set up by the Directory such as the Cisalpine, Cispadine and Parthenopean Republics (Italy), the Batavian Republic (Holland), the Helvetic Republic (Switzerland) and the Grand Duchy of Berg (Germany).

When Napoleon assumed the imperial title in France in May 1804, republican rule elsewhere in Europe also gave way to a form of monarchy, though in this case the new rulers were drawn from Napoleon's own family or his trusted subordinates. Thus Napoleon himself assumed the title of King of Italy in March, 1805, crowning himself in Milan cathedral. A year later in March 1806 his brother Joseph was made King of Naples, to be followed by his brother Louis, who became King of Holland in May. In 1807 Napoleon's youngest brother, Jerome, was made King of Westphalia. In 1808 Joseph gave up the throne of Naples to become King of Spain and was replaced in Naples by Marshal Murat, himself married to Napoleon's sister Caroline. Napoleon's son-in-law, Eugene de Beauharnais, became Viceroy of Italy. The empire so created contained 88 million subjects.

There was a third category of states all of whom

at one time or another were allied to France (*pays alliés*). They included the south German states of Bavaria, Baden and Württemberg; Prussia; Russia and Sweden. Austria qualified as an ally since in April 1810 Napoleon married Princess Marie Louise, and thus became son-in-law to the Austrian Emperor, Francis II. The rulers of these states could not but be influenced by the example of the man whose success was so evident. In Prussia, for instance, Stein and Hardenburg consciously sought to remodel the system of government in line with French practice. In Russia Alexander I appointed Speransky as his chief minister in 1807 in the hope that he would introduce a new constitution and legal code, again in imitation of the French example.

Thus the impact of French domination was felt in a variety of ways, and it is hardly surprising that it met with so varied a response. When it comes to defining the nature of that impact one encounters an immediate difficulty. The debate as to whether Napoleon's rule in France can be seen as fulfilling or contradicting the ideals of the Revolution is no less relevant to the rest of Europe. Just as the Directory gave way to the Consulate and the Empire, so the sister republics were replaced by the personal rule of Napoleon's relatives. While in 1792 the revolutionary armies offered fraternal assistance to peoples seeking to overthrow their hereditary rulers, after 1806 Napoleon's concerns were less with the liberation of peoples than with their exploitation. Thus in gauging the effects of the French Revolution on Europe one has to balance the liberating impact of revolutionary ideas and institutions against the arbitrary financial exactions, the commercial interference through the continental system, the toll of manpower through conscription and the crushing of opposition which were all characteristic of Napoleon's rule.

The influence of the Revolution

In the first period of French rule there were lasting legacies in the Austrian Netherlands, Holland, parts of Switzerland, the left bank of the Rhine and northern Italy. Orderly systems of administration were introduced. Feudal tenures were abolished. In many of these areas religious orders were also suppressed, their assets confiscated and sold off. Civil marriage was introduced, press censorship relaxed. No fewer than thirteen written constitutions were produced for the 'sister' republics, eleven of which were based on the Thermidorian constitution of the Year III (1795) 'with its elaborate, rigid and ultimately unworkable separation of powers and graduated system of election' (S. Woolf, *Napoleon's Integration of Europe*, London, Routledge, 1991, p. 11). No one, be it noted, favoured the introduction of universal suffrage and the elected assemblies that were provided for rarely met. New groups competed for political power in the Italian republics in particular and temporarily at least the old governing elites were replaced. There was little redistribution of wealth. The properties of the religious orders generally found their way into the hands of existing landowners though in some parts of the Austrian Netherlands 35 per cent of the purchasers were peasants. Unlike France there were few émigrés, so the aristocracy were not as a rule deprived of their lands by the new regimes.

The influence of Napoleon

With Napoleon's advent to power, as we have seen, came changes of regime. Yet in Europe, as in France, this did not necessarily mean a repudiation of the reforms that had taken place. In an important letter to Jerome when he became King of Westphalia in 1807, Napoleon wrote:

What the peoples of Germany impatiently desire is that individuals who are not noble and have talent should have an equal right to your consideration and employment; that all forms of serfdom and intermediary ties between the sovereign and the last class of people should be abolished. ... The peoples of Germany, of France, of Italy and Spain want equality and liberal ideas. I have been leading the affairs of Europe for some years now and I have become convinced that the general opinion is against the buzzing of the privileged. Be a constitutional king. ... This way you will find that you have the strength of opinion and a natural ascendancy over the absolute kings, your neighbours.

(Woolf, *Napoleon's Integration*, p. 127)

Napoleon insisted on the introduction of the Code Napoleon wherever his relatives ruled. It was introduced into Italy in 1806, Naples and Westphalia in 1808, Holland in 1809 and to those parts of Spain which were under French control. Taxes were more efficiently collected, schools promoted and communications improved in many parts of the empire. It has even been claimed that Napoleon's rule was the last manifestation of enlightened despotism.

But it was from the outset fatally flawed by Napoleon's insatiable ambition. This rendered a lasting peace with Britain impossible and saddled Napoleon with the two campaigns he could not win, in Spain and Russia. An inevitable consequence was the exploitation of the empire to sustain his military adventures. There were three particular sources of grievance. The Continental System led to the closing of European ports and the loss of markets, especially in America. Internal tariffs were erected to protect French products and manufactures against competition, for example from Italian textile producers. As well as the Code Napoleon, Napoleon also introduced conscription into all the areas he controlled and levies were imposed on his dependants and allies. Frenchmen constituted less than half the *Grande Armée* of over 600,000 that invaded Russia in 1812. It has been estimated that at least 1 million foreigners served in Napoleon's armies. The costs of warfare had also to be shared with the satellite kingdoms. Their brief periods of solvency following the introduction of financial reforms were followed by mounting indebtedness as the scale of Napoleon's operations grew.

Thus it is impossible to separate the gains from the losses of Napoleon's rule and it met with a variety of reactions. Outright opposition was comparatively rare, and tended to coincide with periods of economic hardship and extra demands for troops. There was a serious rising in Parma in 1805 and a much more extensive one in the Tyrol, against Napoleon's ally, Bavaria, in 1809. In Spain Joseph's rule was challenged from the outset. Violence was endemic in Calabria, both under Joseph and Murat. But the south German states of Bavaria, Württemberg and Baden welcomed the changes brought by Napoleon from which they stood to benefit. Prussia stayed neutral until 1806,

and even after her ignominious defeat and the occupation of Berlin that followed, she was still prepared to sign a treaty with Napoleon in 1812 and to supply 20,000 men for the invasion of Russia. Louis in Holland and Eugene in Italy were each able to recruit distinguished natives into their administrations. Collaboration was as much in evidence as opposition.

Opposition to Napoleon

In three countries, however, Napoleon stirred up an opposition that finally brought him down. In England, whereas there was considerable sympathy for the French Revolution both in intellectual circles and among literate artisans, Napoleon was universally disliked. In 1803 a government survey discovered 500,000 men who were willing to volunteer for armed service. By 1814 the British army had expanded to 250,000 and the navy to 140,000. In Spain a French army of 200,000 was incapable of suppressing a guerrilla movement which enjoyed huge popular support. In Russia Napoleon's fatally mismanaged campaign roused a sleeping giant and the experience of invasion lent a new popularity to the Tsar's government. After the failure of the Russian campaign and the victories won by Wellington in Spain from 1812 onwards the defeat of Napoleon now looked a practicable possibility. Prussia and Austria examined their options.

In March 1813 Prussia, with a keen eye for the main chance, changed sides and declared war on Napoleon. Austria followed suit in August and at the battle of Leipzig in October the armies of Russia, Prussia and Austria won a decisive victory. The new allies entered Paris on 31 March 1814, and Napoleon abdicated, for the first time, on 4 April (see Figure 6.1).

As his authority collapsed in France so it was repudiated elsewhere. Jerome left Westphalia following the battle of Leipzig. Holland regained her independence in November 1813. In Italy Eugene remained loyal to Napoleon, but faced with an Austrian invasion he saw no point in prolonging the war and retired to Munich in April 1814. Murat, on the contrary, played a complicated game, trading his support for Austria in return for

6.1 Napoleon's abdication at Fontainebleau, 4 April 1814. Painted by Gaetano Ferri (1822–96) after François Bouchot (1800–42)

Source: Chateau de Versailles et Trianon © Photo R.M.N.

recognition of his own claim to the throne of Naples. His calculations were upset when Napoleon escaped from Elba in February 1815, but on this distraction, Murat made a bid for the kingdom of Italy, advancing as far as Bologna in April 1815. The gamble failed ignominiously. His absence from Naples allowed the allies to seize control and Ferdinand IV was restored to the Neapolitan throne under Austrian escort. Wellington's victories had ensured the ending of French rule in Spain, and Ferdinand VII returned to the throne in May 1814.

Assessment

What was the long-term legacy of French domination? In one sense it would take the whole of the nineteenth century for the consequences to work themselves out and much of the rest of this book will be concerned with those consequences. Certain signposts can still be discerned which point to the likely directions of change. Nationalism, meaning a strong sense of identity between a state and its people, received a marked boost. This is most evident in France where the experience of victory and the growth in the power and range of the state contributed to a stronger sense of nationhood in which all shared. The same phenomenon may be seen, if not to the same degree, in the states of Britain, Spain and Russia. Elsewhere, the position is not so clear, for as Stuart Woolf has pointed out, 'it is misleading to write of a national identity in a political sense where a nation state had not yet emerged' (*Napoleon's Integration*, p. 236).

Though there were a few intellectuals in northern Italy who were sympathetic to a united and independent Italy, Napoleon would have no truck with this idea and Murat's appeal in 1815 fell on largely deaf ears. In Germany there was a more mixed response, well illustrated by the changing views of a German professor of philosophy, J.G. Fichte. In 1799 he wrote: 'Only the French Republic can be considered by a just man as his true country . . . on its victory depend the dearest hopes and even the very existence of humanity' (N. Hampson, *The First European Revolution*, London, Thames and Hudson, 1969, p. 125). In 1807–08, following the French occupation of Berlin, he delivered a series of lectures entitled *Addresses to the German Nation*, in which he called upon the German nation to become 'the regenerator and the re-creator of the world'. In intellectual circles admiration for the French revolution gave way to a form of cultural nationalism which found the roots of civilisation in German language and literature rather than in the ideas of the French Enlightenment. But here too, such sentiment was confined to the educated elite. Contrasting Germany with Spain, an Alsatian diplomat commented: 'In Germany there is no reason to fear any event similar to those in Spain because there exist neither ideas nor interests that can act uniformly on a great mass of persons' (Woolf, *Napoleon's Integration*, p. 237).

What of those watchwords of the French Revolution, liberty, equality and fraternity? While the sister republics may have enjoyed a limited degree of self-government, Napoleon had a very restricted view of liberty, informing the Italian legislature in 1805: 'Political liberty, which is so necessary to the state, does not consist of this sort of multiplication of authority, but in a visibly stable and secure system of administration' (Woolf, *Napoleon's Integration*, p. 97). Only in Holland did an elected assembly meet with any regularity. But despite

their poor record, written constitutions continued to be seen as mechanisms through which the interests of the governors and the governed could be reconciled. Prior to 1789 only Sweden had a written constitution. One of the consequences of the French Revolution was a belief shared by all who would have described themselves as liberals in a written constitution as a prerequisite of fair and stable government.

The promotion of equality was limited to the sweeping away of feudal systems of land tenure in western Europe and the recognition in the Code Napoleon of the equality of the citizen before the law. There was no significant redistribution of wealth, and while Napoleon certainly believed in the career open to talents, he was equally concerned to integrate the old nobility into his administrations, both in France and in his satellite kingdoms. This merging of elites may indeed have widened the gap between the propertied and the property-less and did nothing to ease the class tensions that industrialisation would bring.

The promise of fraternity looks an even hollower boast. French casualties alone in the twenty-three years of warfare that began in 1792 have been calculated at 1.4 million. The total for France's opponents must have been considerably higher. It is hardly surprising that high on the list of the objectives of those who met to make a peace settlement in the Congress of Vienna was the need to contain France.

It was perhaps in the field of religion that the impact of the French Revolution had least lasting effect, in Europe if not in France itself. The republics established between 1795 and 1800 generally took action to suppress religious orders and to confiscate their property (in Catholic areas). Despite Napoleon's concordat with Pope Pius VII in 1801 and the Pope's willingness to attend the imperial coronation in 1804, relations steadily worsened. In 1808 the Papal States were annexed to the kingdom of Italy and in 1809 Rome itself was annexed to France. Napoleon was excommunicated and in May 1809 the Pope was removed first to Savona and then to Fontainebleau, near Paris. Both in Italy and in Spain the Inquisition and the Index of Prohibited Books were abolished.

With Napoleon's downfall all these changes were reversed. Pius VII, his authority strengthened by his enforced exile, was restored to Rome and to rule over the Papal States. The Inquisition and the Index were restored. Old religious orders were refounded and joined by others, anxious to reverse the slaughter caused by what the bishop of Modena called 'philosophism and incredulity'. Where religion was concerned the one lasting consequence of the revolution was to make the Catholic Church in particular wary of any liberal tendencies, either in church or state, because of the assaults it had suffered.

THE MAKING OF THE PEACE SETTLEMENT

Summary

The changes made to the map of Europe by the Revolutionary and Napoleonic wars inevitably required a redrawing of Europe's frontiers as well as the imposition of peace terms on France. The process of peacemaking, complex enough, was further interrupted by Napoleon's second bid for power, usually known as the One Hundred Days (technically the period from 20 March 1815 to 22 June 1815) when Napoleon reclaimed his imperial position.

Before dealing with the settlement of Europe it would be as well to set out the main stages by which it was reached. Those who were to impose their terms on the rest of Europe were clearly identified in the treaty of Chaumont, signed by representatives of Austria, Britain, Prussia and Russia on 9 March 1814. Under its terms the Allies (as they will now be referred to) agreed to prevent Napoleon or any members of his dynasty from returning to France, and to guarantee any territorial settlement that was reached for the next twenty years. By the end of March the Allies had agreed, largely thanks to British insistence, that the Bourbons must be restored to the French throne. On 12 April Napoleon signed the treaty of Fontainebleau, the instrument of his abdication. He surrendered any claim to France or any other country, but was allowed to retain his imperial title, as was the Empress Marie Louise. He was given the island of Elba to which to retire and an annual income from French funds of 2 million

francs. Despite the generosity of these terms Napoleon still attempted to commit suicide, having signed them.

On 30 May the Allies agreed the terms for the first treaty of Paris with Talleyrand, the French Foreign Minister, who had transferred his allegiance from Napoleon to Louis XVIII. The terms were remarkably generous. France was reduced to the territories she possessed in 1792; she surrendered to Britain Malta in the Mediterranean, Mauritius in the Indian ocean and Tobago and St Lucia in the West Indies. She was allowed to retain the art treasures looted by French armies. It was also provided that Holland would receive an increase of territory, taken from what had been the Austrian Netherlands, that the German states would be independent and united into a federation, and that Italy would be made up of sovereign states, apart from those territories restored to Austria. It became clear during the negotiations that these matters would have to be decided in detail and no agreement could be reached on the problem of Poland, partly resurrected by Napoleon as the Duchy of Warsaw. A further conference was therefore arranged by the Allies to meet at Vienna on 1 October 1814 to resolve these problems.

During September the crowned heads of Europe and their representatives duly assembled in Vienna, but the work of the Congress did not begin until 1 November because of arguments over organisation and procedure.

So serious was the dispute over Poland and Saxony that in January 1815 Britain, Austria and France signed a secret treaty to oppose the ambitions of Russia and Prussia. It was not until this issue was resolved in February 1815 that the real work of the Congress could begin. There was a further interruption when news reached Vienna of Napoleon's escape from Elba on 7 March. At once the King of Prussia, the Emperor of Austria, the Tsar of Russia and the Duke of Wellington departed to lead their respective armies. But their deputies continued their deliberations and the final treaty of Vienna was signed on 9 June, a few days before the battle of Waterloo (18 June) at which Napoleon's fate was finally sealed.

Napoleon's attempt to upset the peace met with a harsh response. By the second treaty of Paris, signed on 20 November 1815, France was reduced to the frontiers of 1789, restoring Chambery and part of Savoy to Piedmont and further territory to Switzerland. She had to pay an indemnity of 700 million francs and support an allied army of occupation in seventeen border fortresses at an annual cost of 250 million francs. She was also required to restore the art treasures she had previously been allowed to keep. In order to reinforce these terms the four Allies signed the Quadruple Alliance, guaranteeing each others' possessions and promising to maintain by armed force the exclusion of the Bonaparte dynasty for the next twenty years. The Allies also undertook to meet at regular intervals for the purpose of discussing what measures would be 'most salutary for the repose and prosperity of nations and for the maintenance of the peace of Europe'. Thus was peace finally made with the country that had so upset the equilibrium of Europe.

The makers of the settlement

The task of restoring that equilibrium, as well as defeating Napoleon, rested mainly on the shoulders of a handful of men, the rulers of the victorious states and their advisers who met at Vienna. Of the rulers, the most significant was Alexander I of Russia, who took an active part in the proceedings and had his own very definite ambitions, primarily the creation of a large but dependent Poland, which might also provide an opportunity for him to experiment with the constitutional ideas to which he was, when the mood took him, sympathetic. Emperor Francis I of Austria was content to leave most of the work to his Foreign Minister, Count Metternich. Metternich, Foreign Minister from 1809 to 1848, hosted the conference and was the chief influence behind the scenes (Figure 6.2). He was accused by some of his contemporaries of indolence and superficiality. Wellington described him as 'a society hero and nothing more' (Harold Nicolson, *The Congress of Vienna*, London, Allen Lane, 1946, p. 35). But the Secretary to the Conference, Friedrich von Gentz, a close associate of Metternich's, gave a more favourable verdict: 'Not a man of strong passions and of bold measures; not a genius but a great talent; cool, calm, imperturbable and calculator par excellence' (Henry Kiss-inger, *A World Restored*, London, Gollancz, 1974, pp. 11–12). A natural conservative, his aim was to protect Austria, and Europe, from any further descent into revolution. Britain was represented initially by Viscount Castlereagh, Foreign Minister from 1812 to 1822. He struck up a natural rapport with Metternich when the two men met, and he shared Metternich's conservative instincts. Castlereagh, perhaps because of the enduring role that Britain had played in the defeat of Napoleon, was more concerned than Metternich by the external threats to Europe's stability. He was primarily determined to prevent any recurrence of French ambitions and was equally suspicious of Russian aggrandisement. While anxious to maintain Britain's maritime rights and to secure the colonial rewards that were her due, he was also a notable advocate for the abolition of the slave trade.

Frederick William III of Prussia took little active part in the negotiations, leaving that responsibility to Prince Hardenberg and Baron Humboldt. He was, however, a strong admirer of the Russian Tsar, and this helped to create a bond between the two countries. Prussian ambitions were focused on the neighbouring territory of Saxony, whose King had been made Duke of Warsaw and stayed loyal to Napoleon too long. His territories in Prussian eyes were clearly to be forfeited. France was represented by Talleyrand, a natural diplomatist, who played the hand he had been dealt with consummate skill. By his insistence that all the powers which had signed the first treaty of Paris should have equal rights, and by exploiting the differences between Prussia and Russia on the one hand, and France and Britain on the other, he was able to secure France's place on the inner council of the Allies. Unfortunately for Talleyrand, Napoleon's escape from Elba cut the ground from under his feet, and he was replaced as Foreign Minister by the Duc de Richelieu in September 1815.

The Congress of Vienna

All the powers who had taken part in the final campaigns against Napoleon were invited to attend the Congress and the big four were joined by the Kings of Denmark, Bavaria and Württemberg,

6.2 The Congress of Vienna, 1814–15, an engraving from a painting by the French portraitist J-B. Isabey (1767–1855). The Duke of Wellington stands at the far left, with Hardenberg sitting in front of him. Castlereagh is seated with his legs crossed in the centre and is looking towards Metternich, who is standing and pointing towards him. In the right foreground sits Talleyrand, with his forearm on the table. Immediately behind him is Gentz, with Humboldt standing to the right of him

Source: Graphische Sammlung Albertina, Vienna

the Elector of Hesse, the Grand Duke of Baden and the Dukes of Saxe-Weimar, Brunswick and Coburg. Portugal, Spain and Sweden were also represented. It became clear at the outset that if progress was to be made, the key decisions would have to be taken by the major powers and that the details of the settlement would have to be delegated to committees. After much initial wrangling, it was eventually agreed that the main work of the Congress should be referred to a Council of Eight, made up of the Allies, France, Spain, Portugal and Sweden. In practice the Council of Eight held only nine meetings and it was the Council of Five (the Allies plus France), formed in January 1815, which finally determined the main features of the settlement. It held forty-one meetings. Ten committees were also established, the most important of which were those on Germany, international rivers, the slave trade and the statistical committee.

As so much power rested with members of the Council of Five, it was their different aims and the compromises needed to win agreement that determined the outcome of the Congress. All the members were agreed on their primary objective, to restore peace and stability to a Europe which had known neither for the past twenty years. Each country also had a more specific agenda. Russia wanted Poland. Prussia wanted Saxony. Austria wanted to recover her influence in northern Italy. Britain wanted the recognition of her maritime rights and the colonies she had been promised and a strengthening of France's neighbours to act as a deterrent to any further aggression. Whether there was any general attachment to the principle of legitimacy, that rulers and dynasties should be restored to the thrones of which they had been dispossessed, seems less likely.

The one issue that threatened to disrupt the Congress had little to do with the French Revolution. The private arrangement made by Alexander I and Frederick William III, under which Prussia would acquire the whole of Saxony while Russia would secure the greater part of Poland, was never acceptable to Austria and Britain. The dispute came to a head in January 1815 and led to a secret treaty, signed on 3 January by Metternich, Castlereagh and Talleyrand under which the three countries pledged mutual support should any of them be attacked 'on account of the proposals to which they had agreed for the completion of the Treaty of Paris' (Nicolson, *Congress of Vienna*, p. 178). The Tsar did not know the exact wording of this treaty until it was revealed to him in September 1815 but he was sufficiently aware of its gist to make him ready to compromise. Agreement was reached on 3 February. A new kingdom of Poland was to be set up in what had been the Duchy of Warsaw, under Russian tutelage. It was to have a written constitution providing for an elected assembly and full rights for peasants and Jews, among other things. Austria was to retain Galicia; Prussia was to retain Posen. Cracow and a surrounding area of 1,000 square kilometres was to become a free city. Two-fifths of Saxony was awarded to the King of Prussia, but the ruling King of Saxony was allowed to keep the rest. Prussia also acquired the fortresses of the Elbe, much of the left bank of the Rhine, Swedish Pomerania and the Duchy of Westphalia (see Map 6.2).

Once this issue was settled progress on other matters was surprisingly rapid. Two areas required particular attention, Germany and Italy. In Germany many changes had taken place during the wars which could not be reversed. Many of the 300 odd states which made up the Holy Roman Empire had disapppeared following Napoleon's

victories over Austria in 1805 and Prussia in 1806. The Confederation of the Rhine and the kingdom of Westphalia had absorbed many minor principalities and free cities. The Holy Roman Empire had itself been dissolved on 6 August, 1806 when Francis I renounced his title, though retaining his imperial status as Emperor of Austria. The rulers of Bavaria, Württemberg and Baden had made territorial gains at Austria's expense and their independent status had been recognised. Many of these changes were accepted in the treaty of Vienna.

The German Committee held many contentious meetings and considered numerous proposals. Eventually agreement was reached on a scheme put forward by Baron Wessenberg of Prussia. A new German Confederation was established, this time with thirty-nine states. The Emperor of Austria was to be its hereditary head. A Federal Diet would be established at Frankfurt which would draft the fundamental laws of the Confederation. Eleven of the larger states would have one vote each. Minor states were grouped into six cohorts, each having one vote. Member states were forbidden to go to war with each other. Major decisions required a two-thirds majority. Significantly, this was a union of governments, not of peoples. It bore more similarity to the European Union than to the United States of America. Its members were free to conduct their own internal affairs on condition that war between them was forbidden, and the consent of the Diet was needed for any foreign war. There was also an ambiguous clause providing that 'Each state will create a constitution based on assemblies'. Metternich interpreted this to mean a revival of a system of Estates, not a parliamentary system (A. Palmer, *Metternich,* London, Weidenfeld and Nicolson, 1972, p. 147). Taken as a whole the German settlement disappointed all those liberals and nationalists who had been hoping for a more united Germany with effective representative institutions, but it satisfied the hereditary rulers who kept their independence and their powers.

Where Italy is concerned it is perhaps worth recalling Henry Kissinger's comment: 'It would have occurred to no one in eighteenth century Europe that the legitimacy of a state depended on linguistic unity' (*A World Restored*, p. 145). Metternich, who first visited the Italian peninsula in

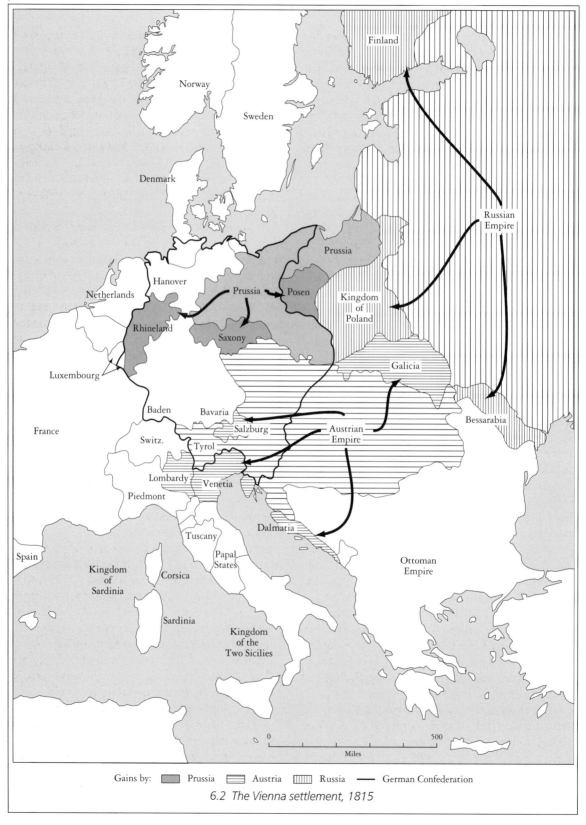

6.2 *The Vienna settlement, 1815*

1815, was convinced in his own mind that the political fragmentation of the peninsula would be 'both natural for the Italians and desirable for the Austrians' (Palmer, *Metternich*, p. 123). Thus when it came to deciding what should be done, the wishes of the Italians themselves were the last consideration to be taken into account. It was agreed that Austria should be compensated for the loss of the Austrian Netherlands to Holland by the granting to her of Lombardy and Venetia. Tuscany and Modena went to other members of the Habsburg family and the properties of Parma, Piacenza and Guastella were conferred on the Empress Marie Louise, who did not accompany Napoleon into exile. The Pope was restored to the Papal States, with the addition of Bologna and Ferrara. Ferdinand I recovered his kingdom of Naples and Sicily. Here, if anywhere, the clock was turned back and the republics and kingdoms established by French intervention were forgotten.

There were other territorial changes which mainly reflected the fortunes of war and the need to balance one gain with another. The cession of the Austrian Netherlands to Holland, provided for in the first treaty of Paris, was confirmed. The King of the Netherlands also became Grand Duke of Luxemburg and, in that capacity, a member of the German Confederation. Switzerland acquired three new cantons, Geneva, Wallis and Neuchâtel. Sweden retained her control of Norway, gained from Denmark in 1812. To the colonial gains made at France's expense, Britain added Ceylon and the Cape of Good Hope, gained from Holland, and Trinidad, gained from Spain.

Perhaps the most positive outcome of the Congress of Vienna was the attempt to abolish the slave trade. This had continued to flourish throughout the eighteenth century and had brought wealth and prosperity to its practitioners, notably in Britain, France, Spain and Portugal. The Enlightenment in France and the Evangelical revival in England had brought about a change in human sensibilities to this appalling traffic. In 1807 the British House of Commons, after a long campaign waged by Wilberforce and his supporters, voted to abolish the slave trade. French revolutionary governments were initially unwilling to go so far, the National Assembly in 1789 ruling that colonial governments themselves

should determine the status of 'people of colour'. But during the most radical phase of the Revolution, under the Committee of Public Safety, slavery was abolished on 4 February 1794. Napoleon, however, restored slavery in the French empire in 1802. When Louis XVIII was restored in 1814 he assured Castlereagh that slavery would cease in France's dominions within five years. During his brief return to power in 1815 Napoleon, conscious of the new image he needed, abolished the slave trade forthwith, a decision that Louis XVIII could not hope to reverse.

Castlereagh still had to overcome opposition from Spain and Portugal and in the end the Congress of Vienna went no further than condemning the slave trade as inconsistent with civilisation and human rights. Though France, Sweden and Holland did abolish it in 1815, Spain continued the trade until 1820, and the Atlantic slave trade lasted in clandestine form until the outbreak of the American Civil War in 1861. It lasted elsewhere in Africa until much later.

Another enlightened gesture, if little more, was made towards the Jews. Many of the German states, under Napoleon's influence, had granted civil rights to Jews. The Congress confirmed these rights and made a vague recommendation that they should be extended. Of more immediate practical effect was the work done on international rivers such as the Rhine, the Moselle and the Meuse. The Congress recommended that navigation should be free on such rivers to the traffic of countries which bordered them, and this became a precedent for many similar international agreements in the future. The Congress also agreed on the minor but thorny question of diplomatic precedence. This was now to be decided by the length of tenure of the diplomats in post, irrespective of the size of the countries they represented.

There is one final agreement to record, prompted chiefly by the religious enthusiasm of Tsar Alexander I. Always susceptible to the idea that it was his duty to bring Christian principles into the political arena, he had been particularly influenced on his journey to Paris from Vienna in 1815 by an encounter he had with a certain Baroness von Krudenar, who called on him at Heilbronn. The Baroness had predicted Napoleon's escape from Elba and convinced the Tsar that he was the predestined instrument of God. In this mood, the Tsar organised a huge religious parade on the Plain of Vertus, some 80 miles east of Paris, on 10 September, and on 26 September presented his fellow sovereigns with what became known as the Holy Alliance. It was addressed particularly to the rulers of Prussia and Austria, and pledged its signatories to use force only in service to one another and to God (see p. 93). All the rulers of Europe eventually added their signatures except for the Pope (who refused to be associated with Protestant powers), the Sultan of Turkey (who had similar reservations about Christians) and the Prince Regent, who was advised that it would be a breach with the British constitution which gave control over foreign policy to the King's ministers. Whether the Holy Alliance was anything more than the brainchild of Alexander I has been much disputed. It did link together the conservative powers of central and eastern Europe and it has also been compared with other blueprints for the peaceful conduct of international relations such as the Kellogg–Briand Pact of 1928, when the powers of Europe renounced war, as a statement of benevolent intent (see Section B).

Thus the peacemaking process came to an end. The statesmen who met, first at Paris, then at Vienna, and finally in Paris again, have been much criticised. They have been accused of ignoring the forces of liberalism and nationalism unleashed by the French Revolution, and of satisfying their particular ambitions at the expense of the interests of Europe as a whole. Section B examines that charge and provides some of the evidence with which to test it.

SECTION B – SOURCES

THE TREATY OF VIENNA: A BACKWARD LOOKING SETTLEMENT?

Among the critics of the settlement, one of the most influential was Sir Charles Webster, whose book on the Congress of Vienna was first published in 1922. He criticised 'the discouragement of the idea of self-government' and the failure to do anything about disarmament, and concluded: 'Yet it cannot be asserted that the statesmen concerned

were equal to the opportunity presented to them. They were limited in outlook, too prone to compromise, lacking in faith and courage' (C.K. Webster, *The Congress of Vienna*, London, 1922, p. 167). A more measured appraisal was given in a popular textbook first published in 1927, *Europe in the Nineteenth and Twentieth Centuries*, which concluded:

It has been customary to denounce the peacemakers of Vienna as reactionary and illiberal in the extreme. It is true that they represented the old regime and were, to a large extent, untouched by the new ideas. But they represented the best and not the worst of the old regime, and their settlement averted any great war in Europe for forty years. According to their lights the settlement was a fair one.

(A.J. Grant and Howard Temperley, *Europe in the Nineteenth and Twentieth Centuries*, London, Longman, 1947, p. 178)

A more enthusiastic endorsement comes in a history of international relations, *The Transformation of European Politics, 1763–1848*:

The Vienna settlement should therefore be judged primarily not on how well it met the demands and desires of rulers, elites and the general populace, but on how well it faced and met the permanent structural problems of international politics. . . . In this sense how well did it establish peace? Judged on this basis, the Vienna settlement comes out with a remarkably positive balance sheet. This is immediately apparent simply from its handling of persistent areas of conflict in Europe. . . . No other general peace settlement in European history – 1648, 1713–14, 1763, 1801–2, 1919–20, or 1945 – comes anywhere close to this record. Everyone failed this test, led almost immediately to new or continued conflict. Only the Vienna settlement got things right; only it genuinely established peace.

(P. Schroeder, *The Transformation of European Politics 1763–1848*, Oxford University Press, 1994, p. 577)

Whether this verdict is justified or not has to be judged by what followed the Congress of Vienna, treated in subsequent chapters, but it is also worth seeing how the statesmen who met at Vienna saw their own roles. Were they simply reactionaries, bent on restoring the Europe they had known before Napoleon's conquests, or were they more concerned to create a new world order which would remove the causes of conflict?

In the extracts which follow you will find Napoleon's vision of Europe, as expressed by him in exile in St Helena (extract A); Castlereagh's approach to peacemaking, reflected in his correspondence and in a speech to the House of Commons (extracts B (i and ii)); and the beliefs of Alexander I, as stated in the Holy Alliance, and subsequently modified by Metternich and Francis II (extract C). You should be aware of the circumstances in which each was spoken or written.

A Napoleon in conversation with his companion, the Marquis Emanuel Las Cases, and his doctor, Barry Edward O'Meara, during his captivity on St Helena. Each man published versions of what Napoleon had said in 1822 and 1823 respectively. Napoleon knew that his remarks were being noted, and expected them to be reported

The first ruler who embraces in good faith the cause of the peoples will find himself at the head of all Europe and will be able to accomplish everything he wishes.

There are in Europe more than 30 million French, 15 million Spanish, 15 million Italians, 30 million Germans. I would have wished to make each of these peoples a single united body.

Europe thus divided into nationalities freely formed and free internally, peace between States would have become easier: the United States of Europe would become a possibility.

F. Markham, *Napoleon*, New York, Mentor, 1963, pp. 256–57)

B Castlereagh's views on the peace settlement

(i) A letter to Lord William Bentinck, British Minister to Sicily, 7 May 1814

It is impossible not to perceive a great moral change coming on in Europe, and that the principles of freedom are in full operation. The danger is that the transition may be too sudden to ripen into anything likely to make the world better or happier. We have new constitutions launched in France, Spain, Holland and

Sicily. Let us see the result before we encourage further attempts. The attempts may be made, and we must abide by the consequences; but I am sure it is better to retard than to accelerate the operation of this most hazardous principle which is abroad.

(J.W. Derry, *Castlereagh*, London, Allen Lane, 1976, p. 158)

(ii) A speech to the House of Commons on 20 March 1815 in which Castlereagh defends the basis on which the peace settlement is being made

With regard to the European powers, if the assembled sovereigns had put forward a declaration to the effect that all the ancient governments of Europe, which time had swept away, should be recreated; that those rude and shapeless fabrics which had been thrown down, and had long ceased to exist in any tangible form, should be reconstructed; if this was to be done without any regard to the corruptions that had grown up under these ruinous institutions, without recollecting that those very governments had produced the calamities by which Europe had been so long and so severely tried, and which might in the end have the effect of recreating the dangers from which we have just escaped; if such a declaration had been issued, I should have felt ashamed that my country belonged to a confederacy founded upon the principle of imbecility.

(ibid, p. 185)

C The Holy Alliance

The text of the Holy Alliance was probably drafted by Alexander I, and certainly approved by him. He submitted it to Francis II, Emperor of Austria, and to Frederick William IV, King of Prussia, about the middle of September 1815. As reported by Castlereagh, Francis II had distinct reservations, as did Metternich, but after verbal alterations had been made by Metternich the text was approved by both monarchs on 26 September. Privately Metternich dismissed the Holy Alliance as 'a high sounding nothing' (J. Droz, *Europe between Revolutions*, London, Collins, 1967, p. 217) and Castlereagh described it in a letter to Lord Liverpool on 28 September as 'this piece of sublime mysticism and nonsense'. It was published in Russia in its original form by Alexander I, who continued to believe in its principles.

In the name of the Very Holy and Indivisible Trinity Their Majesties, the Emperor of Austria, the King of Prussia and the Emperor of Russia . . . solemnly declare that the present act has no other object than to manifest before the universe their unshakeable determination to take as their rule of conduct, whether in the administration of their respective states, whether in political relations with all other governments, no precepts other than those of this holy religion, precepts of justice, charity and peace, which so far from being uniquely applicable to private life, ought on the contrary to bear directly on the resolutions of princes and to guide all their steps, as being the only means of strengthening their human institutions and remedying their imperfections.

In consequence their Majesties are agreed on the following articles:

Article I

In conformity with the words of Holy Scripture which ordain that all men should regard themselves as brothers the three contracting monarchs [in the original 'the subjects of the three contracting parties'] will live united by the bonds of an indissoluble fraternity, and considering themselves as compatriots will in all cases lend one another assistance, aid and help; regarding themselves in relation to their subjects and armies as fathers of families, they will direct them in the same spirit of fraternity by which they are animated in order to protect religion, peace and justice.

Article II

The sole principle of force, whether between the said governments and their Subjects, shall be that of doing each other reciprocal service, and of testifying by unalterable good will the mutual affection by which they ought to be animated, to consider themselves all as members of one and the same Christian nation, the three allied Princes looking on themselves as merely delegated by Providence to govern three branches of One Family, namely Austria, Prussia and Russia, thus confessing that the Christian world of which they and their people form a part, has in reality no other Sovereign than Him to whom all power really belongs, because in Him alone are to be found all the treasures of love, of science and of infinite wisdom, that is to say God, our divine Saviour, Jesus Christ.

Article III

All the powers which wish to affirm the sacred prin-

ciples which have inspired this act and recognise how important it is to the welfare of countries too long disturbed that these truths henceforth exercise all the influence which should properly be theirs on human destinies, will be received into this alliance with equal eagerness and affection.

Francis   Frederick William   Alexander

(F. Ley, *Alexandre 1 et la Sainte Alliance*, Paris, 1975, pp. 149–53, author's translation)

Questions

1 How far can you trust each of these extracts as a true reflection of their authors' real views?
2 How far did Napoleon encourage the goals he sets out for Europe in extract A when he had the power to do so ?
3 Explain 'this most hazardous principle' (extract B (i)) and 'rude and shapeless fabrics' (extract B (ii)).
4 What is the effect of Metternich's changes to the original wording of Article I of the Holy Alliance (extract C)?
5 Explain what the wording of the Holy Alliance actually binds its members to do. How fair was Castlereagh's dismissive verdict of it as 'this piece of sublime mysticism and nonsense'?
6 To what extent do these extracts show that the European powers were able to come to terms with the changes brought about in Europe by the French Revolution and Napoleon?

Further reading

The impact of Napoleon on Europe

Three books are particularly recommended: O. Connelly, *Napoleon's Satellite Kingdoms* (New York, The Free Press, 1969), a lively study of each of the kingdoms and their rulers; G. Ellis, *The Napoleonic Empire* (London, Macmillan, 1991), which has useful statistics, and is particularly good on the army; and S.J. Woolf, *Napoleon's Integration of Europe* (London, Routledge, 1991), an in-depth analysis of the impact of Napoleon's rule, sympathetic to its beneficial effects.

N. Hampson, *The First European Revolution* (London, Thames and Hudson, 1969) a brief survey, contrasts the different impact of the Revolution from that of Napoleon. It is very well illustrated.

The Congress of Vienna

H. Nicolson, *The Congress of Vienna* (London, Constable, 1946) is good on the working of the Congress, lively on the personalities involved.

P.W. Schroeder, *The Transformation of European Politics 1763–1848* (Oxford University Press, 1994) is the most up-to-date account, but written from the narrow perspective of diplomatic history.

H. Kissinger, *A World Restored: Metternich, Castlereagh and the Problem of Peace* (London, Gollancz, 1957) is based on the author's conservative political outlook, and was written at the time when the Cold War was at its height.

J.W. Derry, *Castlereagh* (London, Allen Lane, 1976) is a brief but solid study of his policies.

A. Palmer, *Alexander I* (London, Weidenfeld and Nicolson, 1974) is a full-length biography and study of his personality as well as his diplomacy; A. Palmer, *Metternich* (London, Weidenfeld and Nicolson, 1972) as above.

• CHAPTER SEVEN •

The Industrialisation of Europe and its Effects

• CONTENTS •

Key dates

KEY DATES

	Inventions	Publications
1710	Abraham Darby used coke to smelt iron	
1711	Thomas Newcomen's steam engine used for pumping engines	
1765	James Hargreaves invented the Spinning Jenny	
1768	Richard Arkwright introduced the Water Frame and the first spinning mill	
1776		Adam Smith, *The Wealth of Nations*
1784	Henry Cort's Puddling and Rolling process improved iron production	
1784	James Watt converted steam power to rotary motion	
1785	First French blast furnace opened at Le Creusot	
1794	First German cotton mill opened at Kromford	
1803		J.B. Say, *Traite d'Economie Politique*
1815		B. Constant, *Principes de Politique*
1816–17	Prussian *Zollverein* created	
1830	Liverpool–Manchester Railway opened	
1840		P.J. Proudhon, *What is Property?*
1845		F. Engels, *The Condition of the Working Class in England*
1848		J.S. Mill, *Principles of Political Economy*
1848		K. Marx, *The Communist Manifesto*
1857	Henry Bessemer invented the hot air blast steel furnace	

SECTION A

ECONOMIC CHANGE

The term 'industrial revolution' first came into general use in the 1840s. Among those to use it were Friedrich Engels in his book *The Condition of the Working Class in England* (1845) and John Stuart Mill, in his *Principles of Political Economy* (1848). Since then the term has generally been used by economic historians to describe the transformation of an economy based primarily on agriculture to one based on manufacturing industry. There are pitfalls to be avoided, however, in using the term, particularly in relation to Europe in the first half of the nineteenth century. 'Revolution'

suggests an overwhelming and rapid change. It also implies a once and for all occurrence, rather than a continuing process. Even when the British industrial revolution was at its height it is doubtful whether economic growth rates ever exceeded 2 per cent a year. From the standpoint of the late twentieth century it is only too clear that once the industrial revolution had begun there would be no end to its progress. One must also distinguish carefully betweeen a new and potentially revolutionary technological advance, such as the smelting of iron with coking coal, and its diffusion, which took well over a hundred years.

There are numerous problems in charting economic change. Many vital indices such as industrial output, the size of economic undertakings, the rate at which technological improvements are adopted, for example, are not available until the mid-nineteenth century at the earliest. Even where reliable statistics are available it is not easy to assess their significance. Crude measurements of total output per head may give some idea of how fast a country is growing, but they may well ignore the small but vital qualitative changes that are taking place in particular sectors of the economy. Historians have recently likened the industrialisation of Europe prior to 1850 to a series of lakes dotted with islands, the lakes representing the individual countries, and the islands the industrial centres, whether towns or villages, where mining and manufacturing developed. Such islands were to be found in Manchester, Lille, Rouen, parts of Saxony and Alsace.

Population growth

The fundamental characteristic shared by most European countries in the nineteenth century was the continuing growth in population (see Table 1.1 on p. 4). Europe's population as a whole has been calculated to have risen from 150 million to 400 million between 1750 and 1900, and from one-fifth to one-quarter of the world's population over the same period. One of the consequences of this rise in population was a continued migration from Europe to other continents, notably to North and South America, but also to Australasia, Africa and Asia. Between 1821 and 1924, 55 million Europeans emigrated, of whom 19 million came from the British Isles. In total this represented about one-tenth of Europe's population and because it was mainly the young and active who emigrated, perhaps one-quarter of the labour force.

A rising population also provided an increasing source of consumer demand and a ready supply of labour for the new industries that were coming into existence. The Malthusian fear that the population increase would outstrip the resources needed to support it proved generally unfounded, though there were occasional demographic disasters such as the Irish potato famine from 1845 to 1848, when over 1 million died of hunger. Whatever miseries industrial growth brought in its train, the Irish example and the safety valve of emigration suggest that Europe's growing population was

vitally dependent on the new sources of wealth and employment created by industrialisation, patchy as its impact may have been.

The main areas of industrial growth in Britain

The first industrial revolution was characterised by developments in a few key industries, which because of their particular requirements tended to be highly localised. These industries were textiles, coal, iron and steel and engineering. In most cases improvements in productivity (output per worker) and production (total output) were achieved by a combination of technological improvements and mobilisation of the factors of production: land, labour and capital. Such mobilisation needed the skills and initiative of the entrepeneur, who would have to buy the land, raise the capital and employ the workforce to get production under way. This can best be illustrated in the textile industry. The growth in the demand for cotton prompted first a series of improvements in spinning, achieved mainly through Hargreaves's Spinning Jenny (1765), Arkwright's Water Frame (1767) and Crompton's Mule (1779). Their combined effect was to make possible the spinning of yarn on machines powered first by water and then by steam. Arkwright was the first entrepreneur to use these inventions in factories. By 1780 he was employing over 1,000 hands. The surplus of yarn now produced led to a demand for a power loom, which was duly invented by Edmund Cartwright in 1787, and came into use about 1800. These inventions spread rapidly in Britain and, to a lesser extent, on the continent. In Britain, whereas in 1765 half a million lbs of cotton had been spun by hand in 1784 this figure had risen to 12 million lbs, all spun by machine.

The iron and steel industry depended on a similar combination of technological improvement and entrepreneurial initiative. Hobbled by the limited size of its forests, the British iron industry could not expand so long as it was dependent on charcoal for smelting purposes. Abraham Darby experimented with coke (coal which had previously been baked to rid it of its impurities) in 1710 and by the middle of the century his foundries in Coalbrookdale were producing pig iron smelted with coke in some quantity. The conversion of pig iron into high quality bar or wrought iron, suitable for iron rails, machine parts and so on was improved through Henry Cort's puddling and rolling process, introduced about 1784. Ten years earlier Benjamin Huntsman had improved the production of steel through smelting it at very high temperatures in clay crucibles, adding small quantities of charcoal and ground glass. With ample supplies of coal and iron ore available, entrepreneurs such as John Wilkinson and Richard Crayshaw were able to exploit these inventions and the British iron and steel industry also took off in the 1780s.

The use of coal for all these operations led to a major expansion in the coal industry, which was aided by the use of the steam pump for draining mines, wire ropes, iron rails for the transporting of coal and the invention of the Davy lamp to minimise the dangers of underground explosions caused by fire damp. In other respects coal getting remained a pick and shovel industry, dirty and dangerous for those who worked in it.

All these advances depended on a new source of power and the machinery needed to harness it. The first efficient steam engines were designed and built by Thomas Newcomen, and were used for pumping water out of mines or into reservoirs. Their use spread quickly from 1711 onwards. Further development depended on the many improvements made by James Watt, the most important of which were the introduction of a separate condenser, which cut fuel costs (1774), and rotary motion, introduced in 1781. Once the steam engine could be used to turn a wheel, its applications were virtually unlimited. By 1800 the firm of Boulton and Watt had produced 289 steam engines of which 106 were used in the textile industry, 58 in mines, 31 in canals and water pumping, 30 in metallurgy and 23 in brewing.

The parts for these machines required a high level of accuracy and uniformity in their manufacture. John Wilkinson's iron works at Bradley was able to supply them. An early prototype for the machine tool industry was developed by Mark Brunel (father of Isambard Kingdom Brunel) and Henry Maudsley at Portsmouth in 1803. Their factory was designed to produce blocks (pulleys) for the navy, which needed at least 100,000 a year. A production line of ten unskilled men operated the machines. It attracted the admiration of Sir Walter Scott, who said in 1816 that he had never witnessed 'such wonderful sights'.

Most of these inventions at this time were British, and the commonly held view that the industrial revolution began in Britain and then spread to the continent is substantially correct. It is borne out by the following figures: in 1850 Britain's production of pig iron was three times greater than that of France, Belgium and Germany combined, as was her cotton spinning capacity. Britain had twice the steam power capacity of these countries and her railway mileage also exceeded theirs.

Industrial growth in Europe

Where Britain led, other countries were sure to follow. For if they did not, their own products would be unable to compete with low-cost British ones and there would be no market for their exports. There was a conscious effort to emulate the British experience, sometimes sponsored by governments, as in Prussia, sometimes the result of individual initiative. British craftsmen were lured to the Continent, British inventions copied. In 1785 William Wilkinson helped to design the first French coke blast furnace at Le Creusot in France. The first cotton spinning mill in Germany, using Arkwright's Water Frame, was established at Kromford near Düsseldorf in 1794. The first coke blast furnace in Prussia was built by a Scottish engineer, John Baildon, at Gleiwitz in 1794–96 (see Figure 7.1). By 1870 three countries, France, Germany and Belgium, were well on their way to rival Britain, but as Table 7.1 shows, the gap had still to be closed.

In France the French Revolution and the twenty years of warfare that ensued delayed economic development and the gap between the British and French economies widened, but after 1850 industrialisation proceeded more rapidly. The French cotton industry developed in four main areas: Normandy, Alsace, Picardy and Paris. Mechanical spinning spread quickly in Normandy and Paris, which had forty-four spinning mills by 1814. But the wars interrupted the spread of British inventions and the supply of cotton, and the French cotton industry never looked like rivalling the British one. Iron production, which stood at 200,000 tons

7.1 The Royal Foundry at Gleiwitz in 1841: ironmasters on the coal-fields of Upper Silesia were among the first in Germany to use coke-smelting

Source: Deutsches Museum, Munich

Table 7.1 Economic development in the third quarter of the nineteenth century

		Rail mileage	Coal production (1,000 tons)	Steam capacity (1,000 hp)	Pig iron output (1,000 tons)	Cotton consumption (1,000 tons)
Germany	1850	3,639	5,100	260	212	17.1
	1869	10,834	26,774	2,480	1,413	64.1
France	1850	1,869	7,225	370	406	59.3
	1869	10,518	21,432	1,850	1,381	93.7
Belgium	1850	531	3,481	70	145	10.0
	1869	1,800	7,822	350	535	16.3
UK	1850	6,621	37,500	1,290	2,249	266.8
	1869	15,145	97,066	4,040	5,446	425.8

per annum in the 1820s, rose to 1,262,000 tons in 1865. Coal production which had averaged 1.1 million tons per year in 1820–24 rose to an average of 12.7 million tons per year in 1865–69. There were 625 steam engines at work in 1830, 27,000 in 1870, and 6,250 kilometres were added to French railways between 1850 and 1860. The French industrial revolution was a more gradual process than the British one, but French technology was every bit as advanced.

Germany was already endowed with plentiful reserves of coal and iron ore, a workforce of talented craftsmen and relative ease of communications. There were no significant geographical barriers between the Rhine and the Oder or the Baltic and the Alps. In fact it was political and economic barriers which delayed German industrialisation, and their removal acted as a stimulus to economic growth. The ending of the Holy Roman Empire and its replacement by the German Confederation simplified the political map of Germany. Prussia's acquisitions in the Rhineland prompted her to establish a *Zollverein* (customs union) to link her scattered territories, which she did in 1816–17, abolishing all internal tariffs and adopting a common external tariff. From here it was a logical step to include the intermediate states. Anhalt and Hesse joined in 1826–28. In 1829 the southern states of Bavaria and Württemberg agreed to bring their tariffs into line with Prussia's by 1832, and by 1834 most of the other German states had joined the Zollverein, creating a common market of 23.6 million consumers.

The removal of trade barriers was followed by an improvement in communications. Lacking a good road system (unlike France), there was a boom in railway construction. The 549 kilometres of railway that had been built by 1830 had risen to 5,822 by 1850, much of it with the assistance of the Prussian government, which by 1860 controlled over half the network. Economic integration was also assisted by a monetary union. In 1838 the Prussian *taler* became the statutory unit of currency in the northern states and the rate of exchange between northern and southern states was fixed.

Though the German cotton industry never achieved the same volume of production as the British, mechanisation spread to areas such as the Rhineland and Saxony, and in the 1850s to Bavaria. The woollen industry grew faster and by 1864 woollens provided more than half the value of textile exports from the Zollverein. It was in the coal, iron and steel industries that Germany achieved her greatest gains, though they came relatively late in the day. Production of pig iron within the Zollverein rose slowly from 110,000 tons in 1834 to 184,000 tons in 1845. It reached a figure of 1.4 million tons in 1870 and 7.5 million tons in 1900. The industry in which Germany eventually took the lead was steel. As with other industries it was technology that provided the key to expansion. In 1857 Henry Bessemer revolutionised the steel-making process by blowing air through molten iron in a blast furnace. However, this technique worked only with ores of low phosphoric content. In 1878 Gilchrist Thomas discovered how to remove the phosphorus from iron ore and the Bessemer process could now be used with all types of iron ore. The first Bessemer plant in Germany was opened in 1862 at Essen by the firm of Krupp, and by 1900 the German steel industry had overtaken all its rivals. German production that year was 6.7 million tons, compared with British production of 5 million tons.

The third country to industrialise in the first half of the nineteenth century was Belgium. Surrounded by the Zollverein to the east, France to the west and (after 1830) by Holland to the north, Belgium was always critically dependent on her more powerful neighbours for export markets. France prevented her from joining the Zollverein in 1844, while Britain refused to allow her to join a French customs union in 1842. Fortunately for Belgium her large and accessible iron and coal deposits enabled her to compete in terms of price with French and German producers. The Belgian government also realised the need for good communications. There were 1,600 kilometres of navigable waterway by 1830 and 1,730 kilometres of railway by 1860, more than Russia or Spain could claim. Coke smelting of iron was introduced in 1823 and in 1825 the Seraing ironworks at Liège employed over 2,000 people. Steam power was quickly harnessed. The 354 steam engines employed in 1830 had risen to 2,300 by 1850. Coal production had also almost trebled to reach 6 million tons over the same period of time. The

Belgian textile industry did not expand so fast, but the linen industry was mechanised, with dire consequences for the domestic workers in Flanders, who saw their employment disappear.

By 1850, then, Britain was still very much the largest industrial producer in Europe but her lead was disappearing as France, Germany and Belgium began to develop their industries. On a larger canvas the economic domination of the rest of the world by western Europe and the United States was already visible, if not yet fully realised. Let us now examine the social and political consequences of these changes.

SOCIAL CONSEQUENCES OF INDUSTRIALISATION

The industrial revolution affected every aspect of human existence, and indeed continues to do so. Here we can do no more than touch upon the most obvious and quantifiable ones. The physical aspect of Europe was altered most clearly by the process of urbanisation. This was most noticeable in Britain, where it led to the growth of huge conurbations: in Lancashire around Liverpool and Manchester, in the West Riding of Yorkshire, in the West Midlands around Birmingham, in the North East around Newcastle and in central Scotland around Glasgow (see Figure 7.2).

In Europe there were no such conurbations until the development of the German iron and steel industry in the 1870s in the Ruhr, but a few individual cities grew as quickly as Manchester or Leeds. Manchester's population went up from 20,000 in 1757 to 95,000 in 1801. Lille, Mulhouse, Liège and Rouen would have showed comparable rates of growth. It was still the case that urbanisation proceeded much faster in Britain than it did elsewhere. In 1836 there were seventeen cities in Great Britain with populations of over 50,000. By way of comparison in France there were nine, in the German Confederation (including Prussia) there were also nine. By 1851 half of the population of England and Wales were town-

7.2 The urbanisation of Sheffield, 1858
Source: Sheffield City Art Gallery. Courtesy of Sheffield Galleries and Museums Trust

7.1 The growth of European cities, 1800–50

dwellers. In France and Germany that proportion was only a quarter (see Map 7.1).

The occupational structure of the population showed similar differences. In Britain the share of the actively employed population engaged in agriculture in 1851 was 25 per cent. In Belgium it was 50 per cent. Even by the end of the century over half the employed population of France and Germany still worked on the land. In Russia that figure was 86 per cent. Thus the changes brought about by the industrial revolution varied enormously in their impact on daily life.

The same variation is apparent in the changes

brought to the class structure. In a famous letter to a friend in 1852 Karl Marx argued that 'the existence of classes is only bound up with particular phases in the development of production', and as he put it elsewhere, 'The handmill will give you a society with the feudal lord, the steam engine a society with the industrial capitalist' (D. McLellan, *Marx*, Glasgow, Fontana, 1975, p. 41). Thus, according to Marx, the industrial revolution gave birth to two classes, the manufacturing interest, the owners of capital such as factories, shipyards and coal-mines, and the landless labourers who worked in them. How correct was Marx's formula?

Certainly, there had been nothing quite like the entrepreneurs such as Arkwright, Boulton, Wilkinson and Wedgwood who pioneered the first industrial revolution in Britain, and they had their counterparts in France (the Wendels in Lorraine) and Germany (Caspar Engels, father of Friedrich, who owned cotton mills in Barmen and Manchester). Paul Mantoux, in his celebrated history of the British industrial revolution, went so far as to say that 'With the factory system a new social type came into being' (*The Industrial Revolution in the Eighteenth Century*, London, Jonathan Cape, 1961, p. 376). Dickens was to portray him as the hardhearted employer, Mr Bounderby, in *Hard Times*.

It must always be remembered, however, that factory owners were only one ingredient, if a new one, in a bourgeoisie that already flourished at any rate in western Europe, made up of merchants, bankers, civil servants and members of the professions such as doctors, lawyers and university teachers. When the Frankfurt Parliament met in 1848, 68 per cent of their members were civil servants, 12 per cent were drawn from the professions and a mere 2.5 per cent came from the world of business. Many of these would become shareholders in the new joint stock companies that were used to finance industrial enterprises such as railways in the 1840s and 1850s, and would have shared with employers the same interest in profits. But as the industrial revolution proceeded it led to an expansion of the educational system, a growth in the role of the state, a flowering of service industries such as tourism, leisure and entertainment, all financed out of the greater wealth created by increased production. Thus the Marxist vision of a bourgeoisie, exclusively made up of the exploiters of labour, was blinkered, even in 1848, and has become even more so in later times.

Marx also called attention to the emergence of the proletariat, a term originally used in Ancient Rome to describe those required to lend their offspring to the state because they could not pay taxes. For Marx and his followers, the proletariat were the property-less wage-earners recruited to work in the new factories, having nothing to sell but their own labour power. Again, there is no disputing that such a class came into being wher-

ever factories appeared. Nor is there any doubt that for many of them, their wives and children, working conditions were appalling, hours excessive and wages low (see Figure 7.3). There has been, and continues to be an active debate on whether the industrial revolution made conditions worse for the working classes. In four respects, at least, industrialisation had damaging consequences. Wherever mechanisation replaced the work of handworkers it threatened their livelihoods. This happened to handloom workers in England in the 1830s, with the introduction of the power loom. In West Flanders linen weavers were similarly affected in 1846–48: 'A whole regional economy and a pattern of existence which had survived for over two centuries was thus rendered unviable in a few years' (A.S. Milward and S.B. Saul, *The Economic Development of Continental Europe*, London, Allen and Unwin, 1979, p. 447). Weavers in Silesia rioted in 1844, as their jobs disappeared and hunger or typhus carried them off.

The uncontrolled and unrestricted growth of towns, with inadequate water supplies and sewage disposal, led to the spread of water-borne diseases such as cholera. There were serious epidemics in most European cities until clean water became available. Life expectancy was twice as high in rural Rutland as it was in urban Manchester in the 1840s. Diseases associated with particular occupations such as silicosis (coal-mining) and grinder's disease (steel) spread inevitably with the expansion of these industries. Finally, whereas in agriculture peasant cultivators could rely on the regularity of the seasons and a reasonably constant market for their products, factory workers were at the mercy of economic fluctuations over which they had no control. A financial crisis sparked off by the collapse of a land boom in the United States in 1824–25 led to a serious depression in the British textile industry. Railway building was particularly at the mercy of speculators, and employment correspondingly uncertain.

It may be true that without the additional employment provided by the growth of industry the mass of Europe's population would have been even worse off, as the example of Ireland suggests. But the introduction of new technology, subject only to the unregulated operation of market forces, undoubtedly widened the gap between rich and

7.3 Coal-mining: women and children's employment in a pick and shovel industry, 1842

Source: Mansell/Time Inc./Katz

poor, as it brought into existence factories and towns where industrial workers now congregated. The edges of class conflict were sharpened in consequence.

There was both a conservative reaction against these changes and a radical response which demanded that something must be done to ameliorate their effects. To the hopes and fears generated by the French Revolution were now added the beckoning prospects of increasing wealth tempered by the apprehension of working class revolt.

IDEOLOGICAL RESPONSES TO INDUSTRIALISATION

Liberals

The industrial revolution was generally welcomed, as might be expected, from those who benefited from it. Most were members of the bourgeoisie and whether as employers or shareholders took little convincing that the growth in material progress outweighed any costs there might have been. It was from their ranks that liberal parties, whether in Britain, France or Germany, were generally recruited. Their creed, Liberalism, was grafted on to the optimistic views of the Enlightenment and belief in the possibility of progress. In relation to the industrial revolution perhaps the most influential voice was that of Adam Smith (1723–90), professor of logic and moral philosophy at Glasgow University and later a customs commissioner in Edinburgh. In 1776 he published *The Wealth of Nations*. Its essential message was that man's self-interest would promote the economic well-being of all: 'It is not from the benevolence of the butcher, the brewer or the baker that we expect our dinner, but from their regard to their own interest.' The economic growth he witnessed happening around him would occasion 'in a well-governed society, that universal opulence which extends itself to the lowest ranks of the people' (the trickle-down theory of wealth used today to justify economic inequalities: *The Wealth of Nations*, vol. 1, London, Dent, 1910, pp. 10–13). Smith believed in the beneficent working of the market, the invisible hand, which would ensure the most efficient use of resources. The role of the state should be confined to the maintenance of security at home and abroad, an attitude which became popularly abbreviated in the phrase *laissez-faire* (literally, allow to do). His views were echoed by a French economist, Jean Baptiste Say (1767–1832) who argued in his *Traité d'Économie Politique* (1803) that the economic system was self-regulating. Supply automatically creates its own demand, and thus there should be no crises of over-production and unsold goods. It is probably safe to say that the views of Smith and Say represented the conventional wisdom not only of their day but also throughout the nineteenth century. They have their adherents today.

If liberals were generally optimistic about the workings of the the economy, they did not take such a hopeful view of their fellow human beings. While there was a general belief in the need for written constitutions and representative institutions such as parliaments, democracy was feared as much as absolute monarchy. Benjamin Constant (1767–1830) exemplified these views. His *Principes de Politique*, published in 1815, advocated a two chamber assembly, one hereditary, one elected, but

the supreme guarantee of political liberalism was, in his opinion, the property qualification for the vote. Only property gave a citizen sufficient interest to share effectively in government and the leisure 'to acquire understanding and sureness of judgment' (J. Droz, *Europe between Revolutions*, London, Fontana, 1967, pp. 49–50). When the Charter, calling for universal suffrage, was presented to the British House of Commons in 1839, it was rejected by a large majority (235 to 46) on precisely these grounds. Distrust of the industrial proletariat was characteristic of European liberals while they generally applauded the economic changes which brought it into existence.

Conservatives

The conservative response to the French and industrial revolutions took several forms. One of them was a nostalgic idealisation of the Middle Ages and a rejection of the secular values and the belief in progress characteristic of the Enlightenment. This is well illustrated in the works of Joseph de Maistre and François René de Chateaubriand. De Maistre (1753–1821) came from Savoy and spent most of his life there, but he was a close observer of the French Revolution, which he condemned unreservedly. He believed in the restraining force of religion and in his *Du Pape* (Of the Papacy), published in 1819, argued that all legitimate rulers held their power on the authority of the sole true sovereign, the infallible Pope. Chateaubriand (1768–1848), a Breton aristocrat, who later became Foreign Minister (1822–24), published his *Génie du Christianisme* in 1802 in which he idealised the medieval world and stressed the poetic values of Christianity as well as its dogmatic truths. His book achieved a wide circulation, and had a considerable influence on Tsar Alexander I.

Another response was to condemn the consequences of industrialisation, first voiced, as was to be expected, in England. The writer Samuel Taylor Coleridge was only one among many to condemn child labour. He pressed 'the hopeless cause of poor little white slaves, the children of our cotton factories, against the cruel spirit of trade and the shallow, heart-petrifying self-conceit of our political economists' (P. Johnson, *The Birth of the Modern*, London, Phoenix, 1991, p. 722). Thomas Carlyle in a series of essays, *Past and Present*, equally condemned the evils of industrialism and in his later years called for a return to rule by a landed aristocracy, a view he shared with the Young England movement of which Disraeli was an enthusiastic member. In one of his novels, *Sybil or the Two Nations*, Disraeli deplored the class divisions between the rich and the poor which were a consequence of the industrial revolution. It was significant that the campaign for legislation to restrict the hours worked by children in factories was led by Lord Shaftesbury, who was both a member of the aristocracy and a committed Christian.

Socialists

A more radical response to the industrial revolution was to be found among those who christened themselves socialists. As with all such labels, the origin of the term is impossible to locate but the first socialist is often held to be Gracchus Babeuf. He led a rising in Paris in 1796, and in his *Conspiracy of Equals* advocated absolute equality of incomes. Babeuf created a precedent for conspiratorial violence that was to be imitated by his followers such as Filippo Buonarotti in Italy and Auguste Blanqui in France. Very different was the response of Robert Owen, a factory owner who established what he hoped would be a model community at his cotton mill in New Lanark, where his workers enjoyed the benefits of good housing and education. He attempted to establish a similar community named New Harmony in Indiana. When this failed he returned to England and in 1834 set up the Grand National Consolidated Trade Union (GNCTU) with the intention that producer co-operatives should replace capitalist organisation. Needless to say, within a year the GNCTU had collapsed.

Other early socialists addressed themselves to the problem of inequality. The Comte de Saint-Simon, a French aristocrat who had served in the American War of Independence, wrote prolifically on industry and society. While welcoming the advances brought by technology, he exposed the exploitation of individual by individual which it had brought and his followers attacked the private ownership of productive capital. While Saint-Simon and his followers believed in the role of a strong state to organise the economy and promote equality, Charles Fourier, a man of humble background, proposed a quite different solution. He advocated the foundation of 'phalansteries' (the term is derived from the Greek phalanx), small communities whose members would be rewarded in accordance with the capital invested, the labour expended and the skill employed. Though no such phalansteries were successfully established in Fourier's day, his followers did succeed in applying his ideas later on.

Another French socialist, Pierre-Joseph Proudhon, the son of an artisan and entirely self-educated, produced what was perhaps the most outspoken denunciation of the economic system. To the question 'What is Property?' (the title of his pamphlet published in 1840), Proudhon answered 'Property is Theft'. He also described it as the suicide of society. But Proudhon had little to offer by way of solutions. He favoured a federation of small communes composed of small landowners, equality of wages and the replacement of the state by the workshop.

Not surprisingly, perhaps, these thinkers have become known as Utopian Socialists. Their justifiable critiques of a society based on the free operation of market forces, and the inequalities to which this gave rise, were not matched by a comparable set of realistic objectives. Two works, both produced by Germans, gave Socialism greater intellectual credibility. In 1845 Friedrich Engels produced his *The Condition of the Working Class in England*, based on observations made while he was running his father's cotton mill in Manchester. It was a devastating portrayal of the appalling working conditions and urban squalor he encountered there. Karl Marx, who had met Engels for the first time in 1842, without appreciating his qualities, met him a second time in August 1844, and their cooperation began in earnest. It culminated in the publication in 1848 of *The Communist Manifesto*. This began with the famous declaration 'The history of all hitherto existing societies is the history of class struggles'. It went on to prophesy the downfall of the bourgeoisie: 'What the bourgeoisie produces above all, is its own grave diggers' (the proletariat) and ended with the clarion call 'Workers of the world unite, you have nothing to lose but your chains'. At the time *The Communist Manifesto* had little impact. Only a few hundred copies were printed, and its initial circulation was tiny. But, starting as a cloud no bigger than a man's hand, it was to become one of the most influential books ever written. Thus the industrial revolution came not only to alter material conditions for the majority of Europe's citizens, but also to shape their political life.

SECTION B – SOURCES

LIVING STANDARDS AND THE INDUSTRIAL REVOLUTION

The debate on whether living standards rose or fell for the great majority of the working population as a result of the industrial revolution continues unabated. The pessimistic view, generally embraced by left-wing historians, is well represented by Eric Hobsbawm, who concluded

That the condition of the labouring poor was appalling between 1815 and 1848 was not denied by any reasonable observer, and by 1840 there were a good many of these. That it was actually deteriorating was widely assumed. . . . It is in fact probable that there was some general deterioration over wide areas of Europe, for not only (as we have seen) urban institutions and social services failed to keep pace with headlong and unplanned expansion and money (and often real wages) tended to fall after 1815, the production and transport of foodstuffs also fell in many large cities until the railway age.

(E.J. Hobsbawm, *The Age of Revolution*, New York, Mentor, 1962, pp. 243–44)

Other historians have stressed the benefits brought by industrialisation, without denying the costs:

It was the Industrial Revolution that initiated a cumulative, self-sustaining advance in technology whose repercussions would be felt in all aspects of economic life. . . . The result has been an enormous increase in the output of goods and services, and this alone has changed man's way of life more than anything since the dis-

covery of fire: the Englishman of 1750 was closer in material things to Caesar's legionnaires than to his own grandchildren.

(Landes, *Unbound Prometheus*, p. 5)

There were costs:

For one thing, if mechanization opened new vistas of comfort and prosperity for all men, it also destroyed the livelihood of some and left others to vegetate in the backwaters of the stream of progress. Change is demonic; it creates but it also destroys, and the victims of the Industrial Revolution were numbered in the hundreds of thousands or even millions (On the other hand, many of these would have been even worse off without industrialization).

(Landes, *Unbound Prometheus*, p. 7)

To illustrate these views we have chosen to examine evidence mainly from the British industrial revolution, which, as we have seen, was the first and much the greatest in scale in the first half of the nineteenth century. Evidence to support these views has been of two kinds, statistical and descriptive. The statistical evidence with regard to population, based on the annual censuses introduced in 1801, has shown a steady rise throughout the nineteenth century, though whether this was due to a falling death rate rather than a rising birth rate is still open to question. In most other respects, statistical evidence gives incomplete or ambiguous answers. There are no reliable figures for unemployment before 1911. Attempts to trace the movement of wage rates in relation to prices have been possible for certain occupational groups, for example handloom weavers, but this cannot be done for the working classes as a whole. Similarly, while it is possible to detect certain changes in consumption, such as a shift from bread to potatoes in certain areas, or a decline in the consumption of meat per head of population, it is not possible to quantify the increase in the wearing of cotton, which certainly improved personal hygiene and hence health, or the greater availability of china, pots and pans and carpeting. In the absence of reliable statistical information the historian has to depend on the observations of contemporaries. Among the most acute were Adam Smith, whose *Wealth of Nations* was based upon his own breadth of knowledge as well as his powers of analysis, and Friedrich Engels, whose *The Condition of the Working Class in England* was written on the basis of his experiences while working at his father's spinning mill in Manchester during 1842–44, and on his extensive reading of government blue books and medical reports. Rather than enter the general debate about living standards, we have chosen to focus on two particular aspects of the industrial revolution: wage rates and child labour.

Wage rates

When workers left the land for the town and the factory they became wholly dependent on their money wages, unlike the agricultural labourer who often had at least a garden where he could grow his own produce and possibly a tied cottage where he could raise his children. Thus wage levels were fundamental to his subsistence. In extract A Adam Smith expounds his views on what determines wage rates. In extract B Engels explains why, in his view, a surplus population helps to keep wages down. In extract C industrial workers in Cologne voice their protests at the behaviour of their employers.

A Adam Smith explains how wages are determined

What are the common wages of labour, depends everywhere upon the contract usually made between those two parties [the workmen and the masters], whose interests are by no means the same. The former are disposed to combine in order to raise, the latter in order to lower the wages of labour. It is not, however, difficult to foresee which of the two parties must, upon all ordinary occasions, have the advantage in the dispute, and force the other into a compliance with their terms. The masters, being fewer in number, can combine much more easily; and the law, besides, authorises, or at least does not prohibit their combinations, while it prohibits those of the workmen. We have no acts of parliament against combining to lower the price of work; but many against combining to raise it. [Such acts were repealed

in England in 1824–25, but remained in force in Europe much longer.]

(Adam Smith, *The Wealth of Nations*, vol. 1, London, 1910, pp. 58–59)

B Friedrich Engels explains why competition leads to low wages

Surplus population is engendered rather by the competition among the workers themselves, which forces each worker to labour as much each day as his strength can possibly admit. If a manufacturer can employ ten hands nine hours daily, he can employ nine if each works ten hours, and the tenth goes hungry. And if a manufacturer can force the nine hands to work an extra hour daily for the same wages by threatening to discharge them at a time when the demand for hands is not very great, he discharges the tenth and so saves much wages. This is the process, on a small scale which goes on in a nation on a large one.

(Friedrich Engels, *The Condition of the Working Class in England*, London, Granada, 1969, pp. 113–14)

C Memorial from the workers to Cologne factory owners, April 1848

The time for hypocrisy is over and done with. When you wanted to overcome the competition of foreign rivals you cut down our wages and you made no personal sacrifices. When you wanted to drive the goods of other German manufacturers from the home market it was the factory hands who had to work harder for longer hours. When you aimed at artificially raising the prices of manufactured goods you closed your works without turning a hair even though hundreds of workers were ruined.

Do you want proof? Your own enormous wealth and our extreme poverty – these facts speak louder than words. Our labour – the sweat of our brows and the ruin of our health – has made you rich. So it is to you that we look for redress. It is to you that we make the following demands:

(i)   All factory workers dismissed since April 8 shall be reinstated at once unless it can be proved that they have violated the law.

(ii) The hours of work shall be from 6 a.m. to 6 p.m. Workers shall have half an hour for breakfast in the morning, half an hour for lunch at midday, and half an hour for coffee in the afternoon. . . .

(v) The wives and children of workers absent from the factory owing to sickness shall receive half-pay for three months.

(vi) The minimum day wage of an adult worker shall be 20 silver groschen.

(W.O. Henderson, *The Industrial Revolution on the Continent*, London, F. Cass, 1961, pp. 38–39)

Questions

1 What according to Adam Smith determines the common wages of labour, and why do advantages generally rest with the employer?

2 How convincing do you find Engels' argument in extract B that it is the forces of competition that keep wages down?

3 How far does extract C support the views expressed in extracts A and B of how employers are likely to behave?

4 Using these documents and your wider knowledge, comment on the view that the main cause of poverty among nineteenth century workers was the greed of employers.

Child labour

Child labour was not a product of the industrial revolution. Children were employed on the land in a wide range of tasks as soon as they were capable of them. They took part in spinning and weaving under the domestic system from the age of 6 in some parts of England. The children of paupers had always been set to work. What the industrial revolution did was greatly to increase the numbers at work, lengthen the hours and herd children together in unhealthy factories where they were employed on repetitive and physically damaging tasks.

A Report by Dr Percival for the Manchester Board of Health, 1796

(1) It appears that the children and others who work in the large cotton factories are peculiarly disposed to be affected by the contagion of fever, and that where such infection is received it is rapidly propagated. . . . (2) The large factories are generally injurious to the constitution of those employed in them even where no particular diseases prevail, from the close confinement which is enjoined, from the debilitating effects of hot and impure air, and from the want of the active exercises which nature points out as essential in childhood and youth to invigorate the system and fit our species for employment and for the duties of manhood. (3) The untimely labour of the night, and the protracted labour of the day, with respect to children, not only tends to diminish future expectations as to the general sum of life and industry, by impairing the strength and destroying the vital stamina of the rising generation, but it too often gives encouragement idleness, extravagance and profligacy in the parents, who, contrary to nature, subsist by the oppression of their offspring. (4) It appears that the children employed in factories are generally debarred from all opportunities of education, from moral and religious instruction. (5) From the excellent regulations which subsist in several cotton factories, it appears that many of these evils may in a considerable degree be obviated.

(Paul Mantoux, *The Industrial Revolution in the Eighteenth Century*, London, Jonathan Cape, 1961, p. 481)

B Joseph Farington, a member of the Royal Academy, visits one of Arkwright's factories, 12 August, 1801

In the evening I walked to Cromford and saw the children coming from their work out of one of Mr. Arkwright's Manufactories. I was glad to see them look in general very healthy and many with fine, rosy complexions. These children had been at work from 6 or 7 o'clock this morning and it was now near or about 7 in the evening. The time allowed them for resting is at 12 o'clock 40 minutes during which time they dine. One of them, a boy of 10 or 11 years of age, told me his wages were 3s 6d. a week, and a little girl said her wages were 2s 3d. a week.

August 23 – We went to Church at Cromford where is a Chapel built about 3 years ago by Mr. Arkwright. On each side the organ a gallery in which about 50 boys were seated. These children are employed in Mr. Arkwright's work in the week-days, and on Sundays attend a school where they receive education. . . . To this school girls also go for the same purpose, and alternately with the boys go to Church, the boys on one Sunday, the girls on the next following . . . . The whole plan appears to be such as to do Mr. Arkwright great credit.

(T. Charles-Edwards and B. Richardson (eds) *They Saw it Happen, 1689–1897*, Oxford, Blackwell, 1958, pp. 239–40)

C Dr Andrew Ure describes child labour in Lancashire

I have visited many factories, both in Manchester and in the surrounding districts, during a period of several months, entering the spinning rooms unexpectedly and often alone, at different times of the day, and I never saw a single instance of corporal punishment inflicted on a child . . . . The scene of industry, so far from exciting sad emotions, in my mind, was always exhilarating. It was delightful to observe the nimbleness with which they pieced broken ends, as the mule carriage began to recede from the fixed roller beam, and to see them at leisure after a few seconds' exercise of their tiny fingers, to amuse themselves in any attitude they chose, till the stretch and winding were once more completed. The work of these lively elves seemed to resemble a sport, in which habit gave them a pleasing dexterity. Conscious of their skill, they were delighted to show it off to any stranger. As to exhaustion by the day's work, they evinced no trace of it on emerging from the mill in the evening; for they immediately began to skip about any neighbouring playground, and to commence their little games with the same alacrity as boys issuing from school.

(Dr Andrew Ure, *The Philosophy of Manufactures*, cited in F. Engels, *The Condition of the Working Class in England*, London, Granada, 1969, p. 196)

Questions

1 Which of these three extracts would you regard as most accurate in its portrayal of child labour?
2 How would you account for the very different images of child labour conveyed by extracts A, B and C.
3 Using these extracts and your wider knowledge, account for the widespread acceptance of child labour in the industrial revolution and the growing objections to it.

Further reading

The British industrial revolution

There is a huge literature on the British industrial revolution. Here are three standard works: P. Mathias, *The First Industrial Nation: an Economic History of Britain, 1700–1914* (London, Methuen, 1969) is the best summary. E.J. Hobsbawm, *Industry and Empire* (London, Penguin, 1990) is written from a Marxist perspective, but is lively and soundly based. M.W. Flinn, *Origins of the Industrial Revolution* (London, Longman, 1966) examines various explanations of why the industrial revolution began when it did.

The industrial revolution in Europe

A.S. Milward and S.B. Saul, *The Economic Development of Continental Europe* (2nd edn, London, Allen and Unwin, 1979) provides useful studies of particular industries and countries. W.O. Henderson, *The Industrial Revolution on the Continent* (London, F. Cass, 1961) is mainly confined to France, Germany and Belgium. C. Trebilcock, *The Industrialisation of the Great Powers 1780–1914* (London, Longman, 1981) is a strongly analytical comparative study of reasons for industrialisation. D.S. Landes, *The Unbound Prometheus: Technological Change and Industrial Development in Western Europe from 1750 to the Present* (Cambridge University Press, 1969) puts industrial changes 1750–1850 in perspective.

The effects of industrialisation

E.J. Hobsbawm, *The Age of Revolution, 1789–1848* (New York, Mentor Books, 1962) is a stimulating comparison of the effects of the French and industrial revolutions on living conditions, ideology, the arts and science. See also essays on the challenge of industrialisation and the growth of population in P.M. Pilbeam (ed.) *Themes in Modern History* (London, Routledge, 1995). P. Johnson, *The Birth of the Modern* (London, Phoenix, 1991) is a vivid if quirky panorama of the world between 1815 and 1830, with much fascinating source material. J. Droz, *Europe between Revolutions* (London, Fontana, 1967) has useful chapters on Liberalism and Socialism.

• CHAPTER EIGHT •

Nationalism and the Breakdown of the Concert of Europe, 1815–56

• CONTENTS •

Key dates

KEY DATES

1818	Sept.	Congress of Aix-la-Chapelle
1820	Jan.	Outbreak of rebellion in Spain
	July	Outbreaks of rebellion in Naples and Palermo
	Oct.	Congress of Troppau; Troppau Protocol
1821	Jan.	Congress of Laibach; Austria authorised to intervene in Italy
	Feb.	Austrian aid to King of Naples
	March	Outbreak of Greek revolt
	March	Constitutional rising in Piedmont
	April	Austrian troops help suppress rising in Piedmont
1822	10 Jan.	Greeks declared their independence at Epidaurus.
	August	Canning succeeded Castlereagh as British Foreign Minister
	Oct.	Congress of Verona; France authorised to intervene in Spain
1823	April	French invasion of Spain, opposed by Britain
	Dec.	Monroe Doctrine opposing European intervention on American Continents
1824		Britain recognises independence of new republics in South America
1827	5 June	Turks enter Athens
	6 June	Treaty of London between Britain, France and Russia to secure autonomy for Greece within the Turkish empire
	20 Oct.	Turkish fleet destroyed at Navarino
1829	14 Sept.	Treaty of Adrianople between Turkey and Russia
1830	Feb.	Greek independence guaranteed by main powers
	Aug.	Belgian revolt against Dutch rule begins
	Nov.	Polish revolt v. Russian rule begins
	Dec.	London Conference agrees to support Belgian independence
1831	Feb.	Belgian constitution proclaimed
	Sept.	Polish revolt finally crushed
1832	Jan.	'Young Italy' founded by Mazzini
	April	Sultan declares war on his Egyptian vassal, Mehemet Ali
		Greek boundaries agreed
1833		Prince Otto of Bavaria chosen to be the first king of Greece
	June	Treaty of Unkiar Skelessi between Russia and Turkey: Dardanelles closed to all foreign warships
1839	April	Mehemet Ali invades Syria
	June	Sultan Mahmud defeated at Nezib; succeeded by Abdul Majid; European powers agree to support new Sultan
1840	15 June	Quadruple Alliance (Britain, Russia, Prussia and Austria) impose terms on Mehemet Ali
1841	July	Straits Convention closes Dardanelles to all warships when Turkey at peace
1850		Louis Napoleon asserts French rights to guard Holy Places
1852	May	French warship passes through Dardanelles
	Dec.	Nicholas I asserts claim to protect all Orthodox Christians in Turkish empire
1853	Jan.	Prince Menshikov arrives in Constantinople
	3 June	Russian troops occupy Moldavia and Wallachia
	24 July	Vienna Conference
	1 Aug.	Vienna note agreed; Turks reject it
	Oct.	State of war between Russia and Turkey
	30 Nov.	Turkish fleet destroyed at Sinope
1854	March	Britain and France declare war on Russia
1854–56		Crimean war
1856	30 March	Treaty of Paris signed; Black Sea to be demilitarised

SECTION A

NATIONALISM AND ITS SUPPORTERS

Nationalism, meaning a strong sense of identity between a state and its people, as we have seen, was greatly strengthened in the established states of Europe as a result of the French Revolution. French people felt a new sense of pride in their achievements, despite Napoleon's defeat, while his enemies in Britain, Russia and Spain enjoyed a corresponding sense of pride in their successful resistance to him. It was no accident that Trafalgar Square and Nelson's Column were put up in the 1830s. In the nineteenth century nationalism was to become an even more powerful sentiment in two ways. First, what has been called civic nationalism, loyalty to the state, was enhanced by the extension of natural rights to all its citizens, if only in an abstract sense. The French Declaration of Rights of 1789 stated that 'the principle of all sovereignty resides essentially in the nation'. To the question who constitutes the nation, the French revolutionaries would have replied that all who subscribed to its political creed had the right to belong, whether they lived in the departments annexed to France or in Paris itself. As greater numbers were included in the political nation through the extension of the franchise, so their sense of belonging to it was strengthened. Civic nationalism was thus very bound up with the extension of political rights. In practice, universal manhood suffrage did not become a feature of western European states before 1870 at the earliest, and of eastern Europe before 1919, so that nationalism as a conscious belief tended to be largely confined to the educated middle class until the late nineteenth century. With the coming of the popular press and compulsory education, both towards the end of the ninteenth century, it became a much more widely shared sentiment.

Second, a very different answer as to what constitutes the nation was given by German philosophers at the end of the eighteenth century. To men like Herder and Fichte the nation was made up of those who shared a common race, language and culture. It was Herder who first emphasised the links between language and nationality. He claimed to find the soul of the German *Volk* (people) in its folklore and popular songs. It was those united by the same language who constituted for Fichte the German nation which he addressed in his series of lectures in 1807–08. This link between language, race and nationality was to be a powerful and often destructive force.

Problems arose whenever there was a clash between existing political boundaries and ethnic nations. In post-Congress Europe this was most obvious in the Habsburg empire, which included Italians, Poles, Hungarians, Czechs, Slovenes, Serbs (after 1878) and Croats as well as German speaking Austrians. Similar problems arose in the Turkish and Russian empires. The Balkan peninsula under the nominal rule of the Sultan was populated by a variety of ethnic groups – Serbs, Croats, Bulgarians, Romanians, Montenegrins and Greeks – all of whom would come in time to demand their independence. The Russian empire was to be faced with similar challenges from Poles, Ukrainians and Finns in the west and from a host of other ethnic groups in the south and east. In these cases nationalism acted as a dissolvent, helping to cause the break-up of empires. Where Italy and Germany, were concerned, on the other hand, nationalism acted as a bonding agent, bringing together peoples who were united by language, culture and religion (in the case of Italy) into sovereign and united states.

It will be remembered that at the Congress of Vienna ethnic nationalism was barely recognised as a concept, let alone a principle to be applied in the determining of frontiers. Within a generation nationalist movements had taken root in many parts of Europe and within two generations two new nation-states, Italy and Germany, had appeared on the map of Europe. Initially, however, progress was slow and nationalist revolts where they occurred, were contained with relative ease.

In seeking to explain the spread of nationalism one must first identify its supporters. It was overwhelmingly a movement of the educated classes. This was at a time when secondary education was confined to a tiny minority. In France 70,000 children a year attended secondary schools in 1842. In Russia it was a mere 20,000. The university population was naturally even smaller. There were 1,500 university students in Prussia in the 1840s and the total student population of Europe in 1848 has been calculated at 40,000. It was in this educated elite, nonetheless, that ethnic nationalism first made its appearance. In 1840 Hungarian was adopted as the official language of the Diet (parliament). In the 1830s textbooks written in Romanian rather than Greek appeared for the first time. In 1835 the *Croatian Gazette* was first published. The early supporters of Italian and German unification tended to be drawn from student and university circles. Mazzini, founder of Young Italy in 1832, might be described as a perpetual student, and moved in intellectual circles when he was in exile. Professors from Kiel university championed Prussia's claims to Schleswig and Holstein in 1846.

Nationalism could also count on the support of disadvantaged groups such as the minor gentry in Hungary and Poland. Popular support was much less common. At a time when literacy rates were very low (0 per cent among the Southern Slavs, 2 per cent in Russia) it was only when economic conditions were particularly bad that nationalist risings were likely to attract much support among the peasantry, whose concerns were much more basic than the language of textbooks. The bourgeoisie, too, were generally more interested in economic stability and political security than in the redrawing of political frontiers. Both in Germany and Italy there was an initial reluctance on the part of the middle classes to get involved in revolutionary disturbances. In northern Italy, for instance, there was little sympathy for Mazzini's call for a united Italy in upper class circles. The monarchies and aristocracies of Europe very often had more in common with each other than with their subjects and tenants. The cousinhood of kings was a reality. Queen Victoria was related through her ancestry and progeny to every European dynasty. For these reasons, it is not surprising that nationalist revolts initially met with little success. Where they did succeed it was only because they had the support of one or more of the major powers.

CHALLENGES TO THE VIENNA SETTLEMENT

There were numerous challenges to the international order established at Vienna between 1815 and 1856, in which nationalism was the main if not the only ingredient. Italy was the scene of many abortive revolts: a rebellion in Naples in 1820–21, a rising in Piedmont in 1821, disturbances in the Papal States in 1831 and again in 1832. In April 1821 fighting broke out in the Morea (Greece, south of the Gulf of Corinth) which proved a prelude to the Greek War of Independence. This lasted intermittently until September 1831. In August 1830 the Belgians claimed their independence from the Dutch, a problem that was not finally resolved until 1839. Final challenges to the status quo, though not strictly in Europe, were mounted by Mehemet Ali, ruler of Egypt and nominally the Sultan's vassal, who declared war on the Sultan and invaded Syria in 1839; and by Tsar Nicholas I and Louis Napoleon, whose competing claims to guard the Holy Places in Palestine helped to produce the Crimean war in 1855.

In their reactions to these challenges the powers of Europe responded in different ways. Initially there was a serious attempt to display a united front and to take joint action to quell any revolutionary disturbance. It had been agreed under the terms of the Quadruple Alliance of November 1815 that its members would meet at regular intervals to discuss whatever measures would be 'most salutary . . . for the maintenance of the peace of Europe'. Between 1818 and 1825 a number of conferences took place to discuss such measures. Initially, the main threat was still seen to be a resurgent France, but before long it was the threat of revolution which became the dominating concern. The first such meeting took place at Aix-la-Chapelle in 1818. Here it was agreed to end the military occupation of France (two years earlier than the treaty of Paris had specified) and to admit France to all future Congresses. Almost from the outset Britain was a reluctant participant, and unwilling to intervene in other countries' affairs on the side of autocratic governments, as soon became apparent.

In 1820 the outbreak of a rebellion in Spain which forced King Ferdinand to grant a democratic constitution provoked a demand from Alexander I for joint action to restore Ferdinand to his rightful position. This prompted Castlereagh to detach Britain from any such initiative. In a celebrated State Paper, dated 20 May 1820, he voiced Britain's reservations: 'No country having a

Representative system of govt. could act upon it [the principle of one state interfering by force in the internal affairs of another], and the sooner such a Doctrine shall be distinctly abjured, as forming in any Degree the basis of our Alliance, the better'.

When the Congress convened at Troppau in November 1820 a circular was agreed by the rulers of Russia, Prussia and Austria proposing joint action against any revolutionary changes:

States which have undergone a change of government due to revolution, the results of which threaten other States, *ipso facto* [by that fact itself] cease to be members of the European Alliance and remain excluded from it until their situation gives guarantees for legal order and stability. If, owing to such alterations, immediate danger threatens other States, the Powers bind themselves, by peaceful means, or if need be by arms, to bring the guilty state into the bosom of the Great Alliance.

(*Cambridge Modern History*, vol. 10, Cambridge University Press, 1907, p. 28)

Castlereagh again dissented, dismissing the Troppau circular as 'devoid of common sense'. He wrote privately to his brother Lord Stewart, the British observer at Troppau,

It is singular . . . that it should have occurred to the three Courts to reform an Alliance which has been found to adapt itself to all the exigencies (demands) of affairs upon the exploded doctrine of divine right and passive obedience. . . . We cannot adhere to their principles and if they will be theorists, we must act in separation.

(H. Kissinger, *A World Restored*, London, Gollancz 1957, p. 266)

The division between Britain and the other powers was now quite explicit. When the next Congress met at Verona in 1822, Canning, who had now replaced Castlereagh after the latter's suicide, made it clear that Britain would not be party to the invasion of Spain. His opposition did not prevent a French army marching to Madrid in April 1823. In his speech to the House of Commons explaining British neutrality, Canning made no secret of his support for Spain and 'earnestly hoped and trusted that she would come triumphantly out of the struggle' (Wendy Hinde, *George Canning*, London,

Collins, 1973, p. 329) and there was much popular support for the Spanish cause (see extract D).

Britain refused to send a representative to a Congress convened to discuss the fate of Spain's colonies in the New World in January 1824, and at the end of the year Britain recognised the independent republics of Buenos Aires, Mexico and Colombia. In December 1826 Canning, recalling his failure to intervene in 1823, made his famous boast:

I looked another way – I sought materials of compensation in another hemisphere. Contemplating Spain, such as our ancestors had known her, I resolved that if France had Spain, it should not be 'Spain with the Indies'. I called the New World into existence to redress the balance of the Old.

(Hinde, *George Canning*, p. 422)

Britain was not represented at a Congress which met at St Petersburg in 1825. The experiment in European cooperation came to an inglorious end, partly because of British refusal to cooperate, but also because one of its purposes was the suppression of any opposition to the status quo, whether justified or not.

With the breakdown of the Congress system European responses to revolution were more clearly determined by the balance of national interests, rather than the need to impose common solutions. This explains why some revolutions were allowed to succeed while others were not. In their response to rebellion in Italy the powers were generally prepared, at this stage, to allow Austria to act as the police officer of Europe. Austrian troops were dispatched to Naples in 1821 and to the Papal States in 1831 and 1832 to help in the restoration of order. With the failure of these rebellions, opposition to Habsburg rule in Italy became confined to expatriate groups who settled in Paris, London and Geneva, where they were generally tolerated, if not encouraged.

The Polish revolt of 1830 met with much the same response. Though Poland had been granted its own constitution in 1815, it was declared indissolubly linked to Russia and power rested effectively in the hands of the Russian commander-in-chief, Grand Duke Constantine. In November 1830 a group of army officers seized public buildings in Warsaw. The Russian army withdrew, a Supreme National Council was set up which in January 1831 declared the deposition of Nicholas I. A Russian army invaded Poland in May, and by September had overcome all opposition. Isolated voices were raised in support of the Poles in France and Britain, but to no avail. Such autonomy as Poland had enjoyed in 1815 was removed, and Russian rule was more strictly imposed.

The first revolt to succeed took place in Belgium. Following the July Revolution in France in 1830 a group of Belgian patriots demanded separation from Holland, if not yet from the House of Orange. However, when Dutch troops entered Brussels they encountered fierce opposition and withdrew after three days. A provisional Belgian government now demanded full independence. The Dutch king, aware that this would directly conflict with the treaty of Vienna, appealed to the powers for a solution. Only France and Britain had a direct interest in the outcome, and the eyes of Russia, Prussia and Austria were fixed on events in Poland rather than the Low Countries. Britain was naturally anxious to minimise French influence in any newly created state there, while Louis Philippe, the new French king, could not be seen to be less patriotic than his new subjects in pressing for a French ruler. The trial of strength was resolved in Britain's favour. Though Belgium's frontiers were not finally agreed until 1839, the essential steps were taken in 1831. Belgium's permanent neutrality was to be guaranteed by the five major powers; the new hereditary ruler was to be Leopold of Saxe-Coburg-Gotha, husband of the late Princess Charlotte of England, and therefore uncle by marriage to Queen Victoria. These arrangements were confirmed by treaty in 1839, the 'scrap of paper' which helped to lead to the British declaration of war in 1914 (see p. 353). On this occasion a revolution was allowed to succeed because it had British support and because it posed no threat to the principle of monarchical rule.

THE NEAR EAST

Throughout the nineteenth century the concert of Europe was threatened by the force of nationalism in the Ottoman empire, where a number of different ethnic and religious groups jostled both against their Turkish overlord and against each other. In 1815 the boundaries of the Ottoman empire extended up to Hungary's southern frontier. Present-day Serbia, Bosnia, Romania, Bulgaria, Montenegro, Albania and Greece were all nominally under Turkish rule. Ethnic divisions were reinforced by religious differences. There were 12 million members of the Greek Orthodox Church within the Ottoman empire. While Christianity was officially tolerated, in practice religious fanaticism was always likely to lead to massacres and reprisals when Turkish rule was challenged.

All the major powers had vested interests in the fate of the Ottoman empire. Russia's main ambition was to secure control over the Dardanelles, but she also claimed to the right to protect all Orthodox Christians in the empire, whether they were the monks who guarded Holy Places in Jerusalem or ordinary worshippers in the villages of Bosnia. Austria came to see the Ottoman empire as a shield against Russian expansion, and feared that if the Balkan races were to be granted their independence by the Sultan the example would not be lost on Austria's own racial minorities.

France had traditional claims to protect Latin Christians in Palestine, enjoyed strong commercial links with the empire, and since Napoleon's Egyptian expedition in 1798 had begun to take a close interest in North Africa. Britain feared the loss of her naval dominance in the Mediterranean, should Russian warships be given the right of passage through the Dardanelles, and was also concerned about the security of the sea route to India, especially after the opening of the Suez Canal in 1869.

Whereas in the sixteenth and seventeenth centuries when Turkish power was expanding, European powers generally united to check it (France was an exception), after 1815 when Turkish power was on the wane, Britain and Austria were more concerned to see the Ottoman empire preserved. Russia, while not consistently opposed, was the power most likely to benefit from the empire's collapse. France's policy varied with circumstance. These clashing interests, coupled with the inherent weaknesses of the empire and the challenges to its rule, produced a series of crises which culminated in the Crimean war, and the final breakdown of the concert of Europe.

The first such threat materialised when the cause of Greek independence was raised in March 1821 by a group of wealthy expatriate Greeks, living in Odessa, who named themselves the *Philiki Etairia* (Society of Friends). Actual fighting broke out in the Morea and on 10 January 1822 an assembly at Epidaurus proclaimed Greek independence. A provisional government was established at Nauplion. The initial reaction of the powers was to stay well clear. But two factors compelled them to intervene. First, sympathy for Greek nationalism ran deep in Britain and France because of the links with Greek culture forged through centuries of classical education. It was no accident that Lord Byron, the leading romantic poet of his generation, should go to Greece as an unofficial emissary to the Greek government in the hope of raising a British loan. Second, the new Tsar of Russia, Nicholas I, was not prepared to see fellow members of the Greek Orthodox Church being killed and persecuted by the efficient but ruthless Ibrahim Pasha, the Turkish general dispatched to subdue the revolt.

Mutual suspicions compelled the powers to keep an eye on each others' policies, and when Russia threatened to intervene Britain and France could not afford to stand aside. On 4 April 1826 Britain and Russia agreed to bring pressure on Turkey to sign an armistice with the Greek government and to concede some form of home rule. On 2 June France joined in and the three powers signed the treaty of London, authorising the use of force should the Turks reject the course of action suggested to them. By 1827 no progress had been made towards peace and on 12 August a joint allied fleet under the command of a British admiral, Sir Edward Codrington, entered Navarino Bay where the Turkish fleet was anchored. Shots were fired and a full-scale naval battle ensued in which the Turkish fleet was destroyed and 8,000 Turks were killed. Neither Britain nor France had wanted the humiliation of Turkey. The battle of Navarino was referred to as 'this untoward event' in a subsequent debate in the House of Commons and Codrington was deprived of his command. The battle of Navarino was followed by a Russian declaration of war on Turkey in 1828 (without Britain or France) and the treaty of Adrianople, signed the following year, secured the recognition of Greek autonomy. This became full independence in 1830 and the first king, Otto of Bavaria, was crowned in 1833. Russia also gained autonomy for Serbia and the right to occupy Moldavia and Wallachia (present-day Romania) until an indemnity had been paid. Russia's forward policy in the Balkans had clearly begun, and this added to the strains that were pulling the powers apart.

The next threat to Europe's stability came about in the Near East. Russia built upon the dominant position she had achieved in the war with Turkey in 1828–29, and in 1833 signed the treaty of Unkiar Skelessi, under which the Dardanelles were to be closed to all foreign fleets, thus protecting Russia's Black Sea coasts. In June 1839 the Turkish Sultan faced a further challenge. The ruler of Egypt, Mehemet Ali, declared war on his nominal overlord, Sultan Mahmud, and defeated him at the battle of Nezib in Syria. Before news of the defeat reached him, Mahmud died, leaving as his successor a 16-year-old boy, Abdul Majid. Aware of the threat which this power vacuum might pose, the five major powers agreed to settle the dispute between Mehemet Ali and the new Sultan themselves. Before they could do so there was a change of government in France, and the new Prime Minister, Adolphe Thiers, decided to champion the claims of Mehemet Ali. In July 1840 the other four powers agreed on terms to be imposed on him. He was to remain hereditary ruler of Egypt and to be ruler of Syria in his own lifetime. Mehemet Ali initially rejected these terms, but after the bombardment of Acre by the British navy, he gave way. He now had to surrender Syria to the Sultan, but was allowed to remain ruler of Egypt. The French could do nothing, and reluctantly added their assent. As a coda to this agreement another Straits Convention was signed in 1841 by the five major powers under which the straits would be closed to all warships while Turkey was at peace.

The next crisis owed more to French and Russian ambitions than it did to internal stresses within the Ottoman empire. It began in 1850 with the assertion by the newly elected French President, Louis Napoleon, of France's right to protect certain Holy Places in Jerusalem, in particular the keys to the north and south gates of the Church of the

Holy Sepulchre and the grotto of the Holy Manger. In asserting this claim Louis Napoleon was making a bid for Catholic support in France. The Sultan tried unavailingly to please both sides but Nicholas I objected to any changes. In May 1852 Louis Napoleon ordered a French warship through the Straits. In November Nicholas mobilised two army corps in southern Russia. In December he announced his right to protect not only the Orthodox religion but also the 12 million members of the Orthodox Church within the empire. In February 1853 a Russian general, Prince Menshikov, was sent to Constantinople to secure formal recognition of the Tsar's claims. The Turks refused to agree. On 27 May diplomatic relations were broken off and on 3 July Russian troops entered the principalities of Moldavia and Wallachia.

With war threatening, a conference was summoned at Vienna on 24 July to find a solution. On 1 August 1853 the Vienna Note, drawn up by the Austrian Foreign Minister, Count Buol, laid down that the existing position would not be changed without French and Russian consent. This time the Turks, who were not represented at Vienna, refused its terms. By October a state of war existed between Russia and Turkey and on 30 November at the battle of Sinope another Turkish fleet was destroyed. Britain and France, alarmed at the threat now posed to the survival of the Ottoman empire, declared war on Russia on 28 March 1854. Much to Nicholas I's dismay, neither Austria nor Prussia were prepared to come to his support. Austria pressed for Russian withdrawal from the principalities as the price of her neutrality, a price which Russia duly paid. The Holy Alliance was well and truly dead, killed finally by rivalries in the Balkans and Russian ambitions.

Though Russian withdrawal from the principalities had removed the prime cause of the war, Britain and France were still determined to fight, their aim now to destroy Russia's naval base, Sebastopol on the Black Sea. A campaign lasting two years was undertaken in the Crimea. It caused half a million casualties, 300,000 of them Russian. In September 1855 Sebastopol finally fell to the British and French. Faced with the threat of Austrian intervention in December, the Russians began negotiations in February 1856. The treaty of Paris was finally signed on 30 March. It guaranteed the integrity and independence of the Ottoman empire. The Sultan promised religious equality to all his subjects. Serbia and the principalities of Moldavia and Wallachia were to enjoy protected status, and the Black Sea was to be permanently demilitarised, neither naval bases nor warships being permitted there. The Straits Convention of 1841 was reaffirmed.

The Crimean war settled nothing. It left Russia disgruntled and humiliated, determined to pursue her goals in the Balkans when the opportunity arose again, as it did in 1875. Christians continued to be at risk in the Ottoman empire, suffering severely in Bulgaria and Bosnia in 1875–78, and having to endure the Armenian massacres in 1914–15. The failure of the concert of Europe and the Holy Alliance paved the way for a series of wars from 1859 to 1871, as nationalist aspirations in Italy and Germany took precedence over the search for security.

SECTION B – SOURCES

NATIONALISM AND ITS OPPONENTS

Attitudes to nationalism in Europe in the first half of the nineteenth century varied widely. At one extreme to a man like Mazzini nationalism was a redemptive force which had a greater claim on his loyalty than religious belief, locality or family (see Figure 8.1). He devoted his life to the cause of a united Italy. Where nationalism was associated with escape from an oppressive regime, as in the Greek and Belgian revolts, it could generally call upon the sympathy of middle class liberals, who supported the idea of 'small nations struggling to be free'. Conservatives, on the other hand, associated nationalism with revolution. Nationalism had no appeal for the signatories of the Holy Alliance. Britain, which did not sign it, took a more pragmatic view, prepared to support nationalist revolts which favoured British interests. The Papacy as head of a religion which claimed to be universal, after a brief flirtation with the idea of a united Italy in 1848, was generally to be found in opposition to nationalist

8.1 *Giuseppe Mazzini (1805–72), apostle of nationalism*

Source: AKG London

movements. The following extracts illustrate these varying attitudes.

A The writings of Giuseppe Mazzini explain the goals he set himself during the course of his imprisonment in 1830

(i) Mazzini

It was during these months of imprisonment that I conceived the plan of the Association of Young Italy (*La Giovane Italia*). . . . The worship of Rome was a part of my being. The great Unity, the One Life of the world, had twice been elaborated within her walls. Other peoples – their brief mission fulfilled – disappeared for ever. To none save to her had it been given twice to guide and direct the world. . . . Why should not a new Rome, the Rome of the Italian people – portents of whose coming I deemed I saw – arise to create a third and still vaster Unity; to link together and harmonize earth and heaven, right [law] and duty; and utter, not to individuals but to peoples, the great word Association –

to make known to free men and equal their mission here below?

(Denis Mack Smith, *The Making of Italy*, London, Macmillan, 1988, pp. 48–49)

(ii) A letter which Mazzini wrote to a British friend, James Stansfeld, who was an MP in 1860

The principle of nationality is sacred to me. I believe it to be the ruling principle of the future. I feel ready to welcome, without any fear, any change in the European map which will arise from the spontaneous general manifestation of a whole people's mind as to the group to which it feels naturally, not only by language, but by traditions, by geography, by tendencies, to belong.

(Denis Mack Smith, *Mazzini*, New Haven, CT, Yale University Press, 1994, p. 15)

B The Proclamation of Independence issued by the Greek National Assembly which met at Epidaurus on 27 January 1822

We, descendants of the wise and noble peoples of Hellas, we who are the contemporaries of the enlightened and civilised nations of Europe, we who behold the advantages which they enjoy under the protection of the impenetrable aegis (defence) of the law, find it no longer possible to suffer without cowardice and self-contempt the cruel yoke of the Ottoman power which has weighed on us for more than four centuries. . . .

The war which we are carrying on against the Turk is not that of a faction or the result of sedition. It is not aimed at any single part of the Greek people; it is a national war, a holy war, a war the object of which is to reconquer the rights of individual liberty, of property and honour, – rights which the civilised peoples of Europe, our neighbours, enjoy today; rights of which the cruel and unheard of tyranny of the Ottomans would deprive us – us alone – and the memory of which they would stifle in our hearts.

J.H. Robinson, *Readings in European History*, London, Ginn, pp. 519–20)

C The address read at the opening session of the Belgian Congress on 10 November 1830

In the name of the Belgian people, the provisional

government opens an assembly of the representatives of the nation. The nation has confided to these representatives the august mission of founding, on the broad and solid basis of liberty, the edifice of the new social order which will be the beginning and guarantee of durable happiness to Belgium . . .

There follows a list of complaints against the Dutch government: 'freedom of conscience was violated, education fettered, the press condemned to be nothing more than an instrument of the government or forced into silence. . . . The despotic imposition of a privileged language, . . . and an enormous debt which Holland brought to us at the time of our deplorable union. Add to these grievances taxes, overwhelming in their amount and still more in the manner in which they were apportioned . . . in a word all Belgium treated as a conquered province, as a colony, – everything rendered a revolution necessary and inevitable and hastened its approach. Such just and real grievances could lead only to one result.'

(ibid., pp. 521–22)

D British zeal in the cause of Spanish liberty or a hint to legitimate despots

The contrast between the British attitude to popular revolution and that of the signatories to the Troppau Protocol is well illustrated in the words of the following song opposing the French invasion of Spain to restore Ferdinand. It was printed in March 1823 and sung to the tune of *Scots wha hae* at the London Tavern at a dinner given to the Spanish and Portuguese ambassadors on 7 March, 1826.

> Spain awaked from slavery's trance
> Spain who spurned the yoke of France
> Saw Napoleon's hordes advance
>   Flushed with victory.
>
> Spain in native valour strong
> Backward drove th'invading throng
> Bold her songs and this their song
>   Death or Liberty!
>
> Proud Iberia, gallant land,
> Reared the pile by freedom planned,
> Fired the torch by freedom fanned
>   Scorned to bend the knee.

> Shall (forbid it, Heaven!) the men
> Who, from mountain, rock and glen
> Baffled France as France was then
>   Now defeated be?
>
> Shall they break their patriot vow?
> Who master'd strength to weakness bow
> Yield to France as France is now?
>   No, they shall be free!
>
> Britons, you whose patriot train
> Oft has spurned oppression's reign
> You whose hearts beat high for Spain
>   Pledge one cup with me.
>
> Urged by foreign despots, Gaul
> Flies to arms adventuring all,
> Forced to fight, but fights to fall
>   Leagued 'gainst liberty.
>
> Soon may Spain in justice strong
> Backward drive th'invaders' throng
> Bold her sons, and this their song –
>   Death or liberty!

(Wendy Hinde, *George Canning*, London, Collins, 1973, facing p. 328)

By comparison, elsewhere in Europe nationalism was seen as a destructive and corrosive force by those in authority, particularly the rulers of Austria and Russia. Their chief spokesman was Prince Metternich, Chancellor of Austria from 1821 to 1848 (see Figure 8.2). In his treatment of Austria's Italian provinces Metternich was prepared to concede the use of Italian in education and as the medium of government, but he regarded the unification of Italy as a dangerous and pointless objective, dismissing Italy as late as 1849 as 'a geographical expression'. He applied to Europe the same principles he applied to Italy:

'Nations' existed only in so far as they had shown themselves capable of maintaining their political independence over centuries. 'Subjects' were not interested in chimeric [illusory] ideas of nationalism proposed by revolutionary sectarians, but only in their material well-being and the efficient administration of just laws. Hence all threats to these true interests of subjects must be suppressed, by censorship, secret

8.2 Prince Metternich (1773–1859), opponent of nationalism

Source: AKG London

police (and Metternich maintained a private spy service in Germany and Italy) or international intervention.

(S. Woolf, *A History of Italy 1700–1860*, London, Methuen, 1979, p. 232)

E Prince Metternich's comments made to the Austrian ambassador to London, Prince Esterhazy, in connection with the Greek Revolt

(i) Metternich to Paul Esterhazy, 2 December 1828

We look on the Ottoman Empire as the best of neighbours: since she is scrupulously true to her word, we regard contact with her as equivalent to contact with a natural frontier which never claims our attention or dissipates our energies. We look on Turkey as the last bastion standing in the way of the expansion of another Power.

(ii) Metternich to Paul Esterhazy, 2 December 1829

What do we mean by the Greeks? Do we mean a people, a country, or a religion? If either of the first two, where are the dynastic and geographical boundaries? If the third, then upwards of fifty million men are Greeks; the Austrian Empire alone embraces five million of them. . . . The Emperor Our August Master, will never consent that the Greeks, his subjects, should consider themselves at the same time to be citizens of the new Greece. In this respect he can only follow the rules of public justice which prevent him from considering his Milanese and Venetian subjects as members of the Italian body politic, or his Galician subjects as belonging to a kingdom of Poland. Long experience has taught us that in racial denominations there may lie elements of trouble between empires and bones of contention between people and governments. And what a powerful and ever hostile weapon such denominations become in the hands of those who overthrow, or seek to overthrow, the existing order!

(A.L. Macphie, *The Eastern Question*, London, Longman, 1996, pp. 88–89)

Questions

1 To what was Mazzini referring when he stated 'To none save to her had it been given twice to guide and direct the world' (extract A, (i))?

2 In the light of extracts A (i and ii) what do you think Mazzini meant by 'the principle of nationality'?

3 What evidence can you find in extracts B and C that nationalism was a sentiment that appealed particularly to the middle classes?

4 Explain the lines 'Urged by foreign despots, Gaul/Flies to arms adventuring all' (extract D)

5 What light does extract D shed on the connection between nationalism and liberty?

6 Compare Metternich's opinion of the Ottoman empire in extract E (i) with that expressed in extract B. How do you account for the difference?

7 What reasons does Metternich give in extract E (ii) for opposing Greek independence? How valid are his objections?

Further reading

On the idea of nationalism see E. Hobsbawm, *The Age of Revolution* (New York, Mentor, 1962), E. Kedourie, *Nationalism* (London, Hutchinson, 1960) and J. Breuilly, *Nationalism and the State* (Manchester, Manchester University Press, 1980). For a more recent view see M. Ignatieff, *Blood and Belonging: Journeys into the New Nationalism* (London, Chatto & Windus, 1994). It is Ignatieff who draws a distinction between civic and ethnic nationalism.

The breakdown in the Concert of Europe is well covered in the works by Henry Kissinger and P. Schroeder cited at the end of Chapter 6. To the biographies of Alexander I, Castlereagh and Metternich cited there should be added Wendy Hinde, *George Canning* (London, Collins, 1973). There are useful essays on the period in P.M. Pilbeam (ed.) *Themes in Modern European History* (London, Routledge, 1995). The Eastern Question is well covered in A. Macphie, *The Eastern Question* (London, Longman, 1996).

• CHAPTER NINE •

Restoration Europe, 1815–48, and Challenges to Authority

• CONTENTS •

KEY DATES

France

1814	May	Bourbon restoration; King Louis XVIII
	June	Constitutional Charter issued by Louis XVIII
1815	March–June	Napoleon returns for One Hundred Days
	8 July	Louis XVIII's second restoration
1818		Indemnity paid off; Allied occupation troops withdrawn
1820	Feb.	Assassination of Duc de Berry; Ultra reaction follows
1823		French army intervenes in Spain and restores Ferdinand VII
1824		Charles X succeeds Louis XVIII
1830	26 July	Charles X issues Four Ordinances and dissolves new Chamber
	31 July	Louis Philippe and Lafayette appear at Hôtel de Ville after Charles X abdicates
	9 Aug.	Louis Philippe proclaimed King of the French; revised Charter
1831	Nov.	Lyon silk-weavers' insurrection suppressed
1839	April	France signs treaty of London guaranteeing Belgium's neutrality
1840	Aug.	Louis Napoleon imprisoned after attempting a rising at Boulogne
	Nov.	France's former ally Mehemet Ali accepts treaty of London and peace with Turkey
1847		Opposition starts banqueting movement

The Habsburg empire and the German Confederation

1806	Aug.	Holy Roman Empire abolished; Holy Roman Emperor renamed Emperor Francis I of Austria
1809	Oct.	Metternich appointed Chief Minister
1814	Sept.–	Congress of Vienna; Austria
1815	June	given presidency of German Confederation
1817		Wartburg Festival; expression of German nationalism
1819		Carlsbad Decrees following murder of Kotzebue
1821		Metternich made Chancellor of Habsburg empire
1830		Risings in Hesse, Brunswick and Saxony; constitutions follow
1832		Metternich's Six Acts or Articles
1834		*Deutscher Zollverein* established by Prussia; Austria excluded
1835		Ferdinand I becomes Emperor on Francis I's death

Russia

1801	Alexander I becomes Tsar on assassination of Paul
1810	Council of State set up
1812	Napoleon's invasion of Russia
1815	Alexander I sets up Holy Alliance alongside Quadruple Alliance; Kingdom of Poland set up
1819–20	Kazan University purged
1825	Alexander I's death occasions Decembrist Revolt; Nicholas I now Tsar
1826	Imperial Chancery developed; Third Section set up
1826–35	Speransky codifies laws
1830–31	Polish Rising suppressed; constitution revoked
1833	Treaty of Unkiar-Skelessi with Ottoman empire; Münchengrätz agreement with Austria
1841	Straits Convention; closure to Russian and other warships

SECTION A

FRANCE 1815–48

During the thirty-three years which followed Napoleon's second abdication, a succession of three monarchs ruled France, which experienced two revolutions, in July 1830 and in February 1848. The restored Bourbon King Louis XVIII had an uphill task to establish a constitutional monarchy following the upheaval of the Revolutionary and Napoleonic period, and his task was complicated by the One Hundred Days of Napoleon's return in 1815. However, he stuck to the Constitutional Charter and helped the French recovery. He was succeeded in 1824 by his brother, the Comte d'Artois, who as Charles X tried to re-establish most of the authority that the throne had had before 1789 (see Figure 9.1). Old divisions were reopened. Only the extreme Ultras supported him, and when he attempted to rule by using the emergency powers in article 14 of the Charter he lost control of Paris and fled into exile. The power-vacuum of July 1830 was filled quickly by Louis Philippe, Duke of Orleans, who came from the branch of the Bourbon family which had embraced the Revolution. Styling himself 'King of the French' to emphasise that he accepted the progress of popular sovereignty since the fall of the *ancien régime*, his regime became known as the bourgeois monarchy because it confirmed the rights of property and office claimed by the middle classes. However, Louis Philippe's regime became unpopular; it offered no glamour, no reform, and excluded most of the middle class from the franchise. Poor harvests and dreadful living conditions in the cities added to the revolutionary mixture which exploded in February 1848. It was now Louis Philippe's turn to flee, and a second Republic was proclaimed at the Hôtel de Ville by a city which had finally abandoned monarchy for good.

The Constitutional Charter and the Ultra-royalists

Louis XVIII approved the Charter in June 1814. Its seventy-four articles accepted many of the legal and social changes which had taken place during the Revolutionary and Napoleonic period. Equality before the law, freedom from arbitrary arrest (which the *lettres de cachet* of the *ancien régime* had infringed) and property rights (including rights to church land which the revolution had sold off) were all guaranteed. The legislature consisted of two chambers, one of which was elected on a narrow franchise which gave the vote to about one-half of 1 per cent of the population. The constitution echoed some features of the *ancien régime* by stating that the Roman Catholic faith was the state religion, by allowing the King to appoint ministers who were not responsible to the Chambers, and by giving the King power to rule by ordinances (decrees) in an emergency (Article 14).

In 1814 Louis XVIII inherited an efficient government and legal machine from Napoleon, and could look forward to peace bringing prosperity and refilling the treasury. Altogether the restored Bourbon regime, if it were managed carefully and the Ultra-royalist ambitions of the Comte d'Artois were kept in check, seemed to have a reasonable chance (see extract A (i)). But mistakes such as replacing the *tricolore* with the white flag of the Bourbons, combined with the hardships of demobilised soldiers and officers, gave Napoleon his chance to grab power in March 1815. His wild adventure cost dearly and made the task of restoration doubly difficult. Louis XVIII was made to appear the puppet of the victorious Allies, returned to the throne 'in the baggage train' of their armies. His hold on the loyalties of French people had been proved feeble and was poisoned further by the persecution of Napoleon's supporters which followed Waterloo. Marshal Ney was shot, Fouché and Talleyrand, who had done so much to install Louis on the throne, were banished, and royalists murdered several hundred opponents in the countryside in a White Terror. The terms of the second treaty of Paris saddled the regime with the punishment for Napoleon's last campaign, and France was humiliated by a brutal occupation force of over 1 million soldiers, and required to pay an indemnity of 700 million francs.

To cap it all, the small electorate had reacted after the One Hundred Days by returning a large Ultra-royalist majority to the Chamber in August 1815. But Louis XVIII stuck to the Charter and a

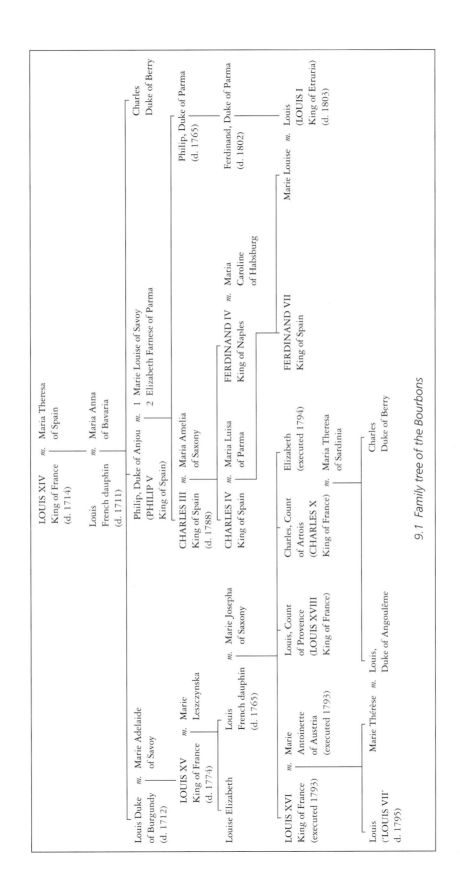

9.1 Family tree of the Bourbons

middle course, appointing a moderate ministry headed by Richelieu and including Decazes, men who had no support from the majority in the Chamber of Deputies. A year later Louis XVIII dissolved the Chamber and called new elections which returned a Constitutionalist majority, and this gave Richelieu's ministry its chance to pass legislation which would stabilise the regime.

Recovery and the expedition to Spain

Government finances were overhauled, and this produced an efficient system for controlling expenditure and raising revenue. The indemnity was paid, the allied armies of occupation left French soil in November 1818, and France was admitted to the Congresses of the powers; the stigma of defeat was lifted from the regime. Conscription for a small, professional army signalled France's gathering recovery. Alterations were made to the electoral system in 1817 and 1818 which helped the moderates who supported the constitution. Richelieu developed a good relationship with Metternich, the Habsburg Chancellor, and they reassured each other about the good sense of avoiding both Ultra and liberal policies (see extract B).

The liberal disturbances in Spain in 1820 helped France to crown her escape from the burdens imposed on her in 1815. Ferdinand VII of Spain, faced with growing problems with constitutionalists limiting his power, appealed to his fellow sovereigns for help in 1822. Tsar Alexander I was eager to send a Russian army to his aid, an expedition which would set a dangerous precedent for Russian intervention in Europe and risk inciting the populations of the countries it crossed. Metternich, at the Congress of Verona in October 1822, cleverly avoided these problems by inviting France, as the country most immediately threatened by disturbances in Spain, to intervene. The French force re-established Ferdinand VII's authority in 1823, at the same time re-establishing her own ability to project her power beyond her frontiers. Canning, the British Foreign Minister, described the French move as 'an affront to the pride of England' because of her role in liberating Spain from French rule during the Peninsular War

(K. Bourne, *The Foreign Policy of Victorian England 1830–1902*, Oxford University Press, 1970, p. 210). There was nothing Britain could do directly, but Canning was quick to lend British recognition to the republics which were Spain's former colonies in South America to prop them up against Spanish claims and United States influence, and he sent a naval expeditionary force to Portugal in 1826 to protect the constitutionalist regime there from Spanish attack. Britain's break from her former continental allies was complete, and mirrored the rehabilitation of the former enemy, France.

The revival of the Ultras

In 1820 the Duc de Berry, the son of the Comte d'Artois, was assassinated by a man sworn to destroy the Bourbons. The result was an outcry from the Ultras who argued that government policy had lacked firmness; one publicist claimed that the dagger itself was 'a liberal idea'. Richelieu's more royalist government tightened the press laws, allowed double voting for the wealthiest and altered the electoral system to *scrutin d'arrondissement* which tended to favour Ultra and church influence. Louis XVIII was ageing quickly and lacked the appetite to repeat the moderating role he had played after 1815. Richelieu was replaced by Villèle at the head of an Ultra ministry, and it seemed that the Ultra-royalists would have their hopes fulfilled when Louis XVIII was succeeded by the Comte d'Artois in 1824. However, his son's assassin would have his sworn wish fulfilled indirectly, for the Ultra reaction he had helped provoke would produce a revolution which would sweep the Bourbons from power.

The coronation of Charles X purposely echoed the form of the *ancien régime*, and it was followed by several measures confirming the new direction. Instead of a proportion of the Chamber of Deputies facing elections each year, all deputies in the Ultra-dominated Chamber had a seven-year term ahead of them. Monsignor Frayssinous was created Minister of Education, restoring Catholic influence in the educational system with a vengeance. Sacrilege became punishable by death, an extraordinary revival of a bygone age. In 1825 an indemnity was voted for émigrés who had been dispossessed by the Revolution, to be funded by reducing the interest paid on government loan stock from 5 per cent to 3 per cent. The main holders of the stock were the bourgeoisie, including many who had risen under Napoleon. In fact, all of these steps played on old divisions and kindled opposition. The Republican and Napoleonic periods had diminished church power and created a system of secular education, but the Ultra government was trampling on this achievement. The Ultra aim to revive the 'alliance of throne and altar' was an essential part of eroding the Constitutional Charter and restoring the *ancien régime*, and was supported by enthusiasts who belonged to the *Chevaliers de la Foi* and the Jesuit-dominated *Congregation*.

Bonapartist sympathies were kept alive, very often by disgruntled officers who were maintained on half-pay in charge of National Guard units. These were disbanded in 1827, and the preference given to former émigrés created further ill-feeling towards the regime. Republican conspiratorial organisations such as the *Chevaliers de la Liberté* and the *charbonnerie* kept alive a selective memory of the Revolution's achievements. They were not serious threats to the state but rather warnings of the divisions in France, divisions which Charles X was doing more to make worse than to heal. Pilbeam concludes:

Bonapartism and republicanism were blended together and leavened with a healthy regard for the practical and finally emerged as a vaguely liberal sentiment. The military glories were remembered, the economic disasters put on one side. The constitutional promises of the Hundred Days were recalled, the reality of dictatorship forgotten.

(P.M. Pilbeam, *Republicanism in Nineteenth century France, 1814–1871*, London, Macmillan, 1995, p. 93)

The 1830 Revolution

Charles X called new elections in November 1827, and was surprised that over sixty opposition deputies were returned. In January 1828 Villèle resigned and Martignac was appointed to head a conciliatory government. Controls on the press were eased, but liberal support fluctuated and the ministry was destabilised. In August 1829 Charles X lost patience with compromise and appointed Prince Jules de Polignac, an 'Ultra of the deepest dye' (J.P.T. Bury, *France 1814–1940*, London, Methuen, 1985, p. 38) to head a no-nonsense Ultra-royalist ministry. Fears of a monarchical *coup d'état* grew, and there was increasing talk of England's constitutional monarchy and the suitability of the Duke of Orleans for the role in France. In January 1830 the newspaper *Le National* was founded to voice liberal opposition, and the fact that the astute Talleyrand was a sponsor was surely significant. In March 1830 a vote of no confidence in the ministry passed the chamber, and the constitutional crisis broke. Was the King entitled to appoint ministers who had no support in the chamber?

Charles X decided to insist that he was. He called new elections, but government influence failed to stop the return of a large opposition majority (extract E (i) shows his position). Persuaded that this amounted to a state of emergency, the King used the power given to him by article 14 and issued the four Ordinances on 26 July; the press was censored, the chamber dissolved, the franchise made more exclusive, and a new election was scheduled. Having set in motion a *coup d'état*, the King left to go hunting. Paris was weakly garrisoned, and many troops had yet to return from their victory in Algeria. Opposition mounted but Pilbeam points out that the 'revolutionary fighters were not the wealthy politicians but artisans, at odds with the government over economic problems, but also concerned over political questions and themselves alert to the gains and expectations of the 1789 Revolution' (P.M. Pilbeam, *Republicanism*, p. 94).

The barricades went up and decisive fighting took place on the streets of Paris on 29 July. Charles X abdicated in favour of his grandson 'Henri V', who had been born after the Duc de Berry's death, and fled, retracing his path into exile. It is often said the Charles X, above all of the émigrés, had learned nothing and forgotten nothing since 1789, and Bury seems to agree in placing the blame for events: 'Thus ingloriously and unnecessarily the restored Bourbon monarchy came to an end through the folly of the monarch'. (Bury, *France*, p. 41).

Louis Philippe and the July Monarchy

The 'Three Glorious Days' of the 1830 Revolution did not produce a Bonapartist revival nor a republic. There was no candidate for the first, and Thiers and Laffitte at *Le National* energetically backed Louis Philippe, the Duke of Orleans, for the throne not least to head off the republic which some of the street-fighters wanted. The compromise was sealed on 31 July when Louis Philippe appeared on the balcony of the Hôtel de Ville and was embraced by Lafayette, the old revolutionary; Republican opposition to another monarchy was stifled by this signal of approval, and by the reintroduction of the *tricolore*. The Charter of 1814 was modified and offered to Louis Philippe. He was invited to become 'King of the French', the procedure and the title designed to make clear that the monarch had limited powers which rested on the will of the people (see Guizot's comment, extract E (ii)).

Some republican opposition continued underground. Royalists were divided between loyalty to the Orleanist branch of the Bourbon family, which had cooperated with the 1789 Revolution originally, and the 'Legitimists' who upheld the Carlist succession of 'Henri V', under a regency of his mother, the Countess de Berry. The Roman Catholic faith was recognised simply as the majority religion, and the Church lost its place in the establishment. But if it was neither republican nor fully royalist, was it really the 'bourgeois monarchy' as it is sometimes called? The franchise was extended, but it remained restricted to wealthy property owners to such an extent that, by 1846, only 2.8 per cent of the adult male population (about 240,000) were entitled to vote (see Marx's comment, extract E (iii)). The King himself appeared like a wealthy banker rather than a king, talking incessantly to everyone, enjoying the Parisian social scene, and often walking the streets virtually unaccompanied.

The limits of reform

Lafayette, Lafitte and the 'Party of Movement' wanted to see extensive reform, including the abolition of the hereditary peerage, a large increase in the electorate and the election of officers in the National Guard (which would make it a citizens' army, not a government force). Following a ferocious anti-clerical riot in February 1831 which wrecked the archbishop's palace, Lafitte's government was replaced by a more conservative ministry led by Casimir Périer. It was supported by Guizot and the 'Party of Resistance' who wanted to limit the changes brought in by the 1830 Revolution; significantly, a tax threshold was applied to membership of the National Guard which turned it into a bourgeois force for the protection of property.

France was undergoing great economic and social change at this time. Industry was developing, but recession (which began in the late 1820s) fuelled discontent. Cities were growing and bringing under-nourished and sometimes unemployed workers to live alongside the wealthy merchants and factory owners. Paris added to the potentially dangerous mixture a lively press (which was restricted but not silenced under Louis Philippe) and the institutions of government. These circumstances help explain the revolutionary potential which was realised in 1830, and the central challenge for Louis Philippe's regime was to prevent a recurrence.

Social reform was one way to ease the stresses and strains of economic change. Apart from some limited state funding for primary schools after 1833, and a Factory Act in 1841, virtually nothing was done. In fact the government quickly showed where its sympathies lay when it intervened in the Lyon silk-weavers' strike in November 1831. Higher wages had been agreed by the Chamber of Commerce and the Prefect, and only 104 of some 1,400 employers opposed the deal. Suspecting Republican influence, the government abandoned negotiation and used force to crush the disturbances. Collective bargaining by workers was declared to be illegal. It seemed that the government had failed the test and turned its back upon the pressing needs of the urban poor.

One consequence was that the appeal of Republicanism increased. Some 6 million Republican pamphlets were distributed during the three months after the Lyon insurrection, and the Society of the Friends of the People developed. When Napoleon's Marshal Lamarque died in June 1832 it became the occasion for an insurrection in Paris (featured in Victor Hugo's *Les Misérables*). There were other signs of discontent with the regime too. Attempts on Louis Philippe's life were quite frequent (six between 1835 and 1846), the Legitimists staged a revolt in the Vendée in 1832 when the white flag of the Bourbons was raised for 'Henri V', and in 1836 and 1840 Louis Napoleon staged two comical attempts to copy his uncle's seizure of power in 1815. A series of conservative ministries dominated government, and in the 1840s Guizot rose to power through the foreign ministry as the favourite of Louis Philippe. The preference was for tighter press controls and tougher policing of disturbances, rather than for social or political reform to broaden the base of support.

Foreign policy

While the July Monarchy used and developed France's new status in Europe, its caution won little enthusiasm at home. A Polish rising in 1830 attracted enthusiastic support from the 'Party of Movement' which wanted to extend *fraternité* to the rebels, but Louis Philippe resisted the temptation to make gestures which would alienate the Tsar. The Belgian revolt against Dutch rule in 1830 was much nearer to home in every sense, and France supported Britain's policy of protecting Belgian independence. This meant resisting Russian demands for the revolt to be crushed, but it also required the July Monarchy to work with France's former opponent, Britain. French troops intervened to protect Belgian independence against Dutch forces, and captured Antwerp in 1832. By the treaty of London (1839) Britain, France, Austria, Prussia and Russia guaranteed Belgian neutrality. The Vienna settlement had been eroded by giving France a small friendly neighbour in place of a larger, tougher state (the kingdom of the Netherlands) which had contained her. However, this subtle and cautious change lacked appeal at home to French people who remembered their country ruling over Belgium. To them, an opportunity to expand had been lost when French forces were withdrawn.

When the Vatican called on Austrian forces to intervene to put down liberal disturbances in the Papal States in 1832, French forces were sent to Ancona to give a clear warning to Austria to limit her role. Sympathy with independence movements in Italy was strong in France where they were seen as sister movements to the French Revolution, fostered by Napoleon's campaigns which rid the Italian peninsula from Austrian power, but Louis Philippe's ministers avoided escalating matters in the 1830s. Austrian forces were withdrawn in 1838, and the French went home too.

The most serious anti-climax arose over the Ottoman empire's clash with an over-mighty subject, Mehemet Ali of Egypt. France supported Mehemet Ali as a way of extending her influence in the Mediterranean and in Egypt, but his defeat of the Ottoman forces on land (in Syria) and sea in 1839 set alarm bells ringing in London and Vienna. The problem was that if the ailing Ottoman empire (the 'sick man of Europe') collapsed, chaos in the Balkans would threaten Habsburg control of the Slav peoples, and might allow Russia to menace Britain's route to the East. British intervention forced Mehemet Ali to agree to the treaty of London in 1840 by which Britain, Russia, Austria, Prussia and eventually France guaranteed the Ottoman empire, restored her rule in Syria, and closed the straits to non-Ottoman warships. This particular episode of the Eastern Question was settled as Britain and Austria wanted, but France had abandoned her ally Mehemet Ali. There had been some excited talk in France of war to protect her ally, and the humiliation of the climb-down was felt strongly. Even the close understanding with Britain which had been obtained was broken in 1846 over a silly wrangle about who should marry the Queen of Spain and her sister. 'France is bored', commented Lamartine, and his verdict may be applied generally to the regime which lost all its glamour during the 1840s.

This lack of respect for the regime, its reluctance to pursue social reform, and its failure to extend the franchise, left the July Monarchy increasingly isolated at home. A 'bourgeois monarchy' which represented only a small section of the bourgeoisie was easily blown away when liberal protest, economic hardship and street disturbances combined in 1848, as we shall see.

THE HABSBURG EMPIRE AND THE GERMAN CONFEDERATION

At Vienna in 1815 the victorious powers constructed a post-war settlement designed to make Europe safe from revolution. Castlereagh, the British Foreign Secretary, and Metternich, the Habsburg Minister (he was named State Chancellor in 1821), designed a central European bloc which would prevent both French expansion and Russian intervention. The key to achieving this lay in the power and central position of the Austrian empire. As the Holy Roman Empire it had taken a battering during the Revolutionary and Napoleonic wars, and the last Holy Roman Emperor, Francis II, took the title Francis I, Emperor of Austria, in 1806.

The empire itself was a supra-national bloc containing a collection of different nationalities, Austrians, Magyars (Hungarians), Romanians, Slovaks, Slovenes, Croats to name but some (see Map 19.1 on p. 309). National self-determination or liberal reform which would encourage it would poison the empire, and the Habsburgs relied upon a system of 'divide and rule'; Francis I remarked famously: 'My people are strangers. Out of their dislike order is born, and out of their hatred universal peace' (cited in A. Wood, *Europe 1815–1945*, London, Longman, 1964, p. 33). The Vienna settlement confirmed this system; it ignored national self-determination and backed the *ancien régime* idea of legitimate rule on the hereditary principle. It also gave the Austrian empire great influence in the Italian states (Habsburg princes ruled in the central duchies) and created the German Confederation of states under her presidency.

Metternich is credited with the central role in managing this system until he fell victim to revolution in 1848. Was he really the reactionary whose repressive policies and exaggerated suspicions made a revolutionary explosion inevitable, or was he a skilled manipulator who kept Europe stable until 1848 despite the steady crumbling of the power of his own empire?

Governing the empire

Metternich frequently complained that the empire was administered rather than governed. Francis I 'had little sympathy for organized government' in Sked's judgement (A. Sked, *The Decline and Fall of the Habsburg Empire 1815–1918*, London, Longman, 1989, p. 26). He intervened in matters great or small, as the inclination took him, he called for reports from many sources, and then he took his time in making a decision. Metternich complained that reports he submitted in 1817 were still in the Emperor's desk drawer at the time of his death in 1835. His successor, the simple-minded Ferdinand I, made things worse as he seemed to be incapable of understanding a document; he refused to see Metternich until twenty white horses came through the gate, and he refused to sign state documents when he was put on a diet to protect his health!

Metternich wanted there to be a Council (*Staatsrat*) which would offer advice to the Emperor, who would then come to a decision with the help of discussion in an executive Ministerial Conference (*Ministerkonferenz*). Francis I never used the Council in this way, and never developed a Ministerial Conference at all. After Francis I's death Metternich manoeuvred to set up the system, and to cut down the influence of Count Kolowrat, who had dominated the Council and managed the government's finances. But his plan was foiled by the return of Archduke John, and a new Ministerial Conference was set up. The Archdukes Louis and Francis Charles, together with Kolowrat (who kept control of financial and internal matters) and Metternich now operated a type of regency to enable Ferdinand I to rule the empire.

It is clear therefore that the machinery of government and Metternich's place in it left much to be desired as far as the Chancellor was concerned. A further complication was financial weakness. The empire had large debts by 1815 (it had been bankrupt in 1811), and until 1848 annual interest payments cost about 30 per cent of the state revenue. Kolowrat reckoned that the army budget accounted for about 40 per cent of the revenue. With troops being paid double wages when they were on war readiness, and with about one-third of the army placed on leave to save money in peace time, it was difficult for Metternich to afford to threaten let alone use force convincingly. In 1830, when war with France seemed possible, the empire could offer only

170,000 troops to go alongside the 250,000 of her junior partner, Prussia. It is important to judge the preservation of the empire's control and Metternich's system of repression in the context of these handicaps.

Hungary had a unique status within the empire. Her own constitutional tradition meant that laws had to pass the Hungarian Diet, and the lower house of this Diet was indirectly elected on a broader franchise than existed in France. This gave the reform movement a means of developing. Metternich hated the power of Magyar public opinion and he used some of the sharpest repression to destroy the reform movement. The press was tightly controlled, voters were influenced, police surveillance and a network of informers were set to work, and leaders like Kossuth spent periods in prison. Metternich's efforts to tame the Hungarian Diet provide perhaps the strongest example of his method of rule within the whole empire and keep central authority; did it work? In Hungary a Liberal party was constituted in 1847 demanding that ministers should be responsible to the Diet, that the franchise should be extended to include more of the middle classes, and that serfdom should be abolished. In Bohemia-Moravia the German speaking Bohemian nobility remained loyal to the Habsburgs, but the Czech people were developing a national consciousness. In 1830 Palacky set up the 'Czech Mother' movement to develop awareness of Czech history and literature, and in 1844 students with artisan support set up the secret 'Repeal' organisation which modelled itself on Daniel O'Connell's movement for the repeal of the Act of Union which tied Ireland to Britain. Metternich despised the middle classes whose arrogance he believed stirred up liberal and nationalist ambitions (see extract C). He argued that these ambitions misled the ordinary people, and he believed that his repressive system protected the ordinary people and kept their best interests at heart. With the benefit of hindsight which reveals the economic, social and educational developments that gave the middle classes such political power in Europe during the nineteenth century, it would seem that Metternich was out of date and doomed to fail. Yet the Habsburg empire survived until 1918, the nationalisms it tried to contain created many problems, and

Metternich's system helped to ensure European stability.

Governing the German Confederation

Set up by the Vienna settlement in 1815, representatives of the thirty-nine German states met in the Federal Diet of the Confederation in Frankfurt under Austrian presidency. The idea was to stabilise the central area of Europe against external threats from French expansion or Russian intervention, and against the internal threats of liberal reform or German nationalism.

There were various different parliamentary traditions in some of the states of the Confederation. Bavaria and Baden gained limited constitutions in 1818, Württemberg in 1819, and in Prussia the provincial assemblies (*Landtage*) were recognised in 1823. Metternich's system of control here used a restrained version of the methods we have seen used in Hungary. Spies and a network of informers played their part. The imperial postal system intercepted the correspondence of liberals. The universities were held in great suspicion because they encouraged a sense of German nationalism through the study of history and German literature, and because they were home to the arrogant and 'presumptuous' middle classes. The Wartburg Festival of 1817 confirmed Metternich's worst fears of universities, and when the right-wing Kotzebue was assassinated in 1819, Metternich seized the moment to hit back. The Carlsbad Decrees were to be applied throughout Germany, controlling the press and political meetings, and of course tightly restricting university teaching and behaviour (see extract B).

The 'particularism' of the states benefited the Habsburgs who stood as protectors of princes against reform pressures, and defenders of one state's rights against a powerful neighbour. Prussia was of course the most powerful state in Germany, with extensive territories, a developing economy and a growing middle class. Her challenge to Habsburg domination of Germany came through the expansion of the Prussian *Zollverein* (customs union). Most internal duties in Prussia were abolished by the tariff law of 1818, but a transit duty was placed on goods passing through which encouraged neighbouring states to join what by 1828 was the Prussian *Zollverein*. The rival Mid-German Union (encouraged by Metternich) collapsed soon afterwards, and in January 1834 Prussia was able to launch the *Deutscher Zollverein* of eighteen states (with a population of 23 million). The remaining states of the Confederation soon joined because of the economic advantages of membership, but Prussian power was regarded with suspicion by many. Prussia energetically but politely excluded the Austrian empire, her more sluggish and less industrialised economy being left further and further behind partly as a result. One sign of her relative weakness was that in the crisis of 1830, and again in 1840 when French pressure on the Rhineland was feared, Prussia was able to call upon a considerably larger military force than was available to the poverty-stricken Habsburg empire. Despite this growing reversal of the junior–senior partnership of Prussia and Austria in the Confederation, it was destined to remain in existence until Bismarck confronted Austrian control of Germany in the 1860s.

The series of revolutionary disturbances in 1830 touched several of the German states, including Brunswick and Saxony, but Metternich's system and the Diet of the Confederation contained the situation. The Six Acts or Articles of 1832 reinforced the repressive surveillance of the Carlsbad Decrees. In France, Belgium, Poland and Italy, as we have seen, the situation was more challenging, and the results more enduring in France and Belgium, but Metternich's diplomacy continued to dominate Europe as his government dominated the Empire and the Confederation. He liked to claim that he was not simply a man of 'order'. He argued that popular sovereignty which flew the flag of nationalism or *liberté* was just a disguise for tyranny, while the best and most benevolent government relied upon the hereditary principle and the dominance of a ruling class. This ruling class was truly European, its members often had more in common with each other than the various ethnic groups over which they ruled. Order at home went with order throughout Europe, and the key was in recognising a community of European interests which were more important than the petty concerns of various nationalities. If this was the heart of Metternich's system, it tried to keep a European equilibrium through the idea of community, rather than by manipulating a balance of power which depended upon competition and conflict. On the other hand, Metternich boasted that he could bore a man to death and it is possible that all this was just a façade; Napoleon may have been right about him; 'Everyone lies sometimes, but to lie all the time, that is too much' (cited in Sked, *Decline and Fall*, p. 11).

RUSSIA

Tsar Alexander I's reign (1801–25) appeared confusing to the rest of Europe. At home it began with a series of reforms, including one which made it possible for serfs be freed (1803), and the role played by Russia in defeating Napoleon from 1812 added to her new image. But then things seemed to change. Alexander I created the Holy Alliance, which Castlereagh dismissed as 'a piece of sublime mysticism and nonsense' but which created the fear among almost everyone, from Metternich to the Belgium liberals and Spanish constitutionalists, that Russia would intervene anywhere in Europe to destroy liberalism and revolutionaries. At home Arakcheyev and the Military Colonies, and the management of the educational system, made it appear that the Tsar had turned away from his earlier interest in reform. Part of the explanation for these changes lies with the problems which confronted Alexander I, but from the outside it is easy to agree with Napoleon's description of him as 'the Northern Sphinx'.

His successor, his younger brother Nicholas I, began his reign in 1825 amidst a confrontation with a strange conspiracy, the Decembrist revolt. Aristocratic and badly organised, it had wildly liberal aims and yet avoided recruiting popular force. It left its mark upon the reign, for Nicholas I's measures were acutely concerned to suppress liberalism while trying to improve the efficiency of government administration and finances. Abroad he gained the reputation of being 'the Gendarme of Europe' for his reliable policing of liberal and revolutionary threats.

The inheritance of Alexander I

Alexander, born in 1777, was brought up in the court of his grandmother, Catherine the Great, to be a ruler. While his main tutor was a Swiss republican (La Harpe), he was exposed to a completely different environment when he visited his father Paul's remote court at Gatchina which was obsessed with military drill and Prussian-style discipline. Paul became Tsar in 1796, but Alexander's own succession in 1801 was poisoned by two things. First, there was some doubt that his own father was really the son of Tsar Peter III (Catherine took many lovers). Second, Alexander had supported the palace coup by the Guards to remove Paul on condition that his father's life was spared, but he was murdered. Not only was Alexander's personal and psychological background complex, so too was the empire he came to rule.

Several features of Russia made her a land apart from the rest of Europe. The peasantry comprised 83 per cent of Russia's population. Many were serfs, the property of their landlord, while 'state peasants' lived on state-owned lands. Their lives altered little from one generation to another and the sense of remoteness in the vast expanse was more acute than in many other countries. The *mir* (village community) was the key authority, dealing with the allocation of peasant land, the landlord's labour requirements, and the collection of taxes and rents. The Tsar was regarded as 'the little father' whose God-given authority was concerned to look after his people, and his status was thoroughly supported by the Orthodox Church. But communications were difficult, the bureaucracy corrupt, and the cruelties of life were blamed on advisers who misled the Tsar rather than on the Tsar himself.

Peter the Great had transformed the idea of nobility from an inheritance into something which could be earned by progressing, usually in the army or civil service, through the great table of ranks which structured Russian society. High rank brought estates from state lands and conferred a title which would be inherited. A great gulf separated this elite (comprising about 10 per cent of the population) from the rest. The gulf was spanned by some of mixed rank (*Raznochintsky*) from the elite, and some merchants, together comprising about 4 per cent of the population. This group produced the intellectuals and liberals known as the 'intelligentsia' in Russia, and also the few home-grown entrepreneurs and technocrats for commercial and industrial development (many were immigrants), but the small size of the group indicates another important difference which distanced Russia from the developing European middle classes. Industrial development was occurring (particularly in cotton production), and the economy was growing, but development of new industries and growth by comparison with parts of Europe was slow. Population was growing too, and this put pressure on food supplies and would contribute, in due course, to the growth of towns and industry (see Figure 9.2).

Alexander I and reform

Alexander began his reign by repealing much of the repressive legislation passed by his father, and releasing many political prisoners. He also began a process which looked as though it might lead to fundamental change and which went beyond the abolition of torture and legalising the voluntary emancipation of serfs by their masters (1803). First, he set up a commission to create a clear and fair legal system from the contradictory complexities of the present. Second, he appointed Speransky to propose a restructuring of government, which amounted to a proposal for a constitution.

There were great difficulties in the way of such plans. The Tsar ran an autocracy, but to govern Russia he depended upon the support of the nobility, the civil service, and (as he knew well) the Guards. Conservative critics of his reforming energy called the legal reform group the 'Committee of Public Salvation' as though it was something invented by the French Revolution, and they secured Speransky's dismissal in 1812. While reform of the legal system made little progress, Speransky produced a reform plan in 1809 and as a result the Council of State was developed (in 1810) to advise the Tsar. New ministries were created with clear responsibilities, staffed by a system which attempted to reward merit rather than seniority.

War with Napoleon during 1812–15 took Alexander's attention away from domestic affairs,

9.2 Procession in the province of Kursk, by I.E. Repin
Source: Edimedia, Paris

but it had important effects. The French invasion failed to spark domestic rebellion, and it actually created a unity of purpose in Russia which was rare; it was rightly called the 'Patriotic War'. Would Alexander be able to exploit this after 1815? But victory against Napoleon had lured the Tsar's troops as far as Paris, and Alexander himself was becoming convinced of his God-given mission to destroy revolutionary conspiracies. The Holy Alliance which he launched in 1815 was an expression of this mission. Not only did it take Alexander's attention away from his own country, but also it made him more preoccupied with restraint and order than with reform.

Alexander I: reaction or reform after 1815?

Alexander spent the majority of his time out of the country between 1816 and 1820, but the policies of two key advisers characterised the rest of his reign. General Arakcheyev was responsible for the development of Military Colonies. These involved regiments, complete with families, being combined with peasant communities in carefully planned new villages. New housing, medical provision and schooling improved the conditions for all. However, peasants were now expected to become part-time soldiers and parade after working in the fields, officers and soldiers were to take their turn at the plough, girls were directed who they should marry, and wives who failed to produce the regulation one baby per year, or who miscarried or gave birth to girls, were fined. It is no wonder that this early version of a planned economy was unpopular, but agricultural production was improved, maintaining the army became cheaper, and by 1825 one-quarter of all soldiers were military colonists. The whole system (which continued until 1857 in places) perhaps reflected Arakcheyev's description of himself as 'a truly Russian uneducated gentleman' – sentimental, religious, authoritarian, brutal and cruel. He agonised over how severely to punish those responsible for a colonists' rebellion in 1819 before sending them to run the gauntlet of one thousand men twelve times; twenty-five died from the blows they received, and Alexander sympathised with Arakcheyev's 'sensitive soul' (cited in J.N. Westwood, *Endurance and Endeavour: Russian History 1812–1992*, Oxford University Press, 1993, pp. 22–23).

Golitsyn, appointed Over Procurator of the Holy Synod in 1803, kept this influential post overseeing the Orthodox church when he was made head of the Ministry of Spiritual Affairs and Education in 1817. Alexander's choice of this close friend and spiritual adviser to invigorate and direct the reform of education tells us a great deal about his aim to make Christian piety the basis of education. If the Tsar's and Golitsyn's intentions were liberal, to enable people to read the Bible and think for themselves about it, the civil servants operated quite differently in practice and earned the description 'the ministry of darkness'. For instance, a book on poisonous mushrooms was banned on the grounds that it was sacrilege to write this about mushrooms which were the sacred food of the Orthodox during Lent. More seriously Magnitsky inspected Kazan University in 1819 and recommended that it should be demolished because of the radical thinking he found there. Instead he was put in charge of purging it, a task he performed with such ludicrous vigour that he and those like him put would-be students off university life altogether. Despite these developments which helped to destroy Alexander's reputation as a reformer, new schools and universities were opened and by 1825 there were some 1,700 students at the universities, 5,000 at the gymnasiums and 60,000 at the district and parish schools. Military schools and those run by the Church and other institutions educated about twice as many pupils again as the ministry's schools, but even so only a tiny fraction of the population was involved.

Alexander's reputation in Europe as a reactionary seemed well deserved. The Holy Alliance which he created in 1815 encouraged vigorous suppression of liberal rebellions, but (as we have seen) Metternich did not need the Tsar's prompting to issue the Carlsbad decrees in 1819 or to engineer French intervention in Spain. Alexander's reputation was partly the result of the religious fervour which he brought to his European mission, and to his growing belief in the existence of a revolutionary conspiracy. Even the mutiny of his elite Semeonov Guards in 1820 failed to redirect his attention to the home front. When a rebellion in Greece against Turkish rule broke out in 1820, Alexander backed Russia's traditional enemy, Turkey, despite his great sympathy for the Greeks; the murder of the Patriarch of the Greek Orthodox Church intensified Russian anger, but the Tsar kept to his unpopular policy of condemning rebellion.

In Poland, however, Alexander gained a different reputation. Feeling shamed by Catherine's role in the partition of Poland in 1795, Alexander obtained the former Napoleonic creation of the Duchy of Warsaw in 1815 and created the kingdom of Poland. It was given a parliament and a constitution, and Alexander made himself King of Poland. Westwood comments that he 'regarded his Polish constitution as a pilot-project for an eventual constitution for Russia proper', and in 1818 Novosiltsev was instructed to produce a draft. He presented this remarkable proposal in 1820. Civil liberties and elected regional and national assemblies would give representation to the people, although the Tsar would remain in charge of legislation. But Alexander believed that the starting-point for such reform was the emancipation of the serfs, and the opposition of landowners made it impossible for the time being. As a result 'Russia would remain an old-fashioned benevolent despotism, enjoying a chronic shortage of first-rate benevolent despots' (Westwood, *Endurance*, pp. 26–27). The draft constitution was sufficiently dangerous for Nicholas I to order all copies to be burned, but the fact that Alexander called for it and handled Poland as he did means that he cannot be dismissed as a blind reactionary.

The Decembrist Revolt, 1825

Alexander's death, like his reputation in life, has a curiosity about it. He decided to spend the winter in the remote southern town of Tagnarog where he became ill and died quickly, on 19 November 1825. Rumours that it was staged so that he could slip into obscurity as a travelling holy man, or retire to the banks of the Rhine as he had considered doing once, were sustained later when Alexander III had his coffin opened and found it empty. The other curiosity is that his death prompted a liberal conspiratorial revolt of the sort which he had so feared in other countries.

Russian officers who had served in Europe during the Napoleonic war had collected revolutionary ideas about representative government and civil rights. The masonic lodges, which many officers joined, were often the channel for these ideas to reappear in Russia. The Union of Welfare was one important expression of this new thinking which drew much comfort from the way Alexander had dealt with Poland, but in 1821 it closed itself, fearing correctly that it was being spied upon. The members immediately restarted the group on a secret basis as the Northern Society and the Southern Society. The Northern Society (led by Muravyov) wanted the separation of powers on the model of the United States, a Tsar reduced to presidential powers, and civil rights. The better organised Southern Society (which was powerful in the Ukraine among army officers) was led by Colonel Pestel and wanted a republic. There were extremists and moderates in both societies, but there existed the beginnings of a plot to assassinate the Tsar in 1826.

When news of Alexander's death reached St Petersburg, the confusion over who would succeed him made the Northern Society decide that this was the moment to rebel. On Alexander's death Nicholas, his younger brother, proclaimed the elder brother Constantine as Tsar. There were two problems about this. First, Constantine had renounced the succession secretly, which Nicholas knew, as his heirs could not inherit the throne, but he needed to do so publicly to make Nicholas's position safe. Second, Constantine was in Poland and it took a week for a message from one brother to reach the other. So it was that the officers of the Northern Society planned to lead their men and the garrison of St Petersburg into proclaiming Constantine and accusing Nicholas of treason. They lacked a plan beyond this. The extraordinary plot was played out in the Senate Square of St Petersburg on 14 December. There had been

moments of comedy with a betrayal of the plot, a confession of the betrayal, Nicholas directing opposing soldiers where they should assemble, and the aristocratic rebel officers turning away popular supporters (they did not want to encourage a mob). But towards evening, with some three thousand rebels surrounded by ten thousand troops who had already sworn allegiance to the new Tsar Nicholas I, the artillery was used to destroy the revolt. The Southern Society's rebellion was crushed within a week as well.

The Decembrists were aristocrats, officers and members of the gentry who had tried to make a revolution out of an idea. In Russia in 1825 this was indeed 'an echo of distant happenings' as Pipes has called it (R. Pipes, *Russia Under the Old Regime*, London, Penguin, 1984, p. 188). But it was no mere palace coup that they intended – their aim was a better society for many, not just for themselves. This is why they were celebrated as the first to take a step towards real revolution in Russia.

Nicholas I, 'Gendarme of Europe'

Nicholas had been brought up to be a soldier. He liked parades, routine and a clear line of command. His attitude to reform was less complex than Alexander I's; he disliked it unless it increased the control and authority of his centralised government. The Decembrist revolt, and the detailed investigations which followed, affected him and he became greatly concerned to prevent another conspiracy.

Nicholas recognised that the cumbersome bureaucracy was corrupt (bribe-taking and promotion through connection were common) and obstructed his personal authority. His solution was to expand his own civil service, the Imperial Chancery. The First Section was his own Secretariat. The Second Section (1826) started a colossal reform and codification of the legal system under Speransky, which was put in place in 1835. The Third Section (under General Benckendorf) was the secret police. It began life in 1826 with sky-blue uniforms and white gloves, investigating corruption and injustice, but it became the key agency for censorship, control of education, detention without trial, and repression.

The Fourth Section controlled education, and operated with the Third Section to censor books. Uvarov was made Minister of Education in 1833 and operated a system which tried to ration education carefully according to rank, and insulate Russia from the influence of the wrong sort of western ideas. Uvarov's famous summary of his ideas as 'Orthodoxy, Autocracy, Nationality' characterised more than just the system of education. The role of the Orthodox Church as a supporter of Tsarism was natural to such a conservative institution which saw its role simply as the keeper of eternal truths. Autocracy focused on the Tsar's own authority. Nationality meant the promotion of Russian culture and patriotism over others, and may be seen most clearly in the 'russification' of Poland after the revolt of 1830–31; martial law was imposed and Alexander's model constitution revoked.

Other aspects of Nicholas I's rule were perhaps more 'progressive'. The Fifth Section of the Chancery was created in 1836. Under Kiselev new lands were opened up, new farming techniques and crops introduced, and hospitals and schools built, but the resettlement of some 200,000 peasants met with opposition and the elements of compulsion and control were never far away. Kankrin as Minister of Finance (1823–44) 'was both reactionary and progressive' in Sherman's view (R. Sherman, *Russia 1815–81*, London, Hodder and Stoughton, 1991, p. 38). Technical studies were encouraged, bullion reserves were built up, the budget balanced and inflation brought under control. On the other hand he disliked the development of railways, presided over industrial production which fell further behind European standards, while overseas trade increased no further than to allow Russia to maintain her 3.7 per cent stake in world trade.

In foreign affairs Nicholas I and his adviser Nesselrode pursued similar objectives to Alexander I, but they were framed more clearly and without talk of a mission from God. Leaving his predecessor's opposition to the Greek rebellion, Nicholas I joined with Britain in pressing the Ottoman empire to allow Greek independence. At the battle of Navarino in 1827 British, Russian and French fleets destroyed the combined Turkish and Egyptian force. War between Russia and Turkey followed, concluded profitably for Russia in 1829 with the Treaty of Adrianople. Greek independence was secured for 1830.

Britain was especially alarmed about Russia's growing power in the Balkans, so near to the Mediterranean line of communications with India, but Russian policy was interested in stabilising the area rather than in gaining more turbulent provinces. When Turkey was threatened by Mehemet Ali in the early 1830s, Russian forces intervened in strength, afterwards obtaining the treaty of Unkiar-Skelessi (1833) which promised mutual defence. This meant that Turkey would close the Straits in time of war, but Britain was highly suspicious that Russia would be allowed access. Metternich succeeded in clarifying Russian policy, and gaining Habsburg influence in the process, by the Münchengrätz Agreement (1833) to prop up the Ottoman empire. But the clearest expression of Nicholas I's interest in achieving stability rather than control in the region came in 1839 when he cooperated with Britain in defending Turkey against Mehemet Ali. The treaty of London (signed by Britain, Russia, Austria and Prussia) of 1840 guaranteed the Ottoman empire and the Straits Convention cleared up suspicions about access to the straits (they were closed to foreign warships). Not only had Nicholas I forged closer links with Britain, and united Russia with Austria and Prussia, but also he had forced the questionable regime of Louis Philippe to abandon her support of the rebel Mehemet Ali and toe the line.

Nicholas I's regime weathered the revolutionary storms of 1830 and 1848 easily, finding only the Petrashevsky circle to arrest in 1849. This was only partly because the system was so effectively repressive. Primarily it was because Russia was so different from the other nations which were rocked by trouble in 1848; her government, her traditions and thinking, the stage of her social and economic development all meant that the challenges faced in Paris and Vienna had yet to arrive in St Petersburg and Moscow. Nicholas I and Alexander I before him tried in slightly different ways to anticipate and contain these challenges, and they and their successors arguably succeeded in postponing them; what cost was paid in trying to modernise an autocracy in the nineteenth century?

SECTION B – SOURCES

REACTION, CHANGE, AND THE FAILURE OF THE FRENCH MONARCHY

Napoleon abdicated in 1814 and the first Bourbon restoration followed immediately. The victorious allies understood that the *ancien régime* could not be restored as though nothing had happened since 1789, and Louis XVIII's powers were limited by the Constitutional Charter. The influence of the Ultra-royalists was strong, focusing on the King's brother, the Comte d'Artois (who became King Charles X in 1824), and fear that they would bring about a complete restoration of the *ancien régime* helps to account for Napoleon's favourable reception when he returned to France in March 1815 for the One Hundred Days (extracts A (i and ii)). After the battle of Waterloo and the second restoration, Louis XVIII maintained Richelieu at the head of a moderate government despite the election of a Chamber with an Ultra majority; the King and the ministry seemed to be upholding the constitution against Ultra wishes for a full-blown restoration of the throne's authority (extract A (iii)). Under Charles X the Ultras got their way, and by 1830 the King had moved into a position of confrontation with the constitution. The chamber was dissolved and new elections held in the summer (extract E (i)), but the chamber remained opposed and Charles tried to rule by decree.

Revolution followed and brought in the 'July Monarchy' of Louis Philippe, who was careful to accept the title 'King of the French' to show that he owed his position to popular sovereignty and not the hereditary principle of the Kings of France of the *ancien régime* (extract E (ii)). The franchise, originally moderate, remained unchanged until the end of the regime in 1848. This created growing resentment from many including the bourgeoisie who did not have the vote. Guizot became the key minister during the 1840s, pursuing increasingly repressive policies to defend what had become a narrow franchise (extract E (iii)). The fall of the regime in February 1848 sparked a series of revolutions which raised the hopes of republicans and socialists throughout Europe.

The turmoil of 1848 was of course Metternich's worst nightmare. As Chancellor of the Habsburg empire since 1812 he had laboured to create stability in Europe. This made him appear reactionary on some matters, in particular signs of nationalism within the German Confederation (of which Austria was president) (see extract B). He despised the middle classes for their arrogance and their readiness to overturn traditional government (extract C), and he saw this class as being the starting-point for liberalism and nationalism which would unravel the Habsburg empire. But he was also a realist: he understood that the Ultras were a threat in France (extract A (ii)) and he developed a close relationship with Richelieu through the French ambassador at Vienna. From the time of the Congress of Vienna, Metternich also feared Russian intervention in Europe (which a weakened Habsburg empire would be unable to prevent), so his solution to the constitutionalist revolution in Spain headed off Tsar Alexander I's wish for Russian intervention by allowing France to restore the situation there (extract D). Russia was contained, but France escaped from the restrictions imposed on her after Waterloo and the distance between Metternich and the Tsar's reactionary attitude was clear.

A Reaction in Restoration France

(i) Louis Philippe, then Duke of Orleans, writing in his Memoirs *of 1814*

Louis XVIII recognised . . . that everything that had been accomplished in France since 1789 . . . were maintained in full force. . . . Yet, what proved damaging to him, and to France, was that he did not perceive that the purpose of all the new laws was, invariably, to weaken royal authority . . . France, exhausted by everything it had endured . . . called in one voice for the establishment of a constitutional monarchy, which was not to be the old order, but a new monarchy adapted to the spirit of the age.

(*Archives national de Paris*, cited in M. Broers, *Europe after Napoleon*, Manchester University Press, 1996, pp. 128–29)

(ii) From Metternich's letter to Richelieu, 25 January 1818

Time will weaken one of the parties in France, that of

the Ultra-royalists. . . . It is regrettable that the party was ever formed. . . . It was the Ultras and weak men who found themselves at the head of government during the ten months of the first Restoration who made the king stumble in his tracks. That party can claim much of the credit for bringing about the crisis of 1815. The only reproach which could perhaps be brought against the ministry [i.e. Richelieu's government] is that of having attached too much importance to fighting that same party since the 1816 session.

(iii) From Richelieu's letter to Metternich, 17 March 1818

By obstinately refusing to join us, that party [the Ultras] . . . have forced us to remove them from positions of any importance and to entrust these positions to men who agreed to cooperate with us, even if they had not given quite such striking proofs of loyalty. It was a sad but inevitable result of the situation. . . .

. . . Do not believe, my dear Prince, that I am unconcerned by the growth of these revolutionary principles. On the contrary, I am much alarmed by them and should like to see all royalists unite to oppose them. . . . this revolutionary spirit cannot be blamed on the actions of the administration. . . . If no way is found of limiting the freedom of the press, it will destroy the social order in Europe . . . Bonaparte knew this.

(translated from text cited in G. de Bertier de Sauvigny, *France and the European Alliance 1816–21*, Indiana, University of Notre Dame Press, 1958, pp. 38, 50 and 53)

B The Carlsbad Decrees, 20 September 1819

The University Law
The duty of this commissioner shall be to watch over the most rigorous observation of the laws and disciplinary regulations; to observe carefully the spirit with which the professors are guided in the scientific courses, or in the method of instruction, to give the instruction a salutary direction . . . and to devote constant attention to everything which may tend to the maintenance of morality, good order and decency among the youths. . . .

The Press Law
. . . no daily paper or pamphlet of less than twenty sheets shall be issued from the press without the previous consent of public authority.

(G.A. Kertesz (ed.) *Documents in the Political History of the European Continent, 1815–1939*, Oxford 1968, pp. 67–69, cited in P. Jones, *The 1848 Revolutions*, London, Longman, 1981, pp. 68–69)

C Metternich's letter to Tsar Alexander I at the Congress of Troppau, December 1820

From the time that men attempt to swerve from . . . [morality, religious as well as social] society suffers from a *malaise* which sooner or later will lead to a state of convulsion. . . .

. . . experience has no value for the presumptuous man; faith is nothing to him. . . . Laws have no value to him, because he has not contributed to make them. . . . Power resides in himself . . . Presumption makes every man the guide of his own belief. . . .

It is principally the middle classes of society which this moral gangrene has affected. . . .

For the great mass of the people it has no attraction and can have none. . . . The people know that the happiest thing for them namely to be able to count on the morrow, for it is the morrow which will repay them for the cares and sorrows of to-day.

(*Memoires of Prince Metternich*, trans. A. Napier, 1880–82, vol. 3, pp. 453–76, cited in R.C. Bridges, P. Dukes, J.D. Hargreaves and W. Scott (eds) *Nations and Empires: Documents on the History of Europe and its Relations with the World since 1648*, London, Macmillan, 1969, pp. 122–26)

D Metternich at the Congress of Verona justifies intervention in Spain, from his letter to the Austrian *Chargé d'Affaires* in Madrid, 14 December 1822

A just repugnance . . . to meddle with the internal affairs of an independent nation would perhaps influence those sovereigns not to pronounce on the situation in Spain, if the evil operated by her revolution was concentrated, or could be concentrated, within her territorial limits. But this is not the case . . . by the contagion of its principles and of its example, and by the intrigues of its principal partisans, created revolutions in Naples and Piedmont . . . [and] would have excited insurrections throughout Italy, menaced France, and compromised Germany, but for the intervention of the Powers.

(*Annual Register* 1822, pp. 569–76, cited in Kertesz (ed.)
Documents in the Political History of the European Continent,
1815–1939, pp. 25–26)

E The nature of the 'July Monarchy' of Louis Philippe

(i) *Proclamation of Charles X of France before the election, 14 June 1830*

listen to the voice of your King, and maintain the Constitutional Charter, . . . but to obtain this object, I must freely exercise, and cause to be respected, the sacred rights which belong to my Crown, which are the guarantee of public peace and of your liberties.

(Kertesz (ed.), *Documents in the Political History of the European Continent, 1815–1939*, p. 50)

(ii) *Guizot's views on the authority of Louis Philippe, King of the French*

The duty of this royal personage is to govern only in harmony with the other great authorities of state instituted according to the charter; to govern with their approval, their allegiance, their support. The duty of the counsellors of the crown is to win the support of the crown for the ideas, the measures and the policy for which they are sure of support in the chambers.

(Guizot's *Memoirs*, in E.L. Woodward (ed.) *Three Studies in European Conservatism: Metternich, Guizot and the Catholic Church in the Nineteenth Century*, London 1929, p. 145, cited in Jones, *1848 Revolutions*, p. 70)

(iii) *Karl Marx's contemporary view of the 'bourgeois monarchy' of Louis Philippe*

It was not the French bourgeoisie that ruled under Louis Philippe, but one faction of it: bankers, stock-exchange kings, owners of coal and iron mines and forests, a part of the landed proprietors associated with them – the so-called finance aristocracy.

(K. Marx, *The Class Struggle in France*, 1850, cited in Broers, *Europe after Napoleon*, p. 126)

F M. Broers's summary of Metternich's policy

Metternich based much of his strategy to preserve a conservative Europe on stressing the potential – if not always the imminence – of revolution by radical or nationalist elements. This was aimed less at an active repression of subversive forces (except in times of outright crisis), than at keeping reactionary regimes mindful of the need for conservative reform, and consequently, at keeping reactionaries and conservatives from each others' throats. For the forces of the Right, this desired unity usually came after the event, but was stressed by Metternich and his supporters at all times. Nevertheless, when the forces of the Right could act in unison, the results were momentous.

The military activities of the Holy Alliance in Spain and Italy, in the suppression of the revolutions of 1820–23 were the chief manifestations of this.

(Broers, *Europe after Napoleon*, p. 107)

Questions

1 Explain Metternich's meaning in context:
   (a) 'It is regrettable that the [Ultra-royalist] party was ever formed' (extract A (ii))
   (b) 'experience has no value for the presumptuous man' (extract C)
   (c) 'the contagion of its principles' (of the revolution in Spain) (extract D).
2 Read extracts A (i–iii). How effectively does Richelieu's attitude to the Ultras and the press answer the criticisms made by Metternich and by the Duke of Orleans earlier?
3 Consider extracts A (ii), B, C and D. To what extent do they support Broers's analysis of Metternich's policies in extract F?
4 What is meant by 'the sacred rights which belong to my Crown' in extract E (i)? What light does this extract shed upon the fall of the Bourbon monarchy in 1830?
5 How useful are extracts E (ii and iii) for assessing the strengths and weaknesses of the 'July Monarchy' of Louis Philippe (1830–48)?
6 To what extent does the 1830 Revolution in France confirm Broers's analysis in extract F? You should refer to the relevant extracts and use your own knowledge in your answer.

Further reading

France

K. Randell, *France: Monarchy, Republic and Empire 1814–70* (London, Hodder and Stoughton, 1986) is a clear and well-structured student text, while J.P.T. Bury, *France 1814–1940* (London, Methuen, 1984) seems to have been deservedly in print for over forty years for it is a model – well phrased, concise, sensibly detailed and scholarly. G. Wright, *France in Modern Times* (New York, Norton, 1981) contains a well-written overview. More focused studies include: P.M. Pilbeam, *Republicanism in Nineteenth century France, 1814–1871* (London, Macmillan, 1995), R. Magraw, *France 1815–1914: the Bourgeois Century* (London, Fontana, 1983), which is a detailed social history, H.A.C. Collingham, *The July Monarchy* (London, Longman, 1988), which is unusually focused on Louis Philippe's reign, and W. Fortescue, *Revolution and Counter-Revolution in France, 1815–52* (Oxford, Blackwell, 1988), a fairly short but detailed survey.

The Habsburg empire and Germany

A. Sked, *The Decline and Fall of the Habsburg Empire 1815–1918* (London, Longman, 1989) is clear and sharply argued, while J. Lowe, *International Relations 1814–70* (London, Hodder and Stoughton, 1990) is a useful student text which deals with the international system. The relevant sections of R. Gildea, *Barricades and Borders: Europe 1800–1914* (Oxford University Press, 1996) provide a clear and scholarly blend of detail and analysis. W. Carr, *A History of Germany 1815–1985* (London, Arnold, 1987) is a helpful study. Useful works with a particular focus or theme include: A. Sked (ed.) *Europe's Balance of Power 1815–48* (London, Macmillan, 1979), A. Palmer, *Metternich, Chancellor of Europe* (London, Weidenfeld and Nicolson, 1972) and M. Broers, *Europe after Napoleon: Revolution, Reaction and Romanticism, 1814–48* (Manchester University Press, 1996).

Russia

R. Sherman, *Russia 1815–81* (London, Hodder and Stoughton, 1991) is a clear, concise student text which includes quotes from primary sources. J.N. Westwood, *Endurance and Endeavour: Russian History 1812–1992* (Oxford University Press, 1993) is a scholarly blend of detail, analysis and anecdote. H. Seton-Watson, *The Russian Empire 1801–1917* (Oxford University Press, 1988) is more solid and detailed, very useful for researching particular points, while R. Pipes, *Russia under the Old Regime* (London, Penguin, 1984) is a classic which repays some selective reading. D. Saunders, 'Alexander I of Russia: Reformer or Reactionary?' in P. Catterall and R. Vinen (eds) *Europe 1815–1870* (Oxford, Heinemann, 1994) is a usefully compact article on this key question.

Documentary material is to be found in G.A. Kertesz (ed.) *Documents in the Political History of the European Continent, 1815–1939* (Oxford University Press, 1968) and R.C. Bridges, P. Dukes, J.D. Hargreaves and W. Scott (eds) *Nations and Empires: Documents on the History of Europe and its Relations with the World since 1648,* (London, Macmillan, 1969). The works by Sherman and Broers, already listed, contain some useful excerpts.

• CHAPTER TEN •

1848: The Year of Revolutions

• CONTENTS •

Key dates

1848	12 Jan.	Revolution in Palermo, Sicily
	24 Feb.	Louis Philippe abdicates
	26 Feb.	French Second Republic proclaimed
	5 March	Liberals in Heidelberg call Frankfurt *Vorparlament*
	13 March	Fall of Metternich
	15 March	Hungarian Diet demands independence
	18 March	Frederick William IV of Prussia agrees to allow a constitution
	23 March	War between Piedmont and Austria
	31 March	Frankfurt *Vorparlament* meets
	11 April	Habsburgs allow constitutional progress in Hungary, Bohemia and Moravia
	23 April	French Constituent Assembly meets
	17 May	Habsburg court flees from Vienna to Innsbruck
	18 May	Frankfurt meeting of German National Assembly
	22 May	Berlin meeting of Prussian National Assembly
	2 June	Prague meeting of Slav Congress
	16 June	Prague bombarded by Windischgrätz
	23–26 June	'June Days' repression in Paris
	22 July	Vienna meeting of Austrian Constituent Assembly
	23 July	Piedmontese forces defeated by Austrians at Custozza
	Aug.	Habsburg court returns to Vienna
	26 Aug.	Prussia and Denmark sign Malmö cease-fire
	Sept.	Jellacic begins campaign against Hungary
	Sept.	Serfdom abolished in Austria
	Oct.	Austria declares war on Hungary
	6–31 Oct.	'October Days' repression in Vienna
	21 Nov.	Schwarzenberg becomes Habsburg Chancellor
	24 Nov.	Pope Pius IX leaves Rome
	2 Dec.	Francis Joseph replaces Ferdinand as Habsburg Emperor
	5 Dec.	Prussian National Assembly dissolved; new constitution decreed; troops occupy Berlin
	10 Dec.	Louis Napoleon elected President of French Second Republic
1849	9 Feb.	Roman Republic established by Mazzini
	7 March	Austrian Constituent Assembly dissolved
	23 March	Piedmontese forces defeated by Austrians at Novarra; Victor Emmanuel II replaces Charles Albert as King of Piedmont-Sardinia
	3 April	Frederick William IV rejects Frankfurt Assembly's invitation to be Emperor of Germany
	27 April	New Prussian assembly dissolved
	May	French Legislative Assembly elected; 'Party of Order' majority
	3 July	French occupy Rome after Republic falls; Pope restored
	13 Aug.	Hungarians surrender to joint Austrian–Russian force
1850	Jan.	New Prussian constitution imposed; ministers and army responsible to King
	March	*Loi Falloux* allows Catholic Church to run schools in France
1851	1–2 Dec.	Louis Napoleon's *coup d'état* sets up ten-year presidency
1852	2 Dec.	Second Empire proclaimed under Napoleon III

SECTION A

In January 1847 the Prussian Count Galen wrote: 'The old year ended in scarcity, the new one opens with starvation. Misery, spiritual and physical, traverses Europe in ghastly shapes – the one without God, the other without bread. Woe if they join hands!' (M. Traugott, 'The mid-nineteenth century crisis in England and France', *Theory and Society*, 12, 1983, cited in A. Price, *The Revolutions of 1848*, London, Macmillan, 1988, p. 20). These prophetic words touch several of the important features of the revolutions of 1848. Poor harvests, high food prices, terrible urban conditions affecting the poor, combined with the frustration felt by the middle classes at the lack of reform and careers, required only a spark or an example to catch fire. The sense of foreboding in Galen's words helps explain why the governments, when faced with disorder, believed they faced a massive conspiracy. They gave way, and only later regained their nerve and used their armies to restore control. But Metternich, the Habsburg Chancellor, and Louis Philippe, the last king to reign in France, were swept away by the tide of 1848. There was now a new point of reference for the future; governments would try to avoid a repetition, and those who wanted change would try to improve on the method and results.

THE POLITICAL AND ECONOMIC BACKGROUND

The population of Europe grew quickly over the hundred years before 1848, roughly doubling, and food supplies came under pressure. The poor harvests of 1845 and 1846 drove prices up (see extract A (i)) and meant starvation threatened the urban poor. Normally 50 per cent of an urban worker's income was spent on food, so there was nothing to spare to cope with a price increase. Purchases of manufactured goods fell, workers were laid off and unemployment increased, making destitution more common. Typhoid and cholera epidemics added to the death toll in 1847 and 1848, and up to half of the deaths recorded in parts of the Habsburg empire in 1847 were of children. In Ireland the potato blight destroyed the principal food crop in 1846, leading to the deaths of half a million and widespread emigration. However, it is possible to argue that the worst of the starvation conditions were over before 1848, and hunger and disease provide only part of the circumstances which made revolution.

There were many other miserable features of urban life which led to anger and disorder. Cities brought wealth and poverty close together, and the poor inevitably became aware of their numbers and more open to political ideas and agitation. Was a class consciousness emerging as the workers came to realise that it was the middle classes who owned the capital and made the profit? While there is evidence to show this growing awareness (for example extracts C and D), it is much harder to show that such an awareness *caused* the outbreak of revolution in 1848. Other factors came in to play when life was so desperate and short (32 years was the life expectancy in Lille in 1848). Freed of the constraints of a village community, lawlessness and violence were commonplace among the poor of the cities, so it is perhaps unsurprising that it should overflow into the smarter streets during 1848. Unemployment, caused by the trade cycle or mechanisation, was another feature of life and machine-breaking was a popular crowd activity in 1848 as a result.

Cities, especially the capital cities, were the key points in the revolutions of 1848, but peasant unrest was destabilising because it threatened the landowning nobility and reminded them of 1789. In 1844 there was a revolt of the Silesian weavers, and in 1846 Metternich called upon the Galician peasantry to put down a revolt by their Polish masters. The enthusiasm with which this was done taught an important lesson for everyone. Any increase in food prices affected the peasantry just as badly as the urban workers, and in eastern Europe the feudal burden of labour on the landowners' estates (called the *robot* in the Habsburg empire) was an additional grievance. The plight of the peasantry was another contributory factor in the revolutionary mixture, not least because the landowning class felt threatened and was aware of a 'malaise'.

The middle classes also sensed this 'malaise' or sickness in the state of affairs in several countries. Metternich had always suspected this class of causing the problem, and in 1820 he had written to the Tsar blaming their arrogant pushiness for undermining the social and religious morality which held society together (see Chapter 9, extract C). Metternich's solution had been control and repression which may have made the liberal middle classes the allies of more radical and working class movements in 1848, as we shall see. But Metternich's policies were not the only cause of middle class resentments, of course.

In Louis Philippe's France, where 1 per cent of the middle class owned 30 per cent of the wealth of the middle classes, the *grande bourgeoisie* of wealthy manufacturers, bankers and merchants were the key supporters of the regime and especially prominent. The electorate was virtually restricted to this group which enjoyed investing in land as a symbol of status as well as a safe asset. On the other hand, the professional middle class of doctors, lawyers, officials, professors and teachers represented about 10 per cent of the middle classes in Europe and were more aware of a 'malaise'. They did not have the money to become 'landed wealth', and they tended to be the most important advocates of liberal reform, including free trade (see extract A (ii)). Often their education and ambitions were frustrated; in France most of this group did not have the vote, and in Prussia the civil service was dominated by sons of the aristocracy and it was very hard to find a career open to talent. The 'banqueting movement' in France was an important vehicle for middle class opposition to Louis Philippe and his chief minister, Guizot, in 1847. It attracted especially the professional class to political meetings which were thinly disguised as expensive banquets, run along the lines of the Anti-Corn Law League's events in Britain, and helped to engage this class in the revolutionary events which followed.

The lower middle class of shopkeepers, small employers and the most affluent craftsmen were the most numerous segment of the middle classes. The lower middle class shared some of the frustrations and reform interests of the better-off professional class, but they were close in every way to the urban workers; they sympathised with their difficulties, and feared their power – many from this class of shopkeepers and small employers had been careful to call themselves *sans-culottes* in Paris in the early 1790s! In France by the 1840s this class included many republicans, and they feature noticeably among those arrested during the June Days fighting in Paris (see extract B).

All of these factors help to explain why there was a possibility of revolution in Europe in the 1840s. These factors affected many parts of Europe too, making it easier to understand why disturbances in one capital would find an echo in another. However, they do not explain why events got out of the control of so many governments in 1848. Who, then, were the leaders of revolution? Karl Marx had just published the *Communist Manifesto* in January 1848 with its stirring call for workers of the world to unite, but he and Bakunin (the anarchist) were in Brussels when revolution began in Paris, Mazzini was in London, and they were all taken by surprise by the sequence of events. It seems that the disturbances which broke out in so many European cities were spontaneous, their leaders unknown or non-existent, and the words of the republican Ledru-Rollin may stand for all: 'I am their leader, I must follow them' (cited in A. Wood, *Europe 1815–1945*, London, Longman, 1964, p. 133). What then sparked the disturbances, and what turned riots into revolutions?

THE COURSE OF REVOLUTION

The fall of the July Monarchy in France

The Austrian monopoly on trade in tobacco prompted some ugly incidents in Milan in January 1848 when rioters (presumably smokers) confronted Radetzky's troops, but the real curtain-raiser was the rebellion in Palermo, Sicily. By the end of the month Neapolitan troops had been pulled out of Sicily and King Ferdinand II had granted a constitution to the whole of his kingdom for his own safety. During February Charles Albert of Piedmont drew up a constitution, and Tuscany adopted a representative government. These changes would perhaps have been relatively insignificant and quickly reversed had not the barricades gone up in Paris soon afterwards.

Louis Philippe's government rested upon a very narrow electoral base and the unpopularity of the King and his Chief Minister, Guizot, was further increased by the economic hardships of the past eighteen months. The Bank of France had been forced to raise 1 million through Barings from the Bank of England, and scandals like the Teste affair (a minister who accepted bribes) gave the widespread impression of government incompetence and sleaze. An opposition press had started up as well, and *Le National* and *La Réforme* gave some encouragement and direction to the street protests which took place from 22 February. Guizot was replaced by Molé, but demonstrations continued on the evening of 23 February. Victor Hugo witnessed the events which helped turn a demonstration into a revolution:

> The crowds which I had seen start cheerfully singing down the boulevards, at first went on their way peacefully and without resistance. . . . But . . . infantry and cavalry was . . . guarding the Ministry of Foreign Affairs and its unpopular minister, M. Guizot. Before this impassable obstacle, the head of the popular column tried to stop . . . but the irresistible pressure of the huge crowd weighed on the front ranks. At this moment a shot rang out, from which side is not known. Panic followed and then a volley. Eighty dead or wounded remained. . . . And in a few hours Paris was covered with barricades.
>
> (cited in A. Cobban, *A History of Modern France*, vol. 2,
> London, Penguin, 1970, pp. 130–31)

The next day the 75-year-old Louis Philippe replaced Molé with Thiers, but events were really beyond his power to control. Disheartened by the cold reception given to him by the National Guard he reviewed, he abdicated in favour of his grandchild and followed Charles X into exile in England. The chamber was inclined to accept the succession, but it was invaded by a mob on 26 February and quickly proclaimed a republic instead. The crowds on the streets and at the barricades were mostly working class, in some cases organised from the newspaper offices or by republican groups such as the Society for the Rights of Man and the Family, while the bourgeoisie 'came and went' according to a contemporary (Lucien de la Hodde, *Histoire des sociétés secrètes et du parti républicain de 1830 à 1848*, Paris, 1850, cited in R. Price (ed.) *1848 in France*, London, Macmillan, 1975, p. 58), but republican government was not the result of planning but came about by accident. The pattern of rioting developing into revolution was to be repeated in other capitals within months.

There were other features of this revolution which would be repeated too. The army, which was in Paris in large numbers, was not used. The loyalty of the soldiers was doubted, and it is understandable that Louis Philippe, the King of the French, recoiled from pitting his forces against a city of about 1 million citizens. However, the Republican government which succeeded him did make use of these same forces just four months later. The fall of the July Monarchy therefore showed another feature which was common to the 1848 revolutions: a failure of nerve by governments when they were confronted by violence on the streets.

The Second Republic set up a broad-based Provisional Government. Moderate republicans such as Lamartine, Marrast and Garnier-Pagès were connected with the newspaper *Le National*, while Louis Blanc, Albert and the editor of *La Réforme* aimed for a social republic which would redistribute wealth. For the time being there was consensus and compromise. Universal adult male suffrage was agreed as the basis for elections in April to a Constituent Assembly. Demands for equal rights for women were limited and ignored. The *tricolore* was retained in preference to the red flag which the more eager social reformers wanted. Press controls were lifted. No help was offered to the Poles in their struggle against Russian authority. But the most dramatic gesture was the decision to set up National Workshops (under Émile Thomas) to give meaning to the right to work. By April 70,000 unemployed people had enrolled in the National Workshops in Paris and were being paid to undertake various schemes of work such as levelling the Champs de Mars. Not only was this a very costly project which further drained the reserves and damaged the new government's creditworthiness, but also it began attracting the unemployed from far and wide, making Paris yet more crowded and turbulent. Worse still for bourgeois and provincial taxpayers was that the scheme reminded them of the fanatical republicanism of the Jacobins.

Revolution in the German states

The shock waves set off by the events in Paris had an immediate effect throughout much of Europe. In neighbouring Belgium the liberal ministry led by Rogier doubled the electorate and moderate liberals won a victory in the June elections, reaping the reward for making changes early. In Holland William II allowed ministerial responsibility to the elected chamber. The impact of the French Revolution of February had a more spectacular effect in Germany. Changes were made to the constitutions of a number of states, including Württemberg, Bavaria, Baden and Brunswick, and the demands of the citizens of Nassau were fairly typical and included a clear reference to the precedent set by France. On 5 March an important meeting of some fifty liberals from a number of states, under von Gagern (from Hesse-Darmstadt), took place at Heidelberg. They took the revolutionary step of issuing invitations to representatives from all the states of the German Confederation to meet at Frankfurt. This *Vorparlament* (before-parliament) of 600 delegates assembled on 31 March and began arranging elections throughout Germany for a Constituent Assembly.

The 1848 Revolution in Germany was quickly taking on a middle class and nationalist character which threatened to dilute Prussian power and to confront Habsburg domination of the Confederation. Neither of these two powers was in a position to answer the challenge, however. In 1847 Frederick William IV of Prussia had called a United Diet in order to raise the tax revenue needed to build a railway to open up East Prussia. When faced with demands for regular meetings, the King refused, but on 18 March 1848 serious disturbances broke out in Berlin and about three hundred people were killed. Frederick William IV backed down quickly, probably remembering the fate of Louis Philippe. Ordering a cease-fire, he appeared on the streets himself showing the German flag and pledging Prussia's solidarity with the German revolution (see extract E (ii)). He was greeted with tumultuous applause and his timely surrender allowed him to weather the storm.

The fall of Metternich

In the Habsburg empire itself dissolution threatened. In March the Hungarian Diet at Pressburg took up Kossuth's demands for national independence and the abolition of serfdom, and these were echoed in Bohemia. More serious still were events in Vienna itself. The university presented a petition on 12 March, and the representatives of the estates of Lower Austria were preparing to do the same on 13 March when a mob, mostly students but with working class involvement, interrupted them and proceeded to the imperial palace. The police had lost control of the situation, and Metternich discovered that no one in the Ministerial Conference would support his policy of resistance. He was easily the most unpopular figure in the government (the Emperor was able to appear in his carriage at the height of the troubles to general applause) and after thirty-nine years in office (he was now aged 74) his grip on events was not what it used to be. It made sense to the Imperial family and his rival, Kolowrat, to offer the rioters (and the Hungarians) the convenient concession of removing him. Metternich resigned on 13 March and began the journey into exile in England.

Neither Metternich's resignation nor the progress to constitutional government in Austria (and Galicia, Bohemia and Moravia) quite satisfied popular demands. In May further rioting broke out in Vienna, mostly student led. The Imperial court fled to Innsbruck having granted a Constituent Assembly, now on the basis of universal manhood suffrage. P. Jones comments that this 'was a further indication of the profound shock and loss of confidence experienced by the dynasty' (P. Jones, *The 1848 Revolutions*, London, Longman, 1981, p. 43). What had provoked such paralysis, concessions and flight without calling upon the army? One reason may have been that the Habsburg government, in common with others, actually believed that, with food prices falling by later in 1847, the worst danger was past and they were therefore taken by surprise. Another important consideration was the widespread belief that they were facing a European-wide conspiracy, a belief which the progressive spread of revolution from one capital to another seemed to confirm. No evidence of the conspiracy was found then, despite the vast machinery of surveillance run from Vienna, and none has been found since to suggest that there were international (or even national) leaders of a conspiracy. However, to ministers and kings who witnessed the collapse of one stable regime after another, like so many dominoes, the belief that there was a plot at work seemed plausible and hastened their own surrender.

Revolution in Italy

While the Habsburg empire was being shaken at home, events in Italy added to its loss of confidence. In Piedmont, Charles Albert accepted a liberal constitution in March which allowed a chamber of deputies to be elected on a limited franchise (about 2 per cent of the population). In addition civil rights were guaranteed, press freedoms established, and while Roman Catholicism was the only religion of the state, others were tolerated. Pope Pius IX granted a constitution in the Papal States, and in Venice Manin's revolt led to Austrian forces withdrawing and the proclamation of a Republic. When an uprising in Milan forced Radetzky's troops out, Charles Albert made common cause with the rebels and advanced against the Austrians in Lombardy.

To begin with, Charles Albert's Piedmontese forces made progress against the Austrians. But Pius IX withdrew his support for the campaign in April, and in May Austrian forces defeated the rebels in Tuscany. Following the Austrian victory at Custozza in July, Charles Albert signed a ceasefire. Hopes of creating a northern Italian kingdom had been undermined by Lombardy's and Venetia's preference for keeping their new-won independence, by the withdrawal of support from the Papal States, and by King Ferdinand II of Naples re-establishing control and revoking the constitution he had granted in February.

Metternich used to say that Italy was only a geographical expression, and by the late summer of 1848 the collapse of unification seemed to prove him correct. But the hope had not yet died, and Austrian power was far from being re-established. In November 1848 Rossi, the premier of the Papal states who wanted a northern Italian federation under the Pope, was assassinated; his scheme had created fierce opposition from radicals and nationalists. The Pope fled from the Eternal City, and in February 1849 a Roman Republic was proclaimed with Mazzini playing a key role. The possibility that Rome would focus Italian nationalism as the Frankfurt *Vorparlament* hoped to do for German

nationalism was hindered by the reluctance of Tuscany and Lombardy to send deputies to Rome.

The revolutions lose their way: the June Days in France

Elections to the Constituent Assembly in April attracted a high turnout, but the victory was overwhelming for moderate Republicans, former Orleanists and Legitimists. The fears of the bourgeois property owners, and the influence of the priests in the countryside (polling took place on Easter Sunday) ensured that radical republicanism was rejected. In Paris several demonstrations occurred, but the National Guard dispersed the occupants of the Hôtel de Ville and arrested the ringleaders.

Inevitably, the government moved against the National Workshops which were proving expensive, unable to employ properly the 100,000 who had enrolled who were endangering the safety of Paris. Later in June it was announced to the workmen that young bachelors would be dismissed or enlisted in the army, and the rest would either find employment privately in Paris or work on public enterprises in the provinces. This announcement was greeted with fury. It seemed that the government was going back on the very principles which the new republic had just proclaimed, the right to work, and that it was betraying the hopes of the working classes who had made the revolution. Many of the workmen enrolled in the National Workshops determined to resist, and they were joined by the eastern working class faubourgs of Paris where the barricades went up.

The National Guard (including one hundred thousand from the provinces) were prepared for a show-down and, on 24 June, the Assembly took the fateful step of making General Cavaignac Chief of the Executive Power with authority to use the army. There were no leaders to this insurrection of about a hundred thousand who fought (according to de Tocqueville) 'without a war-cry, without chiefs, or a standard, and yet with a cohesion and a military skill which surprised the oldest officers' (cited in J.P.T. Bury, *France 1814–1945*, London, Methuen, 1985, p. 77). Women and men fought side by side, infuriated that the gains they had won in February were being stolen from them. The struggle had the character of a class conflict (see extract B); most, but not all, of those arrested were from the working classes. By 27 June the insurrection was crushed and many had been killed (see Figure 10.1). Fifteen thousand were arrested, the clubs were now placed under surveillance, the press restricted, and the working day increased to twelve hours in Paris.

Many felt that the republic had been hijacked by the middle classes and the reform agenda was betrayed (see extract D); Lamartine remarked sadly that 'the Republic is dead', but the middle classes and many in the provinces felt reassured that events would not slide towards a Jacobin dictatorship. Significantly, the newly elected Assembly had called upon the very same forces to arrest the revolution in June which Louis Philippe had not dared to use to stop it in February.

The revolutions lose their way: divide and rule in the Habsburg empire

The Hungarian Diet in Pressburg expressed its nationalism by demanding that the Magyar language was to be used by members of the parliament and seemed to want to replace Austrian with Hungarian supremacy. This alarmed the several minority groups within Hungary. Czech nationalism, expressed in June 1848 in the Slav Congress in Prague, took a different direction. Palacky, who chaired the Congress, supported the Habsburg empire which he argued was vital for the protection of the infant Czech nation from Russia (see extract E (i)). However, Palacky's programme was unacceptable to the large German speaking minority in Bohemia, and it was unacceptable to the Habsburg governor of Moravia, Windischgrätz,

10.1 Barricade at the corner of Boulevard and Rue Masagran, near the Porte St. Denis, Paris.

Source: AKG London

who used a student rising in Prague on 16 June as the pretext for bombarding the city and crushing the Slav revolution.

In Austria itself the revolution was becoming divided between middle class professionals who wanted a constitutional monarchy, the Student Academic Legion which had republican sympathies, and the demands of the working classes for radical reform. Each faction was suspicious of the other. The Constituent Assembly met in Vienna in July and it was very anxious to arrest a drift towards a republic, and to halt Magyar and Slav independence. Clearly, the Habsburg monarchy was the best instrument to do both. The middle class liberals in the Assembly therefore invited the Court to return to Vienna, and began planning the reinforcement of General Jellacic (the governor of Croatia) so that the Hungarian National Assembly could be crushed. The abolition of serfdom and the *robot* (in September) helped to defuse revolutionary pressures by removing peasant support from the urban radicals.

In September 1848 Jellacic invaded Hungary and Kossuth became president of the Committee for National Defence. At the beginning of October the Emperor formally dissolved the Hungarian National Assembly and declared war. Polish forces came to help the Hungarians; their revolution needed to destroy both Austrian and Russian authority to survive. Hungarian resistance was effective to begin with, however, and the whole affair prompted a serious rising in Vienna itself just as the decision to close the National Workshops had done in Paris. Students and workers combined against the pro-Habsburg Austrian Constituent Assembly, the Minister for War was lynched and the Court withdrew to Olmütz. But the 'October Days' were to continue to parallel the 'June Days' in France. Windischgrätz's forces crushed the rising brutally, killing up to five thousand inhabitants. Revolution was halted in Vienna in October by using the force which Metternich had recommended in March.

The revolutions lose their way: the Frankfurt Assembly

The Constituent Assembly which met at Frankfurt on 18 May 1848 was dominated by liberal, middle class, professional delegates. The voting had been decided within the various states, but the *Vorparlament* had backed the idea of a property-based franchise to exclude any whiff of mob-rule. One consequence was that the working classes felt excluded from the whole business; demonstrations occurred, and assemblies of artisans met in Frankfurt and Hamburg. Their main concerns were to protect employment (which often made them hostile to machinery and free trade) and the trade guilds (see extract A (iii)), and they were often hostile to the Jews.

Meanwhile the Frankfurt Assembly moved on a different level. Under von Gagern's presidency the debates dragged on for weeks. There was discussion about the rights of citizens, about whether the state should have a federal or a centralized structure and whether or not it should be a republic. There was division over whether Austria should be included (*Grossdeutschland*) or excluded (*Kleindeutschland*), many of the southern states fearing that Prussia would overwhelm them if her authority in a united Germany was not counterweighted by Catholic Austria. The deliberations lacked appeal to the working classes and the peasantry, but the Frankfurt Assembly committed a more serious error. Wishing to counter the claims of King Frederick VII of Denmark, the Frankfurt Assembly approved the inclusion of the Duchy of Schleswig (Holstein was already a Confederation member) within the new Germany in August 1848. Not only had moderation been replaced by nationalist ambitions, but also the action which the Assembly approved against Denmark was undertaken by the soldiers of Prussia.

Prussian soldiers had already intervened on behalf of German nationalism. In April 1848 they had seized part of the Duchy of Posen to save the German minority there from becoming swallowed up in a new Poland (which looked as intolerant of minorities as the Hungarian nationalists). Prussian forces helped Russia to contain the Polish revolt.

Prussia's use of force against Denmark undermined the authority of the Frankfurt Assembly in the Schleswig-Holstein question. On 26 August, responding to British concerns for Denmark's independence, Prussia signed a cease-fire with Denmark at Malmö and abandoned the campaign. The Frankfurt Assembly felt betrayed and it had been humiliated. Powerless in the face of Prussia's loss of interest in the German revolution, it had no option but to accept the position. When the delegates voted their approval (narrowly) on 16 September, Prussian and Austrian troops from the fortress of Mainz were rushed in to save the Frankfurt Assembly from rioters.

The last chapter in the Frankfurt Assembly's existence was fairly predictable. The delegates continued to debate, and by March 1849 they produced a constitution. There were to be two chambers, the one representing the states (Austria was excluded) and the other elected by universal manhood suffrage through a secret ballot. The executive was to be an hereditary emperor, and Frederick William IV of Prussia was invited to do the job. But the King of Prussia was not at all interested in the invitation from an elected assembly, 'from the gutter' as he put it. His official reply of 3 April 1849 was more polite, but it was a refusal nevertheless to accept the Assembly's offer (see extract E (iii)). With no force of its own, and very limited popular interest behind it, the Frankfurt Assembly now disintegrated. Armed resistance from radicals in Saxony, Baden and several other states was crushed in May by a military alliance of the rulers of the states with Prussia; the leaders were executed. German national unity would have to await Prussian leadership.

THE RE-ESTABLISHMENT OF AUTHORITY

The short life of the revolution in Prussia

What had caused Frederick William IV to reverse his earlier support of the cause of German nationalism? In March 1848 he had embraced it. The answer seems to be either that the King was frightened into the original gesture, or that he was acting to divide the middle class liberals from the radical reform demands of the working classes (who wanted a minimum wage and a shorter working day). The Prussian liberals were allowed to develop their constitutional ideas (they assembled in May) while the Berlin working classes, whose leading spokesman was Stephan Born, were confronted in the March demonstrations. Further-

more, the radical reform demands frightened the liberal middle classes badly, and the King was able to exploit this division and recover his authority.

The Prussian National Assembly began work on a liberal constitution in May 1848. Meanwhile, opposition was focused on the conservative, military, court circles and the landowners (*Junkers*) decided to set up a Society for the Protection of the Interests of Landowners. They successfully won Frederick William IV back to a traditional position. In November the National Assembly was moved out of the capital to Brandenburg, and in December it was dissolved while von Wrangel's troops occupied Berlin. As a sop to liberal opinion a new constitution was decreed and elections held (in January 1849), but the new assembly was dissolved in April 1849. The revised constitution of January 1850 made ministers responsible to the King and required no oath of allegiance to the constitution from the army; Gildea concludes: 'The Prussian military monarchy was back in business. After all, the revolution had been defeated by the military' (R. Gildea, *Barricades and Borders: Europe 1800–1914*, Oxford University Press, 1996, p. 91).

President Bonaparte

The French Second Republic's Constitution of November 1848 separated the power of a President, elected every four years, from the Legislative Assembly which was elected, also by universal manhood suffrage, every three years. The right to work was not included. Was a throne being prepared under the disguise of the elected presidency? Possibly the monarchist sympathisers hoped that evolution to a constitutional monarchy may happen. What actually happened disappointed both the monarchists and the republicans. In the December elections for the president, Cavaignac attracted just over 1 million votes, the left-wing republican Ledru-Rollin gathered some 370,000, while Louis Napoleon Bonaparte won an easy victory with over 5 million votes. We shall look at the nature of this Bonapartist revival later, but he was acceptable to many diverse groups. To the middle classes, President Bonaparte was the strong man who would prevent Republican excesses; to the monarchists, he was a stop-gap; to republicans, he was better than Cavaignac; and for some, memories of earlier glories were stirred. The appeal of his name (he was Napoleon's nephew) attracted the peasantry in an extraordinary way. Magraw comments: 'Peasant France ... put its trust in a saviour, a resurrected legend, a name made famous since 1815 in the villages by the stories of army veterans' (R. Magraw, *France 1815–1914: the Bourgeois Century*, London, Fontana, 1983, p. 136).

Elections to the Legislative Assembly were held in May 1849 and consolidated Louis Napoleon's position. About 500 of the 750 deputies were Bonapartists or monarchists of the 'Party of Order'; it had indeed become 'a Republic without republicans'. Louis Napoleon now proceeded to use his powers as president to strengthen his own position and popularity. A French expedition to Rome was approved for the purpose of defending the sister republic against Austrian forces. Louis Napoleon altered its mission completely. To court domestic support from the Catholics, the expedition now needed to restore the Pope. To do this, the Roman Republic had to be destroyed, and an appeal was made to patriotic (and Bonapartist) feelings by presenting the French occupation of Rome as traditional and necessary to keep Austrian forces out. Republicans at home were not fooled, and Ledru-Rollin inspired an insurrection in Paris on 13 July 1849, but it was crushed and Louis Napoleon's position became even stronger as the guardian of law and order.

Louis Napoleon continued to appeal to Catholic opinion in 1850 with the *Loi Falloux* which allowed the Roman Catholic Church to run schools alongside department or state schools; the secularisation of education was checked and reversed. He toured the country, building up his reputation, and in November 1851 he proposed repealing the Electoral Law (of May 1850) which had imposed a three year residence requirement on voters and which effectively disenfranchised the poorest workers who tended to vote republican. Arguably this was yet another device to gain popularity as a man of the people as he must have realised that the Assembly would keep the law in place. All these steps were not in readiness for the presidential election campaign but to prepare the ground for a

military backed coup on 1–2 December 1851. The Assembly chamber was occupied, arrests were made, and it was announced that Louis Napoleon would remain president for ten years and that he had acted to prevent civil war. The Second Republic survived in name for another year; the Second Empire was proclaimed on 2 December 1852. The Emperor Napoleon III was the real inheritor of the 1848 Revolution in France.

The collapse of the Italian revolution and the fall of the Roman Republic

In March 1849 Piedmont broke her truce with the Austrians and attacked without the support of other Italian states; she was defeated heavily at the battle of Novarra, and Charles Albert abdicated. His son, Victor Emmanuel II, became King of Piedmont-Sardinia. Austrian forces went on to re-establish their authority in Tuscany, Modena and Parma, and by August they had occupied Venice and Manin had fled. But progress towards constitutional government and Italian unification was not completely destroyed. Victor Emmanuel II's powers were constitutionally limited as taxation had to be approved by an elected assembly and ministers needed a majority there. Furthermore, he was sympathetic to Italian unification and prepared to face the opposition of the Papacy.

The Roman Republic provided a more difficult problem, not least because French rather than Austrian forces intervened in April 1849 (see Figure 10.2). Among the motives behind the French expedition was to please Roman Catholic opinion at home by restoring the Pope, and preventing an Austrian force from occupying the city. Mazzini took the hopeless but symbolic decision to fight the forces sent by the sister French Republic, and Garibaldi's defence of the city in April and throughout June 1849 created a great inspiration for Italian patriotism in future. Important precedents had been established. A Republic had ruled in Rome and made a patriotic claim to lead Italian unification from there. The Pope had set his face against such a development, as indeed he was to oppose 'every idea that the nineteenth century spawned', as Gildea put it, after his return to the Vatican in July 1849 (Gildea, *Barricades*, p. 88).

FIRST ATTACK OF THE FRENCH TROOPS AT ROME NEAR THE PORTA CAVELLEGIERE.

10.2 French troops capturing Rome, 1849

Source: ©BBC Hulton Picture Library

The Habsburg recovery

Following the 'October Days' Schwarzenberg was placed in charge of the government in Vienna. The Emperor Ferdinand, who had made the concessions in the spring, was persuaded to abdicate and on 2 December his 18-year-old nephew, Francis Joseph, became Emperor. He was determined to recover his authority. The successful suppression of the revolutions in Italy lent him the prestige to ignore the Constituent Assembly (which had been sent away to talk in Kromeriz since November), and he closed it in March 1849.

The Hungarian revolution still had to be crushed, for it had reignited by May 1849 and recovered Budapest, which had fallen to Jellacic in January. If Kossuth hoped for the support of Britain or France, he was disappointed. British inter-

ests lay in a stable central Europe which would keep Russia well away from the Balkans, and President Louis Napoleon was unwilling to provoke the anger of France's old enemies Austria and Russia by supporting rebels. The Emperor Francis Joseph appealed to Tsar Nicholas I for help in crushing the Magyar revolution, and a combined Austrian–Russian force defeated the Hungarians in August at Világos. Kossuth fled and his nation's bid for independence ended.

Francis Joseph had recovered his inheritance in August 1849, and the verdict of P. Jones reflects how this came about: 'Liberal constitutionalism had experienced a short and unsuccessful life. It was easily consumed by more vigorous national rivalries – a desire for Germanic ascendancy over Magyars as well as a Germanic–Magyar ascendancy over Slavs' (Jones, *Revolutions*, p. 46). In these circumstances the old imperial formula that used the divisions of the subject peoples to keep the Habsburgs in power still worked – or perhaps it all showed the value of the empire in keeping the peace of Europe.

The revolutions in perspective

Revolution touched most of Europe in 1848, but Russia and Britain remained quiet. Effective repression in Russia was only part of the explanation, for Metternich's repressive system had not kept the Habsburg empire under control. Russia's circumstances separated her. Russia had negligible industrial development and a tiny middle class. Her agricultural economy meant that there was a great gulf between the peasantry, the vast majority of the population, and the class which comprised landowners, priests, civil servants and nobility, and therefore the social conditions were quite different. Russia's cities were also at an isolating distance from the wildfire excitement which enabled news and revolt to spread between other European capitals.

If this is the explanation for the absence of revolution in Russia, it cannot explain Britain's peacefulness. Parliamentary reform in 1832 had given the vote to the middle class, and the repeal of the Corn Laws in 1846 seemed to demonstrate that parliament was responsive to middle class pressure (the Anti-Corn Law League) and the demand for cheap bread (which many of the urban poor believed repeal would bring). Furthermore, a certain chauvinism assumed that England had had her revolution in the seventeenth century, and the French version was regarded with horror. There was therefore little desire to copy what foreigners were doing in 1848. Even the Chartist petition had a touch of comedy about it, with forged signatures, and the mass meeting succeeded only in frightening Queen Victoria into travelling to the Isle of Wight; the military authorities were ready and quite able to contain any trouble, as the Chartists knew well.

The revolutions of 1848 had much in common. Social and economic circumstances which affected much of Europe were important in sustaining the spirit of revolt. The example set by the dramatically fast fall of Louis Philippe in France set things in motion, inspiring liberals and radicals, and striking monarchical regimes with fear and paralysis. Once governments recovered their nerve and realised that the conspiracy was imaginary, they were able to use the forces which they had not dared to use at the outbreak.

Governments exploited the divisions of the revolutionaries to recover power. In France the middle classes used Cavaignac's army to destroy the radical revolution, and in President Louis Napoleon they found a substitute for the bourgeois monarch who had let them down. In Prussia King Frederick William IV separated the liberals from the radicals, and recovered most of his authority. In Austria a similar cycle of events took place, the October Days supplying the decisive defeat of the radical revolution.

Nationalism was a more prominent revolutionary aim than liberalism in Germany, the Habsburg empire outside Austria herself, and in Italy. However, nationalism proved a divisive force. In Italy it did not produce unity; neither Piedmont nor the Roman Republic was able to attract the wholehearted support of the other states. The Frankfurt Assembly, absorbed in liberal debate, was deserted by Prussia and its aim of unification came to nothing. Within the Habsburg dominions themselves, Hungarian nationalism mounted a strong challenge to Vienna's authority yet the Slav Congress wanted to find independence within Habsburg protection; nationalisms which headed in such different directions were crushed separately.

What then did the revolutions achieve? Louis Philippe and Metternich had gone, but they were replaced by Louis Napoleon and Schwarzenberg, and the forces of reaction seemed to recover. But things could never be quite the same again. Metternich's system had failed to predict or prevent the revolutions. Governments had actually to use force, not merely threaten its use. The 'presumptuous' middle classes had shown their power, and the teeming industrial cities had made their challenge to authority felt. In future, governments would pay more attention to popular pressures and conditions, while those who wanted change would try to avoid repeating the mistakes of the revolutionaries of 1848.

SECTION B – SOURCES

The 1848 revolutions: common features and failures

The role of economic and social factors in causing widespread political discontent in 1848 has been much debated by historians. A very large proportion of the workers' income was used to buy food, so changes in the price of grain would have had a great impact on hunger (extracts A (i and ii)). Economic discontent affected the bourgeoisie also, shown in their demand for free trade in Germany (extract A (ii)). In this context, a spark was sufficient to ignite revolutions throughout Europe.

In Paris the so-called 'bourgeois monarchy' of Louis Philippe had excluded most of the bourgeoisie from the franchise and from office, and the bourgeois-dominated National Guard did nothing to stop the protests becoming a revolution on the streets of Paris. Working class hopes were high that the new Republic would bring social reform and a fairer distribution of wealth (extract D), and National Workshops were set up in Paris to fulfil the promise of the right to work. However, the Church, the monarchists and many of the property-owning bourgeoisie feared Republicanism. The secret societies and clubs, and extremists like Blanqui, who hoped to cash in on the Revolution and drive it towards the Jacobinism of 1793 (extract C), all increased bourgeois fears. The National Workshops were a great expense, they attracted vagabonds to Paris from all over France, and they represented an extreme republican idea; the newly elected 'Republican' government closed them and in the 'June Days' many protesters were arrested, mostly but not all from the working class (extract B).

The fall of Louis Philippe encouraged revolutions throughout the Habsburg lands, but while the bourgeoisie often dominated events, as they did in France, the demands were focused more on national self-determination than on purely liberal aims. Nationalism often produced competing rather than complementary pressures (extract E (i)). In the end Frederick William IV of Prussia rejected the Imperial crown, symbol of the new German nationhood, offered by the Frankfurt Assembly of delegates who had been elected by the German states (extract E (iii)). Prussia was not to be submerged in a new Germany.

A The standard of living and free trade

(i) Grain prices (Table 10.1)

Table 10.1 Grain prices in Hamburg, 1843–49 (1841 = 100)

	Wheat	Rye	Barley	Oats
1843	103.1	83.3	105.2	94.9
1845	89.5	59.5	113.0	91.5
1847	151.8	120.8	185.7	149.1
1848	134.0	82.7	124.7	110.2
1849	100.0	53.5	103.9	69.5

(ii) From the Heppenheim Programme of German Liberals, 10 October 1847

The Diet [of the German Confederation] has not so far fulfilled the tasks set it by the Act of Confederation in the fields of representation by estates, free trade, communications, navigation, freedom of the press. . . . The only expression of the common German interest in existence, the Customs Union, was not created by the Confederation, but negotiated outside its framework.

(G.A. Kertesz (ed.) *Documents in the Political History of the European Continent, 1815–1939*, Oxford University Press, 1968, pp. 79–81, cited in P. Jones, *The 1848 Revolutions*, London, Longman, 1981, p. 71)

(iii) From a petition by the tradesmen of Karlsruhe to the Frankfurt Assembly, 1848

Only theoreticians who do not know the internal conditions of industry and its needs, only people who find nourishment in unlimited freedom for their own flightiness without thinking of the future, only speculators and the aristocrats of money who snatch some advantage for themselves out of the frivolity and need of others, speak with scorn of a legal order in industry and praise unlimited freedom of trade as a means of higher development.

(P.H. Noyes, *Organisation and Revolution: Working-Class Associations in the German Revolutions of 1848–9*, Princeton, NJ, 1966, p. 240, cited in M. Broers, *Europe after Napoleon*, Manchester University Press, 1996, p. 131)

B The June Days in Paris, 1848 (Table 10.2)

Table 10.2 Participation in the insurrection of June 1848: professions of those arrested

Profession	No. arrested	Total arrested (%)
Building	1,725	14.82
Food and drink	438	3.76
Furniture	1,004	8.62
Clothing and shoes	1,225	10.52
Textiles	351	3.01
Skin and leather	157	1.35
Coach building, saddlery and military equipment	223	1.92
Chemicals and ceramics	116	1.00
Metal, engineering and metal products	1,312	11.27
Precious metals and jewellery	231	1.98
Coopers and basket-makers	68	0.58
Printing workers	433	3.72
Labourers and navvies	1,093	9.39
Cultivators, gardeners and herdsmen	141	1.21
Transport workers	522	4.48
Concièrges, servants, cooks and waiters	282	2.42
Proprietors, rentiers	47	0.40
Clerical workers	438	3.76
Liberal professions	208	1.79
Artistic professions	72	0.62
Commercial professions (including shopkeepers)	450	3.77
Students	39	0.33
Garde mobile	163	1.40
Police and soldiers	216	1.86
Ragpickers, pedlars, etc.	297	2.55
Others	297	2.56
Occupation not specified	94	0.81
	11,642	99.90

C Blanqui's speech to the Club du Prado, 25 February 1848

France is not Republican. The Revolution that has just passed is nothing more than a happy surprise. . . . The national guard itself has only been an unwilling accomplice; it is composed of timid shopkeepers. . . . Leave the men in the Hôtel de Ville to their impotence; their feebleness is a sure sign of their fall. Their power is but ephemeral: we – we have the people and the clubs [250 appeared in Paris alone February–March 1848] where we shall organise them in revolutionary fashion, as was the way of the Jacobins of old.

Let us have enough sense to wait a few days more – then the revolution will be ours!

(A. Lucas, *Les Clubs et les clubistes*, Paris 1851, cited in Price, *Revolutions of 1848*, p. 72)

D The trial of an engineering worker, 27 August 1848

Prosecutor: What do you mean by a social Republic?

Accused: I mean a Republic with social reforms. Universal suffrage has been decreed, but that doesn't do the people any good. It is an instrument that the people do not use. . . . I want to ensure that the worker receives the product of his labour, a proportion of which is at present taken away from him by the man who provides the capital.

(*Le National*, cited in Price, *Revolutions of 1848*, pp. 111–12)

E National self-determination in 1848

(i) Palacky, chairman of the Prague Slavonic Congress, refuses to attend the Frankfurt Assembly, 11 April 1848

The object of your federation is to establish a federation of the German nation in place of the existing federation of princes, to guide the German nation to real unity . . . I cannot, precisely for the reasons that I respect it, participate in it in any manner whatsoever. I am not a German . . . I am a Czech of Slavonic blood. . . .

. . . The second reason which prevents me from taking part . . . is your . . . purpose to undermine Austria as an independent empire . . . whose preservation . . . is . . . a great and important matter not only for my own nation but also for the whole of Europe, indeed for humanity and civilisation itself. . . .

[Russia] has become . . . a menace to its neighbours . . . [threatening] to establish a *universal monarchy* . . . [which] has no more determined opponent or foe than myself – not because that monarchy would be Russian but because it would be universal.

(W. Beardmore (trans.) *Slavonic and East European Review*, 27, 1947–48, pp. 303–08, cited in R.C. Bridges, P. Dukes, J.D. Hargreaves and W. Scott (eds) *Nations and Empires: Documents on the History of Europe and on its Relations with the World since 1648*, London, Macmillan, 1969, pp. 136–40)

(ii) From the declaration of Frederick William IV of Prussia in March 1848

From this day forth the name of Prussia is fused and dissolved into that of Germany.

(iii) From Frederick William IV of Prussia's rejection of the Imperial Crown offered by the Frankfurt Assembly, 3 April 1849

It will now lie with the several Governments of the German States to examine the constitution which the national assembly has drawn up, and declare ... whether the rights it confers on me will place me in the position to guide the destinies of Germany. . . . But of this Germany may be certain . . . that if it needs the protection of the Prussian sword I will, even without a summons, not hesitate to follow that course from which my royal House has never departed – the course of fidelity and honour.

(*Annual Register*, 1848, pp. 380–81 and 1849, pp. 347–8, cited in S. Brooks, *Nineteenth Century Europe*, London, Macmillan, 1983, pp. 35–6)

F From A. Sked's analysis of the causes of the 1848 Revolution in the Habsburg empire

Did the revolutions of 1848 cause the fall of Metternich or did the fall of Metternich cause the revolutions? This is not a trivial question. It is rather an invitation to pause and think before falling into the traditional trap of assuming that Metternich's liberal critics were correct and that the Habsburg Monarchy in 1848 was overwhelmed by profound forces of revolution which swept away the Metternich System. . . . A more plausible explanation of events is simply that when a street riot took place in Vienna on 13 March, the imperial family lost its nerve, sacked the Chancellor and there-

after lost control of events as the Monarchy plunged into a power vacuum.

(A. Sked, *The Decline and Fall of the Habsburg Empire, 1815–1918*, London, Longman, 1995, p. 41)

Questions

1 What light is shed on the causes of the 1848 revolutions in the German Confederation by extracts A (i–iii)?
2 How useful are the statistics of those arrested (extract B) for evaluating the nature of the June Days rising in Paris in 1848?
3 How much importance should be attached to Blanqui's comment that 'The Revolution that has just passed is nothing more than a happy surprise' (extract C)?
4 Compare and contrast the political aims of the engineering worker at his trial (extract D) with Blanqui's political aims (extract C).
5 Using extracts A–D and your own knowledge, explain how far the events of 1848 justify the description of 'class war'.
6 How useful are extracts E (i–iii) for assessing the contribution of national self-determination to the direction and outcome of the 1848 revolutions?
7 Use your own knowledge and any relevant extracts to evaluate Sked's argument (extract F) that the Habsburgs 'lost their nerve' and 'lost control of events'.

Further reading

Two compact studies of the course of the 1848 revolutions are R. Price, *The Revolutions of 1848* (London, Macmillan, 1988), which provides detailed information and a good review of scholarly work, and P. Jones, *The 1848 Revolutions* (London, Longman, 1984), which is very concise and contains a useful selection of documentary excerpts. R. Pearson (ed.) *The Longman Companion to European Nationalism*, (London, Longman, 1994) is an extremely useful reference book. A recent scholarly treatment of the revolutions is to be found in R. Gildea, *Barricades and Borders: Europe 1800–1914* (Oxford University Press, 1996), while A. Wood *Europe 1815–1945* (London,

Longman, 1970) offers a clear, fluent and detailed survey of events. Highly readable and authoritative coverage of the Revolutions as they affected individual countries may be found in A. Sked, *The Decline and Fall of the Habsburg Empire 1815–1918* (London, Longman, 1995), A. Palmer, *Metternich, Chancellor of Europe* (London, Weidenfeld and Nicolson, 1971), J.P.T. Bury, *France 1814–1940* (London, Methuen, 1985) and R. Magraw, *France 1815–1914: The Bourgeois Century* (London, Fontana, 1983).

Useful also because they contain documentary excerpts are R. Price (ed.) *1848 in France* (London, Thames and Hudson, 1975), G.A. Kertesz (ed.) *Documents in the Political History of the European Continent, 1815–1939* (Oxford University Press, 1968) and P. Jones's work mentioned above.

• CHAPTER ELEVEN •

The Second Empire in France, 1851–70

• CONTENTS •

Key dates

KEY DATES

1840		Louis Napoleon imprisoned after Boulogne coup fails
1851	1–2 Dec.	Louis Napoleon's coup sets up ten-year presidency
1852	Jan.	Constitution of what became the Second Empire
	Oct.	Napoleon at Bordeaux says 'the Empire is peace'
	Dec.	Second Empire proclaimed under Napoleon III
		Press law requires financial deposits from newspapers; Crédit Mobilier founded
1853		Napoleon marries Eugénie, Countess de Montijo
1854	March	Crimean war begins; France and Britain ally with Ottoman Empire against Russia
1856	March	Treaty of Paris ends Crimean war
1858	Jan.	Orsini's attempt to assassinate Napoleon III
	July	Meeting at Plombieres between Napoleon III and Cavour of Piedmont
1859	June	France and Piedmont defeat Austria at battles of Magenta and Solferino
	July	France abandons Piedmont and makes peace with Austria at Villafranca
1860		Cobden–Chevalier tariff reduction agreement
		Nice and Savoy plebiscites confirm French rule after partial reconciliation with Piedmont
1861	Feb.	Legislative Body debates may be published in full
1861	Dec.	Legislative Body able to consider separate items of budget
1862		French expedition to set up Emperor Maximilian in Mexico
1863		Elections to Legislative Body; fifteen Republicans returned
1864		Thiers and 'Third Party' propose 'necessary reforms'; peaceful strikes legalised
	Oct.	Biarritz meeting between Napoleon III and Bismarck
1866	3 July	Battle of Sadowa (Koniggrätz); Prussia defeats Austria
	Aug.	Bismarck rejects French demands for territorial gains; French forces withdraw from Mexico
1867	Jan.	Legislative Body able to question government; Maximilian executed in Mexico; Crédit Mobilier collapses
1868		Trade unions legalised; press controls eased; legislative body refuses funds for army reserve and forces Rouher to promise to keep troops in Rome
1869	May	Elections produce large 'Third Party' demanding reforms
1870	Jan.	Ollivier appointed to replace Rouher; 'Liberal Empire' begins
	May	Constitution of 'Liberal Empire' makes ministers accountable
		Plebiscite approves liberal reforms by 7 million votes to 1.5 million
	13 July	France demands Prussian guarantee against renewal of the Hohenzollern candidature for the Spanish throne
	19 July	France declares war on Prussia
	2 Sept.	Napoleon III captured at Sedan
	4 Sept.	Third Republic proclaimed in France

SECTION A

Napoleon III's regime brought a degree of stability and glory to France which she had not experienced since 1815. However, the period of the Second Empire is difficult to disentangle and the conflicting elements have produced many different historical assessments. Louis Napoleon had great confidence that it was his destiny to rule France and carry on where his uncle had left off. This meant that he wanted to build upon the 1815 amendments to the Imperial constitution and the Napoleonic legend and create a system of authority from above with confidence from below. Quite how this could be achieved was a little vague, but the 1852 constitution made the attempt and also contained signs that it would be liberalised in future. However, the *coup d'état* of December 1851 was sufficiently violent to damage Napoleon III's claim that he had acted for the people, and it was not until the 1860s that the liberalisation of the regime began. It went slowly to begin with, giving the appearance that it was driven more by the need to conciliate opposition out of weakness rather than being from principle and out of strength.

The 1850s were encouraging years for Napoleon III. Great projects were begun such as the rebuilding of Paris and the mass-banking initiative of the Crédit Mobilier, and the 1815 settlement was overturned when France, in alliance with Britain, successfully challenged Russia in the Crimea. Napoleon III's support for Italian nationalism against Austrian power was complicated by his continued support for the Pope, and this episode set the scene for foreign policy failures in the 1860s in Mexico and in dealing with Bismarck. The sense of muddled purpose extends to domestic affairs where concessions on freedom of the press and the power of the Legislative Body seemed to be made reluctantly, spurred on by foreign policy failures and economic problems, and the creation of the 'Liberal Empire' of 1870 is often seen in this context rather than as 'liberty crowning the edifice' of Empire according to Napoleon III's idea. The debate about the coming of the 'Liberal Empire' is sharpened by its speedy destruction in the Franco-Prussian war which broke out in July 1870. The status of the 'Liberal Empire' as either a last desperate expedient or the culmination of the evolution of the regime into a stable parliamentary system was left open to debate by the last in a series of foreign policy failures.

LOUIS NAPOLEON BONAPARTE AND POWER

The character of Louis Napoleon and his rise to power provide important clues about the Second Empire. Born in Paris in 1808 to Hortense Beauharnais and Louis Bonaparte, King of Holland and brother of the Emperor Napoleon, he was brought up by his mother, after 1815 in comfortable exile, usually in Switzerland. Although he felt his Bonapartist inheritance keenly, he had other relatives who took precedence over him in any succession. But no Bonapartist succession was in prospect while Metternich remained in office, and Louis Philippe prudently banned Louis Napoleon and his mother from returning to France after 1830. It was the excitement of being in Italy in 1830–31 that thrilled Louis Napoleon with the taste for military adventure in a popular cause, together with the death of Napoleon I's son by Marie Louise (the Duc de Reichstadt) in 1832, which encouraged Louis Napoleon to start preparing himself for what he believed was his destiny to re-establish the Empire.

Failed coups and pamphlets

Louis Napoleon, like Hitler, began his bid for power by trying to seize it in a coup or *putsch*. First he advertised himself and between 1832 and 1836 he wrote several pamphlets, including one on Switzerland and one on the artillery, before attempting to copy his uncle's return from Elba (in 1815) by seizing Strasbourg one October morning in 1836. Despite attracting some support for his band, the garrison commander kept control and Louis Napoleon was exiled to the United States by the July Monarchy which wanted to avoid giving him the status of a martyr. By 1838 he was back in London, working on his pamphlet *Des idées napoléoniennes*. This was his political manifesto, and it was widely sold (in six languages) from 1839. Louis Napoleon argued that the Revolution had made proper government the instrument for improving society and civilisation, and that Napoleon I had reconciled what was positive in the Revolution with the *ancien régime*. Only Britain's mistaken enmity had stopped Napoleon I from establishing liberty and European peace based upon national self-determination. Louis Napoleon signalled clearly that France might look to him as the heir to the Napoleonic legend.

With this publicity behind him, Louis Napoleon and his supporters staged another coup attempt at Boulogne in August 1840. It failed dismally, and with elements of farce such as a tame vulture standing in for the imperial eagle and

Louis Napoleon being dragged from the surf, his imprisonment for the next six years seemed likely to destroy this Napoleonic pretender. But his faith in his destiny remained undaunted (see extract A), and in 1844 he published *L'Extinction du paupérisme* which argued along the lines of Saint-Simon's economic theory that the government should take an active role in funding work schemes for the poor, and developing capital enterprise as well to get wealth percolating down to the wage-earner. This pamphlet provides an important clue to Louis Napoleon's thinking: well meaning, populist, with elements of both socialism and an active, authoritarian state. Was it another political manifesto, a blueprint for his government, or just an essay in self-advertisement?

Seizing power

Louis Napoleon escaped in 1846 and enjoyed a sociable life in London. When revolution broke out in Paris in February 1848, his arrival embarrassed the Republicans and he withdrew to England, keeping his hands clean from the massacre of the 'June Days'. His agents and friends were busy on his behalf in Paris during the summer and autumn of 1848, and he became the ideal candidate for President of the Second Republic in the eyes of several different groups by December, as we have seen in Chapter 10. Clearly he took many of his friends of convenience by surprise with the extent of his popularity. At the time he appeared to Thiers and others in the 'Party of Order' to be dull, inarticulate and easy to handle. But he possessed a name which guaranteed instant and favourable recognition to the peasantry, he had no blood on his hands from the 'June Days' and many workers were aware of his pamphlet on *paupérisme* (which had run to six editions by 1848) and all this told in his favour.

The story of Louis Napoleon's seizure of power is the story of the Second Republic's collapse (see Chapter 10). We have seen how Louis Napoleon used his authority as president to develop his power by appealing to Catholic opinion, with the *Loi Falloux* and the restoration of the Pope, and to the working class with his proposal to repeal the electoral law which had imposed a residence

qualification. In October 1849 he dismissed Barrot's ministry which commanded a majority in the Legislative Assembly from the 'Party of Order', and replaced it with his own men who could command similar support but who would not simply use him as a front. Besides publicising himself through speaking tours and appointing supporters to office, Louis Napoleon entertained lavishly (especially generals) and organised military pageants where soldiers were well supplied with wine and sausages. It was clear that Louis Napoleon did not plan that his return to power should end with the expiry of his presidential term, and when the Assembly rejected his proposal in July 1851 to allow him to be re-elected by amending the Constitution, a military coup became only a matter of time. After several postponements, it went ahead on 2 December 1851 under the meticulous planning of the Duc de Morny (Louis Napoleon's half-brother). Blood was shed, especially on 4 December when about sixty protesters and bystanders were shot down on the street, and a large number of people, including peasants, were arrested in the provinces for opposition or due to their Republican sympathies. About 9,500 were exiled to Algeria. Louis Napoleon was troubled then and throughout his reign by the human cost, and typically he intervened to reduce punishments and even secretly tried to help the families of victims. This might be seen as authoritarianism combining with humanitarianism into a benevolent dictatorship, but it may also evidence a muddled purpose. McMillan comments, 'Paradoxically a coup perpetrated allegedly to protect the people against the machinations of the Assembly quickly came to be justified as a preventative measure to quell rural disorder' (J.F. McMillan, *Napoleon III*, London, Longman, 1991, pp. 47–48). Martyrs were created by the coup, and Republicans like Gambetta were never reconciled to the Second Empire as a result (see extract C); Louis Napoleon's wish to unite all French people was doomed from the start.

The Constitution of 1852

A plebiscite was called after the coup of 2 December 1851 which registered nearly 7.5

million votes in favour of the action and for the Prince-President continuing in office for ten years, while careful management of the ballot helped to ensure that only 647,000 voted against. The Constitution of 14 January 1852 continued to reflect this blend of authority and populism. The Executive was the Prince-President, ministers were responsible only to him, and he had command of foreign policy and the army. The Legislative Body comprised 260 deputies (a big reduction from the 750 of the Second Republic) elected by manhood suffrage every six years. They met for only three months of each year to discuss the Prince-President's measures; they had no power to raise issues, to question ministers or publish their debates, and the Prince-President could always go over their heads by calling a plebiscite. The Senate was appointed by the Prince-President for life and provided a means of amending the constitution. A Council of State was created to advise and support the Executive, and it was to this body that Louis Napoleon made clear, as part of the constitutional proclamation, that there was a flexibility to allow future change in the system of government (see extract B (i)).

The system of government set up by the constitution of January 1852 was for the personal and authoritarian rule of Louis Napoleon. In December 1852 the constitution was amended to proclaim the Second Empire with the Prince-President taking the title Emperor Napoleon III (acknowledging Napoleon II's right of succession before his death in 1832), and a plebiscite duly confirmed this change (7.8 million in favour, 253,000 voting against). Yet the system was representative to some extent, as the role of plebiscites showed. Furthermore, the election of the Legislative Body in 1852 produced 5.2 million votes for government candidates through local incentives and encouragements, and by a voting system which made it much easier for the semi-literate to use the white ballot paper supplied for the official candidate rather than the more rarely available and embarrassingly obvious coloured paper of an opposition candidate.

Was this benevolent dictatorship, 'leadership from above, support from below'? Or were such claims hypocritical nonsense from a regime which

closed political clubs and operated a tough system of press controls involving newspapers forfeiting deposits and risking closure if they published critical articles? Victor Hugo, writing just before the Second Empire was proclaimed, was in no doubt about the petty nastiness and hollowness of Louis Napoleon:

Though he has committed enormous crimes, he will remain paltry. He will never be other than the nocturnal strangler of liberty; he will never be other than the man who has intoxicated his soldiers, not with glory, like the first Napoleon, but with wine; he will never be other than the pigmy tyrant of a great people. Grandeur, even in infamy, is utterly inconsistent with the character and calibre of the man. As Dictator, he is a buffoon.

(from V. Hugo, *Napoleon the Little*, cited in K. Randell, *France: Monarchy, Republic and Empire, 1814–70*, London, Hodder and Stoughton, 1986, p. 123)

But we have already seen how Louis Napoleon's background and his clumsy and unprepossessing appearance fooled many who wanted to use him in 1848 and 1849, and Victor Hugo's condemnation written in 1852 may be equally mistaken.

THE FLOURISHING OF THE SECOND EMPIRE: THE 1850s

Immediately the Second Empire was proclaimed, Napoleon III faced a problem of reconciling different expectations. Tsar Alexander I took exception to a Bonapartist revival, especially Napoleon III's claim to be the third when Russia had not recognised any Napoleon II, and it was essential for Napoleon III to make it quite clear that 'the Empire is peace' (as he said at Bordeaux in October 1852) to avoid reawakening a hostile European coalition. But many of his supporters at home wanted to see the revival of French glory and a forceful foreign policy which would assert French power in Europe after the humiliations piled upon her since 1815. Additionally, the prestige of the army had been restored after its role in the 1851 coup. How might the public and the army be satisfied without arousing the hostility of Europe?

Prosperity at home

'Bread and circuses' was the formula of Imperial Rome to keep the populace quiet, and parallels may be drawn with Napoleon III's technique. Political liberty was at a minimum, with press controls, police surveillance, opponents exiled, and elections manipulated through the prefects and mayors. To compensate for this the benefits of the regime needed to be tangible in economic well-being, with foreign policy and other spectacles providing the 'circuses'.

The ideas in Napoleon III's earlier pamphlets were put into practice in the 1850s. Public works programmes were funded, and an ingenious scheme which guaranteed a return for investors in railway building produced a tenfold increase in the system between 1848 and 1870. By the end of the Second Empire, France had a railway network which was not so far behind Britain's, a considerable achievement from a lower starting-point. Railways, and the development of harbours, boosted industry, trade and employment, which in turn increased the spending power of the consumer market. The Paris exhibition of 1855 (following the fashion set by the Crystal Palace exhibition of 1851) and the Suez Canal project (1859–69) reflected the confident progress of French industry, design and investment.

Perhaps the most spectacular project was the rebuilding of Paris under Baron Haussmann (who became Prefect of Paris in 1853), whose energy and questionable financial methods powered through slum-clearance schemes and established the pattern of broad boulevards, radiating from central points which is to be seen today (see Figure 11.1). Haussmann in some ways typifies the self-advertising monied brashness which became the unacceptable face of capitalism in the Second Empire. Vast employment was provided for workers from far afield who built the new apartment and office blocks just as the slum clearance schemes were making affordable housing increasingly scarce for the working class, the famous drains were built not for sewerage (which was still carted away by night) but for rainwater, and the fund raising was conducted with so little regard for the law that Haussmann was lucky to keep his post until 1870, when he was finally forced into luxurious retirement. Successful though the change was, it was not deep; one block behind many of the new buildings, the slums remained.

Funding for many of these projects came from new sources. The government itself raised loans quite effectively outside the banking system. The Crédit Foncier raised money and made loans for urban development, but the most important innovation was the Crédit Mobilier. This bank was set up by the Péreire brothers, whose close friendship with Napoleon III showed the way private enterprise and the Second Empire operated in mutual support. The Crédit Mobilier found a whole new source of funds by paying interest on the savings of small investors, and it prospered by taking more risks with its lending. In both respects it was quite different from the elite and cautious banking of houses such as the Rothschilds', but the whole venture relied upon economic confidence continuing; when projects it had lent to ran into difficulties and savers felt their savings were at risk, the glittering growth and prosperity looked skin deep. The old-fashioned banking houses felt justified in their caution when the Crédit Mobilier failed in 1867, but of course by then it had achieved much.

Saint-Simonism and the ideas in Napoleon III's own pamphlets may be seen in these economic changes, but there is a patchiness about them which shows that there was not a detailed economic plan. The structure of the economy was not transformed, and although the infrastructure was improved both industrial and agricultural productivity developed only slowly. Although free trade was an economic and moral cause in which Napoleon III believed, bourgeois producers and manufacturers preferred to have their domestic markets protected from British competition and the Legislative Body opposed tariff reduction in 1856. Napoleon III instead concluded a tariff-reduction deal with Britain in 1860 (the Cobden–Chevalier agreement) which upset many who felt their interests would be harmed, but the effects were less clear-cut and on balance it seems that trade may have been encouraged. However, the affair was typical of how the Second Empire tended to operate piecemeal, pleasing some supporters while upsetting other interests, its initiatives (some good, some

11.1 Haussmann's rebuilding of Paris involved pulling down narrow, winding streets of old buildings. The rebuilding of the Rue Soufflot in 1876. Engraving by Stablo after Chegaray

Source: © Collection Viollet, Paris

bad) stopping short of being a tightly planned progression.

The destruction of the 1815 settlement

Napoleon III's supporters included Orleanists, former Legitimists who had given up any hope of a monarchical restoration, old Bonapartists, and eventually a handful of Republicans – Ollivier came across in the 1860s once he saw the Second Empire might move towards a liberal parliamentary regime. There was no Bonapartist party as such after 1851 – Napoleon III saw parties as being divisive factions. In terms of economic groups, the regime's most reliable supporters were the peasantry (out of loyalty to a legend many had grown up with), and the bourgeoisie, out of con-

cern for order and prosperity; the urban working class showed a growing republican sympathy by the 1860s. The Second Empire found new men to be its prefects, mayors and officials regardless of their background (although wealth was an important qualification); such men did not need to be Bonapartists, but they had to accept the regime wholeheartedly. In this way the Second Empire tried to grow its roots as widely as possible. For instance, as we have seen in 1849–50 with the expedition to Rome, Louis Napoleon made an appeal to Catholic sentiment as a way of attracting a broad support within France.

Continuing with this seems to have been his primary motive for getting the Ottoman empire to give the Catholic Church control of the Holy Places in Palestine. The immediate consequences in 1852 and 1853 were to provoke counter-claims from Russia on behalf of the Orthodox Church. To be facing further Tsarist anger helped Napoleon III's standing with the liberals at home, and drew France closer to Britain and Austria, who both feared Russian intervention in the Ottoman empire. But there was little calculation or foresight in this manoeuvre, and Napoleon III seemed unable to control the slide towards war which resulted (see extract E (i)). Despite claiming in 1852 that 'the Empire is peace', war broke out in March 1854 with the Crimea as the unlikely ground for a trial of strength between the British and French allies of Turkey on the one hand, and Russia on the other. The campaign was marked by blunder and inefficiency on all sides, but the French army proved itself (despite one British general, presumably of the Waterloo era, persisting in referring to the Russian enemy as 'the French'). Once Sebastopol fell in September 1855 it was possible for the western powers to end the war, and the new Tsar Alexander II was anxious to withdraw and remodel his forces. Paris became the setting for the peace conference in 1856, which was of spectacular importance for showing the French public that Napoleon III had made the Second Empire the hub of European diplomacy, broken the coalition of Waterloo and humbled the Russian empire.

Supporting Italian nationalism

The way was clear for a new phase in Napoleon III's foreign policy, and friendship with Russia developed, along with investment. More important, Napoleon III was now able to take up the theme of a Europe of nationalities which the St Helena period had approved. National self-determination could be supported in Italy, and the Austrian empire's hold there might be challenged without fear of provoking an anti-French coalition. Napoleon III had a long-standing fascination for the idea of an Italian nation-state, seeing its origins in his uncle's campaigns in northern Italy, but the restoration of Pope Pius IX in 1849 by French troops had badly wounded his standing in Italian eyes. When Orsini tried to assassinate him in 1858 for abandoning the cause, it strangely rekindled Napoleon III's interest especially if France might

gain Nice and Savoy as the price of her involvement against Austria.

The domestic benefit of a successful campaign against Austria, on behalf of Italian self-determination, with some territorial gain was intoxicating to Napoleon III. He negotiated with a conspirator's love of secrecy with Cavour, the artful Prime Minister of Piedmont, at Plombières in July 1858. A secret treaty followed in January 1859, with Nice now included with Savoy as the price for French support, and in March Russia promised France that she would remain neutral (see Chapter 12). Was Napoleon III carried away with the excitement of the adventure? At Plombières he was ready to forget Nice as part of the price (see extract E (ii)), and risk that Prussia would exploit France's distraction by moves in the Rhineland. Most seriously he appeared to ignore the fact that the Pope would oppose the kind of Italian state which would result. It seems unlikely that Napoleon III actually calculated that he was exchanging the support of the Catholic faithful at home for liberal and nationalist opinion instead, but that was to be the outcome.

There was a short but costly war with Austria in the summer of 1859, and after the bloody victories at Magenta and Solferino (in June), Napoleon III negotiated peace at Villafranca on 11 July. Napoleon III had been upset by the bloodshed (Magenta gave its name to a bloody crimson colour), and he had become concerned by Prussia's manoeuvres and the threat to the Pope's control of the Papal States, so he abandoned the deal with Piedmont prematurely. The outcome, detailed in Chapter 12, left Venetia in Austrian hands, removed eastern Romagna from the Pope's control, and enlarged Piedmont, but both Italian nationalists and French Catholics felt badly let down by Napoleon III. France had not obtained Nice or Savoy and her policy seemed a muddled collection of half-measures.

It is often said that to govern is to choose, and only belatedly did Napoleon III make his choice. The Pope's rule of the Papal States was attacked in a pamphlet which appeared in France, improved relations with Austria were abandoned, and in January 1860 Napoleon III came to terms with Cavour and accepted the expansion of Piedmont in return for Nice and Savoy. These territorial changes were confirmed by plebiscite, easily arranged to polish up a widely acceptable alteration. But even now Napoleon III had not made a decisive change. French troops remained in the city of Rome to protect the Pope until 1864, and returned in 1867. Not only was this a futile attempt to conciliate Catholic opinion at home, but also it damaged French relations with the newly united Kingdom of Italy created under Victor Emmanuel II in 1861.

The 1850s were years of optimism for the Second Empire, symbolised by Napoleon's marriage to the beautiful Spanish Countess Eugénie in 1853, the lively gaiety of the court, and birth of the Prince Imperial. But J.P.T. Bury is not alone in seeing 1860 as the turning-point in the fortunes of the regime (J.P.T. Bury, *France 1814–1940*, London, Methuen, 1985, p. 96). Relations with the Catholic Church became distant, a trend confirmed by Victor Duruy's secular reforms to the educational system in the 1860s. Commercial interests were shaken by the Cobden–Chevalier agreement. Enticing liberal support as an expedient or as part of a principled evolution towards a 'Liberal Empire' would prove difficult, not least because the Empress was a traditionalist and Catholic and so many senior ministers and officials disliked the idea of giving the legislature more authority and the people more political liberty. Had Napoleon III left choosing his policy too late to control the events which now began to control him?

FAILURE OR FULFILMENT: 1860–70

The path of reform

In 1859 an amnesty released some political prisoners, and in 1860 press controls were eased. In 1861 two constitutional amendments were announced allowing the publication of debates in the Legislative Body (provided they were published in full) and for the budget to be voted in sections (see extract B (ii)). Coming so long after the establishment of the Second Empire, but so soon after Catholic criticism of the policy in Italy, these modest concessions seemed to be gestures of expediency and not the beginning of a process which would crown the Second Empire with liberty. Social reforms took place, and working class support was cultivated by legalising peaceful strikes, to the dismay of bourgeois employers, and by permitting trades unions in 1868. Toleration was shown to working class demands (see extract D).

Although liberalism as policy or design may well be questioned, it is clear that Napoleon III's attitude permitted such developments which were part of what Bury calls his 'idealistic humanitarianism'; Émile de Girardin commented: 'If surnames were given to Princes, Napoleon would be called Napoleon the well-meaning' (Bury, *France*, p. 92). Certainly to dismiss these changes, and the constitutional reforms which followed in 1867 and 1870, as expedients to stave off criticism would be to miss an important characteristic of the Second Empire.

If the changes were mere expedients, they failed to conciliate republicanism. Five Republican deputies (including Émile Ollivier) were elected in 1857, and this number grew to fifteen in 1863 despite the electoral arrangements which helped government candidates. Republicanism proved a durable and attractive cause in the big cities. There were more moderate calls for reform. In 1864 the 'Third Party' which gathered around Thiers supported the call for 'necessary reforms' which included greater freedom for the press and the individual, and ministerial responsibility to the Legislative Body. Buffet's proposal in 1866 for a constitutional amendment giving the Legislative Body more powers attracted sixty votes.

Napoleon III's half-brother, the Duc de Morny, was the key supporter for liberal changes and as President of the Legislative Body his political skills were crucial. Things became more difficult after his untimely death in 1865, and soon afterwards the Emperor's failing health (he suffered bouts of great pain from gall-stones) made it more difficult for him to press for further change against the wishes of the Empress. The devoted Persigny was in retirement, and the Empire increasingly was run by civil servants and conservatives. One such was Rouher, whose authority as Minister between 1866 and 1869 earned him the nick-name 'the Vice-Emperor'. Consequently, change appeared to come piecemeal and reluctantly as concessions made following government failures.

Foreign policy failures

In 1863 the Poles rose in revolt against Tsar Alexander II's rule. Despite the fact that Russia was France's chief ally since the Crimea, and there was no prospect of French forces crossing Prussian or Austrian territory to help the Poles, Napoleon III chose to make a noisy protest upholding the national self-determination of the Poles. It was no mere gesture, and the Russian alliance was destroyed. But French pressure was doomed to fail and both Catholic (Poland was a Catholic country) and liberal sentiment in France was bound to feel the humiliation keenly.

In fact Bismarck gained from Napoleon III's mistake, for Prussia made a point of siding with Russia during the repression of Poland. This was the first of a series of moves which ultimately left France isolated and at war with Prussia and the North German Confederation in 1870. Chapter 12 explains the details of Bismarck's policy and the unification of Germany, and our concern here is to register Napoleon III's unhappy involvement and the consequences for the Second Empire.

In informal conversations at Biarritz in 1865, Bismarck sounded Napoleon III out on his attitude should Prussia come to war with the Austrian Empire in the cause of German unification. No treaty was signed, but Napoleon III showed that he was more interested in removing Habsburg control from Venetia, and transferring this state to Italy, than he was in protecting Austria against a challenge from Prussia.

Was Napoleon III negligent in abandoning the traditional French fear of a united Germany? Was he perhaps too fond of the nationality principle and in awe of Prussia? While these considerations may have influenced his policy, it must be remembered that few people expected Prussia to achieve the speedy and decisive victory against the might of the Habsburg empire that she did in July 1866, and Napoleon III could feel confident in 1865 that he was keeping his options open at Biarritz. A stalemate between Austria and Prussia would permit French mediation and the acquisition of Luxembourg for France and Venetia for Italy, with the Paris of the Second Empire in a central role again (see also extract E (iii)). Two developments confirm these aims. First, Napoleon III encouraged Italy to accept the secret treaty with Prussia in 1866 which would give her Venetia if she launched war on Austria from the south when Prussia did in the north, while shortly afterwards he made room for mediation by promising Austria that he would discourage Italy from such conflict. Second, in August 1866 he secretly demanded Bismarck's approval for France taking possession of Luxembourg and Belgium, following up the claim on Belgium in 1867 with a draft treaty. But it was hopelessly ill-timed, coming after Prussia's decisive defeat of Austria at Sadowa, and Bismarck contemptuously dismissed the claim for payment after the event as a 'hotel-keeper's bill' – he kept the draft and published it in 1870 to isolate France. The Second Empire had miscalculated and had been outmanoeuvred. The remaining states of south Germany looked to her to protect them against Prussia, but it was clear to many French people that Prussia after Sadowa was a formidable potential adversary now.

The Mexican adventure

Colonial gains were made outside Europe. The conquest of Algeria was completed in the late 1850s, but brought little prestige for the Empire and commercial competition upset some interests. France extended her hold in Senegal, established a claim in Madagascar, joined Britain in an expedition to Peking in 1859–60, and established French interests in the Levant by an expedition into Syria in 1860. By the early 1860s French control was established in Saigon (captured in 1859), Cochin China and Cambodia. Important though these gains were, they attracted little enthusiasm at home. Napoleon III hoped the Mexican campaign would be different, and would distract attention from the disappointments experienced in Italy by 1861.

Mexico was a former Spanish colony, vast and with considerable economic potential, but lapsed into chaos. With the United States preoccupied with civil war, the new Republican government under Juárez became vulnerable to a joint expedition by France, Britain and Spain to recover debts. But with an opportunism typical of him, Napoleon III made bigger plans. By 1862 France was on her own in Mexico, determined to create a Latin Catholic empire under the Habsburg Archduke Maximilian and to overthrow Juárez's anticlerical regime. The Empress Eugénie was enthusiastic, the good opinion of Catholics would be restored, and commercial benefits would follow in Latin America to rival the Anglo-Saxon wealth of the north. It went horribly wrong. At vast cost France deployed some 38,000 troops, losing 6,000, and the Mexican republican cause was boosted ferociously by the foreign invasion. Once the American civil war ended and Prussia threatened in Europe in 1866, France had no option but to withdraw. Maximilian was abandoned to his fate; he was eventually caught and shot in 1867 (see Figure 11.2). With some justice Manet's painting in the National Gallery shows the firing squad in French uniforms. An ill-planned and opportunistic adventure, invented largely to win support at home, had backfired badly and darkened the prestige of the Second Empire beyond repair.

The Liberal Empire

The Second Empire's failures in Mexico and on the Rhine, and the economic recession which took

11.2 The execution of Maximilian of Mexico, June 1867. Painted by Manet (Louvre)

Photo: © BBC Hulton Picture Library

hold in 1867, prompted concessions at home. As McMillan points out, Napoleon III instinctively 'tried to conciliate opponents rather than crush them' (McMillan, *Napoleon III*, p. 57). In response to the reform programme advanced by the 'Third Party', in 1867 the Legislative Body was given the power to table questions for ministers, called interpellations (see extract B (iv)), and in 1868 the press was allowed greater licence to criticise. The legitimacy of the regime was again scrutinised because of the 1851 coup. The Legislative Body became increasingly assertive, in 1867 blocking spending to expand the army reserve in an ill-timed bid to economise, and forcing Rouher to promise that French troops would never again be withdrawn from Rome.

The elections of May 1869 showed mounting opposition to the regime in the towns, while the peasantry remained substantially loyal. Although republicanism was in evidence, it was the moderate demands of some 116 deputies of the 'Third Party' for ministerial responsibility which were the most significant. Napoleon III did not meet these demands wholeheartedly to begin with, although he made some concessions. Illness damaged his concentration and energy, and he got no support from the court circles, but his reluctance to move to parliamentary government at this point may indicate that the 'Liberal Empire' of 1870 was more an expedient to appease than an attitude of mind.

In January 1870 Napoleon III asked Émile Ollivier (one of the five Republican deputies of 1857) to replace Rouher and establish a government which would answer to the Legislative Body as well as to the Emperor. The new constitution appeared in May 1870 (see extract B (v)) and was subjected to the traditional device of approval by plebiscite. Two ministers resigned over this extra-parliamentary procedure, but it worked like a charm. Over 7 million approved the liberal changes made since 1860, particularly those just announced, and only 1.5 million opposed the well-phrased question. It seemed that the Second Empire had reinvented itself and regained the popularity it had claimed in 1851, but it may be suggested that the approval was really for launching a new regime rather than for reconditioning the old one.

War with Prussia

War ended the Second Empire before the real nature of the liberal reforms could be seen, but by making ministers more open to parliamentary pressures these changes opened the way for France to enter a fatal conflict with ill-judged enthusiasm.

Chapter 13 details Bismarck's diplomacy. He was opportunistic in using the Hohenzollern candidature of Leopold for the Spanish throne to incite French protests and persuade the southern German states that Prussian protection was desirable. The whole affair was really such an unlikely pathway to war that we need to investigate how it was that France actually declared war on Prussia on 19 July 1870 *after* Leopold had turned down the Spanish invitation to take up the throne.

France had become highly sensitive to Prussian expansion since the spectacular defeat of Austria in 1866. Anti-Prussian feeling ran high, especially among those who realised the Emperor had been short-changed for his neutrality then, emerging with nothing to show from the Biarritz conversations in 1865 and his interest in Luxembourg and Belgium. Furthermore, in trying to install a member of the Prussian Royal family on the throne of Spain, where France had intervened in the 1820s, was not merely 'encirclement' to French opinion but clear evidence of Prussia's arrogance and cheek in reaching over France to influence the politics of a country with which she had no common border. In addition to all this, the anti-Prussian attitude of the Empress Eugénie, as a Spanish Catholic, was incited to fury by the very idea of Prussian Protestant influence in her homeland, and she quickly came to personify the war party in Paris.

On 12 July Leopold withdrew from the candidacy, following discreet pressure from King William of Prussia in response to a French request, but tempers in France were not to be so easily cooled. Gramont, the anti-Prussian Foreign Minister, caught the public mood and focused it. The French ambassador was instructed to obtain a formal guarantee from William (who was at Ems) that the matter would not be renewed. The King's tactful rejection of this unsubtle request became the basis for Bismarck's published version of 'the Ems telegram', making the French demand appear overbearing and the King's response humiliating to France.

The rest followed automatically. Amidst great patriotic enthusiasm which could easily be mistaken for a rebirth of Imperial confidence, France declared war. Troops assembled and such was the buoyancy of mood that the slogan became 'To Berlin' and the army was issued with maps of Germany only. But France had no allies; Britain and Belgium had been horrified when Bismarck produced the French draft treaty to absorb Belgium, Italy was more interested in getting France to withdraw from Rome than in helping her, and neither Austria nor Russia had any interest in helping by confronting Prussia. Worse still for France was the well-planned efficiency of the German mobilisation; in eighteen days, Prussia had 380,000 troops at the front, whereas French forces numbered at the most 250,000 in badly supplied confusion. Alsace and most of Lorraine fell to the invader during the first part of August, and the gallant but outmanoeuvred French forces had to requisition school maps to fight on their own soil. The mood in Paris became grim, and the Emperor, hunched up with pain, departed to lead his soldiers and left the government in the hands of the Empress. Ollivier, who had entered the war 'with a light heart', resigned; the ministry had failed to modify public enthusiasm for the war and committed the dreadful mistake of going to war 'on a mere point of etiquette' as the *Illustrated London News* saw it (cited in R. Christiansen, *Tales of the New Babylon: Paris 1869–1875*, London, Minerva, 1996, p. 139). A new ministry under General Palikao followed a cautious policy, avoiding confrontation with the radical opponents of the Second Empire. Support evaporated quickly, the Empress became more unpopular than ever, and military reverses destroyed the regime's own confidence.

With Metz blockaded by 20 August, everything depended upon MacMahon's force and the outcome of the battle on the Belgian frontier. On 2 September the Emperor was captured at Sedan, even his obvious attempt to die in battle at the head of his troops having failed. MacMahon's army of 87,000 (including thirty-nine generals) surrendered. Napoleon met with Bismarck at a roadside cottage, and later with King William, but there was little prospect of ending the struggle at this stage; Prussia wanted to annex Alsace-Lorraine and to establish the German empire through the total defeat of France (the empire was proclaimed at Versailles in January 1871) not merely after a Sadowa-type trial of strength (see Chapter 13). But the Second Empire gave up the struggle now. The Empress Eugénie fled Paris in an American dentist's carriage, and forgot to thank the English aristocrat who took her across a squally Channel in his yacht. Napoleon joined her and the Prince Imperial in England the next year. He died in 1873. In France the Third Republic was proclaimed on 4 September 1870 and continued the war with Prussia, unsuccessfully as we shall see.

Assessment

The speed with which the Second Empire collapsed suggests that its real enthusiasts were few and that its support was lightly rooted as acceptance only. This should not detract from the great changes which had occurred in France since 1848. The economy had grown, the small investor had been discovered, the infrastructure had developed, and political stability had been imposed sufficiently effectively to allow important reform to take place in the end without a revolutionary explosion. The regime of Napoleon III should be given due credit for its role. It was not a tyranny, but it was certainly authoritarian. Yet it had the capacity to change, in marked contrast to the inflexibility shown by the restored Bourbon regime or the July Monarchy as they aged.

The flexibility of the Second Empire owed much to Napoleon's own character and ideas; opportunist that he was, he was inspired by certain ideals – his sense of destiny, his support for the nationality principle, his humanitarianism. But his uncle famously said that it was all in the execution, and here the nephew earned the reputation of a buffoon. His escapades at Strasbourg and Boulogne, the sentimentality he showed over the coup of 1851, the lack of resolve which prompted him to back out of the Italian campaign, the miscalculation which led him into Mexico, and the muddled incompetence of his dealings with Bismarck all seem to support the judgement of Victor Hugo that he was 'Napoleon the Little'. While the 'Liberal Empire' served as a belated expedient to appease criticism in the wake of so many failures, it was not the response of a tyrant, nor was the step towards parliamentary government an obvious one for a mere buffoon to take.

SECTION B – SOURCES

LIBERAL AT HOME AND ABROAD?

Louis Napoleon Bonaparte had great confidence that it was his destiny to rule France and continue the development of his uncle's Empire. This sense of destiny led him to make two attempts to overthrow Louis Philippe's government, in 1836 and 1840, which failed with so many touches of farce that many of his contemporaries looked on him as a joke. However, he kept his faith and defended himself, for example in extract A. Once Louis Philippe's July Monarchy had fallen and Louis Napoleon had been elected President of the Second Republic (in December 1848) he had the opportunity to fulfil his destiny, and staged a *coup d'état* in December 1851. Contemporaries like Victor Hugo contrasted him with his 'Great' uncle, and the republican Gambetta condemned Louis Napoleon's regime for the bloodshed in the coup (see extract C). Louis Napoleon, or Napoleon III as he called himself from December 1852, claimed that the Second Empire was a continuation of the first Napoleonic Empire (see extract B (i)) and he appeared to want the constitution to evolve along the lines suggested by the changes Napoleon I had introduced during the One Hundred Days. During the Second Empire there were a series of amendments to the 1852 constitution (see extracts B (ii–v)) which suggested that the progress towards the so-called 'Liberal Empire' of 1870 was planned rather than conceded due to failures and weakness. This is the heart of the debate about Napoleon III's regime.

There are other points of reference in the debate about Napoleon's aims and liberalism. The regime operated an elaborate system for getting the 'official candidates' elected to the Legislative Body and to other positions. Controls placed on political activity were part of this system, but they do not

seem to have been particularly powerful, as extract D indicates, but they caused protest and opposition, as extract C illustrates. Foreign policy has a double importance in the debate about how liberal the Second Empire was. First, in confronting Russia in the Crimea in alliance with 'liberal' Britain (extract E (i)), and in supporting Italian national self-determination against Habsburg opposition, Napoleon could claim to be following liberal principles in foreign policy. On the other hand, foreign policy failures such as the expedition to Mexico, the half-hearted pursuit of Nice and Savoy in return for fighting Austria alongside Piedmont (extract E (ii)), and above all the failure to anticipate the threat to France from Bismarck's unification of Germany (extract E (iii)) helped to force the regime into making political concessions at home. Would the Second Empire have moved towards the 'Liberal Empire' if foreign policy had proved triumphant, any more than Napoleon I's Empire had done?

A From Louis Napoleon's letter to a childhood friend, London 1847

In all my adventures, I have been guided by a single principle. I believe that, from time to time, providential men are born, in whose hands the destinies of a country are inevitably to be entrusted. I further believe that I am such a man. . . . if I am right, Providence will see to it that I fulfil my mission.

(C. Seignobos, 'The magic of a name', 1921, in S. Osgood (ed.) *Napoleon III*, Boston, MA, D.C. Heath, 1965, p. 15)

B The changing constitution

(i) From the constitutional proclamation, 14 January 1852

since France makes progress in the last fifty years in virtue alone of the administrative, military, judicial, religious and financial organisation of the Consulate and Empire, why should we not also adopt the political institutions of the epoch? . . .

. . . our present state of society is nought else than France regenerate by the revolution of '89, and organised by the Emperor. . . .

The Emperor [Napoleon I] said to the Council of State: 'A constitution is the work of time: it is impossible to leave in it too large a margin for ameliorations.' Accordingly, the present Constitution has only settled that which it was impossible to leave uncertain. It has not shut up within insurmountable barriers the destinies of a great people. It has left for change a margin sufficiently large to allow in great crises other means of safety than the disastrous expedient of revolution.

(*The Political and Historical Works of Louis Napoleon Bonaparte*, vol. 1, London, 1852, pp. 146–52, cited in G.A. Kertesz (ed.) *Documents in the Political History of the European Continent, 1815–1939*, Oxford University Press, 1968, pp. 162–64)

(ii) From 2 February 1861 amendment to article 42 of the Constitution

The debates in the sessions of the Senate and the Legislative Body shall be taken down in shorthand and inserted, in full, in the official gazette of the following day.

(iii) From 31 December 1861 amendment to articles 4 and 12 of the Senatus Consultum of 25 December 1852

The estimates of expenditure shall be presented to the Legislative Body set out in sections. . . . The estimates of each ministry shall be voted by sections.

(iv) From 19 January 1867 Imperial Decree

1 Members of the Senate and Legislative Body may address interpellations to the Government.
2 All requests for interpellations must be in writing and signed by at least five members.

(v) From 21 May 1870 proclamation of the new constitution after the plebiscite

The Senate and Legislative Body as well as the Emperor now have the initiative in introducing legislation;
   A Council of Ministers is established; the ministers are responsible; they may be members of the Senate or the Legislative Body.

(F-A. Hélie, *Les Constitutions de la France*, Paris, 1880, cited in Kertesz (ed.) *Documents in the Political History of the European Continent, 1815–1939*, pp. 166–69)

C Gambetta condemns the *coup d'état* of 1851

you have never dared to say: 'We will celebrate, we will put among the solemnities of France the 2nd of December as a national anniversary.' . . . there are only two anniversaries, the 18th Brumaire [Napoleon I's seizure of power] and the 2nd December, which have never been placed among the ranks of the festivals of birth, because you know if you wanted to put them there they would be repulsed by a universal conscience. . . . it will be the anniversary of our dead until the day when this country, once again its master, will impose a great national expiation on you in the name of liberty, equality, and fraternity.

(E. Ollivier, *L'Empire Libéral*, vol. 11, Paris, 1895–1915, pp. 94–95, cited in W.H.C. Smith, *Second Empire and Commune: France 1848–1871*, London, Longman, 1985, p. 77)

D Varlin, founder of the Consumers' Cooperative, on the toleration of societies in January 1870

All our societies are outside the law. They only exist because the administration tolerates them. But this tolerance has become such a habit, and is now so deeply engrained in people's behaviour that it would be impossible for the administration to reverse it. We claim to enjoy the natural right of association. For our General Assembly meetings we simply inform the prefect of police at least twenty-four hours beforehand. He sends a policeman along who makes his report, but that doesn't stop us saying whatever we want to say.

(cited in A. Rifkin and R. Thomas (eds) *Voices of the People*, London, Routledge and Kegan Paul, 1988, p. 196)

E Louis Napoleon's diplomacy

(i) From Napoleon III's letter to Tsar Nicholas I, 24 January 1854

If Your Majesty desires as much as I do to find a peaceful solution, what could be simpler than to declare that an armistice will be signed today [between Russia and the Ottoman empire], that diplomatic negotiations will be resumed. . . . In this way the Russian troops would evacuate the Principalities and our squadrons would evacuate the Black Sea.

(Napoleon III, *Oeuvres*, Paris, 1869, pp. 373–74, cited in Smith, *Second Empire and Commune: France 1848–1871*, p. 80)

(ii) From Ollivier's account of the meeting at Plombières between Napoleon III and Cavour, July 1858

This enlargement of Piedmont would be balanced by the cession of Savoy to France. The Emperor asked for Nice as well, but Cavour objected and the matter was left in suspense. The Emperor, stroking his moustache, said this was for him a 'secondary question' which one would have time to think about later.

(Ollivier, *L'Empire Libéral*, vol. 3, pp. 489–91, cited in Smith, *Second Empire and Commune: France 1848–1871*, p. 82)

(iii) From Napoleon III's letter to King William of Prussia, 7 March 1866

If serious events should arise in Germany, my formal intention is to observe neutrality, meanwhile preserving the friendly relations which have for long existed between us. Later, if extraordinary circumstances should alter the balance of Europe, I should ask permission to examine the new bases with your Majesty in order to secure the interests of my country.

(in Sir V. Wellesley and R. Sencourt, *Conversations with Napoleon III*, London, 1934, p. 246, cited in Smith, *Second Empire and Commune: France 1848–1871* p. 83)

F From J. Garland's reassessment of Napoleon III

What did he give to France? He gave France her railway network, . . . broad boulevards . . . the Crédit Mobilier. . . . He launched France into the Industrial Revolution. . . . He founded the late nineteenth century French colonial empire . . . he realised the folly of antagonising Britain and strove, with some success, to keep on friendly terms with her. He fostered and supported the national principle . . . unlike his uncle, he preferred diplomacy by congress to diplomacy by war. In every major international crisis of the 1850s and 1860s Napoleon III's opening gambit was to propose a meeting of the powers to find a way out. . . . And three months before his regime collapsed he submitted to the French people his new 'liberal empire', which they endorsed. . . .

. . . He had made many mistakes [by 1870]: the Mexican gamble, his apparently contradictory policies on Italy. . . . But the lasting achievements of his rule would appear to be at the very least on a par with those of his glorious uncle. . . . Yet, for the French nation, the nephew failed to live up to the standards of the uncle. . . . Because of his name he is fated to be compared only with Napoleon I; and after Sedan there was for most Frenchmen and many others just no comparison. The tragedy of Napoleon III is that without his name he would never have been able to achieve supreme power in France, and yet because of that same name he will forever be condemned to having his achievements judged by a false and unreal standard. The genius of Louis Napoleon hangs over the Paris he built, but his bones will remain in Britain.

(J. Garland, 'Is there a case for Napoleon III?', *History Review*, 21, March 1995, p. 35)

Questions

1 Explain the meaning of this description of the constitution in extract B (i): 'It has left for change a margin sufficiently large to allow in great crises other means of safety than the disastrous expedient of revolution.'

2 To what extent do extracts A and B (i–v) show that progress towards the Liberal Empire was always Louis Napoleon's aim?

3 How useful is the evidence in extracts C and D for showing the real nature of the Second Empire?

4 Consider extracts E (i–iii), together with extract D in Chapter 12. Does the evidence show that Napoleon III's foreign policy failed to protect French national interests?

5 To what extent is Garland's judgement about the importance of Louis Napoleon's name in extract F supported by extracts A, B (i) and C?

6 Do you agree with Garland's evaluation of the achievements of Napoleon III's regime? Use your own knowledge and any relevant extracts in your answer.

Further reading

Modern works in English take a balanced view of the Second Empire, but the topic has created much controversy in the past. There is a good historiographical essay in Chapter 1 of J.F. McMillan, *Napoleon III* (London, Longman, 1995), while S.M. Osgood, *Napoleon III: Buffoon, Modern Dictator, or Sphinx* (Boston, MA, D.C. Heath, 1965) contains samples of an excellent range of writing, from Victor Hugo to Theodore Zeldin. McMillan's study is clear and very helpful, but for those seeking a more concise treatment, J.P.T. Bury's *France 1814–1940* (London, Methuen, 1985) and A. Cobban's *A History of Modern France*, vol. 2 (London, Penguin, 1970) remain unbeatable. A. Plessis, *The Rise and Fall of the Second Empire, 1852–77* (Cambridge University Press, 1985) provides substantial and scholarly analysis for the more ambitious. K. Randell, *France: Monarchy, Republic and Empire 1814–70* (London, Arnold, 1986) is clear and carefully structured to help with student essays, while W.H.C. Smith, *Second Empire and Commune: France 1848–71* (London, Longman, 1985) aims at a similar readership but provides more detail and documentary excerpts. J.M. Thompson, *Louis Napoleon and the Second Empire* (Oxford, Blackwell, 1980) was first published in the 1950s but it remains a scholarly and sympathetic study, while R. Christiansen, *Tales of the New Babylon: Paris 1869–75* (London, Minerva, 1996) provides a colourful wealth of anecdote.

Useful documentary material may be found in G.A. Kertesz (ed.) *Documents in the Political History of the European Continent, 1815–1939* (Oxford University Press, 1968), F-G. Dreyfus and R. Marx (eds) *Documents d'histoire contemporaine*, vol. 2, 1851–1971 (Paris, Librairie Armand Colin, 1964), and in W.H.C. Smith's work mentioned above, while useful but more anecdotal material appears in A. Rifkin and R. Thomas (eds) *Voices of the People* (London, Routledge and Kegan Paul, 1988) and R. Christiansen's work (see above).

• CHAPTER TWELVE •

The Unification of Italy, 1849–71

• CONTENTS •

Key dates

SECTION A

The Nationalist Movement prior to 1860

Italian unification, 1850–61

Remaining problems

SECTION B – SOURCES

The roles of Mazzini and Cavour in the making of Italy

Key dates

1849	23 May	Battle of Novara, defeat of Piedmont; abdication of Charles Albert, succeeded by Victor Emmanuel II
	4 July	French troops enter Rome
	28 Aug.	Surrender of Venice to Austrians
1852	4 Nov.	Cavour becomes Prime Minister of Piedmont
1855	26 Jan.	Piedmont enters Crimean war on side of Britain and France
1856	25 Feb.–16 April	Paris Peace Congress to end Crimean war
1857	July	Landing by Pisacane at Sapri
	August	Founding of National Society by La Farina and others
1858	14 Jan.	Orsini's attempt to assassinate Napoleon III
	July 20	Meeting between Cavour and Napoleon III at Plombières
	Sept.	Marriage of Clotilde, daughter of Victor Emmanuel II, to Jerome Bonaparte
1859	Jan.	Secret treaty signed between France and Piedmont
	March.	Promise of Russian neutrality to Piedmont
	19 April	Austrian ultimatum to Piedmont
	April–June	War between Austria and Piedmont
	3 May	France joins Piedmont
	4 June	Battle of Magenta
	22 June	Battle of Solferino
1859	11 July	Treaty of Villafranca; Cavour's resignation
	Aug.–Nov.	Independent governments in Parma, Modena and Tuscany
1860	Jan.	Cavour returns to power
	12 March	Treaty between Cavour and Napoleon III; France to get Savoy and Nice in return for recognising accessions of Parma, Modena and Tuscany to Piedmont if approved by plebiscite

	March–April	Plebiscites held in Parma, Modena, Tuscany, Savoy and Nice
	2 April	Meeting of first 'Italian' parliament at Turin
	April	Rising in Sicily
	11 May	Landing of Garibaldi at Marsala in Sicily
	22 May	Fall of Palermo to Garibaldi
	18 Sept.	Battle of Castelfidardo
	21 Oct.	Plebiscite in Naples
	25 Oct.	Meeting between Garibaldi and Victor Emmanuel at Taena
	26 Oct.	Garibaldi proclaims Victor Emmanuel King of Italy
	4–5 Nov.	Plebiscite in Sicily
1862	29 Aug.	Garibaldi defeated at Aspromonte by Piedmont army
1864	Sept.	Convention with France; Italy promises not to attack Rome; Florence to be new capital; Syllabus of Errors proclaimed by Pius IX
1866	8 April	Treaty between Bismarck and La Marmora
	15 June	Prussia invades Saxony
	16 June	Italy declares war on Austria
	24 June	Battle of Custozza; Piedmont defeated by Austria
	3 July	Battle of Sadowa; Austria defeated by Prussia
	20 July	Battle of Lissa; Piedmontese navy defeated by Austria
	23 Aug.	Treaty of Prague; Venetia handed over to Prussia and then to Italy
1867	3 Nov.	Garibaldi defeated at Mentana
1870	19 July	Outbreak of Franco-Prussian war
	July	Papal Infallibility declared
	1 Sept.	Battle of Sedan
	5 Sept.	Proclamation of French Republic
	20 Sept.	Occupation of Rome
1871	2 July	Victor Emmanuel II takes up residence in the Quirinal Palace in Rome

SECTION A

THE NATIONALIST MOVEMENT PRIOR TO 1860

The legacy of 1848

Italy, it will be remembered, had been made a virtual province of the Habsburg empire in 1815. The two northern territories of Lombardy and Venetia were ruled directly from Vienna. Members of the Habsburg family were placed at the head of the Duchies of Parma, Modena and Tuscany. The Bourbon King Ferdinand I was restored to the kingdom of Naples and Sicily in 1815, but only on condition that he signed a permanent defensive alliance with Austria. The two remaining territories in the Italian peninsula, the kingdom of Piedmont (which also incorporated Savoy and the island of Sardinia) and the Papal States, while nominally independent, were linked by their shared Catholicism to the Habsburg empire, and conservative elements in both states continued to favour the Austrian connection.

Austrian rule had indeed been challenged in 1820, 1830, 1831 and much more seriously in 1848 (see p. 180). But with the defeat of Piedmont at the battles of Custozza (1848) and Novara (1849), the overthrow of the Roman Republic by French troops in 1849 and the surrender of Venice to Austrian troops also in 1849, it looked as if Italian unification was as far away as ever. The 1848 revolutions had not been a complete failure, however. As has already been noted the new regime in Piedmont gave a guarantee of basic civil rights, established religious toleration and provided for an elected parliament with powers over legislation and taxation. The new constitution, the *Statuto*, accepted by Charles Albert in March 1848 was to be the basis of the Italian constitution adopted in 1861, which lasted, in theory at any rate, until 1946.

The replacement of Charles Albert by Victor Emmanuel II brought to the throne a man now sympathetic to Italian unification who was prepared to face the antagonism of the Papacy. While the King still possessed considerable executive powers, including command of the army, because legislation and taxation now required the consent of parliament this meant that he had to appoint ministers who could command a majority there.

Another significant consequence of the 1848 revolutions was the experience of the Roman Republic. Even though this had lasted only from November 1848 to July 1849 a significant precedent had been established. While in one sense the setting up of the Republic and the flight of the Pope meant that the papal influence would now be exerted against rather than for a united Italy, the relative success of Republican rule and the cooperation established between Mazzini and Garibaldi proved a source of inspiration to Italian patriots everywhere and encouraged them to keep the flame burning.

In the 1850s there were, too, significant shifts in the international arena. The alliance of the three conservative eastern states, Austria, Prussia and Russia, had held up reasonably well in the 1848 revolutions, Russian troops assisting in the crushing of the Hungarian revolt. But the Crimean war (1854–56) did irrevocable damage to this alliance (see pp. 118–19). While Austria did not join Britain and France in attacking Russia, her neutral stance offended Russia. More significantly, Louis Napoleon's accession to power in France upset all previous calculations. For while he was committed to the defence of the Papacy by his need to keep the support of Catholics in France, he was sufficiently his uncle's heir to wish for territorial gains for France and military glory on the battlefield. He shared too the belief in nationality which Napoleon I had somewhat belatedly advanced on St Helena. As a young man Napoleon III had participated in a rebellion in the Romagna in 1831 and he continued to have a sentimental attachment to the idea of a united Italy. The events of the 1830s and 1848 had made it clear to most, if not all Italians, that Italy could not overcome Austrian rule unaided. From 1852 onwards there was now a vital potential source of support in Paris.

Possible scenarios for a united Italy

Four men are popularly credited with the achievement of Italian unification and their statues are to be seen all over Italy. They are Giuseppe Mazzini, Giuseppe Garibaldi, Count Camillo Cavour and

King Victor Emmanuel II of Piedmont. Each man had a different vision of the Italy he wished to see and the final outcome did not match any one of them. Thus in explaining the nature of the Italian state that came into existence in 1870, it is necessary to take into account both the ambitions of those who worked towards that goal and the play of events which determined the shape and structure of the new Italy.

Mazzini (1805–72) was above all the prophet of unification. He was born in Genoa, the son of a professor of pathology at Genoa university, it was his experiences as a student in that city which converted him to the vision of a united liberal republic which remained his constant objective. Mazzini's patriotism was not aggressive. He believed that the principle of nationality should be extended to all peoples and looked forward to the day when there would be a United States of Europe. As a good liberal he believed in a free press, civil rights and liberty of conscience. As a Democrat he believed in a wide franchise. 'The right to vote', he said, 'is a necessary part of political education'. He hoped that unification would be achieved through popular insurrection rather than through diplomacy and foreign support. Mazzini was never a socialist and quarreled fiercely with Marx on this issue. Nor was he anti-clerical, unlike Garibaldi, though his Catholicism was certainly unorthodox.

His main role in the unification of Italy was to spread the idea and make it popular. He kept up an enormous correspondence and personally edited and produced numerous publications, the best known of which were *Young Italy* (1831), *Italia del Populo* (1848) and *Friends of Italy* (1851), which was directed at an English audience. In 1831 he founded the association Young Italy which became the first organised Italian political party, with its own programme, subscriptions and a distribution system for its publications. When in exile in England, he tried to organise Italian émigrés into a National Italian Committee, based in London, in 1850. This later became the National party and its manifesto urged the principle of popular sovereignty in a democratic Europe. Though his weapon was the pen rather than the sword, Mazzini was quite ready to condone the use of violence and personally took part in several conspiracies, for one of which – an attempt to seize the arsenal in Genoa –

he was sentenced to transportation in 1857. Wrongly suspected of being involved in the Orsini bomb plot in 1858, he was sentenced to death *in absentia*, a sentence that was never revoked by Cavour, who disliked him intensely.

If Mazzini's main weapon was the pen, Garibaldi's was unquestionably the sword. Garibaldi (1807–82) was born in Nice in 1807 into a seafaring family. He ran away to sea himself in 1822 and by 1832 was skipper of a merchant ship trading in the Mediterranean. Attracted by Mazzini's ideas when he met him at Marseilles in 1832, he was involved in a plot against Charles Albert of Piedmont in 1834 and condemned to death. He took refuge in South America, fighting first for a separatist movement, the Rio Grande di Sul, against the newly established government of Brazil, and then for the government of Uruguay in a border struggle with Argentina. During this time he kept in touch with events in Italy, and news that a pope with the reputation of being a reformer, Pius IX, had come to the papal throne in 1846 persuaded him to return to Italy. He arrived at his birthplace, Nice, in June 1848 and played an active part in the 1848 revolution, both in Lombardy and the Papal States. Garibaldi was no less a supporter of a united Italy than Mazzini, but he differed from him in two important respects. Garibaldi had no time for the Catholic Church, apart from the handful of renegade priests and friars who joined his movement. He was also much readier than Mazzini to accept the need for foreign intervention, and hence the Piedmontese dynasty as monarchs of a united Italy. Garibaldi's natural magnetism won him support wherever he appeared. His personal bravery and shrewd military tactics enabled him to achieve astonishing success, even when greatly outnumbered by regular troops, as in the Sicilian campaign of 1860. But he was distrusted by conservative elements in Piedmont, who feared that his very successes might undermine the existing balance of power and wealth.

The third man, often seen as the real architect of a united Italy, was very different from the previous two. Count Camillo Cavour (1810–61) was born the younger son in a noble family. Destined for the army, he instead chose to travel widely and read extensively. In 1850 he was appointed Minister for Agriculture, Marine and Commerce in the

Piedmont government and two years later, on the strength of his proven ability, was made Prime Minister. Politically Cavour stood well to the right of both Garibaldi and Mazzini. He believed in a limited monarchy of the kind established in 1848, but had no wish to see the franchise extended. He was not opposed to Catholicism and wished to see 'a free Church in a free state', but he was sufficiently anti-clerical to introduce civil marriage and abolish the ecclesiastical courts in Piedmont. As a disciple of Adam Smith he believed firmly in the principle of free trade, and a large tariff free market was one of the attractions of a united Italy. How committed Cavour was to this goal is not easy to establish. He certainly wanted an end to Austrian rule in Lombardy and Venetia, and the fusion of those provinces with Piedmont. Whether he would have taken the initiative in seeking to include also the states of central and southern Italy, had others not pushed him in this direction, seems less likely. Unlike Mazzini, Cavour distrusted popular insurrection which could lead only too easily in his view to mob rule. Conversely, he had no reservations about using the weapon of diplomacy to achieve the expulsion of Austria from northern Italy and indeed made that his primary objective.

The fourth man who played a critical role was King Victor Emmanuel II (1820–78) who succeeded his father Charles Albert in 1849. Victor Emmanuel, according to the French ambassador in Turin, writing in 1852, 'does not like the existing constitution, nor does he like parliamentary liberties, nor a free press'. He had little option but to work with the constitution, however, and appointed able ministers, notably D'Azeglio and Cavour, whom he may have disliked but was still prepared to trust. He was more interested in hunting and amorous pursuits than in statecraft, but a British ambassador, Sir John Hudson, reported in 1861 that 'For a mere soldier and hunter he is rising into a politician'. As a fellow soldier, he struck up a warm rapport with Garibaldi that was of vital importance at critical moments.

In 1849 it was far from clear what form a united Italy might take. Would it stretch from Sicily to the Alps, as Mazzini and Garibaldi wanted? Would it take the form of a federation, under the Papacy, as men like Gioberti wanted? Would it be divided into three, as Napoleon III would have preferred?

Would it be a monarchy or a republic? Only one thing was certain. After the experiences of 1848 neither the Habsburg emperor nor the Pope would surrender an inch of their territories without a fight. Ferdinand II of Naples was equally determined to keep his political opponents in his unsavoury gaols. Some external stimulus was going to be needed to revive the momentum lost in 1849.

ITALIAN UNIFICATION, 1850–61

The intervention of France

In the 1850s there was a significant shift in the attitudes of European states towards the prospect of a united Italy. Whereas in the 1820s and 1830s, and in 1848, Austria had been given a free hand in suppressing nationalist revolts in the 1850s there was a much greater readiness to work with the grain of nationalism than against it. Napoleon III was positively, if not consistently, in favour of Italian unification. British governments became more and more critical of misgovernment in Naples and the Papal States, especially after Gladstone's denunciation of Neapolitan prisons in 1851. Even Russia was prepared to tolerate a united Italy provided there could be some compensation for her elsewhere.

It was after the Crimean war that these changes became apparent. Cavour and Victor Emmanuel both supported Piedmont's participation in the war, Cavour because he hoped to gain a seat at the conference table when the war ended, Victor Emmanuel because he wanted to display his military prowess. In the event Piedmont contributed little. Of the 18,000 troops sent, 2,000 died of cholera and a handful were killed in the only military engagement in which they took part. At the Paris Congress which ended the war, although the question of Italy's future was raised by Cavour, nothing was promised; however, Cavour claimed that he had secured the guarantee of 'enthusiastic and energetic help' from England in any future war between Piedmont and Austria. This claim, needless to say, was furiously denied by the British foreign secretary, Lord Clarendon. The consequence of this misunderstanding was that Cavour now turned to France for help.

Two further events helped to promote French intervention. In June 1857 Mazzini sponsored an ill-advised attempt to promote a rising in Naples. A Neapolitan supporter, Carlo Pisacane, managed to release a number of political prisoners and ordinary convicts, and with this motley group landed at Sapri on the west coast of Naples. The force was easily overcome by the local peasantry and Pisacane was killed. Mazzini's attempt to seize arms from the arsenal at Genoa to support Pisacane was equally disastrous. This failure convinced many of Mazzini's former supporters that it was time for a more realistic policy. In August 1857 the National Society was formed, mainly by Giuseppppe La Farina and the Marquis Giorgio Pallavicino. It was also joined by Garibaldi. The Society stated in its political creed that it would support Piedmont so long as Piedmont would embrace the cause of Italian independence. There was now a vital link between Cavour and Italian nationalists, sustained by the secret visits which La Farina now began to make to Cavour.

The second event was the attempt by Felice Orsini to assassinate Napoleon III on 14 January 1858. The bomb he detonated failed to harm the emperor, but wounded 150, of whom eight subsequently died. Paradoxically, in the letter Orsini was permitted to write to justify his action, he pleaded with the man he had just attempted to kill: 'As a single individual, I dare to raise my voice from prison, to ask you to give Italy again the independence that Frenchmen helped her to lose in 1849.' Even more paradoxically Napoleon III allowed the letter to be published in France and encouraged Cavour to publish it in Piedmont.

Not surprisingly, overtures from Cavour followed, and on 20 July a critical meeting took place between Cavour and Napoleon III at Plombières, a small town in eastern France. Although no treaty was signed, a firm understanding was reached whereby if Austria could be induced to attack Piedmont, France would come to Piedmont's help. Cavour expected to gain Lombardy and Venetia from Austria, while Napoleon III would be rewarded with Savoy, and possibly Nice. Napoleon also put in a strong plea for the hand in marriage of Clotilde, Victor Emmanuel's 15-year-old daughter on behalf of his dissolute middle-aged cousin, Jerome, the son of Napoleon I's brother Jerome. The future of Italy was also discussed (see Section B).

The marriage requested between Clotilde and Jerome duly took place in September 1858, and a treaty embodying the terms agreed at Plombières was signed secretly in January 1859. It differed only in promising Nice as well as Savoy to France. Piedmont was to provide 100,000 troops, France 200,000, and an enlarged kingdom of Upper Italy was to bear the whole cost of the war by annual payments amounting to one-tenth of her revenues. Rumours of the treaty reached Mazzini, who condemned the possibility of French intervention unreservedly (see Section B). Garibaldi, now a general in the Piedmont army, was much more enthusiastic at the prospect.

On 3 March 1859 Napoleon III's cousin Jerome, now a member of the family, secured a promise from Tsar Alexander II of benevolent neutrality in the event of a war between Austria and France. England's neutrality was assured. How Prussia would react remained in doubt. This proved a severe handicap and discouragement to Napoleon III. Cavour, however, was still bent on war and did his best to provoke an Austrian attack on Piedmont. This proved more difficult than Cavour expected, and he was on the point of resigning when the Austrian government played into his hands. On 19 April 1859 it demanded that Piedmont should place its army on a peace time footing, and allowed only three days for Piedmont to respond. The Italian minister D'Azeglio commented: 'It was one of those jackpots you win only once in a century.' Cavour rejected the Austrian ultimatum on 26 April and the war began. On 3 May Napoleon III announced his determination to go to Piedmont's assistance.

The war was brief but bloody. French troops were brought to Piedmont by train and the first major battle was fought at Magenta (4 June). Milan fell to the allied army. A further battle was fought at Solferino on 22 June, another expensive victory. At this point Napoleon III decided to call a halt. He was apprehensive of Prussian intervention on the Rhine. He had no wish to encourage further insurrection in the Papal States, and he was genuinely appalled by the bloodshed he had witnessed on the battlefield. The Austrians were equally ready to negotiate and at the treaty of Villafranca, signed on 11 July, it was agreed that Lombardy should be ceded to France who would hand it on to Piedmont. Venetia would remain under Austrian control. Cavour resigned in disgust. He had gained only half his share of the bargain.

The extension of Piedmont

With the withdrawal of Austrian troops from northern Italy there was now an opportunity for Italian patriots in the duchies of Parma, Modena and Tuscany to seize power on their own account. In a series of complicated manoeuvres local oligarchies replaced the old rulers. In Modena representatives of the National Society took control until La Farina was made temporary dictator. In Parma local notables took over when the Duchess Maria Luisa withdrew. In Tuscany rival factions contested for power until a moderate landowner, who also believed in a united Italy, Baron Ricasoli, asserted his authority. Even though it had been agreed in the treaty of Villafranca that the rulers of Modena and Tuscany should be restored, neither Napoleon III nor the Austrians were prepared to renew the war for this purpose. There were also changes of regime in the Romagna, the eastern part of the Papal States. Provisional governments were formed in Bologna and in the neighbouring cities of Ferrara, Ravenna and Forli. Papal control, however, was reasserted through Swiss mercenaries in the Marches and Umbria.

Clearly these newly independent areas could not survive on their own and a common pattern emerged under which elected assemblies petitioned for annexation to Piedmont, to be confirmed by local plebiscites. This outcome was initially strongly opposed by Napoleon III, who did not want to see too powerful a state on France's borders. In January 1860, however, Cavour returned to office and he succeeded in persuading Napoleon III to accept what had happened in return for Savoy and Nice. It was agreed that should plebiscites confirm the annexations by Piedmont of Parma, Modena and Tuscany, France

would accept them in return for similar arrangements for Savoy and Nice to become part of France. These terms were finally agreed in a treaty signed on 12 March 1860. This concession on Cavour's part infuriated Garibaldi, himself a citizen of Nice, and marked a further breach between the two men.

Plebiscites were duly held in each of the territories concerned: Parma, Modena, Tuscany and the Romagna (18–22 March 1860), and in Savoy and Nice (15–22 April). It has been calculated that in the areas to be annexed by Piedmont 80 per cent of the 1 million registered voters turned out, and of these 97 per cent voted for annexation. Similar results were obtained to support annexation by France in Savoy and Nice. Not surprisingly, perhaps, doubt has been cast on the validity of these results. There was no secret ballot, landlords unquestionably brought pressure to bear on their tenants and the National Society monopolised the election campaigns. It would be wrong to conclude from this, however, that the policy of annexation lacked overwhelming popular support. Thus by the spring of 1860, Piedmont had acquired Lombardy, Parma, Modena, Tuscany and the eastern part of the Papal States. Within a year they would be joined by Sicily, Naples and the rest of the Papal States.

The campaigns of Garibaldi

While Cavour had never expected, or wanted, to extend Piedmont as far as Naples and Sicily, he found himself impelled to accept the achievements of Garibaldi, unwelcome as they might be. While Sicily remained relatively quiescent in 1859, a rising broke out in Palermo in April 1860. It was crushed in the city, but resistance continued in the countryside and an urgent appeal was delivered to Garibaldi to lead an expedition in support of the rising. Garibaldi, whose fingers had already been burned in 1831 and 1849, was initially reluctant to go, but on 30 April he was persuaded that he must. Cavour and Victor Emmanuel met at Bologna on 1 May, and agreed to allow Garibaldi to recruit his own volunteers, but not to support him with regular troops. Garibaldi succeeded in raising a force of about 1,100, about half from the professional classes (there were 150 lawyers and 100

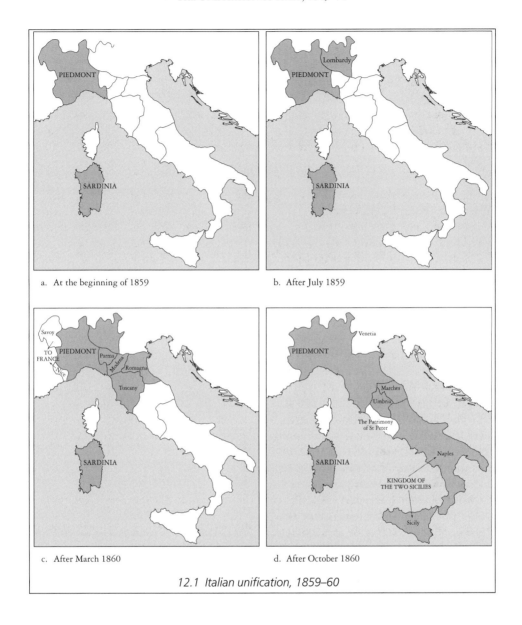

a. At the beginning of 1859

b. After July 1859

c. After March 1860

d. After October 1860

12.1 Italian unification, 1859–60

doctors in his impromptu force). Most came from northern towns such as Milan, Bergamo and Brescia, Bergamo alone providing 160. Inadequately supplied with arms, ammunition or maps, Garibaldi nonetheless achieved astonishing success. He landed at Marsala, a little harbour on the western extremity of Sicily, on 11 May. He fought his first engagement at Calatafini on 15 May, losing 30 killed, and by a successful feint, managed to occupy Palermo on 22 May. The Bourbon army of 20,000 capitulated and agreed to evacuate

the island. On 22 August Garibaldi crossed the straits of Messina to the mainland and on 7 September occupied Naples (see Map 12.1).

Cavour was now placed in something of a dilemma. If Garibaldi continued his successful progress up the Italian peninsula he was likely to attack Rome, which would almost certainly provoke the intervention of France and possible Austria. Furthermore, though Garibaldi always claimed to be fighting for Italy and Victor Emmanuel, his growing popularity could not but weaken Cavour's position. In fact Garibaldi sought to have Cavour dismissed. Cavour's ingenious solution was to pre-empt an attack by Garibaldi on what was left of the Papal States. In September he provoked risings in Umbria and the Marches, which provided a pretext to invade Umbria. On 18 September papal troops were defeated at Castelfidardo and Piedmontese troops joined Garibaldi at the battle of Volturno on 1 October, which though a victory, still left the Bourbon army intact. Garibaldi was in no position to refuse a summons by Victor Emmanuel to meet him at Taena on 25 October, where he acknowledged the King's authority. It had already been agreed by Garibaldi and Cavour that Naples and Sicily and all of the Papal States except for Rome and its immediate surroundings should be incorporated into the kingdom of Italy, once plebiscites had taken place. These were duly held on 21 October and 4–5 November. They produced massive majorities in favour of incorporation. The *Statuto*, Piedmont's written constitution, was applied to the rest of Italy. This meant that the first Italian parliament which met in March 1861 at Turin was elected on a very narrow franchise and that power rested with the upper and middle classes. The first King of a united Italy was Victor Emmanuel II. The fact that he retained his Piedmontese title was proof, were it needed, of Piedmont's dominant role in the new state. Those who had hoped for a republic or a federation were to be disappointed.

Unfinished business

Two areas remained to be included: Venetia and Rome. There was little obvious enthusiasm among the citizens of either to take the initiative themselves, though Garibaldi was always ready to chance his arm. One Venetian commented in 1863: 'It is not for us to judge of opportunities; that is Victor Emmanuel's business; but when the King makes his sign we will rise as one man.' In fact it was not Victor Emmanuel but Bismarck who made a sign, and Venetia's fate was determined by European power politics. Bismarck, who was contemplating a war with Austria in 1866, was naturally anxious to secure Italy's sup-

port, and on 8 April 1866 he signed a treaty with the Italian Prime Minister, La Marmora, under which Italy was pledged to go to war with Austria should Prussia do so. The treaty was to remain in force for three months, and Italy's reward would be Venetia. Napoleon III advised the Italians to accept the offer. Though Austria offered to cede Venetia to France in return for Italian neutrality in a war with Prussia, the offer came too late. Italy wanted to acquire Venetia herself and by plebiscite. On 15 June Prussian troops invaded Saxony, well within the three-month time limit. On 16 June Italy duly declared war on Austria. Italian arms did little to justify the determination to fight. The Austrians inflicted a defeat on the Italian army at Custozza on 24 June and on the Italian navy at Lissa on 3 July, but to no avail. Austria suffered a comprehensive defeat by Prussia at Sadowa on 3 July, and made peace at Prague on 23 August. Italy gained Venetia but nothing else.

The acquisition of Rome, similarly, owed more to Prussia than to the efforts of Italians. So long as Napoleon III kept a French garrison there the Italians were in a cleft stick. Twice Garibaldi attempted to win Rome for Italy with the covert acquiescence of the Italian government. On the first occasion in 1862 his venture was stopped by the Italian government at Aspromonte, once it became clear that he was unlikely to be successful. Garibaldi was wounded by Piedmontese troops. On the second occasion in 1867 he failed to defeat the papal army, and was himself defeated by French troops at Mentana on 3 November.

The Italian government, meanwhile, signed a secret convention with France in 1864 in which it promised not to attack any territory held by the Papacy, and moved the capital from Turin to Florence. In return Napoleon agreed to withdraw his troops, but they returned in 1867 after Garibaldi's second assault, and stayed there.

The outbreak of the Franco-Prussian war on 19 July 1870 compelled France to withdraw its garrison from Rome, thus providing an obvious opportunity for Italy to occupy Rome. The government was initially reluctant to act for fear of antagonising Catholic opinion, and out of a residual loyalty to Napoleon III. Garibaldi even offered his services to the French emperor. But

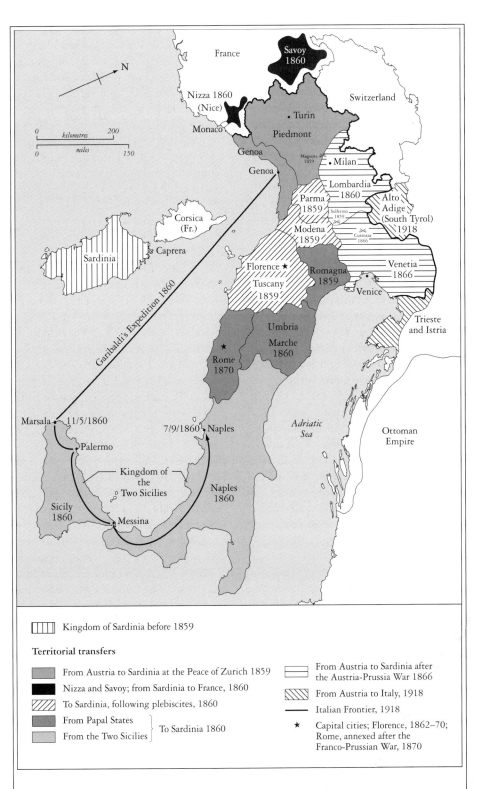

France

Savoy
1860

Switzerland

Nizza 1860
(Nice)

Monaco

• Turin

Piedmont

Genoa

Genoa

Magenta
1859

• Milan

Lombardia
1860

Alto
Adige
(South Tyrol)
1918

Parma
1859

Solferino
1859

Modena
1859

Custozza
1866

Corsica
(Fr.)

Caprera

Florence ★

Tuscany
1859

Romagna
1859

Venetia
1866

Venice

Sardinia

Umbria
Marche
1860

Trieste
and Istria

★
Rome
1870

*Adriatic
Sea*

Ottoman
Empire

Marsala • 11/5/1860

7/9/1860 • Naples

Palermo

Kingdom of
the
Two Sicilies

Naples
1860

Sicily
1860

Messina

N

0   kilometres   200

0   miles   150

Garibaldi's Expedition 1860

Kingdom of Sardinia before 1859

Territorial transfers

From Austria to Sardinia at the Peace of Zurich 1859

Nizza and Savoy; from Sardinia to France, 1860

To Sardinia, following plebiscites, 1860

From Papal States

From the Two Sicilies — To Sardinia 1860

From Austria to Sardinia after
the Austria-Prussia War 1866

From Austria to Italy, 1918

Italian Frontier, 1918

★   Capital cities; Florence, 1862–70;
Rome, annexed after the
Franco-Prussian War, 1870

12.2 The unification of Italy, 1859–70

with the battle of Sedan on 1 September, the capture of Napoleon III and the proclamation of a French Republic on 4 September all doubts were ended. A brief assault on the city took place, the Pope refusing to abandon Rome without a show of resistance, and on 20 September the city was finally occupied. The Risorgimento was completed (see Map 12.2).

REMAINING PROBLEMS

'The idea of unity is the sole one to have been inculcated and understood. Cavour has driven down the lines laid by Mazzini' (Carlo Cattaneo, an Italian political economist, 1859, quoted by S. Woolf, *A History of Italy*, London, Methuen, 1979, p. 466). Though the new Italy was united politically, it faced many problems. The first and fundamental weakness was the remoteness of the new government from the majority of its subjects. Out of a population of 23 million in 1861, 17 million were illiterate. Only 2.5 per cent spoke the form of Italian dialect that became the national language. Only 2 per cent had the right to vote. Most of the new leaders were recruited from the north and the centre. This remoteness was most marked in the south. Despite the apparently overwhelming support for the new Italy expressed in the plebiscites held in Sicily and Naples in 1860, there was little sympathy for the new government. In Sicily in particular peasant disturbances broke out which by 1863 required the presence of 90,000 Piedmontese troops to bring them under control. The mafia was already making its presence felt, using its influence on behalf of landowners to collect rents and on behalf of the government to win elections.

Another serious problem was the attitude of the Catholic Church. As the temporal power of the papacy declined, so its spiritual claims expanded. The Syllabus of Errors, issued by Pope Pius IX in 1864, condemned a number of what he defined as modernist heresies, many directly affecting Church-state relations, for example Proposition 15: 'Every man is free to embrace and profess the religion he shall believe true, guided by the light of reason' and Proposition 77 : 'The abolition of the temporal power, of which the Apostolic See is

possessed, would contribute in the greatest degree to the liberty and prosperity of the Church.' That such propositions were condemned as heretical indicates how far Catholicism still had to move to come to terms with the modern world. In 1870 the Pope buttressed his spiritual authority by proclaiming the dogma of papal infallibility, under which when defining matters of doctrine or morals he was deemed infallible, i.e. his teaching could not be in error. Not surprisingly, Pius IX found it impossible to recognise the new Italian state and forbade Catholics to do so either. In 1868 by the decree *Non Expedit* Catholics were forbidden to vote in national elections or take part in Italian political life. In 1871 the Italian government tried to heal the breach by the Law of Papal Guarantees under which the Papacy was promised diplomatic immunity and a revenue equivalent to that which it had received from the Papal States. This still did not satisfy Pius IX or his successors, and it was not until the Lateran Accords of 1929, signed by Mussolini and Pope Pius XI that the Catholic Church was reconciled to the Italian state.

A third problem arose from the divisions between Left and Right. Republicans like Mazzini were disillusioned by the new Italy, which they saw being ruled by a narrow and privileged elite. When Mazzini died in 1872 no speeches of tribute were allowed in the Italian parliament. While Republicanism ceased to be an issue, there was a growing gulf between rich and poor, made worse by the taxation policies of the government which raised indirect taxes on consumer goods, especially that on the grinding of flour. In southern Italy there was little change in methods of land tenure and the peasantry continued to be exploited.

Finally, Italy, unlike Britain, France or Germany, was under-endowed with the raw materials on which industry depended, coal and iron. Though there was industrial development in the north, it was not on a sufficient scale to absorb the increasing population. Emigration became an increasingly important way out. In the 1890s annual figures averaged 300,000. After 1900 this rose to 500,000. While to many Italians, the achievement of political unity between 1859 and 1870 did seem like a miraculous rebirth, the integration of all Italians into the new state would take much longer.

SECTION B – SOURCES

THE ROLES OF MAZZINI AND CAVOUR IN THE MAKING OF ITALY

Both Cavour and Mazzini have been hailed as the founders of a united Italy. While Mazzini left no doubt in the minds of his readers as to the kind of Italy he wished to see created, a united, democratic republic, or in the methods by which he wished to see it achieved, by popular insurrection, Cavour's ambitions and methods continue to be much more open to question. He has been described as 'a supreme pragmatist' (Spencer M. di Scala, *Italy from Revolution to Republic*, Oxford, Westview Press, 1995, p. 95). Denis Mack Smith sees him as 'a diplomat who had, as he himself said, a fairly elastic conscience and thus could do many things which were outside both Mazzini's competence and his code of morality' (D. Mack Smith, *The Making of Italy, 1796–1866*, London, Macmillan, 1988, p. 12).

Stuart Woolf takes a more critical view of both men: 'It was Mazzini who had preached the need to subordinate and delay all political problems until after the achievement of independence. It was Cavour, after the Paris Congress who enacted this policy with disastrous consequences for united Italy' (Woolf, *History of Italy*, p. 434). In the extracts which follow you can see the aims and policies of Mazzini and Cavour as reflected in their own writings and those of some of their contemporaries.

A Mazzini sets out his aims in a letter to a British sympathiser, Joseph Cowen, November 1857

The question of Italy is not one of more or less security or administrative improvement in one or another corner of our country; it is a question of Nationality; a question of independence, liberty and unity for the whole of Italy; a question of a common bond, of a common flag, of a common life and law for twenty-five millions of men belonging between the Alps and the sea – to the same race, tradition, and aspiration. Everybody is free to approve or blame this one aim of ours....

And for the question of means, the practical question,

it is not one between republic and royalty; it is one between action and inertness. I am a republican, and such are almost all those who support me in a struggle now lasting twenty-five years and which will be carried on until crowned by victory....

Lastly, as to Piedmont, we are not adverse to it; how could we be so? Is not Piedmont an Italian province? Nor are we refusing the help of its government in the struggle. We do only say that a National revolution is never achieved without an appeal to arms; that neither the Austrians, nor the King of Naples, nor the Pope can ever be driven away from Italy by protocols or memoranda; that an open struggle cannot be initiated by the Piedmontese government; and that only a popular insurrection can offer an opportunity for action to Piedmont.

Denis Mack Smith, *The Making of Italy, 1796–1866*, London, Macmillan, 1988, pp. 220–21

B G. Pallavicino to D. Manin, 24 August 1856

Foresti write again to me as follows:

'Our Garibaldi went to Turin on the thirteenth and I went with him. Cavour welcomed him with courtesy and friendliness and hinted that he could rely on considerable official help. Cavour even authorised Garibaldi to pass on these hints to others. It seems that he is seriously thinking about the great political redemption of our peninsula. Garibaldi took his leave of the minister on very friendly terms and with these encouraging promises of help for our cause.

It was all an act! What Cavour wants, and I am sure of it, is just for Piedmont to be enlarged by a few square miles of Italian soil.'

(Ibid, p. 216)

C Cavour explains his position to La Farina, Sicilian secretary of the National Society, September 1857

'I have faith,' said Cavour, 'that Italy will become one State, and will have Rome for its capital. But I do not know whether it is ready for this great change, for I do not know the other provinces of Italy. I am minister to the King of Piedmont, and I cannot, I ought not to say or do anything prematurely to compromise his dynasty. Make your National Society and we shall not have long to wait for our opportunity. But remember that among my political friends no one believes the enterprise (viz. the union of Italy) possible, and that haste would compromise me and the cause.'

(G.M. Trevelyan, *Garibaldi and the Thousand,* London, Cassell, 1989, p. 74)

D Cavour's account of the negotiations with Louis Napoleon at Plombières, in his letter to Victor Emmanuel II, 24 July 1858

The Emperor readily agreed that it was necessary to drive the Austrians out of Italy once and for all, and to leave them without an inch of territory south of the Alps or west of the Isonzo. But how was Italy to be organised after that? After a long discussion, which I spare your Majesty, we agreed more or less the following, recognising that they were subject to modification as the course of the war might determine. The valley of the Po, the Romagna, and the Legations [Bologna, Ferrara, Ravenna and Forli] would form a kingdom of Upper Italy under the House of Savoy. Rome and the immediate surroundings would be left to the Pope. The rest of the Papal States, together with Tuscany, would form a kingdom of central Italy. The Neapolitan frontier would be left unchanged. These four Italian states would form a confederation on the pattern of the German Bund, the presidency of which would be given to the Pope to console him for losing the best part of his estates.

(D. Mack Smith, *The Making of Italy*, pp. 239–40)

E A Public Declaration by Mazzini in London, 28 February 1859 in which he attacks the prospect of a war between Austria on one side and France and Piedmont on the other

Our party believes that without Unity there is no Country; that without national sovereignty there is no Nation; that without liberty, true liberty for all, there can be no real National independence.... We also believe that any war fought by Italians for national independence disjoined from that of liberty would lead to tremendous disillusionment and the mere substitution of new masters for old.... We believe that Louis Napoleon Bonaparte cannot without self-destruction establish by force of arms the liberty that at home he has drowned in French blood. For us to ally with despotism would be to deny those principles which justify and render sacred the Italian cause.... We think that an alliance between the Piedmontese monarchy and Napoleon would render

inevitable a European coalition against what would be seen as a war of conquest, and this prospect has already deprived Italy of much of the favour she has hitherto received in Europe.

(D. Mack Smith, *Mazzini*, New Haven, CT, Yale University Press, 1994, pp. 129–30)

F Cavour praises Garibaldi's conquest of Sicily, in a letter to Count Nigra, Cavour's representative in Paris

Garibaldi has rendered to Italy the greatest service that a man could render: he has given the Italians confidence in themselves.... As long as he is faithful to his flag, one has to march along with him. This does not alter the fact that it would be eminently desirable for the revolution in Naples to be accomplished without him.

(S. Woolf, *A History of Italy, 1700–1860*, London, Methuen, 1979, p. 465)

G Cartoons

UN FRUTTO PROIBITO

Serpente – O lo mangiate voi, o lo mangio io – o ce lo mangiano a tutt' e due.

12.1 Cavour, Garibaldi and Sicily: 'Forbidden fruit'. The snake (Garibaldi) is saying to Eve (Cavour): 'Either you eat it, or I eat it – or they will eat up both of us' ('they' evidently being the great powers of Europe)

Source: cartoon published in *Lampione*, 19 May 1860, © Moro Roma, Rome

RIGHT LEG IN THE BOOT AT LAST.

GARIBALDI. "IF IT WON'T GO ON, SIRE, TRY A LITTLE MORE POWDER."

12.2 Garibaldi and Victor Emmanuel II: 'Right leg in the boot at last'. Garibaldi is saying: 'If it won't go on Sire, try a little more powder!'

Source: reproduced by kind permission of *Punch* Ltd

Questions

1 What, in your view, did Mazzini mean by Nationality (extracts A and E)?
2 In the light of extracts C, D and F, how justified is the view expressed by Pallavicino that all Cavour wants is 'a few square miles of Italian soil' (extract B)?
3 What light does extract D shed on Napoleon III's Italian policy?
4 Explain the phrase 'the liberty that at home he has drowned in French blood' (extract E).
5 What messages are the cartoons in source G intended to convey?

6 In the light of these extracts and your wider knowledge, how far is it true that Cavour pursued the goals advocated by Mazzini?
7 What do you think were 'the disastrous consequences' which according to Stuart Woolf followed from the subordination of all political problems to the achievement of independence?

Further reading

The best introductions to Italian unification are to be found in D. Beales, *Italy and the Risorgimento* (London, Longman, 1982) and D. Mack Smith, *Italy, a Modern History* (Ann Arbor, University of Michigan Press, 1959). S. Woolf, *A History of Italy, 1700–1860: the Social Constraints of Political Change* (London, Methuen, 1979) is very useful on the social and economic background. A recent overview which takes into account recent Italian scholarship is provided by Spencer M. Di Scala, *Italy from Revolution to Republic: 1700 to the Present Day* (Oxford, Westview Press, 1995).

There are good biographical studies of Cavour, Garibaldi and Mazzini in D. Mack Smith, *Cavour and Garibaldi in 1860* (Cambridge University Press, 1954) and *Mazzini* (New Haven, CT, Yale University Press, 1994). For a briefer account of Cavour, see H. Hearder, *Cavour* (London, Historical Association, 1972).

For a vivid and still reliable narrative account of various episodes in the Risorgimento, see G.M. Trevelyan, *Garibaldi and the Defence of the Roman Republic*, *Garibaldi and the Thousand* and *Garibaldi and the Making of Italy* (London, Cassell, 1988).

The best source book is D. Mack Smith, *The Making of Italy, 1796–1866* (London, Macmillan, 1988), and there is a useful collection of documents in D. Beales, *The Risorgimento and the Unification of Italy* (London, Allen and Unwin, 1971). Trevelyan's three books also have much eye-witness material. A.J. Whyte, *The Early Life and Letters of Cavour, 1810–1848* (Oxford, University Press, 1925) and *The Political Life and Letters of Cavour, 1848–1860* (Oxford University Press, 1930) are still worth consulting.

• CHAPTER THIRTEEN •

The Unification of Germany, 1849–71

• CONTENTS •

KEY DATES

1849	18 June	Forcible dissolution of the German Assembly at Stuttgart
1850	29 April	Opening of Erfurt Parliament
	May	German Diet reassembles at Frankfurt
	20 Nov.	Convention ('humiliation') of Olmütz
1851	Jan.	Dresden Conference; failure of Habsburg empire to enter German Confederation
1853		Zollverein renewed; Austria not admitted
	Oct.	Outbreak of Crimean war
1858	Oct.	William I became Regent in Prussia
1859	11 Dec.	Albert von Roon made Prussian Minister of War
1862	Aug.	Refusal of Prussian Landtag to vote funds for military reorganisation
	22 Sept.	Bismarck appointed Minister-President in Prussia
	30 Sept.	Bismarck's 'Iron and Blood' speech
	7 Oct.	Military budget rejected in Prussian Landtag
1863	Jan.	Outbreak of Polish Revolt
	Nov.	Schleswig-Holstein crisis begins
	16 Jan.	Austro-Prussian alliance v. Denmark
	18 April	Prussian victory at Duppel over Danish forces
	April–June	London Conference on Schleswig-Holstein question
	30 Oct.	Treaty of Vienna: Schleswig and Holstein ceded to Austria and Prussia
1865	14 Aug.	Convention of Gastein: Holstein to Austria, Schleswig to Prussia
	4–11 Oct.	Conversations between Bismarck and Napoleon III at Biarritz
1866	8 April	Prussian–Italian alliance for three months

	9 April	Bismarck suggests elected parliament for German Confederation
	21 April	Austria mobilises southern armies v. Italy
	1 June	Austria asks Diet to decide future of Schleswig and Holstein
	7 June	Prussian troops occupy Holstein
	12 June	Napoleon III signs secret treaty with Austria
	14 June	Confederation votes by nine to six for mobilisation v. Prussia
	16 June	Outbreak of Austro-Prussian war
	3 July	Battle of Koniggrätz (Sadowa)
	26 July	Preliminary peace terms agreed at Nikolsburg
	13–22 Aug.	Peace treaties between Prussia and Baden, Bavaria and Württemberg
	23 Aug.	Treaty of Prague ending Austro-Prussian war
	Sept.	Compensation for France in Luxemburg and Belgium discussed
1867	16 April	Constitution of North German Confederation approved
1868	March	Elections to the Customs Parliament
	Sept.	Deposition of Queen Isabella of Spain
1869	Sept.	Marshal Prim suggests candidacy of Leopold of Hohenzollern-Sigmarinen for Spanish throne
1870	Feb.	Leopold's candidacy renewed
	9 March	Bismarck urges acceptance of Spanish candidacy
	21 June	Leopold accepts offer of Spanish throne
	3 July	France informed of Leopold's acceptance
	6 July	Angry French protest voiced
	12 July	Withdrawal of Leopold's candidacy announced
	13 July	French seek guarantee that candidacy will never be renewed;

		Ems telegram sent, edited and published
15 July	France decides on war
19 July	War declared by France
1 Sept.	Battle of Sedan
2 Sept.	Napoleon III captured
4 Sept.	French Republic proclaimed
6 Sept.	Bismarck decides on annexation of Alsace-Lorraine
1871 18 Jan.	Proclamation of German Empire at Versailles
26 Feb.	Peace terms agreed between France and Prussia
14 April	Imperial Constitution adopted
10 May	Treaty of Frankfurt signed

SECTION A

POSSIBLE SOLUTIONS TO THE GERMAN PROBLEM

There must be some special magic in the word 'German'. One can see that each person calls German whatever suits him and whatever suits his party's standpoint. Thus the use of a word changes according to requirements.

> Bismarck, in a speech to the Prussian Landtag [elected assembly], 1864, cited in J. Breuilly, 'The national idea in modern German history', in J. Breuilly (ed.) *The State of Germany*, London, Longman, 1992, p. 3)

The main problem facing central Europe in the nineteenth century hinged upon the problems of defining Germany and how Germans were to be incorporated into a single, sovereign state. There were at least three possible solutions. The first, both in conception and reality, was the *grossdeutsch* (Great German) solution. To be German meant primarily but not exclusively to be German speaking. Thus the German Confederation of 1815 included the German speaking provinces of the Habsburg empire, Prussia and the thirty-seven other states which made it up (see Map 13.1). However, the Confederation did not include German speakers in East and West Prussia or Germans in the Danish province of Schleswig. Contrariwise there were non-German speakers in Bohemia,

Moravia, Styria, Slovenia and the South Tyrol. Some parts of the Confederation were ruled by foreigners, notably Holstein, ruled by the King of Denmark; Hanover, ruled by the King of England (until 1837); and Luxemburg, ruled by the King of Holland. Furthermore, the German Confederation was hobbled from the start by its lack of power. It had no independent source of revenue and therefore no army. After 1848 it was increasingly threatened by the rivalry between Prussia and Austria, muted by the fear of revolution during the era of Metternich, but all too evident thereafter. Every attempt to reform the Confederation ran into the obstacle of this rivalry. So long as the Kings of Prussia retained a residual veneration for the emperor, the Confederation could survive, but once this disappeared the Confederation's days were numbered unless it could be reformed.

The *kleindeutsch* (Small German) solution aimed to include all German speaking areas outside the Habsburg empire. This meant excluding Germans in Bohemia and Austria, but for historical reasons including Poles in Posen and East Prussia, Danes in Schleswig and (after the Franco-Prussian war), French people in Alsace and Lorraine. While this variant was acceptable to Prussia and to most Protestant opinion, it met with a good deal of opposition in the south German states of Baden, Bavaria and Württemberg, which were largely Catholic; it was also bitterly opposed by the Habsburg empire.

The third solution was canvassed by Prince Schwarzenburg at a conference of German princes held at Dresden early in 1851. Schwarzenburg suggested a vast *Mitteleuropa* of some 70 million people, to be formed by linking the Habsburg empire with the German Confederation. The idea died in 1851, but it was to surface again in the 1890s when the Pan-German League suggested something similar, and it became one of the League's war aims in 1914. Hitler's Anschluss (connection) with Austria in 1938 saw a partial realisation of Schwarzenburg's ambitions.

Of these three variants it was the second, the *kleindeutsch*, that was to succeed in the form of Imperial Germany, or the Second Reich. But, contrary to what Bismarck often claimed, there was nothing preordained about this outcome and it did not solve in the long term the problem of how to

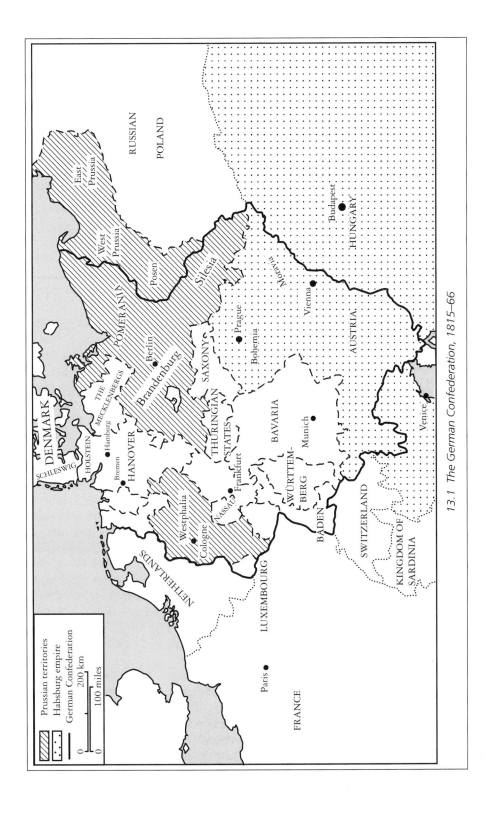

13.1 *The German Confederation, 1815–66*

create a Germany whose frontiers would include all ethnic Germans while excluding all racial minorities.

There was a further difficulty to be resolved. The failure of the 1848 revolutions in Prussia and Austria and Frederick William IV's refusal to accept the throne of a new Germany at the invitation of the Frankfurt parliament (see pp. 152–53) dashed the hopes of those who wanted to see a republic, or at the very least a constitutional monarchy. Princely authority survived in every German state after 1848, largely unhindered by elected parliaments. This was truer of north Germany than the south, but even where parliaments had effective power, as in Baden and Bavaria, their members were elected on a very narrow franchise. There was to be a serious contest for power in Prussia between 1862 and 1867, won by Bismarck, and this had an important bearing on the Constitution that was framed for the North German Confederation in 1867, and extended to the German empire in 1871. The constitution of the Frankfurt parliament would have given Germany a government, headed by an hereditary ruler, but answerable to an assembly elected by universal suffrage. When it came to devising a constitution in 1867, Bismarck was prepared to gamble with the idea of universal suffrage, in the expectation that the peasantry and workers would vote for their natural superiors. He would not tolerate the idea of a government responsible to an elected parliament. Thus the process of unification determined not only the boundaries of the new Germany but also its form of government.

PRESSURES TO UNITE

Three reasons have conventionally been advanced to explain why Germany became united on the *kleindeutsch* model between 1864 and 1871: the growing economic integration of north Germany; the development of ideological support for a stronger and more united Germany; and the rise to power in Prussia of Otto von Bismarck, a political genius whose diplomatic skills matched his commitment to German unification along *kleindeutsch* lines.

It was a British economist, J.M. Keynes, who remarked in 1919 that 'the German empire was built more truly on coal and iron than blood and iron' (W. Carr, *A History of Germany, 1815–1945*, London, Arnold, 1979, p. 78). Industrialisation prior to 1870 was largely confined to Prussia's Rhineland provinces. Prussia controlled the great arteries of the Rhine, the Elbe and the Oder. It was Prussia which took the lead both in the creation and subsequent direction of the Zollverein. One of its founders, Friedrich von Motz, remarked: 'The more natural the attachment to a customs and commercial system is . . . the more intimate and deep will be the attachment of those states to some political system' (W. Carr, 'The unification of Germany', in J. Breuilly (ed.) *The State of Germany*, p. 86). Significantly, Prussia rebuffed all Austrian attempts to join the Zollverein and rejected an Austro-German customs union suggested by the Austrian Minister of Commerce, Karl Bruck, in 1851. As Prussia industrialised, the economic gap between Prussia and the Habsburg empire widened. Not only did Austria lack the raw materials for an industrial revolution, but also her public finances were so badly managed that 40 per cent of revenue went in debt interest, whereas Prussia was able to sustain a large army out of ordinary revenue. The failure to integrate the economies of the Habsburg empire and the German Confederation was therefore a major reason for the political divisions that arose between Prussia and Austria.

The 1850s and 1860s also witnessed growing ideological support for a united Germany based on Prussian leadership. This was reflected in intellectual circles by the writings of historians such as Heinrich von Treitschke (1834–96), Heinrich von Sybel (1817–95) and Johann Gustav Droysen (1808–94). All of them extolled the virtues of Prussia, and argued in favour of a dominant role for their state in a united Germany. In commercial and judicial circles there was similar sympathy for greater unity. In 1858 the Congress of German Economists was founded, to be followed by the German Jurists Congress (1860) and the German Commercial Association (1862). Most significant was the formation in August 1859 of the *National Verein* (National League). This organisation, based on the Italian National Society, owed its inception both to the Italian example and to the warning presented by the Franco-Austrian war of 1859. This is made clear in the League's programme:

1 In the present position of the world we see great dangers threatening the independence of the German Fatherland – these are increased rather than diminished by the peace just concluded between France and Austria.
2 These dangers have their ultimate origin in the faulty constitution of Germany and they can be countered only by a speedy alteration of it.
3 For these purposes it is necessary that the German Federal Diet should be replaced by a firm, strong, permanent central government and that a German national assembly should be summoned.
4 In the present circumstances effective steps for the attainment of this aim can originate only in Prussia. We shall, therefore, work to the end that Prussia may take the initiative (cited in M. Gorman, *The Unification of Germany*, Cambridge University Press, 1989, p. 56).

Though the League's membership did not reach more than 25,000 its speakers appeared frequently at the popular festivals organised by groups such as the German Sharpshooters League (1861) and the German Singers League (1862).

When Bismarck came to power in Prussia in 1862 he thus inherited a situation that was inherently favourable to his purposes. What those purposes were and how far he can be credited, or blamed, for the path which German unification took will be examined in Section B. It is first necessary to outline the course of events which culminated in the proclamation of the German empire in 1871.

THE PROCESS OF UNIFICATION, 1848–61

The aftermath of the 1848 revolutions

On 14 May 1849 Prussia ordered its representatives to leave the Frankfurt Assembly. A radical remnant moved to Stuttgart where they attempted to maintain a show of authority, but on 18 June the King of Württemberg ordered their dispersal from the town hall and the Frankfurt Assembly came to an inglorious end. What would replace it was far from clear. Schwarzenberg, the new Minister President in Vienna, was determined to re-establish the German Confederation under Austrian primacy. Frederick William IV and his new Foreign Minister, Radowitz, were anxious to salvage something from the attempt to unite Germany in 1848 and in May 1849 Radowitz suggested the formation of the League of Three Kings (Prussia, Saxony and Hanover) which was eventually joined by seventeen states. This initiative was supported by 150 ex-members of the Frankfurt Parliament, who gave their approval in a meeting held at Gotha in June. In the meantime, Schwarzenburg and Radowitz signed an interim agreement providing for the joint administration of Germany by Austria and Prussia until 1850.

In March 1850 representatives of the states which had joined the League of the Three Kings met at Erfurt in the so-called Erfurt Parliament. In May Schwarzenburg summoned a meeting of the German Confederation at Frankfurt which Prussia refused to attend. The two gatherings were clearly incompatible and a trial of strength ensued. It nearly broke into armed conflict when the elector of Hesse-Cassel (a state which divided Prussia from its Rhineland provinces) appealed for help from the German Confederation to subdue his rebellious subjects. Bavaria and Württemberg mobilised their forces. Prussia could hardly tolerate such intervention on her borders and was prepared to resist. But Russia was prepared to support Schwarzenburg and Frederick William decided that war under such conditions was unacceptable. Radowitz resigned and on 29 November the Convention of Olmütz was signed. In Prussia it became known as 'the humiliation of Olmütz'. Both armies were to demobilise, but the Prussian one was to do so first, and the Erfurt Union was to be abandoned. The right of the Confederation to intervene in the affairs of Hesse Cassel and Holstein was recognised. The German Confederation was re-established. Schwarzenburg had triumphed. But when the Diet met at Dresden in December (it continued into 1851) his ambitious plans to include the whole of the Habsburg empire in the Confederation were defeated, and the best he could achieve was a three-year alliance with Prussia under which each side agreed to defend the other's territories.

On the surface, Austro-Prussian relations remained reasonably amicable, but when Bismarck became the Prussian delegate to the Confederation, as he did in 1851, he lost no opportunity to assert Prussia's equality, even insisting on the right to smoke which had previously only been permitted to the Austrian president of the Diet. More seriously, Austria's attempt to join the Zollverein was turned down in 1853, and she had to be satisfied with a commercial treaty with Prussia instead. When the Crimean war broke out in 1853 Prussia insisted firmly on neutrality and would have nothing to do with Austria's efforts at armed mediation. Thus the rivalry which had bedevilled Austro-Prussian relations in the eighteenth century recurred.

Developments in Prussia

It was internal changes in Prussia which precipitated the next crisis. In October 1858 Frederick William IV suffered an incapacitating stroke and Crown Prince William became Regent. He succeeded to the throne in 1861. He immediately embarked on an ambitious reform of the army, appointing a strong conservative who was also an administrative genius, Albert von Roon, to be Minister for War. Von Roon made plans for an immediate increase in the size of the army, raising the annual intake from 40,000 to 63,000. He also planned to improve the army's standard of efficiency by lengthening the time of active service from two to three years and the period in the front-line reserve from two to four years. This entailed a down-grading of the *Landwehr*, the citizen army to which Prussian liberals attached so much importance because it mitigated the 'cadaver [corpse] obedience' which had characterised the armies of Frederick the Great. William supported the reforms on the grounds that 'Discipline, blind obedience are things which can be inculcated and made permanent only by long familiarity' (W.E. Mosse, *Liberal Europe*, London, Thames and Hud-

son, 1974, p. 137). It was on these grounds, rather than the increase in the size of the army, that Prussian liberals opposed the projected reforms. So intense was their opposition that many of them broke away from the main party to form the Progressive Party, and in elections held in December 1861 they gained 110 seats. In a subsequent election held in May 1862 this figure rose to 135, making the Progressives the largest party in the Landtag. In August the Lower House rejected von Roon's proposals. It was at this point that von Roon recommended to King William that he should send for Bismarck, one of the most critical summonses to office in the history of Europe.

Otto von Bismarck

The man who was to preside over the destinies first of Prussia and then of Germany for the next twenty-eight years was 47 when he took office. Bismarck was born into a Prussian landowning family in 1815, but his mother came from the educated bourgeoisie, and Bismarck did not have a typical *Junker* upbringing. He went to university first at Göttingen and then at Berlin, where he gained sufficient legal qualifications to become a civil servant. He took posts first in Aachen, and then in Potsdam from 1834 to 1839, but on his mother's death took over the running of the family estates at Kniephopf and Schonhausen in Prussian Pomerania. Here he lived the life of a country squire, acquiring a reputation for wildness and debauchery. In 1843 he met the religious minded daughter of a neighbour, Marie von Thadden, who though engaged to someone else, evidently had a profound effect on Bismarck and caused him to adopt a more sober lifestyle. Her death in 1846 affected Bismarck greatly, and her dying wish that he should marry a friend with similar views, Johanna von Puttkamer, undoubtedly helped to determine Bismarck's choice of bride. They were married in 1847, and though Bismarck's affections were to stray from time to time, the marriage survived intact. Bismarck acquired a wife in whom he could confide and on whose uncritical support he could always rely. In the same year Bismarck entered political life almost by accident, deputising for an ill colleague in the Prussian Landtag. Bismarck was a conservative by instinct, but his views were reinforced by his experiences of the 1848 revolution. He was appalled by the street fighting he witnessed in Berlin, opposed all concessions by the King, attacked the Frankfurt parliament as 'the German swindle', and advised Prussia 'to avoid all dishonourable connections with democracy'. But he was also a realist, and defended the convention of Olmütz in the Landtag on the grounds that 'it is unworthy of a great state to pick a quarrel for a cause that does not serve its own interests' (Werner Richter, *Bismarck*, London, Macdonald, 1964, p. 58).

In 1851 Bismarck became Prussian ambassador at the Diet of the German Confederation in Frankfurt where, as we have seen, he insisted on what he called a dualistic equality of rights. In this capacity he made his first visit to Vienna in 1852. He also visited Paris for the World Trade Fair in 1855 and again in 1857 when he met Napoleon III. In 1855 he turned down a proposal from the Austrian ambassador to the Diet, Count Bernhard von Rechberg that Austria would lay before the Diet only such bills as had previously been agreed with Prussia, and continued to insist that it was his task to represent the interest of Prussia, not the Confederation. It may have been Bismarck's intransigence that caused Prince William, as Regent, to have Bismarck transferred from Frankfurt to St Petersburg in January 1859. He spent the next three years in Russia, apart from a ten-month interval from August 1860 to May 1861. In May 1862 he was transferred to Paris. From here he took the opportunity to visit London (see extract D) and to holiday in Biarritz, where he met the extremely attractive wife of the Russian ambassador in Brussels, Katherine Orlow. Bismarck was smitten, and was accompanying the Orlows in their travels in the Pyrenees when a letter reached him from von Roon on 12 September, urging his return. Bismarck could not make up his mind to leave France, and on his return to Paris, received a curiously worded telegram from von Roon in a mixture of Latin and French: *Periculum in mora. Dépechez vous* (Danger in delay. Hurry up). Bismarck took von Roon's advice, and arrived in Berlin on 20 September 1862.

THE PROCESS OF UNIFICATION, 1862–66

Austro-Prussian relations

Within four years of Bismarck's coming to power Austria and Prussia were at war. How far Bismarck intended this outcome remains a matter of dispute, the evidence for which is considered in Section B. Bismarck's actions certainly helped to provoke war, but they were not always consistent with this objective.

He had first to assure his position in Prussia, both by dealing with the Landtag and winning the King's confidence. He dealt with the Landtag essentially by ignoring it. His attitude can be gauged by the speech he made to the Budget Commission on 30 September 1862, within a week of his becoming Minister-President. In a celebrated extract he said: 'Prussia's boundaries according to the Vienna Treaties are not favourable to a healthy political life; not by means of speeches or majority verdicts will the great decisions of the time be made – that was the great mistake of 1848 and 1849 – but by iron and blood' (cited in Gorman, *Unification of Germany*, p. 63). When the lower house of the Landtag refused to approve the budget, Bismarck continued to collect taxes as though it had been passed, arguing that if, as the Prussian constitution stated, the consent of both houses and the crown was needed to approve the budget, the refusal of one house could not bind the other two parties, and that 'whoever has the power at hand goes ahead with his views' (Gorman, ibid., p. 65). Taxes continued to be collected without the Landtag's approval until 14 August 1866, when in the euphoria of victory, Bismarck secured the passage of an indemnity bill by 230 votes to 75, justifying all the taxes that had been collected illegally in the mean time. For good measure on 1 June 1863 Bismarck introduced a Press Ordinance giving him the power to close down any periodical that was too critical of the government.

Grateful to Bismarck for restoring his princely authority at home, William I gave him virtually a free hand in the conduct of foreign policy, though William still had misgivings at times. Bismarck took every opportunity to isolate Austria diplomatically and he resisted any attempts to reform the Confederation. In January 1863 he used the opportunity of the Polish Revolt which broke out that year to demonstrate Prussia's goodwill towards Russia, offering Prussian assistance in subduing the revolt. In August of the same year he successfully torpedoed an Austrian initiative to reform the Confederation. When Emperor Francis Joseph suggested a meeting of all German princes at Frankfurt to take place in August, Bismarck used all his powers of persuasion to discourage William I from attending. William reluctantly took Bismarck's advice, and without a Prussian presence the meeting was doomed to failure.

In November 1863 the reopening of the Schleswig-Holstein question gave Bismarck the opportunity first to invade the duchies and then to exploit the divisions with Austria to which their acquisition gave rise (see extract E). Under the London Protocol of 1852 Denmark's sovereignty over the two duchies had been recognised subject to the condition that their administrative privileges and German character were respected, a solution that satisfied no one. In November 1863 two things happened to upset this uneasy compromise. On 13 November a new constitution was approved, incorporating Schleswig into Denmark. On 15 November King Frederick of Denmark died, to be succeeded by Christian IV. At this point a third claimant stepped in, Frederick, Duke of Augustenburg, who claimed both duchies in his own right. Protests erupted in Germany, and on 16 January 1864 Bismarck secured an alliance with Austria providing for joint military action against Denmark. The Danes were given forty-eight hours to rescind the new constitution, and on their failure to do so Austrian and Prussian forces invaded Schleswig. On 18 April Prussian forces won a minor battle at Duppel, and faced with the threat of invasion, Denmark agreed to a conference which opened in London later in the month. The conference ended on 25 June without reaching agreement, and the fighting resumed. In October Denmark capitulated and by the treaty of Vienna both duchies were surrendered to the joint rule of Austria and Prussia. Austria, now aware that she had been outmanoeuvred, supported the claim of Frederick, Duke of Augustenburg, to the duchies, the last thing Bismarck wanted. Tension mounted, but was temporarily eased by the Convention of Gastein, signed on 14 August 1865, which awarded

Holstein to Austria and Schleswig to Prussia. Prussia was also allowed to have naval and military bases in Holstein. Bismarck had gained his immediate but not his long term objective.

On 1 October 1865 he met Napoleon III at Biarritz, and though no formal agreement was reached, Bismarck came away from the meeting with the conviction that Napoleon would not support Austria in any war with Prussia – 'he would not go and stand beside a target' (A.J.P. Taylor, *The Struggle for Mastery in Europe*, Oxford University Press, 1954 p. 159). For his part, Napoleon was given to understand that Prussia would not continue to support Austria's claim to Venetia. Vague hints of compensation for France in the event of Prussian gains in northern Germany were also offered. Assured of French neutrality, Bismarck turned up the pressure on Austria. On 1 January 1866 he protested vigorously when Austria permitted a demonstration in favour of Duke Frederick at Altona in Holstein. More seriously, on 8 April he signed the alliance with Italy which committed Italy to come to Prussia's assistance in the event of a war with Austria should it occur within the next three months (see p. 186). Napoleon III was fully aware of this treaty. On 9 April, to the surprise of both his friends and opponents, Bismarck proposed the election of a parliament based on universal suffrage to discuss reform of the Confederation. He also encouraged the Hungarian nationalist leader Kossuth to form a Magyar legion to attack Austria.

The next few weeks were punctuated by various initiatives to avert the war which so obviously threatened. Early in April Austria offered to stop her military preparations if Prussia did the same. At William's behest, Bismarck reluctantly agreed. But on hearing news of Italian troop movements, Austria ordered the mobilisation of her southern armies on 21 April, and this was the signal for Prussian mobilisation. On 24 May Napoleon, now reluctant to see war break out, suggested a Conference at Paris to which Prussia, Austria and the other members of the German Confederation were invited. Bismarck accepted, but Austria agreed to attend only if she was assured that there would be no territorial changes as a result of the conference. No conference met and Napoleon III sought to cover himself instead by a secret treaty with

Austria signed on 12 June under which he promised to remain neutral providing France would get Venetia (for transfer to Italy) in the event of an Austrian victory.

The final steps to war began on 1 June when Austria asked the Diet to decide the future of Schleswig and Holstein. Prussia declared the alliance of January 1864 at an end and terminated the Convention of Gastein. On 7 June Prussian troops occupied Holstein. Austria's riposte was to urge in the Diet that a federal army be mobilised against Prussia for revoking the Convention of Gastein. On 14 June this proposal was carried in the Diet by nine votes to six. On 15 June Prussia ordered Saxony, Hesse-Cassel and Hanover to demobilise their forces, and receiving no satisfactory reply, on 16 June Prussian forces invaded Hanover. The Austro-Prussian war had begun.

The Austro-Prussian war

Bismarck was only too well aware that his own fate was bound up with that of Prussia in the days that followed. He remarked to the British ambassador on the day war broke out : 'The fight will be bitter. If we are beaten, I shall not return here. Or I shall fall in the final attack' (Richter, *Bismarck*, p. 127). As it transpired such a sacrifice was not required. Within a week the Hanoverian army was surrounded and their forces forced to surrender. On 3 July the Austrian and Prussian armies clashed at Königgrätz (also known as Sadowa) in Bohemia and within a few hours the Austrian army had been driven from the battlefield. On 5 July Napoleon III telegraphed his congratulations to William I, announcing at the same time that Austria had surrendered Venetia, and offering his services as a mediator. Negotiations continued for three weeks, while Bismarck relayed his terms to Paris. They included the surrender to Prussia of Schleswig and Holstein, the annexation by Prussia of Hanover, Hesse-Cassel and part of Hesse-Darmstadt and the exclusion of Austria from the German Confederation. Napoleon insisted for his part on the independence of the three south German states, Baden, Bavaria and Württemberg, and the continuation of the kingdom of Saxony. Both William I and the Prussian generals thought these terms far

too generous. Austria was to suffer no loss of territory and there would be no triumphal parade in Vienna. But Bismarck's view prevailed. He wrote in a letter to his wife : 'If we are not excessive in our demands and do not believe we have conquered the world, we will attain a peace that is worth our effort. . . . I have the thankless task of pouring water into bubbling wine and making it clear that we do not live in Europe alone but with three other Powers that hate and envy us' (G.A. Craig, *Germany 1861–1945*, Oxford University Press, 1978, p. 4). On 26 July preliminary terms were initialled by Prussia, Austria and Napoleon III at Nikolsburg and finalised in the treaty of Prague on 23 August. Bismarck also used the opportunity when making peace with the south German states to insist on offensive and defensive alliances with them which required them to hand control over their railway systems and armed forces to Prussia in the event of war.

The battle of Königgrätz and the peace of Prague produced a *kleindeutsch* solution to the German problem, but only at the expense of excluding permanently the 10 million or so Germans who lived in Austria and Bohemia. It left the status of the south German states in the air; and it put the future of the Habsburg empire in jeopardy. Viennese ambitions now turned to the Balkan peninsula where they would sow the seeds of future conflict.

THE PROCESS OF UNIFICATION, 1866–71

The North German Confederation

Bismarck was now faced with the task of giving a constitutional structure to the group of territories which Prussia now controlled. The North German Confederation was essentially his creation, though he took advice from men such as Max Duncken, one-time professor at Halle university, and Karl von Savigny, previously the Prussian representative at the Diet. The new constitution was drafted in the six months from July to December 1866 and it was finally approved by a constituent assembly elected for the purpose by a vote of 230 to 53 on 16 April 1867. Its main provisions underlined the primacy of Prussia. The King of Prussia was to become hereditary president and the Prussian Chancellor was to become chancellor of the Confederation, as well as its Foreign Minister. The King of Prussia retained control over all the armed forces and over foreign policy. There was to be a two-chamber assembly: a Reichstag, for which all males over 25 would be eligible to vote, and a Bundesrat on which delegations from each of the states would be represented. Prussia, with four-fifths of the population, had seventeen votes out of forty-three, sufficient to block any reform to the constitution. Critical to the way the constitution operated was the relationship between the Reichstag and the Prussian government. All legislation relating to the Confederation required the assent of the Reichstag, which also had limited control over the budget. But under a compromise struck in the early months of the constitution, it was agreed that the Reichstag would have no control over military spending for the next four years. Many of these provisions were copied directly into the constitution of the German empire which replaced the Confederation in 1871, and thus they shaped the political structure of Germany between 1867 and 1918. The two most significant features were first the dominant role given to Prussia, both in the composition of the government and in the Bundesrat, and second the lack of any direct connection between the Reichstag and the government (see Figure 13.1). Germany might have a parliament elected by universal manhood suffrage, but ministers owed their posts to the favour of the king and later the emperor.

The Franco-Prussian war and the acquisition of the south German states

There can be little doubt that Bismarck expected and worked for the union of the south German States with the North German Confederation (see Map 13.2). To the military treaties he had imposed in 1866 he added in 1867 the offer of representation in a new Customs Parliament which he introduced into a reorganised Zollverein. This parliament was to have the right to regulate tariffs and certain indirect taxes and customs duties. The southern states were given generous representa-

tion. When the first elections took place in the early months of 1868 Bismarck received a shock. So far from returning members eager to link up with the north, the southern states elected a majority hostile to any such move. Twenty-six out of forty-eight delegates in Bavaria were opposed, there was a slender majority in favour in Baden, and none out of seventeen delegates in Württemberg. Altogether fifty-seven delegates from these states opposed any closer links with the north and on 7 May 1868, joined by Old Conservatives, Catholics, Poles and Guelfs (from Hanover), they succeeded in defeating a motion in the Customs Parliament which called for 'complete unification of the whole German fatherland in a peaceful and salutary manner' (Craig, *Germany 1866–1945*, p. 19). On 9 March 1869 Baron von Rosenberg, Württemberg's representative in Berlin reported to Bismarck that when electors were asked whether they wished to remain Württembergers or become Prussians they said of the North German Constitution that it contained only three articles: 1 Pay, 2 Serve in the army, 3 Keep your mouth shut (H. Bohme (ed.), *The Foundation of the German Empire*, Oxford University Press, 1971, p. 202). Bismarck evidently accepted these reverses philosophically and declared his readiness to wait until the fruit was ripe (see extract F).

As well as lack of enthusiasm in the south, Bismarck also had to face opposition from Napoleon III who had already been strongly criticised for permitting France to be faced by two strong neighbours, Germany and Italy. In September 1866 Napoleon initiated a clumsy attempt to secure Luxemburg and Belgium for France in compensation for Prussia's gains under the treaty of Prague. Nothing came of these discussions except a copy of the French proposals (undated) which Bismarck published to embarrass France when war broke out in 1870. But while Bismarck would do nothing to appease Napoleon there is little evidence to suggest that he would have initiated such a war had not events played into his hands.

In September 1868 Queen Isabella of Spain was deposed, leaving the Spanish throne vacant. The head of the provisional Spanish government, Marshal Prim suggested as a possible successor Leopold of Hohenzollern-Sigmaringen, the son of

13.1 Germany's future: 'Does it come under a hat? I believe it will more likely come under a spiked helmet'

Source: Bildarchiv Preussicher Kulturbesitz, Berlin

Prince Charles Anthony, who was related to William I of Prussia and a good friend of the King. The offer was made initially in September 1869, and turned down by Leopold. When it was renewed in February 1870 Bismarck decided to press for acceptance. On 9 March he wrote a strongly worded memorandum urging this course to William I, including this argument:'It is desirable for Germany to have on the far side of France a country on whose sympathy she can rely and with whose susceptibilites France would be obliged to reckon' (Bohme (ed.), *Foundation of the German Empire*, p. 219) It has been suggested, notably by

William Carr, that Bismarck was anxious to provoke a crisis as a way of mobilising internal support, with elections pending in north Germany and the emergence of strong Catholic political parties in Bavaria and Baden. Whatever his motives, there can be no question of the storm Bismarck aroused. Leopold was eventually induced to accept the Spanish throne and telegraphed his decision to Madrid on 21 June, promising to arrive there on 26 June. Unfortunately a Spanish cipher clerk misread this for 9 July. The Spanish Cortes who were to 'elect' the King were allowed to leave the capital, to reconvene in July, and Leopold arrived to

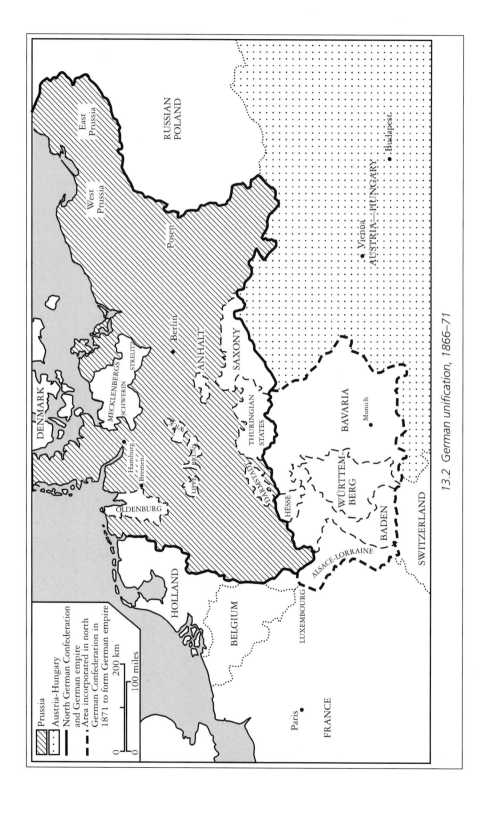

13.2 *German unification, 1866–71*

Legend:

- Prussia
- Austria-Hungary
- North German Confederation and German empire
- Area incorporated in north German Confederation in 1871 to form German empire

0 — 100 miles
0 — 200 km

Labels on map: RUSSIAN POLAND, East Prussia, West Prussia, Posen, DENMARK, MECKLENBERG SCHWERIN, STRELITZ, Berlin, ANHALT, SAXONY, THURINGIAN STATES, BRUNS..., LIPPE, OLDENBURG, Hamburg, Bremen, HOLLAND, BELGIUM, LUXEMBOURG, HESSE, DARMSTADT, ALSACE-LORRAINE, WÜRTTEM-BERG, BADEN, BAVARIA, Munich, SWITZERLAND, AUSTRIA–HUNGARY, Vienna, Budapest, FRANCE, Paris find Madrid empty. Instead of being faced with a *fait accompli*, the French government learned of the proposed candidacy on 3 July through a Spanish news agency. A change of goverment in France in May 1870, following a successful plebiscite approving Napoleon III's recent constitutional changes, had brought the Duc de Gramont to the foreign ministry. He was well known as a hardliner, and in favour of a Franco-Austrian alliance.

His reaction was predictable. On 6 July he delivered an inflammatory speech, threatening force if the Prussian and Spanish governments did not abandon the Hohenzollern candidacy at once. On 7 July Gramont wrote to the French ambassador, Benedetti, to this effect, and included the ominous words: 'we are pressed for time, because we must strike first. In the event of an unsatisfactory reply, and for the campaign to begin in a fortnight, the troops must begin to march on Saturday' (Bohme, *Foundation of the German Empire*, p. 225).

On 9 July Benedetti, the French ambassador, sought assurances from William I, who was taking the waters at Bad Ems, that he would withdraw his consent to the Hohenzollern candidature. William, who had never shown much enthusiasm for the idea, discusssed the matter with his relatives, and on 12 July Prince Charles Anthony announced that his son Leopold had withdrawn.

There, but for French obstinacy, the matter might have rested. Fatally for France, Benedetti was instructed to demand further that Leopold's claim to the Spanish throne would never be renewed. This demand William firmly but politely refused in a discussion held with Benedetti on 13 July. An account of the interview, drafted by Heinrich Abeken, one of Bismarck's assistants, was telegraphed as a matter of routine to Bismarck, in Berlin. Bismarck, who had been shattered by Leopold's withdrawal, saw his opportunity. He edited the telegram to make it appear that Benedetti had been snubbed (extract H (i)) and released it to the press and to foreign embassies. In his Memoirs Bismarck makes no secret of his intentions (extract H(ii)). On 15 July, in the fever for war that had been provoked by Bismarck, abetted by Gramont, the French government decided on war, and four days later on 19 July a declaration of war was delivered to Berlin.

The Franco-Prussian war

Whereas the Austro-Prussian war was over in six weeks, the Franco-Prussian war lasted six months and left much deeper scars. The military history of the war has already been dealt with in Chapter 11. Here we are concerned with its impact on Germany. Its first and most immediate effect was to generate a wave of nationalist sentiment which extended to the south German states as well as to Prussia. Arnold Ruge expressed a common view when he wrote: 'Any German, whoever he may be, who is not now on the side of his people, is a traitor' (Craig, *Germany 1866–1945*, p. 27). The military alliances with Bavaria, Baden and Württemberg came into effect immediately and within one month 1.8 million men had been mobilised, of whom 462,000 were deployed on France's borders.

After the battle of Sedan and the proclamation of a French Republic, Bismarck announced to Russia and Austria that the three eastern monarchies must stand together against the contagion of revolution spreading outwards from France, and Germany must protect herself by the annexation of Alsace and Lorraine. This now became a German war aim, and it proved astonishingly popular. The military argued for annexation on the grounds of security and those in the south German states, who were most vulnerable to a French invasion also backed this demand. When Johann Jacoby, a lifelong democrat, opposed the idea in a speech made in the autumn of 1870, he was imprisoned. Once the aim had been stated it could not be abandoned, and it had the inevitable effect of prolonging the war.

The war also helped to influence the character of the German empire, most visibly in the extraordinary scene that took place in the palace of Versailles on 18 January 1871. It was on this occasion that the German empire was proclaimed and that King William I of Prussia assumed the imperial title. In a conscious reference to the Holy Roman Empire, William declared that he had been unanimously called upon by the German Princes and the Free Cities 'to revive and assume, with the restoration of the German Empire, the German imperial office, which has not been occupied for more than sixty years' (L.L. Snyder, *Documents of German History*, New Brunswick, NJ, Rutgers

University Press, 1958, p. 222). The deliberate choice of the palace of Versailles in which to make this proclamation could not have been more explicitly designed to humiliate France, and to associate the new empire with military power. The terms of the treaty of Frankfurt, agreed on 26 February 1871, and signed on 10 May, underlined the extent of the German victory. Alsace-Lorraine was ceded to Germany in perpetuity. France was to pay an indemnity of 5 billion francs (Prussia's estimate of what the war had cost her); and she was to submit to a German army of occupation until such time as the debt had been paid. The acquisition of Alsace-Lorraine, popular as it was with the Germans, proved a thorn in Germany's side. For as J. Jacoby said in the speech for which he was imprisoned: 'Even the most ardent and insensate partisan of annexation allows that the inhabitants of Alsace and Lorraine are in heart and soul French' (T.S. Hamerow, *The Age of Bismarck*, New York, Harper and Row, 1973, p. 108). The recovery of these lost provinces would become the cardinal aim of French foreign policy from now until 1919.

The final and most obvious consequence of German victory was the inclusion of Baden, Bavaria and Württemberg in the new German empire. All three states recognised that they had no viable future outside the empire. Baden joined without making any conditions, on the same terms as other members of the German Confederation. Bavaria and Württemberg were more concerned to retain a measure of independence. Both states retained control over their armed forces in peacetime and were given certain rights in the fields of taxation, transport and other local affairs. In all other respects the constitution of the German empire mirrored that of the North German Confederation. Bavaria was given six votes, Württemberg four and Baden three in the Bundesrat, but the primacy of Prussia was unaffected. The King of Prussia was now the German Emperor rather than President of the North German Confederation but his powers remained the same. The most significant change occurred in the composition of the Reichstag where a Catholic Centre party emerged to represent the greatly increased numbers of Catholic voters. It soon became the second largest party.

There has been much argument as to whether Imperial Germany was simply an extension of Prussia in the same way that Italy had become an extension of Piedmont. Bismarck believed that there was no contradiction between an expanded Prussia and a united Germany: 'Whether one considered the issue from the Borussian angle to be the leading role of Prussia or from the national angle to be the unification of Germany, both objectives coincide' (W. Carr, 'The unification of Germany', in J. Breuilly (ed.), *The State of Germany*, p. 97).

Certainly, Prussia now accounted for three-fifths of Germany's land area and three-fifths of its population. Those facts, and Prussia's hold on the monarchy and the imperial government, meant that the character of the German empire would inevitably reflect the character of the state, and the statesman, who had done most to create it.

SECTION B – SOURCES

BISMARCK'S ROLE IN THE UNIFICATION OF GERMANY

'Men make their own history . . . they do not make it just as they please, but under circumstances directly encountered, given and transmitted from the past' (Karl Marx, *The Eighteenth Brumaire of Louis Napoleon*, 1852). The question of how far the German empire of 1871 was the product of Bismarck's ambition and influence has exercised historians for generations, and continues to do so. The answer is not made any easier by the gloss Bismarck placed on his career in his retirement. Politicians' memoirs are notoriously unreliable, and Bismarck's were written in a mood of disillusion and resentment, after his dismissal by William II in 1890. They were published under the title *Gedanken und Erinnerungen* (Reflections and Recollections), three years after his death, in 1898. They are a curious mixture of detailed reminiscence, with conversations precisely recalled, and self-justifying comments on the policies Bismarck pursued. Thus while they cannot be taken at face value, they do contain much essential if unreliable evidence.

Bismarck was also a prolific writer. His collected works run to some fifteen volumes and in his correspondence, speeches and memoranda there is plenty of material by which to judge what he said or wrote at the time against the interpretation he placed on his policies in retirement. The following extracts have been selected to shed light on the three wars in which first Prussia and then the North German Confederation were involved, and Bismarck's responsibility for starting them.

A Bismarck recalls his support for the wars of 1864, 1866 and 1870

During the time that I was in office I advised three wars, the Danish, the Bohemian [Austro-Prussian] and the French; but every time I first made myself clear whether the war, if it were successful, would bring a prize of victory worth the sacrifices which every war requires, and which are now so much greater than in the last century.

(*Otto von Bismarck, the Man and the Statesman, being the Reflections and Reminiscences of Otto Prince von Bismarck, Written and Dictated by Himself after his Retirement*, vol. 2, ed. A.J. Butler, London, Smith, Elder, 1898, p. 290)

B A Memorandum written by Bismarck in 1856 when he was Prussian representative at the German Confederation

the traditional policy of Austria and its jealousy of us cannot be removed, and I would trust the old fox in his new coat as little as in his summer bristles . . . I will express my conviction that in no long time we shall have to fight for our existence against Austria, and that it is not in our power to avoid the fight, because the course of events in Germany admits of no other development.

(C. Grant Robertson, *Bismarck*, London, Constable, 1918, p. 95)

C Bismarck's suggestions as to how Prussia should respond to the Austro-French war, given in a Memorandum to Regent William, May 1859

the present situation has put the winning card in our hands provided we allow Austria to become deeply involved with France and then march southwards with our entire army carrying frontier posts in our big packs. We can then plant them either on the Bodensee [Lake Constance] or as far south as Protestantism is the dominant faith.

(W. Carr, 'The unification of Germany', in J. Breuilly (ed.) *The State of Germany*, London, Longman, 1992, p. 84)

D Bismarck in conversation with Disraeli at a dinner given in the Russian embassy in London, in the summer of 1862 when he was still ambassador to France.

This account comes from the memoirs of Count Eckstadt, the Saxon ambassador, published in 1887

'I shall soon', said in effect the Prussian statesman, 'be compelled to undertake the conduct of the Prussian Government. My first care will be to organise the army, with or without the help of the Landtag. The King was right in undertaking this task, but he cannot accomplish it with his present advisers. As soon as the army have been brought into such a condition as to inspire respect, I shall seize the first best pretext to declare war against Austria, dissolve the Diet, subdue the minor states, and give national unity to Germany under Prussian leadership.'

(M. Gorman, *The Unification of Germany*, Cambridge University Press, 1989, p. 61)

Count Eckstadt also reported that Disraeli had said: 'Take care of the man. He means what he says'.

(W. Carr, *A History of Germany, 1815–1945*, London, Arnold, 1969, p. 87)

E Bismarck and the Schleswig-Holstein question: the Austro-Prussian alliance of January 1864

Nor was the alliance designed as a trap for Austria. There was no reason to suppose that joint control of the duchies would necessarily lead to a quarrel. . . . The alliance was a test for Austria rather than a trap. Bismarck answered the criticism of Goltz, his ambassador in Paris: you do not trust Austria. Nor do I; but I think it is right to have Austria with us now; we shall see later whether the moment of parting comes and from whom.

(A.J.P. Taylor, *Bismarck*, London, Arrow, 1955, pp. 73–74)

F Von Moltke's views of the reasons for the Austro-Prussian war; Von Moltke had been appointed Chief of the Prussian General Staff in 1857

The war of 1866 did not take place because the existence of Prussia was threatened, or in obedience to public opinion, or to the will of the people. It was a war which was foreseen long before, which was prepared with deliberation and recognised as necessary by the Cabinet, not in order to obtain territorial aggrandisement, but in order to secure the establishment of Prussian hegemony in Germany.

(Grant Robertson, *Bismarck*, p. 204)

G Albert Baron von Suckow, Minister for War in Württemberg, recalls a conversation with Bismarck in May 1868, when Bismarck said the following

Our whole sympathy belongs to our south German brother to whom we stretch out a hand, but we neither wish nor ought to force him to grasp it. Rather let us thirty million Germans build our house, then the other eight million will become reconciled in time, especially if we commit no act of force against them and so give the lie to their prejudices. I have always told the National Liberals that I consider the thing like a hunter, who has laid his bait. He does not shoot the first doe that comes, but waits until the herd has taken the food.

(H. Bohme (ed.), *The Foundation of the German Empire*, Oxford University Press, 1971, pp.200–01)

H Bismarck and the Ems telegram

(i) The original and edited versions of the Ems telegram

Abeken (one of Bismarck's assistants) to Bismarck, 13 July 1870 3.40 p. m.
His Majesty [William I] writes to me:
'Count Benedetti [the French ambassador] spoke to me on the promenade, in order to demand from me, finally

in a very importunate manner, that I should authorise him to telegraph at once that I bound myself for all future time never again to give my consent if the Hohenzollerns should renew their candidature. I refused at last somewhat sternly, as it is neither right nor possible to undertake engagements of this kind *à tout jamais* [for all time]. I told him that I had as yet received no news, and as he was earlier informed from Paris and Madrid than myself, he could see clearly that my government had no more interest in the matter.' His Majesty has since received a letter from Prince Charles Anthony [father of Leopold]. His Majesty, having told Count Benedetti that he was awaiting news from the Prince, has decided with reference to the above demand, on the suggestion of Count Eulenberg and myself, not to receive Count Benedetti again, but only to let him be informed through an aide-de-camp: 'That his Majesty has now received from the Prince confirmation of the news which Benedetti had already received from Paris [that Leopold had withdrawn his candidature], and had nothing further to say to the ambassador.' His Majesty leaves it to your Excellency [Bismarck] to decide whether Benedetti's fresh demand and its rejection should be at once communicated to both our ambassadors, to foreign nations, and to the Press.

Bismarck's version for publication

After the news of the renunciation of the hereditary Prince of Hohenzollern had been officially communicated to the Imperial government of France by the Royal government of Spain, the French Ambassador further demanded of his Majesty at Ems, that he would authorise him to telegraph to Paris that his Majesty, the King, bound himself for all time, never again to give his consent, should the Hohenzollerns renew their candidature. His Majesty, the King, thereupon decided not to receive the French ambassador again, and sent the aide-de-camp on duty to tell him that his Majesty had nothing further to communicate to the ambassador.

(Grant Robertson, *Bismarck*, pp. 496–97)

(ii) Bismarck recounts his response to the Ems telegram, made to von Moltke and von Roon

If in execution of his Majesty's order I at once communicate this text, which contains no alteration in or addition to the telegram, not only to the newspapers, but also by telegraph to all our embassies, it will be known in Paris before midnight, and not only on account of its contents, but also on account of the manner of its distribution, will have the effect of a red rag upon the Gallic bull. Fight we must if we do not want to act the part of the vanquished without a battle. Success, however, essentially depends upon the impression which the origination of the war makes upon others; it is important that we should be the party attacked and this Gallic overweening and touchiness will make us if we announce in the face of Europe, so far as we can without the speaking trumpet of the Reichstag, that we fearlessly meet the public threats of France.

(*Otto von Bismarck, The Man and the Statesman*, vol. 2, p. 100)

I The proclamation of the German empire at Versailles (Figure 13.2)

13.2 This celebrated painting, commissioned in 1871 to commemorate the proclamation of the German empire at Versailles on 18 January 1871, is here reproduced in its third version, which was ordered to celebrate Bismark's seventieth birthday in 1885. The artist, Anton von Werner, was present at the original occasion, which he remembered as short and drab. His first rendering of it was criticised for its emptiness, and the inconspicuous place given to Bismark. In the second and third versions, Bismark was moved to the centre, dressed in the white uniform of the Cuirassiers and joined by the War Minister, Roon (seen here on Bismark's left), who had not been present on the actual day

Source: Bildarchiv Preussicher Kulturbesitz, Berlin

Questions

1 What can you infer about Bismarck's attitude to war from extract A?
2 What was 'the winning card' to which Bismarck refers in extract C?
3 In the light of extracts B, C and D, what did Bismarck hope to gain from a war with Austria?
4 How far does extract E weaken the argument advanced in extract F that the war of 1866 'was prepared with deliberation'?
5 With reference to extract H (i) comment on the following lines in extract H (ii): 'If in execution of his Majesty's order I at once communicate this text, which contains no alterations or additions to the telegram'.
6 In view of extracts G and H, and your wider knowledge, assess Bismarck's responsibility for causing the Franco-Prussian war.
7 What message was illustration I painted to convey with reference to the unification of Germany?
8 How far do these extracts and the historical record support Bismarck's claim to have 'advised three wars' (extract A)?

Further reading

The best introduction to German history during this period is W. Carr, *A History of Germany, 1815–1945* (London, Arnold, 1969). For fuller coverage consult J.J. Sheehan, *Germany History, 1770–1866* (Oxford University Press, 1989) and G.A. Craig, *Germany, 1866–1945* (Oxford University Press, 1978). A useful collection of essays is to be found in J. Breuilly (ed.), *The State of Germany: the National Idea and the Making, Unmaking and Remaking of a Modern Nation State*, (London, Longman, 1992). The unification of Germany is covered specifically in A. Stiles, *The Unification of Germany, 1850–1890*, (London, Arnold, 1986).

There are many biographies of Bismarck. The best brief introduction is by B. Waller, *Bismarck* (Oxford, Blackwell, 1985). On the personal level see W. Richter, *Bismarck* (London, Macdonald, 1964) and A.J.P. Taylor, *Bismarck, the Man and the Statesman* (London,

Arrow, 1955). For a fuller and more recent account see Lothar Gall, *Bismarck the White Revolutionary* (2 vols, London, Unwin Hyman, 1982). C. Grant Robertson, *Bismarck* (London, Constable, 1918) has much valuable documentary material.

Two useful collections of source material are H. Bohme (ed.), *The Foundation of the German Empire*, (Oxford University Press, 1971) and M. Gorman, *The Unification of Germany* (Cambridge University Press, 1989).

• CHAPTER FOURTEEN •

Reform and Reaction in Russia, 1849–94

• CONTENTS •

Key dates

SECTION A

Defeat under Nicholas I

Alexander II, 1855–81

Alexander III and the return to reaction, 1881–94

SECTION B – SOURCES

The limitations of Alexander II's reforms

KEY DATES

1849	Nicholas I (r. 1825–55) helps Habsburgs suppress Hungarian rebellion
1853	Russia claims protectorate over Orthodox Christians in Ottoman empire and occupies Danubian Principalities
1854	Crimean war; Britain and France join Ottoman empire against Russia
1855 Feb.	Nicholas I dies; Alexander II (r. 1855–81)
Sept.	Fall of Sebastopol
1856 March	Peace of Paris ends Crimean war; Russian defeat; Alexander II asks nobility to consider emancipation of the serfs
1861	Emancipation of the serfs
1863	Universities reformed by Golovnin (Minister of Education 1861–66)
1863–64	Polish rising crushed
1864	*Zemstva* set up; judicial system reformed
1865	Press law sets up system of warnings; Jewish artisans freed from restrictions
1866	State peasants emancipated; entitled to redeem land
1874	Universal Military Service law by D. Miliutin (Minister of War 1861–81); *Narodnik* campaign in countryside
1877–78	Russia intervenes against Ottoman empire, most gains removed at Congress of Berlin
1881 Feb.	Loris-Melikov reform plan approved by Alexander II
1 March	Alexander II assassinated by People's Will terrorists; Alexander III (r. 1881–94)
29 April	Alexander III's manifesto proclaims autocracy; reform plan rejected; Statute on State Security increases repression
1882–86	Finance Minister Bunge sets up Nobles' and Peasants' Land Bank
1890	*Zemstva* Act restricts powers; Land Captains introduced
1887–92	Finance Minister Vyshnegradsky exports grain; gold reserves built up
1891–92	Famine and cholera
1892–94	Russian–French alliance concluded

SECTION A

The last years of Nicholas I's reign were overtaken by the humiliating defeat of Russian forces in the Crimea. The 1848 Revolutions had left the Tsar's throne untouched and given Nicholas I a sense of security and confidence which was rudely shattered by the intervention of French and British forces in Russia's own backyard. He died in 1855, leaving his son Alexander II to accept defeat in 1856.

The shock of defeat and the opportunity provided for a fresh start by the new reign together prompted a period of great reform in Russia, and comparisons have been made with the Gorbachev era of *perestroika* (reform) and *glasnost* (openness). The reforms began with the emancipation of the serfs. Serfs belonging to private landowners comprised 31 per cent of the total population of 74 million in 1858, and emancipating them was a colossal social reform. It involved a bitter struggle between the Tsar, supported by some liberal bureaucrats, and the nobility, and Westwood makes another comparison: 'the autocracy succeeded, where transatlantic democracy [the United States] failed, in ending bondage without civil war' (J.N. Westwood, *Endurance and Endeavour; Russian History 1812–1992*, Oxford University Press, 1993, p. 78). But there were limitations to emancipation which caused problems and complicate the assessment of the impact of the reform. Other important changes followed during the 1860s. The judicial system was transformed, elected bodies (called *zemstva*) were set up with responsibilities for local government, more schools and universities were opened, the press was given greater freedom, and, perhaps the key objective for Alexander II, the state was strengthened by military and financial reform, and by economic development.

But was Alexander II taking a terrible risk in trying to reform the autocracy in this way? His critics (such as Pobedonostsev) saw his measures as westernising modernisations which did more harm than good. Significantly, Alexander II's enthusiasm for reform seemed to decline during his reign, perhaps under the weight of disappointments such as the Polish rebellion and assassination attempts, and his death in 1881 after a bomb was thrown at him finally ended the last period of voluntary reform 'from above'. Alexander III (1881–94) pursued a reactionary policy, restricting many of his father's changes, while the last Tsar, Nicholas II (1894–1917) would take up reform unwillingly only when he was compelled to do so by pressure 'from below'. Did Alexander II's great reforms help to preserve the autocracy, only to be thwarted by his reactionary successors, or did they begin to weaken the state by admitting the possibility of change? Perhaps Lenin's analysis is accurate, that it was incomplete reform which raised hopes only to dash them down, that created the potential for revolution.

DEFEAT UNDER NICHOLAS I

As we have seen, Nicholas I ran an efficient and centralised state (see Chapter 9). Dealing with the Decembrist revolt in 1825, when he came to power, probably contributed to his 'siege mentality'. Certainly he was reactionary in most of his policies, fond of military drill and parades, and almost obsessive in his need to inspect and check up on the process of government. But his policy seemed to work, for his throne was unshaken by the 1848 Revolutions and he was able to help the Habsburgs suppress the Hungarians in 1849, again deserving the title of the 'gendarme of Europe' (see Chapter 10).

Although Nicholas I felt secure and confident in the correctness of his policies, there were stresses and strains which made it impossible for the regime to remain motionless in time. Nicholas I recognised one of the looming problems, telling the Council of State in 1842: 'There is no question that serfdom in its present state in our country is an evil, palpable and obvious to everyone. How-

ever, to attack it now would be, of course, an even more disastrous evil. . . . The Pugachev rebellion [of peasants in the 1770s] showed how far mob violence can go' (cited in R. Sherman, *Russia 1815–81*, London, Hodder and Stoughton, 1991, p. 42). The Tsar felt that the time was not right to address the problem, but perhaps it never would be right for him because his mentality was so defensive.

Nicholas I treated other pressures in a similar way. The threat of the 1848 Revolutions spreading was increased by a cholera epidemic and food shortages, so 400,000 troops were moved to the western borders to prevent this from happening. Censorship was tightened up too, and universities became more rigidly controlled under Shikmatov (who replaced Uvarov). These measures certainly restricted the spread of ideas and alienated the intelligentsia, but they did not prevent debate about the future from occurring within this tiny group. One important area of debate divided liberal 'Westernisers', who wanted Russia to have western parliamentary institutions and social reform, and the 'Slavophiles' who wanted Russia to develop along traditional lines. These would build on the spiritual importance of the Orthodox Church, the fraternalism of the *mir* (peasant commune), and the mystical unifying paternalism of the autocratic Tsar. Nicholas I naturally felt more at ease with this Slavophile philosophy, but he preferred to stifle the debate rather than further it.

Ironically for such a cautious Tsar, he became sucked into the disastrous Crimean war largely through miscalculation. Russia had a long-standing interest in maintaining influence in the Ottoman empire, but this became a drive for greater control when France demanded Catholic rights in the Holy Places (see Chapter 11). Early in 1853 Nicholas I sent his emissary, Menshikov, to persuade the Ottoman empire to reject French demands. Not content with succeeding in this, Menshikov demanded that the Ottoman empire should recognise Russia's right to protect Christians of the Orthodox Church who lived there too. Neither France nor Britain could allow Russia to win such authority, so why was Nicholas I taking such a risk? Besides Menshikov's over-confidence in negotiations in Constantinople, the Tsar himself was placing much faith in the support of the

Habsburgs. After all, Russia had helped them suppress the Hungarians in 1849. But Nicholas I could not see matters from the perspective of Vienna. The Austrian empire would be dangerously exposed if the Ottoman empire were to collapse, and if Russian influence grew in the Balkans it might destabilise Austria's authority over her own Slav minorities. So the Russian plan to occupy the Danubian Principalities threatened Austria's interests, and there was no prospect that Austria would support Russia in the war with the Ottoman empire, which began on 22 September 1853 (see Map 14.1).

International conflict developed only slowly, allowing ample time for peace to be restored had the political will and diplomatic expertise been available. The Turkish fleet was destroyed by a Russian counter-attack at Sinope in October 1853, which the British press reported as a 'massacre', but Britain and France waited until March 1854 before joining the Ottoman empire and declaring war on Russia (see Chapter 11, extract E, (i)). In July 1854 Britain, France and Austria agreed the 'Four Points' for peace demanding the replacement of Russian control in the Danubian Principalities by a European guarantee, and joint five power protection for the Ottoman Christians. But this diplomatic front was weakened as Austria lost interest – Russia's troop withdrawal from the principalities, and the suggestion that Britain would replace Russian naval power in the Black Sea, saw to that.

Austria therefore remained in doubtful neutrality, the object of British and French suspicion and the Tsar's astonished disappointment. But neither side would back down from the regional trial of strength. In September 1854 Anglo-French forces landed in the Crimea, and by the end of the year had fought at the Alma, Balaklava and Inkerman, and laid siege to the Russian fortress-port of Sebastopol. Early in 1855 diplomacy came to nothing, and the war effort became more earnest when Palmerston became Prime Minister and the Tsar dismissed his commander in the Crimea. Reinforcements were slow to arrive from Russia, the commander-in-chief (Paskevich) defying the Tsar by holding forces back to guard against an Austrian attack. Relying on ox-drawn carts to supply her troops and evacuate her wounded, Russian forces faced superior western rifles and logistics which supplied their forces over a greater distance by sea – the French even built a railway in the Crimea.

With Russian fortunes at their lowest point, Nicholas I developed pneumonia after inspecting his troops in sub-zero temperatures and died on 18 February 1855 (see Figure 14.1). His son, the 36-year-old Alexander II, decided to continue with the war. But the main port of Sebastopol fell on 27 August 1855, and early in 1856 Alexander II agreed to an armistice. Britain and France, fearful of the escalating costs of a prolonged war, were quite ready for peace as well.

14.1 The Crimean war

Alexander II, 1855–81

The new Tsar's inheritance

The Peace of Paris, signed in March 1856, was a humiliation for Russia. In 1815 her forces had been among the victorious allies. Now, isolated and defeated, she had to accept her loss of power on the Danube, the Ottoman rejection of any foreign interference in her internal affairs, and the demilitarisation of the Black Sea, which meant the end of the Russian Black Sea fleet.

Alexander II was personally well equipped to face up to this difficult inheritance. He had received a fairly broad-minded education, he had

'GENERAL FÉVRIER" TURNED TRAITOR.

Russia has Two Generals in whom she can confide—Generals January and February."—Speech of the late Emperor of Russia

14.1 'General Février turned traitor': Punch cartoon showing Tsar Nicholas I's death from winter conditions, 18 February 1855

Source: Reproduced by permission of Punch Ltd

a palace coup or civil war, and if he was too vigorous in his impact, he might destroy the regime entirely.

But the necessity for reform was generally accepted, as Saunders points out: 'A regime that could not win a war on its own soil was ripe for reform' (D. Saunders, *Russia in the Age of Reaction and Reform, 1801–1881*, London, Longman, 1992, p. 201). Defeat and the reversal of her international position since 1815, together with the opening of a new reign, triggered the 'great reforms', but we need to consider why it was that emancipation of the serfs was the first great undertaking.

The emancipation of the serfs

The immensity of the change which emancipation would bring becomes clear once the scale of serfdom is seen. In 1858 there were just under 23 million serfs belonging to private landowners, together with about 27.4 million 'state peasants' who were tied to land which belonged to the state, 1.5 million 'household serfs' who worked in their masters' homes, and about 800,000 'appanage peasants' tied to the Imperial family's estates. Landowners had immense power over their serfs, who were treated as their property, buying and selling them, punishing them, banishing them to the army, giving permission (or not) to marry or travel (see Figure 14.2). The serfs were obliged to work on their master's land or in his factories

travelled (he was the first Romanov to visit Siberia), he had a knowledge of European languages, and in 1842 he had married a German princess. His father had also given him experience of government on the Council of State and various committees including those dealing with serfdom and railways. Westwood concludes: 'He inherited from his father and his tutors an honesty of character and loyalty to his subordinates, but he was milder, more sensitive, more patient than his father. He was still, however, an autocrat rather than a ruler' (Westwood, *Endurance*, p. 71). It is important to remember this limitation on the new Tsar's capacity for reform. Alexander II knew that Russia needed to reform, but the means available to him as autocrat were potentially dangerous; if he was too domineering in his methods, he might provoke

14.2 Serfs for sale at the annual fair on the river Volga

Source: M. Perrie, *Alexander II: Emancipation and Reforms in Russia* (London, Historical Association, 1989)

(*barshchina*), or pay feudal dues (*obrok*) from their earnings from cultivation, handicrafts or factory work, or a combination of both. The serfs had an allotment of land with their cottage, and they farmed strips which the *mir* periodically reallocated on the basis of the size of the family. 'State peasants' tended to be better off in terms of the amount of land allotted to them and the greater freedom they enjoyed.

The law of 1649 established the institution of serfdom. In return for serving the state as an army officer or civil servant, the nobility were granted total authority over their labour force. The autocracy was in fact using the nobility to control most of its subjects through serfdom, leaving tsarism free of interference from the nobility in its central affairs of state. But the mutual self-interest of tsarism and nobility in maintaining serfdom began to break up when the nobility were freed from their obligation of state service by Peter III (in 1762) and Catherine the Great (in 1785). Consequently the institution of serfdom fell into question. Alexander I made it possible for serfs to become free (in 1803) (see Chapter 9) and Nicholas I referred to it as an evil, as we have seen, but powerful reasons would be needed to abolish it.

As military defeat occasioned emancipation, was its main purpose to improve the army? Serfs who became soldiers served up to twenty-five years before they were released and given their freedom, if they survived. Shortening the period of service might create trouble by returning more and more free men back to village or factory life. Not only did the length of service make it impossible to maintain a trained reserve for the army, but also it involved maintaining a vast standing army which cost about one-third of the government's income. Emancipation of the serfs would open the way to reducing the period of military service and creating a reserve, but there is no clear evidence that this was what spurred Alexander II on.

The economic argument that emancipation was the necessary precondition to free the labour force and enable industrialisation to go ahead is perhaps more convincing, and it is certainly stressed by Marxist historians. However, industrialisation was going ahead anyway, with serfs working either in their masters' factories or, for example, labouring in the expanding cotton industry and paying their *obrok* from their wages. Furthermore, government was worried by the prospect of a totally free labour force, and feared the unrest which large industrial centres had brought in the west, so again it is not possible to see the economic argument as the key reason for emancipating the labour force.

The incentive for emancipation may be understood as a necessary modernisation. Russia's weakness had been proven in the Crimea against the industrial and commercial power of Britain and France. Serfdom distinguished Russia as a backward nation to many who could make a comparison, and peasant expectations that it would end often appeared ready to provoke revolt. A new reign offered the right psychological moment for emancipation. It seems that Alexander II exploited all these feelings in March 1856 when he first spoke to the nobility of Moscow province and urged emancipation 'from above', and he referred to them again two years later (see extract B). But the Tsar needed the support of his own family, in particular his wife, his younger brother the Grand Duke Constantine, and the Grand Duchess Elena (widow to one of his uncles) to encourage him to face the opposition of the nobility. He also needed the help of a group of liberal bureaucrats to drive through the reform, as they saw it in the interests of the state, in particular Minister of the Interior Lanskoy, N. Miliutin (nephew of former Minister of State Domains Kiselev and brother of Minister of War 1861–81 Count D. Miliutin) and General Rostovtsev.

The process of emancipation was very long drawn out, the nobility's opposition being profound. Alexander II chaired the Secret Committee from January 1857, but its proposals were framed cautiously and slowly. Meanwhile the governor of the Lithuanian provinces pushed the landowners into a proposal for emancipation of the serfs which gave them no land. But this was the breakthrough Alexander II had been awaiting, and he responded with the Rescript of 20 November 1857, instructing that the Lithuanian peasants would be emancipated and given land in return for payment (in labour or money) over many years. This Rescript was widely published and the nobility of other provinces made their counter-proposals to the

Main Committee (as the Secret Committee was now publicly called).

Despite the obstructionist efforts of some of the nobility, the idea of giving emancipated serfs land to be paid for (by 'redemption payments') over a period of years took hold. Rostovtsev's plan, based on Nikolai Miliutin's draft, received the support of the Tsar. A great struggle followed, but on 4 December 1858 the Main Committee under Rostovtsev accepted this and Miliutin soon became reconciled to the General whom he had once regarded as a reactionary. In 1859 the preparation of the legislation was placed before the Editing Commission (chaired by Rostovtsev, including many liberal bureaucrats), charged with the task of reviewing the mostly opposing proposals of the nobility (see extracts A and C). Two convocations of deputies from the provinces were held in St Petersburg (in August 1859 and February 1860), but the basic shape of emancipation with land was kept despite criticism. Miliutin was made Deputy Minister in 1859, a position which increased the strength of the reformers. In October 1860 the Editing Commission sent the draft to the Main Committee, which approved it in January 1861. But in the Council of State the majority was opposed and had to be overruled by the Tsar, and on 19 February 1861 Alexander II signed the Act of Emancipation.

The impact of emancipation

Emancipation was to be a slow process, to the disappointment of many serfs. After at least two years, the peasant's 'temporary obligation' to the landlord would end. The peasant would receive the cottage and allotment, and a share (allocated by the *mir*) of that portion of the landowner's land which the Arbitrator decided was the village's entitlement. In return the peasant made redemption payments for forty-nine years (through the *mir*) to the state to repay the compensation which the state had given to the landlord. Sometimes this took until 1881 to set up. Separate legislation freed household serfs (who received no land), those employed in mines and factories, and in 1863 'appanage peasants' and in 1866 state peasants became entitled to redeem their land.

The limitations of this emancipation were considerable. Most peasants believed that those who worked the land really owned it, so the forty-nine year debt of redemption payments seemed to be theft. High expectations had been raised by talk of emancipation, and these were dashed by the debt, the complexity of the law and by wrangles with some Arbitrators (who generally did a fair job). Suspicion that the Tsar Liberator's great reform was being hidden by greedy landlords sparked some serious peasant disturbances (see extracts D (i and ii)). In addition, the burden of redemption payments and hold of the *mir* over the peasantry restricted the emergence of the labour mobility which rapid industrialisation would require. Landowners themselves generally did well from the over-valuation of the land they lost, but as they were paid in government bonds which could not be cashed (the government could not afford this), and which were often swallowed up in mortgage repayments, only some were able to transform their estates into efficient farms producing a surplus for market. Some leased out their land to successful peasant farmers and lived off the rent, or sold up altogether, and there was no rapid agricultural revolution from a subsistence to a market economy. Economic problems were thus stored up for the future. Population growth continued (1812, 41 million; 1858, 74 million; 1897, 125 million) and made increasing demands on food supplies, while the peasant family's average landholding declined from the barely adequate to the level of 'land-hunger'.

It is easy to register these limitations, but the scale of the legal and social reform was formidable. The nobility had been driven to accept change which most saw as being against their interests, but there was no palace coup nor civil war. Russia was clearly beginning a process of modernisation and regeneration. Was it perhaps the start of revolution? The Tsar was careful to dismiss some key architects of emancipation afterwards, including Nikolai Miliutin, and a great social upheaval was contained because peasants continued to be tied to the land and the landowning class had not been destroyed, so it may be argued that tsarism was potentially strengthened by weathering the storm successfully.

Continued reforms

In 1864 Alexander II began the reform of local government by introducing *zemstva* at a district and provincial level. Representatives were elected by each social group to the lower district level *zemstva*, the nobility and peasantry each holding about 40 per cent of the seats, and the merchants, clergy and towns people about 20 per cent (see extract E (i)). Representatives for the provincial *zemstva* were elected by the district *zemstva*, and the nobility predominated at this level, not least because they had the time and money to spare. The rationale behind this reform, which was developed in parallel with emancipation, was quite calculated. First, it harnessed the energies of the nobility and townspeople in worthwhile local government projects and diverted them from meddling in central government. Second, it provided a way of looking after the welfare of former serfs who were no longer the direct responsibility of their former masters. Many important projects resulted from *zemstva* activity, with local hospitals, schools, welfare, business projects including road building tailored to local needs in a way which was well beyond the capacity of the remote central bureaucracy. In 1870 a similar reform was allowed to city government. The *zemstva* continued to operate until the Bolshevik Revolution, and many of their creations continued to serve generations afterwards, but the autocratic regime was careful to restrict such progressive reform to local government. The history of France served as a suitable warning against extending the powers of elected assemblies or municipal authorities.

Zemstva elected Justices of the Peace who dealt with small cases in an inexpensive way, and this was part of a total reform of the judicial system. Once a resort to the courts was financially disastrous for anyone involved and had nothing to do with justice; the process took years, bribery was essential, the judges were often untrained and sometimes illiterate, and the rules of evidence so weighted that the word of a nobleman had to be given preference over anyone else's. Written evidence only was considered, giving the secretary great influence when the judges could not read. All of this was swept away by the Judicial Reform of 1864. The court system was streamlined with a clear appeals procedure. Cases were heard in open court before a jury. Lawyers had to be properly qualified, and judges received a salary intended to make them bribe-proof and were appointed for life to give them proper independence. The public was admitted to courts, and this in itself made the new system respected. But problem areas remained. Church courts continued to deal with divorce, and the government discovered the dangers of a transparently open judicial system in 1878 when Vera Zasulich was acquitted after shooting and wounding General Trepov, the Governor of St Petersburg. In court she was able to demonstrate the governor's brutality to political prisoners and create such sympathy, at the expense of the regime, that in future the autocracy dealt with political trials in military courts. For some observers, the regime stood condemned by the light of its very own judicial reforms, and its authority was being eaten away from within.

Conservatives feared that the educational reforms carried out under Golovnin (Minister of Education) after 1861 would also cause embarrassment to the autocracy by creating liberal-minded citizens who would demand a say in government. In 1863 the Tsar approved new university regulations which gave them considerable autonomy, while a liberal curriculum allowed any literature to be imported. At the other end of the educational scale, primary education was soon handed over to the *zemstva*, while many new secondary schools were built. These new schools were outside the control of the church and taught a modern curriculum which emphasised science and languages. Between 1855 and 1865, the number of pupils in school doubled, and between 1861 and 1881 the number of schools multiplied fourfold. But in 1866 a former student of Kazan university fired a pistol at the Tsar, and conservative fears about the dangers of all this education seemed justified. Golovnin was replaced by Dmitri Tolstoy, university discipline became a police matter, school inspections became vigilant, and the school curriculum became more classical; rote-learning replaced enquiry (see extract G (i)).

A similar thaw, followed by a cautious qualification, occurred with the censorship of the press. Nicholas I's controls had been severe and complex, but these were greatly relaxed during the early years of Alexander II's reign. In 1863 Valuev became Minister of the Interior, and his Press Law of 1865 was progressive in that newspapers did not have to submit copy to a censor before publication, but they would forfeit a deposit or be closed for a time if they published inflammatory articles (see extract F). Papers and journals were warned, and in 1866 *The Contemporary* was prohibited, but generally there was a great flourishing of literature and some of the most famous works of Turgenev, Tolstoy and Dostoevsky were published.

Military and economic progress

One argument behind these 'great reforms' was to restore the power of the Russian state which had been shown to be enfeebled in the Crimea. They do indeed form part of the picture which included army reform, but were they a necessary part of the military and financial regeneration or merely superficial 'extras'?

Dmitrii Miliutin remained Minister of War from 1861 to 1881, his length of service indicating clearly that Alexander II set a priority on the great military reforms which he carried through. To begin with the command structure was reformed by creating military districts which took on decentralised responsibilities for command and supply. The harsh code of discipline was altered, and with emancipation the period of military service in the 1860s became fifteen years. Military education was transformed, academic and military subjects were taught alongside each other, civilian teachers were employed, and some establishments admitted non-nobles to be trained as future officers. An elite Staff College was created, training many of the future army and ministry chiefs, and specialist schools for engineers, artillery officers and military lawyers were created, and recruits were taught to read and write from the 1870s.

This may be seen to be in harmony with the other reforms which were taking place, but Miliutin's proposed change to conscription caused friction. Miliutin proposed the recruitment of about one-quarter of all young men from every social class to serve for seven years full time and another eight as reservists. There would be no buying out by hiring substitutes. Of course the nobil-

ity were appalled at the prospect of their sons serving alongside peasants, but the plan to allow the better educated to serve for a shorter period met with fierce opposition from another direction. Dmitri Tolstoy, the Minister of Education, objected to Miliutin giving privileged status to students, fearing it would increase their power to destabilise society. However, Prussia's victory over France showed the value of a well-trained professional army, with a reserve, and Miliutin's fear that the Tsar had turned against him proved groundless (see extract H). Alexander II agreed to the law on Universal Military Service in 1874, and Miliutin continued in his post until he was forced to resign under Alexander III.

It seems impossible that these great military reforms could have been accomplished without first removing the physical and psychological barrier of serfdom, and they do form part of a pattern which undermined class privilege in education, the judicial system and the economy.

Raetern served as Minister of Finance from 1862 until 1878, his long period in power reflecting the priority given to his work. Taxation and expenditure controls became streamlined and budgets were published, but economic development held the key to the recovery of Russia's power and this was recognised. Railway expansion was seen to be of central importance in starting matters off, and Alexander II's government actually planned the network and encouraged private investors by guaranteeing the return. French investment also contributed greatly. In 1851 the line between Moscow and St Petersburg was opened. Fifteen years later, there were 3,000 miles of track, and by 1883 the network had expanded to 14,700 miles. Improved transport and the vast growth of the banking sector boosted investment and trade. Grain exports increased from about 26 million tons in 1866 to 86 million tons in 1880. The cotton industry developed strongly, the American civil war prompting Russia to become virtually self-sufficient by growing her own. Iron and steel production began to develop following the example set by John Hughes and his fellow Welsh pioneers in the Donets basin, and the Nobel brothers founded the oil industry based around Baku. The more vigorous and open-minded commercial emphasis helped to revise another long-standing restriction, that preventing Jews from living outside the Pale of Settlement on the western border. In 1865 Jewish artisans joined Jewish merchants and foreign Jews in being allowed to live and work anywhere in the Empire, a change which exemplifies the way that the post-emancipation 'thaw' cleared the way for economic development.

Minorities, unrest and the question of consistency

Alexander II aimed to reconcile Finland to Russian rule through a most liberal policy. In 1863 he personally opened the Diet in Helsinki, gave equality to the Finnish language, and in 1867 granted a Fundamental Law which created a constitutional government of Four Estates. In Poland, however, liberal reforms encouraged popular demonstrations against Russian rule and an attempt on the life of the Governor-General, the Tsar's brother Constantine. When recruitment for service in the Russian army began in 1863, Poland rose in revolt. By early in 1864 Alexander II's forces had crushed the revolt, and the Tsar returned to the earlier policy of 'russification' in an attempt to stamp out Polish nationalism. Poland was renamed the Vistula Region.

The case of Poland stands as a good example of the Tsar's difficulty with reform. It needed to be a compromise between necessary modernisation and keeping power, and it is not surprising that Alexander II became steadily more cautious as his reign moved on. Herzen, a socialist, exiled in London, welcomed emancipation to begin with but returned to angry criticism when the compromise with the landowners became clear. Chernyshevsky, writing for *The Contemporary* (soon to be banned) argued the need for a federal democracy in all aspects of government (not merely at local level). The *zemstva* began to call for central representation in the mid-1860s, but of course the Tsar rejected it.

Students, owing much to the educational reforms, joined the populist *Narodnik* movement (meaning movement to the people) in 1874 and tried to mobilise the peasantry to make political demands. Most peasants were highly suspicious of these educated youngsters and turned them in to

the authorities. In the late 1870s the group divided between those like Plekhanov, who emphasised the role of education and propaganda to provoke change, and the People's Will who used assassination. A series of bomb attacks on ministers and the Tsar followed, and the dining room in the Winter Palace was blown up in 1880.

These were not the only signs that reform was bringing an unhappy harvest. Russia's successful intervention against the Ottoman empire in 1877, again on the pretext of protecting the Christians, came close to restoring her military prestige, but in 1878 the Congress of Berlin robbed her of her gains. Public dismay was acute. Therefore, by the end of the decade, it would be understandable for Alexander II to feel a growing sense of disappointment and isolation as his concerns with the great reforms of the 1860s were replaced by threats to his person and challenges to his state.

Alexander II's response to the situation in 1879–81 has provoked great debate because his assassination left matters unconcluded. Repression was fierce but brief. Changes in government gave the edge to the liberal Loris-Melikov, who became Minister of the Interior in 1880. But concessions were made to the right (including the Tsarevich, the future Alexander III), and the reactionary Pobedonostsev was made Procurator of the Holy Synod. However, soon after the death of the Empress in 1880, the Tsar married his mistress Catherine Doloruky, and Loris-Melikov had the support of the Tsar's new Princess Yurievskaya, as she became. This helped Loris-Melikov succeed where others had failed, and he obtained the Tsar's consent to a significant step towards constitutional reform. In February 1881 Alexander II approved calling a General Commission as a consultative body, which would include some elected representatives from the *zemstva*. Was this merely a gesture which developed the reforms to local government, or the beginnings of a popular constitution? This remains an open question, for on 1 March 1881, before a proclamation could be issued, the People's Will took the Tsar's life with their second bomb in their last-ditch attempt to destroy the regime. Perhaps they achieved their goal indirectly, for by destroying reform they made revolution more likely.

As the reign drew towards its unexpected close,

the comments of a French observer seem perceptive:

'The task was to build a new Russia, [but] the edifice was constructed upon the old foundations. Building operations were carried out without … a general plan.… By introducing here and there particular innovations while neglecting near-by indispensable repairs … Alexander in the end succeeded after immense labours in making of the new Russia an incomplete and uncomfortable dwelling where the friends and opponents of innovation felt almost equally ill at ease.'

(1881, cited in W.E. Mosse, *An Economic History of Russia, 1856–1914*, London, I.B. Tauris, 1996, p. 52)

ALEXANDER III AND THE RETURN TO REACTION, 1881–94

Pobedonostsev's policy

As the Tsarevich watched his father die from his wounds, his belief that liberal policies were counter-productive must have been confirmed. However, to begin with it seemed that Alexander III might continue with the Loris-Melikov reform plan because he felt a loyalty to the path his father had approved. Pobedonostsev, the famously reactionary Procurator of the Holy Synod (in charge of the Orthodox Church), had no such concerns. To him the great reforms of Alexander II had been a 'criminal mistake'. He believed that parliamentary government was a great fraud, giving power to those who could manipulate public opinion, and a free press wielded power without responsibility. Rightful power came from God, and its proper use was in God's service. In Pobedonostsev's carefully reasoned view, the Tsar Autocrat of all Russia was the instrument of God's power, sanctioned by the Orthodox Church, and anyone who tried to alter it, or who stood outside the Church (for example the Jews), was an enemy. As his former tutor and close adviser, Pobedonostsev carried weight with Alexander III.

Pobedonostsev argued fiercely against the reform plan in the Council of Ministers on 8 March 1881 (see extract I). But he won only minority support that day. Alexander III took several weeks to make up his mind and back him. He may have been strengthened in his decision as it became clear that the terrorists had ceased to be a threat for the moment. On 27 April the Tsar approved Pobedonostsev's draft manifesto which vigorously proclaimed the principles of autocratic government, and it was published on 29 April (see extract J). Loris-Melikov and Miliutin resigned, the Princess Yurievskaya packed up and left Russia, and the period of reform ended with a purge of the bureaucracy. Pobedonostsev and the terrorists had won.

The reaction

Repression intensified under the 1881 Statute on State Security, which enabled political trials to be heard in special courts outside the reformed judicial system. The *Okhrana*, the secret police, had its powers increased and censorship of the press became more intrusive. Universities became more closely controlled by the government, and the new Minister of Education, Delyanov, created horror among liberals in 1887 by telling schools in the Moscow district to exclude the children of cooks and laundresses who would only cause trouble if they were educated above their place in society (see extract G (ii)). The *Zemstva* Act of 1890 limited the powers of these elected bodies which had dared to seek influence in the Tsar's government (see extract E (ii)).

In the countryside Land Captains were appointed by the Minister of the Interior from the ranks of the nobility or army officers after 1890. They were given wide powers to control the peasantry, overrule the *mir* and direct the police. Not only did this go a long way to restoring the levels of supervision which had existed under serfdom, but also it helped to reaffirm the authority of the nobility. However, emancipation could not be undone, and the policies of Bunge (Finance Minister 1882–86) sought to develop the agricultural economy by reducing redemption payments and setting up the Nobles' and Peasants' Land Bank to provide loans to the more enterprising.

Economic progress was one area where Alexander III was only too eager to build on his father's achievements. Stabilising the currency (by fixing its value against gold reserves) had been Raetern's aim, and it was also Bunge's, because an unstable currency deterred foreign investment in Russia, handicapped her trade, and threatened political stability if purchasing power was damaged. He hoped to stabilise the rouble by strengthening the economy. Bunge struggled to stimulate production, but exports grew slowly, and government income from taxation failed to cover spending – over 30 per cent went on the military and nearly 30 per cent went to pay interest on debts between 1881 and 1886.

Bunge's failure led to his replacement as Finance Minister in 1887 by Vyshnegradsky. Single-minded and tough, he resolved to use Russia's great asset of grain to export. Provided imports were kept to a minimum, the trade surplus would boost Russia's gold reserves, attract inward investment and allow the rouble to go onto the gold standard. He was called 'the looter' because his ruthless collection of tax arrears forced the peasantry to sell grain. Preferential rates on state-owned railways encouraged grain exports which reached their highest level of the century in 1888. In 1891 tariffs on many imports improved Russia's balance of trade further. However, the policy was ruthlessly exploitive and probably stifled industrial and agricultural development. The harvest failed in 1891, cholera struck in 1892 but Vyshnegradsky stood firm: 'We ourselves will not eat, but we shall export' (cited in Mosse, *Economic History*, p. 91). The death toll mounted, the eventual cost of relief was 150 million roubles, grain exports ceased and Vyshnegradsky suffered a stroke and resigned. However, Russia's gold reserves had increased by 281 million roubles since 1886 to reach 581 million in January 1893, and the foundation had been laid for the rouble to be put on the gold standard in 1897 by his successor, Sergei Witte.

Pobedonostsev's attitude to non-Russian minorities and those outside the Orthodox Church was profoundly hostile. 'Russification' was pursued with great energy, with Russian being declared the official first language throughout the empire, and minorities such as the Poles (7.9 million in 1897), Armenians (1.2 million) and Ukrainians (22.4 million) being subjected to bullying interference in administrative, educational and religious matters.

Undoubtedly, hostility was created where there had been coexistence. There were about 5 million Jews in the empire, and by the 1890s they were the subject of renewed economic and social restrictions, while a blind eye was turned to the increasingly popular pastime of attacking the Jewish quarters of towns. These 'pogroms' as they were called were the speciality of a sinister group of Russian ultra-nationalists, the 'Black Hundreds', who blamed Jews for the assassination of Alexander II. Many Jews emigrated, while others became more active in fighting tsarism by joining the revolutionary Jewish 'Bund', so Pobedonostsev's ferocious suspicion of the disloyalty of this minority became self-fulfilling.

The key achievement of Alexander III's reign was probably to keep out of war, tempting though it was over the Coburg candidature to the Bulgarian throne in 1885–88. The economic progress and improvement in the government's financial position would have been wrecked by the cost of war. In this context, the forging of the alliance with France during 1892–94 was an important and successful realignment for Russia, bringing her a reliable partner with funds to invest in Russia (see Chapter 17). But in other respects it is difficult to escape the conclusion that Alexander III's reign, which ended in 1894, was a period of dangerously wasted opportunity. After the 'thaw' of Alexander II's great reforms, the period of reaction created new enemies and encouraged liberals and revolutionaries to become fellow-travellers, allies of convenience in their campaigns to change tsarist autocracy.

SECTION B – SOURCES

THE LIMITATIONS OF ALEXANDER II'S REFORMS

Russia's defeat in the Crimean war made reform urgent if she was to match the industrial and military strength of the European powers and protect her interests in future. Reform from above occurred periodically in Russia, and emancipation of the serfs had been long recognised as the necessary starting-point. It seemed that economic development could come only when the system which made serfs the property of the nobility was ended. But ending the centuries-old institution of serfdom aroused great hostility from the nobility who obstructed the reform, and Alexander II had to perform the leading role in powering the change through (see extracts A, B and C). He was assisted by some liberal bureaucrats, and in 1859 set up the Editing Commission to draw up the emancipation statute after hearing representations from the provinces. General Rostovtsev was placed in charge, but in his previous post on the Main Committee on Peasant Affairs he had acquired a reputation as a reactionary, and the extent of his conversion to the idea of emancipating the serfs and giving them land rested on his loyalty to the tsar (extract C). Emancipation in 1861 created some disappointment among the peasantry over the land allocations by the Arbitrators, the time-scale and because redemption payments were required from them to compensate the landowners (see extracts D (i and ii)).

Other reforms followed: of the press (extract F), the judiciary, education (extract G (i)) and by creating provincial and district *zemstva* (extract E (i)). Some commentators argue that Alexander II's reforms were piecemeal and superficial, or that he lost enthusiasm for them during his reign (see extract H). Clearly he stopped short of changing the autocracy fundamentally. However, before he was assassinated in 1881, he approved reform proposals giving representatives from the *zemstva* a consultative role in the legislation of central government. The suddenness and the tragic circumstances in which Alexander III came to the throne increased the power of those who argued that liberal change created instability. Alexander III seemed to hesitate briefly about which course to follow, but the advice of the famously reactionary Pobedonostsev, his old tutor, was strongly opposed to the reform package (extract I). The new Tsar soon made up his mind to stand by autocracy with its overtones of God-given authority and paternal responsibility for the land and the people (see extract J). During his reign universities, schools, the press and the *zemstva* were all restricted (see extracts E (ii) and G (ii)) and Land Captains were appointed from the ranks of the nobility to control the peasantry. Was autocracy strengthened by the

time of Alexander III's death in 1894? Did his policy 'stop the rot', as Pobedonostsev hoped, or by standing against change was tsarism doomed? Was there in fact a middle way, as Alexander II seemed to follow for some of his reign, or was it impossible to pursue modernisation and keep an autocratic system of government intact?

A Emancipation: the recollections of a member of the Editorial Commission

(Solov'ev was Head of the Land Department of the Ministry of Internal Affairs 1857–59, then a member of the Editorial Commission 1859–60)

The great initiative in the sacred matter of freeing the serfs belongs entirely to the sovereign emperor Aleksandr Nikolaevich himself. From the moment that the sovereign announced to the Moscow nobility his intention to free the serfs, there began a struggle between the liberal and the conservative elements. . . .

. . . Although not quite consciously, the representatives of the conservative estate-owners' party began to strive to carry out a plan seemingly prepared beforehand. The aims of the group were either to block the reform completely or, if that proved impossible, to free the serfs without land and to receive compensation for having granted them personal freedom. As a means of achieving one of these aims they launched a scare campaign threatening peasant unrest and democratic revolution. . . .

. . . There is not the slightest doubt that the information received at the time from the Third Section . . . was just as one-sided. . . . The chief of the gendarmes at that time was Prince V. A. Dolgorukov. . . . He was one of the fanatical enemies of the serf reform. The campaign to frighten the sovereign was worked out especially beginning in (1856) and was then put into operation.

(from 'notes' by Senator Ia. A. Solov'ev, written 1873–75,
Zapiski Senatora Ia. A. Solov'eva in *Russkaia starina* 27
(February 1880), cited in G. Vernadsky (ed.) *A Sourcebook for Russian History from Early Times to 1917*, vol. 3, New Haven, CT, Yale University Press, 1972, pp. 590–91)

B From Alexander II's address to the Moscow nobility, 31 August 1858

I find it pleasant, gentlemen, when I can thank the nobility, but I cannot say what I do not believe. . . . You will remember that when I spoke to you here . . . two years ago I told you that sooner or later it would be necessary to change serfdom and that it would be better for this change to begin at the top than at the bottom. . . . I expected the Moscow nobility to be the first to respond; but Nizhnii-Novgorod responded and the guberniia of Moscow was not the first, not the second, nor even the third. This made me sad, for I am proud that I was born in Moscow.

(from Tatishchev, *Imperator Aleksandr II*, vol. 1, pp. 310–11, cited in Vernadsky (ed.) *Sourcebook for Russian History from Early Times to 1917*, vol. 3, 1972, p. 591)

C Rostovtsev reports to the Tsar on opposition to emancipation, 23 October 1859

(Rostovtsev was chairman of the Editorial Commission)

From the standpoint of civil law the entire reform . . . is unjust from beginning to end, since it is a violation of the right of private ownership; but, as a state necessity and on the basis of state law, the reform is legitimate, sacred, and essential.

A large number of enemies of the reform who are unable to see its urgency accuse the Editorial Commissions . . . of a desire to fleece the nobles, and others . . . accuse them of wanting to cause anarchy.
The efforts of the commissions have been and are still:
First, *to save Russia*. . . .
Second, to carry through *rational and not palliative* changes, that is to say, not for a certain period or by halves, but forever and completely, in order to spare both Russia and Your Majesty's heirs from future upheavals.

(from Semenov, *Osvobozhdenie krest'ian*, vol. 2, pp. 298–32, cited in Vernadsky (ed.) *Sourcebook for Russian History from Early Times to 1917*, vol. 3, 1972, p. 595)

D Peasant reactions to emancipation

(i) A western observer records peasant disappointment

many believed that the nobles would receive salaries from the Tsar, and that *all* the land would be given to the Communes. . . .

Instead of this the peasants found that they were still to pay dues, even for the Communal land which they regarded as unquestionably their own! . . . Either the proprietors must be concealing or misinterpreting the law, or this was merely a preparatory measure, which would be followed by the real Emancipation. Thus were awakened among the peasantry a spirit of mistrust and suspicion.

(from D.M. Wallace, *Russia*, London, 1912, pp. 500–05, cited in W.B. Walsh, *Readings in Russian History*, vol. 2, New York, Syracuse University Press, 1963, p. 393)

(ii) From the report of the marshal of the aristocracy of Podolski province, August 1861

The peasants expect everything to come direct from the Tsar, to whom they give the character of a natural force, blind and implacable. They have completely given up believing in the simplest rules of respect for the property of others and for the general economic rules . . . in the manifesto of 19 February . . . because for once fate has turned the natural force of supreme power to their advantage, they now have the right to expect from it every kind of benefit and generosity.

(from *The Peasant Movement in 1861*, 'Kolokol' 1862, p. 174, cited in F. Venturi, 'The peasant movement', in T. Emmans (ed.) *Emancipation of the Russian Serfs*, New York, Holt, Rinehart and Winston, 1970, p. 94)

E The *Zemstva*

(i) From a western observer's record of the zemstvo *in Novgorod in the early 1870s*

In form the institution is parliamentary – that is to say, it consists of an assembly of deputies which meets at least once a year, and of a permanent executive bureau elected by the assembly from among its members. . . .

What surprised me most in this assembly was that it was composed partly of nobles and partly of peasants – the latter being decidedly in the majority – and no trace of antagonism seemed to exist between the two classes.

(from Wallace, *Russia*, pp. 500–05, cited in Walsh, *Readings in Russian History*, vol. 2, pp. 461–62)

(ii) From the new Zemstvo *Act, 12 June 1890*

5 The governor shall have supervision over the correctness and legality of the actions of the *zemstvo* institutions. . . .

87 The governor shall halt the execution of an ordinance of the *zemstvo* assembly in cases where he ascertains that it: (a) is incompatible with the law or was enacted in violation of the sphere of jurisdiction . . . of *zemstvo* institutions; or (b) does not correspond to the general welfare and needs of the state or clearly violates the interests of the local inhabitants.

(*PSZRI*, 3rd series, vol. 10, pp. 496, 499, 501, 505–06, 509, cited in Vernadsky (ed.) *Sourcebook for Russian History from Early Times to 1917*, vol. 3, pp. 688–89)

F From the press laws, 6 April 1865

16 Guarantees are deposited . . .

19 The guarantee is used to pay monetary penalties imposed on a periodical publication.

29 The minister of internal affairs is accorded the right to issue warnings to periodical publications, indicating the articles giving cause for this. A third warning suspends publication for a period of time designated by the minister . . . but not exceeding six months.

(*PSZRI*, 2nd series, vol. 40, pt 1, pp. 396, 398–400, cited in Vernadsky (ed.) *Sourcebook for Russian History from Early Times to 1917*, vol. 3, p. 617)

G Education

(i) Tolstoy's ministry of education explains its new aims, November 1872

(D. A. Tolstoy replaced the more liberal Golovnin as Minister of Education after 1866)

Western Europe cannot be indifferent as to whether the colossal state to its east will assume . . . a European character or will . . . become a half-European, half-Asiatic state. Now it was precisely . . . [this] that was being decided at the time the educational reform of 1871 and 1872 was under discussion, and, thanks to the wise decision of the sovereign emperor . . . this question was definitively resolved in principle . . . in favour of a European education and a European character for Russia.

(*Zhurnal Ministerstva Narodnogo Prosveshcheniia* 164 (November 1872): 1–2, cited in Vernadsky (ed.) *Sourcebook for Russian History from Early Times to 1917*, vol. 3, p. 624)

(ii) From Minister of Public Education Delyanov's circular to Moscow schools, June 1887

I find it necessary, in order to improve the student body of the gymnasia to admit to these institutions only those children who have adequate guidance and supervision at home. The strict application of this rule will free the gymnasia and progymnasia from enrolment in them of the children of coachmen, lackies, cooks, laundresses, petty shopkeepers, and similar persons. . . . Many years of experience show that attempts to educate such children cause them to neglect their parents, to become discontented with their way of life, and arouse in them an animosity against the existing and naturally inevitable disparities in wealth.

(in *Khrestomatiya*, vol. 3, pp. 467–68, paraphrased in Walsh, *Readings in Russian History*, vol. 2, p. 486)

H From D.A. Miliutin's diary on Alexander II's change of mind, 31 December 1873

(Field Marshal and Count D.A. Miliutin was Minister of War 1861–81 and a close adviser of the Tsar)

What an amazing and lamentable comparison with the situation as it was when I entered the top echelons of the government thirteen years ago! Then everything surged forward; now everything drags back. Then the sovereign was sympathetic to progress, he moved things forward himself; now he has lost confidence in everything he himself created. . . . With such a state of affairs is it possible for me alone to keep my footing amidst the debris of the shipwreck?

(P. A. Zaionchkovskii (ed.) *Dnevnik D.A. Miliutina 1873–82*, Moscow 1947–50, vol. 1, pp. 119–20, cited in Vernadsky (ed.) *Sourcebook for Russian History from Early Times to 1917*, vol. 3, p. 625)

I Pobedonostsev argues against further change, 8 March 1881

A week after Alexander II's assassination, Alexander III presided over the Council of Ministers which was considering Minister of the Interior Loris-Melikov's proposal – approved by Alexander II – to summon elected representatives from the *zemstva* and give them a consultative legislative role. This is from the diary of Peretts, chief secretary of the State Council, recording the comments of the Chief Procurator of the Holy Synod.

They want to introduce a constitution in Russia . . . And what is a constitution? Western Europe provides us with the answer to this question. The constitutions existing there are tools of every kind of falsehood, the tools of every kind of intrigue.

. . . Russia was strong thanks to autocracy, thanks to the boundless mutual trust and close ties between the people and their tsar. . . . The so-called representatives of the *zemstvo* only alienate the tsar from the people. In the meantime the government ought to provide for the people; it should come to know their real needs and should help them contend with their often desperate poverty. This is the destiny toward which we must strive; this is the task of the new reign.

But instead they propose to organize a chatter shop for us, something like the French Estates General. . . .

. . . new judicial institutions were established – new chatter shops, chatter shops for lawyers. . . .

Freedom was finally given to the press, the most fearful chatter shop of all, which to every corner . . . sows the seed of discord and dissatisfaction among peaceful and honest men, inflames passions, and incites the people to the most flagrant lawlessness.

In such a terrible time, Sire, we must not think of instituting a new chatter shop, in which new corrupting speeches will be delivered; we must think of action. We must act.

('Iz dnevnika E.A. Perettsa', in *Krasnyi arkhiv*, vol. 8, 1925, cited in Vernadsky (ed.) *Sourcebook for Russian History from Early Times to 1917*, vol. 3, p. 678)

J Alexander III upholds autocracy, 29 April 1881

Amidst our great sorrow the voice of God enjoins us to take up firmly the reins of government, with trust in divine Providence, with faith in the strength and veracity of autocratic power, which we have been called upon to maintain and defend, for the good of the people, against all encroachments upon it.

Consecrating ourselves to our great task of service, we call upon all our faithful subjects to serve us and the state with fidelity and truth, for the eradication of the vile sedition disgracing the Russian land . . . and for the establishment of order and integrity in the activity of the institutions granted to Russia by her benefactor, our beloved father.

(*PSZRI*, 3rd series, vol. 1, p. 54, cited in Vernadsky (ed.) *Sourcebook for Russian History from Early Times to 1917*, vol. 3, p. 680)

Questions

1 Use extract C to evaluate Rostovtsev's attitude to the emancipation of the serfs.
2 To what extent do extracts B, C and D (i and ii) support the evidence of Solov'ev in extract A?
3 How useful is extract E (i) to an historian studying the development of *zemstva* under Alexander II?
4 Use extracts E (i and ii), F, G (i and ii), and your own knowledge, to evaluate Miliutin's analysis in extract H that reform policy changed well before Alexander III came to the throne in 1881.
5 In extract I, explain Pobedonostsev's meaning in:
   (a) his description of constitutions as 'tools of every kind of falsehood'
   (b) his description of 'the boundless mutual trust and close ties between the people and their tsar'.
6 To what extent does extract J suggest that Alexander III accepted the advice of Pobedonostsev in extract I?

Further reading

Detailed and authoritative treatment of this period is provided by D. Saunders, *Russia in the Age of Reaction and Reform 1801–81* (London, Longman, 1995) and H. Rogger, *Russia in the Age of Modernisation and Revolution 1881–1917* (London, Longman, 1985).

Interesting and perceptive analysis, especially of the great reforms and the politics behind them, is provided by W.E. Mosse in the slightly misleadingly entitled *An Economic History of Russia 1856–1914* (London, I.B. Tauris, 1996); it was originally published in 1992 as *Perestroika Under the Tsars*. Very useful and concise treatment of the great reforms is provided in the pamphlet by M. Perrie, *Alexander II, Emancipation and Reform in Russia, 1855–1881* (London, Historical Association, 1989), while A. Wood, *The Origins of the Russian Revolution 1861–1917* (London, Methuen, 1987) provides a clear and short review. Helpful student texts are R. Sherman, *Russia, 1815–81* (London, Hodder and Stoughton, 1991) and M. Lynch, *Reaction and Revolutions: Russia 1881–1924* (London, Hodder and Stoughton, 1992), valuable not least because they include documentary excerpts and statistical information. J.N. Westwood, *Endurance and Endeavour: Russian History 1812–1992* (Oxford University Press, 1993) combines scholarship, perspective and anecdote in highly readable proportions.

Obtaining original source material in translation may be problematic because most of the collections have been published in the United States; of particular value are G. Vernadsky (ed.) *A Sourcebook for Russian History from Early Times to 1917*, vol. 3 (New Haven, CT, Yale University Press, 1971) and W.B. Walsh, *Readings in Russian History*, vol. 2 (New York, Syracuse University Press, 1963).

• CHAPTER FIFTEEN •

The Age of Imperialism

• CONTENTS •

Key dates

SECTION A

Economic growth in Europe

The imperialist impulse

Africa and the Far East

SECTION B – SOURCES

Colonial expansion and European rivalries

KEY DATES

1833	Slavery abolished in the British empire
1842	Britain annexes New Zealand; treaty of Nanking, Britain and China
1857	Indian troops mutiny against Britain
1865	Russia annexes Tashkent
1869	Suez Canal opened
1872	Disraeli's speech at Crystal Palace begins popularisation of empire
1873	Death of Livingstone in Africa
1874	Britain claims protectorate on Gold Coast and annexes Fiji Islands
1875	Queen Victoria created 'Empress of India'; Disraeli purchases 45 per cent of Suez Canal shares for Britain
1876	Leopold II of Belgium begins development of Congo
1879	Zulu victory at Isandhlwana followed by British victory in Zulu war
1881	France occupies Tunis; Boer victory over Britain at Majuba Hill; Convention of Pretoria allows qualified independence for Transvaal
1882	Britain bombards Alexandria and occupies Egypt
1883 Feb.	Germany enquires what claim Britain has in South West Africa
1884 April	Germany claims protectorate over Angra Pequena, South West Africa
Nov. – 1885 Feb.	Berlin Colonial Conference; 'rules' of 'Scramble for Africa' set out
	French seizure of Madagascar complete. Germany claims Tanganyika; death of Gordon at Khartoum
1886	Royal Niger Company formed by granting Charter to Goldie's United African Company. Britain claims Bechuanaland; Britain,

	France and Germany agree division of East Africa
1889	Rhodes awarded Charter for Bechuanaland Exploration Company
1890	Britain, France and Germany settle east Africa boundaries; Britain cedes Heligoland (in North Sea) to Germany
1891	Britain's claim to Northern Rhodesia recognised by Germany
1894	Japan defeats Russia and claims Korea
1895	Jameson Raid into Transvaal fails
1898	Russia gains lease on Port Arthur from China
1898–1900	Boxer rebellion in China
1899–1902	Anglo-Boer war
1902	Alliance between Britain and Japan
1904–05	Russo-Japanese war

SECTION A

Industry and empire are in a way the dominating aspects of Europe between the Napoleonic and First World Wars. Certainly they affected far more people in their ordinary lives, health, careers and expectations than any of the great political milestones of Europe's nineteenth century. When one stands back from the details, the connection between a growing population, industrialisation, and the European colonial empires is obvious and exists at many levels; commercial, emotional and patriotic, competitive, to name just a few. Different theories about the nature of the connection, and complex analysis about economic growth and imperialism, should not obscure the fact that these are basically parallel developments. But industry and empire in the nineteenth century reached their most obvious crescendo in Great Britain herself; the first industrial nation established an empire 'over which the sun never set' so extensive was its dominion, making her the first and in some sense the only world power in modern history. With much comic patriotism, Rudyard Kipling reflected on the great power which had at its head the small figure of the widow Queen Victoria:

Walk wide o' the Widow at Windsor,
For 'alf o' Creation she owns:
We 'ave bought 'er the same with the sword an' the flame,
An' we've salted it down with our bones. . . .
Hands off o' the sons o' the Widow,
Hands off o' the goods in 'er shop,
For the Kings must come down an' the Emperors frown
When the Widow at Windsor says 'Stop!'

(cited in D. Judd, *Empire: the British Imperial Experience from 1765 to the Present*, London, Fontana, 1997, p. 125)

ECONOMIC GROWTH IN EUROPE

Population growth

Malthus published his *Essay on the Principle of Population* in 1798, and revised it in 1803, warning that population would increase geometrically and quickly outstrip the arithmetic growth in resources. The future looked dismal, and Malthus warned that individuals would have to postpone having families, and keep the size of their family strictly within their capacity to provide for it, if famine and starvation were to be avoided. However, economic development occurred and sustained the European population growth of the nineteenth century.

The population of Europe west of the Urals grew from 187 million to 401 million over the century. Emigration lightened the load on European resources and increased European domination of the world; at the beginning of the century, about one-fifth of the world's population was European, and by the end of the century the proportion had grown to one-third (M.S. Anderson, *The Ascendancy of Europe*, London, Longman, 1985, pp. 121–22). The growing population supplied both the labour force for the industrial economy, and an important slice of the market for its products. Economic growth meant that the growing population could afford to buy food and the necessities of life. The exact relationship between population growth and economic growth is complicated, as each was both a cause and an effect of the other.

A glance at Tables 15.1 and 15.2 shows the vast rise in the population of both Germany and Brit-

Table 15.1 Population of selected European countries (millions), 1801–1911

	1801	1851	1881	1911
Britain	10.5	20.82	29.71	40.83
France	27.35	35.78	37.4	39.19
Hungary	8.5	13.19	15.74	20.89
Spain	10.54	15.45	16.62	19.93
Germany	20	33.41	45.23	64.93
Austria		17.53	22.14	28.57

Table 15.2 Coal, iron and steel production (millions of metric tons) and railway mileage (thousand statute miles) of selected European countries, 1850–1910

		1850	1873	1880	1910
Britain	Coal	57		149	268
	Pig iron	2.2		7.8	10
	Steel			1.3	5.9
	Railway	6.6	16		
France	Coal	5		19.4	38.4
	Pig iron	0.4		1.7	4
	Steel			0.4	3.4
	Railway	1.9	11.5		
Germany	Coal	6		59	222
	Pig iron	0.2		2.5	9.5
	Steel			0.7	13.8
	Railway	3.6	14.8		

ain, and the equally impressive growth in the key indicators of their industrial economies. France's population grew comparatively slowly and caused mounting anxiety as she was eclipsed by Germany as the premier power within Europe. Britain, the first industrial nation, found her lead steadily eroded later in the nineteenth century by competition from Germany and the United States, but she was cushioned by income from her large overseas investments and the resources of her empire. As we shall see, Britain sought to expand and safeguard her empire with increasing vigour as her European and transatlantic competitors muscled in on the available territory.

What caused the population explosion? Large families were the order of the day, despite

Malthus's warning. The birth rate in England and Wales peaked in the 1860s at thirty-five per thousand of the population; in Germany the peak came during the 1870s at thirty-nine per thousand. In France the rate fell steadily from just over twenty-eight per thousand of the population in the early 1840s to just under twenty between 1906 and 1910. The fall in death rates was a more important reason behind the population explosion (see Table 15.3).

The result was a surplus of births over deaths which was most striking in the two or three decades before the First World War. There were several reasons for this. Cleaner water supplies were perhaps the most important factor reducing the number of deaths from epidemics, especially among children. In Britain, for example, the deaths from the great killers typhoid, smallpox and typhus fell dramatically between the 1870s and the early 1900s. Vaccination, improvements in public health controls, and the use of antiseptics all helped as well. A better diet made an important contribution, and some research has drawn particular attention to improved milk supplies (partly due to improved processing methods so that it could be kept longer) which were more plentiful in northern Europe than in the south and east where fewer cattle were kept (S.J. Kunitz 'Speculations on the European fertility decline', *Economic History Review*, 2nd series, 36(3), 1983, pp. 152 and 360, cited in Anderson, *Ascendancy*, p. 124)

Urbanisation

The growth of cities, urbanisation, went hand in hand with the population explosion and industrialisation. The 21 European cities of 1800 which had

over 100,000 inhabitants each, about 4.5 million altogether, had by 1900 swollen to 147 cities and some 40 million people in total, roughly 10 per cent of Europe's total population. Berlin grew twice as fast as any other European capital (Anderson, *Ascendancy*, pp. 155–56). The rate of growth of towns of over 20,000 outstripped the rate of population growth as well; Prussia's population, for example, grew by an average 1.5 per cent each year between 1849 and 1890 while her towns and cities grew by 4.2 per cent each year on average (Gildea, *Barricades*, p. 142).

The growth of the towns and cities was caused mainly by the two changes which we have noticed already – economic development and falling death rates. During the second half of the nineteenth century health and conditions in the towns and cities began to improve, although in a patchy and slow way. This helped to attract people from the countryside to the towns and cities, and it also meant that cities grew not simply because of this movement of people but also because the birth rate in the cities exceeded the death rate. The economic attraction of the towns and cities for factory hands, craftsmen, traders and the professions, together with the amusements and excitements which were available, supplied the other main reason for urbanisation.

It should be noted that there were positive attractions for people to move to the towns and that this movement was not simply the result of land hunger or rural unemployment. In France before the 1870s urbanisation was driven by rural poverty, but Italian cities later in the century lacked the economic attractions and the surplus rural population emigrated. Urbanisation depended upon a developed transport system. Canals and navigable rivers, roads and above all railways provided the vital arteries for food supplies to reach the towns and for the products of industry to be moved to their markets. International trade depended upon efficient seaports and merchant fleets, of which Britain's was by far the largest, providing in itself an important area of employment and production in shipbuilding.

M.S. Anderson concludes: 'This urban growth made more immediate difference to the lives of more people than anything else which happened during the nineteenth century' (Anderson,

Table 15.3 Death rates in selected European countries (per 1,000 of population), 1846–1910

	1846–50	1876–80	1906–10
England and Wales	23.4	20.8	14.7
France	23.9	22.4	19.2
Germany	27.4	26.1	17.5
Austria	36.5	30.5	22.4

Ascendancy, p. 155). It not only altered the way people lived and died, but also shattered forever the timeless cycle of agrarian life which one generation inherited from another. The clock began to rule as punctuality from the workforce was vital to keep the factories profitable. The spendthrift drinking binges on payday, and absenteeism afterwards, slowly gave way to more sophisticated budgeting, and some workers would pay into insurance schemes or friendly societies. Decent clothing became more generally affordable, and travel became possible. Seaside holidays became commonplace for the mill-workers of Lancashire by the 1900s. Before the First World War spectator sports (such as football and the Tour de France) and the cinema became important leisure activities. Expectations for a better life were gradually raised through growing prosperity and education. Politics was altered as well. The growth of towns and cities also made the urban poor more conscious of their numbers and strength. Trade unions emerged and reflected the new socialist politics of the working classes (see Chapter 16). The authorities became more fearful of these vast cities in which governments often had to live uncomfortably close to the powerful body of the working classes, and as a result policies became more responsive to their wishes and needs.

Industrialisation

Industry was the engine which sustained the growing population and the process of urbanisation. The Revolutionary and Napoleonic wars increased Great Britain's economic lead. Before the war with Revolutionary France, she had the coal resources, access to supplies of raw cotton, spare capital for investment and the entrepreneurial spirit to set the pace. The wartime dislocation, including the damage done to Dutch banking, increased Britain's lead which she then continued to build up over the post-war decades. Britain's position as the leading industrial nation is clear when we look at the employment of the active population (see Table 15.4).

Equally clear from these figures, and from the key industrial indicators of coal, pig iron and steel production and railway mileages shown in Table 15.2, is that Britain's industrial lead was being successfully challenged by Germany before the First World War. Great Britain's economic hegemony lasted for most of the nineteenth century, but her competitors benefited first from her example and later by pioneering new industries themselves.

In the years after Waterloo (1815) British textiles and manufactured metal goods flooded the European markets and showed new manufacturers what might be achieved. The future iron and steel magnate, Alfred Krupp, came to study Britain's metallurgical industry in person in the late 1830s. The booming trade in British machine-tools soon equipped continental factories to follow in Britain's footsteps, and British engineers and patented designs were employed as well. During the second half of the century, technological breakthroughs such as the Bessemer process (1855) greatly boosted steel production, but they also opened up new industries. Synthetic dyestuffs from the 1860s, and electrical products from the 1880s, powered great new sectors of industry in Germany especially where the electric companies of Siemens and Rathenau acted to boost other areas of production. Electric trams, electricity generation from coal (which now had a new market), and improved manufacturing methods in many products all followed. This so-called 'multiplier effect' meant that the annual rate of economic growth in Europe rose from 2 per cent on average between 1860 and 1890, to 3.7 per cent between 1890 and 1914. Britain's industrial lead had been founded on the textile industry and powered forward by coal, iron and shipbuilding, but in the new industrial sectors she was the latecomer and her dominant position was eroded.

The challenge of German industry

Emigration and empire-building increased the markets for European manufactured goods in the middle decades of the century. Britain's trade with India became increasingly important to her as she faced mounting competition for her world market share. By the beginning of the twentieth century the larger industrial base of Germany and the United States was powering the rapid growth of

Table 15.4 Structure of the active population of selected European countries in 1850s, (1880s) and *c.* 1910 (percentages)

	Agriculture, forestry	Manufacturing, mining, building	Trade, banking, transport	Services, armed forces	Other
Britain	21.9	48.1	5.8	18.4	5.5
	(13.3)	(48.5)	(9.7)	(21.1)	(7.4)
	8.8	51.1	14.2	21.4	4.6
Belgium	46.8	37.4	4.9	10.9	—
	(36.5)	(36.3)	(10)	(14.2)	—
	23.2	45.5	14	16.3	—
France	51.7	26.9	6.8	14.6	—
	(47)	(25.7)	(10.2)	(17.1)	—
	41	33.1	13.2	12.8	—
Austria	52.3	17.6	1.6	10	18.5
	(55.6)	(20.6)	(3.9)	(11.9)	(8)
	56.9	24.2	8.9	8.3	1.7
Germany	(46.7)	(35.4)	(7.3)	(9.2)	(1.3)
	36.8	40.9	10.5	11.1	0.6
Italy	(51.4)	(25.4)	(3.6)	(9.3)	(10.5)
	55.4	26.9	8.9	8.5	0.5

their exports, a performance which Britain could not match (see Table 15.5).

Although Britain's Gross National Product per head of her population was still the highest in Europe in 1913, she was being overtaken in terms of exports and total production in many sectors. In Europe, Germany was clearly the dominant challenger, and the potential resources of Russia had yet to be harnessed competitively (see Chapter 20). The reasons for Britain's relative decline and Germany's rise are complex and the subject of debate. The big banks, such as the Darmstadter Bank (founded in 1853) played a central role in financing later industrial development in Germany and shaping the concerns on a far greater scale than was the norm in Britain. In the 1870s Krupp's iron and steel works employed 16,000 and was the largest concern in Europe, while twenty years later new steel mills in Britain were built on one-quarter or one-third of the scale of most existing German plants. In the early twentieth century a very high proportion of British companies were still privately owned and relatively small concerns, in sharp contrast to many German enterprises which had the investment banks behind them.

But it was not simply differences of funding and ownership which gave Germany her edge. British technological improvements in steel were often put to speedier use in Germany. Furthermore, German enterprise developed whole new industries, as we have seen, and well before the First World War her chemical industry was producing more benzol than France, Belgium and Britain together, and about one-third of the world output of the fertiliser sulphate of ammonia (Anderson, *Ascendancy*, p. 134). Even in her traditional market sector Britain lost her place. Her early century dominance of machine-tool making was lost to the United States in the 1880s, but between 1861 and 1907 employment in Germany's machine-building industry rose from 51,000 to over 1 million people.

There are at least three other factors which may have contributed to Germany's rise and Britain's decline. First, while Britain remained attached to free trade and the relatively open competition between firms which went with it, Germany under Bismarck adopted protection in 1879 and her industrial life became closely regulated by cartels which fixed prices and agreed market sharing

Table 15.5 Exports from UK and other industrial countries, 1899 and 1913 (million dollars at 1913 prices)

Exports from		Totals	
		Manufactured goods	All exports
UK	1899	1,327	1,978
	1913	1,970	2,556
% increase		47.7	29.2
Germany	1899	782	1,121
	1913	1,726	2,405
% increase		120.7	114.5
USA	1899	423	1,661
	1913	846	2,484
% increase		100	49.6
UK, USA, Canada, Japan, all major western European countries in total	1899	3,677	7,006
	1913	6,497	11,230
% increase		76.7	60.3

arrangements. As a result, German industry and her economy became dominated by a body of powerful industrial magnates and bankers. The effect is difficult to quantify, but the difference was marked and may have contributed to the crushing scale of German industrial enterprises.

Second, Britain had extensive colonial markets, and traditional areas of capital investment in Latin America, which became increasingly important to her export and import business. She was also successful in the late nineteenth century expanding her empire in Africa and her trade in the Far East. India in particular was immensely important to Britain. By 1911–14 India's trade and bullion surplus with industrial Europe, the USA and China and Japan averaged over £60 million a year, but her trade and bullion deficit with Britain averaged over £52 million each year. This situation meant that India financed about 40 per cent of Britain's total international trade deficits and helped her to survive the protectionist policies of Europe and the USA (S.B. Saul, *Studies in British Overseas Trade 1870–1914*, Liverpool University

Press, 1960, pp. 62 and 204). It may be suggested that these markets cushioned British industry from competition and protected it from the need to modernise until it was too late (see C.P. Kindelberger, *Economic Growth in France and Britain, 1851–1950*, Cambridge MA, Harvard University Press, 1964).

Third, and perhaps most important of all, British society continued to regard entrepreneurship, engineering and the management of industry as inferior to professional occupations, politics or landowning. Often the sons of successful 'self-made men' would lose interest in the family firm (see Landes, *The Unbound Prometheus*). In Germany the educational system and society did not look down on people of industry, technology and science, and her industry employed them enthusiastically. M.S. Anderson argues starkly: 'The superior efficiency of German industry was in the last analysis the outcome of an intellectual and educational superiority. In particular the lead of Germany over all her competitors in applied science was very marked' (Anderson, *Ascendancy*, p. 32).

THE IMPERIALIST IMPULSE

Was European imperialism in the nineteenth century the product of industrialisation and economic growth? Obviously technology gave Europeans the decisive capability to conquer and dominate; a few men with a Maxim gun or some light artillery could face overwhelming numbers and win. Medical advances too enabled white men and women to survive in the tropics. But having the knowledge and the seapower to build empires does not explain why the colonial empires were built, and the search for the answer to this question has produced many versions of history.

Stages of colonial imperialism

Colonial imperialism in the nineteenth century seems to have occurred in several stages. Up to about 1870 there were five powers with overseas colonies, the Netherlands, Spain, Portugal, Britain and France. Britain made the most significant gains during this period. The Dutch lost the Cape

Colony to Britain during the Napoleonic wars. Natal was added in 1843. New Zealand was annexed (by the treaty of Waitangi) in 1840. In 1819 Britain acquired Singapore, in 1839 Aden, in 1842 Hong Kong, while in 1825 and 1852 British rule was extended to parts of Burma. The treaty of Nanking (1842) allowed Britain to impose her trade and exercise extraterritorial rights over China. Control of India was steadily increased, for example with the conquest of the Punjab by 1849, and the Indian Mutiny (viewed by some historians as a war of independence) of 1857 was put down, paving the way for more direct control of the subcontinent by the government in London. The Persian Gulf became dominated by Britain, and Bahrain placed itself under British protection in 1861. France gained less during this period. Algeria was conquered slowly during the 1830s and 1840s. Tahiti became a protectorate in 1843, and French power in Cochin China and Cambodia grew steadily during the 1860s. Russia's Asian empire grew at the expense of China in 1858 and 1860, including the site of what became Vladivostok. Russia also expanded southwards, taking Tashkent in 1865 (forming Russian Turkestan), Bukhara in 1868 and Khiva in 1873.

But these gains were made with little pride or enthusiasm. The Duke of Wellington wrote in 1829: 'We have possession of nearly every valuable port and colony in the world, and I confess that I am anxious to avoid exciting the attention and jealousy of other powers by extending our possessions' (quoted in Anderson, *Ascendancy*, p. 256). Many feared that colonial empires would soon follow America's example, and the pattern of Spain's South American possessions, and break loose. In addition, moral objections to empire were quite strong in Britain where they also led to the abolition of slavery in 1833. In France, the conquest of Algeria brought no popular acclaim to Louis Philippe's monarchy, Napoleon III's 'Mexican adventure' blackened the Second Empire, and suspicion of colonialism remained so powerful that Ferry's government was defeated in 1885 when the French colonial venture in China met with a temporary setback at Tonkin (see Chapters 9, 11 and 17). Even in the Tsar's empire, it may be suggested that the government was pushed into expansion by ambitious men on the spot; the conqueror of

Tashkent was quickly recalled, and foreign ministers and finance ministers in the 1850s and 1860s regarded expansion in Asia as money-draining distractions from the pressing concerns in Europe and the Ottoman empire.

From the 1870s until the First World War, colonial imperialism became more open, chauvinistic and competitive. The so-called 'Scramble for Africa' during the 1880s was the most striking example of this change of gear, but great colonial gains were made in the western Pacific rim, and elsewhere. Germany made her entry into the race in the 1880s, and the United States joined in the competition, making the phenomenon of imperialism part of a world struggle not simply for colonies but also for domestic prestige and regional power in Europe and the Pacific. What then changed the attitude to colonial imperialism from the 1870s?

J.A. Hobson and 'the highest stage of capitalism'

One answer was provided in 1902 when Hobson published his important study of *Imperialism*. He was most concerned about Britain's domestic economic and social problems, which he saw as limiting the spending power of the domestic market. He believed that wealth had piled up in the hands of a few capitalists who were disappointed by the returns on investment in the British market, and Hobson argued that they sought higher returns in colonial investment. These capitalists then put pressure on the British government to protect their investments by extending their colonial rule. Did the flag follow capital investment in this way? Lenin, in his *Imperialism: the Highest Stage of Capitalism* (1916) adopted much of Hobson's analysis in concluding that 'the economic quintessence of imperialism is monopoly capitalism', that this led to the division of the world into colonies and spheres of influence, which in turn produced rivalries and hostility between the capitalist powers (V.I. Lenin, 'Imperialism, the highest stage of capitalism', in H.M. Christman (ed.) *Essential Works of Lenin*, New York, Dover Publications, 1987, p. 265).

This analysis is useful because it draws attention to the economic importance of the colonies, and we have noticed already the great value of India to

Britain. However, the evidence does not support it as an explanation for imperialism after 1870. In the first place, British domestic investment often exceeded lending abroad (Table 15.6).

Furthermore, the distribution of Britain's overseas investments by 1914 do not show much support for the theory that capitalism eagerly created a colonial empire in the search for profitable investments. In 1914 Britain held investments totalling $1,850 million in India, and $2,450 million in all of Africa, out of a total of $20,000 million of overseas investments. Her investments in Europe totalled over $1,000 million, in North America over $7,000 million, and in Latin America $3,700 million (from W. Woodruff, *Impact of Western Man*, 1967, pp. 154 and 156, cited in P. Mathias, *The First Industrial Nation*, London, Methuen, 1972, pp. 469–70). Investment which did take place in the new colonies was often risky; the British East Africa Company failed in 1895, the Royal Niger Company collapsed in 1899, and Cecil Rhodes's British South Africa Company paid shareholders no dividends at all while it administered Rhodesia. Unsurprisingly, capital investment preferred the safer returns from older colonies and the developed or developing economies.

Economic opportunism

There was certainly an economic dimension to the colonialism of the period 1870–1914, but there is no evidence to support the idea that capitalists forced the European governments into their bout of imperialism in order to protect new investment opportunities. E.J. Hobsbawm argues with authority:

Economic development is not a sort of ventroliquist with the rest of history as its dummy. For that matter, even the most single-minded businessman pursuing profit into, say, the South African gold- and diamond-mines, can never be treated exclusively as a money-making machine. He was not immune to the political, emotional, ideological, patriotic or even racial appeals which were so patently associated with imperial expansion.

(E. J. Hobsbawm, *The Age of Empire, 1875–1914*, London, Abacus, 1996, p. 62)

For Cecil Rhodes and for Bismarck alike there were powerful mixtures of reasons which created the imperial opportunities, which they seized with great vigour.

One contributing economic factor was the increasing importance of certain raw materials which were crucial to particular new technologies. The internal combustion engine needed oil from the USA, Russia, Romania and the Middle East, and rubber from the jungles of the Amazon and the Congo. The electrical industry needed copper from Latin America and central Africa. The western market for gold and diamonds made South Africa a great prize. But the importance of raw materials was not alone enough to explain the extension of colonial rule by the industrialised world, but when the ingredient of competition for survival is added then the importance of establishing spheres of influence and staking claims becomes more logical.

A related point may be made about markets for industrial products. In the French and British empires of the later nineteenth and early twentieth centuries, the colonial claims were generally made before investment and business grew; trade followed the flag. It was similar with Germany's gains in 1884–85 which were made well before her domestic market had peaked; 'in so far as any rational economic calculation underlay it,' Anderson argues, the German colonial empire 'was much more a guarantee for the future than a response to

Table 15.6 UK average annual net investment, 1870–1913 (constant 1912–13 prices) (£ million)

	Net domestic capital formation	Net lending abroad	Total net investment
1870–74	81	65	146
1875–79	77	28	105
1880–84	96	63	159
1885–89	85	100	185
1890–94	84	78	162
1895–99	169	54	223
1900–04	174	46	220
1905–09	127	138	265
1910–13	128	202	330

any immediate needs' (Anderson, *Ascendancy*, p. 273). Hobsbawm develops this reasoning, pointing out that simultaneous concerns among the industrialised nations made them abandon their ideal of 'open door' competition and resort instead to intervention and territorial claims to protect their position in the future (see extract F (ii)) (Hobsbawm, *Empire*, pp. 66–67). This involved political issues as well, and the explanation for imperialism in the later nineteenth century needs to include factors which are remote from economics and capitalism.

Popular patriotism

Benjamin Disraeli began the process of popularising imperialism in Britain. In his Crystal Palace speech (1872) he damned the prospect offered by Gladstonian Liberalism as 'a comfortable England, modelled and moulded upon Continental principles', by contrast with his Conservative vision of 'a great country, an imperial country, a country where your sons, when they rise, rise to paramount positions, and obtain not merely the esteem of their countrymen, but command the respect of the world' (cited in D. Judd, *Empire: the British Imperial Experience from 1765 to the Present*, London, Fontana, 1997, p. 121). Disraeli saw electoral advantage for his party in appealing to what today sounds like a chauvinistic patriotism. But there were many in Victorian Britain who believed that her economic lead reflected a God-given superiority, which in turn brought with it the duty and the obligation to bring the benefits of Christianity and the rule of law to less civilised peoples. Ruskin (who was not a Disraelian Conservative) in 1870 spoke of England's destiny to 'found colonies as fast and as far as she is able, formed of her most energetic and worthiest men' (from J. Ruskin's lecture at Oxford, 1870, cited in Judd, *Empire*, p. 121). Rudyard Kipling called this duty 'The White Man's Burden'.

Once in power, Disraeli greatly advanced the British empire. In 1874 he settled a long-standing dispute with France by establishing a protectorate in the Gold Coast of Africa, safeguarding British trading interests there. In 1875 he seized the opportunity to buy a major holding of shares in the Suez Canal, on his own authority, and created

Queen Victoria 'Empress of India' – a master stroke of flattery which also developed the colonial myth of the 'Great White Queen' across the ocean. At home, it raised the profile of empire. India surely played a crucial role in popularising empire, and because she paid her own defence costs and more besides, she helped to remove any lingering doubts in the official mind that the empire was a liability. Disraeli was not embarrassed by Britain's imperial power, as Gladstone was, and he was not slow to use the advantages it gave, as Wellington had been. At the Congress of Berlin in 1878, called to pressurise Russia into cutting the size of her new Bulgarian satellite, Disraeli moved a token force of Indian troops to the Mediterranean. The point was not lost on any of the powers meeting in Berlin. Although Britain had no serious continental army herself, she ruled a subcontinent of nearly 300 million which was ideally placed to bring decisive pressure to bear on Russia, something which neither Austria-Hungary nor even the new unified Germany could do with such imperial confidence. Disraeli made imperialism popular, and tied its patriotic appeal tightly to the Conservative party. Although there were moments when imperial reverses damaged the appeal, as after the Zulu victory at Isandhlwana in 1879, imperialism remained a widely popular idea, as Queen Victoria's Diamond Jubilee celebrations of 1897 showed (see Figure 15.1). Imperialism had yet to collect the flavour of disapproval which is commonplace today.

The British empire and its expansion encouraged France and Germany to make their own colonial claims, but there are some other ingredients in imperialism which should be registered. Disraeli hoped that people would become less concerned with class barriers and differences in wealth as a common patriotic pride in empire helped build 'One Nation Conservatism' at home. Later Cecil Rhodes wrote in a more practical vein:

In order to save the forty million inhabitants of the United Kingdom from a bloody civil war, our colonial statesmen must acquire new lands for settling the surplus population of this country, to provide new markets. . . . The Empire, as I have always said, is a bread and butter question.

(from a letter by C. Rhodes in 1895, cited in Anderson, *Ascendancy*, p. 267)

15.1 'Queen Victoria outside St Paul's Cathedral, Jubilee 1897'

Source: AKG London

This idea that empire might provide a solution to dangerous pressures at home was adopted by Joseph Chamberlain and helped to persuade him to abandon Liberalism and become a powerful Conservative Colonial Secretary in 1895.

The solution empire might provide was in part economic and practical, in part by providing a glorious patriotic sideshow which would distract attention from problems at home and help to maintain social stability. It has been suggested that Bismarck's sudden pursuit of colonies in the 1880s was exactly this 'social imperialism' (see H-U. Wehler, 'Bismarck's imperialism, 1862–1890', *Past and Present*, 48, 1970, pp. 119–55, or the outline of the arguments in J. Lowe, *The Great Powers, Imperialism, and the German Problem, 1865–1925*, London, Routledge, 1994). A competitive element crept into the mixture, especially through popular patriotism, for Germany's pursuit of 'a place in the sun' as Foreign Minister von Bülow was to call it in 1897. In 1882 the *Kolonialverein* (Colonial League)

was formed with powerful backing which included some leading bankers and industrialists. It argued the colonial cause and may have been the product of jealousy at existing colonial empires and fear of being left behind in the race. This type of pressure mounted as the imperial cause became more popular and connected with the chauvinistic nationalism of the Pan-German League in the 1890s (see Chapter 18). Jules Ferry argued that colonies were needed to protect markets from other colonial powers and maintain social peace (see extract F (i)), while the notion of another Frenchman that 'there has never been a great power without extensive colonies' was a typical patriotic way of looking at empire and arguing that France needed to keep up with Britain (cited in Anderson, *Ascendancy*, p. 264). Basically, in adopting an open and competitive imperialism, British, German and French governments were reflecting public pressures and attitudes. Neither Germany, under Bismarck or after his departure from office (1890), nor French governments, could allow their prestige to be damaged in the eyes of their own electorates by a rival power winning colonies while they sat idly by.

AFRICA AND THE FAR EAST

There were clearly many ingredients to Europe's colonial imperialism of the late nineteenth and early twentieth centuries, and the proportions of the mixture varied according to the time and place. However, it is clear that competition played an important part, as did the contributions made by the 'men on the spot' and local circumstances, as we shall see when we look at the course of the 'Scramble for Africa' and the race for the Pacific markets.

The partition of Africa: Egypt and the Sudan

In 1870 European colonial claims were around the coastal periphery of what the Victorians called 'the Dark Continent' (see Map 15.1). A glance at the map of 1914 shows only the Ethiopian empire and Liberia as independent. Livingstone, one of the most famous explorers of the interior, died in 1873, and he and others like Stanley had aroused the curiosity of the European public about Africa. However, it was not curiosity but strategic and financial concerns which drew Britain into Egypt in the 1880s, ironically when the Liberal leader William Gladstone was Prime Minister.

The opening of the Suez Canal in 1869 sharpened Britain's concerns about the safety of the route to India, for the strategists in London soon became highly sensitive to the possibility that it would fall into hostile hands. This helps explain Disraeli's opportunist purchase of 45 per cent of the shares in 1875. But these shares were sold by Ismail, the ruler of Egypt, because bankruptcy was threatening the stability of the country. During Ismail's reign (1863–79) Egypt's foreign debt rose from £3 million to over £100 million (M.E. Chamberlain, *The Scramble for Africa*, London, Longman, 1995, p. 37). The danger of financial collapse prompted Britain and France (who invaded neighbouring Tunis in 1881 and also had

financial interests in Egypt and the Canal) to set up Dual Control of Egypt's finances which lasted, on and off, from 1876 until 1882.

This overt foreign interference (in what was nominally part of the Ottoman empire) created an Egyptian nationalist movement (led by Arabi Pasha) which undermined Ismail and he was deposed in 1879. A clash between this movement on the one hand, and the feeble successor government of Tewfik and his Anglo-French backers on the other, became inevitable. Rioting in Alexandria in June 1882 (when about fifty Europeans were killed) led Gladstone's government to send in the navy to bombard the fort at Alexandria. Initially this was a joint Anglo-French operation. In Britain Bright resigned from the Cabinet rather than support such imperialist aggression, but otherwise the Liberal party held firm. However, in France the Freycinet government fell and Britain was left to push on alone. A military operation to protect the Canal went according to plan, but Gladstone knew the unwelcome consequences: 'We have done our Egyptian business, and we are an Egyptian government' (cited in M.E. Chamberlain, *Scramble for Africa*, p. 42).

The famous analysis of Gallagher and Robinson argues that informal empire in Egypt sucked the government into establishing formal control by strategic and financial concerns, and by local 'proto-nationalism' which arose in reaction to the European presence (R. Robinson and J. Gallagher, *Africa and the Victorians: the Official Mind of Imperialism*, London, Macmillan, 1981). A parallel analysis may be applied to the Sudan where the Mahdi's Islamic movement was reacting with growing hostility to foreign influence. General Gordon was sent to arrange an evacuation, but he allowed himself to become besieged in Khartoum. Public pressure at last forced Gladstone's government to send a powerful rescue force, which arrived shortly after Gordon's death in January 1885. To a large number of people, Gordon became a martyr to the cause of empire, and Gladstone his executioner. But the action of the 'man on the spot' had forced the hand of the British government into intervening in the Sudan, although Britain did not reconquer the Sudan at this stage but left it in theoretical Egyptian possession. In due course Britain felt her interests threatened by rival French claims which might

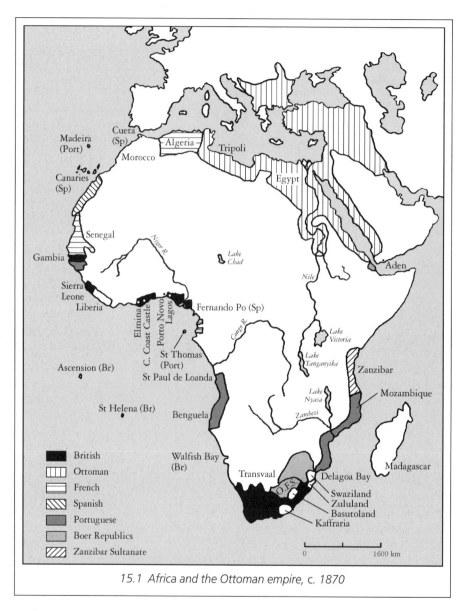

15.1 Africa and the Ottoman empire, c. 1870

Map labels:
Madeira (Port), Cueta (Sp), Algeria, Tripoli, Morocco, Egypt, Canaries (Sp), Senegal, *Niger R.*, Lake Chad, *Nile*, Aden, Gambia, Sierra Leone, Liberia, Elmina, C. Coast Castle, Porto Novo, Lagos, Fernando Po (Sp), *Congo R.*, Lake Victoria, Lake Tanganyika, Zanzibar, Ascension (Br), St Thomas (Port), St Paul de Loanda, Lake Nyasa, Mozambique, St Helena (Br), Benguela, *Zambezi*, Madagascar, Walfish Bay (Br), Transvaal, Delagoa Bay, O.F.S., Swaziland, Zululand, Basutoland, Kaffraria

Legend:
British
Ottoman
French
Spanish
Portuguese
Boer Republics
Zanzibar Sultanate

0   1600 km

gain control of the upper Nile and damage the Egyptian economy which depended upon it (see Figure 15.2). Marchand's spectacular march east from the Congo confronted Kitchener at Fashoda in 1898. But by then the British conquest of the Sudan was nearly complete (the battle of Omdurman was won in September 1898, a few days before the meeting). Kitchener's force was partly Egyptian, and the whole thing was presented as an Egyptian reconquest of the Sudan and went forward with all the signs of permanent authority being established; a railway and the telegraph were

laid. After some diplomatic blustering (see extract E) the French government accepted Britain's claim to the Sudan formally in March 1899. All this showed how Britain was led into the interior by internal disturbances and European rivalries which threatened the safety of her original object of concern, Egypt. While the Gallagher and Robinson thesis as applied to the partition of Africa as a whole has been extensively challenged since 1961 when it first appeared, it remains an elegant and cogent account which is most revealing in the context of Egypt and the Sudan.

THE FORMULA OF BRITISH CONQUEST

PEARS SOAP IS THE BEST

REG^D COPYRIGHT

PEARS' SOAP IN THE SOUDAN.

"Even if our invasion of the Soudan has done nothing else it has at any rate left the Arab something to puzzle his fuzzy head over, for the legend PEARS' SOAP IS THE BEST, inscribed in huge white characters on the rock which marks the farthest point of our advance towards Berber, will tax all the wits of the Dervishes of the Desert to translate."—Phil Robinson, *War Correspondent (in the Soudan) of the Daily Telegraph in London*, 1884.

15.2 Advertisement in 1887 for 'The formula of British conquest' – in this case trading Pear's soap in the Sudan

Source: The Illustrated London News Picture Library

The Berlin colonial conference and the partition of West Africa

Trade, competition and the pressure of the 'men on the spot' seem to have been the different mixture which prompted the scramble in this part of the continent. Leopold II, King of the Belgians, had a great interest in setting up a colonial empire, a dream which he pursued with little support from his own parliament. He created the Association Internationale Africaine (AIA), with himself as president, in 1876 to open up the Congo river basin and suppress the slave trade. By 1884 the British government was becoming suspicious of its activities in exploiting the rubber traders there, and the personal fortune which Leopold made began to damage his reputation. In 1884 Leopold announced treaties with African chiefs which gave him sovereignty in the Congo. These treaties were probably obtained under false pretences, but Leopold was anxious to beat the growing French competition in the area. Operating out of French Gabon, de Brazza had been staking out a French claim to part of the Congo basin under Makoko's jurisdiction. The French government accepted this treaty as valid in 1882, partly to appease public opinion which had been angered by the decision to drop out of the Egyptian operation and leave it all to Britain. By this stage Britain was becoming alarmed about France's claims as well as Leopold's activities, and the British government was anxious to settle the vague and ancient claim which Portugal had to the mouth of the Congo river. But before the Anglo-Portuguese treaty of 1884 could be ratified by parliament, two fresh factors emerged.

First, British commercial interests, led by the Manchester cotton lobby, reacted furiously against the cripplingly high tariff which Portugal would impose on British goods going to the Congo. The diplomats had misjudged the impact it would have when they negotiated the treaty with Portugal. Faced with this outcry, the British government was quite happy to abandon the treaty with Portugal, using as the excuse the outcry from France and Germany at being excluded from the original Anglo-Portuguese arrangement.

German involvement was the second fresh factor in the early 1880s. The reasons for Bismarck's new interest in Africa have been much debated by historians, and we have mentioned earlier some possible domestic pressures which range from 'social imperialism' to placating the interest of commercial and colonial pressure groups (see also Chapter 18). He had obvious diplomatic interests in keeping France isolated after Germany's annexation of Alsace-Lorraine in 1871, and anything which would further Anglo-French or Franco-Belgian friction was worth a try, even if it meant dabbling in colonialism (see Chapter 18).

Bismarck had encouraged the French occupation of Tunis to stimulate Franco-Italian friction, and he had supported Britain's lone operation in Egypt to divide her from France (see extract A). An angry wrangle developed between Germany and Britain over South West Africa in 1883–84. In 1878 Britain annexed the Walfisch Bay trading station, and in February 1883 Berlin enquired whether Britain had any regional claims. Chamberlain explains the misunderstanding which followed:

the British thought that they were seeking protection for the [German] missionaries and returned a polite but evasive reply. It only very slowly dawned on the British that the Germans, who had previously insisted that they had no colonial interests in Africa, wanted to take control of the region themselves. In fact, the Germans may only have reached that conclusion themselves in the course of the negotiations.

(Chamberlain, *Scramble for Africa*, p. 58)

While the British government dragged its feet and consulted the Cape Colony government about a German claim, Bismarck became more angry. In April 1884 Germany declared a protectorate over Angra Pequena, a German trading station near Walfisch Bay, and later extended this to the whole of South West Africa while at the same time withdrawing German support for Britain in the closing stages of the London conference on Egyptian finances (see extracts B and C). This made a good impression within Germany, but if it was intended to intimidate Britain and impress on her that she was isolated, it failed. The British government resented Bismarck's discourteous grabbing, but accepted the claim which it would have been an easy matter for the Royal Navy to render meaningless. When Bismarck acted alongside France later in the year to intervene against the Anglo-Portuguese treaty on the Congo, it quite suited the British government to take this way of backing out of the treaty she now realised was commercially damaging, at the same time as diluting the French claims in the Congo with international involvement.

Bismarck and Ferry, the French Prime Minister, persuaded Portugal to place the whole question of the Congo in the hands of an international conference at Berlin. This met between November 1884 and February 1885 and ruled on several other issues as well. Freedom of commerce in the Congo basin was established, and the area was under the administrative control of King Leopold's Congo Free State. However, it was a victory for the AIA and acceptable to Britain. France's high-tariff policy and her wrangling to get counter-concessions over Alsace-Lorraine and in Egypt began to offend Bismarck and persuade him that Germany could reach a colonial settlement with Britain more easily.

This helped Britain to secure an advantageous settlement in the Niger river basin where her dominant position in the middle and lower Niger were internationally recognised at the Berlin Conference. However, the Berlin Conference also laid down the rule that there had to be 'effective occupation' of new territories which were claimed (extract D). This really established the rules for the way the 'Scramble for Africa' was to be conducted. Of course it would make it more difficult to repeat the sort of claim Bismarck had recently made to South West Africa, and it also sharpened the awareness of the British government about its claim in the Niger basin. For decades British commercial interests had competed with rival French claims in the Niger basin, but the British government was prepared to step in and support the traders' lobby when French competition and international involvement threatened what became seen as the only national interest. In 1886 the National African Company (founded by Goldie in 1879 as the United African Company) became the Royal Niger Company, and British rule of a vast area was to be exercised through a chartered company. In this case, the flag was following trade. Germany's claim to a protectorate over the Cam-eroons in 1884 had provided another point of concern for British trading interests in the region, but the government had accepted it. The Anglo-German agreement at the Berlin Conference over the Niger helped restore relations, and after Ferry's fall from power (March 1885) French governments lost their taste for colonial adventure with Germany. But matters could never be restored as they had been before Bismarck pursued colonialism, as Medlicott and Coveney point out; 'however much Bismarck might seek to minimize the significance of his essay in imperialism, the fact remains that he had departed from the purely continental conception of German policy and of Germany as a completely "saturated" state' (W.N. Medlicott and D.K. Coveney, *Bismarck and Europe*, London, Arnold, 1971, p. 136).

The British lion's share: southern and eastern Africa

Besides Egypt with the Sudan in due course, the Niger basin and large claims on the Gold Coast and west coast, Britain gained huge territories in south and east Africa during the 'scramble' (see Map 15.2). To some extent the aims were strategic, to prevent a foreign presence competing with or threatening the trade with India. Significantly, the British government of India controlled British diplomacy in Zanzibar until 1883. However, this emphasis by Gallagher and Robinson does not explain Britain's readiness to accept the aggressive French seizure of Madagascar (1883–85), nor the Admiralty's lack of interest in the port of Mombasa.

In the late 1870s commercial interests, led by Sir William Mackinnon, suggested that the territory between Lake Victoria and the coast could be developed into another India. The Foreign Secretary, Salisbury, undermined the scheme; indeed Conservative and Liberal governments were equally reluctant to expand government responsibilities in east Africa. German claims to what became Tanganyika were announced in 1885, immediately after the Berlin colonial conference, and transformed the attitude of the British government. By October 1886 Britain, France and Germany had agreed on a division of the area, with German

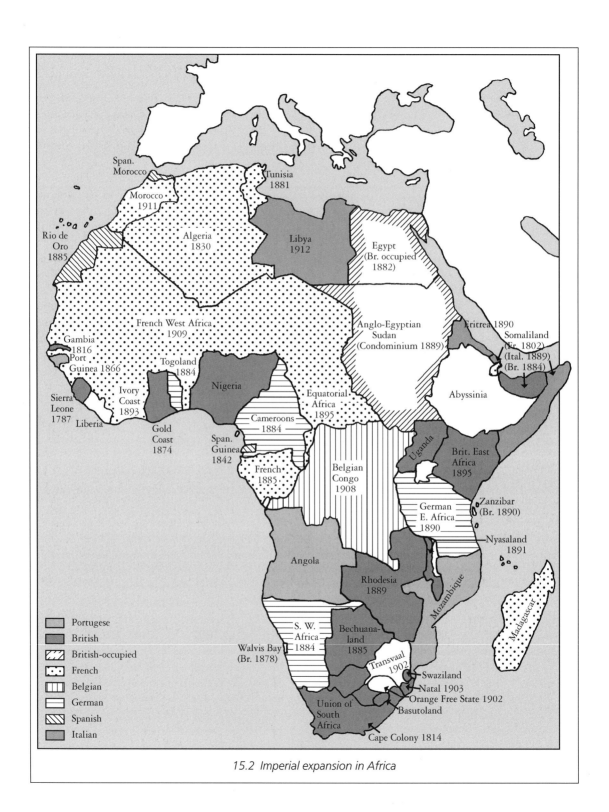

Span.
Morocco

Tunisia
1881

Morocco
1911

Rio de
Oro
1885

Algeria
1830

Libya
1912

Egypt
(Br. occupied
1882)

French West Africa
1909

Anglo-Egyptian
Sudan
(Condominium 1889)

Eritrea 1890

Somaliland
(Fr. 1802)
(Ital. 1889)
(Br. 1884)

Gambia
1816
Port.
Guinea 1866

Togoland
1884

Nigeria

Equatorial
Africa
1895

Sierra
Leone
1787

Ivory
Coast
1893

Liberia

Gold
Coast
1874

Span.
Guinea
1842

Cameroons
1884

Abyssinia

Uganda

Brit. East
Africa
1895

French
1885

Belgian
Congo
1908

Zanzibar
(Br. 1890)

German
E. Africa
1890

Nyasaland
1891

Angola

Rhodesia
1889

Mozambique

Madagascar

Portugese

British

British-occupied

French

Belgian

German

Spanish

Italian

S. W.
Africa
1884

Walvis Bay
(Br. 1878)

Bechuana-
land
1885

Transvaal
1902

Swaziland

Natal 1903

Orange Free State 1902

Basutoland

Union of
South
Africa

Cape Colony 1814

15.2 Imperial expansion in Africa

claims being accepted in return for the British claim to the area which became known as Uganda and Kenya. But neither the Imperial British East Africa Company nor the German chartered companies which tried to develop the region were able to attract settlers or investment, and by the 1890s they were in financial trouble. Although it was politically impossible to give up the claims, the notion that surplus capital in industrialised Europe had produced these colonial ventures was obviously incorrect here.

The British expansion from south Africa was mainly the achievement of Cecil Rhodes. He made his fortune at an early age in the diamond mines of Kimberley in the 1870s, but his burning obsession was not with making money but with his vision of the destiny of the Anglo-Saxon peoples. He believed fervently in the value of the British empire as a force for peace and prosperity. He dreamed not only of a Cape to Cairo railway, but also of a federal empire which would include the United States. By the time he entered the Cape parliament in 1880, relations between the English government of the Cape, and the Boer states of the Transvaal and the Orange Free State, were already poisoned.

In the 1870s the British annexed to the Cape Colony the diamond-mining region claimed by the Transvaal. Later, faced by Zulu hostility, the Boers had been persuaded to accept British protection and annexation. Initially the British force met with a shattering defeat at Isandhlwana in 1879, redeemed in Victorian mythology by the truly heroic stand at Rorke's Drift, but Cetewayo's Zulu force was soon worn down and defeated. The Transvaalers quickly demanded their independence back, claiming with some justice that they had agreed to give it up under duress. Before Gladstone's Liberal government agreed to this, a Boer force inflicted a defeat on the British army at Majuba Hill in 1881. The agreements which followed (the Convention of Pretoria, 1881, and the Convention of London, 1884) stopped short of plainly restoring independence to the Transvaal, but British authority over foreign policy and to intervene in domestic affairs was claimed by Joseph Chamberlain, Colonial Secretary from 1895 to 1903.

Rhodes countered Boer expansion, and the chal-lenge of German South West Africa, by pressing the British claim to Bechuanaland which he argued was vital to keeping the route north open. In 1886, Britain staked her claim. But gold had been discovered in the Transvaal by then, and a new opportunity for northerly expansion was materialising. Rhodes invested heavily in the Witwatersrand goldfield through the De Beers Consolidated Mines Company. He used this company to secure Marshonaland and Matabeleland (the future Rhodesia) which lay to the north of the Boer republics. Deals were struck with King Lobengula, and Rhodes then secured a political triumph in October 1889 by obtaining a charter from the British government for his Bechuanaland Exploration Company. The government secured control on the cheap, and beat off rival claims from the Boers, the Germans and the Portuguese. Armed with this authority, Rhodes furthered his scheme for a Cape to Cairo link, and extended the territory to found the town of Salisbury in 1890. Excited investors in the venture, which failed to find gold, saw their shares fall in value, but the empire had been expanded vastly by a combination of the zeal of a 'man on the spot', foreign competition, and the hope of profitable investment in raw materials.

Much of the 'scramble' of the 1880s was resolved by the agreements of 1890 which ended the rivalry over new claims. Britain's position in Uganda, Kenya and protectorate over Zanzibar was recognised by Germany, who in return had her position in Tanganyika confirmed, and gained both the 'Caprivi Strip' connecting South West Africa with the Zambesi river and Heligoland, in the North Sea (which Britain had gained during the Napoleonic Wars). France accepted these arrangements in return for British recognition of her claim to Madagascar. Portugal recognised British claims in Nyasaland and Marshonaland in return for boundary concessions which affected Portuguese East Africa (the future Angola). In 1891 Rhodes's Chartered Company claims to Northern Rhodesia and Nyasaland were accepted by Germany. The only unfinished business for Rhodes and Britain were the Boer Republics, which were now virtually surrounded.

In 1895 Rhodes, as Prime Minister of the Cape Colony, plotted to annex the Transvaal on the pretext of protecting the non-Boer goldfield workers. The conspiracy required the workers to rise in revolt, and for his old friend Dr Jameson to lead an invasion force which would topple the Boer government. The rising failed to occur, Jameson's force was arrested, Rhodes was forced to resign and Colonial Secretary Joseph Chamberlain, who was involved to some extent, was lucky to survive politically. Worse, the Kaiser sent Kruger, the President of the Transvaal, a telegram congratulating him on the victory he had won without having to appeal to friendly powers for help. The British government took note that German competition had returned, and sent a naval squadron to the Cape to demonstrate her attitude to the suggestion that Germany could 'help'. However, the Transvaal bought German arms and moved them in along the new railway from Delgoa Bay in Portuguese Mozambique. Given this level of hostility, the Anglo-Boer war of 1899–1902 was inevitable. But it was won at such cost, and for such controversial motives, that the British public's enthusiasm for the kind of adventurous imperialism which Cecil Rhodes personified was killed. So too was Britain's confidence in her 'splendid isolation'.

The Pacific and China

Bismarck showed an interest in the Far East before his colonial intervention in Africa. Between 1875 and 1877 he cooperated with Britain to oppose a Spanish claim to the Sulu islands in the southern Philippines. He asserted the rights of German traders in Tonga and Samoa with commercial treaties, and protested at Britain's treatment of German settlers when Disraeli annexed the Fiji islands in 1874.

However, the central area of competition lay in China, an increasingly enfeebled power which was preyed upon by western and Japanese imperialism (see Map 15.3). Russia claimed Vladivostok in 1860, France claimed the tributary states of Annam and Tonkin (1884–85), and Britain claimed Burma (1886). In 1894 Japan defeated China in her bid to control Korea. Following this, China's need for loans from the western powers allowed them to gain important railway and mining concessions. Russia used French capital, and

obtained a lease on Port Arthur in 1898 (see Chapter 20), but Germany had already seized Kiaochow as a coaling station following a Chinese attack on two German missionaries. Salisbury reluctantly retaliated with a British claim on Wei-hai-wei, and France followed suit with Kwangchow.

Russia's position in Manchuria made her the dominant colonial authority in China. This position was intensified by the Boxer rebellion, a violent Chinese nationalist protest which targeted foreigners in China between 1898 and 1900. A joint force of all the interested colonial powers, British, French, Japanese, Russian, American and German cooperated to crush the movement and relieve Peking. The affair swelled the number of Russian troops in Manchuria to 100,000 by 1901, and allowed Russia to establish what was effectively a protectorate there. British alarm at this situation helped to prompt her alliance with Japan in 1902, and it was Japan's defeat of Russia in the war of 1904–05 which halted the further expansion of Russia in the Far East (see Chapter 20). After this, the competitive pressure among the western powers and Japan fell away; there seemed to be enough trade for everyone, provided no single power was staking a protectionist claim which would exclude others. The value of China's foreign trade grew about threefold between 1895 and 1914, and the foreign presence in Shanghai became stronger.

Appraisal

It seems impossible to produce a single explanation for the 'Scramble for Africa', let alone a theory of imperialism which would explain the competition in the Pacific and China as well. Russia's interest in the Far East was partly the product of her relative weakness in Europe. Clearly, pressure from rival European countries was an important ingredient in Africa too, and it is reasonable to argue that Leopold's action in the Congo set the ball rolling. Bismarck's intervention, for a mixture of reasons, certainly intensified the race. Britain's existing responsibilities in south Africa and Egypt, her imperial concerns about the routes to India, and the lobbying of her own trading interests – and to a lesser extent her financial

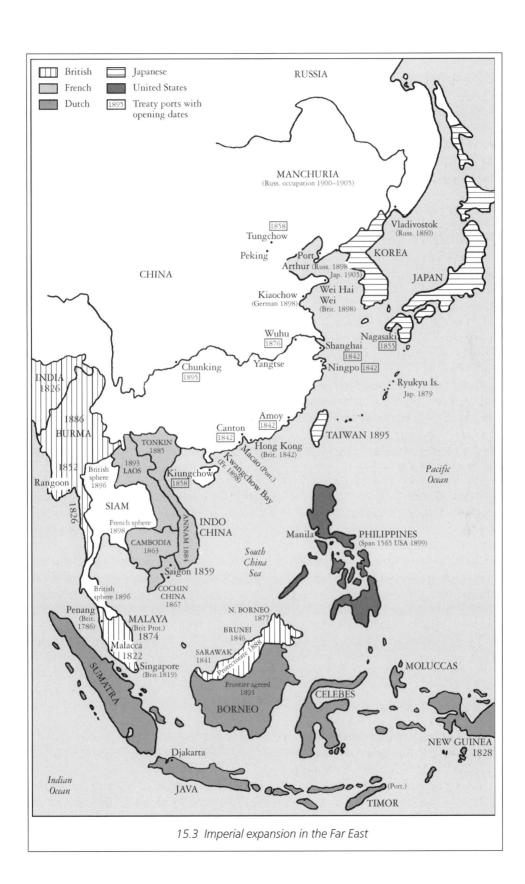

Legend

British		Japanese	
French		United States	
Dutch		1895	Treaty ports with opening dates

RUSSIA

MANCHURIA
(Russ. occupation 1900–1905)

Vladivostok
(Russ. 1860)

1858
Tungchow

Peking

Port
Arthur (Russ. 1898
Jap. 1905)

KOREA

JAPAN

CHINA

Kiaochow
(German 1898)

Wei Hai
Wei
(Brit. 1898)

Wuhu
1876

Nagasaki
1855

Shanghai
1842

INDIA
1826

Chunking
1895

Yangtse

Ningpo 1842

Ryukyu Is.
Jap. 1879

1886

BURMA

Amoy
1842

Canton
1842

TAIWAN 1895

1852

TONKIN
1885

Hong Kong
(Brit. 1842)

Macao (Port.)

Rangoon

1893
LAOS

British
sphere
1896

Kiungchow
1858

K.wangtchow Bay
(Fr. 1898)

Pacific
Ocean

1826

SIAM

French sphere
1898

ANNAM 1884

INDO
CHINA

Manila

PHILIPPINES
(Span 1565 USA 1899)

CAMBODIA
1863

Saigon 1859

South
China
Sea

British
sphere 1896

COCHIN
CHINA
1867

Penang
(Brit.
1786)

MALAYA
(Brit Prot.)
1874

N. BORNEO
1877

BRUNEI
1846

MOLUCCAS

Malacca
1822

Singapore
(Brit.1819)

SARAWAK
1841

Protectorate 1888

SUMATRA

Frontier agreed
1891

CELEBES

BORNEO

NEW GUINEA
1828

Djakarta

Indian
Ocean

JAVA

(Port.)

TIMOR

15.3 Imperial expansion in the Far East

stakeholders – all made her sensitive to the claims of other European powers. The force of circumstances, often created by 'men-on-the-spot' like Rhodes, Goldie, de Brazza and Gordon, was a powerful factor. Underpinning both the 'scramble' and the competition in the Far East was the economic strength and technological superiority of an industrial and populous European continent which had the energy, the incentive and the means to project its power across the oceans.

SECTION B – SOURCES

COLONIAL EXPANSION AND EUROPEAN RIVALRIES

The 'Scramble for Africa' during the 1880s resulted in the division of almost the whole of the 'Dark Continent' among the claims of the European powers. This transformed the map of Africa and extended the process of major economic change. The alteration in the attitude of the colonial powers was dramatic; before this period governments had usually shown the greatest reluctance to extend their responsibilities in this way. The reasons behind the scramble are the subject of much debate. Some arguments focus upon the need to protect capital investment, for example in driving Britain (and originally France) to intervene in Egypt in 1882 (extract A). Others argue that it was the commercial interests of traders who lobbied successfully for government support. Yet another argument focuses on strategic concerns, especially of Britain to protect her routes to India, and Germany, to use colonial policy as another dimension to European foreign policy (see Chapter 18) (extracts B and C). Most of the arguments rest upon the economic strength of Europe (and the emergence of the United States' economic power) making it possible and desirable for industrial countries to extend their trade and influence overseas. There are variations on these analyses, but what soon becomes clear is that competition between the European powers played an important part, if not in starting the scramble, then certainly in shaping its progress (extracts A, D, E and F (i and ii)).

A Britain's occupation of Egypt: from a dispatch by the British ambassador in Berlin (Lord Ampthill) to the Foreign Secretary (Lord Granville), 15 July 1882

Let me congratulate you most sincerely and heartily on having so tactfully steered out of the inevitable complications of 'entangling alliances' into the independent prosecution of a truly British national policy. Everybody I meet seems overjoyed that we are asserting our right to protect our own interests, and have taken the lead of the concert into our own hands. Everybody congratulates me on your policy, with the exception of my French colleague, who is quite broken down with disappointment at Freycinet's weakness, and the absence of national pride in the French Chambers. Münster [German ambassador in London] is probably right in thinking that Bismarck will now be reticent and reserved.

(Lord Edmond Fitzmaurice, *The Life of Lord Granville 1815–91*, London, 1906, vol. 2, pp. 268–69, cited in M.E. Chamberlain, *The Scramble for Africa*, London, Longman, 1995, p. 117)

B From Bismarck's dispatch to the German ambassador in London (Münster), 5 May 1884

A further criterion for England's intentions to foster permanent friendly relations with us, concerns Heligoland. As an English possession this ancient German island is nothing more than a foothold for making attacks on the Elbe estuary. . . . Our friendship can be very useful to England. It cannot be a matter of indifference to her whether the power of the German Reich stands by her ready and willing to cooperate, or coldly holds back. The effect which our example had on the continental powers with the latest invitation to the conference, the probability of a completely opposite effect, if Germany had sought an understanding with *other* powers over the Egyptian question, are illuminating.

[The reference to a conference was apparently Gladstone's attempt to withdraw British forces from Egypt by getting European recognition of Britain's dominant interest there and guarantees about the free use of the Suez Canal. France was proving uncooperative, so Gladstone was aiming to internationalise the matter in order to get Bismarck's support.]

(J. Lepsius *et al.* (ed.) *Die Grosse Politik der Europäischen Kabinette 1871–1914*, Berlin, 1922, cited in W.N. Medlicott and D.K. Coveney, *Bismarck and Europe*, London, Arnold, 1971, p. 141)

C A German protectorate over Angra Pequena: from Bismarck's speech to the Budget Commission of the Reichstag, 23 June 1884

If it were asked what means the German Reich possessed for protecting German undertakings in far-off places, the answer first and foremost would be the desire and interests of other powers to preserve friendly relations with her. If in foreign countries they recognized the firm resolve of the German nation to protect every German with the device *civis Romanus sum*, it would not cost much effort to afford this protection. But of course if other countries were to see us disunited, then we should accomplish nothing and it would be better to give up the idea of overseas expansion.

[Angra Pequena was a German missionary station in South West Africa, which Germany proclaimed as a protectorate in April 1884. It was not far from Walfisch Bay which Britain claimed; see p. 242)

(H. von Petersdorff *et al.* (eds) *Bismarck: Die gesammelten Werke*, Berlin, 1923, xii, pp. 473–74, cited in Medlicott and Coveney, *Bismarck and Europe*, p. 142)

D From the Berlin Conference agreement between Germany, Austria, Belgium, Denmark, Spain, the USA, France, Britain, Italy, the Netherlands, Portugal, Russia, Sweden, Norway and Turkey, 26 February 1885

Article 34. Any Power which henceforth takes possession of a tract of land on the coasts of the African Continent . . . as well as the Power which assumes a protectorate there, shall accompany the respective act with a notification thereof, addressed to the other Signatory Powers . . . to enable them, if need be, to make good any claim of their own.

Article 35. The Signatory Powers . . . recognize the

obligations to insure the establishment of authority in the regions occupied by them on the coasts of the African continent sufficient to protect existing rights, and . . . freedom of trade . . . under the existing conditions agreed upon.

(*Parliamentary Papers*, lv (1884–85), 438, cited in Chamberlain, *Scramble for Africa*, p. 125)

E Fashoda: from the telegram by the British ambassador in Paris (Monson) to the Prime Minister (Salisbury), 28 September 1898

For the circumstances of the Anglo-French confrontation at Fashoda, see Section A.

his Excellency [Minister for Foreign Affairs, Delcassé] was just as determined as ever upon the right of France to occupy territory practically abandoned by Egypt and contested the right of Great Britain to warn off other Powers which had not recognized her sphere of influence or to assert that France was committing an unfriendly act in advancing on the Upper Nile. . . . He reiterated that it is the desire of the present French Government to make a friend of England, adding that between ourselves he would much prefer an Anglo-French to a Franco-Russian alliance. . . . He said: 'You surely would not break with us over Fashoda?' To which I answered that it was exactly that which I feared.

(Gooch and Temperley, *British Documents on the origins of the war, 1898–1914*, vol. 1, p. 171, cited in Chamberlain, *Scramble for Africa*, pp. 139–40)

F The motivations behind colonialism

(i) Jules Ferry's published argument for colonialism, 1885

Colonial policy is the daughter of industrial policy. . . . exports are an essential factor of public prosperity. The spread of capital, like the demand for work, is measured by the extent of the foreign market. . . .

. . . The European consumer market is saturated. New layers of consumers must be brought in from other parts of the globe. If this is not done, modern society will go bankrupt . . .

It is because England was the first to perceive those distant horizons that she has headed the modern industrial movement. It is because of possible setbacks which her industrial hegemony could suffer through the detachment of Australia and India, after the separation of the United States from North America, that she is laying siege to Africa on four fronts . . . In order to prevent British enterprise from capturing for its exclusive profit the new markets that are opening up for western products, Germany is opposing England at all points of the globe with a rivalry which is as inconvenient as it was unexpected. Colonial policy is an international manifestation of the eternal laws of competition. . . .

(cited in K. Randell, *France: The Third Republic 1870–1914*, London, Arnold, 1986, pp. 52–54)

(ii) E.J. Hobsbawm's view (published originally in 1987)

But the crux of the global economic situation was that a number of developed economies simultaneously felt the same need for new markets. If they were sufficiently strong their ideal was 'the open door' on the markets of the underdeveloped world; but if not strong enough, they hoped to carve out for themselves territories which, by virtue of ownership, would give national business a monopoly position or at least a substantial advantage. Partition of the unoccupied portions of the Third World was the logical consequence. In a sense, this was an extension of . . . protectionism. . . .

At this point the economic motive for acquiring some colonial territory becomes difficult to disentangle from the political action required for the purpose, for protectionism of whatever kind is economy operating with the aid of politics. . . . Once rival powers began to carve up the map of Africa or Oceania, each naturally tried to safeguard against an excessive portion (or a particularly attractive morsel) going to the others.

(E.J. Hobsbawm, *The Age of Empire 1875–1914*, London, Abacus, 1996, pp. 66–67)

Questions

1 What light is shed by Bismarck's comments about Britain's intervention in Egypt (extract B) on the British ambassador's earlier account (extract A)?

2 To what extent does Bismarck's speech to the Budget Commission of the Reichstag (extract C) suggest that his rivalry with Britain over Angra Pequena was governed by domestic political considerations? You should use extracts A and B, and your own knowledge, in your answer. (You may also refer to Chapter 18, extract A.)

3 Explain the significance of the commitment of the powers at the Berlin Conference 'to insure the establishment of authority in the regions occupied by them' (extract D).

4 Use extracts A, B, C and D to evaluate the French claim to Fashoda described in extract E.

5 Compare and contrast the explanations for colonial expansion presented by Ferry and Hobsbawm (extracts F (i and ii)).

6 Use all of the extracts and your own knowledge to evaluate the accuracy of the analyses of the causes of the 'Scramble for Africa' offered by Ferry and Hobsbawm (extracts F (i and ii)).

Further reading

The overall subject of economic development and imperialism is covered very well in M.S. Anderson, *The Ascendancy of Europe 1815–1914* (London, Longman, 1995) which provides a wide-ranging and detailed study. R. Gildea, *Barricades and Borders: Europe 1800–1914* (Oxford University Press, 1996) contains several useful chapters. E.J. Hobsbawm's classic *Industry and Empire* (London, Penguin, 1969) covers the two hundred years from 1750, while *The Age of Empire 1875–1914* (London, Abacus, 1996) is more specifically focused and both scholarly and readable. H. Gollwitzer, *Europe in the Age of Imperialism, 1880–1914* (London, Thames and Hudson, 1969) aims to explain the imperial impulse. The economic history which provides the important backdrop to colonialism in the nineteenth century may be approached through P. Mathias, *The First Industrial Nation: an Economic History of Britain 1700–1914* (London, Methuen, 1972), while D.S. Landes, *The Unbound Prometheus: Technological Change and Industrial Development in Western Europe from 1750 to the Present* (Cambridge University Press,

1972) sets Britain's development in the European context.

Among the studies which concentrate more specifically on colonialism, M.E. Chamberlain, *The Scramble for Africa* (London, Longman, 1995) provides a clear and concise analysis aimed at A-level and undergraduate students, and includes some documentary excerpts and a helpful bibliography. B.Waller's chapter on 'Europe in the wider world', in B. Waller (ed.) *Themes in Modern European History 1830–90* (London, Routledge, 1990), provides a concise and scholarly overview (with a useful chronology). D.K. Fieldhouse, *The Colonial Empires: a Comparative Survey from the Eighteenth Century* (London, Weidenfeld and Nicolson, 1971) provides scholarly detail across the full range of events.

Germany's colonial policy is covered briefly in D.G. Williamson, *Bismarck and Germany 1862–1890* (London, Longman, 1986) and W. Simpson, *The Second Reich* (Cambridge University Press, 1995), both of which include some documentary material, while more detailed cover is provided in G.A. Craig, *Germany 1866–1945* (Oxford University Press, 1978). A useful documentary collection, which includes a chapter on colonial policy, is W.N. Medlicott and D.K. Coveney, *Bismarck and Europe* (London, Arnold,

1971). More specifically focused material includes J. Lowe, *The Great Powers, Imperialism, and the German Problem, 1865–1925* (London, Routledge, 1994). British imperialism is covered in a stylish and accessible way by D. Judd, *Empire, the British Imperial Experience from 1765 to the Present Day* (London, Fontana, 1996). Both D.C.M. Platt, *Finance, Trade and Politics in British Foreign Policy, 1815–1914* (Oxford University Press, 1968) and P.J. Cain and A.G. Hopkins, *British Imperialism: Innovation and Expansion 1688–1914* (London, Longman, 1993) are scholarly and important studies. J. Gallagher and R. Robinson, *Africa and the Victorians: the Official Mind of Imperialism* (London, Macmillan, 1981) remains a stylish and revealing account which has continued to be debated by historians since it first appeared in 1961. French colonial policy is discussed briefly in the student texts by W.H.C. Smith, *The Second Empire and Commune: France 1848–1871* (London, Longman, 1985) and K. Randell, *France: The Third Republic 1870–1914* (London, Arnold, 1986), both of which provide some documentary excerpts, while more substantial studies are provided by H. Brunschwig, *French Colonialism, 1871–1914* (London, Pall Mall Press, 1966) and R. Aldrich, *Greater France, a History of Overseas French Expansion* (London, Macmillan, 1996).

CHAPTER SIXTEEN

Marxism and the Growth of Working Class Organisations

• CONTENTS •

Key dates

SECTION A

Karl Marx, his life and works

Varieties of Marxism

Working class movements

International organisations

SECTION B – SOURCES

Left-wing alternatives

KEY DATES

SECTION A

KARL MARX, HIS LIFE AND WORKS

Between 1871 and 1914 a powerful challenge emerged to the prevailing distribution of wealth and power in most of western Europe. Ironically, perhaps, it was in the much less developed countries of eastern Europe, notably Russia, that this challenge was to meet with success. But the revolutionary creed that sustained the communist revolution was written by people inspired by the western example of the French Revolution and who had themselves witnessed the impact of the industrial revolution above all in Britain. Such was the impact of Marxism that not only did it dominate the thinking of socialist parties in all parts of Europe but also with the triumph of the Bolshevik revolution in Russia it was to become a world-wide ideology, and the inspiration behind anti-imperialist movements in China, South East Asia, parts of Latin America and Africa. Ironically, just as the last quarter of the nineteenth century marked the point at which Europe's domination of the globe reached its zenith, so it was European thinkers in the first decade of the twentieth century such as J.A. Hobson and Lenin who provided the strongest case against imperialism. From the standpoint of the twenty-first century Marx's relevance may not seem so apparent as it was during the height of the Cold War. Few are likely to repeat Khrushchev's boast that 'History is on our side'. But the problem of poverty in the midst of wealth, which Marx addressed, is still with us, and the hold which his ideas had both on individuals and on political movements for much of the late nineteenth and twentieth centuries means that any study of socialism and working class organisations must begin with Marx.

Marx's life and ideas

Karl Marx was born in Trier in 1818, the son of a Jewish lawyer who had adopted the Protestant faith in order to be able to practise law. Marx went first to Bonn University in 1835, but then moved to Berlin in 1836, where he was strongly influenced by the works of Georg Hegel (1770–1831), professor of philosophy at Berlin from 1818 to 1831. After completing his thesis on the atomic theories of Democritus and Epicurus, Karl Marx became a journalist on the *Rheinische Zeitung* in 1842. Its inflammatory articles, such as one by Marx on the plight of German wine growers in the Moselle valley, led to its suppression, and Marx moved to Bad Kreuznach where he married Jenny von Westphalen, daughter of a civil servant who was also a minor aristocrat. In 1844 Marx moved to Paris where he met other left-wing thinkers such as Proudhon, Bakunin, and notably, Engels. Expelled from Paris, he went to Brussels. On a visit to London in 1847 he met a group of émigré German workers. These men had formed themselves into a revolutionary group called the League of the Just, and it was for them that Marx and Engels produced *The Communist Manifesto*, first printed in January 1848.

With the outbreak of the 1848 revolutions Marx moved first to Paris and then to Cologne, where he edited the *Neue Rheinische Zeitung*. Its last issue was published in May 1849, and Marx became once again a political exile. Expelled a second time from Paris, he arrived in London in August 1849, where he was to spend the rest of his life. He died in 1883. His early years were a constant battle against poverty, as much the consequence of his own improvidence as lack of income. Three of his six children died before they reached maturity. For a time he was London correspondent for the *New York Herald Tribune*. In 1864 he became the main organiser of the First International Working Men's Association, based in London, until its demise in 1872. His main energies, however, were devoted to research in the British Museum and writing *Das Kapital*. When Engels gave up his partnership in the family firm in 1869 he was able to subsidise Marx more generously, and Marx's last years were spent in reasonable comfort. He invested on the stock exchange, went on cures to the continent and sent his daughters to a private school.

Marx's writings

Though Marx built up a large acquaintance among fellow socialists, it was through his writings that he exerted his main influence. Of these *The Communist Manifesto* was unquestionably the most important. By 1888 it had been translated from its original German into French, English, Spanish and Russian. Marx never retracted any of the views he expressed there, and the vigour and simplicity of its language made it immediately accessible. His second most important book was *Das Kapital* (*Capital* in its English form), the first volume of which was published in 1867. The second and third were published by Engels after Marx's death in 1892 and 1894 respectively. *Capital* was very different from *The Communist Manifesto*. It was addressed to an academic readership and sought to provide by its exhaustive economic analysis the intellectual proofs for the revolutionary prophecies he had made in the Manifesto.

Marx was also a considerable journalist. A set of articles he wrote on the 1848 revolutions was republished as *The Class Struggle in France*, and he wrote articles on Napoleon III's seizure of power (*The Eighteenth Brumaire of Louis Bonaparte*, 1852) and on the Paris Commune (*The Civil War in France*, 1871). These were the publications by which Marx was best known in his lifetime. After his death his disciples and critics disinterred all his other writings, notably his early philosophic works such as *The Theses on Feuerbach*, *The Holy Family* and *The German Ideology*, all produced between 1845 and 1846. Many unpublished manuscripts came to light in the 1930s and these continue to be studied and edited by Marxist scholars. It is therefore no easy task to summarise Marx's leading ideas. From the historian's point of view what matters most is how they were perceived, and here we are on safer ground.

Perhaps the most significant of Marx's ideas was his new view of the whole historical process as an evolutionary one. Marx was a great admirer of Darwin and wanted to dedicate the first English translation of *Das Kapital* to him (Darwin politely declined the honour). Marx borrowed from Hegel the idea that the history of humankind had an inner logic to it, which proceeded by the clash of opposing principles to a desired goal. For Hegel this goal was 'the consciousness of freedom', achieved through the ancient Greeks, the Protestant Reformation and the Prussian state of his day (*Lectures on the Philosophy of History*). For Marx it was the classless society, to be achieved through the class struggle. He put it most cogently in the opening words of *The Communist Manifesto*:

The history of all hitherto existing society is the history of class struggles. Freeman and slave, patrician and plebeian, lord and serf, guild-master and journeyman, in a word, oppressor and oppressed, stood in constant opposition to one another, carried on an uninterrupted, now hidden, now open fight, a fight that each time ended, either in a revolutionary reconstitution of society at large, or in the common ruin of the contending classes.

The commercial and industrial revolutions beginning in the sixteenth century had reduced this struggle to 'two great classes directly facing each other – bourgeoisie and proletariat'.

In a letter to a friend, written in 1852, Marx indicated that he had no doubts about the outcome:

What I did that was new was to prove (1) that the existence of classes is only bound up with particular phases in the development of production (2) that the class struggle necessarily leads to the dictatorship of the proletariat. (3) that this dictatorship itself only constitutes the transition to the abolition of all classes and to a classless society.

Marx elaborated these ideas in *Capital*. In particular he stressed the contradictions within the capitalist system that were bound to lead to its downfall. He argued first that because the capitalist's profits depended on the surplus value he derived from his workers (their wages needed only to be sufficient to keep the workers alive), as industry became more capital intensive, the numbers of workers relative to machines would decline. This would lead to falling profits, reduced wages and greater competition. Small businesses would be forced to the wall. Their owners would join the ranks of the proletariat and the growing misery of the working class would inevitably bring about a revolt. The first volume of *Capital* concluded with this melancholy prediction:

Along with the constantly diminishing number of the magnates of capital, who usurp and monopolize all advantages of this process of transformation, grows the mass of misery, oppression, slavery, degradation, exploitation; but with this too grows the revolt of the working class, a class always increasing in numbers and disciplined, united, organized by the very mechanism of the process of capitalist production itself . . . . Centralization of the means of production and socialization of labour at last reach a point where they become incompatible with their capitalist integument [skin]. This integument is burst asunder. The knell of capitalist private property sounds. The expropriators are expropriated.

This was the Marxist message at its starkest. It also raises a problem that would divide his followers. If the downfall of capitalism was inevitable, what, if anything, should be done to hasten the process? To this problem Marx gave varying answers. He was himself generally an active supporter of revolution. In 1847 he had said in his *Theses on Feuerbach*: 'Philosophers have only given different interpretations of the world. The important thing is to change it.' He admired the Jacobin dictatorship of 1793–94. He bemoaned the failure of the 1848 revolutions. Most significantly, perhaps, he praised the Commune rising of 1871, which had resulted in the loss of at least 18,000 lives among the insurgents and the lives of several hostages, including that of the archbishop of Paris, taken as reprisals for the brutal way in which the rising was being suppressed. In a letter to a friend, Dr Kugelmann, Marx wrote:

Working-man's Paris, with its Commune, will be celebrated for ever as the glorious harbinger [forerunner] of a new society. Its martyrs are enshrined in the great heart of the working class. Its exterminators History has already nailed to that eternal pillory from which all the prayers of their priests will not avail to redeem them.

(E. Wilson, *To the Finland Station*, London, Collins, p. 291)

On other occasions Marx appeared to concede the possibility that in a country with an established parliamentary system of government such as England the workers might gain power peacefully. In 1881 he wrote: 'My party considers an English revolution not necessary, but – according to precedents – possible' (D. McLellan, *Marx*, London, Fontana, 1975, p. 64). Thus when Marx died it was not clear whether he still believed in the inevitability of revolution. He certainly had no reservations about its legitimacy.

VARIETIES OF MARXISM

It has been necessary to discuss Marx at such length because he is the reference point to which all other socialists and socialist parties can best be related, if only, as with the British Labour party, by rejecting him. By 1914 three main variants of Marxism can be distinguished. First there were the moderate orthodox Marxists best represented by the leaders of the German Social Democratic party, notably Theodor Bebel and Karl Kautsky (see Section B). In the Erfurt programme of 1891 the German SPD (Sozialdemokratische Partei Deutschland) accepted the Marxist diagnosis of capitalism and pledged itself to a full socialist programme of nationalisation of the means of production, distribution and exchange. It refused to cooperate with other parties in the German Reichstag and rejected the possibility of reform within the capitalist system. At the same time Kautsky accepted the possibility that a social and economic revolution might be achieved by democratic means. To the right of Kautsky was the school of thought associated with Edward Bernstein who in 1899 challenged some of the basic premises of Marxism. To Bernstein it was all too clear that capitalism was not on the point of collapse. So far from the workers' economic position getting worse, real wages were increasing, as was the number of small businesses. Bernstein argued that his party should 'appear what it really is today: a democratic-Socialist reform party' and should seek to improve the position of the working classes through parliamentary reform rather than through revolution. At the time Bernstein announced his ideas in his *Die Voraussetzungen des Sozialismus und die Aufgaben der Sozialdemokratie* (The Prerequisites of Socialism and the Tasks of Social Democracy) they represented an unacceptable departure from Marxism, and at the party congress held in Dresden in 1899 they were rejected by a massive major-

ity. In practice many members of the German SPD tacitly accepted them.

Bernstein's ideas found echoes in the British Labour party. The Fabian Society, founded in 1884, accepted much of the Marxist indictment of capitalism but its supporters too believed in an evolutionary kind of socialism, to be achieved by the gradual conversion of public opinion.

To the left of orthodox Marxists were the Bolsheviks. Coming from a totally different soil, where opposition to the regime was not permitted and where there was no national parliament, their version of Marxism developed quite differently from the German one. The first Marxist programme was adopted in 1883 by a group headed by Georgy Plekhanov, Vera Zasulich and Paul Axelrod, and the Russian Social Democratic party was founded at Minsk in 1898. Its leading members were soon either arrested or driven into exile but it did succeed in holding a conference which started in Brussels, and then to avoid the attentions of the Belgian police, moved to London in the summer of 1903. It was at this conference that Vladimir Ilyitch Lenin introduced the political strategy he had already spelled out in his highly important pamphlet, *What is to be Done?* written in 1902. Lenin argued that in the political circumstances prevailing in Russia in 1903 the only kind of political party that could succeed was a small conspiratorial party of dedicated revolutionaries. The notion of a mass party, aiming to achieve political power through the ballot box, as suggested by Bernstein, was wholly unrealistic (see Section B). Lenin's concept of the party did not meet with immediate acceptance, but on one crucial vote relating to the composition of the editorial board of the party's official publication, *Iskra* (The Spark), Lenin had a majority. This was sufficient for him to claim the right to call his faction *Bolsheviki*, the majority party. It was far from clear in 1903 that Lenin would carry the day, but he had drawn a very significant dividing line between his concept of Marxism and that of Kautsky, let alone Bernstein.

Outside the Marxist tradition but related to it were the Anarchists and Syndicalists. Anarchism is first associated with the name of Bakunin (Figure 16.1). Bakunin came from a Russian landowning family and, like Marx, came under the influence of

16.1 Michael Bakunin (1814–76), one of the founders of anarchism

Source: ©BBC Hulton Picture Library

the Young Hegelians at Berlin in 1840. He met Marx in 1842, took part in the 1848 revolutions and was arrested for his part in an uprising in Dresden in 1849. He spend the next eight years in prison, but eventually reached London in 1861 where he renewed his contacts with Marx. In 1869 he cooperated with a Russian student of extreme views, Nechaev, in producing *The Catechism of a Revolutionist*. This demanded of the would-be revolutionary complete dedication to the cause of the workers and complete ruthlessness in dealing with their opponents. Bakunin and his followers saw the state not as a potentially useful instrument to be used by the proletariat but as an evil in itself (see Section B). Authority could come only from below and would depend on the spontaneous action of the workers once the state had been destroyed.

Anarchism was closely linked to Syndicalism, which took its name from the French word for a trade union, Syndicat. Syndicalists shared with Anarchists their distrust of the state and a belief in the need for direct action. For Syndicalists the preferred weapon was the general strike which would lead, so it was hoped, to workers' control of industry.

Anarchism made little progress in northern Europe, but it had considerable appeal in Italy and Spain, where it made a significant impact in Barcelona in 1907, and again in the Spanish Civil War. One of its later exponents, a retired French engineer called George Sorel, produced in his book *Reflections on Violence*, written in 1906, a justification of violent acts of revolution which would alone be capable of transforming society. Assassination was seen as a perfectly legitimate tactic by some anarchists. Four leading political figures met their deaths at the hands of anarchists between 1890 and 1901: President Sadi Carnot of France (1891), Prime Minister Canovas of Spain (1897), King Umberto of Italy (1900) and President McKinley of the United States (1901). The Empress Elizabeth, wife of the Habsburg Emperor Francis Joseph, was assassinated in 1898 by a young Italian labourer who claimed to be an anarchist, though he had no links to any political party.

WORKING CLASS MOVEMENTS

National parties

By far the largest and best organised working class party was the German one, the Socialdemokratische Partei Deutschland, usually abbreviated to SPD. This began life as the German Working Men's Association, founded by Ferdinand Lassalle in 1862. Lassalle was a German nationalist as well as a socialist and differed in this respect from Wilhelm Liebknecht and August Bebel, both of whom came from southern Germany and were active in organising the League of Workers' Clubs, which drew its support from Saxony and parts of Bavaria. The two movements came together after the Franco-Prussian war. Lassalle had died in 1864 and in 1875 the two groups merged to form the SPD at a conference held in Gotha where they adopted the Gotha Programme, pledged to the achievement of a socialist society 'through all legal means'. Bebel and Liebknecht had voted against the acquisition of Alsace-Lorraine in 1871. They had also voiced their support for the Paris Commune, arousing Bismarck's ire on both counts. Two assassination attempts on Kaiser William II's life in 1878 gave Bismarck the opportunity he was looking for and he persuaded the Reichstag to pass an Anti-Socialist Law which effectively prevented the SPD from undertaking any serious political activity.

When the law expired in 1890 it was not renewed, and the SPD took on new life. In 1891 it met at Erfurt and drew up a new programme, along more explicitly Marxist lines. It accepted without question the Marxist critique of capitalism but confined its party programme to limited objectives such as a democratic franchise in Prussia and protection for industrial workers. This created, as George Lichtheim has put it, 'a yawning gap between its theoretical analysis and its practical demands' (G. Lichteim, *Marxism*, London, Routledge, p. 262). This was an unfortunate legacy. It prevented any links being established between the SPD and the moderate bourgeois parties such as the Progressives and frightened off some of the academic elite, who might otherwise have been tempted to give social democracy their support. The adoption of a Marxist ideology did not damage its standing in the eyes of the workers however. Popular support rose steadily from 1890 onwards, with the exception of the 1907 election, until by 1912 the SPD's share of the vote had risen to over a third and its representation in the Reichstag had risen from 35 in 1890 to 110 in 1912 out of a total of 397 seats. The SPD, despite being the largest single party in the Reichstag was never able to exploit its numerical superiority over other parties, however, partly because it refused to go into coalition, but more seriously because under the constitution of the German empire the Reichstag itself was denied an effective voice in many areas of policy making.

Socialism in France had to contend with the damaging impact of the Paris Commune. Adolphe Thiers, Prime Minister at the time, went so far as to say in 1871: 'Nobody talks of Socialism any more, rightly. We are rid of it' (J. Joll, *The Second International*, London, Routledge, 1974, p. 12). In 1872 a law was passed banning membership of the First International (see p. 260) and over 9,000 people who had taken part in the Commune rising were sentenced to death, prison or deportation. However, Thiers spoke too soon. In 1880 an amnesty was declared. Exiled and imprisoned leaders returned to political life, and workers' parties made their reappearance. Unlike Germany, French parties lacked the disciplined organisation and doctrinal unity of the German SPD. In 1879 a Marxist party, the Parti Ouvrier Français (French Workers' party) was founded at Marseilles. This was followed in 1882 by the Fédération des Travailleurs Socialistes (Federation of Socialist Workers), founded by Paul Brousse, who had anarchist sympathies. Another group, the Parti Socialiste Revolutionnaire, represented the believers in direct revolutionary action in the tradition of Babeuf and Auguste Blanqui. Such divisions weakened the socialist cause and in 1889 only seven socialists of various persuasions were elected to the French Chamber. However, in 1905 under the pressure of the Dreyfus Affair (see pp. 274–76) the socialist parties came together, and by 1914 they had seventy-six seats in the Chamber. They had also acquired an effective and popular leader in the person of Jean Jaurès whose reputation stood high in Europe as well as in France.

Socialist parties also developed in most other western and central European countries. The Partito Socialist Italiano was founded in Italy by Filippo Turati, an orthodox Marxist, in 1892. The Parti Ouvrier Belge dates from 1885. The Austrian Social Democratic party came into existence in 1889, led by Victor Adler, a distinguished Jewish doctor who also acquired an international reputation. Social democratic parties also developed in Scandinavia: the Danish one in 1878, the Swedish one in 1889 and the Norwegian one in 1904.

The British Labour party was formed out of four distinctive groupings: the Social Democratic Federation (1883), which was Marxist in its approach; the Fabian Society (1884), mainly supported by middle class intellectuals such as George Bernard Shaw and H.G. Wells; the Independent Labour party (1893), one of whose leaders, Keir Hardie, described socialism as 'the embodiment of Christianity in a social system'; and the Trades Union Congress (1868). These four groups came together in 1900 to form the Labour Representation Committee. By 1910 the Labour party, as it had by then become, had won 40 seats in parliament with 8.1 per cent of the vote.

The party which was to have the largest impact on European history, the Russian Social Democratic party, had, as we have seen, split into two distinctive factions after the Brussels-London Congress of 1903. All attempts to heal the breach failed, largely it would seem because Lenin was not prepared to make any compromise. Plekhanov commented acidly: 'Lenin desires unity as a man desires unity with a piece of bread. He swallows it' (cited in J. Joll, *The Second International*, p. 121). The breach between the two factions became final at a conference held in Prague in January 1912 at

which Lenin appointed a 'Central Committee' consisting exclusively of Bolsheviks.

Trade unions

The rise of workers' political parties was paralleled by the growth of trade unions. In a free labour market the individual worker had no bargaining power and the determination of hours and wages was left to the employer's discretion. It was in the employer's interest to keep the wage bill as low as possible, and it was only when demand for labour exceeded the available supply that workers could expect an improvement in their wages. Trade unions developed in all industrialised countries to redress the balance. This was to be done through collective bargaining, under which wage rates would be negotiated with employers through workers' representatives. Unions derived their bargaining power through the weapon of the strike. The threat of a collective withdrawal of labour could force an employer to concede wage demands rather than face the shut down of his undertaking.

Hardly surprisingly, unions were bitterly opposed by employers, and by the political parties which represented them. Unions were banned in England by the Anti-Combination Acts of 1799 and 1800, by the Le Chapelier Law of 1791 in France and by the Russian penal code of 1845. Bit by bit they won the right to exist. In Britain the Anti-Combination Acts were repealed in 1824, union funds were given protection in 1871, the right to picket peacefully was conceded in 1875 and unions were protected against claims for civil damages caused by strike action in 1906. In France unions were legalised in 1868, and again in 1884 after legal recognition had been withdrawn following the Commune in 1871. In Germany the Anti-Socialist Law of 1878 curtailed the activities of any Social Democratic unions, but in 1890 these restrictions were repealed. In Russia unions were officially permitted in 1906, though the right to strike was still denied.

Union membership grew slowly at first, but then accelerated as the industrial workforce expanded. Originally confined to craft workers, unions spread in the 1880s to manual workers in the mines, textiles, engineering and transport industries. By 1914 British trade union membership had reached 4 million, French 1 million and German 3 million. There were different patterns of membership. In Germany there were 400 different unions, whereas in Britain there were 3,000 and in France 5,000. Each country had developed its own national organisation. In Britain the Trades Union Congress dated from 1868; in Germany the General Commission of Trades Unions was founded in 1890; and in 1895 the French Confédération du Travail (CGT) came into existence.

Most union activity was devoted to the tedious but essential business of collective bargaining, at which German trade unions seem to have been particularly successful. But two tendencies became particularly marked in the years between 1890 and 1914, particularly in Britain and France. There was first the development of the industry-wide strike. Such strikes took place in the railways, mines and docks in Britain between 1911 and 1914: 41 million working days were lost in 1912 alone. In France there were serious strikes in the post and telegraph services in 1909 and a serious rail strike which led to reservists being called up in 1910. The syndicalist threat of a general strike was posed by a committee of the CGT which in 1899 argued that the General Strike was 'the only practical method by which the working class can fully liberate itself from the yoke of capitalism and the government' (W.O. Henderson, *The industrialisation of Europe 1780–1914*, London, Thames and Hudson, 1969, p. 190).

In Britain the formation of the Triple Alliance between miners, dockers and railway workers in 1914 was seen as a serious challenge to the authority of the government. The British General Strike in 1926, though it originated as a sympathetic strike on behalf of the coalminers, was seen in conservative circles as a threat to the constitution.

INTERNATIONAL ORGANISATIONS

A prime feature of Marxism was the belief that loyalty to the working class transcended loyalty to the nation. *The Communist Manifesto* concluded with the appeal: 'Working men of the world

unite!' Two attempts were made to give institutional expression to this sense of class solidarity. The First International, or the Working Men's International Association, to give it its original title, was founded in September 1864 by a group of French and British workers anxious to cooperate. Marx wrote the constitution of the organisation and gave the inaugural address. Designed to appeal to British trade unionists, it praised the efforts which had led to the passage of the Ten Hours Bill, providing for a maximum working day of ten hours, in 1847 and the emergence of the cooperative movement. Marx spelled out the programme for the future: 'To conquer political power has therefore become the great duty of the working classes' (Lichtheim, *Marxism*, p. 104). For the next eight years Marx devoted much of his energy to coordinating and directing the work of the First International. But it was riven by factional disputes, with both the supporters of Proudhon and Bakunin. British workers were appalled by Marx's praise for the Paris Commune. In 1872 Bakunin was expelled from the organisation and Marx transferred its headquarters to New York where it died a lingering death. At its peak, the First International is credited with enjoying the support of 800,000 workers, but it never posed much of a threat to established governments.

The Second International had a longer history and enjoyed a much wider degree of support, partly because it coincided with the growth of mass workers' parties. It was founded in Paris in 1889, the centenary of the outbreak of the French Revolution. It began with an inauspicious division between orthodox Marxists, who met at one venue, the Salle Petrelle, on 14 July, and moderate French socialists, who called themselves Possibilists because of their policy of cooperating with other political parties, who met at another venue. No junction took place in 1889. The Marxists attracted about 400 delegates from twenty countries, and among those attending were Liebknecht and Bebel from Germany, Vaillant and Guesde from France, Keir Hardie and William Morris from Britain and Plekhanov from Russia. Four simple resolutions were passed: the first supported an eight-hour day and improved working conditions; the second condemned standing armies and called for national defence by means of 'the people in arms'; the third supported universal suffrage (still to be achieved in most European countries apart from France and Germany); and the fourth called for 1 May to be made an occasion to demonstrate the solidarity and effectiveness of the working class movement. Though none of the resolutions had any immediate effect apart from the final one (May Day was celebrated in 1890 and thereafter in various ways), the Second International had succeeded in bringing together a significant number of socialist leaders. A Bureau was set up to organise future gatherings; and a basis for future cooperation had been laid.

Successive congresses followed at regular intervals: Brussels (1891), Zurich (1893), London (1896), Paris (1900), Amsterdam (1904), Stuttgart (1907), Copenhagen (1910) and Basle (1912). The International Congress planned for Vienna in August 1914 never met because by then working class solidarity had been irrevocably wrecked by the outbreak of the First World War. All the divisions which plagued Socialism were reflected in these meetings. Thus the Brussels Congress was marked by the unsuccessful attempts of anarchist delegates to force their way in. The same issue arose at Zurich in 1893 when fifteen delegates were expelled. At the Amsterdam Congress in 1904 the revisionist arguments raised by Bernstein were debated and defeated (see Section B). Attempts to end the Bolshevik-Menshevik split were made on several occasions without success.

Perhaps the most critical issue to be discussed was the attitude towards national defence. For French socialists there was a continued suspicion of German ambitions, and Jaurès made it quite clear that any German aggression would have to be met by force. So far as German socialists were concerned, they were equally insistent on the need to resist any aggression from Russia. Bebel said in 1891: 'the soil of Germany, the German fatherland, belongs to us the masses as much and more than to others. If Russia, the champion of terror and barbarism went to attack Germany and destroy it . . . . we are as much concerned as those who stand at the head of Germany' (Joll, *Second International*, p. 114). With these reservations, there was still a strong conviction in socialist circles that any war between the European powers would be to the detriment of the working classes. There

was little enthusiasm for imperialism or spending on armaments, though the German SPD did vote for an increased armaments bill in 1913, when it was coupled with an inheritance tax. At the Stuttgart Congress in 1907 a resolution was adopted calling for 'the working classes and their parliamentary representatives in the countries taking part, fortified by the unifying activity of the International Bureau, to do everything to prevent the outbreak of war by whatever means seem to them most effective'. It concluded, however, with a more ominous sentence, incorporated through the influence of Rosa Luxemburg, a committed Marxist:

Should war break out in spite of all this, it is their duty to intercede for its speedy end, and to strive with all their power to make use of the violent economic and political crisis brought about by the war to rouse the people, and thereby to hasten the end of capitalist class rule.

(Joll, *Second International*, p. 141)

When the first Balkan war broke out in 1912 an emergency congress was summoned at Basle, attended by 555 representatives from twenty-three countries. It was an impressive occasion, with powerful speeches being made in favour of peace (see Section B). The conference opened with a massive gathering in Basle Cathedral at which Jaurès quoted the German poet Schiller in his rousing address.

In retrospect the Basle Conference can be seen as the highwater mark of the Second International. When the First World War broke out two years later all the resolutions in favour of peace counted for little, compared with national sentiment. This was strengthened by the conviction, both in France and Germany, that the war was being fought to defend the homeland, against Germany in the case of France, against Russia in the case of Germany.

By 1914 the world of bourgeois-led capitalism, created by the industrial revolution, was being challenged in a variety of ways. Socialist ideology based on Marxism attacked the very premises on which capitalism rested, and forecast its inevitable downfall. Socialist parties committed to this ideology, at any rate in theory, thrived in Germany and France, had made some progress in Italy and Spain, and to a lesser extent, England. Powerful trade union movements had grown up in Germany, France and England, capable of crippling the economies of these countries should they choose to do so. On the fringes of these movements were the anarchists and the Bolsheviks, prepared to use the weapons of assassination, conspiracy and coup to achieve their ends.

There is no way of telling how these threats would have materialised had the First World War not intervened. Clearly a social democratic movement committed to a revisionist programme, working through a democratically elected parliament would have been a more desirable outcome than the imposition of a socialist dictatorship by a revolutionary minority, which is what happened in Russia, and consequently in most of eastern Europe. Section B illustrates these contrasting alternatives, as they were seen by their adherents, and their opponents, in the years leading up to 1914. While they may do little to explain the cataclysm of the First World War, they will help to explain what happened after it.

SECTION B – SOURCES

LEFT-WING ALTERNATIVES

As we have seen, by 1914 parties of the left embraced a wide spectrum of views, both about the goals of socialism and how they should be achieved. The following extracts have been chosen to illustrate these divisions within the European socialist movement. The first two extracts (A and B) represent the central Marxist position, as laid down by Marx in 1848 and reinterpreted by Engels in 1888. The Anarchist critique of Marxism is reflected in extract C, taken from the writings of Bakunin in 1872. Extracts D and E illustrate the fierce debate on revisionism which went on in the German SPD and the Second International between 1899 and 1904. Extracts F (i and ii) display Lenin's concept of what a Marxist party ought to be and do in Russia around 1900. We begin with Marx and Engels. Extract A comes from *The Communist Manifesto*, extract B from Engels' Preface to the 1888 edition.

A The Communist Manifesto

We have seen above that the first step in the revolution by the working class is to raise the proletariat to the position of the ruling class to win the battle of democracy. The proletariat will use its political supremacy to wrest, by degrees, all capital from the bourgeoisie, to centralise all instruments of production in the hands of the state, i.e. of the proletariat organised as a ruling class; and to increase the total of productive forces as rapidly as possible.

(*The Essential Left*, London, Allen and Unwin, 1967, p. 34)

B Engels' Preface to the 1888 edition

The Manifesto being our joint production, I consider myself bound to state that the fundamental proposition belongs to Marx. That proposition is: That in every historical epoch, the prevailing mode of economic production and exchange, and the social organisation necessarily following from it, form the basis upon which is built up, and from which alone can be explained the political and intellectual history of that epoch; that consequently the whole history of mankind (since the dissolution of primitive tribal society, holding land in common ownership) has been a history of class struggles, contests between exploiting and exploited, ruling and oppressed classes; that the history of these class struggles forms a series of evolutions in which, nowadays, a stage has been reached where the exploited and oppressed class – the proletariat – cannot attain its emancipation from the sway of the exploiting and ruling class, the bourgeoisie – without at the same time, and once and for all emancipating society from all exploitation, oppression, class distinction and class struggles . . . . However much the state of things may have altered during the last twenty-five years, the general principles laid down in this Manifesto are, on the whole, as correct today as ever.

(ibid., pp. 12–13)

C Bakunin, writing in 1872, attacks the dangers of state socialism

The government will not content itself with administering and governing the masses politically, as all governments do today. It will also administer the masses economically, concentrating in the hands of the State the production and the division of wealth, the cultivation of land, the establishment and development of factories, the organisation and direction of commerce, and finally the application of capital to production by the only banker – the State. All that will demand an immense knowledge and many heads 'overflowing with brains' in this government. It will be the reign of scientific intelligence, the most aristocratic, despotic, arrogant and elitist of all regimes. There will be a new class, a new hierarchy of counterfeit scientists and scholars, and the world will be divided into a minority ruling in the name of knowledge, and an immense, ignorant majority. Moreover . . . for the proletariat this will, in reality, be nothing but a barracks: a regime where working men and women will sleep, wake, work, and live to the beating of a drum.

(D. Miller, *Anarchism*, Oxford, Dent, 1984, p. 11)

D The revisionist debate

This came to a head in 1899. Edward Bernstein published his *Voraussetzungen* (Assumptions) that year and his propositions were hotly debated at the next party Congress in Hanover the same year. After a five-day debate they were rejected and Bernstein was subsequently expelled from the SPD. Extracts D (i and ii) are taken from *Evolutionary Socialism*, an English translation of *Voraussetzungen*, published by the British Independent Labour Party in 1903. Extract E comes from the motion accepted by the party congress at Dresden in 1903, reaffirming the rejection of Bernstein's revisionist views.

(i) Evolutionary Socialism

The present social order has not been created for all eternity but is subject to the law of change and a catastrophic development with all its horrors and desolation can only be avoided if in legislation consideration is paid to changes in the conditions of production and commerce and to the evolution of classes. And the number of those who realise this is steadily increasing. Their influence would be much greater than it is today if the social democracy could find the courage to emancipate itself from a phraseology which is actually outworn and if it could make up its mind to appear

what it really is today: a democratic socialist party of reform.

(D. Smith, *Left and Right in Twentieth Century Europe*, London, Longman, 1970, p. 79)

(ii) Evolutionary Socialism

Democracy is at the same time means and end. It is the means of the struggle for Socialism and it is the form Socialism will take once it has been realised.

(P. Gay, 'The Dilemma of Democratic Socialism', in P.N. Stearns (ed.) *A Century for Debate, 1789–1914*, New York, Dodd, Mead, 1969, p. 404)

E Motion put forward and passed at the Dresden Conference of the SPD in 1903 and subsequently passed at the Congress of the Second International at Amsterdam in 1904

The Congress condemns in the most decisive fashion revisionist efforts to change the victorious tactics we have hitherto followed based on the class struggle, in such a way that instead of conquering political power by defeating your opponents, a policy of coming to terms with the existing order is followed. The results of such revisionist tactics would be that instead of being a party which works for the most rapid transformation possible of existing bourgeois society into the socialist social order, i.e. revolutionary in the best sense of the word, the party would become one which is content with reforming bourgeois society. Therefore the Congress is convinced, in contradiction to present revisionist efforts, that class conflicts are not growing weaker but continually becomes more acute, and declares:

1   That the Party disclaims responsibility for political and economic circumstances based on capitalist modes of production, and that it therefore refuses to support any measures calculated to keep the ruling classes in power;
2   That Social Democracy, in accordance with the Kautsky resolution of the International Socialist Congress in Paris, 1900, cannot aim at participating in governmental power within capitalist society.

(Joll, *Second International*, pp. 102–3)

Lenin's theory of the party did not differ markedly from Kautsky's, but went a good deal further.

F Lenin's arguments

In Russia, unlike France, Britain or even Germany after 1890, left-wing parties were not free to organise, debate and canvass their policies and contest elections. Until 1905 none of this was true of Russia. For Lenin, a convinced Marxist, a parliamentary road to socialism in Russia's circumstances was both inappropriate and impracticable. The Social Democratic party should organise itself for revolution, not for electoral success as the following extracts indicate. The first is taken from an article written by Lenin for the first issue of *Iskra* (The Spark) which came out in 1900 and of which Lenin was one of the main editors. The second is taken from Lenin's pamphlet, *What is to be Done?*, published in 1902.

(i) Lenin writes in Iskra

Not a single class in history has reached power without thrusting forward its political leaders, without advancing leading representatives capable of directing and organising the movement. We must train people who will dedicate to the revolution, not a spare evening but the whole of their lives.

(cited in L. Kochan, *The Making of Modern Russia*, London, Penguin, 1962, p. 208)

(ii) Lenin attacks the idea that 'the broad democratic principle of Party organisation must be emphasised, developed and fought for' which was being argued in Rabocheye Dyelo (Workers' Concerns), a party periodical supported by moderate Russian Social Democrats

Just try to set this picture into the frame of our autocracy! Is it conceivable in Russia for all those 'who accept the principles of the Party programme and render the Party all possible support' to control every action of each revolutionary working in secret? Is it possible for all the revolutionaries to elect one or other of these revolutionaries to any particular office, when, in the very interests of the work he must conceal his identity from nine out of ten 'of these all'? Ponder a little over the real meaning of the high-sounding phrases to which *Rabocheye Dyelo* gives utterance, and you will realize that 'broad democracy' in Party organisation, amidst the gloom of autocracy and the domination of gendarme selection, is

nothing more than a useless and harmful toy. It is a useless toy, because, in fact, no revolutionary organisation has ever practised, or could practise, 'broad' democracy, however much it desired to do so. It is a harmful toy because any attempt to practise 'the broad democratic principle' will simply facilitate the work of the police in carrying out large scale raids, it will perpetuate the prevailing amateurishness, divert the thoughts of the practical worker from the serious and imperative tasks of training themselves to become professional revolutionaries to that of drawing up detailed 'paper' rules for election systems.

(V.I. Lenin, *What is to be Done?*, Peking Foreign Languages Press, 1973, pp. 172–73)

Questions

1 What do you think Marx meant by 'the battle of democracy' (extract A)?
2 What evidence is there in extract B that Engels believed in the inevitability of the classless society?
3 Compare the role of the state in a post-revolution society, as it is envisaged by Marx (extract A) and Bakunin (extract B)?
4 On the basis of your wider knowledge, how justified were Bakunin's warnings?
5 What do you think Bernstein meant by 'a phraseology that is actually outworn' (extract D (i)) and 'Democracy is at the same time means and end' (extract D (ii))?
6 On the evidence of extracts D and E, what were the central issues dividing Bernstein from his opponents in the German SPD?
7 What was distinctive about Lenin's concept of political leadership (extracts F (i and ii))?
8 How convincing are Lenin's arguments in extracts E (i and ii) against the 'broad democratic principle of Party organisation'?
9 Compare the very different attitudes towards Marxism taken by working class parties in Britain, France, Germany and Russia. How far are they to be explained by the different political systems in which they grew up?

Further reading

The best guide to Karl Marx is by D. McLellan, *Karl Marx, his Life and Thought* (London, Macmillan, 1973). A briefer version by the same author is available in *Marx* in the Fontana Modern Masters series (London, 1975). Marx's writings are available in various editions, e.g. D. McLellan, *Selected Writings* (Oxford University Press, 1977). *The Communist Manifesto* was published with a stimulating introduction by A.J.P. Taylor (London, Penguin, 1967). There is a useful compilation of sources, including *The Communist Manifesto*, in *The Essential Left, Five Classic Texts in the Principles of Socialism* (London, Allen and Unwin, 1986). The best books on Marxism are G. Lichtheim, *Marxism* (London, Routledge, 1961), E. Wilson, *To the Finland Station* (London, Collins, 1961) and R. Carew-Hunt, *The Theory and Practice of Communism* (London, Penguin, 1963).

For the history of left-wing movements in Europe see D. Caute, *The Left in Europe since 1789* (London, Weidenfeld and Nicolson, 1966), J. Joll, *The Second International* (2nd edn, London, Routledge, 1974) and D. Miller, *Anarchism* (London, Dent, 1984).

There are useful background chapters on working conditions and labour movements in W.O. Henderson, *The Industrialisation of Europe 1789–1914* (London, Thames and Hudson, 1969) and in E. Hobsbawm, *The Age of Empire* (London, Weidenfeld and Nicolson, 1987).

• CHAPTER SEVENTEEN •

The Third Republic in France, 1871–1914

• CONTENTS •

Key dates

SECTION A

Establishing the Republic, 1870–79: a compromise with the past

Challenges to the Republic

French foreign and colonial policy, 1871–1906

SECTION B – SOURCES

The extent of support for the Third Republic

Key dates

1870	4 Sept.	Republic proclaimed; Government of National Defence set up
	23 Sept.	German forces besiege Paris
1871	28 Jan.	Fall of Paris; armistice between German empire and France
	8 Feb.	Elections to National Assembly; Thiers 'Chief of the Executive'
	18 March	Paris Commune set up; government withdraws to Versailles
	10 May	Treaty of Frankfurt, Germany imposes indemnity on France and annexes Alsace-Lorraine
	28 May	Government forces take Paris; Commune ended after 'bloody week' of death and destruction
1873	24 May	Thiers replaced by Marshal Mac-Mahon; 'Republic of the Dukes'
	Sept.	German forces leave France as the indemnity is paid off
1875		Constitutional laws; Wallon amendment adds 'Republic'
1876	Jan.	Elections to Senate; Monarchist majority
	March	Elections to Chamber; Republican majority
1877	16 May	Constitutional crisis; President MacMahon dismisses Republican ministry and calls new elections
	Dec.	MacMahon accepts Republican ministry with majority backing in the Chamber
1879	Jan.	MacMahon resigns presidency, replaced by Republican Grévy; 'Republic of Republicans' now
1881		Tunis made a French protectorate
1882		Ferry's reforms make primary education secular
1885		Fall of Ferry over Tonkin reverse
1886		Boulanger made Minister of War; great popularity
1887	July	Gare de Lyon demonstration fails to stop Boulanger being posted away from Paris
	Dec.	Wilson scandal forces father-in-law President Grévy to resign
1889	Jan.	Boulanger elected for Paris constituency; coup possibility
	April	Boulanger flees arrest; support soon collapses
1892		Panama Canal Company scandal
1892–94		Alliance between France and Russia concluded
1894		Dreyfus court martialled
1898		Dreyfus Affair arises as forged evidence is revealed; Fashoda Incident; France restricted to colonies in West Africa
1899		President Faure's death provokes anti-Dreyfusard plot; Dreyfus reconvicted on lesser charge and pardoned
1901		Law of Associations bans illegal congregations
1902		Elections; majority Republican bloc includes many anti-clerical Radicals
1904		France and Britain agree *Entente Cordiale*
1905	Dec.	Law on separation of Church and State
1905–06		First Moroccan crisis
1906		Dreyfus rehabilitated by Chamber
1906–09		Prime Minister Clemenceau confronts strikes and syndicalism
1907		Britain and Russia agree *entente*
1909–11		Prime Minister Briand continues firm policy and splits Republican bloc
1911–14		Government instability

SECTION A

The collapse of the Second Empire through military defeat at the hands of the Prussians left a power vacuum. When the newly proclaimed Republic was also defeated, the Communards tried to seize power, and parallels may be drawn with both the Jacobins in 1793 and the Bolsheviks in Russia in 1917. The Third Republic was shaken by war, defeat and the suppression of the Commune, and to start with it seemed that it would be replaced quickly by a constitutional monarchy. But the Monarchists' hopes came to nothing, and conservatives and even radical Republicans found they had common ground and a constitution was approved in 1875. 'It was the first constitution', Theodore Zeldin writes, 'not to require an oath of loyalty from those who served it, with the result that it excluded no one unnecessarily from the start. It was essentially a compromise'. The relatively open nature of the constitution permitted great political instability to occur with 'an endless succession of barely distinguishable ministries', yet the crises and arguments failed to provoke revolution (T. Zeldin, *France 1848–1945: Politics and Anger*, Oxford University Press, 1984, pp. 206–07).

The Third Republic survived until 1940, proof enough that it was the regime which divided French people least. Its formative years were the 1870s from the proclamation to the resignation of President MacMahon when the so-called 'Republic of the Dukes' gave way to genuinely Republican ministries. But the Third Republic was unable to get rid of the effects of France's turbulent political history so quickly, and the political culture remained deeply affected by issues of Church and state, the appeal of the Bonapartist figure of General Boulanger (1886–89), and the Dreyfus Affair (1894–1906) which brought to the surface political and social divisions which went back to the first French Revolution. Despite these crises, and the political instability shown in the bewildering succession of ministries (there were nearly fifty between 1870 and 1914), the Third Republic survived. Governments became more radical in the 1900s, and the nature of the extreme Left changed to class-based Marxist parties and syndicalism (which believed in using strike action to overthrow capitalism), but the regime itself survived and even contained these challenges and changes, suggesting perhaps that the political culture had outgrown revolutionary insurrection or the *coup d'état*.

ESTABLISHING THE REPUBLIC, 1870–79: A COMPROMISE WITH THE PAST

Surrender

The mob which invaded the chamber on 4, September 1870 virtually forced the radical Republican deputies Gambetta and Jules Favre to go through 'the usual' form of revolution by going down to the Hôtel de Ville and proclaiming a provisional Republican government. This was called the 'Government of National Defence', under the presidency of General Trochu (the Governor of Paris).

By 23 September Prussian forces had surrounded and cut off Paris, completing what Parisians had encouraged themselves by pretending was 'mathematically impossible'. Preparations for the siege had been made, but the government delegation of three elderly ministers which had been established in Tours proved incapable of effective government. Gambetta made a dramatic escape from Paris by balloon and reached Tours on 10 October. Combining the posts of Minister of War and Minister of the Interior, his energy and the conscious awakening of memories of 1792 galvanised things. He made full use of the Republican prefects he had appointed, and organised an Army of the Loire which relieved Orleans in November. But the surrender of the French General Bazaine at Metz at the end of October had allowed the Prussian forces to be redeployed, and the tide of war was moving in Prussia's favour. The attempt to break through the Prussian lines and relieve Paris failed, and Gambetta's force was split and ineffective. The Delegation left Tours and moved to Bordeaux. Europe watched in amazed horror as military sorties from Paris were beaten back; horse, dog, cat and rat became part of the diet of this once sophisticated city, and the siege guns built by Krupp began their bombardment.

Paris surrendered on 28 January 1871, the government agreeing to an armistice and promising to hold elections to a National Assembly on 8 February to give them a proper mandate for the peace talks. Gambetta felt betrayed. He saw no reason why France could not continue to fight after Paris had fallen. He was highly suspicious that the government was hoping for a right-wing victory (perhaps preparing the way for a monarchical restoration), and he issued a separate election decree banning anyone who had served under Napoleon III from standing. But government ministers confronted Gambetta in Bordeaux, arguing that the armistice required free elections, and Gambetta drew back from the coup which some ardent

Republicans wanted. He resigned, taking what turned out to be an important step towards the evolution of the Republic by non-revolutionary means.

Elections and peace

The elections of 8 February 1871 were clearly a vote for peace. The National Assembly which met at Bordeaux had a large majority comprising Legit-imists (who wanted a Bourbon restoration under the Duc de Chambord), Orleanists and assor-ted conservatives amounting to about 400, with Republican deputies numbering about 200 and some 30 Bonapartists. Gambetta's status as the hero of patriotic defence would soon become a legend, but it was not popular just then.

Adolphe Thiers, now aged 73, had been returned by twenty-six departments and his pres-tige made him the obvious leader of the Monarchist-conservative majority who voted him 'Chief of the Executive Power of the French Republic' on 17 February 1871. The title was careful to avoid prejudicing the future form of government, and Thiers promised (in the 'Pact of Bordeaux') to remain neutral in party terms and organise a coalition government which would allow no party to criticise the peace from outside.

The peace was severe, Bismarck seeing no reason for it to be otherwise (see Chapter 13). The annex-ation of Alsace-Lorraine was a focus of French ambitions for revenge, the large indemnity appeared crippling, while the humiliation of see-ing the German empire proclaimed at Versailles in January was redoubled by the continued German occupation of several departments and by the vic-tory parade through Paris. France's defeat seemed complete and political turmoil highly likely.

The Commune

Reaction to peace took an extraordinary form in Paris. Despite or because of the experience of the siege, 37 of the 43 deputies elected for Paris on 8 February 1871 had wanted the rest of France to continue the war. During the siege there had been signs of this revolutionary patriotic spirit too.

When news of the fall of Metz reached Paris and rumours of peace talks circulated, the government at the Hôtel de Ville was overwhelmed by a mob (led by the National Guard units from the working class district of Belleville) on 31 October 1870. Municipal elections were demanded and the rioters seemed intent on re-enacting some *journée* from 1792 or 1793. It ended peacefully then and the government reasserted control, but it was different on 18 March 1871.

The Prussian victory parade through Paris departed, leaving some angry patriots scrubbing the cobblestones clean where jackboots had trod-den, but the real incitement came from the newly elected government. The National Assembly moved from Bordeaux to Versailles because of the conditions in Paris, but many Parisians saw this as a further sign that France was turning her back on those who had endured the siege. The government decreed that the National Guard would no longer qualify for pay (they had to prove poverty now), and that all rents and other debts which had been unpaid since August 1870 should be paid, thus adding bankruptcy to the grievances of many Parisians (bourgeois as well as working class). Finally Thiers took a risk on 18 March and sent an inadequate military force to Montmartre to collect the 220 cannon which had been bought by public subscription raised by Parisians. The soldiers were overwhelmed (some happily joined the rioters) and the government beat a hasty retreat to Versailles, leaving Paris in the hands of the National Guards' Central Committee, which had set up the Com-mune in the Hôtel de Ville (see Figure 17.1).

These details may explain what triggered the Commune, but its underlying source is to be found in the Parisian *journées* of 1789–93, the February Revolution of 1848 and the June Days which fol-lowed, and the appeal of the Workers' Inter-national of 1865 to some members of the working class. The Belleville Programme drawn up by Gambetta's constituents in 1869 (extract A (i)), and the Communard's Manifesto of the Twenty Arrondissements (of Paris) which was proclaimed on 19 March 1871 (extract A (iii)) both make clear the revolutionary pedigree that fuelled and inspired the Commune. The Communards con-fidently expected France to follow where Paris led, as she had done before. But to the central

FIGURES DU JOUR PAR BERTALL

PARIS CUIT DANS SON JUS.

17.1 Bismarck and Thiers watch 'Paris stewing in its own juice'
Source: Bibliothèque Nationale, Paris

government of France, established at Versailles, the rebels were 'Federalists', a description made more understandable by attempts to set up Communes in other cities including Lyon and Marseilles, and Thiers was quick to organise the second siege of Paris.

The Commune was a ramshackle attempt at government. Moderate elements quickly fled, and a collection of extremists ranging from radical journalists to Anarchist followers of Blanqui argued and bickered. Sorties were dismal failures as government troops and artillery tightened their grip, in the process wrecking some fashionable suburbs which had not supported the Commune. The Communards issued many decrees, for example exempting tenants from back-payments of rent and banning gambling, and during April a Committee of Public Safety was set up. Rigault as Chief of Police pursued a brutal campaign against priests and took many hostages, including the archbishop of Paris. Government troops under Marshal MacMahon were exasperated at having to fight rebels with German soldiers looking on, and

they shot all Communards they caught as they closed in during May, fighting street by street. The Communards fought desperately at the barricades, the final *semaine sanglante* (bloody week) being marked by the execution of fifty-six hostages (including the archbishop) and the firing of many buildings, including the Tuileries. Paris fell into the hands of the government on 28 May 1871, but brutal repression continued. Probably 20,000 died, and 38,000 were arrested; some 13,500 were imprisoned or deported.

It was not only Paris that was wrecked by this bloody episode of civil war, but also the city's capacity to lead a revolution. It was as though all the ghosts of past insurrections had risen again and created some tragic mockery of Parisian 'popular sovereignty' and Revolutionary patriotism, only for these ghosts to be brutally exorcised. It allowed the government to exterminate insurrectionary Republicanism, and over the next few years the National Assembly and Thiers moved more freely towards a regime less dominated by revolutionary ideology.

The constitution of the Republic

History continued to affect matters, however. Thiers carefully appealed to both moderate Republicanism and the Monarchist majority, telling the National Assembly in 1872 that the 'Republic will be conservative, or it will not exist' (extract B (ii)). Gambetta, unconnected with the Commune and leader of the radical Republicans, was highly suspicious that Thiers's talk of a Republic was a front while preparations were made for a constitutional monarchy (see for example extract B (i)). Thiers seemed sympathetic, and the Orleanists were prepared to throw in their lot with the Legitimists because the Duc de Chambord was childless; if he became 'King Henri V' he would be succeeded by an Orleanist. But the Duc de Chambord seemed to want a return to the *ancien régime*, symbolised by his wish to replace the *tricolore* with the White Flag of the Bourbons. Most of his supporters recognised that his proclamation of July 1871 (extract C) needed to change to accept constitutional restrictions to his monarchy, and their hopes of persuading him faded slowly by 1874. There was little prospect of Legitimists switching their support to the despised Orleanist branch of the family, and the possibility of a Bonapartist revival under the Prince Imperial (Napoleon III died in 1873) was never strong (it was finally ended by the young man's death by a Zulu spear in South Africa in 1879). So it was left largely to Thiers to guide matters towards a Republican constitution.

Thiers pursued a conservative policy of which the Monarchist deputies in the National Assembly approved. He rejected income tax, maintained a centralised government structure, abolished the National Guard, began reforming the army, and achieved spectacular success in raising loans from the general public to pay off the indemnity. The last German soldiers left French soil in September 1873, and Thiers was named 'Liberator of the Territory'. But between 1871 and 1873 Thiers's support for a Republican constitution became more obvious and the 'Bordeaux Pact' was broken. Perhaps he was influenced by the elections which took place in July 1871 when 100 of the 118 vacant seats in the Assembly were filled by Republicans who would soon be able to challenge the Monarchist majority. The Monarchists finally turned against Thiers, in March 1873 passing a law preventing him as President from addressing the Assembly, and following this in May with conservative policy demands which immediately prompted his resignation.

Marshal MacMahon, the Duc de Magenta, was elected President on the same day, 24 May 1873. A resolute conservative, devoted to food and hunting, he appointed the Duc de Broglie to head the first ministry of what has been called the 'Republic of Dukes'. It seemed only a hair's breadth away from a monarchical restoration as government pursued 'the restoration of moral order', purged the civil service and judiciary of Republicans, and began the building of the Basilica of the Sacred Heart in Montmartre where the Communards had started their secular rebellion.

The constitutional laws were passed by the Assembly in 1875. The elected Chamber of Deputies would be checked by the power of the Senate and the President, and Monarchists were clearly guarding against a future Republican majority. But with a majority of deputies in the Assembly still hoping to see a restoration of a Bourbon, Orleanist or even Bonapartist regime, the constitutional laws carefully avoided featuring the word 'Republic'. However, by 353 votes to 352 the Wallon amendment was carried, saying that the 'President of the Republic' would be elected by both the chamber and the senate. The work of the National Assembly and of the provisional government was now ended.

Women were not enfranchised by the new constitution, and they were to be denied the vote until 1944. However, a feminist movement did develop during the 1870s. In 1878 Léon Richer and Maria Deraismes organised a feminist congress, with representatives from eleven countries. Generally the movement was careful to avoid extremism, either by association with the prominent role of women in the Commune (e.g. Louise Michel), or in the 1900s by siding with radical socialism. It avoided campaigning for abortion rights and contraception as birth control issues incurred the anger of the Catholic Church and also fuelled the widespread fear in France that her birth rate was falling dangerously behind Germany's. The moderation of the movement helped ensure that it did not fade out, as it had done in the 1790s and after 1848, but it was held back because opportunities for women to work were limited, and the bourgeois model of the role of women became widely accepted (see for example many Impressionist paintings).

The crisis of 16 May 1877

From 1876 the power of the Monarchists was slipping. The elections of 1876 produced a conservative majority for the senate, but in the Chamber of Deputies Republicans polled 800,000 more votes than the conservative parties, winning some 340 seats in the Chamber of Deputies against 153 Monarchists (including 75 Bonapartists), with 22 Constitutionnels in the centre.

President MacMahon reluctantly called Jules Simon, a moderate Republican, to form a ministry in December 1876. Great tension was developing between the Church, supported enthusiastically by the Monarchists, and the Republican supporters, who still united with great enthusiasm around the old anti-clericalism of the Revolution. When the Republicans carried a motion against Roman Catholic influence, MacMahon forced Simon's ministry to resign on 16 May. The protesting Chamber was adjourned for a month, with the senate's approval, and the Duc de Broglie formed a ministry.

There were obvious parallels with the crisis of 1830 when the Bourbon Charles X had tried to rule through a ministry which did not have the support of the Chamber. Furthermore, some detected a Bonapartist flavour in MacMahon's claim that he was exercising a responsibility to France. While French history made the crisis of 1877 heavy with portends, it was not to become a revolution or a coup. Only the election was furious. The Republicans slipped to 321, the conservative groups (Legitimists, Orleanist, Bonapartist numbering 104) and others gaining 207 seats (figures for 1876 and 1877 from R.D. Anderson, *France 1870–1914: Politics and Society*, London, Routledge and Kegan Paul, 1977, Appendix 1).

MacMahon gracefully explained that his actions had been constitutional and in December 1877 appointed the moderate Republican, Dufaure, to head a ministry which included Freycinet, a close colleague of the highly influential Gambetta.

MacMahon's submission to the verdict of the election increased the authority of the chamber, and presidential power to dismiss ministries fell into disuse. More important, conservatives began to see that the Republic provided a safe form of government which would not degenerate into Republican excess. Much of the credit for this should go to Thiers's gradual acceptance of the Republican form of government, and Gambetta's slow movement towards a less radical position.

For MacMahon the last straw came in January 1879 when the Republicans won a majority in the senate and began to reverse the conservative purge of the civil service, judiciary and army. He resigned, remarking 'I've had enough toads to swallow', to be replaced by the moderate Republican mediocrity Jules Grévy (G. Wright, *France in Modern Times*, New York, Norton, 1987, p. 228). French politics seemed to be shaking off the burden of its revolutionary and explosive past at last.

CHALLENGES TO THE REPUBLIC

The 'Republic of the Republicans' is the name sometimes given to describe the political era between the resignation of MacMahon and the fall of the 'Republic of the Dukes' in the later 1870s, and the 'Republic of the Radicals' of the early 1900s. In the 1880s the key political group was the Opportunists who won 457 seats in the 1881 elections. They were moderate Republicans who believed in choosing the opportune moment for reform, as distinct from the more ideologically pure Radical Socialists of the extreme Left. The Right remained an important minority; in 1881 Monarchists and Bonapartists each won 45 seats. It was a period of change for the country. The agricultural depression of the 1880s, prompted largely by cheap wheat from the United States, encouraged a shift in the population towards the towns and cities, while at the same time reduced consumer spending damaged industry. Governments undertook a programme of public works from the late 1870s, and conducted a generally successful foreign and colonial policy, as we shall see, but ministries came and went with bewildering speed.

One cause of governmental instability was the debating rule (called interpellation) which allowed deputies to challenge ministers on any matter, great or small, and force a vote; if the ministry lost, it was obliged to resign. Another source of political instability was the low calibre of deputies who were often solely concerned to protect local vested interests. President Grévy's uninspiring leadership jealously avoided asking Gambetta to form a ministry until November 1881, by which time intrigue had undermined his once towering authority; his ministry fell in January 1882, and he died that same year at the age of 44. But the most severe bouts of political instability each had a distinct character, and they have come to symbolise France in the late nineteenth and early twentieth centuries.

Boulangerism

In the 1885 elections the conservative Right gained ground, winning 201 seats against the 383 won by Republicans (Opportunist, Radical and extreme groups). Freycinet's Opportunist ministry of 1886 needed the support of the Radicals to stay in office and duly appointed their man, General Boulanger, to be Minister of War. Boulanger began a series of army reforms which included making the three-year military service really compulsory for all (including priests!), and he accompanied these with quite extraordinary publicity. His elegant, dashing appearance quickly made him a hero to the crowd, while he slowly won support in establishment circles. The 1887 war scare with Germany only enhanced his reputation as the patriot who would be able to recover Alsace-Lorraine.

President Grévy and the Opportunist deputies had become highly alarmed by Boulanger's popularity. It was no thanks to the general that war with Germany had been averted. His radical appeal was Napoleonic and suggested that many French people were bored with parliamentary Republicanism. Rouvier was appointed to form a ministry in May 1887 and confront the problem. Now that the Radical–Opportunist alliance had been broken over Boulanger, Rouvier had to rely upon the support of the Opportunists and the Right. The ministry excluded Boulanger and posted the general to a distant command, bracing itself for the public outcry.

Absurd scenes took place at the Gare de Lyon on 14 July 1887, where people lay across the railway line to prevent Boulanger's departure, but he slipped away, embarrassed. There the matter might have ended, but the Republican system of government was discredited by a scandal which made the Boulangist alternative appear thrilling again. Grévy's son-in-law, Wilson, who lived at the Elysée as well, was accused of trafficking in honours and using the President's free postal service to carry on a large correspondence. The President was forced to resign in December, but not before the possibility of Jules Ferry becoming President had provoked turmoil. Ferry was a powerful figure, but he had enemies among both the patriotic Right (which included Monarchists and Bonapartists) and the Radical left. This opposition brought Boulanger into some sort of partnership with the Monarchists and Bonapartists, and it was agreed that he should stand for election to the chamber in as many by-elections as possible in order to challenge the corrupt politicians. Sadi Carnot, respectable bourgeois, grandson of the 'organiser of victory' Lazare Carnot of the original Committee of Public Safety, was elected President but his standing was insufficient to halt the challenge of General Boulanger.

Boulanger won six by-elections during 1888, and in January 1889 Paris returned him in preference to a Republican. His appeal was a curious mixture of radicalism and conservative patriotism which was full of Bonapartist passion (see extract D). Alarmed Republican deputies formed a ministry of 'Republican concentration' and banned multiple candidatures, but their fear, and the hope of Boulanger's supporters, was that a *coup d'état* was about to be staged. However, Boulanger was not a Napoleon III, and this was not to be a repeat of the Eighteenth Brumaire of Napoleon the Great. In April it was rumoured that he was to be arrested, and he fled to Belgium with his mistress. His star faded rapidly after this failure of courage, but the expectations he had raised about what he might do showed that the Third Republic lacked popularity and was still vulnerable to threats from the past.

Church and state, and the Dreyfus Affair

Anti-clericalism was a potent Republican cause which dated back to the Revolution. The division between 'the scarlet' of Republicanism and 'the black' of the Church coloured politics throughout the nineteenth century. Furthermore, social reform involving price controls, the right to work and fair rents carried with it the baggage of Jacobinism, the National Workshops (of 1848) and the Commune which had alienated the bourgeoisie. Therefore, when the 'Republic of the Republicans' arrived in 1879, they had to proceed cautiously; an ideologically pure policy of social reform or a campaign against the Church could wreck the delicate compromise between the Third Republic and the past.

Cautiously, then, changes were made. In 1879 the chamber returned to Paris, many Communards were amnestied, and a programme of public works provided employment for many. Jules Ferry was leader of the Left Republican component of the Opportunists and it fell to him, as Minister of Public Instruction for three years, to address what all Republicans saw as the threats to democracy; illiteracy and clerical influence in education. All Republicans were ready to applaud Gambetta's famous battle-cry of 1876; 'Clericalism – there is the enemy!', and education was to be the arena for this campaign (J.P.T. Bury, *France 1814–1940*, London, Methuen, 1985, p. 157). The important education bill was carried in 1882 making primary education compulsory, free, and secular. There were other measures too. For instance Church influence in education was further attacked by the strict enforcement of an existing law which banned 'unauthorised congregations'; this allowed the Jesuits and other congregations to be broken up. These steps confirmed the Catholic view of the Republic as a Godless regime and the Revolution of 1789 as the insurrection of Man against God, an attitude which Pius IX had helped to preserve by his Syllabus of Errors. Some magistrates and officials resigned rather than enforce the measures (to be replaced by Republicans), and Monarchist deputies were infuriated, but the policy was driven through. Division was limited, however, by comparison with the 1790s or 1848. Religious practice was declining (for example the proportion of marriages taking place in the Roman Catholic Church fell from about 78 per cent in 1870 to 60 per cent by 1910) and Pope Leo XIII was conciliatory to the secular authority of government (figures from graph cited in J.-M. Mayeur and M Rebérioux, *The Third Republic from its origins to the Great War, 1871–1914*, Cambridge University Press, 1987, p. 103). The issue might have subsided quietly now, but for the Dreyfus Affair.

Between the measured Republicanism of Ferry's reforms and the Dreyfus Affair, government was disrupted by Boulangerism, as we have seen, and the Panama scandal. The Panama Canal Company ran into financial difficulties in 1888, and eventually went bankrupt. In 1892 accusations were made that deputies and senators had received bribes through Jewish financiers to vote state assistance to prop up the company. While most of the cases were dropped, the mud which had been thrown stuck. Clemenceau, the Radical leader, Floquet, the President of the Chamber, and Rouvier were among those seriously damaged. Not only had politicians been shown to be corruptible, but also anti-Semitism had been boosted.

The Panama scandal was a dangerous prelude to the Dreyfus Affair. Captain Dreyfus was charged with selling military secrets to the Germans, convicted in a closed court martial in 1894, and deported (see Figure 17.2). As Dreyfus was a Jew, the right-wing anti-Semitic press made a fuss. The matter might have been closed but for Dreyfus's family insisting on his innocence, and Colonel Piquart (an intelligence officer) reporting to his superiors in 1897 that another officer named Esterhazy was the real culprit. At this stage the army attempted a cover-up to protect the original conviction. Piquart was posted abroad and a forged document added to the Dreyfus file.

The affair blew up in 1898. Méline's government stood by the conviction, but some senators and deputies became aware of the flimsy evidence against Dreyfus, Clemenceau reasserted himself in the cause and Jaurès, the socialist leader, joined the defence. Zola, the famous novelist, published his open 'J'accuse' letter to the President alleging that Esterhazy's acquittal in a secret court martial was fixed and part of the cover-up.

17.2 Dreyfus the traitor publicly disgraced by his sword being broken

Source: Roget-Viollet, Paris

Although Zola fled from a conviction for slander, a revision of the case became inevitable when the forgery was revealed and Esterhazy slipped away into hiding.

It is hard for us now to appreciate the enormous division which was opening up in French political and educated circles over this affair, and the fascination it held for other countries. On the one side the anti-Dreyfusards stood by the army and the nation's defence priority. They were nationalists, patriots, often anti-Semitic, and vigorously supported by the Catholic Church (see extract E) who all tended to see the whole thing as a Jewish, German or revolutionary conspiracy to destabilise France. The Dreyfusards on the other hand demanded the fair trial of one man who was being 'framed' by the arbitrary authority of a corrupt state. The Revolution's ideal to protect the Rights of Man was under the kind of attack which Hannah Arendt later saw as a chilling 'foregleam of the twentieth century' (cited in L. Derfler, *The Dreyfus Affair: A Tragedy of Errors?*, Boston, MA, D.C. Heath, 1963, p. xvi).

Dreyfus was retried in 1899, found guilty of 'intelligence with the enemy with attenuating circumstances' by five of the seven judges, then pardoned by the President (cited in J.P.T. Bury, *France 1814–1940*, p. 187). A second revision in 1906 quashed the verdict of 1899, and the chamber passed a special resolution rehabilitating Dreyfus at last. The process created a political upheaval which made the Third Republic appear contemptible. In 1899 President Faure died, as Bury puts it 'in the course of an intimate meeting with a lady who was not his wife' (Bury, *France*, p. 186). The anti-Dreyfusard, Déroulède, accused Dreyfus's supporters of his murder and he attempted the '*coup* of Reuilly' during the funeral. The humiliation caused to the Third Republic's stability and prestige by this fiasco was completed by his acquittal by an obviously sympathetic court. Stability was restored by Waldeck-Rousseau's ministry, which lasted for a record three years, and began life in 1899 by arresting sixty-seven suspected anti-Dreyfusard conspirators.

The Dreyfusards had triumphed, but the cost to the Third Republic was high. The '*Ralliement*', the improvement of relations between the Church and the Right on the one hand with the moderate Republicans, which had occurred after the Boulanger affair, was destroyed. Anti-clericalism again became the great unifying Republican battle-cry because the Church had revealed itself to be so opposed to the Revolution's ideals of fairness and individual rights. The moderate Republicanism of the Progressists (as the Opportunists called themselves from the later 1880s) gave way to a radical Republicanism. Waldeck-Rousseau found his ministry needed Radical support and made Millerand Minister of Commerce; he was the first socialist to join a government.

In 1901 the law on associations was passed requiring congregations to be authorised by the chamber, or they would be declared illegal and dissolved. No member of an unauthorised congregation was to be allowed to teach. This was a divisive and severe step against the Church, and helped provoke a 90 per cent turnout in the 1902 elections. The elections gave the opposition about 220 seats and the government Bloc Républicain 370 seats, but Progressists and moderates numbered about 210 and the other support for the government came from among the Radicals (129), Radical-Socialists (90) and Socialists (48). Combes (a socialist and a former trainee priest and Professor of Theology) led the new ministry which was vigorously anti-clerical – this was the key unifying policy. The law on associations was enthusiastically enforced and about 12,000 schools run by unauthorised congregations were closed. The next year religious orders containing about 20,000 monks were dissolved, despite the protests from the Vatican and the dying Waldeck-Rousseau.

Inevitably the total separation of Church and state became the issue, the unravelling of the 1801 Concordat. In 1904 a bill was introduced, but Combes fell soon afterwards. Rouvier's government was less enthusiastic but dared not alienate the Radicals by abandoning the bill. Instead, it was entrusted to the young and inexperienced Briand, who secured its passage by the end of 1905. Freedom of worship was guaranteed, but the state reallocated Church property and ended all financial support. Clergy and the Church became impoverished but free from state interference, and the political arena was at last rid of this divisive issue inherited from the past.

Socialism and the Radical Republic

The threat to the Third Republic from the Right diminished after Boulangerism and with the defeat of the anti-Dreyfusards. But the threat from the extreme Left had not been destroyed with the Commune, and it reappeared later in the nineteenth century quite changed. The amnesty granted to many Communards in 1880 allowed some to take up political agitation again, but the days of erecting barricades were passed. Radicalism was attracted to Boulanger, and Anarchist outrages continued – President Carnot was stabbed in 1894 – but industrialisation created a trade union movement which became the heart of revolutionary socialism from the mid-1880s onwards.

The *syndicats* were trades unions who believed that fundamental social reform would come through direct strike action holding the government and the capitalist class to ransom. Their thinking owed something to anarchism. Syndicalism gained popularity from the mid-1880s onwards, especially in the large industries such as coal-mining, but it also attracted postal workers and teachers. In 1906 the syndicalists proclaimed in their Charter their aim to expropriate the capitalist class by a general strike (extract F (ii)), and they came close to dominating the trade unions and the Confédération Générale du Travail (CGT – the Trades Union Congress, set up in 1895) with about one in forty of the whole population belonging to a *syndicat*.

Strikes and disturbances became serious during 1906–08 among various groups, but the call for a general strike made by the CGT in 1909 failed. Clemenceau, the formidable Radical, journalist and duelist, confronted these disturbances firmly as Prime Minister (1906–09), and he did not hesitate to use troops against the strikers. He had refused to join the Communards in 1871 and he again showed that his radicalism would not tolerate extra-parliamentary action.

But there were extreme socialists who believed that the key questions of social reform (such as the redistribution of wealth and the provision of social security insurance) could be addressed through parliamentary means, and these groups expressed their views in a joint declaration in 1905 (extract F (i)). Syndicalist violence and Clemenceau's confrontational policies forced the parliamentary

Socialists to choose. The eloquent Socialist leader Jaurès became critical of government policy, and the Radical Prime Minister had to rely increasingly on the support of the Progressists, his old enemies. Clemenceau fell in 1909, to be replaced by Briand, and hopes were raised that relations between the Radicals and the Socialists would be mended. The Socialists were certainly gaining ground; in 1906 they attracted just over 1 million votes, while in the 1910 elections this rose to 1.4 million and about 100 deputies as against the Radicals' 252 seats. But the wave of strikes in 1910 was countered by Briand with the same firmness as Clemenceau had shown, and his power-base crumbled. After Briand's ministry fell in February 1911, government instability returned with a vengeance. Seven Cabinets struggled to hold power during the next three years (see Map 17.1).

Social reform had been excluded from the political agenda for years by the political turbulence of the 1880s and 1890s, while the later confrontation between the Left and the Radicals and Progressists had failed to advance the agenda. The law of 1900 secured the gradual reduction of the working day to ten hours, and the introduction of old age pensions by Clemenceau during Briand's ministry in 1910 were the only modest achievements. The 'Radical Republic' had been full of proposals for social reform during the 1900s, but had achieved little through the years of conflict and instability.

FRENCH FOREIGN AND COLONIAL POLICY, 1871–1906

It took France years to become accustomed to her junior status in Europe after the proclamation of the German empire at Versailles in 1871. *Revanche* (revenge) for the defeat and the recovery of Alsace-Lorraine remained the fixed idea of many French people, but the crucial question was timing. Premature confrontation with Germany would result in total humiliation, and this was recognised more clearly by moderate Republicans of the Opportunist and Progressist variety than by hot-headed rightists or Radicals of the sort who flocked to Boulanger. There were also distractions on the route to *revanche* such as colonial successes and

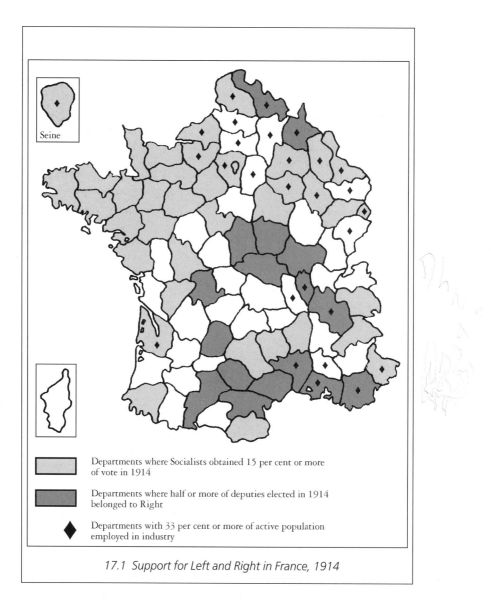

Departments where Socialists obtained 15 per cent or more of vote in 1914

Departments where half or more of deputies elected in 1914 belonged to Right

Departments with 33 per cent or more of active population employed in industry

17.1 Support for Left and Right in France, 1914

failures, and rivalry with Britain who remained the object of great French hostility until the early 1900s. But the treaty with Russia in 1894, and the *entente* with Britain in 1904, marked the recovery of France from her humiliation of 1871 and signalled the approach of war with Germany who was held responsible.

Jules Ferry and imperialism

Empire-building had a bad reputation after Napoleon III's disastrous adventure in Mexico, and acquiring colonies was seen by some Republicans as a distraction from important domestic issues. But Ferry, famous for his secularisation of education, argued that colonial markets were essential if industrial production and employment were to be maintained at home. Tariff barriers to prevent foreign competition were not enough. A prosperous and stable society, with the resources to afford social reform, needed colonies (see Chapter 15, extract F (i)). In the early 1880s his colonial policy had Gambetta's support, and there can be little doubt that colonialism was also seen as a way of boosting France's prestige without pursuing *revanche* and confrontation with the mighty German empire.

At the Congress of Berlin in 1878, called to protect the Ottoman empire and Austria-Hungary from Russia's attempt to create a large Bulgarian satellite state, France re-entered the European stage. Britain acquired Cyprus in the settlement, and was only too anxious to encourage France to seek compensation in Tunisia. Bismarck was happy to divert French ambitions from Alsace-Lorraine too. Therefore Ferry found the international path smoothed, and when some raids were launched from Tunisia into French Algeria, he seized the opportunity. In 1881 the Bey of Tunis agreed to a French protectorate of the country.

Radical deputies were unhappy at this adventure and disliked the way it had been pushed through. Another opportunity occurred in 1882, this time to establish a joint Anglo-French protectorate in Egypt where disturbances threatened the Suez Canal and investments. Ferry was out of office and Freycinet was forced to back out, leaving Britain to undertake some 'gunboat diplomacy' on her own with the prize of establishing a protectorate in Egypt in 1882. France had missed her opportunity, and her resentment at Britain's gain poisoned Anglo-French relations and encouraged colonial rivalry for nearly twenty years.

Ferry's ministry of 1883–85 saw to it that no further opportunities for colonial gains were missed. France's hold in Madagascar was strengthened, and the vast French Congo was won at the cost of a mere 300,000 francs following recognition of France's claim by the International Congress of Berlin (1884–85). The French empire in the Far East was established in Annam, and Tonkin recaptured, but this caused Ferry's fall. When French forces suffered a minor reverse in Tonkin at the hands of the Chinese, and reinforcements were required, the disaster of the Mexican adventure came vividly to mind and Ferry was driven from office in 1885 by an extraordinary panic-stricken over-reaction. A few weeks later, and by a majority of only one vote, the chamber approved staying put in Tonkin. But the whole affair showed clearly the volatility of French politics and the underlying feeling that no risks should be run there when the real enemy occupied Alsace-Lorraine.

The alliance with Russia

In the Franco-Prussian war (1870–71) France had been isolated, and facing Germany single-handed again would be suicidal. If France was ever to recover Alsace-Lorraine, she needed allies. Two war-scares with Germany underlined this point, and fuelled French hatred of Germany. With the French indemnity paid off by 1873 and French army reforms moving ahead, Bismarck encouraged the press to debate 'Is war in sight?' in 1875. His motives may have been to warn France or to try out his allies. This artificial crisis was defused by British and, significantly, Russian diplomacy. The crisis of 1887 was still more obviously one of Bismarck's publicity stunts. Partly to scare off the *revanche* hopes of Boulanger (then Minister of War) and his followers, and partly to get approval for greater spending on the German army, the French police official Schnaebele was arrested on the border as a suspected spy. Bismarck never intended war and French ministers behaved more sensibly than they had done in 1870, so the 'crisis' evaporated, but patriots thought it was all because General Boulanger had scared Bismarck off. Hot-headed patriots therefore kept their taste for *revanche*, but serious politicians saw that Boulanger was a liability and felt France's diplomatic isolation badly.

Deteriorating relations between Germany and Russia were to give France her opening. Soon after the new Kaiser William II removed Bismarck from office (1890) Russia became more clearly excluded from the close partnership of Germany with Austria-Hungary (the Dual Alliance was signed in 1879). Once Tsar Alexander III had shown his suspicions of the atheistic and scandal-ridden Third Republic, but in 1891 he stood bareheaded on the deck of a visiting French warship as the Marseillaise was played. The enthusiastic French reception given to the visiting Russian navy in 1893 showed the intense sense of relief at having found a friend in Europe, and the alliance was concluded in 1894.

Strangely French Republicans felt no embarrassment at this intimacy with the autocratic Russian regime, helped no doubt because the Russian aristocracy spoke French. Considerable investment flowed from France into Russia during the 1890s and early 1900s, especially into railway building. In terms of French foreign policy, the alliance with Russia gave it a new focus and confidence. Although some moderate politicians entertained the distant hope of recovering Alsace-Lorraine, there were no plans for *revanche* and this is shown clearly by the continued bickering with Britain while she was being courted by Germany.

The *Entente* with Britain

French colonial gains continued after Ferry's fall, and a colony was established on the Ivory Coast in 1894 and Madagascar was annexed in 1896. But dislike of Britain was fierce, and many French people felt that British greed and double-dealing had secured Egypt and was busy acquiring a vast line of territory between there and the Cape. The confrontation occurred at Fashoda (in the Sudan) in 1898. A small French expedition, travelling from west Africa to establish a claim to the upper Nile, met Kitchener's larger force moving south from Khartoum. The French were forced to withdraw, and thereafter it was agreed that East Africa should remain mainly British while West Africa (including most of the Sahara) should be French ('rather light soil', as Lord Salisbury remarked sarcastically). This incident might have provoked a serious clash with Britain, but the influential Foreign Minister Delcassé (who served a series of governments) kept a sense of priority; a colonial war with the strongest naval power in the world would not help recover Alsace-Lorraine. Instead bitter dislike of Britain smouldered, and French opinion cheered the Boers on as Britain struggled with the war in South Africa between 1899 and 1902.

But Britain's imperial self-confidence was damaged by the Boer war, and she needed an ally if she was to keep her naval and colonial power. The possibility of an alliance with Germany failed as the German naval building programme moved ahead; in 1902 Britain turned to another offshore island for help and secured an alliance with Japan. Britain's nineteenth century of 'glorious isolation' had ended. But there was a risk that a clash in the Far East between Russia, France's ally, and Japan,

Britain's ally, would bring a confrontation between France and Britain, and this provided one motive for these two colonial rivals to resolve their arguments.

French interests in Morocco provided the other incentive for agreement with Britain. France's hold on Morocco was being damaged by disorder there which was encouraging German and British interference, and a settlement with Britain would enable France to resist German pressure and consolidate her rule. In 1904 the *Entente Cordiale* (understanding) with Britain was concluded which sorted out not only Morocco but also the other points of colonial friction from Newfoundland to Siam.

The *entente* was soon tested. The Russo-Japanese war of 1904–05 caused no tensions between Britain and France, but the crushing defeat of France's ally, Russia, increased the importance of the *entente* partnership with Britain. It also encouraged Russia to reach her agreement with Britain in 1907. In Morocco in 1905–06 disorder led to the Kaiser's intervention and the calling of the Algeciras Conference. But Germany's attempt to split the Anglo-French *entente* and undermine the French position in Morocco failed miserably. Italy, with whom France had repaired relations since 1900, actually deserted her former ally Germany and supported France's claim in Morocco.

By 1906 therefore the alliances were established which were destined to develop into the armed camps of 1914. The Franco-Prussian war was only partly responsible for their emergence. The Third Republic had not planned a war of revenge; the alliance with Russia was defensive and prompted by Russia's growing isolation, and the *entente* with Britain was so long delayed. But two forces are unmistakable in causing the emergence of the Triple Entente. One was the desperate need felt by France to recover her diplomatic place after the isolation and humiliation of the Franco-Prussian war, and this ambition may be seen in her colonial policy as well as in the agreements with Russia, Italy and Britain. The second was German foreign policy after Bismarck's resignation in 1890, a foreign policy which worried Russia, tried to intimidate Britain, depended increasingly on the weakening Habsburg empire, and maintained its hold on Alsace-Lorraine.

SECTION B – SOURCES

THE EXTENT OF SUPPORT FOR THE THIRD REPUBLIC

The three different strands in Republicanism appeared early. The radical Republicanism of Gambetta developed an agenda for social reform before the Second Empire ended, and this was embodied in the Belleville Programme of 1869 (extract A (i)). The Franco-Prussian war, and Gambetta's role in raising a provincial army and resisting peace with the Prussians, gave this radical Republicanism a patriotic element which drew much from the tradition of the defence of the First Republic by the Jacobins in 1793–94. The first Proclamation of the Republican Government in September 1870 reminded the French people of this tradition (extract A (ii)). But the fall of Paris, after a grisly siege, and the shaping of a humiliating peace with the new German empire sparked off the Commune in Paris. This insurrection (March–May 1871) drew on the second strand in Republicanism, the Revolutionary tradition of popular sovereignty justifying the direct intervention of citizens in government. The *journées* of 1789 and the Commune of Paris in the early 1790s had established this tradition, and the Communards of 1871 revived the ideology of the extreme Left in the Manifesto of the Twenty Arrondissements (extract A (iii)).

The Commune was crushed, but it encouraged the moderate Republicans to stick to the conservative formula which Thiers came to embody as the third strand in Republicanism (extract B (ii)). Those who wished to see a monarchical restoration mostly recognised that it would have to be a constitutional monarchy of some sort, but the last Bourbon, the Duc de Chambord, seemed unable to accept this and he wished to replace the glorious *tricolore* with the old White Flag of the Bourbons (extract C). Thiers, who originally saw the provisional Republic (proclaimed in September 1870) giving way to a constitutional monarchy, moved to the centre and accepted the Republic. Gambetta, bitterly critical of Thiers's motives for much of the 1870s (see extract B (i)), moved slowly to a less radical position. Bonapartism was not a spent force until 1879, when the Prince Imperial was killed, but the cross-party appeal of the tradition existed, as the extraordinary support for General Boulanger between 1886 and 1889 showed (see extract D).

Anti-clericalism remained a potent rallying-cry for Radical and insurrectionary Republicanism in the 1870s, and it was revived vigorously by the Dreyfus Affair. The Catholic Church had made its stand against the Revolution (which emphasised the Rights of Man and popular sovereignty), and it was quick to see these 'new' values at work in the defence of Captain Dreyfus (a Jewish officer in the French army, charged with spying for the Germans on doubtful evidence). As a result the Church rose to the defence of the army, which condemned Dreyfus (extract E). As the Dreyfusards gained ground (he was finally acquitted in 1906) so did the move to separate Church and state (the law was passed in December 1905), but it is possible to argue that the influence of the Church was diminished by then.

The tradition of extreme Republicanism which the insurrectionary Commune of 1871 had revived was naturally a terrifying spectre to many. It was also a dated phenomenon to some extent by the end of the century. The growth of industry, and the development of workers' organisations (especially trade unions and *syndicats*) gave reform demands a more obvious Socialist or Marxist content. Reform through parliament was not attractive to the extreme Left in the early 1900s, and the Communards of course acted outside the parliamentary process too. The Revolutionary tradition which took the *sans-culottes* to the barricades might be detected still in the extreme Left's call for class war in the early 1900s (extracts F (i and ii)).

A Radical Republicanism

(i) From the Belleville Programme, 1869

(Gambetta stood for the constituency of Belleville, a suburb of Paris, and asked his radical supporters to draw up this programme, which became the point of reference for the Left Republicans in future years.)

we give our deputy the mandate of affirming the principles of radical democracy . . .

The most radical application of universal suffrage, for the election of mayors and municipal councillors . . . as well as for the election of deputies; . . .

Unrestricted freedom of assembly . . .

. . . separation of Church and State;

Secular, free and compulsory primary education.

(from E. Ollivier, *L'Empire liberal*, vol. 11, Paris, 1907, pp. 497–98, cited in G.A. Kertesz (ed.) *Documents in the Political History of the European Continent, 1815–1939*, Oxford University Press, 1968, pp. 309–10)

(ii) From the first Proclamation of the provisional Republican Government, 5 September 1870

The people have disavowed a Chamber which hesitated to save the country when in danger. It has demanded a Republic. . . .

The Republic vanquished the invasion of 1792. The Republic is proclaimed!

The Revolution is accomplished in the name of right and public safety.

(*Annual Register*, 1870, p. 172, cited in Kertesz (ed.) *Documents in the Political History of the European Continent, 1815–1939*, 1968, p. 311)

(iii) From the Manifesto of the Twenty Arrondissements, 19 March 1871

(This was the manifesto of the twenty districts of Paris which proclaimed the Commune.)

our country again rises, revives, begins a new life, and retakes the tradition of the Communes of old and of the French Revolution. This tradition, which gave victory to France, and earned the respect and sympathy of past generations, will bring independence, wealth, peaceful glory and brotherly love among nations in the future. . . .

To secure the greatest economic development, the national and territorial independence, and security, association is indispensable; that is to say, a federation of all communes, constituting a united nation. . . .

It was the Communal idea . . . which triumphed on the 18th of March, 1871. It implies, as a political form, the Republic, which alone is compatible with liberty and popular sovereignty.

(from P. Vésinier, *History of the Commune of Paris*, London, 1872, pp. 61–65, cited in Kertesz (ed.) *Documents in the Political History of the European Continent, 1815–1939*, pp. 312–13)

B Conservative Republicanism

(i) From Gambetta's Grenoble speech scorning the conservative Republic, 1871

(After the Provisional Government had defeated the Commune in 1871, elections were held. Gambetta toured the country speaking against the kind of Republic he believed Thiers represented – a conservative stop-gap Republic which would allow a constitutional monarchy to return soon.)

Yes, it is likely that, when Parliament meets in Versailles, it will say that there is really no time to waste before establishing a Republic – but what does that mean?

. . . unless they [the deputies] were not personally convinced that dissolution [of the provisional government] was standing there, like a gravedigger, about to throw a handful of earth on the corpse of the Versailles Assembly (this created a sensation), unless they did not feel the pangs of death, you may be sure that there would be no talk of getting married to the Republic *in extremis*.

(cited in D. Halévy, *The End of the Notables*, ed. and trans. by A. Silvera, Middletown, CT, Wesleyan University Press, 1974, p. 133)

(ii) From Thiers's speech to the National Assembly, November 1872

The Republic exists. . . . Let us not waste time declaring it, but use the time to impress upon it desirable and necessary characteristics. A commission appointed by you . . . gave it the title of conservative Republic. Let us seize that title and strive to deserve it. ('*Hear, Hear!*')

Every government must be conservative and no society can live under a government which is not. (*General agreement*) The Republic will be conservative, or it will not exist. (*Exclamations*) . . .

France does not want to live in continual crisis. . . . It may be possible to found a republic which is that of a party, based on the power of the many, thanks to universal suffrage. Such a republic would not last a day.

Even the many need rest, security and work.

(*Journal Officiel de la République Française*, 14 November 1872, pp. 6981–82, cited in R. Gildea, *The Third Republic from 1870–1914*, London, Longman, 1995, p. 90)

C From the Duc de Chambord's proclamation, 5 July 1871

France knows that I belong to her. I cannot forget that the right of the King is part of the nation's inheritance, nor can I refuse those duties towards the nation, which it imposes upon me.

... We will found together, and when you will a Government in conformity with the real need of the nation, widely based on administrative decentralization and local liberties. . . .

On the question of the Flag mention has been made of conditions [replacing his Bourbon White Flag by the *tricolore*] to which I cannot submit.

(from F.H. Brabant, *The Beginning of the Third Republic in France*, London, 1940, pp. 339–40, cited in Kertesz (ed.) *Documents in the Political History of the European Continent, 1815–1939*, Oxford University Press, 1968, p. 318)

D General Boulanger's address to the electors of the Seine, January 1889

The parlementarians, who have done all they could to prevent me standing for election, are panic-stricken at the idea of seeing me elected. My sword upset them. They took it away from me. . . .

In reality, it is not me they are frightened of, but universal suffrage, whose repeated decisions testify to the disgust the country feels at the state of degeneracy to which their incapacity, low intrigues, and tedious debates have brought the Republic. . . .

But I want, and France wants, a Republic composed of something other than a collection of ambitions and greed. . . .

France today is eager for justice, rectitude, and unselfishness. . . .

La Patrie is our patrimony, for all of us. You will prevent it from becoming the prey of a few.

Long live France! Long live the Republic!

(cited in K. Randell, *France: The Third Republic 1870–1914*, London, Arnold, 1986, pp. 61–62)

E From a priest's public appeal to the Army during the Dreyfus Affair

(The speech was delivered at a college festival, presided over by a general.)

When I speak of the necessity for a nation to arm itself with power I mean the material power that does not reason, but imposes itself – the power of which the Army is the most forceful expression, the power of the cannon which is the ultimate argument of statesmen and of nations. . . . The enemy is intellectualism which professes to disdain power. Turn the point of the sword against it. Woe to the government that veils its weakness behind a supposed insufficiency of legal powers and lets the sword drop. . . .

(from N. Halasz, 'Captain Dreyfus, the story of a mass hysteria', New York, 1955, in L. Derfler, *The Dreyfus Affair: Tragedy of Errors?*, Boston, MA, D.C. Heath, 1963, pp. 4–5)

F The extreme Left, 1904–06

(i) From the Declaration of the Union of French Socialist Parties, January 1905

(The Workers Socialist Revolutionary Party, Socialist Party of France, French Socialist Party and six autonomous Federations agreed to this declaration drawn up by the unification commission in December 1904.)

1 The Socialist Party is a class party, whose aim is the socialization of the means of production and exchange, that is, the transformation of capitalist society into a collective or communist society, by the means of the political organization of the proletariat. In its aim, in its ideal, in the means it uses, the Socialist Party is not a party of reform – although it will endeavour to achieve the immediate reforms demanded by the working class – but a party of class war and revolution.

2 Those elected to Parliament shall form a single group opposed to all bourgeois political factions.

(from P. Louis, *Le Parti socialiste en France*, Paris, 1913, pp. 82–83, cited in Kertesz (ed.) *Documents in the Political History of the European Continent, 1815–1939*, pp. 325–26)

(ii) From the Syndicalist Charter of 1906

In the process of making its everyday demands syndicalism seeks to coordinate the efforts of the workers, to better their conditions. . . .

But this activity is only one side of the work of syndicalism. It is preparing that complete emancipation, which can be accomplished only when the capitalist is expropriated; it commends the general strike as a means of action, and it believes that the *syndicat*, which is now the nucleus of resistance, will in future become the nucleus for production and distribution.

(from the charter issued at the annual conference in 1906, cited in Randell, *France*, p. 89)

Questions

1 Explain the meaning of the following phrases and sentences in these extracts:
    (a) In extract A (i): 'radical democracy'
    (b) In extract A (ii): 'The Revolution is accomplished in the name of right and public safety'
    (c) In extract A (iii): 'the tradition of the Communes of old', and 'a federation of all communes'
    (d) In extract C: 'together, and when you will'.
2 Explain the significance of the Belleville Programme's demand for the separation of Church and state (extract A (i)). Why did it take until 1905 for this separation to occur?
3 To what extent does Thiers's speech in 1872 (extract B (ii)) answer Gambetta's warning at Grenoble in 1871 (extract B (i))?
4 Compare and contrast General Boulanger's political position (extract D) with that of the Duc de Chambord (extract C), Thiers in 1872 (extract B (ii)) and the first proclamation of the provisional Republican Government in 1870 (extract A (ii)). To which is the General closest?
5 How useful is extract E for understanding the controversy caused by the Dreyfus Affair?
6 Account for the differences, and any similarities, between the programmes of the extreme Left in 1871 (extract A (iii)) and in 1904–06 (extracts F (i and ii)).
7 According to T. Zeldin, the Third Republic 'was supposed to mark the advent of democracy, but it produced disconcertingly little fundamental change in the structure of the state, which remained monarchical, or even *ancien régime*, in many ways.'

But R. Gildea comments: 'France had made a deliberate choice against both Monarchy and Empire, which at various times since the Revolution had shown contempt for constitutional, parliamentary forms of government. The Third Republic was a parliamentary Republic and designed as such'.

Use the extracts and your own knowledge to explain which view you find to be the more accurate, and why.

(T. Zeldin, *France 1848–1945: Politics and Anger*, Oxford University Press, 1984, p. 206; R. Gildea, *The Third Republic from 1870 to 1914*, London, Longman, 1995, p. 82)

Further reading

Concise and authoritative coverage of this period is provided in J.P.T. Bury, *France 1814–1940* (London, Methuen, 1985) and A. Cobban, *A History of Modern France*, vol. 3, 1871–1962 (London, Penguin, 1970). An excellent and straightforward student text for this complicated period is K. Randell, *France: The Third Republic 1870–1914* (London, Arnold, 1986), which quotes extensively from some important documents. R. Gildea, *The Third Republic from 1870 to 1914* (London, Longman, 1995) is a more academic student text which discusses the key issues in detail and includes documentary excerpts. Thoughtful and perceptive overviews are to be found in G. Wright, *France in Modern Times* (New York, Norton, 1987) and in the famous works by T. Zeldin, *France 1848–1945*, especially the volume entitled *Politics and Anger* (Oxford University Press, 1984). The Commune has a large literature, but the pamphlet by E. Schulkind, *The Paris Commune of 1871* (London, Historical Association, 1971) is concise and useful, while Alistair Horne, *The Fall of Paris: the Siege and the Commune 1870–71* (London, Penguin, 1981) is exciting and full of detail and anecdote. The Dreyfus Affair has also attracted many historians and has an histiography of its own; a concise and useful collection of various sources is L. Derfler, *The Dreyfus Affair: Tragedy of Errors?* (Boston, MA, D.C. Heath, 1963). Important academic monographs include

J.P.T. Bury and R.P. Tombs, *Thiers 1797–1877: A Political Life* (London, Allen and Unwin, 1986), R.D. Anderson, *France 1870–1914: Politics and Society* (London, Routledge and Kegan Paul, 1977) and J.-M. Mayeur and M. Rebérioux, *The Third Republic from its Origins to the Great War, 1871–1914* (Cambridge University Press, 1987).

Documentary material may be found in G.A. Kertesz (ed.) *Documents in the Political History of the European Continent, 1815–1939* (Oxford University Press, 1968), D. Halévy, *The End of the Notables*, ed. and trans. by A. Silvera (Middletown, CT, Wesleyan University Press, 1974), and there are many excerpts in the works by R. Gildea and K. Randell mentioned above.

• CHAPTER EIGHTEEN •

Imperial Germany, 1871–1912

• CONTENTS •

Key dates

SECTION A

The problems of German history

German domestic history, 1871–1918

German foreign policy, 1871–90

German foreign policy, 1890–1912

SECTION B – SOURCES

The links between German domestic concerns and foreign policy

KEY DATES

		Home		Abroad
1871	18 Jan.	Proclamation of Empire	10 Feb.	Treaty of Frankfurt
1873		Passage of May Laws	6 June	Three Emperors' Agreement
1875		Gotha programme agreed by SPD	April	War scare v. France
			May	Outbreak of revolt in Bosnia
1877			April	Russia declares war on Turkey
1878	11 May,	Attempts to assassinate William I		
	2 June	General Election		
	21 Oct.	Anti-Socialist Law passed		
1879		Tariffs imposed on industrial and agricultural products	7 Oct.	Dual alliance signed with Austria
1881			18 June	Three Emperors' League renewed
1881–89		Bismarck's social legislation		
1885			Nov.–March	Berlin Colonial Conference
1887	Jan.	Crisis over army spending; general election		War scare v. France
1888	March	Death of William I	18 June	Reinsurance Treaty signed
	July	Death of Frederick III; accession of William II		
1890	18 March	Bismarck resigns; Caprivi made Chancellor; Anti-Socialist law lapses		Reinsurance Treaty lapses
1891		Erfurt Congress of SPD		
1892				Schlieffen Plan devised
1894	Oct.	Hohenlohe becomes Chancellor		
1896			Jan.	Kruger telegram
1897	June	Bülow becomes Foreign Secretary; Tirpitz becomes Navy Secretary	Nov.	Kiaochow seized
			Dec.	'Place in sun' speech
1898	March	First Navy Law passed; Navy League founded		
1900		Second Navy Law passed		
1902		Tariffs raised		
1904				Anglo-French *entente*
1905			March	First Moroccan crisis
			July	Bjorko agreement
1906				Algeciras conference
1907				Anglo-Russian *entente*
1908		*Daily Telegraph* affair		Bosnian annexation crisis
1909		Bülow's tax proposals defeated; Bethmann Hollweg becomes Chancellor		
1910		Defeat of electoral reform		
1911			July	Agadir crisis
1912	Feb.	SPD gains 110 seats in Reichstag election		Haldane mission to Germany
	8 Dec.	War Council in Berlin		
1913	Oct.	Zabern affair		

SECTION A

THE PROBLEMS OF GERMAN HISTORY

Two fundamental problems have dominated the study of German history between 1871 and 1914: first, why did Germany fail to develop into the kind of parliamentary democracy that evidently prevailed in France, Britain, Belgium, Holland and the Scandinavian countries by the end of the nineteenth century? This concern was voiced and explored in a very influential book by H-U. Wehler, published in its German edition in 1973 under the title *Das Deutsche Kaiserreich, 1871–1918* (The German Empire, 1871–1918). The second question, raised particularly by Fritz Fischer in his book *Griff nach der Weltmacht* (Bid for World Power), published in 1961, examined Germany's responsibility for the First World War and how far that war resulted from the aggressive policies pursued by German governments in the years leading up to 1914. A third question, arising out of the first two, is whether Germany's aggressive stance is to be explained by the nature of the imperial regime and the dilemmas she had to face. It has been argued, for instance, that political power continued to rest with entrenched elites in the army, the civil service and the Prussian land-owning class, and that it was their interests that took precedence in the making of policy. It has been suggested that Germany's bid for colonies, whether under Bismarck or under William II, was a form of 'social imperialism', designed to wean German workers away from the German Social Democratic Party (SPD). An aggressive foreign policy was pursued, it has been claimed, to unite the country. Von Bülow, foreign secretary at the time, wrote in 1897: 'only a successful foreign policy can help to reconcile, pacify, rally, unite' (J.G. Rohl, *Germany without Bismarck*, London, Batsford, p. 252).

Finally, it has been argued, notably by V.H. Berghahn, that an internal political crisis helped to push Germany into war in 1914 as a way of 'overcoming domestic gridlock' (V.H. Berghahn, *Germany and the Approach of War in 1914*, 2nd edn, London, Macmillan, 1993, p. 23).

This chapter will address each of these questions. The first part is devoted to Germany's dom-estic history between 1871 and 1914. The second part examines German foreign policy up to 1912. The years 1912–14 will be considered in Chapter 21 on the origins of the First World War. The connections between home and foreign policy will be considered in Section B.

GERMAN DOMESTIC HISTORY, 1871–1914

The working of the Imperial Constitution

It will be recalled that under the Imperial Constitution adopted on 14 April 1871 the King of Prussia was also Emperor of Germany; that he alone had the power to appoint ministers in Prussia and in the imperial administration; and that he was commander-in-chief of the Prussian army, both in peace and war, and of all the imperial armies in time of war. He also had the power to dissolve the Reichstag and determine, to some extent, the timing of elections. On the other hand, the Reichstag, elected by universal manhood suffrage in a secret ballot, had the right to approve, if not to initiate, legislation and the right to approve, or reject, imperial taxation (see Figure 18.1). The consent of the upper house, the Bundestag, was needed for any declaration of war.

In practice this meant that while the emperor had a free hand in making appointments, and to a large extent in the conduct of foreign policy, his ministers needed to secure majorities in the Reichstag for legislation they wished to enact and taxes they wished to raise. For all the contempt that Bismarck and William II displayed for the Reichstag at different times, they could not afford to ignore it. Bismarck in fact became a consummate political tactician, creating coalitions of supporters by trading concessions, and changing the basis of his support by altering his policies. He also exploited the emperor's right to dissolve the Reichstag as a political weapon, timing elections to suit his purposes.

But while the Reichstag could not be ignored, it had no power to bring down the government. Bismarck's claim to the chancellorship was never challenged. He held office for nineteen years. His successors were more vulnerable, but Bethmann

18.1 The new Reichstag, built 1884–94
Source: Archive Properties, Kent

Hollweg survived two votes of no confidence in 1913, and resigned in 1917 only because he had lost the confidence of the military. There was thus an uneasy balance of power between the Reichstag and the imperial government, but no effective mechanism by which the government could be changed. General elections did not determine who ruled. Nor was there any disposition to change the position on the part of the government. Bismarck privately dismissed the idea of a parliamentary regime with ministers answerable to the Reichstag as 'just impossible', while William II stated categorically: 'My ministers are chosen quite freely by me through the All Highest Confidence; and so long as they enjoy that confidence they do not have to bother about anything else at all' (Rohl, *Germany without Bismark*, p. 150).

So long as imperial goverments could rely on the support of the Conservative and National Liberal parties, it was usually possible for them to get their way. But with the rise of the Catholic Centre party and the SPD German chancellors faced an increasingly difficult task, leading to the state of gridlock to which Berghahn has called attention.

Domestic policy under Bismarck, 1871–90

The period 1871–1914 divides neatly into two. Such was Bismarck's authority that while he was Chancellor, despite recurrent bouts of bad health, and long vacations taken at his country retreat in Pomerania, his was the inspiration behind all policy initiatives both at home and abroad. So convinced was Bismarck of his indispensability that even after his enforced resignation in 1890, at the age of 75, he still tried to influence events from behind the scenes, building up a network of press contacts through which he could air his views. Thus it is impossible to separate Bismarck's personal ambitions from his objectives for Germany.

On a day-to-day level, his main concern was the acquisition and preservation of power, but that power was to be used, as he once put it in a speech to the Reichstag in 1881, for *salus populi*, the good of the people, as he saw it.

In his domestic policies Bismarck was essentially a pragmatist, but if he had a constant objective it was to preserve and consolidate the empire he had created. This meant subduing any forces that threatened the unity of that empire, and this explains his quarrels first with Roman Catholicism and then with socialism. In Bismarck's eyes both groups were *Reichsfeinde*, enemies of the state.

Bismarck and Catholicism

His hostility towards Catholics derives from various sources. He once described himself as a 'Bible believing Christian, but the enemy of priestly rule' (H. Rothfels, *Bismarck und der Staat*, Stuttgart, Kohlhammer, 1958, p. 245). German Catholics were particularly suspect, first, because their loyalties were divided between the German emperor and 'a foreign ecclesiastical prince whose seat is in Rome, a prince who because of the recent changes in the constitution of the Catholic Church [the decree of papal infallibility] is more powerful than he used to be' (speech to the Reichstag in 1873, cited in W.M. Simon, *Germany in the Age of Bismarck*, London, Allen and Unwin, 1964, p. 171). Second, many German Catholics were also Poles or French people, living in West Prussia and Alsace-Lorraine. Bismarck was also bitterly opposed to confessional parties such as the Catholic Centre party, which in his eyes acted as a focus of disunity. These views led Bismarck to attack the privileged status, as he saw it, enjoyed by Catholics. In this attack he was supported by free-thinking members of the National Liberal party. It was one of these, Rudolf Virchow who gave the name *Kulturkampf* (Struggle for Civilisation), to the attempts made to weaken what he took to be an obscurantist Church's authority and independence. In January 1872 Bismarck appointed Adalbert Falk, known for his anti-clerical views, to the Prussian ministry of culture. A School Inspection Law was passed placing all Catholic schools under lay control. The

Jesuit movement, suspected of encouraging Polish nationalism, was banned. In 1873 the so-called May Laws were passed in the Prussian Landtag, laying down the subjects that Catholic priests would have to study, including German history and literature, making civil marriage compulsory and transferring disciplinary authority over the Church to state agencies. In 1875 Pope Pius IX threatened with excommunication all who observed the laws, while Falk responded by suspending or imprisoning those who refused to accept them. By 1876 ten out of twelve Prussian bishops were either under arrest or in exile and 1,400 parishes, nearly one-third of the total, were without incumbents.

Far from weakening the Church's influence, Bismarck's measures had the opposite effect. The Centre party doubled its representation in the Landtag in 1873 and in the Reichstag in 1874 where it had ninety-one seats. A state of deadlock persisted for the next four years, but in 1878 Pius IX died and was replaced by Leo XIII, a man of greater moderation. Equally important, Bismarck now needed the votes of the Centre party to pass his Protectionist legislation. Falk resigned in 1879. Bit by bit the bulk of the May Laws were repealed, the last in 1885. Catholic bishops and priests were restored to the posts from which they had been removed. Jesuits continued to be banned, and civil marriage remained compulsory, but these were the only lasting trophies that survived from the *Kulturkampf*. It was left to Bismarck's successors to continue the task of winning Catholic support for the empire.

Bismarck and Socialism

As Bismarck's hostility to Catholics faded, so his fears of Socialism mounted. Initially, Bismarck had not been wholly hostile. He had some frank exchanges with Lassalle in 1863 and 1864, and the two men were agreed on the need for universal suffrage, if for very different reasons, and on the desirability of a united Germany. But Bismarck could have no sympathy for a party which opposed the cession of Alsace-Lorraine in 1871, supported the Paris Commune and adopted a Marxist programme in 1875. Following the assassination attempt on William I on 11 May, 1878 Bismarck's first Anti-Socialist Bill was defeated by 251 votes to 57. After a second unsuccessful assassination attempt on 2 June, Bismarck called for a general election which was held on 30 June. The conservative parties increased their representation by twenty-nine seats, the National Liberals changed their stance, and on 18 October 1878 the Anti-Socialist Bill was passed by 221 votes to 149. It was a sad reflection on the liberal credentials of the National Liberal party. The bill stayed in force until 1890. Bismarck's hostility to socialism persisted unabated. In 1890 he attempted to have the bill renewed and strengthened. In retirement he never ceased to voice his fears of socialists. In 1893 he went so far as to say to an American journalist-'they are the country's rats and should be exterminated' and in 1897 he wrote: 'The social question could at one time have been solved by using the police. Now it will be necessary to use the army' (L. Gall, *Bismarck, The White Revolutionary*, vol. 2, London, Unwin Hyman, 1986, p. 225).

Despite the Anti-Socialist Law which banned all political meetings, festivals and parades, all socialist publications and the collection of financial contributions, the SPD survived. It continued to contest elections and to hold party congresses in exile. It polled 550,000 votes in 1884 and over 1 million in 1890. Bismarck was no more successful at curbing the spread of Socialism than he had been in curtailing the growth of the Centre party.

Protection

Bismarck was also responsible for initiating the move away from free trade towards a policy of protection. There were both economic and political reasons for such a move. German agriculture was threatened by cheap imports of corn from Russia, and increasingly as transport facilities improved, from North America. German iron and steel producers suffered from the depression which followed a speculative boom in 1873. In 1873 the Association of German Iron and Steel Producers was founded to voice their complaints and in 1876 the Confederation of Fiscal and Economic Reformers emerged with a protectionist programme. In April 1875, 204 votes were cast in the Reichstag urging a policy of protection. Bismarck himself was no economist, but he took a robust view of economic theory. Anxious to win allies on the right, and to support the Junker landowning class to which he belonged, he became a convert to protection himself. In a speech to the Reichstag made on 2 May 1879 he justified his policy on these grounds: 'I make my judgments on the basis of practical experience of the time in which we are living. I see that those countries which have adopted protection are prospering, and that those countries which have free trade are deteriorating' (L.B. Snyder, *Documents of German History*, New Brunswick, NJ, Rutgers University Press, 1958, p. 241). Bismarck also hoped to create another source of revenue for the imperial government from the tariffs he introduced. In this he was thwarted, the Centre party successfully insisting that the bulk of the money raised should go to the individual states as the price of their support. On 12 July 1879 the Tariff Law was duly passed, placing duties on imported corn, cattle, timber and iron while raising the duties on tobacco, salt and luxury goods. It is hard to judge the economic effects of the new tariffs. Grain production was certainly encouraged, at the expense of higher food prices. Iron and steel producers probably owed more to their technical expertise than to the protection they enjoyed.

Politically, the tariff had more tangible results. It created an alliance between 'rye and steel', the Prussian landowners and the industrialists of the Ruhr which would prove a potent combination. On the international front, the introduction of tariffs did nothing to endear Germany to her neighbours and economic rivals.

Social insurance

The most creative aspect of Bismarck's statesmanship was his support for state sponsored insurance schemes designed to protect the worker against the hazards of ill health, industrial injury and old age. In consequence by 1890 Germany had the most advanced system of social welfare in Europe. Bismarck's motives have been questioned. He made no secret of the fact that one of his aims was to keep the worker from running to 'the socialist miracle doctor' and to 'soften the anxiety and hostility of the working classes' (speech on the Second Insurance Bill, 20 March 1884). He also claimed that his policies were 'practical Christianity'. His critics claimed that he was intent on bribing the working classes and undermining the independence of the Reichstag. The SPD treated his policies with initial scepticism, as designed simply to prop up a capitalist regime. Be that as it may, under Bismarck's tutelage and encouragement three significant measures were passed. In 1883 a Sickness Insurance Act provided support for workers who fell ill, employees providing two-thirds and employers one-third of the contributions out of which benefits would be paid. In 1884 an Accident Insurance Act made employers liable to pay compensation to industrial workers who were the victims of industrial accidents. In 1886 these two bills were extended to 7 million agricultural workers. The most ambitious Act of all was passed in 1889, providing pensions for all over the age of 70, paid for by contributions from workers, employers and the state. In his Memoirs Bismarck made no mention of the social legislation he had promoted, but in many ways it was his most enduring legacy.

The change of regime in 1890

In February 1888 William I died. From 1862 until his death he had left the conduct both of domestic and foreign policy very much in Bismarck's hands. His successor, Frederick III, was married to Queen Victoria's eldest daughter, also named Victoria, and her influence strengthened Frederick's liberal and anglophile inclinations. Bismarck greatly feared these tendencies and knew how unpopular he was with Princess Victoria. Tragically, both for the royal couple, and possibly for Germany, his fears proved groundless. Within six months of his accession Frederick III had died from cancer of the throat. He was succeeded by his eldest son, William II, a very different proposition.

William's difficult birth in 1859 left him with a withered left arm and much has been made of this disability; perhaps more important were the

effects on William's personality of the sometimes brutal techniques employed to overcome it. Handicapped by a poor sense of balance, learning to ride entailed many painful falls. In other respects he had a relatively enlightened upbringing which compares favourably with that given to Edward VII. His first tutor was a strict Calvinist named Hinzpeter, but thereafter William went to a Prussian grammar school and then to Bonn University. He then joined the Prussian army, becoming colonel of a crack infantry regiment, the Guard Hussars, where he acquired a lifelong taste for the camaraderie and pomp of peacetime soldiering. Unlike his father, who served in the Austro-Prussian war, William never heard a shot fired in anger until his rare visits to the front in the First World War.

Also, unlike his father, he was, initially at least, a great admirer of Bismarck and both William's personality and Bismarck's influence left him with the conviction that his task was to be the effective ruler of his country, a view he expressed very clearly in a letter he wrote to his cousin Tsar Nicholas II on 25 October 1895: 'The French axiom that "the King rules but does not govern" is basically false and revolutionary. I do not wish to rule in a merely nominal way and I will not do so, but instead intend to be the actual sovereign of my people' (L. Cecil, *Wilhelm II, Prince and Emperor*, Chapel Hill, NC, University of North Carolina Press, 1988, p. 226). Apart from the anachronism of such an ambition in the twentieth century, William lacked the qualities needed to sustain such a role. By temperament he was moody and mercurial, changing from despair to euphoria at a moment's notice. He lacked the application needed to master complex problems and to grapple with the daily routines of government. He was frequently absent from Berlin, regularly enjoying six-week cruises on his yacht, to the point that he was known as *Der Reise Kaiser*, the travelling emperor. One biographer has rightly said of William II: 'He was never the German autocrat, but rather the one constant, unavoidable, unpredictable factor with which all statesmen in Berlin, for better or worse, had to reckon' (Cecil, *Wilhelm II*, p. 261). So far as the working of the German political system is concerned, therefore, the consequence of William's accession was to add a new and destabilising influence to the existing power structure.

This became evident only when Bismarck's term of office came to an end. There were many reasons for friction between Bismarck and William II. The emperor, with all his faults, was genuinely anxious to address the grievances of the working class and in January 1890 insisted on the introduction of measures to reduce Sunday work, to limit hours worked by children under fourteen and to protect women workers who became pregnant. Bismarck, who was pressing for the passage of an even harsher Anti-Socialist Law, grumbled that the social question 'was not to be solved with rose water but called for blood and iron' (Gall, *Bismarck*, vol. 2, p. 209). He also tried to resurrect a Prussian Order of 1852, forbidding the emperor from communicating with his ministers except through his Chancellor. When Bismarck refused to give way on this issue, William insisted on his resignation, which took place on 18 March 1890. All subsequent chancellors now knew that their tenure depended on the emperor's whim.

In practice, Bismarck's successors, though lacking his political flair, were in many respects more enlightened. His immediate successor, General Leo Caprivi (1890–94) was a professional soldier of moderate views. He tried to cooperate with the Reichstag, did his best to meet the wishes of the Catholic Church over the control of schools (without success), modified the high tariffs introduced in 1879 and opposed the reintroduction of an Anti-Socialist Law. It was on this issue that he quarrelled with William II, and resigned in October 1894. He was replaced by Prince Chlodwig zu Hohenlohe-Schillingfurst (Hohenlohe), a Bavarian who had served as ambassador in Paris and as governor of Alsace-Lorraine. He was already 75 when appointed, and was little more than a figurehead. The key figure in his cabinet was the Foreign Secretary, Bernhard von Bülow, appointed to that office in 1897. He was a career diplomat, groomed for high office, who fully expected to be made Chancellor. He wrote to a close friend of the emperor, Philipp von Eulenburg, as early as 23 July 1896: 'I would regard myself as the executive tool of His Majesty, so to speak his political Chief of Staff. With me, personal rule – in the good sense – would really begin' (K.D. Lerman, *The Chancellor as Courtier*, Cambridge University Press, 1990, p. 23). When von Bülow became chancellor in 1900 he certainly tried to be loyal to his master, but was more concerned with his own political survival than the emperor's reputation, as the *Daily Telegraph* affair in 1908 made clear. An indiscreet interview given by William II to the *Daily Telegraph* was submitted to von Bülow for clearance, and von Bülow failed to read it properly, passing it on to a subordinate official. When published on 28 October it caused a storm, both abroad and in the Reichstag. von Bülow joined in the attacks on William's personal government and William was forced to give an undertaking to respect the constitution. His confidence in von Bülow was badly shaken, and when von Bülow's tax proposals were defeated the following year, William gladly accepted his resignation.

The last of Germany's pre-war Chancellors, Theodore Bethmann Hollweg, was in many respects the most responsible. Trained as a civil servant, he was Minister of the Interior both in Prussia and in Germany before succeeding von Bülow in 1909. Aware of the difficulties facing him, he wrote to a contemporary: 'You will find it natural that I accept this office with a heavy heart. Only a genius or a man driven by ambition and lust for power can covet this post. And I am neither. An ordinary man can only assume it when compelled by his sense of duty' (Cecil, *Wilhelm II*, p. 337). By the time he took office Germany's course in both home and foreign affairs had already been set and he was to find his freedom to manoeuvre very limited.

The tasks facing Germany's Chancellors after 1890 was thus no easy one. The political scene was becoming increasingly polarised as the SPD's vote increased in the Reichstag. On the right there were a number of powerful pressure groups, the Alldeutscher Verband (Pan-German League) founded in 1891; the Flottenverein (Navy League) founded in 1897 and the Wehrverein (Defence League) founded in 1911. It was difficult, sometimes impossible, to reconcile the wishes of an unpredictable and volatile emperor with those of a Reichstag in which the Chancellor rarely had a constant majority. Nonetheless, successful initiatives were taken and on certain issues agreement was reached. It is to these we now turn.

Trade and finance

Trade and finance were closely linked. Receipts from tariffs and customs provided the bulk of imperial revenue, over one-third in 1913. Tariffs were also demanded from various pressure groups to protect agricultural and industrial producers. But they could be a two-edged weapon, provoking retaliation from countries where Germany had export markets. It was this threat that induced Caprivi to sign a series of commercial treaties with Germany's neighbours between 1890 and 1894, reducing German tariffs on imported cattle, timber, rye and wheat in return for reciprocal concessions on German manufactures. The Reichstag approved the treaties. But by 1902 pressure from the agricultural interests mounted and duties on agricultural imports were raised again, even though von Bülow was not convinced of the necessity for these increases. Effectively they priced Russian grain out of the German market, and raised food prices in Germany. In the 1903 elections the SPD's vote went up from 2 million to 3 million.

From 1900 onwards the imperial government was faced with mounting deficits as defence spending grew. By 1908 the national debt had doubled since 1900. Every proposal to increase taxes aroused opposition from one quarter or another. Taxes on property were resisted by the Conservatives, indirect taxes by the SPD. In June 1909 Bülow's proposal to raise indirect taxes, coupled with an increase in the inheritance tax, ran into the combined opposition of the Conservative and Centre parties and he took the opportunity to resign. Bethmann Hollweg was able to win over the opposition by some tactical concessions and the taxes in their amended form finally went through in July. Bethmann Hollweg found himself in the same plight as von Bülow in 1913, when huge increases in defence spending were called for. This time it was the SPD's opposition he had to win over. By coupling the increase with the introduction of a capital gains tax, he was able to secure the SPD's support. Significantly, perhaps, while no tax increases were ever welcomed, when linked to expenditure on defence they were usually accepted in the long run.

Armaments

Perhaps William II's most significant influence on the German empire was his decision to create a large German navy. There were several reasons for this. William was a passionate admirer of the British Royal Navy, whose uniform he was proud to wear. He was a keen yachtsman and dabbler in naval architecture, never happier than when drawing diagrams of battleships. He was greatly struck by Captain A.T. Mahan's book, *The Influence of Seapower on History*, which came out in 1890, and which William read in 1894. There were other pressures for a large navy. The Colonial League wanted a navy to protect Germany's newly gained colonies. Merchants engaged in overseas trade supported the idea of a navy to protect Germany's trade routes. Iron and steel producers had an obvious interest in a large navy. There were even those who saw in a large navy a weapon to 'revive the patriotism of the classes and to fill them again with loyalty to, and love for, the Emperor and the Reich' (Berghahn, *Germany and the Approach of War*, p. 44). In 1897 Alfred von Tirpitz was made Secretary of the Navy, and William had an enthusiast and skilled propagandist in a key position. Tirpitz soon converted William to his belief that what Germany needed was not a large cruiser fleet, scattered across the globe, but a battle fleet capable of challenging Germany's most powerful rival on the high seas, Great Britain. This was made quite explicit in the memorandum Tirpitz wrote to the emperor in 1897:

For Germany the most dangerous enemy at the present time is England. It is also the enemy against which we most urgently require a certain measure of naval force as a political power factor ... our fleet must be so constructed that it can unfold its greatest military potential between Heligoland and the Thames. . . . The military situation demands battleships in as great a number as possible.

(P.M. Kennedy, *The Rise of Anglo-German Antagonism, 1860–1914*, London, Allen and Unwin, 1980, p. 224)

Tirpitz was as good as his word. In 1897 he introduced his first Navy Law designed to produce nineteen battleships by 1905. He conducted an active press campaign, and founded the Navy League to support his ideas. By 1906 it had over 1 million members. The Navy Law provided for an automatic building programme, based on three ships a year which would be replaced after twenty-five years' service. Thus, once the bill had passed, the Reichstag would no longer have control over naval expenditure. It was passed in 1898 by 212 votes to 139. A second Navy Law in 1900 greatly expanded the building programme and provided for a fleet of thirty-eight battleships, eight battle cruisers and twenty-four cruisers, seventy ships in all, to be completed by 1917. It was passed by an even larger majority.

Where the army was concerned, there was no such dramatic change. Under the 'iron budget' of 1874, army expenditure was voted every seven years, reduced to five years in 1893. There were no significant increases in the size of the army until 1912, partly because it was already too large to provide adequate training to its regular recruits, partly because the military authorities feared the infiltration of its ranks by SPD members, and the dilution of the aristocratic officer corps by members of the middle classes. As the international situation grew more threatening, especially after the signing of the Franco-Russian alliance in 1894 (see p. 342), there were insistent calls for an increase in the size of the army, especially from the Wehrverein. Bethmann Hollweg responded to these pressures. In 1912 the military budget provided for an additional 29,000 troops. In 1913 the army was planned to increase by 117,000 men, 14,900 non-commissioned officers (NCOs) and 4,000 officers. Total spending on the army doubled between 1910 and 1914.

Other issues

If on defence spending the government usually managed to get its way, on other issues agreement was harder to reach and the gap between a reform-minded Reichstag and a conservative administration grew wider.

Probably the least contentious legislation was that concerned with the extension of Bismarck's system of social insurance and the improvement of working conditions. Under the stimulus of an enlightened Minister of the Interior, Arthur von Posadowsky-Wehner, who held the office from 1897 to 1907, several reforms were introduced. Industrial courts for all towns with more than 20,000 inhabitants were made compulsory in 1901. A widows' and orphans' insurance scheme was adopted in 1902. The prohibition of child labour was extended in 1903. In 1911 social insurance was extended to all salaried employees. By 1913 Germany could boast of having the most comprehensive system of social insurance in the world, providing protection against accidents at work, sickness benefit, and pensions for invalids, widows, orphans and elderly people.

There were some significant political reforms, too. A Polling Booth Law in 1903 guaranteed the secrecy of the ballot. Payments for members of the Reichstag were introduced in 1906, five years before British MPs were paid. In 1911 Alsace-Lorraine gained its own assembly, elected by universal suffrage. In one area, however, the government could not get its way. The three class electoral system in Prussia, with open voting and an indirect system of election, kept right-wing parties in the ascendant and they resisted all attempts to amend the system. Even Bethmann Hollweg's limited proposals to do away with indirect elections and to give greater weight to educational qualifications failed to get through in 1910, and Prussia continued to have an unrepresentative assembly until 1918.

It was in her treatment of racial minorities that imperial Germany showed her least attractive face, the other side of the aggressive nationalism which had helped to create the empire. The common thrust behind all policy was the belief that only true Germans qualified for citizenship. As a very minimum this required all citizens to speak German. In the case of the 2.4 million Poles, German was made compulsory in government, the courts and in schools. A Settlement Law of 1886 enabled a Settlement Commission to buy up Polish land on which German farmers could be settled. In 1908 an Expropriation Law made the sale of Polish estates compulsory, and in 1912 the Prussian decision to implement the law led to an unparalleled vote of no confidence in Bethmann Hollweg's government. The vote had no effect.

Danes living in Schleswig were subjected to

similar pressures. Danes who refused not to be German citizens were deported and the use of Danish in schools was suppressed.

Where Alsace-Lorraine was concerned, two contrasting approaches were evident. The civilian administration tried to encourage assimilation, by giving Alsace-Lorraine the same status as other states in the empire. The military continued to regard Alsace-Lorraine as a conquered province. This became clear in the notorious Zabern incident in the autumn of 1913. It arose out of the insensitive treatment of an Alsatian recruit by a Prussian officer. This led to a group of officers being jeered at on 28 November in the town of Zabern. About thirty of the demonstrators were arrested by the military authorities. Bethmann Hollweg defended the army's actions in a heated debate in the Reichstag on 4 December, and suffered the humiliation of another vote of no confidence.

German Jews were in an anomalous position. Many of them had been in Germany for centuries and German was their native language. They had risen to positions of influence in finance, commerce, the arts and the professions. Gerson von Bleichröder was not only Bismarck's banker, but also his adviser on all financial matters. Most Jews were supporters of the empire and many fought bravely in its defence during the First World War. For all that they still aroused suspicion and prejudice. The influx of 79,000 poverty stricken Jews, victims of Russian persecution, in the 1880s aroused resentment. Anti-Semitism gained a spurious legitimacy through the writings of certain academics and other influential figures. In 1879 the Court Chaplain, Adolf Stoecker, delivered a lecture entitled 'Our demands on modern Jewry' which found an echo in an article written by Henry von Treitschke, the eminent historian, for the *Preussische Jahrbucher* also in 1879. This contained the notorious statement: 'The Jews are our national misfortune'.

Prejudice fed into political life. In 1892 the Conservative party included an anti-Semitic plank in its programme. A rash of anti-Semitic parties emerged in the 1890s which by 1907 had won sixteen seats in the Reichstag. Most worrying of all, in a pamphlet written in 1912 the president of the Pan-German League, Heinrich von Class, called for immediate restriction on any further Jewish immigration and that all Jewish residents be placed under aliens' law. Bethmann Hollweg resisted such suggestions as undeserving of serious consideration, but that they should have been made at all by an influential pressure group is evidence that there was something rotten in the state of imperial Germany.

GERMAN FOREIGN POLICY, 1871–90

A contrast is often drawn between the conciliatory foreign policy supposedly pursued by Bismarck from 1871 to 1890 with the more aggressive and expansionist policy pursued by his successors. Erich Brandenburg, a German historian, stated in 1925 that 'the supreme object of German policy which was constructed by Bismarck until 1890, in spite of various contretemps, was the maintenance of European peace' (E. Brandenburg, *Von Bismarck zum Welktkrieg*, Berlin, 1925, translated as *From Bismarck to the First World War, German Foreign Policy 1870–1914*, London, Oxford University Press, 1927, p. 2). This verdict was echoed by Theodore Hamerow, an American historian writing in 1973, who argued that Bismarck 'laboured unceasingly to maintain harmony among the Great Powers' (T. Hamerow, *The Age of Bismarck*, New York, Harper and Row, 1973, p. 264). Certainly Bismarck appears to have believed that Germany in 1871 was a sated power and had expanded far enough for his generation at least. As with his home policy, his main purpose was to preserve and consolidate the empire. In a note dictated to his son, Herbert, on 15 June 1877, known as the Kissingen Dictate, Bismarck wrote of his fear of the coalitions that might be formed against Germany (particularly a French–Russian–Austrian one), and summarised the picture he had in mind: 'not one of gaining territory, but of a political situation as a whole, in which all the powers except France had need of us, and could thus be deterred as far as possible from coalitions against us by their relations with each other' (W.N. Medlicott and D.K. Coveney, *Bismarck and Europe*, London, Arnold, 1971, pp. 102–03).

As this passage suggests, the one country on whose hostility Bismarck could rely, so long as

Germany retained Alsace-Lorraine, was France. Thus it was Bismarck's main purpose to stay on good terms with all his other neighbours, Russia, Italy and Austria. In an often quoted remark, Bismarck in 1888 said to a well-known German explorer, Eugen Wolf, who had just been demonstrating Germany's gains in Africa, 'Your map of Africa is all very fine, but my map of Africa lies in Europe. Here is Russia and here – pointing to the left – is France, and we are in the middle; that is my map of Africa' (Gall, *Bismarck*, vol. 2, p. 143).

The elaborate alliance system that Bismarck created was intended to keep Russia and France apart and, also, as he put it to the Russian ambassador Saburov in 1880, 'to try to be one of three as long as the world is governed by an unstable equilibrium of five powers' (Craig, *Germany, 1866–1945*, p. 115). The three powers in question were Germany, Russia and Austria. Bismarck's first initiative in this direction was the Three Emperors' Agreement, signed by Francis Joseph, Emperor of Austria, Alexander II, Emperor of Russia, and William I, Emperor of Germany, on 22 October 1873 (see Figure 18.2). It bound the three signatories to consult together over any differences that might arise between them, and in the event of an attack on any one of them by another power to agree on the line of conduct they would follow.

The agreement was strained almost to breaking point by the Near East Crisis of 1875–78. This erupted when the Bosnians revolted against their Turkish rulers. A.J.P. Taylor put the dilemma facing Russia and Austria succinctly: 'Once the Slavs were astir, no Russian government dare let them fail. Austria Hungary dare not let them succeed' (A.J.P. Taylor, *The Struggle for Mastery in Europe, 1848–1918*, Oxford University Press, 1954, p. 229). In June 1876 the revolt spread to Bulgaria and the Turks declared war on Serbia and Montenegro. On 24 April 1877 Russia could be held back no longer, and declared war on Turkey, reaching the outskirts of Constantinople by December 1877. A severe peace treaty, the treaty of San Stefano, creating a large and independent Bulgaria, was imposed on the Turks in March 1878. European dissatisfaction with Russia's success led to the convening of an international Congress which met at Berlin on 13 June 1878.

Bismarck had declared early in the crisis, that he would not advise active participation by Germany 'as long as I see no interest for Germany in it which – forgive the blunt expression – would be worth the bones of a single Pomeranian musketeer' (speech to the Reichstag, 5 December 1876). In February 1878 he offered his services as 'an honest broker, who really intends to do business', and it was under his chairmanship that the Congress of Berlin met for its twenty sessions. The treaty of Berlin greatly reduced the area of the new Bulgaria, separating it from the province of Eastern Rumelia, and gave to Austria the right to occupy and administer Bosnia and Herzegovina. The Russians felt that they had been badly let down by Germany and Austria, and the Three Emperors' Agreement was allowed to lapse. It was this, as much as anything, which persuaded Bismarck to sign a Dual Alliance with Austria on 7 October 1879, providing that each country would come to the aid of the other in the event of an attack by Russia, and promising 'at least a benevolent neutral attitude' should either country be attacked by another power (e.g. France). It was this treaty which tied 'the trim Prussian frigate to the worm-eaten Austrian galleon' (Taylor, *Struggle for Mastery in Europe*, p. 262) and became the keystone of German diplomacy after Bismarck's departure.

Despite the obviously anti-Russian character of the Dual Alliance, Bismarck was still anxious to restore the Three Emperors' Agreement, and in 1881 he succeeded. Russia agreed to recognise Austria's claim to Bosnia and Herzegovina. It was also agreed that Bulgaria might be reunited with Eastern Rumelia.

At the same time Bismarck drew Italy into his security system. Under the terms of the Triple Alliance, signed on 20 May 1882, Austria and Germany were obliged to come to Italy's assistance should she be attacked by France, while the same obligation rested on Italy and Austria should Germany be attacked by France. This, Bismarck hoped, would allow Austria to devote all her military forces to opposing Russia in the event of war, and would deprive France of a potential ally. Bismarck actively supported the two Mediterranean agreements signed by Austria, Italy and Britain in 1887, which were designed to maintain the status quo in that area.

THE THREE EMPERORS;

OR, THE VENTRILOQUIST OF VARZIN!

18.2 The Three Emperors' League: Bismarck is seen manipulating Tsar Alexander III, Emperor Francis Joseph of Austria and the German Emperor William I

Source: reproduced by permission of *Punch* Ltd.

His final diplomatic initiative is the one for which he has been most criticised, the Reinsurance Treaty signed with Russia on 18 June 1887. This replaced the Three Emperors' Agreement, which expired in 1887, and promised that both countries would observe benevolent neutrality should either power be attacked by a third great power; 'this provision would not apply to a war against Austria or France resulting from an attack on one of these two powers by one of the High Contracting Parties', i.e. if Germany attacked France, or Russia attacked Austria. By an Additional and Very Secret Protocol, Germany also promised Russia her benevolent neutrality and her moral and diplomatic support for any measures the Emperor of

Russia found it necessary to take in order to defend the entrance to the Black Sea, 'the key of His Empire'.

The treaty remained secret when it was allowed to lapse in 1890 (see p. 301). It still caused an enormous stir when Bismarck, in a fit of pique, released the text to the press in October 1896. It may not have breached the letter of the Dual Alliance with Austria, but it was hardly in the same spirit.

Bismarck showed much less concern with the maintenance of good relations with France and Britain. Indeed there is a case for saying that he subordinated his relations to both countries to domestic political considerations (see Section B).

The first war scare with France in 1875 arose out of changes in the organisation of the French army. These led to a possibly inspired article in the *Berlin Post* on 8 April 1875, headed 'Is War in Sight'? Bismarck led a diplomatic campaign to have France weakened militarily, which failed miserably. In 1887 there was a second war scare, provoked this time by the militant language used by the new French War Minister, General Boulanger. More relevant in explaining Bismarck's conduct was the defeat in the Reichstag of his military budget in November 1886. In the ensuing election campaign Bismarck raised fears of French aggression, and his supporters won a handsome victory, enabling his Army Bill to go through easily.

Domestic considerations appear best to explain Bismarck's brief flirtation with colonies in 1884–85. As late as 1880 he had refused all talk of colonies, and in 1889 he apparently offered to sell the whole of Germany's colonial empire to the Italian Prime Minister. Yet in the space of two years Germany acquired South West Africa, Togoland, the Cameroons, German East Africa and various Pacific dependencies. At the time Bismarck anticipated the accession of Frederick and the consequent extension of anglophile influence at court. By embarking on a quest for colonies Germany could pick a quarrel with Britain which would reduce the threat. The political climate in Berlin in 1884 thus became violently anti-British. Bismarck was heard to say to one of his colleagues: 'All this colonial business is a sham, but we need it for elections' (Kennedy, *Rise of Anglo-German Antagonism*, p. 172) (see Section B). Germany's colonial empire never fitted in with Bismarck's ambitions for Germany, but it had an important legacy. It provided a tangible basis for the policy of *Weltpolitik*, pursued by Bismarck's successors, to which we now must turn.

GERMAN FOREIGN POLICY, 1890–1912

With Bismarck's departure in 1890, responsibility for German foreign policy now devolved, in theory, upon his successor as Chancellor, Leo von Caprivi. In practice none of Bismarck's successors exercised the same single-minded control as he had done. None of them combined the office of Chancellor with that of Foreign Minister, which had been Bismarck's practice. Caprivi had little experience of foreign affairs, and lacked even a Foreign Secretary in post when he became Chancellor in 1890. The man whom he appointed, Marschall von Bieberstein, was uncertain of his own judgement, and tended to defer to his political adviser in the Foreign Office, Friedrich von Holstein, a man of strong opinions, who exercised a powerful and sometimes malign influence until his resignation in 1906. Von Bülow, who became Foreign Secretary in 1897 and Chancellor in 1900, had plenty of diplomatic experience, and gave the impression of being in control. But his most recent biographer, K.D. Lermann, accuses him of idleness, and of responsibility for the 'virtually anarchic conditions which prevailed by 1908' in the foreign office. (K.D. Lerman, 'Chancellor Bernhard von Bülow and the national idea', in J. Breuilly (ed.) *The State of Germany*, London, Longman, 1992, p. 115). Important aspects of policy making were outside the Chancellor's control: 'The whole areas of naval armaments and military and naval planning were effectively "off limits" for the Chancellor' (ibid.) Thus the influence of men like Schlieffen and Moltke, successive Chiefs of the Prussian Imperial General Staff, between 1891 and 1914, and Tirpitz, Secretary of the Navy from 1897 to 1916, carried greater weight than any of Germany's Chancellors after Bismarck.

There was, too, always the possibility of that loose cannon, William II, firing off a shot in the shape of an ill-considered speech or gesture. He could usually be persuaded to fall in with his ministers' views, but when there were so many potential sources of advice, it was far from certain whose he would take. In these circumstances, it is not surprising that German foreign policy after Bismarck pursued an uncertain course which at times baffled even Germany's own ambassadors.

Some historians have seen, nonetheless, a persistent thread running through German foreign policy after 1890, usually summed up in the phrase *Weltpolitik*. The term is usually attributed to von Bülow with whom it was first associated.

Literally translated as world policy, by implication it came to mean a bid for Germany to become not just a European but a world power. When asked what he meant by the term in a debate in the Reichstag in 1900, von Bülow replied:

by this word I chiefly understood the tasks confronting us in view of the development of our industry, trade and shipping. . . . We have no intention at all of carrying out an aggressive policy of expansion. We intend only to protect the important interests, which, through the natural course of events, we have acquired in all parts of the world.

(Prince von Bülow, *Memoirs*, vol. 1, London, Putnam, 1931, p. 412)

Others gave a wider interpretation to the term and sought the expansion of German power in a variety of ways: through the acquisition of colonies in the Far East and in central Africa; through the construction of a German battle fleet; through informal economic imperialism into areas such as the Balkans and South America; through the construction of a vast trading bloc controlled by Germany in Mitteleuropa; and when war broke out in 1914, through the expansion of Germany both into western and eastern Europe for the sake of German security and greater living space. It is true that these ambitions were shared by only a small minority represented in organisations such as the Pan-German League, the Navy League and the Colonial League. It is also true that a majority could usually be found in the Reichstag to support any policy seen to further German national interests.

In practice, German colonial gains between 1890 and 1914 were surprisingly meagre, despite von Bülow's demand, made in his first speech to the Reichstag as foreign minister in 1897, for 'a place in the sun' (see Section B). In 1897 the murder of two German missionaries in China provided the occasion for Germany to send a naval expedition to Kiaochow, which then became a treaty port under German occupation. In 1899 two islands in Samoa, where there was already a German presence, were secured after negotiations with Britain and the USA. In 1911 Germany acquired a substantial slice of the French Congo, following the second Moroccan crisis (see p. 302). Between 1912 and 1914 hopes were seriously entertained of significant gains in central Africa to link Germany's colonies in West and East Africa, should Portugal and Belgium prove incapable of holding their colonies in Angola and the Congo. In fact Germany gained very little from her colonial empire. Until gold and diamonds were discovered in South West Africa, none of her possessions paid for the costs of their upkeep, and less than 1 per cent of Germany's overseas trade was with her colonies.

The expansion of the German navy, at Tirpitz's insistence, led to a naval race with Britain, who changed the conditions by launching in 1906 the first all big gun, heavily armoured battleship, *Dreadnought*. This, in theory, made all existing battleships obsolete and allowed Germany to start on level terms with Britain. Every attempt to moderate the pace of naval building came to nothing, though this owed as much to British as it did to German intransigence. In fact, by 1914 Tirpitz had lost the race, for by then Britain, thanks to naval agreements with Japan and France, was able to concentrate her heavy ships in home waters and continued to outbuild the German navy.

Where German informal imperialism was concerned, the conquest of overseas markets probably owed more to the superiority of German technology and increases in production than it did to any pressure by German governments. By 1914 Germany was producing two-thirds of Europe's steel and half its coal. Germany had the biggest cotton industry on the continent and had taken the lead in the chemical and electricity industries. Her share of overseas trade grew steadily and she had the second largest merchant navy in the world after Britain. The most deliberate attempt to increase German influence in the Balkan peninsula and the Near East, the building of the Berlin to Baghdad railway, broached in 1898, ran into such problems that only a fraction of it had been built by 1914. Thus the tangible consequences of *Weltpolitik* were much less than the rhetoric surrounding it. It was, ironically, the suspicions that it aroused that did most damage to Germany.

The worsening of Germany's diplomatic position

Between 1890 and 1912 Germany became increasingly isolated, and found herself facing a potentially hostile combination, known as the Triple Entente, made up of France, Russia and Britain. How did this come about? Relations with Russia, so important to Bismarck, were allowed to deteriorate. The Reinsurance Treaty was due to be renewed in March 1890. Unfortunately the Russian ambassador, commissioned to renew it, arrived in Berlin just after Bismarck's resignation. Caprivi was advised by Holstein that its terms were incompatible with the Dual Alliance with Austria, and William II accepted their views. The Reinsurance Treaty duly lapsed. This paved the way for the Franco-Russian alliance (see p. 342) signed in 1894, and Germany now found herself faced with the prospect Bismarck had always sought to avoid, a war on two fronts. In 1902 the restoration of German tariffs on imported grain hit Russia's grain exports. Meanwhile, French loans helped to underwrite Russian defence spending, and the bonds between the two allies grew steadily stronger.

With the defeats Russia suffered during the Russo-Japanese war of 1904–05, William II, who was always well disposed to Nicholas II, saw an opportunity to exploit Russia's vulnerability and in July 1905 he met the Tsar at Bjorko, near Stockholm, where the two men signed a defensive alliance. Von Bülow was not present and threatened to resign, more out of personal pique than objections to the terms. Nicholas was also advised that the terms of treaty were incompatible with the Franco-Russian alliance and on 23 November the treaty was finally buried. It was a lost opportunity.

Relations with Russia took an irretrievable turn for the worse as a result of the Bosnian annexation crisis of 1908. The Austrian Foreign Minister at the time, Count Aehrenthal, decided to change the status of Bosnia-Herzegovina which since 1878 had been an Austrian protectorate. He now sought to annex the territory outright. He held secret conversations with the Russian Foreign Minister, Izvolski, at a country house, Buchlau, near Carlsbad. No record was kept of the six hours of talks, but Izvolski was convinced that in return for recognising the annexation he had secured Aehrenthal's promise to persuade the other European powers to permit the passage of Russian warships through the Dardanelles. When on 5 October Aehrenthal announced the annexation of Bosnia, no progress had been made on the Dardanelles issue, and Isvolski felt betrayed. Russia protested without avail, and war looked a possibility. On 30 October von Bülow promised Germany's unconditional support to Austria: 'I shall regard whatever decision you come to as the appropriate one'. On 2 June 1909 Moltke wrote to his Austrian counterpart, General Conrad: 'The moment Russia mobilises Germany will also mobilise' (Taylor, *Struggle for Mastery in Europe*, p. 453).

Russia, unable to contemplate war so soon after the 1905 rising and the Russo-Japanese war, was compelled to accept the annexation and Germany's unqualified support for her ally Austria set a dangerous precedent that would be repeated in 1914.

Where Anglo-German relations were concerned German policy was also unnecessarily tactless and inconsistent. Trouble began in January 1896 when William II made one of his unfortunate forays ino the diplomatic arena. He sent an open telegram to President Kruger of the Transvaal, congratulating him on his successful handling of the Jameson raid. This had been an ill-advised attempt by one of Cecil Rhodes's lieutenants to provoke a rebellion against Kruger, which would then secure the Transvaal for the British empire.

The two naval laws of 1898 and 1900 were explicitly directed against 'the greatest seapower', a fact which did not escape the British foreign office. Sir Edward Grey, Foreign Secretary from 1905 to 1916, commented before he took office that 'Germany is our worst enemy and our greatest danger' (Z. Steiner, *Britain and the Origins of the First World War*, London, Macmillan, 1977, p. 40). In 1902 Britain emerged from her diplomatic isolation and signed the Anglo-Japanese alliance to safeguard her interests in the Far East. In 1904 she signed a series of agreements with France, settling matters of dispute between the two countries, which became known as the Anglo-French *entente*, and in 1905 embarked on military and naval conversations to explore possible cooperation in any future war with Germany.

In 1907 Britain reached agreement with Russia over their respective interests in Tibet, Afghanistan and Persia. Though friction still arose, especially over Persia, the final link joining France, Russia and Britain was now in place. What remained in doubt was the strength of the link. German initiatives to weaken the link were generally unsuccessful, and had the opposite effect. They both concerned Morocco, a country where France laid claim to a preponderant influence. In 1905 William II was persuaded by Holstein, rather against his will, to make a state visit to Tangier, in order to emphasise Germany's interest in the country and the maintenance of her independence. On 31 March William duly made his visit and demanded free trade and equality of rights with other nations for Germany. When the international conference to settle the issue convened at Algeciras in January 1906 Germany found herself isolated. Britain supported France's claim to be the dominant power, Germany was humiliated and the *entente* was strengthened.

A similar crisis blew up in 1911, this time provoked by the German Foreign Minister at the time, Kiderlen-Wächter. He hoped to extract territory in West Africa to compensate Germany for the gains made by France in controlling Morocco. On this occasion he dispatched the German gunboat *Panther* to Agadir, hoping that 'in possession of such a pawn we can watch quietly and await further developments in Morocco, whether for example France will offer us suitable compensation from its colonial possessions' (F. Fischer, *War of Illusions, German Policy from 1911–1914*, London, Chatto and Windus, 1975, p. 72). Again Germany had badly misjudged British reaction. In a speech made by Lloyd George on 21 July, he warned that if Britain was ignored where her vital interests were concerned, 'then I say emphatically that peace at that price would be intolerable for a great country like ours to endure'. In November Germany secured her reward, 275,000 square miles of jungle in the French Congo. When debated in the Reichstag this result was described as 'wicked' in its failure to take account of Germany's interests by Ernest

Basserman, a leading figure in the National Liberal party. Though there was much sabre rattling, both in the Bosnia crisis of 1908 and the Agadir crisis of 1911, neither led to war. But by 1912, when the next crisis erupted in the Balkans, as a consequence of all that had happened since 1890, Germany would be facing three potentially hostile countries. To set against this combination she could rely only on Austria. Within Germany two dangerous pressures were at work. Groups like the Pan-German League were encouraging unrealistic ambitions while the heads of the armed services were voicing their fears of German vulnerability. For both, a preventive war might come to be seen as the only solution.

SECTION B – SOURCES

THE LINKS BETWEEN GERMAN DOMESTIC CONCERNS AND FOREIGN POLICY

The extent to which German foreign policy was determined by domestic considerations has long been a matter for debate. Two particular links have been identified. It has been argued by historians such as H-U. Wehler that the old elites (the army, the landowning class, the civil service) clung to power by what was called *Sammlungspolitik*, a rallying together of all upper and middle class interests against the threats of Democracy and Socialism. One of the ways this could be done was by pursuing an aggressive foreign policy. Another variant of this policy was social imperialism; through overseas expansion the working classes could be weaned from Socialism by making Germany more prosperous and by encouraging a greater sense of patriotism. Other historians, notably Geoffrey Eley and David Blackbourn, have argued that the power of the old elites was already waning, and that the notion that German governments deliberately pursued an aggressive foreign policy as a way of combating social democracy has been exaggerated. Richard Evans has argued that it was middle class rather than aristocratic values that characterised German society before the First World War and that radical nationalism came from the middle and lower classes rather than from the Kaiser and his ministers (Richard J. Evans, 'Kaiser Wilhelm II and German history', *History Review*, 1991). The following extracts provide some of the evidence in favour of the view that domestic considerations were a major influence in the conduct of German foreign policy. In extract A a British historian cites some of the reasons advanced at the time for Bismarck's colonial ventures in 1884. The advocates of a large navy used similar arguments as extract B indicates.

Von Bülow had no doubt, when he became Foreign Minister in 1897, that his first priority was the building of the German navy. In extract C, written in 1912, he explains the task that was given to him by the Emperor.

When the navy bills of 1898 and 1900 came before the Reichstag, some indication of who supported and who opposed them can be gauged from extracts D and E.

Germany's humiliation after the Agadir crisis of 1911 produced a wave of hostile comment from the right-wing press, which also drew attention to the benefits which a war might have on the domestic situation (see extract F).

A Colonial policy in 1884

'Everything is now bubbling over on account of colonial policy', wrote Herbert Bismarck [Bismarck's eldest son] in August 1884 – so it would 'be wise to hold the elections soon' before there was a swing to the Progressives. Here, as Holstein noted 'both as a means of combating foreign influences' and to check 'liberals and democrats' was a very substantial reason for supporting German interests overseas wherever they appealed for help: 'the best card in the government's hand at present is definitely a harsh move against England. One can hardly believe how popular it is in the business world.'

(P.M. Kennedy, *The Rise of Anglo-German Antagonism*, London, Allen and Unwin, 1980, p. 172)

B Tirpitz argues for an expansion in the size of the Navy: as early as 1895 the later State Secretary of the Navy and Reich Navy Office

(Tirpitz) had been demanding an expansion of the fleet

'In my view' he wrote, 'Germany will, in the coming century rapidly drop from her position as a great power unless we begin to develop our maritime interests energetically, systematically and without delay.' He added that an expansion had become a necessity 'in no small degree also because the great patriotic task and the economic benefits to be derived from it will offer a strong palliative against educated and uneducated Social Democrats.' In other words, Tirpitz's naval policy was nothing less than an ambitious plan to stabilise the Prusso-German political system and to paralyse the pressure for change. The Navy was to act as a focus for divergent social forces which the government hoped to bribe into a conservative Sammlung against 'the Revolution'. Promises of a great political and economic future were made with the aim of maintaining big landowners, the military and the bureaucracy in their key positions within the power structure.

(V.R. Berghahn, *Germany and the Approach of War in 1914*, 2nd edn, London, Macmillan, 1993, p. 42)

C Bülow recalls his task on becoming Foreign Secretary

The task I was set when the conduct of foreign affairs was assigned to me on 26 June 1897 on the *Hohenzollern* [the Imperial Yacht] was to make possible our transition to Weltpolitik (trade, shipping, overseas interests, the consequences of the huge development of our industry, our increasing prosperity, the increase of our population and above all the building of the German navy) without clashing with England, for whom we were in no way a match at seas, but preserving German dignity and our position on the continent.

(K.D. Lerman, 'Chancellor Bernhard von Bülow and the national idea', in J. Breuilly (ed.) *The State of Germany*, London, Longman, 1992, p. 113)

D Bülow comments on the passage of the 1898 Navy Bill

The great Navy Bill, which for years had been the subject of long and careful preparation and had excited public opinion pro and contra more than any other was passed on 28th March 1898 by 212 to 139 votes. The opposition vote was made up of the opponents of all German national claims and aspirations – the Social Democrats, the Poles, the Guelphs (Hanoverians), the Fransquillons of Alsace. The Centre was divided: the majority of the party followed Spahn and Hertling in voting for the Bill.

(Prince von Bülow, *Memoirs*, vol. 1, London, Putnam, 1931, p. 209)

E H-U. Wehler explains how the 1900 Navy Bill was passed

In March 1900, the American naval attaché in Berlin, who was familiar with the hard political bargains struck at home, knew what constellation of forces was necessary to 'get the bill for increased naval estimates through. The agrarians use their support for the bill to wring concessions to protect their own interests and, where possible, to get a tariff on agricultural imports which will be framed in future trade agreements'. For some years previously, government ministries had been preparing for a new increase in protectionism. This came into effect with the Bülow tariff of 1902. In fact, the Supplementary Navy Bill and the customs tariff formed a package put together by the majority of deputies in the Reichstag. The middle classes and heavy industry were given a naval construction programme, the large-scale agrarian producers a more favourable tariff system.

(H-U. Wehler, *The German Empire*, Leamington Spa, Berg, 1985, p. 168)

F Right-wing responses to the Agadir crisis

War, the right-wing Post declared on 26 August 1911 would not only clarify 'our precarious [foreign] political position', but would also bring 'a curing of many political and social ills'. Heinrich Class [founder and president of the Pan-German League], writing at this time about 'the influence of foreign policy on domestic affairs', viewed war as 'the only remedy for our people'. 'A generous passage of arms', the *Deutsche Armeeblatt* maintained, 'should be quite beneficial also for our domestic situation, even if it means tears and grief to individual families'.

(Berghahn, *Germany and the Approach of War*, pp. 108–09)

Questions

1 On the basis of extract A and your wider knowledge, assess the importance of domestic considerations in prompting Bismarck's sudden interest in colonies in 1884.

2 Explain and comment on the phrase 'a strong palliative [cure] against educated and uneducated Social Democrats' (extract B).

3 Compare the arguments advanced in extracts B and C in favour of a large German navy.

4 What can you infer from extracts D and E about which groups supported a German navy, and why?

5 How far would you accept the statement by H-U. Wehler that 'the Supplementary Navy Bill and the customs tariff formed a package put together by the majority of deputies in the Reichstag'?

6 What reliance would you place on extract F as a guide to the state of opinion in Germany in 1911?

7 In the light of these extracts and your further knowledge, how important were domestic political considerations in influencing German foreign policy either between 1871 and 1890 or between 1890 and 1912?

Further reading

See the works by W. Carr, G.A. Craig, Lothar Gall and J. Breuilly cited in Chapter 13. To these should be added H-U. Wehler, *The German Empire 1871–1918* (Leamington Spa, Berg, 1985). This is a radical reinterpretation of the period from a left-wing perspective. It is particularly valuable on the structure of German politics and society. On the working of the political system, see J.C.G. Rohl, *Germany without Bismarck: the Crisis of Government in the Second Reich*, (London, Batsford, 1967). There are good biographies of William II by L. Cecil, *Wilhelm II, Prince and Emperor* (Chapel Hill, NC, University of North Carolina Press, 1989) (up to 1900) and by A. Palmer, *The Kaiser: Warlord of the Second Reich* (London, Weidenfeld and Nicolson, 1978). There is a good biography of Bülow, by K.A. Lerman, *The Chancellor as Courtier: Bernhard von Bülow and the Governance of Germany*

(Cambridge University Press, 1990). On German foreign policy, see W.N. Medlicott and D.K. Coveney (eds), *Bismarck and Europe* (London, Arnold, 1971); V.R. Berghahn, *Germany and the Approach of War* (London, Macmillan, 1993) and P.M. Kennedy, *The Rise of Anglo-German Antagonism* (London, Allen and Unwin, 1980). Two useful collections of essays are G. Martel (ed.) *Modern Germany Reconsidered* (London, Routledge, 1992) and G. Pleuger (ed.) *Essays on German History, 1862–1939* (Bedford, Sempringham Press, 1996). Useful source material can be found in William Simpson, *The Second Reich, Germany 1871–1914* (Cambridge University Press, 1995), and in I. Porter and I.D. Armour, *Imperial Germany, 1890–1918* (London, Longman, 1991), which has an excellent bibliography.

• CHAPTER NINETEEN •

The Habsburg Empire, 1848–1914

• CONTENTS •

Key dates

KEY DATES

		Home		Abroad
1849	March	Dissolution of Reichsrat at Kremsier		
1850			Nov.	Humiliation of Olmütz
1851	31 Dec.	Sylvester Patent, restoration of absolutism	May	Dresden Conference
1854–56				Crimean war
1854			3 June	First ultimatum to Russia
1855			28 Dec.	Second ultimatum to Russia
1856			March–May	Congress of Paris
1859				War between Austria, Piedmont and France
			19 April	Austrian ultimatum to Piedmont
			3 May	France declares war on Austria
			15 July	Peace of Villafranca
1860	20 Oct.	Diploma restoring Reichstag		
1861	11 Feb.	February Patent; Reichsrat widened		
1864–66				Schleswig-Holstein crisis
1864			Feb.	Austria and Prussia declare war on Denmark
1866			June–July	Austro-Prussian war
1867	Feb.	*Ausgleich* agreed in Hungary		
	July	Franz Josef crowned in Budapest		
	Dec.	*Ausgleich* approved in Vienna		
1870		Hohenwart ministry's reforms fail		
1873		Agreement with Poles	6 June	Three Emperors' League
1875		Liberal party formed in Hungary		
1875–78				Near East crisis
1876			8 July	Reichstadt agreement between Andrassy and Gorkachov
1877			15 June	Budapest Convention
1878				Treaty of Berlin: Austria gains Bosnia-Herzegovina
1879–93		Count Taafe Minister President	7 Oct.	Dual Alliance with Germany signed
1881			18 June	Renewal of Three Emperors' League
1883–85				Bulgarian crisis
1887				Three Emperors' League lapses; Reinsurance Treaty signed
1890		Quarrels over military budget between Austria and Hungary		Reinsurance Treaty lapses
1895–97		Badeni reform programme		
1903				Coup in Serbia
			3 Oct.	Mürzteg agreement between Russia and Austria over Macedonia

1903–06		Crisis in Austro-Hungarian relations		
1904–05				Russo-Japanese war
1906–09				Pig war between Austria and Serbia
1907	Jan.	Universal suffrage introduced in Austria		
1908			4 Oct.	Annexation of Bosnia-Herzegovina
1914		March Reichsrat suspended		

SECTION A

THE PROBLEMS FACING THE HABSBURG EMPIRE

'By 1914 the constitutional mission of the Habsburg Empire had everywhere ended in barren failure' (A.J.P. Taylor, *The Habsburg Empire*, London, Hamish Hamilton, 1948, p. 241).

'What happened was that in 1848 the monarchy almost fell apart, but thereafter recovered and in many ways rose rather than declined before 1914. It can even be argued that there was no domestic or even foreign threat to its integrity until 1918' (A. Sked, *The Decline and Fall of the Habsburg Empire 1815–1918*, London, Longman, 1984, p. 6).

These two quotations illustrate the very different views held about the central problem of the Habsburg empire. How, in an age when nationalism was rampant, could a multinational empire be held together? According to Taylor, the problem was never solved and the First World War simply accelerated the empire's collapse. According to Sked it was at least possible that the Empire might have survived had it not been for the First World War. Other historians go further: 'The Austro-Hungarian Empire still looks better as a solution to the tangled problems of that part of the world than anything that has succeeded it' (George Kennan, cited in Sked, *Habsburg Empire*, p. 6).

The Habsburg empire that survived the 1848 Revolutions (see Chapter 10) was plagued by two perennial and related problems. It was an empire brought into existence through a series of dynastic and historical accidents. The Habsburgs acquired Hungary, for instance, through the death in battle of King Louis II of Hungary at the battle of Mohacs against the Turks in 1526. They acquired

Bohemia as a result of the Thirty Years War (1618–1648). The Polish part of the empire, Galicia, became theirs through the three partitions of Poland at the end of the eighteenth century, confirmed in the Congress of Vienna. In 1843 one estimate divided the empire up into these different groupings:

Slavs	15.5 million	Romanians	1.0 million
Germans	7.0 million	Italians	0.3 million
Magyars	5.3 million	Total	29.1 million

A more precise breakdown was made in the Census of 1910:

Germans	12.0 million	Romanians	2.9 million
Magyars	10.1 million	Slovaks	2.0 million
Czechs	6.6 million	Serbs	2.0 million
Poles	5.0 million	Slovenes	1.3 million
Ruthenians	4.0 million	Italians	0.7 million
Croats	3.2 million	Total	49.8 million

(A. Sked, *The Decline and Fall of the Habsburg Empire, 1815–1918*, pp. 278–79)

As can be seen from these figures, two racial groups dominated the empire, the Germans with almost one-quarter of the total and the Magyars (Hungarians) with almost one-fifth (see Map 19.1). Not surprisingly the empire drew its ministers and its bureaucracy almost exclusively from these two groups. The other minorities always felt themselves to be at a disadvantage and liable to be exploited in various ways, inadequately represented, overtaxed, made liable for military service and denied the use at official levels of their own languages, for example. Thus the claims of minority groups within the empire constantly clashed with the interests of the dominant races, the Germans and the Magyars. A partial solution to the

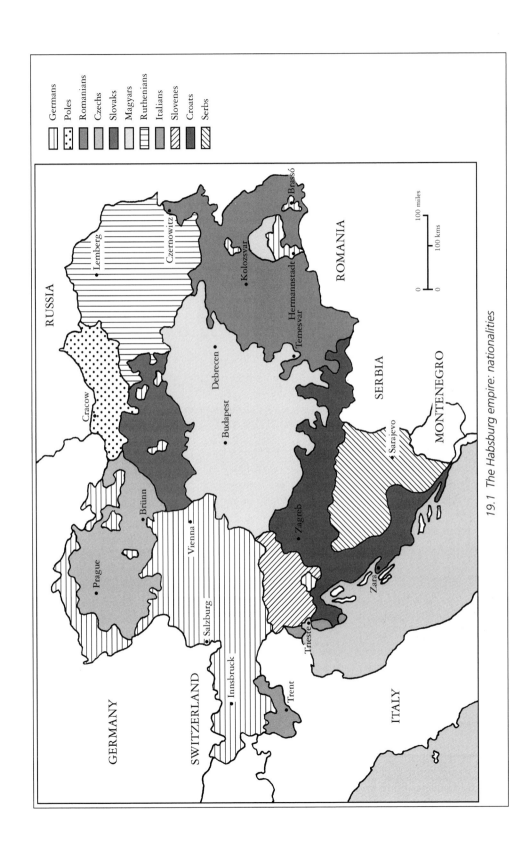

19.1 The Habsburg empire: nationalities

Legend:
- Germans
- Poles
- Romanians
- Czechs
- Slovaks
- Magyars
- Ruthenians
- Italians
- Slovenes
- Croats
- Serbs

RUSSIA

GERMANY

SWITZERLAND

ITALY

ROMANIA

SERBIA

MONTENEGRO

Cracow

Lemberg

Czernowitz

Brassó

Kolozsvár

Hermannstadt

Temesvár

Debrecen

Budapest

Prague

Brünn

Vienna

Salzburg

Innsbruck

Trent

Trieste

Zara

Zagreb

Sarajevo

100 miles

100 kms

rivalry between these two major groups was reached, as we shall see, in the famous compromise of 1867. But the other minorities continued to be dissatisfied to various degrees.

Related to this problem was that facing every other European country after 1848, how to create a system of government that would adequately meet the demands not only of an increasingly large and prosperous bourgeoisie but of an expanding working class too. The transition to parliamentary democracy was never going to be easy, as the histories of Germany and Italy make all too clear. In the Habsburg empire it was peculiarly difficult because of the make-up of the potential electorate. Any elected assembly was liable to reflect not class differences so much as ethnic ones. Any government which reflected the majority of one group, often artificially produced by 'electoral geometry' as the German one was, was likely to be unacceptable to all the others. In these circumstances the only institution that could command the allegiance of all was the Emperor himself. This reinforced the argument for the authoritarian, centralised administration in which the new emperor, Francis Joseph, already believed.

The nationalities problem was thus bound up with the problem of authority. Between 1848 and 1914 a variety of constitutional devices were tried to resolve these problems. They fall into two distinct phases. Up to 1867 the emperor did his best to rule as an absolute monarch, effectively undoing most of the constitutional advances achieved in the 1848 Revolutions. Defeat, first of all in the war against France (1859–60), and second in the Austro-Prussian war of 1866 compelled him to make adjustments and concessions. In 1861 under the February Patent he conceded an elected assembly in which the whole empire was supposedly represented. In 1867 there was the *Ausgleich* (Compromise) with Hungary and the Austrian empire became the Dual Monarchy. Let us look first at the constitutional experiments attempted between 1849 and 1867.

THE RETURN TO ABSOLUTISM

Emperor Francis Joseph was an autocrat by conviction rather than temperament. He could see no

other solution to the problems of his empire than centralised, autocratic rule and he had a strong sense that it was his religious as well as his dynastic duty to devote his life to the empire's preservation. He worked enormously hard, spending many hours every day in his study, reading state papers. He subordinated his private life to his public duties. He judged every political question by the criterion of whether in his judgement it would contribute to the empire's survival.

He had no doubts about the legitimacy of his authority. He insisted that ministers 'are solely responsible to the Monarch' and on hearing of Louis Napoleon's *coup d'état* in 1851, gave his full approval: 'He is perfectly right.' 'The man who holds the reins of goverment in his hands must also be able to take responsibility. Irresponsible sovereignty is, for me, a phrase without meaning' (E. Crankshaw, *The Fall of the House of Habsburg*, London, Longman, 1963, p. 81). As might be expected he showed a particular warmth for the army on whose support his throne rested, and took his duties as its commander-in-chief very seriously. He chose his ministers for preference from the aristocracy, but was quite prepared to appoint civil servants and academics where they had constructive policies to offer. While naturally German in his sympathies, he was equally ready to appoint Hungarians or Czechs to his government when he felt he could rely on their loyalty. It was a Hungarian, Count Andrassy, who was one of his most able Foreign Ministers (1871–79). Only 18 when he took over the imperial title in December 1848, he was to rule with largely undiminished authority until his death in 1916.

He came to the throne at a time of peculiar instability. A constitutional diet was putting the finishing touches to a new constitution at Kremsier, while Hungary had repudiated all links with Vienna. Francis Joseph and his advisers, Count Stadion in particular, wasted little time in getting rid of the assembly at Kremsier. It had already decided to drop the first clause of the new constitution: 'All sovereignty proceeds from the people' but was still prepared to guarantee equality of rights to all nationalities, stating: 'All peoples of the Empire are equal in rights. Each people has an inviolable right to preserve and cultivate its nationality in general and its language in particular'

(C.A. Macartney, *The House of Austria*, Edinburgh University Press, 1978, p. 119). On 6 March 1849 Stadion appeared at Kremsier and announced the dissolution of the Reichstag on the grounds that it had been wasting its time on 'dangerous theoretical discussions'. Instead, Stadion produced his own constitution, which provided for a two house legislature, one legal system for the whole empire and a single customs area. It also promised freedom of conscience and equality before the law.

The Stadion constitution was never implemented. By the time Hungary's resistance had been overcome, with the aid of Russian troops, Stadion himself had resigned and Francis Joseph was relying on the advice of another minister, Karl Kubeck, who attacked the concept of ministerial responsibility. On 31 December 1851 by a document known as the Sylvester Patent, Francis Joseph officially repudiated the Stadion constitution. Locally elected institutions, the Landtage were abolished, as was the office of Minister President. From now until 1867 Francis Joseph was to be his own prime minister. The only body to survive was the Reichsrat, an appointed body of elder statesmen, which was given purely advisory powers. In the next few years the empire was governed from Vienna. Martial law continued in parts of the empire until 1855. Almost the only survival from the Stadion constitution was the establishment of free trade throughout the empire and the extension of the Austrian system of taxation to Hungary. The empire's conservative stance extended to religious questions. In 1855 a Concordat was signed with the Papacy which among other things declared the Catholic Church's property inviolable and protected its control over education.

The new regime may have been acceptable in some parts of the empire but it aroused fierce resistance in Lombardy-Venetia and in Hungary. When war broke out with France in April 1859 Francis Joseph prepared to make concessions. In May 1860 a Reinforced Reichsrat, to which additional members had been invited, was allowed to meet and make recommendations. It produced two reports, one from the Hungarian members, one from the Germans. On 20 October, Francis Joseph promulgated what came to be known as the October Diploma. It conceded the right of the Reichsrat to approve taxation, and its membership was to be raised to one hundred. Hungary was to be given a measure of independence.

These concessions satisfied no one group. Meanwhile the threat to Austrian rule in Italy persisted and the government was running out of money. Further concessions were obviously needed and took the form of a collection of documents known as the 'February Patent', issued on 4 February, 1861. Under its terms there was now to be a Reichsrat made up of two houses, an upper house of notabilities and a lower house of 343 members, chosen by provincial assemblies (Landtage). A curious formula governed the choice of members. Each Landtage was to be made up of four Curias, representing the great landed proprietors, the urban Chambers of Commerce, the urban and the rural communes. The Hungarians boycotted the new assembly from the start. The Czechs and the Poles walked out of its first session. But Franz Joseph did concede, reluctantly, that the ministry owed some responsibility to the Reichsrat as well as to himself. It was at least a start towards dismantling the absolutist system that had prevailed since 1851.

The next concession came about directly as the consequence of another war, that with Prussia in 1866. Even before the war broke out Francis Joseph was anxious to secure his eastern frontier by conciliating Hungary. In December 1865 he convoked the Hungarian and Croatian Diets for the purpose of modifying the February Patent and though negotiations had not been completed by June 1866 when the Austro-Prussian war broke out, a Hungarian committee, chaired by Count Andrassy, had agreed on a set of proposals which became the substance of the *Ausgleich* in 1867. Austria's defeat in 1866 brought a new urgency to the negotiations. With the ending of the German Confederation, Austria had now lost the qualities of a German state and the 'Empire of Seventy Million', which had been Schwarzenburg's ambition, was now a pipe dream. Two possibilities were canvassed. One was a federal system in which each of the provinces of the empire would enjoy similar powers with respect to the central government. Such a scheme was suggested by the Czechs at a 'Slav Conference' held in 1866 under which the empire would be divided into five federal units. This satisfied no one except the Czechs. The new Austrian Foreign Minister, Baron F.F. von Beust, appointed in October 1866, realised that a deal with Hungary was essential. He and Andrassy held a series of meetings in the winter of 1866 as a result of which the terms of the *Ausgleich* were agreed. They were put to the Hungarian Diet on 17 February 1867 and voted through by 257 votes to 117 on 29 May. Francis Joseph was crowned on 8 July in Budapest. The Reichsrat representing the Austrian half of the empire gave its approval in December.

The terms of the *Ausgleich*

The *Ausgleich* divided the Austrian empire into two, the western part known as Cis-Leithanian Austria which now contained about 60 per cent of the population, and an eastern part, the Hungarian Crown Lands, which contained the remaining 40 per cent (see Map 19.2). The river Leitha formed part of the boundary between Austria and Hungary. The essence of the Dual Monarchy as it came to be known was that the two halves of the empire were united only through their common links with the crown. In practice, because the emperor enjoyed so much power, they shared a common government if not a common parliament. There was to be a single Foreign Minister, a single Defence Minister and a single Finance Minister with responsibility for financing the army and the diplomatic service. All questions relating to the army fell within the competence of the crown, though Hungary retained the right to vote the contingent required of her.

The three common ministers reported annually to equal delegations from the two parliaments. The delegations determined the budgets for the three ministries, which then had to be approved by each parliament. The 'quota' required from each country would be determined every ten years by 'deputations' from the two parliaments, which would also have to agree on other matters of joint concern such as tariffs and commercial relationships.

As can be seen, friction was only too likely to occur over such matters as the size of the quota, the language used in the army, tariffs and foreign policy. The Hungarians were naturally more suspicious of their Russian neighbours than the German speakers in Vienna. There have been very mixed verdicts on the *Ausgleich*. Many Germans felt that too much had been sacrificed, one of them, Karl Lueger, writing in 1895: 'I consider Dualism as a misfortune, indeed as the greatest misfortune which my fatherland has ever had to suffer, a greater misfortune even than the wars we lost' (Sked, *Habsburg Empire*, p. 189). Those in the non-German and non-Hungarian speaking parts of the empire felt that their interests had been overlooked and the Dual Monarchy did nothing to address their concerns. Andrassy is supposed to have said to an Austrian colleague: 'You look after your Slavs and we'll look after ours' (Sked, *Habsburg Empire*, p. 190). Finally, it has been claimed that Hungary now exercised a disproportionate influence over the empire as a whole, dragging it into Balkan entanglements that would have been better avoided, as with the annexation of Bosnia and Herzegovina. Despite such criticism the *Ausgleich* clearly worked after a fashion and it gave Hungary a greater degree of autonomy than she had enjoyed since the sixteenth century.

AUSTRIA-HUNGARY UNDER THE *AUSGLEICH*, 1867–1914

Relations between Austria and Hungary

The *Ausgleich* had been constructed to solve, as one Hungarian historian, Zolytan Szasz, has put it, the problem of 'how to cut the Habsburg Monarchy in two while leaving it in one piece' (cited in Sked, *Habsburg Empire*, p. 194). The relationship between Austria and Hungary continued to be fraught at times after 1867, but over the fifty years the *Ausgleich* lasted it never reached the point of armed conflict. Politics in Hungary still revolved round the relationship with the empire, what was known as 'the issue of public law'. In the Diet of 1867 two groups emerged to oppose various features of the *Ausgleich*, twenty deputies on the left who took the name 'Party of 1848' and a group known as the 'Party of the Left Centre'. There was still a con-

19.2 *The Habsburg empire: political boundaries, 1867–1918*

servative majority in favour of the *Ausgleich* and in 1875 the rival groups merged to form the Liberal party which for the next twenty-eight years provided goverments which accepted the *Ausgleich*, at least in principle. For fifteen of those years the Hungarian Minister President was Count Tisza and during his term of office relative harmony prevailed.

Opposition tended to erupt every ten years when the quota due from Hungary had to be reassessed, but there was also friction over the size of Hungary's contribution to the army and the way it was organised. The first such controversy arose in 1890 when an army ordinance requiring reserve officers to take an exam to show their proficiency in German was announced. Though the issue was resolved it led to Tisza's resignation.

A much more serious conflict broke out in 1903. This time it was caused by an increase in the size of the annual contingent required from the Hungarians, which rose from 43,229 to 53, 438 recruits. Opposition parties insisted on various concessions

before they would accept this figure. These included a reduction in the term of service to two years, the use of Hungarian as the language of command in Hungarian regiments and a change in the oath of loyalty required of all soldiers, which was now to be to the Hungarian Constitution. Francis Joseph, on manoeuvres in Galicia, dispatched an Army Order declaring that he would tolerate no infringements of his rights as Supreme War Lord, nor any tampering with the unitary character of the army. In Vienna plans were drawn up for the military occupation of Budapest. In the end a compromise was patched up, which recognised the crown's right to decide the languages of service and command. It did not end the crisis, however. New opposition parties came into existence, and won a substantial majority in the elections held in 1905 as a Coalition of New Parties. Francis Joseph appointed a former Minister of Defence, General Fejervrsary, as Minister President and summoned the leaders of the Coalition parties to an audience where he laid down his terms. A secret agreement was reached and a new Minister President, a Liberal, Wekerle was appointed. Though the Coalition parties won another large majority in the 1906 elections their hands had already been tied.

In the decennial assessments for 1907, Hungary's contribution went up by 2 per cent, to 36.4 per cent. In exchange the economic relationship between Austria and Hungary was now to be called a Customs Treaty, but there was no immediate change in tariffs. Some have seen in this compromise a sign that at last the *Ausgleich* was really working (see Section B) and proof that the arguments over the army that had lasted from 1903 to 1906 could easily have been avoided, with more tact on the part of the emperor. Certainly, when the next great crisis came in 1914, the Hungarians flocked as readily to the colours as their Austrian compatriots.

Cis-Leithian Austria under the *Ausgleich*

When the *Ausgleich* was approved by the Reichsrat in Vienna, a number of constitutional laws were added to it. In sum these left the crown with most of its powers, including the right to appoint the Minister President, a veto over legislation, the power to rule by decree in emergency, known as Paragraph 14, and command of the armed forces. In practice Francis Joseph continued to rule much as he had done before, but a number of guarantees were now written into the constitution. The Austrian citizen was assured of freedom of religious belief and practice, freedom of speech and freedom of the press. All citizens were declared equal before the law and all public offices were made open to them. There were echoes of the old Stadion constitution in a new Nationalities Law which provided that 'All peoples of the State are equal in rights, and every people has an inviolable right to the preservation of its nationality and language' (Macartney, *The House of Austria*, pp. 162–63). Unfortunately such paper guarantees proved almost unworkable in practice, and every attempt to solve the nationalities problem ended in frustration. For a start, the Bohemians and Moravians rejected the *Ausgleich* because of the favourable treatment it gave to the Hungarians. They refused to attend the Reich-

srat, and by 1870 had been joined in their boycott by Poles, Slovenes and Italians. In the face of this opposition the first Minister President of the new regime, Prince Carlos Auersburg, resigned and was briefly replaced by a Polish landowner, Count Potocki, who took office in April 1870. He was no more successful in winning over Czech and Polish opposition and was succeeded by Count Hohenwart, a moderate civil servant. Hohenwart appointed a German professor of political economy, Albrecht Schaffle, to the Ministries of Commerce and Agriculture, and it was he who produced the next blueprint. Schaffle consulted Czech political leaders in Prague and eighteen 'Fundamental Articles' were agreed, giving a considerable measure of autonomy to Bohemia. Though Francis Joseph would have been prepared to accept the Articles, his non-Bohemian subjects were not. The German members of the Bohemian Landtag walked out, German Liberals threatened to leave the Reichsrat and even Andrassy from Hungary advised that the Articles were incompatible with the *Ausgleich*. Hohenwart resigned and was succeeded by Adolf Auersburg, brother of Carlos.

The new ministry introduced two measures which eased the situation. A new Franchise Law in 1873 increased the number of deputies to 353 and arranged that each Curia would elect its deputies directly rather than through the Landtage. The allocation of deputies to each Curia was altered in favour of the urban and rural communes but it still meant that only 5.9 per cent of the population enjoyed the right to vote. A second and more important change was the agreement reached with the Poles in 1873, which gave them almost complete control over Galicia. The contrast with Bismarck's treatment of the Poles in East Prussia could not have been more marked. Polish Deputies to the Reichsrat were now usually to be found on the government's side. Another feature of these years were the anti-clerical measures passed by the German Liberals in the Reichsrat. Secular control of schools was established in 1868. In 1873 the appointment and dismissal of priests was made a government responsibility. The emperor accepted these measures very unwillingly and his opposition to them helps to explain his change of course in 1879.

The occasion for this was the right given to Austria-Hungary by the Congress of Berlin in 1878 to occupy Bosnia-Herzegovina (see p. 297). Many Germans objected to this on the grounds first that it would add to the Slav population of the empire and second that the Reichsrat should have been consulted before any such obligation had been agreed. Auersburg resigned on 5 July 1879 and in his place Francis Joseph appointed Count Taafe. Taafe was a childhood friend of mixed blood (Irish and Austrian) who was also a Bohemian landowner. He was truly a servant of the empire rather than of any racial group and his realistic if unambitious aim in his own words was 'keeping all the nationalities of the Monarchy in a condition of even and well modulated discontent' (C.A. Macartney, *The Habsburg Empire*, London, Weidenfeld and Nicolson, p. 615). His most important concession took the form of three enactments passed between 1880 and 1882 which in effect placed Czech on a footing with German as the language of government, increased Czech representation in the Bohemian Landtag and divided the university of Prague into two distinct foundations, Czech and German.

These concessions brought the Czechs into the Reichsrat at last. Taaf's period in office (1879–93) coincided with that of Tisza in Hungary (1875–90) and while these two men were in power relative stability prevailed. Czech grievances were still not fully met, however, and a conference between the Czech and German parties in Bohemia was summoned to Vienna in 1890. Unfortunately a new and more militant party, the Young Czechs, was not represented. Elections held in February 1891 resulted in their winning thirty-seven seats in the Reichsrat where they adopted a policy of militant obstruction. At this point a member of Taaf's government, Emil Steinbach, suggested that one way out of the impasse might be to extend the vote to the 'lower, politically uncorrupted classes' who were 'sound; they would make social, not national politics; they were dynastically-minded, not irredentist [not seeking independence]; they were reliable, appreciative and easy to rule' (Macartney, *Habsburg Empire*, p. 659). Francis Joseph was easily convinced by this logic, and a suffrage bill was introduced into the Reichsrat which would have given the vote to every male

taxpayer over the age of 25. Nothing, perhaps, is more revealing than the hostile reception of his proposal in the Reichsrat. The German Liberals feared the loss of seats to the Christian Social and Social Democratic parties which had recently come on the scene; the Poles feared the influx of Polish and Ruthenian peasants; the Clerical and Aristocratic parties feared the ending of their privileged status. Faced with this opposition Taaf resigned on 10 November 1893. There followed a long period of political instability.

Francis Joseph turned first to Prince Windischgraetz, grandson of the man who had done so much to defeat the 1848 revolutions. He was replaced in June 1895 by Count Casimir Badeni, a Pole who had been governor of Galicia. Badeni introduced a minor change to the suffrage, giving the vote to all males over 24, but allowing only 72 deputies out of 425 to be elected by popular vote. In 1897 he sought Czech support by introducing a language decree requiring all office holders in Bohemia and Moravia to be conversant with both Czech and German. Most educated Czechs spoke German. Few educated Germans spoke Czech. The decree met with violent protests in Vienna and Graz. It was now the turn of the Germans to adopt obstructive tactics in the Reichsrat. On 28 November 1897 Badeni resigned. He was followed briefly by a bureaucrat, Gautsch, who modified the Badeni decree. Gautsch was followed in March 1898 by Count Thun who was able to carry on the work of government only by invoking Paragraph 14 twenty-eight times.

On 2 October 1899 Thun resigned, to be replaced by Count Clary-Aldringen, who repealed the Badeni-Gausch ordinance on 14 October. This left the Czechs very dissatisfied and Clary resigned himself on 21 December. The sorry story ended with the appointment on 18 January 1900 of Dr Ernst von Koerber, a permanent civil servant. Koerber's rule, which lasted until December 1904, has been described as a period of 'enlightened absolutism' (Macartney), but it reduced the Reichsrat to an irrelevance:

The Reichsrat had no significance except as a meeting place where bargains could be struck between Koerber and the party leaders; it had no influence on policy, and its members had no hope of public careers. They had attained the highest ambition of central European politicians: endless, futile opposition.

(A.J.P. Taylor, *The Habsburg Monarchy*, p. 213)

There is one final experiment to record. News of the 1905 rising in Russia and Nicholas II's decision to grant a Duma, coupled with industrial disturbances in Vienna, prompted Francis Joseph to revert to Steinbach's policy of 1893 and concede universal suffrage. He announced his decision on 3 November 1905, but it was not until 26 January 1907 that the suffrage bill went through. The vote was given to all males over the age of 24 who could establish one year's residence in the same place. Constituencies were divided up on a uni-national basis: 241 German, 97 Czech, 80 Polish, 34 Ruthenian, 23 Slovene, 19 Italian, 13 Croat, 5 Romanian and 3 Serb, making a total of 515. The first elections to the new parliament were held in May 1907. They resulted in an even more complex mixture of parties, with vertical national divisions being criss-crossed by social and political ones. The years from 1907 to 1914 have been described by one Austrian historian, Friedjung, as a period of 'Parliamentary chaos and administrative absolutism' (Macartney, *The Habsburg Empire*, p. 796). There were four different ministries. The first, headed by Freiherr von Beck, previously tutor to the Archduke Franz Ferdinand, endured for a year. Beck became unpopular for opposing the annexation of Bosnia (see p. 319) and for conceding, it was thought, too much to Hungary in the 1907 settlement. He was replaced by another civil servant, Freiherr von Bierneth, who survived until 1911 but failed to secure majority support in the elections he called in May of that year. The emperor turned first to Gautsch, who resigned in despair in October 1911, and then to Count Karl Stürgkh, a Styrian landowner, who formed a cabinet of civil servants and managed to get essential business through by the use of Paragraph 14. In March 1914 obstructive tactics by Czech radicals forced him to suspend the Reichsrat. It did not meet again until May 1917. Stürgkh met an undeserved death at the hands of Friedrich Adler, son of Victor Adler, the leader of the Austrian Social Democratic party on 21 October 1916. As he fired the shots which killed Sturgkh, Adler is credited with shouting 'Down with absolutism!

We want peace!' The Habsburg empire failed on both counts.

AUSTRIAN FOREIGN POLICY, 1849–1908

The Habsburg empire stood on the defensive after 1848. It had to face the challenges of Italian nationalism inside the empire and German nationalism inside the German Confederation. Having failed to defeat these challenges the empire had to resist growing internal pressures from its subject nationalities, as we have seen. These challenges and pressures were inevitable in the context of a Europe where national sentiment was so powerful. The interesting question about Habsburg foreign policy therefore is not so much why these challenges arose but why in almost every case they met with an unsuccessful military response. Lord Clarendon, British Foreign Secretary at the time, remarked after the Austro-Prussian war in 1866 that for the Austrians 'a disastrous war is better than voluntary disgrace' (Sked, *Habsburg Empire*, p. 181). Whatever the reasons, the fact of the matter is that the eventual dissolution of the empire was bound up with its ultimately disastrous choices in its international relations.

Foreign and defence policy were the preserve of the Emperor but he did delegate his responsibilities for much of the time to his Foreign Ministers, who still acted for both halves of empire after 1867. They were immune to the internal wranglings of the Reichsrat and while the ultimate power of decision rested with Francis Joseph several of them were in office sufficiently long to exercise real influence. Their terms of office are summarised below:

Feliz zu Schwarzenburg, 1848–52
Karl Ferdinand von Buol Schauenstein (Buol), 1852–59
Johann Bernhard von Rechberg, 1859–64
Alexander von Mensdorff-Pouilly (Mensdorff), 1864–66
Frederick Ferdinand von Beust, 1866–71
Julius Andrasssy, 1871–79
Heinrich von Haymerle, 1879–81
Gustav Kalnoky, 1881–95

Agenor von Goluchowsky, 1895–1906
Alois Lexa von Aehrenthal, 1906–12
Leopold Berchtold, 1912–15

Austrian foreign policy, 1849–67

Austria's foreign policy has already been encountered in the context of Italian and German unification (see Chapters 12 and 13). Here we will look at it from a different perspective. Viewed from Vienna, what were the possibilities and the objectives? There can be little doubt that Francis Joseph saw his task as the preservation of the empire in its entirety. While he was compelled to surrender first Lombardy and then Venetia, he did this with great reluctance. He and his ministers were equally reluctant to accept the end of Austrian pre-eminence in the German Confederation. Thus from 1848 to 1867 Austria fought a losing battle against the forces of change epitomised by Cavour and Bismarck.

Prince Schwarzenburg met with an illusory success in 1850 when he succeeded in imposing the 'humiliation' of Olmütz on Prussia (see p. 197). His attempt to unite the Habsburg empire with the German Confederation in 1851 at the Dresden Conference never looked like getting off the ground. More serious was Austria's failure to be admitted to the *Zollverein*, an aim that was very clearly dear to Schwarzenburg. Among his papers was a Memorandum which stated 'The Customs Union is a matter of life and death to Austria' (Sked, *Habsburg Empire*, p. 156). At his death in 1852 Austria's destiny in Germany was no nearer to being resolved.

His successor, Buol, has been severely criticised for his handling of Austrian policy during the Crimean war. Austria never declared war on Russia, but delivered two ultimatums, one on 3 June 1854 demanding that Russia evacuate the principalities of Moldavia and Wallachia (Russia did so) and another on 28 December 1855 threatening war unless Russia signed the peace terms on which Britain and France had agreed. While Austria made no tangible gains, she had forfeited Russia's goodwill. Russian troops had assisted in the suppression of Hungary in 1849, and the Tsar had given his support to Austria in 1850. Not surpris-

ingly, perhaps, Nicholas I gave his statuette of Francis Joseph to his valet. In the next crisis, the Franco-Italian war of 1859, Cavour knew that he could count on Russian neutrality. Francis Joseph's ultimatum to Piedmont in April of 1859 was seen at the time as a godsend by Cavour, providing as it did the justification needed to bring Louis Napoleon into the war. Francis Joseph also miscalculated Prussian reaction, writing to his mother before the battle of Solferino: 'I hope that perhaps after all Germany and that ignominious scum of Prussia will come to our aid at the last moment' (Sked, *Habsburg Empire*, p. 173). By the time Prussia mobilised the battle of Solferino had been lost.

Rechberg, whose lot it was to deal with Bismarck between 1859 and 1864, has been accused of underestimating his opponent. The charge here is less justified. After one acrimonious discussion in relation to the future of the German Confederation, Rechberg wrote: 'The task of keeping this man [Bismarck] within bounds, of dissuading him from his expansionistic policy of utility . . . surpasses human powers' (Sked, *Habsburg Empire*, p. 178). Rechberg had few illusions about the man he was dealing with, and it is hard to see how the Austro-Prussian war could have been avoided granted Bismarck's determination to wage it (see p. 200). Where Austrian policy perhaps can be criticised is for its failure to win either French or Italian support. As war approached a secret treaty was signed with Napoleon III, promising Venetia to France (to be passed on to Italy) in the event of an Austrian victory. Had the offer of Venetia been made sooner, Austria might not have had to fight a war on two fronts in 1866. The consequences of Austria's foreign policy between 1848 and 1866 were thus disastrous. She had lost Lombardy and Venetia to Italy. She faced a powerful new neighbour across the river Main in the shape of the North German Confederation, dominated by Prussia. She had forfeited the friendship of Russia.

Austrian foreign policy, 1867–1908

After Austria's defeat in the wars with France and Piedmont (1859–60) and with Prussia (1866) those objectives clearly had to change. Francis Joseph was just as determined to hang on to what remained of his empire but now Austrian ambitions were focused on the Balkans rather than on Germany. Hungary's privileged status within the empire gave their politicians a greater degree of influence, usually in an anti-Russian direction. These factors made a collision with Russia always more likely, but certainly not inevitable. Russia's constant ambition was to secure control over the Dardanelles, Austria's ambitions varied with circumstance and according to who was in office. A minimum condition, however, was that any Russian gain in influence in the Balkan peninsula must be compensated by a corresponding Austrian one. Further, there could be no tolerance for any state outside the empire which gave encouragement to the empire's subject nationalities. Thus Serbian or Russian support for the Slavs in any part of the empire was certain to be resisted.

There were those in both countries who favoured a good working relationship. Both countries, after all, were ruled by conservative minded emperors who had little sympathy for radical nationalists. The history of Austro-Russian relations from 1867 to 1914 is not therefore one of unrelenting rivalry and worsening hostility. Rather it sees periods of mutual cooperation punctuated by moments of high tension, the last of which helped to lead to the First World War.

To begin with, a mood of relative harmony prevailed. In 1873 Andrassy, who admired Bismarck, helped to negotiate the Three Emperors' League, signed in October, with the aim of 'consolidating the peace which exists at the moment in Europe'. Under its terms Francis Joseph, William I and Alexander II agreed to consult together and 'if necessary to impose the maintenance of peace in Europe against all attempts to destroy it' (W.M. Medlicott and D.K. Coveney, *Bismarck and Europe*, London, Arnold, 1971, p. 87). This agreement was put under strain by the Near East crisis which began in 1875 with a revolt in Bosnia against Turkish rule. As in the Crimean war, Russia felt compelled to come to the aid of her co-religionists and fellow Slavs. Andrassy did his best to unite the powers in bringing pressure to bear on the Turks to treat their Christian subjects better, in the Vienna Note of 30 December 1875. His initiative failed to prevent the spread of the revolt to Bulgaria in June

1876. Anticipating possible Russian intervention, Andrassy met the Russian Foreign Minister Gorchakov at Reichstadt on 8 July, and it was agreed that in the event of a Turkish defeat, Russia would recover Bessarabia and Austria would get Bosnia-Herzegovina, the first time this claim was made. On 24 April 1877 Russia finally declared war on Turkey and in the secret Budapest Convention signed on 15 June 1877, Austria's claim to Bosnia-Herzegovina was again agreed with Russia.

However, when Russia finally defeated the Turks and imposed on them the treaty of San Stefano, Austria was alarmed to see that among its terms was the creation of a large Bulgaria, likely to become a Russian satellite. Britain was equally concerned, and on 6 June came to a private agreement with Austria, promising British support for Austria's claim to Bosnia-Herzegovina in return for Austrian backing for a British proposal to reduce Bulgaria's boundaries. The Congress of Berlin, under Bismarck's chairmanship, duly ratified these changes to the treaty of San Stefano in the treaty of Berlin. The exact status of Bosnia-Herzegovina was left dangerously undefined. The provinces were still nominally under the rule of the Sultan, but were to be 'occupied and administered by Austria-Hungary'.

One immediate consequence of the Near East crisis was Russia's sense that she had been victimised, and this led to a further alienation from Austria. This helps to explain the Dual Alliance signed between Austria and Germany on 7 October 1879 which was specifically directed against Russia. But neither Bismarck nor the new Austrian Foreign Minister Haymerle, who replaced Andrassy in 1879, wanted the breach with Russia to be widened. In 1881 the Three Emperors' League was renewed, and in a separate and secret protocol relating to Bosnia-Herzegovina, Austria-Hungary was conceded the right 'to annex these provinces at whatever moment they shall judge opportune'.

A further crisis in Bulgaria which lasted on and off during 1885–87 saw Austria and Russia on different sides. Accordingly the Three Emperors' League was not renewed in 1887. Bismarck nonetheless signed the Reinsurance Treaty with Russia (see p. 299) to show that Germany, at any rate, had no cause to quarrel with Russia. In another secret protocol Bismarck went so far as to promise Russia 'a free hand in order to re-establish a regular and legal government in Bulgaria' and to promise benevolent German neutrality should the Emperor of Russia 'find Himself under the necessity of assuming the task of defending the entrance of the Black Sea'. This treaty was not shown to Austria.

The lapse of the Reinsurance Treaty in 1890 thus had no effect on Austro-Russian relations. In fact between 1890 and 1908 there was remarkably little friction. In 1894 Kalnoky (Foreign Minister from 1881–95) reached an agreement with his Russian counterpart, Giers, that Austria would refrain from meddling in Bulgaria's affairs if Russia would do the same where Serbia was concerned. In 1897 Francis Joseph visited St Petersburg with Goluchowski (Kalnoky's successor) and an informal agreement was reached that both countries would seek to preserve the status quo in the Balkans. Doubts were still expressed over Bosnia-Herzegovina, Russia declaring that annexation by Austria 'would require special scrutiny at the proper time' (Macartney, *Habsburg Empire*, p. 596).

When trouble broke out in Macedonia in 1903 both sides cooperated in restoring order. Under the Mürzteg programme of 3 October they agreed to mount an international police operation there. Russia's involvement in the Russo-Japanese war (1904–05) and the 1905 rising drew her attention away from the Balkans, and had it not been for events in Serbia and changes in Austrian policy there is nothing to suggest that Austro-Russian relations would again have deteriorated. In 1903 a bloodthirsty palace coup caused the assassination of King Alexander Obvenovic, who was on good terms with Austria. His successor, Peter Karajordjovic, owed his position to a group of radically minded nationalists who from now on began to demand a Greater Serbia, to include all those Serbs still under Austrian rule. There were 800,000 of them in Bosnia-Herzegovina, together with 600,000 Muslims and 400,000 Croats. A further cause of difficulty was the Austrian attempt to revise the commercial treaty with Serbia which gave unlimited access to Serb exports. No agreement could be reached on this question and in 1906 all trade between the two countries was suspended. This became known as 'the Pig War', because of the high tariffs to be paid on Serbian agricultural exports to the Habsburg empire, especially pigs, and lasted until 1909.

There were two critical changes of office in Vienna towards the end of 1906. In October Baron Lexa von Aehrenthal replaced the conciliatory Goluchowski at the foreign office. In November Conrad von Hötzendorff replaced Baron von Beck as Chief of the General Staff.

Aehrenthal wanted to embark on an expansionist policy in the Balkans, preferably with Russian approval, but without it if necessary. Conrad wanted a military solution to the problem of Serb nationalism. Of the two, Aehrenthal had much the greater influence at this stage but Conrad was to have a decisive voice in 1914.

By 1908 the situation in Bosnia-Herzegovina was becoming critical. In 1907 the Serbs held a mock parliament in Sarajevo and adopted a resolution demanding complete independence for Bosnia. In July 1908 the Young Turks seized power in Constantinople, forcing the Sultan to issue an order for a parliament to which elected representatives from Bosnia-Herzegovina, along with those from other 'occupied' areas such as Crete, were to be invited.

As luck would have it, on 2 July 1908 the Russian Foreign Minister Isvolski made a highly significant proposal. He suggested that Austria should support Russian control over the Dardanelles in return for Russia's approval for the Austrian annexation of Bosnia-Herzegovina. Aehrenthal responded warmly to the suggestion and the two men agreed to meet at Buchlau, the country house of Count Berchtold, another high-ranking Austrian official. As we have seen (p. 301) no written record has survived of the conversations that took place on 15 September, but Isvolski was certainly left with the impression that Aehrenthal would use his influence in favour of the Russian proposal before taking any unilateral action. Thus when Aehrenthal announced to all the signatories of the treaty of Berlin on 5 October 1908 that the provinces of Bosnia-Herzegovina were to be annexed, Isvolski was outraged, and Austro-Russian relations took a turn for the worse. The annexation went through. Germany gave her unconditional support to Austria. Russia was in no position to fight after the 1905 rising. On

31 March 1909 Serbia recognised the annexation and promised to maintain good relations with Austria. This promise proved hardly worth the paper it was written on, and two Serb nationalist organisations soon emerged, pledged to Serbia's expansion into Bosnia, the *Narodna Obrana* (National Defence) and the *Cerna Ruka* (the Black Hand), whose methods included the assassination of opponents. With hindsight, the annexation of Bosnia-Herzegovina was one of the most fateful mistakes made by the Austrian government, and it paved the way for Austrian entry into the First World War and the destruction of the empire.

SECTION B – SOURCES

THE WEAKNESSES OF THE HABSBURG EMPIRE

Historians have reached very different verdicts about the Habsburg empire's prospects of survival. Two Hungarian historians have pointed out that most of the different nationalities within the empire were not seeking to leave it, at any rate before 1914. Istvan Dioszegi wrote in 1985: 'Nationalism did not work towards the destruction of the Monarchy. Of the nations inside the Habsburg Empire only the Italians aimed consciously at breaking away; the others from considerations of economics, politics and foreign policy were led, not disinclined, to see the Monarchy as the appropriate area in which to fulfil their national aims.' This view is supported by Barbara Jelavich: 'No major leader or party called for the destruction of the monarchy' (1983) (cited in Sked, *Habsburg Empire*, p. 231). With the granting of universal suffrage to Cis-Leithian Austria, though not to Hungary, in 1907 and the successful annexation of Bosnia-Herzegovina in 1908 it appeared to some observers that the empire was about to enjoy a new lease of life (see extract E).

Yet Francis Joseph had concluded as early as 1866, in a letter to his mother: 'One just has to resist as long as possible, to do one's duty to the last and finally perish with honour.' Kaiser William II was reported by Archduke Rudolf, not necessarily a very reliable witness, as saying in 1887 that 'in Austria the whole state was rotten, near to dissolution, and it would break up, that the German provinces would fall like ripe fruit into Germany's lap, that [Austria] as an insignificant duchy would become even more dependent on Prussia than Bavaria was' (cited in Sked, *Habsburg Empire*, p. 229).

Historians also differ about Austrian rule in Bosnia-Herzegovina. To A.J.P. Taylor in 1908:

Even the greatest enthusiasts for the 'Free Trade Empire' had to admit that thirty years of Austrian rule had not brought much benefit to the inhabitants of the two provinces: there were no health services, no railways of normal gauge, no popular schools, no self-government in the provinces'. Annexation brought few improvements. The 'Austrian idea' failed to come to life in the two provinces. There was no 'economic amelioration', no new schools, only a larger bureaucracy and an army of occupation.

(Taylor, *The Habsburg Monarchy*, pp. 232–34)

A more favourable picture is painted by C.A. Macartney, who comments on the rule of Benjamin Kallay, who was in charge of the provinces from 1882–1903:

Kallay's regime was one of enlightened autocracy, and its autocratic nature must be recognised. . . . But the regime also deserves the adjective. . . . Through this instrument [a reformed bureaucracy], Kallay exercised a benevolent dictatorship, which in certain fields achieved a complete transformation of conditions before the occupation. Security became absolute: brigandage was stamped out and the incidence of crimes of violence became the lowest in the monarchy. Justice became completely even-handed and accessible to all. The three local religions were placed on a footing of complete and scrupulously maintained equality. . . . Medical and veterinary services were improved out of all recognition. A considerable number of State primary schools and gymnasia [secondary schools] were constructed, and some exceedingly valuable technical schools of agriculture etc., and a great deal was done to improve local standards of cultivation.

(Macartney, *The Habsburg Empire*, pp. 742–44)

The following extracts echo, and perhaps help to explain, these disagreements. Extract A is taken from Francis Joseph's Proclamation to the peoples of Bosnia-Herzegovina on the occasion of the Annexation. Extract B is taken from a letter of advice given by Count Czernin to the Archduke Franz Ferdinand, Francis Joseph's nephew, and after the death of the emperor's son Rudolf in 1889, heir apparent. Czernin was at the time a high-ranking foreign office official who became Foreign Secretary in 1916. Extract C helps to explain why the Reichsrat had to be suspended in 1914. Extract D, written by the Czech nationalist, Thomas Masaryk, in 1915 is one of the first examples of a bid for full independence by one of the people's of the Habsburg empire and calls attention to its outmoded character. In December 1914 Masaryk, previously a professor of philosophy at Prague university and a founder member of the Czech People's party, left Prague for the west. He began a long campaign to secure international backing for an independent Czechoslovakia. In his Memorandum, dated April 1915, can be seen an explicit rejection of Austrian rule. Extract E expresses the view of a well-respected French observer, Louis Eisenmann, writing in 1910, about the empire's prospects.

A Francis Joseph's Proclamation to the peoples of Bosnia-Herzegovina on the occasion of the Annexation, 7 October 1908

Inhabitants of Bosnia and Herzegovina: Among the many cares of our throne, solicitude for your material and spiritual welfare shall not be the last. The exalted idea of equal rights before the law, a share in the legislation and administration of the provincial affairs, equal protection for all religious creeds, languages and racial differences, all these high possessions you shall enjoy in full measure.

The freedom of the individual and the welfare of the whole will be the aim of our government in the two lands. You will surely show yourselves worthy of the trust placed in you, by attachment and loyalty to us and to our House. And thus we hope that the noble harmony between the prince and the people, that dearest pledge of all social progress, will ever accompany us on our common path.

(R.W. Breach, *Documents and Descriptions in European History*, Oxford University Press, 1964, pp. 78–79)

B Count Czernin offers his advice to the Archduke Franz Ferdinand, Francis Joseph's nephew and heir apparent, 10 February 1909

The duty laid upon the ruler by God is to lead his people, and if the peoples – as in our Monarchy – are not ripe to behave with reason, then they must be compelled. Dictatorship and force are justified, even if they mean a limitation of national right! . . . The Monarchy's way to health lies along the path of Caesarian absolutism! The peoples must first be put under tutelage – then with the passage of time the longing for parliamentarism will once more awake in them, and then they will know how to cherish this priceless gift of the Crown and behave in a manner worthy of it.

(E. Crankshaw, *The Fall of the House of Habsburg*, London, Longman, 1963, p. 357)

C Macartney comments on the suspension of the Reichstag in 1914

The reason why Austria had to enter the World War without a Reichstag was that the Germans had made the Bohemian Landtag [provincial assembly] unworkable by their obstruction and the Czechs had retorted that if the Landtag could not work, neither should the Reichsrat. The Landtage in several other provinces, especially where Southern Slavs and Italians clashed, were little more orderly than that of Prague. One may quote a heartfelt remark by the Landeshauptmann [Governor] of Silesia: 'God forbid that the general franchise should ever be introduced into the Landtage, for if that ever happened, it would have to be extended to the communes, and that would mean reddest anarchy and the ruin of the state'.

(C.A. Macartney, *The Habsburg Empire*, London, Weidenfeld and Nicolson, 1969, p. 797)

D Thomas Masaryk's Confidential Memorandum on the Case for a New State

This Memorandum gives the programme for the reorganisation of Bohemia as an independent state.

Austria, being an aggregate of nine small nations, is quite an artificial State, as she was called by an Austrian politician (Plener, the younger): no nation in Austria is so populous that it would have a ruling majority. The dynasty therefore, tries to maintain its absolutistic position by the principle of divide et impera [divide and rule], by little concessions now to one nation, now to another; the Germans (the dynasty is German) and Magyars are the favourites.

Austria owes her origin to the invasions of the Turks and previously of the Huns (Magyars): Austria means the Eastern Empire, the German provinces, Bohemia and Hungary joined in a federation against Turkey. With the fall of the Turks Austria falls also; Austria lost her ruling idea, and is unable to find a positive idea.

So Austria falls from step to step. The Austrian-Spanish Empire was dissolved. Austria lost the greater part of Silesia and was driven by Prussia to abandon Germany; in 1848, saved by Russia, she lost in 1859 the Italian provinces; in 1866 she was beaten by Prussia. Since then she exists only as a vassal of Berlin, being divided into Austria and Hungary; it is to Berlin that both the Germans and the Magyars owe their dominating position in Austria.

(The Memorandum goes on to sketch out the frontiers of the Independent Bohemian State that Masaryk had in mind. It would have a population of about 12 million and would include Slovaks and those Germans still living in Bohemia.)

(Breach, *Documents and Descriptions in European History*, pp. 152–54)

E The views of a French observer, Louis Eisenmann, writing in 1910 after the sixtieth celebration of Francis Joseph's accession in 1908

It seems as though all the Austrian, Hungarian, and Austro-Hungarian questions could be settled from within. . . .fifty years of national and constitutional life have endowed the people of the monarchy with the strength to enforce their wishes side by side with those of the sovereign, and if necessary in opposition to him. They are of age, and can control their destinies if they wish to do so, provided only that they can agree among themselves. They have come to realise the common interest which keeps them united in the monarchy and in time they will become conscious of the strength by means of which they can govern it in accordance with their own wishes. The monarchy no longer rests on the power of the dynastic tie alone, but on their conscious

desire for union. Herein lies its mighty new strength; this is the great, the enormous result of the reign of Francis Joseph.

(A. Sked, *The Habsburg Empire*, London, Longman, 1984, p. 232)

Questions

1 What specific pledges did Francis Joseph make to the inhabitants of Bosnia and Herzegovina in 1908 (extract A)?
2 Compare and contrast the role of the emperor as it is presented in extracts A and B.
3 Explain and comment on Thomas Masaryk's view that 'with the fall of the Turks Austria falls also' (extract D).
4 How far do the events described in extract C bear out Count Czernin's opinion that the peoples of the Monarchy 'are not ripe to behave with reason' (extract B)?
5 In the light of these extracts and your wider knowledge comment on Thomas Masaryk's description of Austria as 'quite an artificial state' (extract D).
6 How far do extracts A, B, C and D and your wider knowledge support the optimistic view of the empire's prospects presented in extract E?

Further reading

The two most accessible books on the Habsburg empire in the nineteenth century are A.J.P. Taylor, *The Habsburg Empire* (London, Penguin, 1948) and A. Sked, *The Decline and Fall of the Habsburg Empire, 1815–1918* (London, Longman, 1984). Taylor's book takes a somewhat jaundiced view of the empire's prospects, while Sked's is more optimistic. E. Crankshaw, *The Fall of the House of Habsburg* (London, Longmans, 1963), gives a lively narrative account of the empire, and is particularly good on members of the Habsburg family. For a fuller account of the empire see C.A. Macartney, *The Habsburg Empire* (London, Weidenfeld and Nicolson, 1969) and its abbreviated version, *The House of Austria* (Edinburgh University Press, 1978). A.J. May, *The Hapsburg*

Monarchy, 1867–1914 (Cambridge, MA, Harvard University Press, 1951) is particularly strong on social and cultural aspects of the empire. The empire's foreign policy is well covered by F.R. Bridge, *From Sadowa to Sarajevo* (London, Routledge, 1972).

• CHAPTER TWENTY •

Russia, 1894–1914

• CONTENTS •

Key dates

1892–94		Russian-French alliance concluded
1893–1903		Witte as Finance Minister; industrialisation
1903		Social Democratic Party splits into Mensheviks and Bolsheviks
1904–05		Russo-Japanese war; Russian defeat
1905	22 Jan.	'Bloody Sunday' begins revolutionary process
	June	'Potemkin' mutiny
	17 Oct.	Tsar's Manifesto promises liberties and an elected Duma
	Nov.–Dec.	St Petersburg and Moscow soviets suppressed
1906	23 April	Fundamental State Laws define Tsar's powers
	April–June	First Duma
	Aug.	Stolypin appointed chief minister; agrarian reforms and repression
1907	Feb.–June	Second Duma; dissolved; new franchise favours wealthy
1907–12		Third Duma
1911	Sept.	Stolypin assassinated
1912		Disturbances at Lena goldfields
	Nov.–1914	Fourth Duma
1914	July	Bolsheviks organise strike in St Petersburg
	1 Aug.	Germany declares war on Russia
1915	July–Sept.	Duma reconvened; 'Progressive Bloc' formed
	Aug.	Tsar takes command of army at the front
1916	Nov.	Duma reconvened
	Dec.	Rasputin murdered
1917	18 Feb.	February Revolution begins; Putilov workers strike
	27 Feb.	Committee of the Duma meets; Petrograd Soviet meets
	2 March	Nicholas II, prevented from returning to Petrograd, abdicates

SECTION A

The last Tsar, Nicholas II, reigned from 1894 until his abdication on 2 March 1917. At the age of 13 he had watched his grandfather, Alexander II, die from the injuries caused by the assassin's bomb, and he had no illusions about the burden God had laid upon him. His reign began well enough, the famine was receding, the alliance with France provided a source of optimism, and Witte continued as Finance Minister (1893–1903) and helped to modernise the economy with some success. But could an autocracy tolerate modernisation if it produced a turbulent proletariat, peasant demands for land which sometimes seemed eager to seize the property of others, and a set of liberal demands of the sort which *zemstva* leaders were making?

War with Japan (1904–05) was the product of Russia's territorial demands in the Far East. It was seen as providing a patriotic unifying cause, offering an easy victory. Defeat triggered protest, repression and more protest, forcing Nicholas II to concede reform 'from below'. Witte was called back briefly to draw up the October Manifesto in 1905, but the Fundamental Law of April 1906 seemed to show that tsarism was clawing back the powers it had given away. The history of the Dumas suggests that there was little to resemble a constitutional monarchy, but on the other hand the Tsar did not attempt to rule without the Duma and Stolypin, chief minister from 1906 until 1911, tried to govern with its backing. His mixture of repression and reform was astute, but it needed time to prove its worth, and time was in short supply. Stolypin had many enemies and it was unsurprising that one found his mark and murdered him in 1911.

After Stolypin's death, government drifted. The outbreak of war in 1914 briefly boosted the popularity of the regime, but defeat on the battlefield, and dislocation of the economy quickly brought protest and disorder. The significance of the 1905 Revolution may be understood fully from the viewpoint of the February Revolution of 1917. This time defeat and rioting was compounded by mutiny among the soldiers, and the Tsar could no longer hide blameless behind others – he had made himself military commander, and his family had been degraded by Rasputin's influence.

Furthermore the St Petersburg Soviet had asserted itself in 1905, and in 1917 it was to be reborn with a vengeance.

Faced with the demands of economic and social change, and harrassed by events, Nicholas II resorted to stubborn fatalism. In this he was well supported, even led, by his wife Alexandra. As his biographer Marc Ferro has explained, Nicholas 'was one of those individuals who are burdened with a destiny that they have taken upon themselves as a duty decreed for all time, and that separates them from a world undergoing change before their eyes.' It was his duty to his ancestors to maintain the autocracy. The concessions made in the 1905 Revolution were limited, perhaps incidental, and when things got worse abdication was preferable to betrayal (M. Ferro, *Nicholas II, the Last of the Tsars*, trans. B. Pearce, London, Penguin, 1991, p. 4).

WITTE'S REFORMS AND THE 1905 REVOLUTION

Witte as Finance Minister, 1893–1903

Sergei Witte was appointed Finance Minister in 1893, following the problems which had overtaken Vyshnegradsky's policy (see Chapter 14). A tough, confident, bear-like man, he got on well with Alexander III but the more gentle disposition of Nicholas II found the relationship uncomfortable. However, Witte was retained until 1903. He was cautiously supported by Pobedonostsev (Procurator of the Holy Synod; see Chapter 14) in return for Witte funding parish schools, but he remained an outsider to some extent from the court and the bureaucracy where his abilities and policies were not fully trusted.

Witte aimed at economic modernisation through the involvement of government, which is sometimes called state capitalism. Government's role was to plan the areas for economic development and rapidly pilot Russia through industrialisation which would bring her up to western levels. The military objective to be powerful was surely the key motivation in all this for tsarism. Witte's policies focused on stabilising the rouble (against

the gold standard) and attracting foreign investment, developing industry and building the Trans-Siberian railway, and expanding Russia's trade in the Far East.

Foreign investment in Russia was crucial to Witte's plan, but investment would be put off if the rouble kept changing its value. In 1894 he deterred currency speculators from playing with the rouble by a clever manoeuvre on the Berlin stock exchange, and afterwards raised a large loan for the government of 100 million roubles in Paris. All this helped foreign investors feel confident about the stability of the rouble, but getting its value fixed against gold reserves was the prize. Witte faced great opposition in the State Council where his opponents disliked the large debts that Russia was building up, and he had to persuade the Tsar to go over the head of the State Council and issue a decree in 1897 fixing the exchange rate of the paper rouble against gold. Russia was on the gold standard at last, but Witte had made many enemies in the process.

Industrial development went ahead in parallel. Many methods were used. Witte attracted a large number of foreign experts, engineers and managers, to work in Russia and help to modernise the economy. Foreign investors were attracted by the confident and purposeful activity, and high interest rates. Protective tariffs stopped imports from competing with the new industries. Taxation was kept high to support the government's creditworthiness. The key industrial sector was railway building, especially the Trans-Siberian railway which was begun under Witte in 1892, before he became Finance Minister. This was a giant undertaking (the Moscow to Vladivostok route was over 6,000 kilometres) which boosted the metallurgical industry as it went forward, and opened up trade with Siberia and the Far East. Critics point out that it was built 'on the cheap', with lightweight rails which restricted the speed and frequency of the traffic, on a shortened route which cut out some towns. But its completion in 1905 was a landmark.

Commercial relations with northern China, Manchuria and Korea developed under Witte. He intended to beat the Japanese and British competition to monopolise trade with the area, and the building of the Trans-Siberian railway was an important instrument for doing so. Using the opportunity of China's defeat by Japan in 1895, Witte organised a loan (with French backing) to the Chinese government. On the strength of the influence which this gave him he developed trade with Manchuria and agreed a shortcut for the Trans-Siberian railway across Chinese territory. In 1898 China gave its great supporter, Russia, the reward of a twenty-five-year lease on Port Arthur. The prospects for Russian economic development in the Far East were bright.

ment, and this produced concentrations of badly housed, underfed workers. By the early 1900s a depression had set in, and the resulting unemployment produced strikes and protests. Those like the Tsar who had been suspicious of Witte's policies became more inclined to listen to his many enemies who accused him of threatening the very foundations of the autocracy. Witte was dismissed on 16 August 1903, in such an off-hand manner that he nursed a resentment towards the Tsar for the rest of his life.

Appraisal

The economic progress made in the 1890s has been called the 'great spurt', and much credit should be given to Witte. Between 1890 and 1900, key indicators all showed an increase; coal production rose from 5.9 million tons to 16.1 million tons, pig iron production climbed from 0.89 million tons to 2.66 million tons. Exports grew steadily decade by decade from the 1880s, showing a healthy surplus over imports. The foundations were laid for strong development; in 1913 Russia produced more steel than France, and between 1894 and 1913 national income for European Russia grew by 50 per cent by comparison with 58 per cent for Germany, 52 per cent for France, and Britain's 70 per cent (figures from J.N. Westwood, *Endurance and Endeavour: Russian History 1812–1992*, Oxford University Press, 1993, p. 604; M. Lynch, *Reaction and Revolutions: Russia 1881–1924*, London, Hodder and Stoughton, 1992, pp. 23–24; W.E. Mosse, *An Economic History of Russia, 1856–1914*, London, I.B. Tauris, 1996, p. 108).

On the other hand Witte did little to develop the backward agrarian economy, and his reliance on foreign capital made him a target for critics. The real problem, however, was that any minister bent on modernisation was confronted by the suspicion of the autocracy. Industrial modernisation had to be a great compromise with autocratic government. Witte complained that all of Russian thinking was against him, and he faced in more acute form the same basic difficulty with reform that we have seen appearing in the 1860s and 1870s (see Chapter 14). Witte's policies and the world boom boosted urban industrial develop-

Opposition

Opposition to tsarism came in many forms. The populist *Narodnik* movement (see Chapter 14) developed into the Social Revolutionary party, the most prominent revolutionary party during Nicholas II's reign. Its roots lay with the peasantry and their interest in land redistribution to solve the problem of land hunger, but by 1901 under Victor Chernov the party was expanding to attract the support of the proletariat (the industrial working class). The terrorist left of the party (Left SRs as they were called) were the most prominent faction, between 1901 and 1905 assassinating over 2,000 ministers, bureaucrats and officers. The Right SRs believed in a cooperative approach with other parties to develop reform, and they became more prominent after the 1905 Revolution. Land reform remained central to the SR programme and the key to their popularity with the peasantry, but focusing on this to the exclusion of proletarian interests upset the Left SRs and the party became divided into various radical factions.

The Social Democratic party was a smaller group than the SRs, and no more united. Formed in 1898 as a Marxist group, it split in 1903 between the Menshevik and the Bolshevik factions (see Chapter 16 for further details). The Bolsheviks, dominated by Lenin, believed in a small conspiratorial party comprising an elite who would lead the proletariat from mere trade union activity into revolution. Violence would be used to accelerate the process of bourgeois and proletarian revolution which Marx argued was historically inevitable. The Mensheviks (who included Trotsky) believed in a more gradual approach to change with the proletarian revolution awaiting the bourgeois phase, and a mass party membership. The distance between these factions grew, and both remained on the fringe of political opposition right up to 1917.

The demands of the *zemstva* liberals for a say in government did not die after Alexander III's rejection in 1881 (see Chapter 14), but Nicholas II damned such talk as 'senseless dreamings' (Westwood, *Endurance and Endeavour*, p. 152). The activists were excluded from the agricultural committees which were called to investigate the question of agrarian reform, but they set up their own Union of Liberation, which appeared in public in 1904 and demanded a constituent assembly. In the same year the Minister of the Interior, Plehve, permitted a national congress of *zemstva* representatives to go ahead.

Before 1905, therefore, the government was facing a broad range of opposition. It tried repression with them all, and set up a great network of spies to infiltrate the organisations. This was often counterproductive, as Azev's career illustrates vividly. Azev was in charge of the terrorist activities of the SRs, and he was a police agent. To avoid 'blowing his cover', he organised the assassination of various policemen, the Minister of the Interior (Plehve) in 1905, and the Tsar's uncle the Grand Duke Sergei; it seemed that the autocracy was paying a high price to keep its spies in work! Police trade unions were also created to focus workers' demands on politically safe areas such as wages, avoiding revolutionary pressures. This initiative of Zubatov (chief of the Moscow security police) went well until his unions started to call strikes, and the experiment perhaps did more to incite working class demands than to repress them.

Bloody Sunday and the 1905 Revolution

Father Gapon, Orthodox priest and another police agent, set up a police approved trade union movement which got out of control. By 1905 the economic downturn had added serious unemployment to the bad living conditions. The humiliation of defeat by Japan came as the last straw, exposing the careless stupidity of the regime, and provoked Gapon into leading an enormous peaceful proces-

sion to present a petition to the Tsar at the Winter Palace in St Petersburg. The fond hope was that if only the Tsar himself could be told of all that was wrong, all would be put right. Although the Tsar was not in residence, the guards panicked and opened fire. A cavalry charge followed, leaving perhaps several hundred casualties.

The shock waves were enormous and resulted in a revolution of sorts. The Tsar's reputation as the 'Little Father' of his people was rocked. News of the massacre spread fast and provoked strikes in most towns, Plehve and the Grand Duke Sergei were assassinated, and – most worrying portent to the government – the crew of the battleship *Potemkin* mutinied in June, defied the Black Sea fleet, bombarded Odessa, and sought safety in Romania. The Tsar tried to defuse the situation in February by promising to call a consultative assembly, and the August manifesto filled in some details of this consultative Duma.

But the revolution was developing a momentum of its own and could not be bought off so easily. Many peasants had fallen behind with their redemption payments, and the rumour that their land was going to be confiscated provoked widespread and serious disturbances in the countryside. Bourgeois liberals formed the Constitutional Democratic party (Kadet party) and in May, under Milyukov's leadership, they joined with other liberal *zemstva* groups in forming a 'Union of Unions' which demanded a constitution to limit the Tsar's power. By October, the country was in the grip of a general strike. Troops (even those which were reliable) could not be moved because the railway workers were on strike. Soviets (workers' councils) were set up in several cities, and Leon Trotsky (Menshevik) became chairman of the St Petersburg Soviet. The nation was paralysed, and the autocracy faced defiant opposition from everywhere, although it should be noted that few 'professional revolutionaries' played a part.

The October Manifesto and the Fundamental Law

Nicholas II had no choice but to give ground, and in October he appointed Witte chairman of the Council of Ministers. On his advice, the Tsar issued the October Manifesto which gave the Duma legislative authority (with the Tsar), and promised individual and trade union rights. This was sufficient to satisfy some of the liberals, and the Octobrist party of industrialists and land-owners accepted this constitution decreed from above. The peasant disturbances were defused by promising the reduction and eventual abolition of redemption payments. The hard liners in the St Petersburg Soviet declared a strike in November, and they were arrested, but the Moscow Soviet put up a struggle which lasted several days. Having made concessions to the liberals and bought off the peasantry, the regime isolated the urban extremists and repressed the proletariat.

From a combination of courage, stubborness and a sense of duty, tsarism seemed to have kept its nerve, and found sufficient loyal troops to regain control. On 23 April 1906 the Tsar issued the Fundamental Law, setting out his enormous powers (see extract A (ii)) and creating the State Council as an upper house to act as a brake on the Duma. To many this made a mockery of the Octo-ber Manifesto, but Nicholas II seems to have accepted that his autocracy was no longer 'unlimited' (see extract A (i)). Furthermore, although he interfered with elections to the Duma, he did not abolish it. Does this mean that from 1905 a constitutional monarchy existed in Russia?

STOLYPIN'S REFORMS AND THE DUMAS

The Dumas

The first Duma met in April 1906 and was immediately at dagger's drawn with Goremykin, chairman of the Council of Ministers (see extracts B (i–iii)). Witte had already been dismissed and was blamed by the Tsar for creating the problem. In June Nicholas II dissolved the Duma, but two hundred Kadet and SR deputies reassembled in Finland and urged Russians to oppose the govern-ment by refusing to pay taxes (the Vyborg Manifesto). Support for this stand was limited but violent, and Stolypin, the new chairman of the Council of Ministers, had them arrested and put on trial. As a result they were not eligible for re-election to the second Duma. These events confirmed that there were no more gains to be

made by the 1905 Revolution, but had it amended the autocratic system of government?

Stolypin combined ruthlessly efficient repres-sion with a worthwhile effort to reform (see Figure 20.1). To speed up the executions of trouble-makers he used field courts martial; between 1906 and his death in 1911 about 2,500 were hanged by 'Stolypin's necktie'. Naturally this policy compli-cated his relations with the second Duma which met in February 1907. Even the Octobrists were not tempted into cooperation by the offer of a place in the government. Yet Stolypin was clearly anx-ious to govern with the Duma's support, as McK-ean points out: 'He sought to reconcile educated opinion to the Government by co-operation with the Duma in the implementation of moderate improvements' (R.B. McKean, *The Russian Consti-tutional Monarchy, 1907–17*, London, Historical Association, 1977, p. 12).

Stolypin argued that the government's role needed to be a combined one, repressing disorder and addressing its causes through reform (see extract D (i)). His reform plans were not well received in the second Duma in 1907 partly

20.1 Peter Stolypin (1862–1911)
Source: David King Collection

because of the vigorous repression which had begun, and partly because the political groups were becoming polarised (see Table 20.1). The Kadet party had been halved, the extreme Right increased significantly, and the number of Menshevik deputies of the split Social Democratic party rose from eighteen in the first Duma to forty-seven in the second. In this atmosphere it was very difficult for Stolypin to attract support from the weakened centre, and a 'slanging match' developed between the government, cautiously supported by the Octobrists and some conservatives, and the Social Democrats (see extract D (ii)).

The second Duma was dissolved in June 1907 after it angered the Tsar by criticising the way the army was run. Why at this point did the Tsar not abolish the Duma altogether? There seem to have been several considerations which prompted him to call a third Duma. First, the October Manifesto and the existence of a Duma had impressed Russia's existing ally, France, and helped the new *entente* with Britain. Second, rather than abolishing the Duma altogether, it was more discrete to break

article 87 of the Fundamental Law (see extract A (ii)) by changing the franchise for elections to the third Duma. Third, Stolypin would probably be forced to resign if the Duma was abolished altogether, and he designed the new electoral laws for the third Duma so that his policies could proceed with the new Duma's support. This was done, excluding most of the peasantry and proletariat, reducing the representation of troublesome minorities such as the Poles, and packing the third Duma with representatives of the landowners and industrialists. When the third Duma met in November 1907 it was dominated by the Octobrists (154) and Rightist groups (147); it gave no more trouble for some years and lasted until June 1912.

Stolypin's steps to get a Duma which would cooperate with his reform measures was not simply a matter of window-dressing an autocratic regime with the display of representative government. Stolypin believed passionately that reform was needed if the regime was to survive at all. He had few supporters in the bureaucracy or among those who had Nicholas II's confidence, and he needed the support of the Duma to sustain him. But in the third Duma the Octobrists did not have a majority. The majority might have been made up partly from the Kadets, but they had an irreconcilable feud with the Octobrists and they had been severely damaged by Stolypin's prosecutions after the first Duma. Therefore Stolypin needed the support of the Rightists too; it was an uneasy partnership for which he paid a price. For several years things went smoothly and he upheld their interests as Russian nationalists and landowners against Poles, Finns, the Baltic nationalities and the Ukrainian peasantry. But in March 1911 Stolypin persuaded the Tsar, by threatening resignation, to grant the western nationalities separate representation in the *zemstva*, and the partnership with the Rightists was over. His high-handed use of article 87 offended the Octobrists and embarrassed the Tsar as well. His assassination later in 1911 occured before the break-up of his majority in the Duma became obvious.

While the role which Stolypin designed for the third Duma fell well short of the promise of the October Manifesto, it was a departure from the way the autocracy had worked before 1905. Pos-

Table 20.1 Political parties in the Dumas, 1906–17

Party/group	First Duma 1906	Second Duma 1907	Third Duma 1907–12	Fourth Duma 1912–17
SDs (Mensheviks)	18	47	—	—
SDs (Bolsheviks)	—	—	19	15
SRs	—	37	—	—
Trudoviks *	136	104	13	10
Kadets	182	91	54	53
Octobrists	17	42	154	95
Progressists **	427	28	28	41
Rightists ***	8	10	147	154
National parties	60	93	26	22
Others	—	50	—	42
Total	448	518	441	432

Notes:

　* The SRs as a party officially boycotted the elections to the first Duma, but stood as *Trudoviks* (labourists).

　** The Progressists were a party of businessmen who favoured moderate reform.

　*** The Rightists were not a single party; they represented a range of conservative views from right of centre to extreme reaction.

sibly it was a constitutional monarchy in the sense which the last Bourbon King of France, Charles X, would have recognised eighty years earlier. Neither Charles X nor Tsar Nicholas II were comfortable with the arrangement, but the final confrontation took longer to occur in Russia and awaited 1917.

Stolypin and reform

Peter Stolypin is usually regarded as the last great minister of tsarism. Energetic and personally courageous, he was a conservative who believed that reform was essential if tsarism was to live. Just two weeks after surviving a bomb attack on his house (which injured his children), Stolypin outlined a great programme of reform on 24 August 1906. He listed twelve of the most important areas which the government was addressing, including individual liberties, 'the improvement of peasant land tenure', *zemstva* reform and the expansion of *zemstva* to the Baltic region and Poland, reform of education and policing, and an income tax (which was seen as the fairest way of taxation).

Stolypin's period as chairman of the Council of Ministers (1906–11) was chiefly concerned with agrarian reform, the area which Witte had neglected in his drive to industrialise. Stolypin's aim went beyond boosting agricultural productivity, which was certainly needed to feed the population which grew from 125 million in 1897 to 166 million by 1913. He intended to create a class of small peasant farmers, who owned the land they worked and who would therefore have a vested interest in improving it. He hoped that such a class would employ less successful peasants as labourers, and develop their farms beyond subsistence levels and grow crops for market. A property-owning, conservative class would be created which Stolypin

expected would prove loyal to the regime and preserve political stability. This was the nature of Stolypin's 'wager on the strong' (see extract D (iii)).

In order to do this the emancipation settlement of the 1860s would have to be altered (see Chapter 14) and the grievances which provoked the widespread peasant disturbances in 1905 would have to be satisfied. By the Tsar's decree of 9 November, 1906 redemption payments were ended. The peasants were freed from their considerable debt to pay for the land given to the *mir* (the village commune), but most land farmed by the peasantry was still held in common and reallocated to peasant households from time to time by the *mir*. Other important reforms (some of which became law only in 1910 and 1911) ended what remained of the *mir*'s hold on the peasantry. After 1906, peasant households began withdrawing from the *mir* with land, either by unifying their allocated strips into a private holding, or by selling their strips to the new Peasant Land Bank and moving to the towns or purchasing new land (see Table 20.2). New land was available in remote areas, such as Siberia, and settlement there was encouraged.

Stolypin reckoned that twenty years would be needed for these changes to happen properly and give tsarism the political ballast of a conservative, landowning peasant class. The figures show that many peasant households did leave, but by 1915 the proportion who had left (2 million) of the total (10 million to 12 million) revealed the deep conservatism of the peasantry and the colossal and traditional hold exerted by the *mir*. Stolypin's reforms in this and other areas needed time, but it was time which he was denied. He was assassinated on 1 September 1911 by an SR and former police agent, and tsarism itself would survive for only another six years.

Table 20.2 The impact of land reform in Russia, 1907–14

Households (000s)	1907	1908	1909	1910	1911	1912	1913	1914
leaving *mir*	212	840	650	342	242	152	160	120
of whom set up own farms	48	508	580	342	145	122	135	98

Note: There were 10–12 million (est.) peasant households in total. 1907 figures are incomplete

What had he accomplished? Tsarism had recovered well from the 1905 Revolution thanks in part to the revival of the economy from 1908, and to the combination of efficient repression and moderate reform, but balancing the compromise was difficult and made Stolypin distrusted at both ends of the political spectrum. Agrarian reform moved slowly, as we have seen, and left untouched the under-used estates of the nobility. Lenin felt confident that 'Stolypin's "success" in the short term might at best bring about the isolation of a section of consciously anti-revolutionary Octobrist peasants as the majority of the peasantry turned against them.' (V.I. Lenin, *Polnoe Sobranie Sochinenii*, 5th edn, vol. 17, Moscow, 1961, p. 275, cited in M. McCauley, *Octobrists to Bolsheviks: Imperial Russia 1905–1917*, London, Arnold, 1984, p. 144). Eventually Land Captains were abolished and an accident and sickness insurance scheme for industrial workers was established, but these measures were modest and late. The Kadets, hardly revolutionaries, criticised Stolypin for his lack of progress (see extract E(ii)) while the Rightist were alienated by his concessions to the minorities, as we have seen. But perhaps the most telling evidence that Stolypin helped the recovery of tsarism is provided by the number of factors actually needed to destroy the regime after his death, including two and a half years of the First World War.

Unrest on the eve of war

After Stolypin's murder in 1911 government lost its sense of direction. Kokovtsov was chairman of the Council of Ministers until January 1914, but his feeble hold on affairs was undermined further by political in-fighting and because he had abandoned Stolypin's aim to keep the backing of the majority in the Duma. A fourth Duma was elected in November 1912, but the appointment of Goremykin in 1914 as chairman of the Council of Ministers led to open confrontation as he tried to roll back the rights which the Duma claimed to question ministers about their policies. Perhaps a real crisis was about to break as the signs grew that the Tsar wanted to make the Duma purely consultative, but the outbreak of war intervened.

War interrupted another growing confrontation between striking workers and the authorities.

Between 1911 and 1914 the number of strikes which the authorities identified as 'political' increased from 24 to 2,401, and as McKean points out, this was 'an expression of the political awakening of the working class and the latter's growing awareness of the inadequacy of its political rights' (McKean, *Constitutional Monarchy*, p. 23). The most serious incident occurred in 1912 when police arrested strike leaders at the Lena goldfields in Siberia and opened fire on the large number of miners who protested. The shock waves from this incident were felt in a succession of strikes which followed, and they were echoed in the Duma which warned the government that its policy 'threatens Russia with untold dangers' (1914 resolution cited in Lynch, *Reactions and Revolutions*, p. 54).

Marxist historians generally argue that the political and social unrest in the years just before the war amounted to a revolutionary upsurge. They draw particular attention to the Bolshevik inspired strike in St Petersburg in July 1914 which actually led to barricades being built in the streets. The strike was suppressed just days before the war broke out, fuelling the argument that war and the outbreak of patriotism actually postponed the Revolution. On the other hand some historians argue that the Russian economy was actually taking off between 1910 and 1914. The building industry was flourishing, good harvests and large exports of grain produced an inflow of gold, credit was easy to obtain and the iron industry struggled to keep pace with demand. The government revenue from all sources (e.g. taxes, railways, postal services) grew steadily from 2,526 million roubles in 1909 to 3,417 million roubles in 1913, and helped the government boost the economy further by orders for armaments (figures from Mosse, *Economic History*, p. 257). From this type of evidence it would seem that tsarism was more secure on the eve of war than it had been before Stolypin's period in office.

FOREIGN POLICY, 1894–1914

Russia's traditional interest in the Balkans was twofold. First, an exit from the warm waters of the Black Sea via the straits depended upon Russian influence in the Balkans and her leverage with the

Ottoman empire. Second, as 'Mother of the Slavs' and protector of the Orthodox Church, the tsarist state felt that its prestige would be damaged if either the Catholic Habsburg Empire or the Islamic Ottoman empire trampled on the rights of their minority peoples. By the time of Nicholas II's accession to the throne, these traditional interests had become matters of lively concern. Economic modernisation required trade, and trade needed to use the route through the Straits. Furthermore, Bismarck's Germany had supported Austria-Hungary in the Balkans at the Congress of Berlin in 1878, and over the Coburg candidate for the Bulgarian throne (1885–88), at the expense of Russia.

It was in response to this friendship between Berlin and Vienna that Alexander III had sought and obtained a treaty with France by 1894. Russia had protected herself, but eventually would pay the price for joining what became one of the two 'armed camps' which went to war in 1914.

The Russo-Japanese war, 1904–05

The alliance with France did not remove Russia's concerns about her trade route through the Straits. As we have seen, it was Witte who redirected Russian commercial ambitions towards the Far East where the Trans-Siberian railway promised to open up new markets and give access to an ice-free port. Russia's developing interests in Manchuria and Korea brought her into direct competition with Japan, and Richard Pipes notes:

Witte's plans for economic penetration of the Far East were conceived in the spirit of imperialism of the age: it called for a strong military presence, which was sooner or later to violate China's sovereignty and come in conflict with the imperial ambitions of Japan.

(R. Pipes, *The Russian Revolution 1899–1919*, London, Fontana, 1990, p. 13)

In February 1903 Nicholas II accepted the advice of his ministers (including Witte) and agreed to annex the Chinese province of Manchuria. Japan might have accepted this in return for Russian recognition of her dominance in Korea. However, Witte was dismissed, no deal was offered, and

Russian adventurers began exploiting Korea's timber resources. In response, on 8 February 1904, Japan attacked and besieged Port Arthur. The Tsar's government expected such an attack but felt entirely confident that it would serve to unite everyone in a patriotic cause which would quickly triumph against the puny Japanese. Minister of the Interior Plehve has often been saddled with the blame for this conflict (thanks probably to Witte's memoirs), but it is clear that Witte's commercial policy and the whole government were responsible for what followed.

Japanese forces took Port Arthur in January 1905, and news of this humiliation triggered the 'Bloody Sunday' demonstration in St Petersburg. Mukden, the key city in Manchuria, fell soon afterwards and Russia's incomplete Trans-Siberian railway proved unable to supply reinforcements. The final disgrace occurred at sea. In 1904 the Russian Baltic fleet set out for the Pacific, in such a state that they fired on British trawlers off the Dogger Bank, mistaking them for torpedo boats (Britain had an alliance with Japan). Arriving at the Straits of Tsushima in May 1905, the fleet was quickly annihilated by the Japanese. Torn by the mounting tide of revolution at home, the Russian government hastily signed the treaty of Portsmouth in September 1905 and conceded Korea and Port Arthur to Japan, and agreed to pull out of Manchuria.

The Anglo-Russian Entente

Russia paid a high price for blundering into an unnecessary war with Japan. Besides the impetus that defeat gave to the 1905 Revolution, it gravely weakened Russia's diplomatic standing because it demonstrated both weakness and incompetence. France became more reliant upon her *entente* with Britain, now that her Russian ally appeared so broken. This in turn drove Russia to settle her outstanding differences with Britain.

Britain, menaced by German naval development and antagonised by her diplomacy, was quite ready to do a deal with the ally of her ally, France. But Russia was negotiating from a weaker position, and she conceded Afghanistan as a British sphere of influence, as well as a portion of southern Persia.

Russia retained influence in northern Persia, but Tibet was declared neutral and the vague British promise to support Russia over the Straits amounted to nothing.

There was no military alliance involved between Britain and Russia in 1907, nor was the *entente* directed against Germany. However, from Berlin's point of view it appeared that the Triple Entente was encircling Germany, and this drove her into an ever-closer partnership with Austria-Hungary (see Chapter 21). Therefore the agreement between Britain and Russia finalised the basic diplomatic geography of the First World War (see Map 20.1).

Russia played her allotted part in the outbreak of war in 1914. The fuse was lit by the Bosnian crisis of 1908–09. This proved yet another humiliation for Russia in the Balkans when Austria-Hungary announced her annexation of Bosnia-Herzegovina, as agreed with Russia, but failed to support Russia's bid for full access through the Straits. Russian diplomacy therefore supported the protests of the small Balkan state of Serbia against Austria-Hungary, but backed down when Germany stood by Austria-Hungary.

The consequences were twofold. In 1912 Russia's agreement with France was extended to promise French support for Russia if she was confronted by Germany and Austria-Hungary over the defence of Serbia. Armed with this assurance, and quite unable to accept another humiliation in the Balkans, Russia stood by Serbia in the summer of 1914. Partial mobilisation (designed to confront Austria-Hungary alone) would leave Russia exposed to a German attack, so on 30 July 1914 Russia called the full mobilisation of her forces. The German response then needed to follow the dictates of the Schlieffen Plan, and the stage was set for the final phase of Nicholas II's reign.

SECTION B – SOURCES

THE IMPACT OF THE DUMAS AND STOLYPIN'S REFORMS

The 1905 Revolution amounted to a series of concessions by Tsar Nicholas II in the face of widespread disturbances. These disturbances had their roots in peasant land hunger, the appalling urban conditions of the working class, and liberal and *zemstva* demands for some representation in government. The outbreak was triggered by Russia's humiliation in the war against Japan (1904–05), and by the 'Bloody Sunday' massacre of peaceful protesters in January 1905.

Nicholas II was forced into reform by pressure from 'below'. In August 1905 a consultative Duma was promised. Unrest continued and the number of peasant disturbances grew frighteningly. Witte was called back as chairman of the Council of Ministers, and he pressed through the Manifesto of 17 October 1905 pledging individual liberties, elections to the Duma involving classes 'who are at present deprived of voting powers', and the 'unshakeable rule' that legislation required the Duma's approval (cited in McCauley, *Octobrists to Bolsheviks*, pp. 13–14). This satisfied the moderate elements, the peasantry were calmed by the promise to end redemption payments for their land, and the hard-liners like Trotsky in the St Petersburg Soviet were crushed.

In the breathing space between promise and reality, Nicholas II considered how far his autocratic powers had been eroded. The Fundamental Law of April 1906 on the face of it left the Tsar with overwhelming power, yet he had given up the claim to wield 'unlimited' power (see extracts A (i and ii)). The first Duma was hostile to what it saw as a tsarist betrayal of the October Manifesto, and clashed with Goremykin on most issues, including the question of sharing out land so that the peasants could farm more (extracts B (i–iii)). The Kadet party (Constitutional Democrats) were the dominant liberal group spearheading the clash, along with labourists (who were usually SRs, standing unofficially) who had their strongest support from the peasantry (see extract C and Table 20.1). The first Duma was dissolved in June 1906. Stolypin was appointed chairman of the Council of Ministers, immediately repressing trouble but claiming to want reform, a position which made him the object of suspicion to socialists, liberals and reactionaries alike (see extracts D (i) and E (i)).

The second Duma (February–June 1907) was more polarised between Left and Right and highly confrontational towards Stolypin (extract D (ii)). It was dissolved, and article 87 of the Fundamental

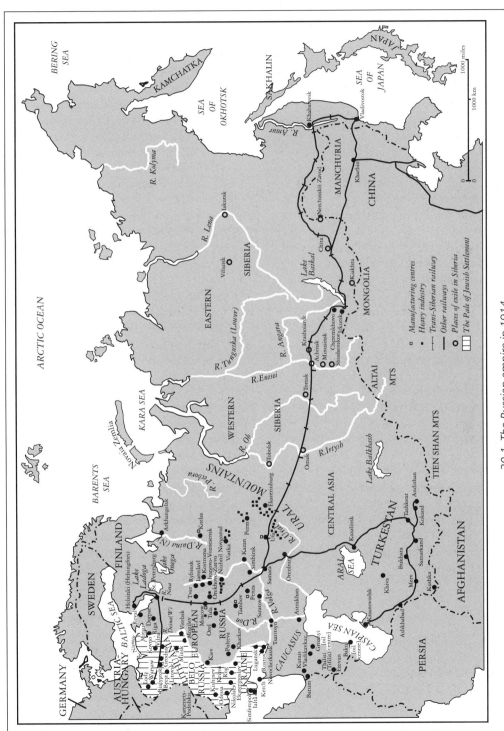

20.1 The Russian empire in 1914

Law (extract A (ii)) was misused to alter the franchise and obtain a more supportive third Duma (November 1907–June 1912). Stolypin's reform programme included agrarian reform allowing peasants to separate from the *mir* and farm their own land independently (extracts D (ii and iii)). His famous 'wager on the strong' was more than an economic gamble that agricultural productivity would increase; it was also an attempt to create a class of small landowning farmers who would provide bedrock loyalty to tsarism. But Stolypin was handicapped by widespread distrust, including that of the Tsar, and by his efforts to work through the Duma which left him dependent on the Octobrists and Rightists, a partnership which was breaking down before his assassination in September 1911. These are among the factors which may be considered when assessing Stolypin's reforms and the extent that this was a period of constitutional government.

A Autocratic power and the Fundamental State Laws of 1906

(i) From discussions between the Tsar and the Council of Ministers, 7–12 April 1906

The Tsar: All this time I have been troubled by the doubt whether I have the right, in the face of my ancestors, to alter the limits of the power I have received from them. . . .

. . . if I were convinced that Russia wanted me to abdicate my powers, I should gladly do so for the sake of its welfare. . . . I am firmly resolved to bring . . . [the Manifesto of 17 October 1905] to completion. But I am not convinced that it is necessary at the same time to abdicate my autocratic powers. . . .

Count Pahlen . . . since October 17, Your Majesty can no longer issue laws by yourself, without the legislative institutions. . . . The word 'unlimited' cannot remain in [article 4 of] the Fundamental Laws.

[on 12 April the Tsar dropped the word 'unlimited']

(ii) From the Fundamental State Laws, 23 April 1906

4 Supreme autocratic power belongs to the emperor of all Russia. . . .

7 The sovereign emperor exercises legislative authority jointly with the State Council and the State Duma.

8 The sovereign emperor possesses the initiative in all legislative matters. . . .

9 The sovereign emperor ratifies the laws, and no law can become valid without his ratification. . . .

87 While the Duma is not in session, if extraordinary circumstances demand a measure requiring legislative sanction, the Council of Ministers shall submit the matter directly to the emperor. Such a measure, however, may not introduce any changes into the Fundamental State Laws, the establishing acts of the State Council or the State Duma, or the laws governing elections.

(cited in G. Vernadsky (ed.) *A Sourcebook for Russian History from Early Times to 1917*, vol. 3, New Haven, CT, Yale University Press, 1972, pp. 771–72)

B The first Duma and the government clash, May 1906

(i) From the first Duma's reply to the Tsar, 5 May 1906

No pacification of the country is possible until . . . all ministers are made responsible before the people's representatives. . . .

. . . the State Duma, faithful to its duty clearly imposed upon it by the people, considers it immediately essential to provide the country with exact laws assuring inviolibility of the individual, freedom of conscience, freedom of speech and of the press, freedom of association. . . .

. . . The most numerous part of the country's population – the toiling peasantry – awaits impatiently the satisfaction of its acute land needs . . . by drawing for this purpose upon state lands . . . lands belonging to the tsar . . . church lands.

(ibid., pp. 776–77)

(ii) From the reply of Goremykin, chairman of the Council of Ministers, 13 May 1906

the solution of this question [of peasant land] on the basis proposed by the State Duma is absolutely inadmissable. The government cannot recognise the right of some people to ownership of land and at the same time deprive others of this right.

(ibid., p. 778)

(iii) From the Duma's reply, carried with only eleven votes against, 13 May 1906

by its refusal to satisfy the people's demands, the government reveals manifest contempt for the true interests of the people and obvious unwillingness to forestall new upheavals in our country. . . .

. . . [Affirms its] complete lack of confidence in the ministry, which is not responsible to the people's representatives.

(ibid., p. 778)

C From V.A. Maklakov's memoirs on the Kadets and the first Duma

(V. A. Maklakov was a member of the Central Committee of the Kadet party)

On the eve of the convocation of the [first] Duma, political leaders said openly that, for the inevitable conflict between the Duma and the monarch to have a successful outcome, it was necessary to provoke a conflict over the *land* question, which *alone* agitated the peasants. Thus the Kadet agrarian bill was inspired not by concern for the welfare of the peasants but by 'politics' . . . As always, the Kadets were straddling the fence: they both stirred up revolutionary sentiments and offered measures for their pacification.

It was absurd . . . to speak of acute land shortage. . . . Resettlement and internal colonisation of these lands should have been encouraged (instead) . . . of seizing the neighbouring landowners' holdings.

(from V.A. Maklakov, *Pervaia Gosudarstvennaia Duma*, Paris, 1939, cited in Vernadsky (ed.) *Sourcebook for Russian History from Early Times to 1917*, p. 781)

D Stolypin and the Dumas

(i) From the communiqué of the government under Stolypin, 24 August 1906

The government cannot, as some groups in society demand of it, call a halt to all reforms, call a halt to the entire life of the country, and direct the entire power of the state toward the struggle with sedition, concentrating on the symptoms of the evil without penetrating to its essence. Nor would the circumstances and the interests of Russia be served by . . . concentrat[ing] exclusively on . . . liberating reforms.

(cited in Vernadsky (ed.) *Sourcebook for Russian History from Early Times to 1917*, **p. 784**)

(ii) The second Duma attacks Stolypin's reform plans, 6 March 1907

Tsereteli [Social Democrat]: All . . . the efforts of the government . . . are but the last desperate attempts of the bureaucracy, with its serf-owning mentality, to halt a historical development . . . Tossing us a few scraps of reforms, long ago outdated by life and incapable of satisfying anyone, the government is attempting by means of unheard-of repressions to smother every sign of life in the country.

. . . As long as the organized force of the government is not opposed by the organised force of the people, the executive power . . . will not submit to the legislative power.

Stolypin [Chairman of the Council of Ministers]: . . . this is the government bench and not a prisoner's dock. . . . These attacks . . . can all be reduced to two words, addressed to those in authority: 'Hands up.' To these two words, gentlemen, the government . . . can answer very simply: 'You will not frighten us.'

(cited in ibid., pp. 786–87)

(iii) Stolypin's 'wager on the strong' speech to the third Duma, 5 December 1908

where the commune [*mir*] as a coercive union constitutes an obstacle to his (the peasant's) independent activity, there must be given the freedom to apply his labours to the land . . . he must be given control over the land, he must be saved from the slavery of the obsolescent communal system. . . . We must, when we write laws for the whole country, keep in mind the judicious and the strong, and not the drunken and the weak. . . . The government . . . by using the provisions of article 87 [of the Fundamental State Laws] in order to enact the law of November 9, 1906 . . . [ending redemption payments and freeing the peasant to take personal land ownership from the *mir*] placed its wager not on the poor and the drunken, but on the firm and the strong.

(cited in ibid., pp. 806–07)

E Contemporary appraisals of Stolypin

(i) Iswolsky's memoirs, 1920

(he was Minister of Foreign Affairs 1906–10, then ambassador to France until 1917.)

His exalted and chivalrous conception of duty made him a servant, devoted to the point of martydom, of his Sovereign and his country, but . . . jealous of his liberty that he ever maintained, toward a Court and a bureaucracy which regarded him in the light of an intruder and were more or less hostile to him from the beginning . . .

Curiously enough, this [agrarian] reform was opposed simultaneously by the two extremes, both Right and Left. The Socialists rejected it because of their communistic theories, and as for the reactionaries, they regarded it as an attack upon the sacrosanct traditions of the past and a step in the direction of the equalization of the classes . . .

Stolypin's agrarian reforms met with extraordinary success. . . . The Russian peasant . . . was not slow in going ahead . . . [with] the ownership of land which he farmed and finding means of acquiring additional land.

(A.P. Izvol'skii, *The Memoirs of Alexander Iswolsky*, London, 1920, cited in ibid., pp. 791–92)

(ii) Izgoev (a leading Kadet) compares Stolypin's promises 1906–07 with his achievements by 1911

1 The granting to the peasantry of state, crown and cabinet lands
   Up to 1 January 1911, only 281,000 desyatinas out of more than 9 million had been sold to the peasantry.
2 'A series of bills . . . [for] unrestricted worship, the building of churches . . .
   Nothing has been accomplished. Most of the bills got bogged down in the State Council, and will meet their death there . . .
3 Personal inviolability . . .
   Administrative arbitrariness rules right across Russia . . .
15 The office of land captain is to be abolished.
   They thankfully exist. . . .
32 Insurance of workers in case of sickness, disability . . .

In reality, nothing was achieved under Stolypin.
42 Income tax.
   Stuck in the Financial Commission of the Duma, from where it is unlikely to emerge.
(A.S. Izgoev, *p. A. Stolypin: ocherk zhizni i deyatelnosti*, Moscow, 1912, pp. 117–23, cited in M. McCauley, *Octobrists to Bolsheviks: Imperial Russia 1905–1917*, London, Arnold, 1984, pp. 51–52)

F From R. Pipes on the constitutional experiment

Nicholas did not regard either the October Manifesto or the new Fundamental Laws as affecting his autocratic prerogatives. In his mind, the Duma was a consultative, not a legislative body. He further felt that in having 'granted' the Duma and the Fundamental Laws of his own free will he was not bound by them: and since he had not sworn an oath to uphold the new order, he could also revoke it at will. The obvious contradiction between the reality of a constitutional regime and the Court's insistence that nothing had changed had bewildering consequences. Thus, even Peter Stolypin, the closest Russia had to a genuine parliamentary Prime Minister, in private conversation insisted that Russia had no constitution because such a document had to be the product of agreement between rulers and subjects whereas the Fundamental Laws of 1906 had been granted by the Tsar.

(R. Pipes, *The Russian Revolution 1899–1919*, London, Fontana, 1992, p. 154)

Questions

1 What light is shed by the discussion in extract A (i) on the terms of the Fundamental State Laws in extract A (ii)?
2 Evaluate Maklakov's explanation (extract C) of the clash between the first Duma and the government shown in extracts B (i–iii).
3 Explain the significance of these phrases in their contexts:
   (a) 'the symptoms of the evil without penetrating to its essence' (extract D (i))
   (b) 'to halt a historical development' (extract D(ii))

(c) 'he must be saved from the slavery of the obsolescent communal system' (extract D(iii))

(d) 'the reality of a constitutional regime' (extract F).

4 How useful are extracts D (i–iii) and Table 20.1 showing political parties in the Dumas, 1906–17 on p. 330 for explaining Stolypin's policies and his relations with the second and third Dumas?

5 Evaluate the accuracy of the two appraisals of the difficulties Stolypin faced, and his achievements, in extracts E (i and ii). Use your own knowledge and any relevant extracts in your answer.

6 Use extract F and the other extracts to assess the significance of the Dumas. Should the term 'constitutional monarchy' be applied to the period opened by the Fundamental Laws in 1906, as McKean does? (R.B. McKean, *The Russian Constitutional Monarchy, 1907–17*, London, Historical Association, 1977, p. 9)

Further reading

There are several clear and concise studies of the last years of tsarism. Alan Wood, *The Origins of the Russian Revolution 1861–1917* (London, Methuen, 1987) is helpful partly because it begins the story earlier than many works. M. Lynch, *Reaction and Revolutions: Russia 1881–1924* (London, Hodder and Stoughton, 1992) chooses a helpful period and covers it systematically, with documentary excerpts. There are many more detailed academic texts. H. Rogger, *Russia in the Age of Modernisation and Revolution* (London, Longman, 1985) is thoroughly detailed, W.E. Mosse, *An Economic History of Russia 1856–1914* (London, I.B. Tauris, 1996) is helpful on the reforms of Witte and Stolypin, and R.B. McKean, *The Russian Constitutional Monarchy* (London, Historical Association, 1977) is a pamphlet focusing on the importance of the Dumas. H. Seton-Watson, *The Russian Empire 1801–1917* (Oxford University Press, 1988) is a detailed and immense text, while R. Pipes, *The Russian Revolution 1899–1919* (London, Fontana, 1992) probably provides the most authoritative recent study. Much briefer and very readable is M. Ferro's biography of *Nicholas II* (London, Penguin, 1992).

Documentary collections include M. McCauley, *Octobrists to Bolsheviks: Imperial Russia 1905–1917* (London, Arnold, 1984), but finding reasonably extensive translated collections on the period before the First World War is problematic; the best is G. Vernadsky (ed.) *A Sourcebook for Russian History from Early Times to 1917*, vol. 3 (New Haven, CT, Yale University Press, 1972). M. Lynch's book (listed above) contains some source material.

• CHAPTER TWENTY-ONE •

International Relations 1890–1914 and the Origins of the First World War

• CONTENTS •

KEY DATES

1890	March	Lapse of Reinsurance Treaty
1891	July	French naval squadron visits Kronstadt
1892	August	Secret military convention between Russia and France; First version of Schlieffen Plan devised
1893	Oct.	Russian naval squadron visits Toulon
1894	Jan.	Franco-Russian alliance signed
1898	March	First German Naval Law
1899	May–July	First Hague Peace Conference
	Oct.	Outbreak of Boer war
1900	June	Second German Naval Law
1902	Jan.	Anglo-Japanese alliance signed
1903		Murder of King Alexander of Serbia
1904	Apr.	Anglo-French *entente*; colonial agreements signed between Britain and France
1905	Feb.–June	First Moroccan crisis
	Dec.	Anglo-French military and naval talks begin
1906	Jan.–Apr.	Algeciras Conference on Morocco; Britain supports France
1907	June	Second Hague Peace Conference
	July	Triple Alliance renewed for six years
	Aug.	Anglo-Russian Convention signed; Triple Entente in place
1908	Oct.	Austrian annexation of Bosnia-Herzegovina announced; German support for Austria
1911	July–Nov.	Second Moroccan Crisis arising out of Agadir incident
	Sept.	Italy declares war on Turkey and invades Tripoli
1912	Feb.	Unsuccessful visit of Haldane mission to Germany to halt naval race
	Apr.	Italian fleet bombards forts off Dardanelles
	Sept.	Balkan League formed by Serbia, Greece, Montenegro and Bulgaria v. Turkey
	Oct.	Outbreak of first Balkan war; Italy makes peace with Turkey
	Dec.	Armistice between Turkey, Bulgaria, Serbia and Montenegro
	8 Dec.	War Council in Berlin
1913	Jan.	Increased military budget accepted by German Reichstag
	May.	Treaty of London ends first Balkan war; Albania created
	June	Bulgaria declares war on Serbia, Montenegro and Greece Turkey and Romania join in against Bulgaria
	Aug.	French army law increases period of conscription from two to three years
	Oct.	Treaty of Bucharest; Serbia gains Macedonia
	Nov.	Liman von Sanders appointed to command of Constantinople District
1914	May	Secret naval talks between Britain and Russia
	28 June	Assassination of Archduke Franz Ferdinand at Sarajevo

For subsequent events see Table of Events on p. 350.

SECTION A

THE BACKGROUND TO 1914

Between 1871 and 1914 Europe experienced an almost unparelleled forty years of peace, while at the same time preparing for war on an unprecedented scale. This is the central paradox which has to be explained in considering international relations between 1871 and 1914. Why, if war was averted for so long, did it erupt with such violence and on such a huge scale, when it finally came? A second and related problem is to explain why the resources of diplomacy, which had successfully resolved crises in 1878, 1905, 1908, 1911, 1912 and 1913 failed in 1914. Finally, was it the case that 'Among the rulers and statesmen who alone could give the final word which caused great armies to spring from the ground and march to and fro across frontiers one can now clearly see that none of them wanted war' (Lloyd George,

War Memoirs, vol. 1, London, Ivor Nicholson and Watson, 1934, p. 55)? Or did war break out in 1914 because policy makers in Germany and Austria in particular were resolved that it should? Section A considers the first two of these problems. The question of responsibility for the outbreak of war is reserved for Section B.

Two armed camps

One obvious explanation for the scale of the First World War is the network of alliances and *ententes* which had been negotiated prior to 1914. Reference has already been made to them in different contexts, but it is worth recapitulating their terms. First in time was the Dual Alliance between Germany and Austria, signed in October 1879, which committed each country to come to the other's assistance should either be attacked by Russia. It is important to note that there was not the same obligation should Germany or Austria be the aggressor. In practice there was a delay of six days between the German declaration of war on Russia on 1 August 1914, and the Austrian declaration of war on Russia on 6 August. The Dual Alliance became the Triple Alliance in May 1882, when Italy joined Austria and Germany. Italy would be supported by both Germany and Austria should she be attacked by France, and would support Germany should she in her turn be attacked by France. Again, this was a defensive alliance and would not operate should either Germany or Austria be the aggressor.

In response to both these alliances and the German failure to renew the Reinsurance Treaty in 1890 France and Russia joined hands in January 1894 when the Franco-Russian alliance was finally signed. Serious negotiations between the military staffs of both countries had begun in 1890 when General Boisdeffre visited Russia. In July 1891 a French naval squadron visited Kronstadt and in 1892 a secret convention was agreed by the military authorities on both sides providing for Russian military support should France be attacked by Germany. In October 1893 a Russian squadron paid a return visit to Toulon, and in January 1894 the treaty of alliance was finally signed. It was specifically directed against Germany. The two armed camps were now in place. In 1892 the Russian General Obruchev who did much to bring about the Franco-Russian alliance, commented presciently in a Memorandum dated 7 May: 'In the face of the readiness of entire armed peoples to go to war no other sort of war can be envisaged than that of the most decisive sort – a war that would determine long into the future the relative position of the European powers, especially Russian and Germany' (cited in George Kennan, *The Fatal Alliance: France, Russia and the Coming of the First World War*, Manchester University Press, 1984, p. 255).

Britain up to this point had been left in the cold, and before 1900 had more cause to quarrel with Russia and France than with Germany or Austria. Britain clashed with France in North Africa, Newfoundland and South East Asia. She had rivalries with Russia in Tibet, Afghanistan and Persia. Among the consequences of Germany's naval building programme and inept diplomacy, as we have seen, was the passage of Britain into the Franco-Russian camp. In 1904 Britain mended her colonial fences with France in the form of the Anglo-French *entente* and she did the same with Russia in 1907. Thus the so-called Triple Entente was created. In neither case did the agreements have the status, or the obligations, of an alliance. Where France was concerned, however, the *entente* was consolidated by a series of military and naval conversations which went on from 1905 to 1912. In 1911 the Committee of Imperial Defence, following the Agadir crisis, agreed to send a British Expeditionary Force of six divisions to France in the event of war with Germany. In 1912 the French agreed to concentrate their battleships in the Mediterranean, so allowing the British to concentrate their heavy forces in the North Sea to counter the German High Seas fleet. Grey, British Foreign Secretary at the time, stated categorically that 'The disposition, for instance, of the French and British fleets respectively at the present moment is not based upon an engagement to cooperate in war' (Sir Edward Grey, *Twenty Five Years*, London, Hodder and Stoughton, 1925, vol. 1, pp. 97–98). In the minds of the French, however, there was now a moral obligation to do so. Relations with Russia continued to be acrimonious at times, particularly over Persia, and though discussions were held in May 1914 on naval cooperation, they did not get very far.

Thus there was a dangerous uncertainty about Britain's likely response in the event of a war involving France and Russia. In February 1914 the Russian Foreign Minister, Sazonoff, wrote to the Russia ambassador in London, Benckendorff: 'One must recognize that the peace of the world will only be assured when the Triple Entente, whose real existence is no more proved than that of the sea serpent, is transformed into a defensive alliance' (D.W. Spring, 'Russia and the coming of war', in R. Evans and H.P. von Strandmann (eds), *The Coming of the First World War*, Oxford, Clarendon Press, 1988, p. 65). It never was transformed into an alliance. The British Prime Minister, Asquith, could even write to his young female confidante, Venetia Stanley, on 24 July 1914, when war between Germany and Austria against Russia and France, was already looming: 'Happily there seems to be no reason why we should be anything more than spectators' (H.H. Asquith, *Letters to Venetia Stanley*, ed. M. and E. Brock, Oxford University Press, 1984, p. 123).

To sum up, by 1914 Germany, Austria and Italy were linked by defensive alliances which would operate automatically only if one of the powers concerned was attacked by either France or Russia. France and Russia were similarly linked. Britain had entered into friendly relations with France and Russia, and had informal naval and military agreements with France.

More significant than the formal alliances were the military preparations that flowed from them. In any future war it was assumed that Germany and Austria and probably Italy would be ranged against Russia, France and possibly Britain. It was upon these suppositions that the war plans of all the major powers were based. Of these, much the most important was the Schlieffen Plan, devised by Count Alfred von Schlieffen, Chief of the German General Staff from 1891 until 1906. The Franco-Russian alliance of 1894 made the prospect of a war on two fronts a virtual certainty, should it ever break out. Schlieffen's solution was to take advantage of the slowness to mobilise and the inefficiency of the Russian army and concentrate on defeating each of Germany's enemies in turn: 'The whole of Germany must throw itself upon one enemy, the strongest, most powerful, most dangerous enemy, and that can only be France' (B. Tuchman, *August 1914*, London, Papermac, 1980, p. 31). Schlieffen calculated that Paris would have to be captured within six weeks of the outbreak of war. Germany could then move the bulk of her armies eastward to meet the Russian threat. To achieve such a quick result, Schlieffen envisaged a huge enveloping movement. Having captured Liège, German armies would sweep through the flat Flanders countryside and would surround Paris from the south and the west (see Map 21.1). The plan went through numerous versions between 1894 and 1914, but retained its essential features. Moltke, who succeeded Schlieffen in 1906, removed two army corps from the right wing in order to strengthen the German defences in Alsace-Lorraine, and in order to ensure Dutch neutrality, planned to channel all his armies through Belgium rather than Holland. Even in its revised form the Schlieffen Plan had two disastrous consequences. It imposed a straitjacket on German diplomacy in that it required any attack on Russia to be preceded by an attack on France; and it necessarily entailed the invasion of Belgium, whose neutrality had been guaranteed by all the powers that had signed the treaty of London in 1839, including Britain.

Though a version of the Schlieffen Plan found its way into French hands in 1904, it was not taken very seriously, and was suspected of being a feint. French military thinking was dominated by the will to recapture Alsace-Lorraine and a belief in offensive tactics. Plan 17, adopted in 1913, postulated two major offensives, one to the south of Metz, one to the north.

Aware of French vulnerability, Russia was persuaded to accelerate her mobilisation and to reduce the pressure on France by launching an offensive in East Prussia. The French government lent huge sums to Russia to improve the railway system in her western provinces. In 1911 General Dubail, Chief of the French War Ministry staff, visited Russia and gained a promise that Russian troops would invade East Prussia within fifteen days of mobilisation. Austria had two war plans, one (Plan B (Balkans)) allowed for a main offensive against Serbia with only nine corps devoted to war against Russia; the other (Plan R), provided for thirteen

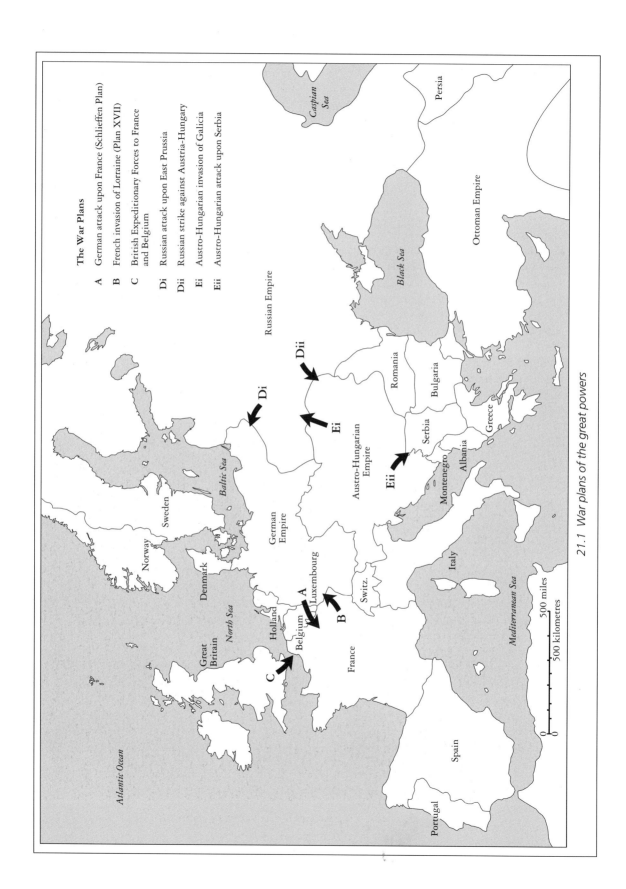

The War Plans

A German attack upon France (Schlieffen Plan)

B French invasion of Lorraine (Plan XVII)

C British Expeditionary Forces to France and Belgium

Di Russian attack upon East Prussia

Dii Russian strike against Austria-Hungary

Ei Austro-Hungarian invasion of Galicia

Eii Austro-Hungarian attack upon Serbia

21.1 War plans of the great powers

corps to be allocated to the Russian front, while remaining on the defensive against Serbia. According to the British plans made in 1911, six divisions were to be deployed on the north end of the French line to defend the Channel ports. Huge armies were needed to excute these war plans. Defence spending and the size of armies both expanded significantly between 1910 and 1914 as the figures in Table 21.1 illustrate.

In 1912 and 1913 German armies were increased significantly to reach a total strength on mobilisation of 2,398,000. Of these 700,000 were earmarked to invade Belgium. The Russian army by 1914 had reached a peacetime strength of 1.4 million, which would be raised to 3.1 million after mobilisation. The French army law of 1913, passed in response to the increases in the German army, extended the length of compulsory military service from two to three years, and raised the fighting strength of French armies on mobilisation to over 3 million (see Figures 21.1 and 21.2).

Table 21.1 Defence estimates of the Great Powers, 1900–14

	1900	*1910*	*1914*
Germany	41	64	110.8
Austria-Hungary	13.6	17.4	36.4
France	42.4	52.4	57.4
Great Britain	116*	68.0	76.8
Italy	14.6	24.4	28.2
Russia	40.8	63.4	88.2

Note: *This figure is accounted for by the Boer war

Military pundits in all European countries drew lessons from the German wars of unification (1866, 1870–71), which had lasted for six weeks in the case of Austria and six months in the case of France, rather than from the American Civil War of 1861 to 1865, which had lasted for four years and resulted in the deaths of 600,000 Americans. Most European generals believed that war on the

21.1 German reservists on their way to the western front, August 1914

Source: Bildarchiv Preussicher Kulturbesitz, Berlin

21.2 Mobilisation of the French army, Paris, August 1914: some 4 million men were affected

Source: ©BBC Hulton Picture Library

scale envisaged could not be sustained for more than a matter of months, and that victory would go to the side which deployed its forces most rapidly and could get its blow in first. Thus every country's war plan was based on an offensive strategy: Germany was to invade Belgium, France was to invade Alsace-Lorraine, Austria was to invade Serbia or Galicia, Russia was to invade East Prussia, all in the expectation of quick victories. These assumptions had disastrous consequences. They made governments readier to contemplate all out war in the expectation that it would be brief. When the crisis came in 1914 they gave a powerful bargaining chip to those military commanders who argued for a rapid resort to force before the resources of diplomacy had been fully exhausted:

These military machines constituted a reality, an irresistible force, and a determining one. The excite-ments of public policy and journalism were only froth, visible on the surface, of those deeply powerful currents that military thinking engendered and upon which the nations were carried, unaware and unsuspecting, to the tragedies of 1914–18.

(Kennan, *Fatal Alliance*, p. 248).

Public opinion and war

Among the visual clichés that accompany any television programme on the First World War are certain to be newsreel shots of cheering crowds greeting the outbreak of war, whether in Berlin, London, Paris or St Petersburg. Every national parliament voted the sums needed to prosecute the war within a matter of weeks. Where conscription was already in force reservists obediently mustered at their assembly points and marched or entrained to their respective battlefronts. Among French reservists, where a 10 per cent desertion rate had been anticipated, it was no more than 2 per cent. In Britain, Kitchener's famous appeal, *Join your Country's Army*, met with an overwhelming response. From such evidence it has been inferred that war, when it came, was universally popular. The assessment of public opinion is notoriously difficult, and in the absence of any scientifically designed polls, the historian has to rely on the comments of individuals and the evidence of what actually happened. While it is clear that national goverments could rely on the support of their citizens in going to war in 1914, the motives of those who went to fight remain in many cases inscrutable.

Every country had its fire eaters. In Germany men like General Friedrich von Bernhardi urged 'the most warlike preparations' for the war he predicted was bound to come (*Germany and the Next War*, London, Arnold, pp. 287–88), published in Germany in 1912. In Britain *The Army and Navy Gazette* called for the German navy to be 'Copenhagen-ed' (i.e. destroyed as the Danish one had been by Nelson in 1801). In France a militant right-wing party welcomed the prospect of war with Germany because it would provide an opportunity to recover Alsace-Lorraine.

At a wider level, patriotism as an ideal made a particular appeal to the youth of most countries, and was sedulously fostered by schools and youth movements such as the Boy Scouts. In Prussia the educational system was specifically charged with the duty of inculcating loyalty, and was warned of the injustice to the state if 'an unpatriotic generation were reared' (P.M. Kennedy, *The Rise of the Anglo-German Antagonism*, London, Fontana, 1989, p. 376). A French history textbook, republished and revised in 1912, included this extract: 'War is not probable, but it is possible. It is for this reason that France remains armed and always ready to defend itself. . . . In defending France we are defending the land where we were born, the most beautiful and the most bountiful country in the world' (cited in J. Joll, *The Origins of the First World War*, London, Longman, 1992, p. 220). Organisations such as the German Navy League and its British equivalent, the Navy League, encouraged an interest in the armed services. Victories such

as Trafalgar, Waterloo and Leipzig were commonly celebrated. It is probably true to say that patriotism was more consciously felt and articulated in upper and middle class circles than among industrial workers and peasants. It is something of a surprise to discover that the eminent psychologist Sigmund Freud wrote in 1914: 'For the first time in thirty years I feel myself to be an Austrian and feel like giving this not very hopeful empire a chance' and that the philosopher Wittgenstein offered his services as an artillery officer to the Austrian army (R.W.J. Evans, 'The Habsburg empire and the coming of war', in *The Coming of the First World War*, pp. 50–51). It is certainly the case that university students and graduates were among the occupational groups to suffer the worst casualties. Manual workers were just as likely to volunteer, but in their cases the discomfort and drudgery of their present employment in mines and factories provided an additional incentive. Whatever the reasons, as Michael Howard has put it,

The vast majority were willing to do what their governments expected of them. Nationalistically oriented public education; military service which, however unwelcome and tedious, bred a sense of cohesion and national identity; continuing habits of social deference; all this helps explain at a deeper level than does the strident propaganda of the popular press, why the population of Europe responded so readily to the call when it came

(M. Howard, 'Europe on the eve of the First World War', in *The Coming of the First World War*, p. 15).

In the face of such pressures, anti-war sentiment proved powerless. Two international conferences did meet at The Hague with the aim of promoting disarmament and providing a mechanism for the peaceful resolution of disputes. The first, summoned on the initiative of Nicholas II in 1899, did succeed in setting up an International Court of Justice at The Hague. Recourse to the court was entirely voluntary and it had heard only fourteen cases by 1914. It made no progress towards disarmament. The Kaiser declared: 'I'll go along with the conference comedy but I'll keep my dagger at my side during the waltz', while the British War Office was equally unenthusiastic: 'It is not desirable to agree to any restrictions upon the employment of further developments in destructive agencies. . . . It is not desirable to assent to an international code on the laws and customs of war' (see Joll, *Origins of the First World War*, p. 202). The second conference, sponsored by the American President Theodore Roosevelt in 1907, achieved even less. Norman Angell's book, *The Great Illusion* (published in 1910) argued cogently that war would bring no gains to any aggressor and that war would bring economic disaster to victor and vanquished alike. It was translated into twenty languages, but though it sold well in Britain it made little impact elsewhere. The efforts of the Second International to preserve working class solidarity against an imperialist war, as we have seen, demonstrably failed in 1914. When European governments mobilised their armies their peoples flocked with remarkably little fuss to their appointed places, ignorant of what lay in store but astonishingly ready to endure it.

THE BALKAN TANGLE

Great power rivalries alone might have precipitated a European war at any time between 1904 and 1914. There had been serious international crises in 1905, 1908 and 1911. It was in the Balkan peninsula that the First World War began, however, and this in itself demands some explanation (see Map 21.2). It was an inherently unstable area where Christianity met Islam. The battle of Kossovo in 1389 where the Turks defeated the last Tsar of Serbia was still commemorated in 1914. In 1529 and again in 1683 Turkish armies had reached the gates of Vienna. The urge to rid Europe of its Turkish occupiers was a continuous and continuing force in Balkan history. In the nineteenth century nationalism added a new dimension to the conflict. It took two forms. It acted as a spur to the existing Balkan states, Serbia, Bulgaria, Montenegro, Romania and Greece to add to their existing territories; and nationalism formed a bond, Pan-Slavism, between Russia and those Balkan states already linked by language and the Greek Orthodox religion. Nationalism also posed a threat to the Austrian empire. It was a Serb Foreign Minister who remarked: 'Ah yes, if the

disintegration of Austria-Hungary could take place at the same time as the liquidation of Turkey, the solution would be greatly simplified (Taylor, *Struggle for Mastery in Europe*, p. 485). If the Serbs were to have their way against the Turks, what was there to prevent the Bosnians, the Czechs, the Poles, the Croats and the Slovenes from demanding independence from the Austrians?

The problem became more acute in 1903. The palace coup, in which the King of Serbia, Alexander Obvenovic, his wife, her two brothers and the Minister for War were all assassinated, replaced Alexander with Peter Karadjordjovic. He was much more sympathetic to Russia than he was to Austria and there ensued a long period of friction with Vienna culminating in the crisis caused by Austrian annexation of Bosnia in 1908 (see Chapter 19).

In September 1911 events in the Mediterranean helped to precipitate war in the Balkans. The Italian government, seeking to win colonies to which the growing Italian population might emigrate, invaded Turkish Tripolitania in North Africa. In April and June 1912 naval attacks were launched on the forts protecting the Dardanelles. The straits were closed for two weeks, badly damaging Russian grain exports. Italy also occupied islands in the Aegean, including Rhodes. A treaty was signed in October 1912, confirming Italy's claim to Tripolitania. The Italian example was not lost on the Balkan states. In March 1912 Serbia and Bulgaria signed a defensive alliance, and were soon joined by Greece and Montenegro. Russia gave its approval to this new Balkan League, which seized the opportunity of the Turkish war with Italy to declare war itself, also in October 1912. Within a month nearly all of Turkey's remaining European territory had been captured. The great powers held aloof from the fighting, and in the last example of constructive diplomacy before 1914 held an Ambassadors' Conference in London at which peace terms were negotiated. The treaty of London, signed in May 1913, shared out the territory conquered among the victors, but at Austria's insistence Serbia was deprived of the stretch of Adriatic coastline she had acquired. This now became the new state of Albania.

Within a matter of days, the victors fell out over the division of the spoils. In June 1913 Bulgaria

N

BOSNIA
(Annexed to
Austria 1908)

Sarajevo ●

Belgrade ●

S
E
R
B
I
A

Nish ●

R O M A N I A

Pruth

Bucharest ●

Danube

DOBRUJA

Varna ●

B U L G A R I A

MONTENEGRO

Cetinje ●

Scutari ●

Durazzo ●

ALBANIA
(Indep. 1913)

Kumanovo ●

Monastir ●

M A C E D O N I A

Florina ●

Janinà ●

EPIRUS

G
R
E
E
C
E

Sofia ●

Kavalla ●

Salonica ●

Adrianople ●
Kirk ●
Kilisse
Lule Burgas ●

T H R A C E

Dedeagach ●

Enos ●

Midia ●

Charalja
Lines

Constantinople ●

Imbros

Lemnos

Mitylene

Chios

Athens ●

Samos

Dodecanese
(Ital. occup.)

Crete

Acquired from Turkey by:

Serbia

Greece

Bulgaria

Montenegro

To Romania from Bulgaria

0   100   200   300 km

21.2 The Balkans, 1912–13

attacked Serbia and Greece. Romania and Turkey seized the opportunity to attack Bulgaria, and by October the second Balkan war was over. Under the treaty of Bucharest which ended it, Serbia gained part of Macedonia, Turkey recovered Adrianople and Romania made gains in the Dobruja. One final episode in the Balkans threatened the peace in 1913. Germany, which had been helping to train the Turkish army since 1882 dispatched another military mission in 1913 after the disastrous Turkish performance in the first Balkan war. It was headed by General Liman von Sanders. William II remarked tactlessly that he hoped that 'the German flag will soon fly over the fortifications of the Bosphorus', and stressed that the mission's first priority was 'the Germanisation of the Turkish army through [German] leadership and direct control of the organisational activity of the Turkish ministry of war' (D.C.B. Lieven, *Russia and the Origins of the First World War*, London, Macmillan, 1983, p. 46). Von Sanders was made commander of the Turkish garrison overlooking the Dardanelles. Russia, already sensitive to what had happened in the Italian–Turkish war, insisted on his removal. Sazonoff, the Russian Foreign Minister, commented at the time to a German journalist : 'You know what interests we have in the Bosphorus, how sensitive we are at that point. All southern Russia depends upon it, and now you stick a Prussian garrison under our noses!' (V.R. Berghahn, *Germany and the Approach of War in 1914*, London, Macmillan, p. 154). Von Sanders was 'promoted' to the post of Inspector General, which took him away from Constantinople, but Russian suspicions of German ambitions in the Balkans were aroused.

Though the Balkan wars ended without involving the major powers they left two damaging legacies. First, Serbia's successes served only to whet her ambitions to acquire Bosnia-Herzegovina, while increasing Austria's apprehension. From 1913 onwards General Conrad, Chief of the Austrian General Staff, began calling for a preventive war against Serbia. Second, the worsening international climate provoked Germany into contemplating a preventive war against France and Russia. On 8 December 1912 a War Council took place in Berlin, attended by William II, Moltke and Tirpitz, among others. Though no official record has survived of this Council, Admiral

Muller, who was also there, recorded that Moltke pressed for war, and 'the sooner the better' (see Section B, extracts A (i–iii)).

An American observer, Colonel House, who was a private emissary of the US President, Woodrow Wilson, reported on 29 May, 1914: 'The situation is extraordinary. It is militarism run staring mad, and unless someone acting for you can bring about a different understanding there is some day to be an awful cataclysm' (L.C.F. Turner, *The Origins of the First World War*, London, Arnold, 1979, p. 69). On the other hand in a speech delivered at the Guildhall on 9 July, Lloyd George said 'In the matter of external affairs the sky has never been more perfectly blue'. The assassination of Franz Ferdinand on 28 June 1914 would show who was the better prophet.

COUNTDOWN TO CATASTROPHE

Table of events, Sunday 28 June to Thursday 6 August 1914

Sunday 28 June	Assassination of Archduke Franz Ferdinand and his wife at Sarajevo by Gabriel Princip
Sunday 5 July	Hoyos mission to Berlin; 'blank cheque' offer of support to Austria
Tuesday 7 July	Austrian Ministerial Council meets
Wednesday 8 July	Ultimatum to Serbia prepared
Thursday 16 July	Poincaré and Viviani leave for St Petersburg
Sunday 19 July	Austrian Ministerial Council approves text of ultimatum to Serbia.
Tuesday 21 July	Franz Josef approves text of ultimatum; text sent to Berlin
Thursday 23 July	Ultimatum sent to Serbia. Poincaré and Viviani leave St Petersburg
Friday 24 July	France, Britain and Russia informed of ultimatum;

	Grey suggests mediation; Russian Council of Ministers requests partial mobilisation
Saturday 25 July	Russia introduces 'Period Preparatory to War'; Grey suggests extending time limit of ultimatum; conciliatory Serbian reply received
Sunday 26 July	Grey proposes Four Power Conference (Germany, Britain, Italy and France) to mediate
Monday 27 July	Bethman Hollweg rejects Four Power Conference
Tuesday 28 July	Austria declares war on Serbia; Belgrade shelled; Russia orders mobilisation of four western military districts
Wednesday 29 July	Germany informed of partial Russian mobilisation; Bethmann Hollweg urges Britain to remain neutral; Moltke demands mobilisation; Tsar orders general mobilisation, but rescinds the order later that evening after letter from William II
Thursday 30 July	Austria agrees to negotiate with Russia but refuses to suspend operations v. Serbia; Tsar finally agrees to full mobilisation
Friday 31 July	Russian mobilisation begins; William II declares state of 'imminent war'; ultimatum to Russia
Saturday 1 August	Germany declares war on Russia at 5.00 p.m.
Sunday 2 August	Germany occupies Luxemburg; German ultimatum to Belgium
Monday 3 August	Germany declares war on France; Britain decides to support Belgium
Tuesday 4 August	German troops invade Belgium; 11.00 a.m. British ultimatum to Germany; 11.00 p.m. British declaration of war on Germany
Thursday 6 August	Austrian declaration of war on Russia

On the afternoon of Sunday 28 June Archduke Franz Ferdinand, heir to the Austro-Hungarian empire, and his wife were assassinated in the streets of Sarajevo. The Archduke was on a ceremonial visit to the city in the course of inspecting imperial troops based in Bosnia. He had chosen an unfortunate day for his visit, the anniversary of the battle of Kossovo, Serbia's national day, equivalent, A.J.P. Taylor comments, to a visit by British royalty to Dublin on St Patrick's Day at the height of the Troubles in 1920. He might expect to be shot at (Taylor, *Struggle for Mastery in Europe*, p. 520). News of the visit had been announced in March, and extreme nationalist groups in Serbia had plenty of time to plan attacks on the Archduke. The successful assassin was Gabriel Princip, a 20-year-old student who had been turned down by the Serbian army because he was too small. He was one of seven known conspirators in Sarajevo that day. The royal party had already survived an earlier bomb attack in the morning and it was on a visit to a member of his entourage, injured in that attack, that the Archduke encountered Princip. The royal car took a wrong turning and presented Princip with an easy target. How far the Serbian government was implicated has never been fully established. Certainly the head of Serbian military intelligence, Colonel Dimitrijevic, who was also head of the terrorist organisation the Black Hand was behind various assassination plots even if Princip acted on his own initiative. It has also been suggested that the Serbian Prime Minister, Pasic, was aware of the plots, and while disapproving of them did nothing to prevent them.

While the assassination sent a shock wave through the capitals of Europe, it had no immediate impact on international relations. As we have seen, two royal heads and several eminent politicians had been the victims of anarchist attacks between 1890 and 1901 without this affecting the European balance of power. Everything depended in this case on how first Austria and then the other European powers reacted. There are two mysteries to be explained so far as timing is concerned. There was a delay of nearly four weeks between the assassination and delivery of the Austrian ultimatum to Serbia, which did not arrive until 23 July. On the other hand there was a mere twelve days between the arrival of the ultimatum and the involvement of all the major powers, Germany, Russia, France, Britain and Austria in a European war. The delayed Austrian response to the assassination can be explained in various ways. Austria needed first to be sure of German support, which she gained on 5 July. The dispatch of the ultimatum to Serbia was deliberately held up until the departure of the French President, Poincaré and his Prime Minister, Viviani, from St Petersburg on 23 July. Finally, there was what R.W.J. Evans has called 'the labyrinthine working of the Austro-Hungarian state apparatus' ('The Habsburg monarchy and the coming of war', in *The Coming of the First World War*, p. 39). The rapidity with which the Austro-Serb conflict escalated into a general war is to be explained partly by the war plans already discussed, but also by the actions of the politicians and their military advisers in the critical days that followed the Austrian ultimatum.

The first important step in the crisis was the dispatch of Count Hoyos, a leading figure in the Austrian foreign ministry to Berlin on 5 July. Here he saw both the Kaiser and Bethmann Hollweg. He obtained what has been described as a 'blank cheque' offer of support, and possibly private encouragement to crush Serbia (see extracts C(i and ii)). When the Austrian Ministerial Council met under the chairmanship of the Austrian Foreign Minister, Count Berchtold, on 7 July opinions were initially divided. Berchtold argued for an immediate settling of accounts with Serbia but Count Tisza, Premier of Hungary, argued that Serbia should first be presented with a list of demands that should be stiff, but not impossible to meet. Tisza's view met with little support, but it was finally agreed to adopt the procedure Tisza suggested, while making the terms so harsh as to make their rejection certain (Berghahn, *Germany and the Approach of the First World War*, pp. 204–05). After much delay the text of the ultimatum was finally produced on 19 July; it was then submitted to the Emperor Francis Joseph on 21 July when it was also sent to Berlin, and finally

delivered to Serbia on 23 July. A mere forty-eight hours was permitted for the Serbian reply.

There can be little doubt that the text of the ultimatum served the Austrian purpose. Grey described it as 'the most formidable document I have ever seen addressed by one state to another' (Z. Steiner, *Britain and the Origins of the First World War*, London, Macmillan, 1977, p. 53). Sazonoff, the Russian Foreign Minister, remarked 'C'est la guerre européenne' when he saw it. The German General Staff worked out the terms of the ultimatum to be delivered to Belgium in accordance with the Schlieffen Plan even before the Serbian reply had been received, while the Austrian ambassador to Belgrade left his post as soon as it reached him. There was no intention to compromise even though the Serbs had accepted all but two of the Austrian demands. On 28 July, three days after receiving the Serbian reply, Austria declared war on Serbia and shelled Belgrade.

All now hinged on the Russian and German responses to Austria's actions. Russia had introduced the Period Preparatory to War on 25 July. As soon as war was declared on Serbia the mobilisation of the four western districts was ordered. On 29 July the Tsar was persuaded to order general mobilisation, but on receipt of a conciliatory telegram from William II he rescinded the order the same evening. However, on 30 July he was finally persuaded by the Foreign Secretary that the risk of delaying general mobilisation could not be accepted (see extracts E(i–iii)). Orders for general mobilisation on 31 July were duly authorised. Moltke, who had agreed to delay German mobilisation so that the blame could be laid at Russia's door, now had the excuse he needed. An ultimatum was sent to Russia on 1 August demanding that Russian mobilisation should cease. When no reply was received Germany declared war on Russia at 5.00 p.m. the same day. How much encouragement the French government gave to Russia to support Serbia is not altogether clear. French politicians were literally and metaphorically at sea when the Austrian ultimatum to Serbia was delivered on 23 July, Poincaré and Viviani having left St Petersburg that day. The French ambassador to Russia, Maurice Paléologue, went beyond his instructions in promising unconditional support to Russia, and a telegram sent on 30 July from Paris urged that 'Russia should not immediately proceed to any measures which might offer Germany a pretext for a total or partial mobilisation of her forces' (J. Keiger, *France and the Origins of the First World War*, London, Macmillan, 1983, p. 160). But all French officers were recalled from leave as early as 26 July and the instructions to French troops on 31 July not to approach any closer than 10 kilometres from the German frontier were designed to reassure Britain that if war came it would not be of France's making, rather than to appease Germany.

In the event the requirements of the Schlieffen Plan took over. On 2 August Luxemburg was occupied and an ultimatum sent to Belgium demanding the unopposed passage of German troops. On 3 August Germany declared war on France on the false pretext that French planes had bombed Nuremberg. The British cabinet up to that point had been bitterly divided on whether to meet the unofficial commitments made to France since 1905. The cabinet had been struggling with a crisis in Northern Ireland when the Archduke was assassinated and it was only when the Austrian ultimatum was delivered on 23 July that its attention was turned to the Balkans. On 27 July five cabinet ministers threatened to resign when Grey voiced the possibility of military intervention. It was the invasion of Belgium that turned the scales. On 3 August the cabinet resolved to come to Belgium's assistance should she be invaded. When German troops crossed into Belgium in the early hours of 4 August Britain delivered a formal ultimatum requiring their immediate withdrawal. German refusal to comply led to a British declaration of war on Germany at 11.00 p.m. that night. On 6 August Austria completed the circle by declaring war on Russia. According to Tirpitz's Memoirs, Moltke remarked to him: 'If Austria had shied away we would have needed to search for peace at any price' (A. von Tirpitz, *Erinnerungen*, Leipzig, 1919, cited in H.P. von Strandmann, 'Germany and the coming of the First World War', in *The Coming of War*, p. 116). It was a revealing comment.

Of the statesmen who headed their respective countries in 1914, Bethmann Hollweg in Germany, Berchtold in Austria, Sazonoff in Russia, Poincaré in France and Asquith in Britain, it is probably true to say that none of them wanted war, yet each when it came to it felt it was the only option open to them. Aided and abetted by their military advisers each believed in the possibility of a rapid victory. With the exception of Austria, whose parliament had been suspended, every parliament supported its government's decision to go to war. The British Labour party as well as the German Social Democrats gave their official backing to the war. In a wave of patriotic euphoria, men responded to the call to arms all over Europe as compulsory military service was implemented. In Britain, the only major country where conscription did not apply, recruiting offices were overwhelmed by the numbers of volunteers for whom they had neither weapons nor uniforms. While the immediate responsibility for the war must rest with the politicians who declared it (see Section B), in the longer term the war was a culmination of deep-seated trends in European history. The growing force of nationalism, provoked at least in part by the French Revolution, had helped to produce a united Italy and a united Germany, upsetting the existing balance of power. Nationalism lay at the root of the many crises in the Balkan peninsula and Austria's paranoid fear of Serbia.

In the last quarter of the nineteenth century nationalism took on a more aggressive guise in the form of imperialism, leading to growing tensions between the major powers. Germany and France clashed over rival claims in North Africa, while the Anglo-German naval building race reflected a wider rivalry for economic dominance.

In the conduct of international affairs there was a growing readiness to reach for the sword, as indicated in the sequence of wars between 1900 and 1914: the Boer war, 1899–1902; the Russo-Japanese war, 1904–05; the Italo-Turkish war, 1911–12; the Balkan wars, 1912–13. Threats of war had been uttered during the Bosnian annexation crisis in 1908 and after the Agadir incident in 1911. The German War Council in 1912 actively contemplated war. The question of Germany's immediate responsibility for the outbreak of war in 1914 is considered in Section B. Whatever conclusion is reached there, seen in a longer perspective responsibility must surely rest not only with those who acted in 1914 but with some of their predecessors as well, and with a climate of opinion in which the claims of the nation-state took precedence over all other loyalties.

SECTION B – SOURCES

RESPONSIBILITY FOR THE OUTBREAK OF WAR

The debate over who was to blame for the First World War has continued unabated since its outbreak. Three broad phases of interpretation can be discerned. At the outset, perhaps not surprisingly, blame was laid at the door of the defeated. This was made very clear in article 231 of the treaty of Versailles which blamed the war on 'the aggression of Germany and her allies'. When the German delegation protested at this charge the Allied powers went further:

The terrible responsibility which lies at her [Germany's] door can be seen in the fact that not less than seven million dead lie buried in Europe, while more than twenty million others carry upon themselves the evidence of wounds and sufferings because Germany saw fit to gratify her lust by resort to war.
(Allied response to German counter proposals, 16 June 1919, printed in A. Luckau, *The German Delegation at the Paris Peace Conference*, New York, Columbia University Press, 1941, p. 415)

Not surprisingly the German Foreign Office did its best to refute this charge. Forty-two volumes of documents were published in Germany between 1922 and 1927 with this end in view. Most German historians placed the blame for the war on Serbia for the assassination of the archduke and upon Russia for coming to Serbia's assistance. The most they would admit to was a misguided belief on the Kaiser's part that the Tsar would never bring himself to support a government guilty of regicide.

In British circles there was a reaction against the vindictiveness of the treaty of Versailles, first represented by J.M. Keynes's *The Economic Consequences*

of the Peace (first published in 1919) which led to a more sympathetic interpretation of German policy in 1914. In his *War Memoirs* (published in 1934) Lloyd George identified no villains: 'the nations in 1914 slithered over the brink into the cauldron of war without any trace of apprehension or dismay', a verdict that was supported by R.H. Lutz, who wrote in 1930: 'All the powers in 1914 put their own interests, true or supposed, and their own ambitions before the peace of the world. . . . No belligerent except Britain was blameless and none the sole culprit' (cited in M.C. Morgan, *Foreign Affairs, 1886–1914*, London, Collins, 1973, p. 121).

This interpretation tended to hold sway until well after the Second World War. A committee of French and German historians concluded in 1952 that 'the documents do not permit attributing to any government or nation a premeditated desire for European war in 1914' (cited in R. Henig, *The Origins of the First World War*, London, Routledge, 1993, p. 43). However, in 1961 Friz Fischer, professor of History at Hamburg at the time, published the first of two ground-breaking books which reasserted Germany's particular responsibility for the war. In the first, *Griff nach der Weltmacht* (Bid for World Power) published in Germany in 1961 and in its English edition under the title *Germany's Aims in the First World War* (London, Chatto and Windus) in 1967, Fischer argued that Germany's annexionist ambitions led Germany to provoke a war in order to realise them. This claim he sustained in a second book, *Krieg der Illusionen: die deutsche Politik von 1911 bis 1914* (*War of Illusions: German Policy between 1911 and 1914*), published in Germany in 1969 and translated into English (London, Chatto and Windus) in 1975. Based upon extensive archival research, especially in the files of the foreign and war ministries, his second book was quite unequivocal in its conclusions. Not only did he state that 'Historians are in 1969 in general agreement that in the summer of 1914 the German empire risked a preventive war'. He argued that after the assassination of Franz Ferdinand 'the German government was determined in early July 1914 onwards to use this favourable opportunity for a war against France and Russia' (F. Fischer, *War of Illusions*, pp. 461, 480). Since then the argument has not gone entirely Fischer's way.

His German critics, notably Gerhard Ritter, have argued that German aims in 1914 were essentially defensive and that what Bethmann Hollweg hoped for was at best a diplomatic victory which would split the *entente* and at worst a localised war in the Balkans (for a fuller discussion of these views see F. McDonough, *The Origins of the First and Second World Wars*, Cambridge University Press, 1997). In 1984 George Kennan, an American foreign policy expert published a book entitled *The Fateful Alliance: France, Russia and the Coming of the First World War* (Manchester University Press). As its name suggests, the book traces responsibility for the war back to the Franco-Russian alliance and more specifically to the Russian decision to mobilise in 1914. The following extracts have been selected to examine the strength of the Fischer case that Germany bears the main responsibility for the outbreak of war.

The first three extracts relate to the War Council held on 8 December 1912 in Berlin. The meeting was convened, according to Bethman Hollweg, because the German ambassador in London, Prince Lichknowsky, having met the British War Minister, Haldane, reported that England would stand by France should she be attacked by Germany. Other reasons may have been the planning of a new army bill and the dangers raised by the first Balkan war. Those in attendance included Tirpitz, Moltke and Admiral Muller, whose diary provides a record of the meeting. The Chancellor, Bethmann Hollweg, was not there and his reactions are also recorded.

A War Council in Berlin, 8 December 1912

(i) Admiral von Muller's account of the War Council, 8 December 1912

The Chief of the Great General Staff (Moltke) says: war the sooner the better, but he does not draw the logical conclusions from this which is to present Russia or France or both with an ultimatum which would unleash war with right on our side. . . . The result was pretty well zero.

(F. Fischer, *War of Illusions: German Policy between 1911 and 1914*, London, Chatto and Windus, 1975, p. 162)

(ii) A report dated 12 December by the Saxon military attaché, Leuckart, on information given to him by the Prussian ministry of war

His Excellency von Moltke wants war because he believes that at the moment it would not be convenient to France as is shown by the advocacy of a peaceful solution. Admiral von Tirpitz, on the other hand, would prefer it to come in a year's time when the Canal [the Kiel Canal] and the submarine harbour in Heligoland will be ready.

(ibid., p. 163)

(iii) Bethmann Hollweg's comments on the War Council

Bethmann denounced the impromptu meeting as an impetuous creation of fear. 'Haldane's communication to Lichknowsky was not nearly that serious. It only affirmed what we have long known: now as before England follows a policy of balance of power and therefore will stand up for France if the latter is in danger of being annihilated by us. . . . Demanding that England throws herself around his neck, despite his policy H.M. has gotten terribly excited about this and immediately held a war council with his stalwarts of army and navy behind my and Kiderlen's back, ordered the preparation of army and navy increase and broadcast the Haldane conversation over the whole world. . . . Britain wants no continental war because it would be drawn into it and does not want to fight. In that light its obligations toward France have their positive side. But we must not conduct a nervous jumping-jack policy; otherwise the others' patience will run out one day.

(K.H. Jarausch, *The Enigmatic Chancellor, Bethmann Hollweg and the Hubris of Imperial Germany*, New Haven, CT, Yale University Press, 1973, pp. 134–35

B Jagow records his impressions of Moltke's thinking, May 1914

Moltke continued to be worried by the prospects facing Germany in the face of French and Russian rearmament. In May 1914 he expressed his fears to Jagow, the German Foreign Secretary at the time.

The prospects of the future seriously worried him [Moltke]. Russia will have completed her armaments in 2 or 3 years. The military superiority of our enemies would be so great then that he did not know how we might cope with them. Now we would still be more or less a match for them. In his view there was no alternative to waging a preventive war in order to defeat the enemy as long as we could still more or less pass the test. The chief of the General Staff left it at my discretion to gear our policy to an early unleashing of a war.

(V.R. Berghahn, *Germany and the Approach of War*, 2nd edn, Macmillan, 1993, pp. 181–82)

C Support for Austria

Much has been made of the unconditional support given to Austria at the meetings at Berlin between Hoyos, the Austrian minister, the Kaiser and Bethmann Hollweg on 5 July 1914. Bethmann Hollweg also saw the Austrian ambassador Szogyeni on 6 July. The nature of that support can be gleaned from the following two extracts.

(i) Bethmann Hollweg's dispatch to Tschirschky, German ambassador at Vienna, 6 July 1914

Finally, as far as concerns Serbia, His Majesty, of course, cannot interfere in the dispute now going on between Austria-Hungary and that country, as it is not a matter within his competence. The Emperor Francis Joseph may, however, rest assured that His Majesty will, [under all circumstances], faithfully stand by Austria-Hungary, as is required by the obligation of his alliance and ancient friendship.

(The phrase 'under all circumstances' in the original draft, the work of Zimmerman, acting foreign secretary, was omitted in the final version by Bethmann Hollweg.)

(L.L. Snyder, *Documents of German History*, New Brunswick, NJ, Rutgers University Press, pp. 310–11)

(ii) Szogyeni reports on his interview with Bethmann Hollweg on 6 July

Although he had always advised us to get along with Serbia, after the recent events he understood this was well nigh impossible. In the course of further conversation I realized that the chancellor, like his imperial master, considers our immediate intervention against Serbia the most radical and best solution of our difficulties in the Balkans.

(K.H. Jarausch, *Enigmatic Chancellor*, p. 156)

D Reactions to the Serbian reply to the Austrian ultimatum

While Germany promised full support to Austria in the early stages of the crisis there is some evidence to suggest that as the prospect of Russian intervention became more likely, Germany wanted to restrain rather than encourage Austria. The two following extracts indicate the responses first of the Kaiser and then of Bethmann Hollweg to the conciliatory Serbian reply to the Austrian ultimatum.

(i) The Kaiser's comments on seeing the Serbian reply on 28 June

A brilliant performance for a time limit of only forty-eight hours. This is more than one could have expected! A great moral victory for Vienna; but with it every reason for war drops away, and Giesl [the Austrian ambassador to Serbia] might have remained quietly in Belgrade. On the strength of this I should never have ordered mobilisation.

(I. Geiss, *July 1914*, London, Batsford, 1967, pp. 222–23)

(ii) Telegram from Bethmann Hollweg to Tschirschky, 28 July 1914

The reply of the Serbian government to the Austrian ultimatum, which has now been received makes it clear that Serbia has agreed to the Austrian demands to so great an extent that, in case of a completely uncompromising attitude on the part of the Austrian government, it will become necessary to reckon upon the gradual defection from its cause of public opinion throughout all Europe ... if it [the Imperial government] continues to maintain its previous aloofness in the face of such proposals [of mediation], it will incur the odium of having been responsible for a world war, even, finally among the German people themselves. A successful war cannot be commenced and carried on on any such basis. It is imperative that the responsibility for the eventual extension of the war among those nations not immediately concerned should, under all circumstances, fall on Russia. . . .

You will have to avoid very carefully giving the impression that we wish to hold Austria back. The case is solely one of finding a way to realize Austria's desired aim, that of cutting the vital cord of Greater-Serbia propaganda, without at the same time bringing on a world war, and if the latter cannot be avoided in the end, of improving the conditions under which we shall have to wage it, in so far as is possible.

(Snyder, *Documents of German History*, pp. 330–31)

E Russian mobilisation

There can be little doubt that once it looked as though Russia was prepared to back Serbia, the aim of German policy was to persuade Russia to mobilise first, thus throwing the blame for a war now seen as inevitable on Russia. On 28 July Bethmann Hollweg saw Sudekum, the right wing leader of the Social Democrats whose support would be vital. He advised the Kaiser that 'In all events Russia must ruthlessly be put in the wrong' (Berghahn, *Germany and the Approach of War*, p. 216). The Russian decision to mobilise was thus no surprise to Germany. Extracts E (i–iii) and F illustrate the reasons for Russian policy and the German response to it.

(i) Conclusions reached at the Ministerial Council at St Petersburg on 24 July 1914

Goremykin [Chairman of the Council of Ministers] summed up by saying 'that it was the Imperial Government's duty to decide definitely in favour of Serbia'; that firmness rather than conciliation was likely to secure peace; but that if it failed to do so 'Russia should be ready to make the sacrifices required of her'. The Council resolved that Vienna should be asked to extend her time limit; that Belgrade should be urged 'to show a desire for conciliation and to fulfil the Austrian Government's requirements in so far as they did not jeopardize the independence of the Serbian state', and that the defence ministers should request Imperial permission, if events should require it, of the mobilisation of the Odessa, Kiev, Kazan and Moscow Military Districts.'

(Lieven, *Russia and the Origins of the First World War*, London, Macmillan, 1983, p. 144)

(ii) Memorandum of the day of the Russian ministry for foreign affairs, St Petersburg, 29 July 1914

The Russian decision to proceed with full mobil-isation, made on 29 July when the Tsar gave his initial consent, is explained in the following extract:

His Majesty gave permission to S.D. Sazonoff to discuss the question of our mobilisation at once with the Minister for War and the Chief of our General Staff. At this moment [the afternoon of 29 July] news was received of the commencement of the bombardment of Belgrade by the Austrians . . . .

After examining the situation from all points, both the Ministers and the Chief of the General Staff decided that in view of the small probability of avoiding a war with Germany it was indispensable to prepare for it in every way in good time, and that therefore the risk could not be accepted of delaying a general mobilisation later by effecting a partial mobilisation now. The conclusion arrived at at this conference was at once reported by telephone to the Czar, who authorised the taking of steps accordingly.

(Geiss, *July 1914*, pp. 297–98)

(iii) Memorandum of the Day of the Russian ministry for foreign affairs, St Petersburg, 30 July 1914

Though the Tsar rescinded his order that evening, on the following day the Russian military authorities, Adjutant-General Sukhomlinov and General Yanushkevich telephoned the Tsar to persuade him to 'revert to his decision of yesterday to permit a general mobilisation. His Majesty decidely refused to do so, and finally declared that the conversation was at an end.' When Sazonoff saw him in the afternoon, however, Nicholas reluctantly agreed to return to general mobilisation. Sazonoff's arguments were as follows:

During the course of nearly an hour the Minister attempted to show that war was becoming inevitable as it was clear to everybody that Germany had decided to bring about a collision, as otherwise she would not have rejected all the pacificatory proposals that had been made and could easily have brought her ally to reason. Under these circumstances it only remained to do everything that was necessary to meet war fully armed and under the most favourable circumstances. Therefore it was better to put away our fears that our warlike preparations would bring about a war, and to continue these preparations carefully rather than by reason of such fears to be taken unawares by war.

(ibid., p. 311)

F Admiral Muller comments on the mood in Berlin, 1 August 1914

The morning papers reprint the speeches made by the Kaiser and the Reich Chancellor to an enthusiastic crowd in front of the Schloss and the Chancellor's Palace. Brilliant mood. The government has succeeded very well in making us appear as the attacked.

(Berghahn, *Germany and the Approach of War*, p. 217)

Questions

1 From your reading of extracts A(i–iii), how serious were Moltke and Tirpitz in advocating a preventive war in 1912?

2 What can you infer from the same extracts about who was responsible for German foreign policy at this time?

3 From the evidence of extracts A and B discuss the argument that German foreign policy up to 1914 was motivated more by fear than ambition.

4 Compare extracts C (i) and C (ii) as evidence of Germany's attitude to the Austrian-Serb question after the assassination of Franz Ferdinand.

5 How did the Kaiser and Bethmann Hollweg differ in their response to the news of the Serbian reply to the Austrian ultimatum (extracts D (i and ii)) and how do you account for their differences?

6 From the evidence of extracts D, E(i–iii) and F what responsibility would you attach to Russia for provoking the First World War?

7 Using all these extracts and your wider knowledge, comment on the Fischer argument that the German government was determined 'early in July to use this favourable opportunity for a war against France and Russia'.

Further reading

There is an enormous literature on the origins of the First World War. Two useful introductions are pamphlets by F.R. Bridge, *The Coming of the First World War* (London, Historical Association, 1983) and by R. Henig, *The Origins of the First World War* (Lancaster University, 2nd edn, London, Routledge, 1993) which has a useful summary of the debate on the origins. Two good overall surveys are provided by J. Joll, *The Origins of the First World War* (London, Longman, 1984) and by L.C.F. Turner, *The Origins of the First World War* (London, Arnold, 1970). F. McDonough, *The Origins of the First and Second World Wars* (Cambridge University Press, 1997) has an admirable summary of current interpretations. The diplomatic background to the whole period after 1871 is covered exhaustively, if sometimes perversely, by A.J.P. Taylor, *The Struggle for Mastery in Europe* (Oxford University Press, 1984). A collection of essays, R.W.J. Evans and H. Pogge von Strandmann (eds)*The Coming of the First World War*, (Oxford University Press, 1991) provides an invaluable study of the 1914 crisis on a country-by-country basis. This approach has also been followed in a series of books, all published by Macmillan, which now cover all the major powers involved. They are V.R. Berghahn, *Germany and the Approach of War* (2nd edn London, 1993); J. Keiger, *France and the First World War* (London, 1983); D.C.B. Lieven, *Russia and the Origins of the First World War* (London, 1983); S. Williamson, *Austria-Hungary and the Origins of the First World War* (London, 1991) and Z.S. Steiner, *Britain and the Origins of the First World War* (London, 1977). There are valuable collections of documents in I. Geiss, *July 1914* (London, Batsford, 1967) and in L.L. Snyder, *Documents of German History* (New Brunswick, NJ, Rutgers University Press, 1958). The Fischer thesis is best studied in his own writings, *Germany's Aims in the First World War* (London, Chatto and Windus, 1967) and *War of Illusions: German Policy from 1911 to 1914* (London, Chatto and Windus, 1975). Valuable commentaries on Fischer are to be found in essays by James Retallack and Holger H. Herwig in G. Martel (ed.) *Modern Germany Reconsidered*, (London, Routledge, 1992) and in H.W. Koch (ed.) *The Origins of the First World War: Great Power Rivalry and German War Aims* (London, Routledge, 1984).

On war plans see P.M. Kennedy (ed.) *The War Plans of the Great Powers 1880–1914* (London, Allen and Unwin, 1979), G. Ritter, *The Schlieffen Plan: Critique of a Myth* (London, Oswald Wolff, 1958) and B. Tuchman, *August 1914* (London, Macmillan, 1980).

• CHAPTER TWENTY-TWO •

Europe in 1914: Retrospect and Prospect

• CONTENTS •

EUROPEAN STATES AND EMPIRES

The dimensions of Europe in 1914 did not differ significantly from those of 1780. There had been a retreat of Turkish power from the Balkans where the independent states of Greece, Romania, Bulgaria, Serbia, Montenegro and Albania had emerged. The Russian empire had extended westwards to include much of Poland. But in other respects Europe's boundaries were much as they had been before the French Revolution. The really significant changes had occurred in terms of population and industrialisation. If Russia is included as a European state, then Europe's population amounted to 423 million in 1900, nearly four times what it had been in 1780. More significant than this share, however, was the degree of economic dominance exercised by Europe, which in the nineteenth century had become the powerhouse of the world. In 1900 Europe accounted for 62 per cent of world manufacturing output. European empires dominated the rest of the world. By 1900 the whole of Africa had been partitioned between the European powers with the exception of two small states: Liberia, founded in 1822 to provide a refuge for liberated slaves from the USA, and Abyssinia, which successfully resisted an Italian attempt to colonise it in 1896 only to succumb to Italian conquest in 1935.

A similar position prevailed in the Far East. Most Pacific islands had been acquired by European powers or the United States by 1900. The Dutch ruled Indonesia, the French Indo-China, the British Malaya and Singapore. China was divided up into different spheres of influence, and when a nationalist movement, the Boxer rebellion, challenged European interference in 1900 a joint European expedition forced its way to Peking (Beijing) to relieve the legations besieged there. Britain, France, Portugal, Holland and Germany all had substantial overseas empires which they would retain or divide among themselves, until the end of the Second World War. Thus in 1900 the world was dominated by Europe, and Europe's concerns.

By 1900 the long established states of Britain, France, Spain and Portugal had been joined by Italy in 1861 and by Germany in 1871. In all these states the overwhelming majority of their citizens spoke a common language, and were united by a common culture. Regional loyalties still persisted, however, and in some cases were so strongly felt that integration into the mother country was fiercely resisted; this was the case with Catholic Ireland's opposition to British rule and Basque opposition to Spain. Imperial Germany included Danes, Poles and Frenchmen whose loyalties lay elsewhere. But such minorities did not generally threaten the unity of the states concerned, and their boundaries, if not fixed for ever, were subject only to minor adjustments.

It was very different with the multinational empires of Austria-Hungary, Russia and Turkey. Austria, as we have seen, was made up of the lands inherited by the house of Habsburg, headed in 1914 by the Emperor Francis Joseph. It included present-day Austria, Czechia, Slovakia, Hungary and parts of Poland, Slovenia, Serbia, Bosnia, Romania and Italy. Since 1867 the empire had been divided into two parts, Austria and Hungary, each with its own parliament, but sharing a common emperor, a common foreign ministry and a common army. Each of the racial minorities within the empire jostled for influence and a greater degree of self-rule, if not yet full independence. The task of keeping this empire together had been the main task facing all Austria's rulers, and the most important consideration in the making of both foreign and domestic policy.

Russia, too, contained racial minorities both in the west and the east. In the west the Russian empire had included since 1815, present-day Finland, the Baltic states of Latvia, Lithuania and Estonia and much of Poland. In the south and east Russia included the Ukraine, Siberia and a whole range of remote Muslim dominated provinces such as Turkestan, Azerbaijan and Khazakstan. Here, too, the need to keep this mixed empire together had been a major concern and a lasting problem.

The long retreat of Turkish power in Europe was marked by the loss of Greece in 1830, Serbia and much of Bulgaria in 1878, the cession to Austria of the provinces of Bosnia and Herzegovina also in 1878 and the losses following the first and second Balkan wars in 1912–13. Turkish power was further weakened by the loss of Algeria to France in 1830 and of Egypt to Britain in 1882. This still left the Turks in control of much of the Middle East, including the Arabian peninsula and present-day Syria, Lebanon, Israel, Jordan and Iraq. But Arab nationalism, barely noticeable in 1900, was to become a significant force in the First World War, and the Ottoman empire suffered from the same disruptive forces as those which plagued Austria and Russia.

FORMS OF GOVERNMENT

With the exception of Switzerland and France all the states of Europe were still headed by monarchies. 'The cousinhood of kings' was still a reality, and most European dynasties were related to each other, if only by marriage. How powerful these families were varied from state to state. In Britain the reigning monarch's powers rested on precedent. In an often quoted book on the English constitution, written by Walter Bagehot, editor of *The Economist* at the time, and published in 1867, the monarch was credited with 'the right to be consulted, the right to encourage, the right to warn'. In practice Edward VII (1901–10) and George V (1910–36) accepted the advice given by their ministers and performed what was essentially a ceremonial role. Their technical right to appoint the Prime Minister could occasionally be significant, as it was in 1922 and 1931 when there was no obvious candidate.

In Germany William II (1887–1918) had the exclusive right to nominate his ministers, who were not answerable to the Reichstag, and was commander of all the armed forces in time of war. This gave him considerable powers, when he chose to exercise them. Francis Joseph (1848–1917) enjoyed similar powers in Austria, and because he had been in power so long had the benefit of experience to buttress his authority.

In Russia Nicholas II (1894–1917) inherited a throne which in theory was subject to no constitutional restraints whatever, but in 1905 even he had to accept a Duma whose powers were defined. For one of the consequences of the French Revolution had been to introduce the concept of a written constitution, one of whose purposes was to limit the powers of the ruling monarch. Whereas in

1780 the only European state to have a written constitution was Sweden, in 1914 Britain was the only one without one, and in Britain's case the powers of the monarchy were already limited by statute, custom and convention. The desirability of some form of representative assembly was universally admitted, even where its powers might be very limited. If one applies the now accepted tests of a democratic system of government, universal suffrage (the right of all adults to a vote) and responsible government (i.e. a government which is answerable to an elected assembly, and through that to the people) only France would have passed both tests. Since the establishment of the Third Republic in 1875 all Frenchmen over the age of 25 had the right to vote for an assembly which in its turn chose the President and to which the Prime Minister of the day was answerable. In practice this meant that French governments, resting on temporary majorities in the Chamber of Deputies, were very vulnerable to votes of no confidence. There were nearly fifty ministries between 1870 and 1914.

In Britain any government defeated on an important vote in the House of Commons was also expected to resign, and general elections really did determine which of the two major parties (Conservative and Liberal) had the right to form the next government, as in 1900, 1906 and 1911. But even after the Reform Acts of 1832, 1867 and 1882 two-fifths of adult males did not qualify for the vote, and the will of the elected House of Commons could be, and was at times, frustrated by the hereditary peers who dominated the House of Lords. In Germany universal manhood suffrage was introduced in 1871 for elections to the Reichstag. This body, however, had no way of influencing the composition of the government, and failed to develop into a significant check on government policies. In Austria universal suffrage for elections to the Reichsrat (the Austrian parliament) was introduced in 1907 to counter agitation in Vienna and in the vain hope that a conservative minded peasantry might return conservative minded politicians. So limited were the Reichsrat's powers, however, that it was suspended in March 1914 because of irresponsible behaviour of Czech radicals and it did not meet again until 1917. Something approaching universal suffrage was reached in Italy in 1912, where all males over 21 were allowed to vote, providing they had served in the army. Those who had not served gained the right to vote when they were 30.

Thus methods of government varied widely from state to state. Parliamentary democracy, a tender plant at the best of times, was generally recognised as a desirable objective, but in 1914 it had barely been tried and the soil in which it might take root was in many parts of Europe barely cultivated.

THE EUROPEAN ECONOMIC SYSTEM

Europe's dominating place in the world economy has already been noted. What were the relative positions of the main European states in that economy? In 1850 Britain was rightly described as 'the workshop of the world'. In that year she produced more than half the world's coal, iron, cotton and steam engines. By 1914, she had just been overtaken by Germany, as Table 22.1 indicates.

If one sets aside the astonishing growth of the American economy during this period, it is clear that Britain's chief rival was Germany. Not only did German steel production exceed that of Britain from about 1900 onwards, in the chemical and electrical industries, which were to be so important in the future, but German technology was also far in advance of any other country. What these figures do not show, however, is the almost universal increase in the levels of industrialisation. This can most easily be measured in terms of energy consumption (coal, petroleum, natural gas and hydro-electricity). By this index all the major powers showed rapid increases between 1890 and 1913 (see Table 22.2).

This growth in energy consumption and manufacturing was matched by an equally rapid growth in international trade, aided by a huge increase in railway mileage and steamship tonnage. By 1914 for instance Britain's railway mileage was 38,000 kilometres, France's 49,500, Germany's 61,000 kilometres and Russia's (thanks to the opening of the Trans-Siberian railway) was 70,000. British and German merchant shipping had each expanded rapidly to carry their dominating shares of international trade. In 1913 the value of British exports and imports was £1,186 million, compared with a German value of £1,021 million. This growth in international trade was made possible only through the development of a sophisticated system of international finance. Countries needed to be able to trade with a wide range of trading partners, and to be able to settle their debts with each other with an acceptable medium of exchange. This was made possible through the development of two currencies which were universally acceptable. The first was gold. In 1821 Britain went on to the gold standard, that is to say the pound now had a fixed value in terms of gold, in effect £3.90 to the ounce. By 1897 most other European countries had also tied their currencies to gold: Germany in 1872, France in 1878, Russia in 1897. Because Britain was the world's largest exporter and importer the City of London developed a wide range of financial institutions for the settlement of international debts, and the pound sterling also became an acceptable

Table 22.1 Relative shares of world manufacturing output, 1880–1913 (percent)

	1880	1900	1913
Britain	22.9	18.5	13.6
United States	14.7	23.6	32.0
Germany	8.5	13.2	14.8
France	7.8	6.8	6.1
Russia	7.6	8.8	8.2
Austria-Hungary	4.4	4.7	4.4
Italy	2.5	2.5	2.4

Table 22.2 Energy consumption of the powers, 1890–1913 (in million tons of coal equivalent)

	1890	1890	1900	1913
United States	147	248	483	541
Britain	145	171	185	195
Germany	71	112	158	187
France	36	47.9	55	62.5
Austria-Hungary	19.7	29	40	49.4
Russia	10.9	30	41	54
Italy	4.5	5	9.6	11

international medium of exchange. The period from 1880 to 1913 saw the operation of what was in effect an international gold standard, which enabled international trade to expand even faster than world output.

Thus the general picture is one of rapid industrialisation, in which Germany was wresting the lead from Britain. Russia was beginning to exploit her industrial potential, while across the Atlantic the American industrial revolution was proceeding at such a pace that the United States would soon achieve the position she was to hold for the rest of the twentieth century, that of the world's leading industrial power. A sophisticated world monetary system enabled capital to flow from developed to undeveloped countries and to sustain an expanding volume of trade between them.

SOCIETY

Every European society was highly stratified, though, to different degrees. A landowning aristocracy had survived the challenges of the French and the 1848 revolutions with remarkable resilience, least successfully in France where it had lost much of its political influence but still retained its social prestige. In Britain, too, while something like half the country's land was still owned by 8,000 landowners, the political influence of this class was in serious decline, as the decision to remove the House of Lords veto in 1911 indicated. In Germany, particularly in Prussia, the German *Junker* class still dominated local government and through its over representation in the Prussian Landtag (assembly) was still able to exert its leverage in domestic politics. In the Austro-Hungarian empire, too, the government and the higher civil service was dominated by the aristocracy. It was in Russia that the landowning class retained most influence, where it still owned 53.1 per cent of privately held land, and dominated both central and local government. The industrialisation of much of western Europe, coupled with other changes such as the growth of the professions (engineering, law, accountancy, medicine, the civil service, education) produced a middle class or bourgeoisie, to use Marx's language, from whose

ranks most political leaders were drawn. In 1914 for instance, Bethmann Hollweg, a civil servant, was Chancellor of Germany; Poincaré, President of France, had been a lawyer, as had Asquith, who was the British Prime Minister. Parliamentary assemblies in most countries were generally recruited from the middle class.

In numerical terms, the majority of Europe's population belonged to what would now be conventionally described as the working class. It was made up of two substantially different groups: those who drew their living from the land either as peasant proprietors or landless labourers, and an industrial proletariat which staffed the mines, factories and transport systems that were features of any industrialised economy. The proportion varied greatly. In Russia up to 75 per cent of the population were engaged in agriculture. In England the figure was 10 per cent. The industrial proletariat in Russia, while growing rapidly in Moscow and St Petersburg, still made up only a small fraction of the labour force.

Characteristic of Europe as a whole were the wide inequalities which resulted from these social divisions. In England it was calculated that in 1914 0.04 per cent of the population owned 65 per cent of the nation's wealth in the form of land, property and investments. At the other end of the social spectrum, according to Charles Booth's ground-breaking social survey, *Life and Labour of the People of London* (published in 1902) one-third of the population did not earn enough to achieve 'physical efficiency', and this was in the country which had pioneered the industrial revolution. Such inequalities were equally characteristic of western Europe, and were even more marked in Russia.

In every European country there was a growing perception among the working classes of these inequalities, reflected in the rise of socialist political parties and the spread of trade unions. At the same time, conditions were improving. The foundations of a welfare state had been laid in Germany, where old age pensions, sickness benefit and unemployment benefit had already been introduced by Bismarck, to be copied in Britain by Lloyd George between 1908 and 1912. Consumer goods were becoming more widely available. Mortality rates were dropping.

Whether these favourable trends could have taken the sting out of the revolutionary forces which threatened Russian society, in particular, without the First World War, is one of those questions to which history can provide no answer. Suffice it to say that in 1914, despite the growing prosperity which industrialisation brought with it, there were few countries where the existing division of wealth and property was accepted without protest.

Europe was still a man's world. In political terms, the only country in Europe to allow women the vote was Norway, where it had been conceded in 1912. Elsewhere the male monopoly of political power was being challenged in various ways. In Britain two influential movements were founded at the turn of the century, the Union of Women's Suffrage Societies in 1897 and the more militant Women's Social and Political Union in 1903. There were movements for women's emancipation in Germany going back to the 1840s. Socialist parties were generally sympathetic to the cause of women's suffrage. But in Britain the campaign to give women the vote had failed to convert either of the two major political parties and in Germany only the Social Democrats were prepared to give whole-hearted support to women's suffrage. In France there was even less enthusiasm for the idea.

A handful of enterprising and adventurous women took a direct part in political activity. In 1878 Vera Zasulich shot and killed Trepov, the governor of St Petersburg, because he had ordered a political prisoner to be flogged for refusing to take off his cap to him. Zasulich was acquitted by the jury which tried her. In Ireland Constance Gore-Booth was an active supporter of the Sinn Fein movement, and under her married name Countess Markiewicz was the first woman MP to be elected to the British House of Commons in 1918, though she refused to take her seat. Born in Russian Poland in 1870, Rosa Luxemburg became a German citizen and took a leading part in German and Russian socialist politics up to 1914 when she was imprisoned for her activities. Such women were exceptional.

The First World War had an obvious effect in advancing women's rights, if only because so many women had shown that they could fill men's places in the world of work. Opposition to women's suffrage crumbled in Britain and in 1918 women over the age of 28 were granted the vote. Under the Weimar Constitution of 1919, drawn up after the collapse of the German empire, German women were given the vote on the same terms as men. This formula was adopted for most of the new European states which came into existence under the treaty of Versailles. In France, however, women did not get the vote until 1944.

In terms of the careers open to women, there was slow progress throughout the nineteenth century and the process was one of gradual infiltration rather than sudden change. Women were first admitted to higher education in Britain in 1871, when Owen's College in Manchester opened its doors to them. At Oxford five women's societies were founded between 1879 and 1893, and in 1884 women were allowed to take university examinations. Even so it was not until the 1950s that full equality at Oxford and Cambridge was achieved. Some of the professions, such as medicine, the law and accountancy, gradually admitted women, but the Christian churches, with rare exceptions, continued to bar women from the priesthood. In their view of the roles they were prepared to allow women to play, the men of 1914 were not very different from their eighteenth century predecessors.

THE INTELLECTUAL CLIMATE

It is impossible to summarise in a few lines the enormous variety of ideas and beliefs held by the inhabitants of Europe in 1914. Certain dominant tendencies can be identified, however. Stemming from the Enlightenment there was a growing belief in the power of reason, as applied to the material world. This was reflected in the growth of scientific knowledge and its application in the huge technological achievements associated with the industrial revolution. With the publication in 1859 of Darwin's *The Origin of Species* the theory of evolution upset the traditional Christian view of Creation and with its emphasis on the struggle for survival as the key to progress it also cast doubt on the notion of a benevolent Creator. Many of the best minds in the nineteenth century grappled with these problems without finding a solution. Equally powerful in eroding traditional beliefs was the work of Karl Marx, for whom religion was the product of man: 'the sigh of the oppressed creature, the feeling of a heartless world, and the soul of soulless circumstances, it is the opium of the people' (Karl Marx, *On the Jewish Question*, cited in D. McLellan, *Marx*, London, Fontana, 1975, p. 31). It is hardly surprising that Christianity in Europe ceased to be the dominant intellectual influence it had been in the eighteenth century.

Yet there were important religious revivals in many parts of Europe throughout the nineteenth century. In England the Evangelical and Oxford movements enlivened the Anglican Church.

In Germany there were similar revivals in the Lutheran churches and in France traditional Catholicism survived the attack made upon it during the French Revolution and during anti-clerical ministries of the Third Republic. The Pope was twice driven from Rome, in 1809 by Napoleon and in 1848 by Italian revolutionaries. But the Papacy's spiritual authority survived, and was indeed enhanced in 1870 by the Decree of Papal Infallibility. While Christianity was challenged in Europe the number of its adherents actually increased because of the extension of European rule in Africa and the Far East. Missionaries accompanied the traders and soldiers who settled the African continent and there was also an upsurge of missionary activity in India, China and other parts of the Far East. The long term consequences of these endeavours have still to be seen, and the association of missions with white rule was bound to have some damaging side-effects. But clearly whatever the intellectual challenges to Christian belief at the end of the nineteenth century, there was still sufficient vitality in the European churches, both Catholic and Protestant, to fuel missionary enterprises on a large scale.

Among the paradoxes of these endeavours was the extension of Europe's domestic religious divisions into the mission field. The worst example occurred in Buganda where rivalry between the French Catholic White Fathers and the Protestant English Church Missionary Society exacerbated a complicated power struggle. Thus national and religious divisions in Europe were sometimes transmitted where they were least appropriate.

CHALLENGES TO EUROPE'S STABILITY

In 1914 Europe was threatened by the two major divisions which have plagued it throughout the twentieth century: national rivalries between the major (and minor) powers and social conflicts between rich and poor. Nationalism at the start of the twentieth century had many strands. In its most innocent form it was the same thing as patriotism, a love of one's country. Where the state coincided with a people, as in England or France, the attachment was as much to a place as to an idea or a group of people. It may be summed up in Rupert Brooke's famous lines,

> If I should die, think only this of me:
> That there's some corner of a foreign field
> That is for ever England.

Where the people and the state did not coincide, as was the case for the Poles, the Southern Irish, the Armenians or the Czechs, for example, nationalism took the form of a belief in the right to self-determination, the right of a people or race to rule itself. The demand for an independent Poland had led to revolutions in 1830 and 1863 and became one of the Allies' war aims in 1918. The Sinn Fein movement, founded in 1905, was committed to the achievement of an independent Ireland. The Armenians rebelled against their Turkish masters in 1894 and were to be constantly at the mercy of their oppressors, whether Turks or Russians in the twentieth century. The Czechs, ruled by the Habsburgs since 1620, never fitted happily into the Austro-Hungarian empire and made their bid for independence during the First World War. The right of national self-determination was to be explicitly asserted by President Wilson in a speech to the United States Congress in February 1918, when he asserted that ' "self-determination" is not a mere phrase. It is an imperative principle of action which statesmen will henceforth ignore at their peril' (*Messages and Papers of the Presidents*, vol. 17, 1925, p. 8450). The prevailing approval of this form of nationalism is to be seen in the twenty-six states into which Europe came to be divided after the First World War.

A less acceptable form of nationalism can be seen in the belief that some racial groups were superior to others, and were therefore entitled to establish their dominance over them. This idea was first clearly expounded by Comte Philippe de Gobineau, an aristocratic French politician and writer, who in his *Essay on the Inequality of the Human Races*, published between 1853 and 1855, argued that the Aryan, or Germanic, peoples represented the summit of civilisation. Gobineau was more interested in cultural differences than in racial dominance but one of his successors, Houston Stewart Chamberlain, took Gobineau's ideas a stage further. Chamberlain left England for Europe at the age of 16, and became a fervent admirer of all things German. He married one of Wagner's daughters and adopted German citizenship in 1916. Kaiser William II was one of his admirers and Hitler attended his funeral. Chamberlain emphasised the peculiar virtues of the German race which according to him had saved European civilisation 'from the clutches of the everlastingly bestial', whereas the Jews were an alien element which threatened all that Europe had accomplished (Houston Stewart Chamberlain, *Foundations of the Nineteenth Century*, vol. 1, London, John Lane, 1909, pp. 494–95).

The superiority of the white races in general was a widely shared conviction, and became a convenient justification for imperialism. After the United States had acquired the Philippine islands in the Spanish-American war of 1898, Rudyard Kipling, one of imperialism's most powerful prophets, urged his American cousins to:

> Take up the White Man's burden:
> Send forth the best ye breed
> Go, bind your sons to exile
> To serve your captives' need;
> To wait in heavy harness
> On fluttered folk and wild
> Your new-caught, sullen peoples
> Half-devil and half-child

Cecil Rhodes, who had the ambition of extending the British empire in Africa from Cape Town to Cairo, believed that 'We [the British] happen to be the best people in the world with the highest standards of decency and justice, liberty and peace, and the more of the world we inherit, the better it is for humanity' (cited by James Morris, *Farewell the Trumpets*, London, Penguin, 1980, p. 124).

If these were the views expressed at least by a minority of well-educated men, whose standing was high in their respective countries, how widely shared were their beliefs? There is some evidence that support for the more aggressive forms of nationalism came from the middle classes. The members of the Pan German League were overwhelmingly middle class, as were the readers of the imperialist-minded *Daily Express*, launched in 1900 with the declaration: 'Our policy is patriotism, our policy is the British Empire'. With the advent of universal primary education, usually paid for by the state, the ideal of loyalty to one's country of birth was encouraged by such symbols as the flying of the national flag or the singing of the national anthem on formal school occasions. The readiness of all the populations of European states to respond to the call to arms in 1914 must be related in some way to the cult of patriotism which was fostered by governments and the media. Equally, those minorities who could not identify with the states to which they reluctantly belonged had a corresponding attachment to the cause of their independence. Patrick Pearse, one of the leaders of the Easter Rebellion against British rule in Ireland in 1916, was to write in December 1915:

The last sixteen months have been the most glorious in the history of Europe. Heroism has come to earth. . . . The old heart of the earth needed to be warmed with the red wine of the battlefields. Such august homage was never before offered to God, the homage of millions of lives given gladly for love of country. What peace Ireland has known these latter days has been the devil's peace, peace with dishonour.

(cited in G. Dangerfield, *The Damnable Question*, Constable, London, p. 182)

Nationalism was a peculiarly heady brew in 1914.

The other main challenge to Europe's stability came from the consequences of rapid economic change. The emergence of a large industrial working class in Britain, Germany, France and to a lesser but still significant extent in Russia brought with it the potential for class conflict. In all the countries of western Europe, and in Russia, there were active socialist parties (see Chapter 16) committed to a lesser or greater extent to the overthrow of the capitalist system and the redistribution of wealth. Socialism embraced a wide spectrum of beliefs, both in terms of objectives and methods. At one extreme Lenin believed in the nationalisation of the means of production, distribution and exchange, to be achieved through revolutionary violence if need be; syndicalists such as George Sorel argued for the use of the general strike as a political weapon which would achieve its effects by bringing economic life to a standstill; while German Social Democrats and the

British Labour party were generally prepared to work through parliamentary institutions. In 1914 it was impossible to say which way the working classes of Europe would go. There were serious strikes in France, England and Russia in the years leading up to 1914, and the ruling classes in each of these countries were at the very least apprehensive, even if they did not tremble as Marx predicted.

Thus the two forces of nationalism and socialism threatened Europe's stability in the decade leading up to the First World War. Nationalism manifested itself in a heightened sense of national pride, reflected for instance in celebrations of battles such as Trafalgar, Sedan and Kossovo and in an armaments race which reached a climax in 1914 (see Figures 22.1 and 22.2). Socialism showed its mili-

22.1 A postcard to commemorate the battle of Sedan, 1895
'What a change through the guidance of God'

Source: Bildarchiv Preussicher Kulturbesitz, Berlin

22.2 A souvenir of the centenary of Trafalgar, 1905
Source: The British Library

tant side in the strikes in the Lena goldfields in Russia in 1912. When an international crisis erupted in July 1914 the forces of moderation proved incapable of resisting the pressures of nationalism and the imperatives of war plans. Europe plunged into a war which none of its leaders really wanted. That war lasted from August 1914 until November 1918 and cost the lives of some 10 million Europeans. During its course it led first to the abdication of the monarchy in Russia and then to the collapse of the Provisional government which replaced it. These events in their turn led to the establishment of a communist dictatorship in Russia that was to dominate eastern Europe for much of the century. The German, Austro-Hungarian and Ottoman empires also collapsed between 1918 and 1920. The map of Europe which resulted from the Paris Peace Conference was no nearer to providing a permanent settlement of Europe's frontiers than the one which was agreed at the Congress of Vienna. In 1939 another war broke out, caused at least in part by frictions generated by that settlement. These developments cannot all be ascribed to the mistakes of the politicians who were in power in 1914 or in 1918. At a deeper level, however, the changes generated in Europe by the French and industrial revolutions helped to shape a continent which, while it dominated the rest of the world, could not resolve the national rivalries and class tensions that divided it.

• INDEX •

Numbers in *italic* refer to pages containing illustrations.